I like to learn.

It's true^^

D0079061

Entrepreneurship
Owning Your Future
Eleventh Edition

Steve Mariotti
**Founder,
Network for Teaching Entrepreneurship**

With Tony Towle
Edited by Neelam Patel

Prentice Hall

Boston   Columbus   Indianapolis   New York   San Francisco   Upper Saddle River

Amsterdam   Cape Town   Dubai   London   Madrid   Milan   Munich   Paris   Montreal   Toronto

Delhi   Mexico City   Sao Paulo   Sydney   Hong Kong   Seoul   Singapore   Taipei   Tokyo

Editor in Chief: Vernon R. Anthony
Acquisitions Editor: Gary Bauer
Editorial Assistant: Megan Heintz
Director of Marketing: David Gesell
Campaign Marketing Manager: Leigh Ann Sims
School Marketing Manager: Laura Cutone
Senior Operations Supervisor: Pat Tonneman
Text and Cover Designer: Amy Rosen
Manager, Visual Research: Beth Brenzel
Photo Researcher: Pamela Ross
Manager, Rights and Permissions, Image Resource Center: Zina Arabia

Image Permission Coordinator: Vicki Menanteaux
Cover Art: Jose Luis Pelaez/Blend Images/Jupiter Images
Content Reviewer: Rupa Mohan
Full-Service Project Management: Gleason Group, Inc., Norwalk, CT
Composition: PDS Associates, Ocean Township, NJ
Printer/Binder: R.R. Donnelley & Sons Company/Willard
Cover Printer: Lehigh-Phoenix Color
Text Font: ITC Galliard Std

This book is dedicated to:
Raymond Chambers; Landon Hilliard; Elizabeth, Charles G., and David H. Koch; James Lyle; and the Honorable John C. Whitehead

Special dedication to:
Diana Davis Spencer, Art Samberg, Mary Myers Kauppila, and the late Bernard A. Goldhirsh

Entrepreneurship: Owning Your Future is the 11th edition of this textbook. The 10th edition was titled *How to Start & Operate a Small Business*. The Network for Teaching Entrepreneurship was previously named the National Foundation for Teaching Entrepreneurship.

Copyright © 2010 NFTE (Network for Teaching Entrepreneurship), 120 Wall St., 29th Floor, New York, NY 10005 and published by Pearson Education, Inc., 1 Lake St., Upper Saddle River, New Jersey 07458. All rights reserved. Manufactured in the United States of America. This publication is protected by Copyright, and permission should be obtained from NFTE prior to any prohibited reproduction, storage in a retrieval system, or transmission in any form or by any means, electronic, mechanical, photocopying, recording, or likewise. To obtain permission(s) to use material from this work, please submit a written request to NFTE (Network for Teaching Entrepreneurship), Permissions Department, 120 Wall St., 29th Floor, New York, NY 10005.

Many of the designations by manufacturers and seller to distinguish their products are claimed as trademarks. Where those designations appear in this book, and the publisher was aware of a trademark claim, the designations have been printed in initial caps or all caps.

10 9 8 7 6 5 4 3

Prentice Hall
is an imprint of

www.pearsonhighered.com

ISBN 10:   0-13-512844-7
ISBN 13:   978-0-13-512844-2

RICHARD ADAMO
Independence High School
New York, NY

STACEY ALDERMAN
Carroll County High School
Hillsville, VA

ANN CARRANZA
Miami Southridge Senior High School
Miami, FL

JAMES G. HAWKINS
North East High School
Kansas City, MO

MICHAEL IACARELLA
Thomas Alva Edison High School
N.E. Minneapolis, MN

GWEN KASSEP
Mt. Lebanon High School
Pittsburgh, PA

DEB MOORE
Sunrise Mountain High School
Peoria, AZ

CONNIE MORAN
Ariel Community Academy
Chicago, IL

ANGELA POWELL
H. Grady Spruce High School
Dallas, TX

SUSI PRICE
Dixon High School
Holly Ridge, NC

BLAIR SAWYERS
Western International High School
Detroit, MI

MONICA SMALLS
Brighton High School
Brighton, MA

SCOTT STEWARD
Gwendolyn Brooks College Preparatory Academy
Chicago, IL

KENE TURNER
EpiLife Consulting
New York, NY

ROBINETTA WEST
Bowsher High School
Toledo, OH

EDWARD YOUNGBLOOD
Silver Creek High School
San Jose, CA

Steve Mariotti

Steve Mariotti, founder of the Network for Teaching Entrepreneurship (NFTE), is an expert in education for at-risk youth He has been helping young people develop marketable skills by learning about entrepreneurship for more than 25 years.

Steve received an M.B.A. from the University of Michigan, Ann Arbor, and has studied at Harvard University, Stanford University, and Brooklyn College. His professional career began as a Treasury Analyst for Ford Venezuela, Mexico, Caribbean, Argentina, Peru, Chile, South Africa, and the Export Division (1976–1979). He introduced financial systems that saved the company over $5 million per annum via interest-expense reduction and improved cash management. After leaving Ford, Steve founded—and for the next three years operated—Mason Import/Export Services in New York, eventually acting as sales representative and purchasing agent for 32 overseas firms.

In 1982, Steve made a momentous career change and became a Special Education/Business Teacher in the New York City school system, choosing to teach in such at-risk neighborhoods as Bedford-Stuyvesant in Brooklyn and the "Fort Apache" section of the South Bronx. It was at Jane Addams Vocational High School in the Bronx that Steve had the idea of bringing entrepreneurial education to low-income youth. This inspiration led to the founding of the National Foundation for Teaching Entrepreneurship in 1987 (now the Network for Teaching Entrepreneurship), with 501(c)(3) nonprofit status granted by the IRS the following year.

Steve Mariotti and NFTE have received numerous awards—including the 2004 Ernst & Young National Entrepreneur of the Year Award, the Golden Lamp Award from the Association of Education Publishers (2002), and the National Federation of Independent Businesses—Best Business Teacher 1988—as well as major media exposure that includes pieces in the *New York Times* and other prominent publications and profiles on ABC News and CNN. Steve has coauthored some two dozen books and educational manuals that have sold a total of over half a million copies.

Tony Towle

Tony Towle has worked with Steve Mariotti and NFTE since its inception. In addition, he has written about art, and is a poet whose books include *A History of the Invitation* (New & Selected Poems 1963–2000), *Memoir 1960–1963*, and most recently, *Winter Journey*. He has received a National Endowment for the Arts Fellowship and a New York State Council on the Arts Fellowship, among other prizes and awards.

Neelam Patel

Neelam Patel joined NFTE in 2006 with over 10 years of experience in the field of education, professional development, and curriculum design. Neelam's current responsibilities at NFTE include creating text- and digital-based entrepreneurship curricula, managing the unit responsible for supporting and creating NFTE's program elements, and providing the organization with short- and long-term programmatic strategic goals. She oversees NFTE's curriculum design, teacher professional development, alumni services, and research initiatives.

Prior to coming to NFTE, Neelam taught in public schools within the Los Angeles Unified School District and the New York City Board of Education. In addition, she has been an instructor and supervisor for Education students in the Master's programs at Mercy College and at Teachers College, Columbia University.

Neelam has a B.A. from the University of Southern California, and an M.S. in Educational Leadership from Pepperdine, and is currently pursuing a doctoral degree at Teachers College, Columbia University, in Curriculum Studies. She is also a 2003 National Board Certified Teacher.

The NFTE Story

From one program in the Bronx, NFTE has expanded its mission into an international movement for teaching entrepreneurship, academic, and technology skills to young people worldwide, and has been recognized with many awards and honors. So, too, has NFTE founder Steve Mariotti, who has been consistently recognized for his leadership and contributions to the nation's youth. Although still an emerging curriculum, entrepreneurship education has enjoyed tremendous growth in acceptance by K–12 educators and in popularity among young adults. NFTE believes that entrepreneurship could and should be added to school programs nationwide.

To fulfill its mission, NFTE focuses on four goals:

- **Engage young people in school** by teaching math, reading, writing, and communication within the motivating context of starting and operating a small business.

- **Teach young people about the market economy** and how ownership leads to wealth creation.

- **Encourage an entrepreneurial mindset** so young people can succeed whether they pursue higher education, enter the workforce, or become entrepreneurs.

- **Make young people financially literate** so they are able to save and invest to meet their life goals.

NFTE is widely viewed as a world leader in promoting entrepreneurial literacy—helping youth achieve greater academic, personal, professional, and financial success. Nearly 50,000 young people will participate in NFTE programs in the 2008–2009 school year. Through a growing network of influential partners and affiliated organizations, NFTE is leading the way in expanding the field of youth entrepreneurship education. Relationships of note include World Economic Forum, Aspen Institute, Council on Foreign Relations, New York Economics Club, Philanthropy Roundtable, Ewing Marion Kauffman Foundation, John Templeton Foundation, Atlantic Philanthropies, McKinsey & Co., and many top institutions of

"NFTE's vision is that every young person will find a pathway to prosperity."

higher learning, including Harvard, Yale, Columbia, Stanford, and Babson College.

Working in partnership with schools, community-based organizations, and teachers, NFTE impacts students' basic academic and life skills through a hands-on entrepreneurship curriculum that reinforces math, reading, and writing, and develops skills in critical thinking, teamwork, communication, and decision-making.

NFTE programs are taught in a variety of settings, including public schools, community-based organizations, and summer BizCamps, and range from 20 to 100 hours. The NFTE program emphasizes learning by doing. Experiential learning activities include visiting local wholesale districts or discount stores, attending selling events, interacting with local entrepreneurs, and participating in a business plan competition, usually judged by outside professionals. NFTE classes may be offered as stand-alone entrepreneurship programs or infused into economics, math, or other relevant subjects.

All programs consistently emphasize the connections between personal motivation, succeeding in the real world, and personal and financial independence. Equally important, NFTE teaches young people to think like entrepreneurs: to take risks, to be open to learning, and to be empowered to own their futures.

ACKNOWLEDGMENTS

This book would not have been possible without the contributions of many people.

First I would like to thank my writing partner, Tony Towle, who from NFTE's very beginning has helped me organize my thoughts and experiences. I would also like to thank Neelam Patel, without whose talent and expertise this eleventh edition would not have been possible.

I must single out the help of two outstanding NFTE executives, Rupa Mohan and Daniel Rabuzzi, whose leadership and insights are deeply appreciated. In addition, I would like to acknowledge the efforts of additional NFTE executives Darlene Ajayi, Luke Anderson, Cathy Blanchard, Del Daniels, Gary Giscombe, Julie Kantor, Erin Koblitz, Deidre Lee, Clare McCully, Estelle Reyes, Nicole Rottino, Victor Salama, Laura Scarlett, Keri Teplitzky, Jane Walsh, and Katerina Zacharia.

Special thanks to Jerry Gleason at Gleason Group, Inc., for helping NFTE put together this extremely complex project. Also, thanks to Gary Bauer, Vernon Anthony, Robin Baliszewski, Leigh Ann Sims, and the entire team at Pearson Prentice Hall for their professionalism and support.

Special thanks to Amy Rosen, whom NFTE is thrilled to have as our new president and CEO. She is sure to take NFTE to a new level of success.

In addition, I would like to recognize the efforts and contributions of members of NFTE's National Board of Directors: Albert Abney, Patricia Alper, Bill Daugherty, Phillip A. Falcone, Michael L. Fetters, Lawrence N. Fields, Donald Friedman, Thomas P. Hartocollis, Landon Hilliard, Sanford Krieger, James Lyle, Consuelo Mack, Alan Patricof, Marsha Ralls, Donna Redel, Robert Reffkin, Arthur J. Samberg, Diana Davis Spencer, Peter B. Walker, and Tucker York.

I would like to acknowledge the inspired guidance provided by our National Executive Committee: Bart Breighner, Steven Brenninkmeijer, Kathryn Davis, Lewis M. Eisenberg, Theodore J. Forstmann, Sir Paul Judge, Mary Myers Kauppila, the late Hon. Jack Kemp, Elizabeth B. Koch, Abby Moffat, Jeffrey S. Raikes, Kenneth I. Starr, and the Hon. John C. Whitehead.

I am deeply grateful as well to the many philanthropists who have supported our work, including Raymond Chambers, Charles G. and David H. Koch, Joanne Beyer of the Scaife Family Foundation, Barbara Bell Coleman of the Newark Boys' and Girls' Clubs, Chris Podoll of the William Zimmerman Foundation, Stephanie Bell-Rose of the Goldman Sachs Foundation, The Shelby Cullom Davis Foundation, Jeff Raikes and the Microsoft Corporation, The Nasdaq Educational Foundation, and Ronald McDonald House Children's Charities.

Further, I would like to acknowledge Essye Klempner, Curtis DeBerg, John Harris, Erika Humphrey, Deborah Reinerio, Karl Boedecker, Steve Alcock, Harsh and Aruna Bhargava, Lena Bondue, Dawn Bowlus, Shelly Chenoweth, Janet McKinstry Cort, Erik Dauwen, Clara Del Villar, Christine Chambers Gilfillan, Kathleen Kirkwood, Michael Simmons, Sheena Lindahl, Cynthia Miree, Henry To, Carol Tully, Dilia Wood, and Elizabeth Wright, as well as Peter Cowie, Joseph Dominic, Paul DeF. Hicks, Jr., Ann Mahoney, David Roodberg, Phyllis Ross Schless, Remi Vermeir, and Jackson, Sienna, and Nina Mariotti who have contributed countless insights into providing entrepreneurial opportunities to young people.

Thanks are due to all of the teachers, students, experts, and friends who were kind enough to look over this book and help me improve it.

In addition, I would like to thank my brother, Jack, the best CPA I know, and my father, John, for financing much of NFTE's early work, and for their continuing love and guidance. Finally, I want to thank my mother, Nancy, a wonderful special education instructor who showed me that one great teacher can affect eternity.

— *Steve Mariotti*

BRIEF TABLE OF CONTENTS

TABLE OF CONTENTS

TABLE OF CONTENTS

TABLE OF CONTENTS

TABLE OF CONTENTS

TABLE OF CONTENTS

Content Overview

Entrepreneurship: Owning Your Future provides you with all the tools you need to become a successful entrepreneur.

- ## Unit 1: What Is an Entrepreneur?
  After an introduction to entrepreneurship, you examine the characteristics of an entrepreneur and are introduced to the role entrepreneurship plays in the economy. You also learn about the basic types of business (such as retail and manufacturing) and the types of business ownership (sole proprietorship, partnership, and so on).

- ## Unit 2: Preparing for Business
  To succeed as an entrepreneur, you need well-developed communication and negotiation skills. You also need to understand business ethics and consider the relationship between business and social responsibility. This unit helps you with all this, and includes special features on time management and goal setting.

- ## Unit 3: Opportunity Recognition & Market Analysis
  Now you begin the real work of starting a business! The first thing you learn is how to write a business plan. The rest of the textbook focuses on fleshing out the various parts of your business plan. This unit also shows you how to spot a business opportunity and how to do market research to evaluate whether an opportunity has sufficient potential.

- ## Unit 4: Marketing Plan & Sales
  In this unit you learn how to develop a marketing plan and how to promote your product. You also learn the principles of successful selling and how to estimate sales.

- ## Unit 5: Analyzing Finances
  This is the "meat" of the textbook. You're introduced to the basics of business finances, including essential financial documents and ratios. Without these tools, you wouldn't know whether you could expect your new business to make a profit.

- ## Unit 6: Starting Your Business
  This unit introduces such basic concepts as financing, recordkeeping and accounting, hiring staff, insurance, and taxes—all critical when starting a business.

- ## Unit 7: Managing Your Business
  Will you be able to manage your new business? This unit walks you though all the important aspects of business management: expenses, cash flow, production, distribution, operations, purchasing, and inventory.

- ## Unit 8: Growing Your Business
  Finally, you consider how to grow your business and how to successfully leave it when the right time comes.

Preview of Your Textbook

Units

Each **Unit** focuses on a group of important entrepreneurship concepts. From the first Unit on, you will work on your business plan.

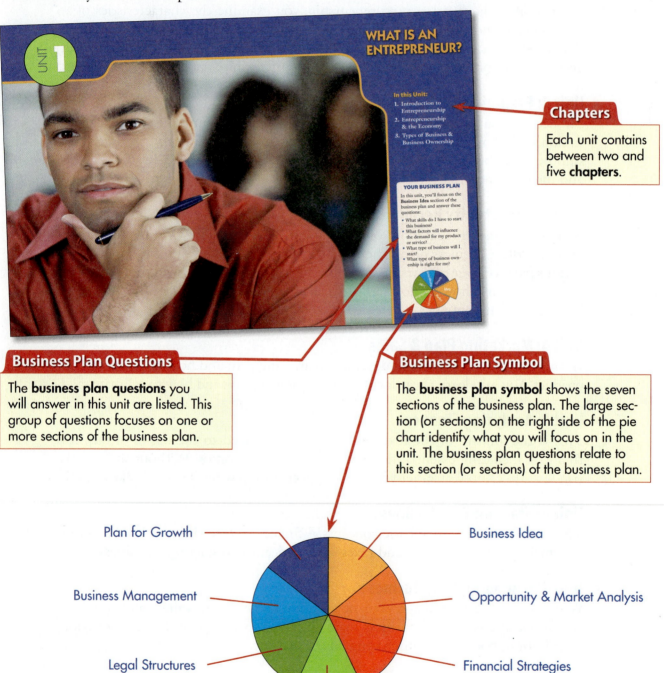

Chapters

Each unit contains between two and five **chapters**.

Business Plan Questions

The **business plan questions** you will answer in this unit are listed. This group of questions focuses on one or more sections of the business plan.

Business Plan Symbol

The **business plan symbol** shows the seven sections of the business plan. The large section (or sections) on the right side of the pie chart identify what you will focus on in the unit. The business plan questions relate to this section (or sections) of the business plan.

Plan for Growth

Business Idea

Business Management

Opportunity & Market Analysis

Legal Structures

Financial Strategies

Organizational Structures

Chapters & Sections

Each chapter in the textbook has two **sections**.

Section Objectives

The easy-to-understand **section objectives** identify the key concepts in each section.

Vocabulary

The **vocabulary** introduced in the section are listed for easy review at the beginning of each section.

Question

Each section begins with a **question** that you will discuss in class. These questions usually require a simple answer, but your class discussion will focus on the thinking behind it.

Working within a Section

To help you focus your learning, important class content is presented in each section with a minimum of interruptions.

Heads Relate to Objectives

The **heads relate specifically to the objectives** listed at the beginning of each section.

Vocabulary

Vocabulary terms are highlighted in the text and defined when they first occur. These terms are listed at the beginning of the section, reviewed at the end of the chapter, and included in the Glossary.

Pronunciation

For vocabulary terms you may not know how to pronounce, the **pronunciation** is shown when the term is first introduced. It's also included in the Glossary.

Figure Questions

After important figures, an open-ended **figure question** asks you to consider relevant issues related to the figure and text.

Reading Checkpoints

Reading checkpoints allow you to make sure you understand key points of each objective.

Entrepreneurship Issues & Your Business Career

Each chapter includes two unique features. The Entrepreneurship Issues feature focuses on specific contemporary topics related to entrepreneurship. In the Your Business Career feature, you develop the techniques and attitudes you will need in business and life.

Entrepreneurship Issues

Entrepreneurship Issues includes such topics as Serial Entrepreneurship, Peace through Entrepreneurship, Focus Groups, Customer Word-of-Mouth, Carbon Credits, Entrepreneurship Blogs, Micro-Loans, Paperless Offices, and Socially Responsible Investing.

Thinking Critically

Both features include open-ended **Thinking Critically** questions that extend your learning.

ENTREPRENEURSHIP ISSUES

Elevator Pitches

Entrepreneurs often need funds from outside sources to start their businesses. To obtain financing, entrepreneurs have to explain the idea for a new business to a bank loan officer, a venture capitalist, or other potential investor. This is called a "pitch."

Entrepreneurs often don't have much time to make their case. This led to the "elevator pitch" (so named because the pitch has to be succinct enough to be delivered during an elevator ride). In an elevator pitch, an entrepreneur has only 30 seconds. He or she must communicate in fewer than 150 words what the product does and how the consumer will benefit. Venture capitalists may ask entrepreneurs for an elevator pitch to weed out bad ideas immediately.

Now, with the advent of micro-blogging Websites such as Twitter—in which readers post updates of 140 characters or less—the "twitpitch" is the newest type of elevator pitch. Entrepreneurs post two-sentence business ideas to their accounts, efficiently getting through to time-crunched consultants and venture capitalists.

THINKING CRITICALLY

Applying Concepts. Think of a new idea for a small business. Can you communicate that idea in 30 seconds? How about in 140 characters or less? Start by practicing an elevator pitch in a small group and then take turns writing your own twitpitches and sharing them with the class.

To read more about pitches, including elevator pitches and twitpitches, go to "Entrepreneurship Issues" on the Student Center at entrepreneurship.pearson.com.

YOUR BUSINESS CAREER

Career Orientation

Some high school students have a good idea about what type of work they want to do after graduation. Others may be undecided about their future plans. They need to know more about careers that suit their skills.

If you know the field you hope to work in, you can plan a career pathway while still in high school. If you intend to go on to college, you will need to think about what to study. Your college major may require you to take specific math, science, or foreign language courses in high school. If you haven't taken these courses, you will have to take them in college before you can actually begin taking the courses that interest you. If you want to follow a specific career, ask your guidance counselor for help in choosing courses that fit with your prospective plans.

If you are not sure about a career path, ask your guidance counselor about tests designed to match your interests and abilities to specific occupations. The results may lead you to some possibilities for which you are especially suited.

THINKING CRITICALLY

Analyzing Information. Take a career aptitude test online (at www.careerkey.org). List the career options suggested by the test and then describe your reaction to these options.

To read more about career orientation, go to "Your Business Career" on the Student Center at entrepreneurship.pearson.com.

Your Business Career

In **Your Business Career**, you'll find such topics as Self-Awareness, Empathy, Respect, Dressing for Success, Self-Esteem, Positive Attitude, Responsibility, Sense of Purpose, Honesty, Self-Control, and Comfort with Diversity.

Student Center

More material about each feature is included on the **Student Center** at entrepreneurship.pearson.com.

Entrepreneur Profile

Each chapter ends with an Entrepreneur Profile, the true story of a young entrepreneur, someone about your age, who started a successful business. These may inspire you to pursue your entrepreneurial dreams.

Thinking Like an Entrepreneur

The **Thinking Like an Entrepreneur** questions ask you to consider situations that would have been faced by the profiled young entrepreneur.

ENTREPRENEUR PROFILE

It's All in the Details

When Marcus Craft was 15 years old, he wasn't legally old enough to drive a car. But, as he puts it, "I could certainly clean them." That's what detailing is. It involves everything from vacuuming the vehicle to buffing and compounding to make the car look as good as possible.

Marcus had always loved cars and anything that involved them. His father passed on his own love of cars to Marcus, as well as teaching him how to clean and preserve a vehicle to keep it in pristine condition. It was the perfect pick for a business for Marcus, and Mac's Auto Detail was born. "I absolutely love cleaning cars," said Marcus. "It really helps to have passion in your chosen field. It keeps you motivated toward always improving your performance and makes the work fun."

Competing for Business

Getting customers wasn't easy at the beginning. "I spent a lot of time making and printing business cards, flyers, and brochures to give to every person I saw or met," said Marcus. It's a time-proven way to increase business—and it worked for Marcus.

He also needed to find a way to make his business unique, to give it a competitive advantage. He relied on pricing (which he kept as low as possible) and his positive attitude. He would do whatever it took to make a sale, and he would go the extra mile to make the client satisfied: "Excellent customer service doesn't just mean providing a good product or service. It needs to be reflected in everything you do."

Planning His Time

Marcus started his business as he completed his sophomore year at William Boone High School, in Orlando, Florida. He was able to work full-time during the summers. However, during the school year, he was extremely busy with various activities. He was a member of a school music ensemble, played on the tennis team, and was an active member of his church. But he still had a business to run and phone calls to return from prospective customers and current clients.

▲ Marcus Craft

When he got his homework done, he would return the calls and schedule times for detailing. "I would also leave time in my schedule to clean cars for my neighbors," said Marcus, "because they always see me working and want theirs done too. I always made sure to leave a slot for them." For Marcus, having a workable plan and sticking to it was important for long-term success. But the bottom line in business, Marcus believes, is dealing with people. If customers see the value of your product or service, you will be successful.

Thinking Like an Entrepreneur

1. What is a competitive advantage?
2. What did Marcus use as a competitive advantage?
3. How would you show customers that your services or goods have value?

Market Research ● 187

Entrepreneurs & Technology

Technology is playing an increasingly important role in business—and particularly in new businesses. That's why there is an Entrepreneurs & Technology feature at the end of every chapter. These features discuss various aspects of technology in simple-to-understand language.

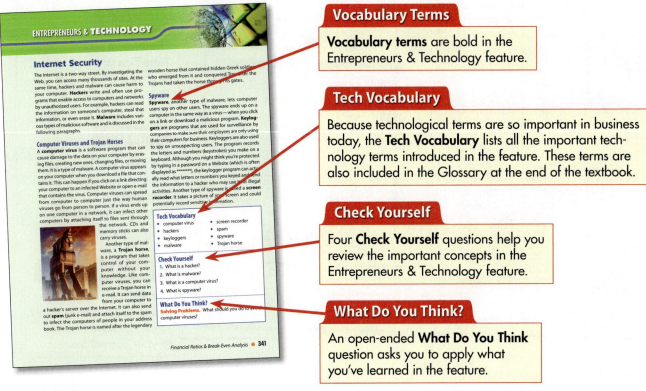

Vocabulary Terms
Vocabulary terms are bold in the Entrepreneurs & Technology feature.

Tech Vocabulary
Because technological terms are so important in business today, the **Tech Vocabulary** lists all the important technology terms introduced in the feature. These terms are also included in the Glossary at the end of the textbook.

Check Yourself
Four **Check Yourself** questions help you review the important concepts in the Entrepreneurs & Technology feature.

What Do You Think?
An open-ended **What Do You Think** question asks you to apply what you've learned in the feature.

Section Assessment

Each section ends with a Section Assessment that provides you with a chance to review important concepts and extend your knowledge.

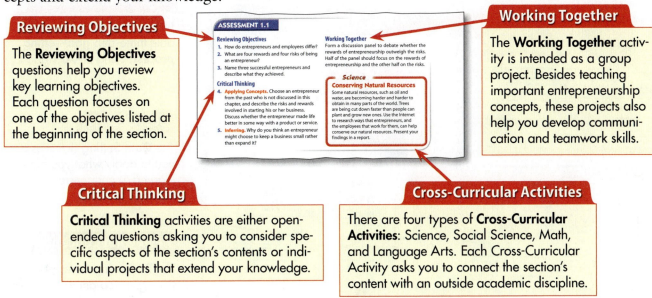

Reviewing Objectives
The **Reviewing Objectives** questions help you review key learning objectives. Each question focuses on one of the objectives listed at the beginning of the section.

Working Together
The **Working Together** activity is intended as a group project. Besides teaching important entrepreneurship concepts, these projects also help you develop communication and teamwork skills.

Critical Thinking
Critical Thinking activities are either open-ended questions asking you to consider specific aspects of the section's contents or individual projects that extend your knowledge.

Cross-Curricular Activities
There are four types of **Cross-Curricular Activities**: Science, Social Science, Math, and Language Arts. Each Cross-Curricular Activity asks you to connect the section's content with an outside academic discipline.

Time Management

Time management is a critical skill for entrepreneurs. In the early stages of growing a business, the entrepreneur may be the only employee and must use time wisely to accomplish all the critical activities associated with starting a new business. The two-page Time Management feature in Unit 2 will help you develop better time-management skills.

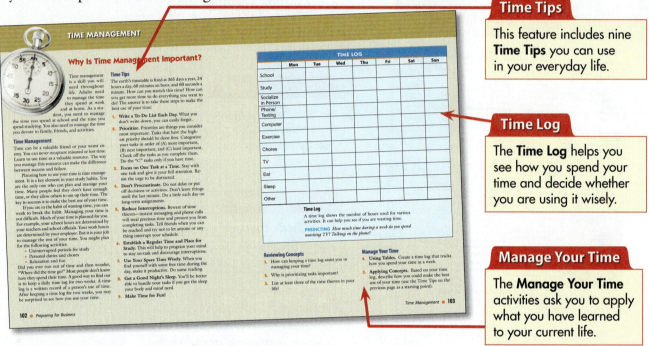

Time Tips

This feature includes nine **Time Tips** you can use in your everyday life.

Time Log

The **Time Log** helps you see how you spend your time and decide whether you are using it wisely.

Manage Your Time

The **Manage Your Time** activities ask you to apply what you have learned to your current life.

Goal Setting

Perhaps just as important as time management for an entrepreneur, goal-setting allows you to determine the direction of your business and your life. The two-page Goal Setting feature in Unit 2 will help you set short- and long-term goals.

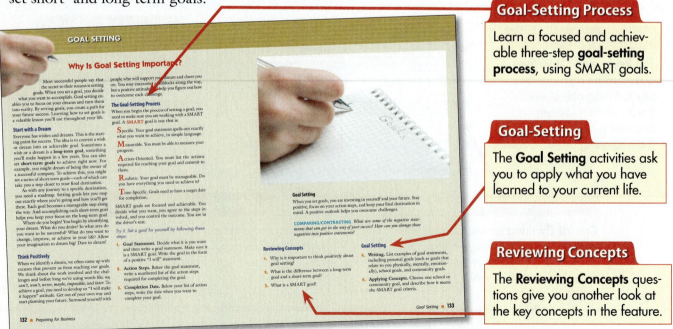

Goal-Setting Process

Learn a focused and achievable three-step **goal-setting process**, using SMART goals.

Goal-Setting

The **Goal Setting** activities ask you to apply what you have learned to your current life.

Reviewing Concepts

The **Reviewing Concepts** questions give you another look at the key concepts in the feature.

Chapter Review and Assessment

The three-page Chapter Review and Assessment is designed to help you review, use, and expand on the basic concepts presented in the chapter.

Check Your Understanding

You can use the **Check Your Understanding** questions to make sure you understand the main ideas presented in the chapter.

Chapter Summary

The **Chapter Summary** provides an overview of the key concepts in the chapter.

Review Vocabulary

Review Vocabulary is an open-ended activity that provides an opportunity to use the vocabulary you learned in the chapter. Typically, you will be describing what you have learned in the chapter to a specific audience who will be unfamiliar with the vocabulary.

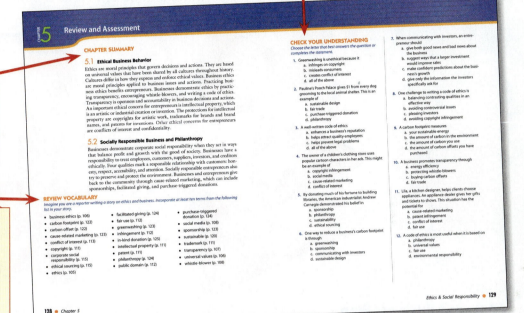

Business Communication

Three **Business Communication** questions ask you to sharpen your communication skills—sometimes alone, sometimes in a group. You will focus on concepts presented in the chapter.

Business Ethics

The **Business Ethics** questions typically present an ethical dilemma in a business setting. Most of these don't really have a correct answer. Consider them from all points of view, and try to determine the role that ethics plays in the scenario.

Business Math

Three **Business Math** questions help you work on your math skills in a business context.

In Your Community

The two **Business in Your Community** activities typically ask you to interact with people, businesses, or organizations in your community. Some will require working in a group or with a partner, others can be done individually.

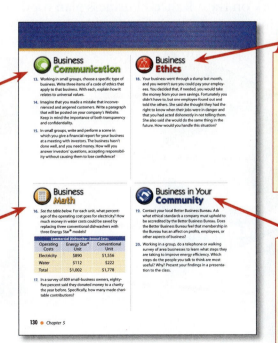

TO THE STUDENT

Standard Business Plan

The ability to prepare a **Standard Business Plan** is the most important learning objective in this textbook and in any entrepreneurship course. You start work on your business plan immediately in Chapter 1. By Chapter 14 you will have created a standard business plan. The standard business plan has three parts. Each part is represented in the business plan symbol and described in the business plan summary.

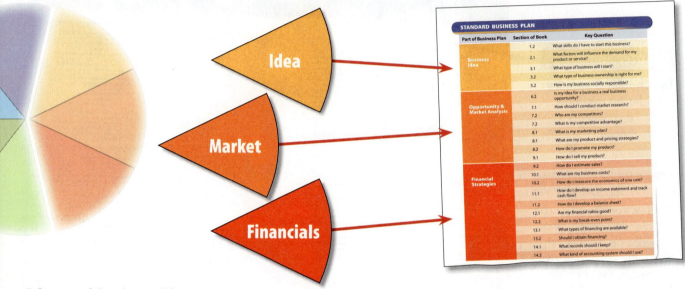

STANDARD BUSINESS PLAN

Part of Business Plan	Section of Book	Key Question
Business Idea	1.2	What skills do I have to start this business?
	2.1	What factors will influence the demand for my product or service?
	3.1	What type of business will I start?
	3.2	What type of business ownership is right for me?
	5.2	How is my business socially responsible?
Opportunity & Market Analysis	6.2	Is my idea for a business a real business opportunity?
	7.1	How should I conduct market research?
	7.2	Who are my competitors?
	7.2	What is my competitive advantage?
	8.1	What is my marketing plan?
	8.1	What are my product and pricing strategies?
	8.2	How do I promote my product?
	9.1	How do I sell my product?
Financial Strategies	9.2	How do I estimate sales?
	10.1	What are my business costs?
	10.2	How do I measure the economics of one unit?
	11.1	How do I develop an income statement and track cash flow?
	11.2	How do I develop a balance sheet?
	12.1	Are my financial ratios good?
	12.2	What is my break-even point?
	13.1	What types of financing are available?
	13.2	Should I obtain financing?
	14.1	What records should I keep?
	14.2	What kind of accounting system should I use?

Advanced Business Plan

Not every business will require all of the **Advanced Business Plan** topics, but any young entrepreneur would be wise to study them for possible future use. Some may be critically important for certain types of businesses. You will start work on the advanced business plan topics in Chapter 15. Each of the four parts is represented in the business plan symbol and described in the business plan summary.

ADVANCED BUSINESS PLAN

Part of Business Plan	Section of Book	Key Question
Organizational Structures	15.1	What organizational structure is right for my business?
	15.1	How should I staff my business?
	15.1	Do I need the help of outside experts?
	15.2	How do I train and motivate employees?
Legal Structures	16.1	Does my product involve intellectual property rights?
	16.1	What contracts will my business require?
	16.2	How will I protect my business by using insurance?
	17.1	How will taxes affect my business?
	17.2	How will government regulations affect my business?
	17.2	How will government regulations affect employees?
Business Management	18.1	How will I manage my business?
	18.2	How do I manage expenses, credit and cash flow?
	19.1	How do I manage production and distribution?
	19.2	How will I manage my operations?
	20.1	How do I manage purchasing?
	20.2	How do I manage inventory?
Plan for Growth	21.1	How can I plan for business growth?
	21.2	What are the challenges of growth?
	22.1	Can I franchise or license my business?
	22.2	When and how should I leave my business?

Case Study

At the end of each unit is a case study that develops through the entire textbook. The case study involves Eva Tan, beginning when she was a high school student in Westerville, Ohio. Watch Eva as she starts her business, makes mistakes, has success, grows her business, and eventually leaves it.

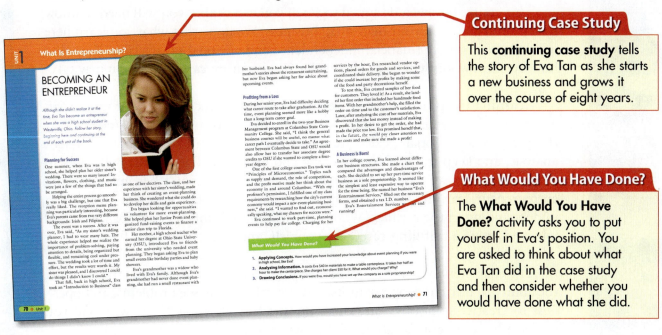

Continuing Case Study

This **continuing case study** tells the story of Eva Tan as she starts a new business and grows it over the course of eight years.

What Would You Have Done?

The **What Would You Have Done?** activity asks you to put yourself in Eva's position. You are asked to think about what Eva Tan did in the case study and then consider whether you would have done what she did.

Business Plan for the Case Study

Because developing a business plan is a critical skill for this course, Eva Tan's initial Business Plan is provided after Unit 3. You get a chance to see what a business plan looks like.

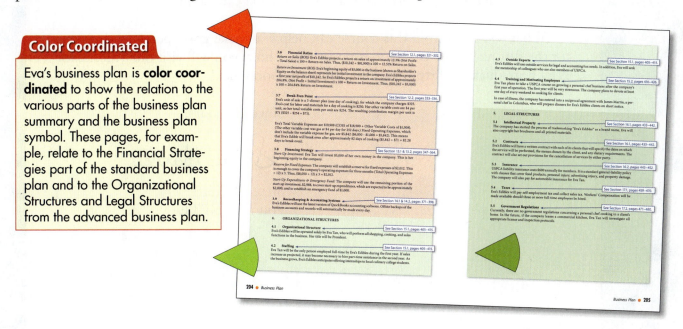

Color Coordinated

Eva's business plan is **color coordinated** to show the relation to the various parts of the business plan summary and the business plan symbol. These pages, for example, relate to the Financial Strategies part of the standard business plan and to the Organizational Structures and Legal Structures from the advanced business plan.

Dear Student,

This course has been designed to teach you everything you will need to know to start and maintain your own small business. We hope that what you learn here will help you achieve financial independence and personal satisfaction. Knowing how business works will be of great value in any future career path you may take.

Learning the principles of entrepreneurship will teach you about more than just business and money, however. In this textbook, you will learn, among other things, how to negotiate, calculate return on investment, perform cost/benefit analysis, and keep track of your income and expenses. These skills will apply to your personal as well as your business life. Even if you don't become a lifelong entrepreneur, learning how to start and operate a small business will give you an understanding of the business world that will make it much easier for you to get jobs and create a fulfilling career for yourself, and thus "own your future."

The characteristics of the successful entrepreneur—a positive mental attitude, the ability to recognize opportunities where others only see problems, and openness to creative solutions—are qualities worth developing. They will help you perform better in any situation life throws at you.

Owning your future will be the key to happiness. You can do so much good for your family, friends, and community by being aware of the opportunities and resources around you. Entrepreneurship is a way to do that—to make your dreams come true and help support the goals of those you care about.

What you learn from this course can help you make good personal decisions for the future. NFTE is here to support you. I hope you will visit our Website for NFTE graduates—http://alumni.nfte.com. Good luck!

Sincerely yours,

Steve Mariotti

Steve Mariotti
Founder, NFTE

BEFORE YOU BEGIN...

Here are some thoughts for you to consider. Thoughts are the foundation for everything you create—your education, your business, and, ultimately, your life.

The secret of success in life is for a man to
be ready for his opportunity when it comes.

– Benjamin Disraeli

If I had eight hours to chop down a
tree, I'd spend six sharpening my ax.

– Abraham Lincoln

When there's nothing to lose and
much to gain by trying, try.

– W. Clement Stone

What really matters is what you
do with what you have.

– Shirley Lord

You must do the thing you
think you cannot do.

– Eleanor Roosevelt

You are equal to anyone, but if you
think you're not, you're not.

– Jake Simmons

Everyone lives by selling something.

– Robert Louis Stevenson

All businesses were launched by
entrepreneurs, and all were once small.

– Nat Shulman

Many a small thing has been made
large by the right kind of advertising.

– Mark Twain

You don't get what you deserve,
you get what you negotiate.

– Chester L. Karrass

Your most unhappy customers are
your greatest source of learning.

– Bill Gates

In the midst of difficulty lies opportunity.

– Albert Einstein

WHAT IS AN ENTREPRENEUR?

YOUR BUSINESS PLAN

In this unit, you'll focus on the **Business Idea** section of the business plan and answer these questions:

- What skills do I have to start this business?
- What factors will influence the demand for my product or service?
- What type of business will I start?
- What type of business ownership is right for me?

CHAPTER 1

INTRODUCTION TO ENTREPRENEURSHIP

1.1 What Is Entrepreneurship?

OBJECTIVES

- Define what it means to be an entrepreneur
- Compare the pros and cons of being an entrepreneur
- Identify successful entrepreneurs and their achievements

VOCABULARY

- apprenticeship
- business
- employee
- entrepreneur
- entrepreneurial
- entrepreneurship
- green company
- internship

? *Think about the following question:*

Have you ever considered starting your own business?

Write your answer (yes or no) on a piece of paper. Be prepared to discuss your answer in class. If you answered "yes," think about what kind of business you'd like to create.

What Is an Entrepreneur?

Most of us earn a living by working in a **business**. A business is an organization that provides products or services, usually to make money. A person who works in a business owned by someone else is an **employee** of that business. On the other hand, someone who creates and runs a business is called an **entrepreneur** (on-tra-prih-NER). To be **entrepreneurial** (on-tra-prih-NER-ee-uhl) means to think or act like an entrepreneur.

How Employees and Entrepreneurs Differ

When an entrepreneur starts a new business, risk is involved. Risk is the chance of losing something. An entrepreneur makes an investment of money, time, and energy in the hope of receiving greater rewards, or benefits. The saying "Nothing ventured, nothing gained" relates to this concept.

Because employees work for someone else and entrepreneurs work for themselves, entrepreneurs risk more than employees. Employees may risk losing a job if they do not perform their work well, but they are paid for their work. Entrepreneurs risk not being able to pay their employees or themselves if business is "slow."

The rewards employees and entrepreneurs get from their work can also be different. A reward can involve money, but it also might be personal satisfaction or independence. As business owners, entrepreneurs are in control of the money made by the business. They also have the final say in all business decisions. As a result, entrepreneurs are ultimately responsible for the success or failure of their businesses.

For example, Carla Hernandez started a fruit smoothie shop. She invested money, time, and effort to start the business. One of her employees created a new smoothie that Carla put on the menu. By doing so, Carla risked the money spent on ingredients and she risked a drop in sales if customers didn't like the new item. But it was a hit. Sales increased. Her employee received a small raise as a reward, but Carla was the one who benefited the most because she owned the business.

Big Business versus Small Business

When people think of business, they tend to focus on large companies such as Ford, Microsoft, and Nike. In reality, more businesses are considered small than big. Small firms employ about half of the U.S. private work force, and they create around 64 percent of all new jobs. The Small Business Administration (SBA), an agency of the U.S. government that provides aid and advice to small businesses, defines a small business as having fewer than 100 employees (fewer than 500 employees in the case of manufacturing companies).

According to the SBA, over 600,000 new businesses are started in the United States every year—and about 500,000 close. Even though

▼ **Figure 1-1**

Internship
Working as an intern or apprentice provides practical experience for students.

Predicting. *What kinds of useful business knowledge might you learn through an internship?*

most businesses begin small, they obviously don't all stay that way. An entrepreneur's goals affect how large a business becomes. For example, suppose someone starts a neighborhood restaurant. The entrepreneur may not want to expand the business to include more than one restaurant, if personal and financial needs are being met. Not everyone is interested in increasing the size of the business.

In other cases, a business may become so successful that it grows beyond the wildest expectations of its owners. That is exactly what happened to Whole Foods Market, Inc. It started in 1980 as one small store in Austin, Texas. Four businesspeople decided the natural food industry was ready for a supermarket format. And they were right! Beginning with a staff of 19, Whole Foods Market was an immediate success. Now Whole Foods Market is the world leader in natural and organic foods, with more than 270 stores in North America and the United Kingdom and over 54,000 employees worldwide.

One way you can gain a sense of what business is like is by taking an **internship**. These work programs provide practical, on-the-job training in a business setting. An internship is similar to an **apprenticeship**. In some apprenticeships, a technical or trade skill is taught, such as carpentry or plumbing. Internships and apprenticeships are usually short-term programs that can last from a few weeks to a year. During this time, an apprentice may or may not be paid. Even so, the experience gained is helpful, for either an employee or an entrepreneur.

 **READING CHECKPOINT**   *What is an entrepreneur?*

Why Be an Entrepreneur?

You might think of many reasons to start your own business. Before doing so, however, it's a good idea to consider the pros and cons of being an entrepreneur. The key is evaluating whether the potential rewards are worth more to you than the risks you will take.

Rewards of Being an Entrepreneur

You may think most people become entrepreneurs to make money. After all, making a good living allows people to provide for their needs and wants instead of depending on others. But more often the biggest reward of becoming an entrepreneur is the feeling of self-sufficiency it brings. Often there is a personal satisfaction that comes from having the freedom to make your own business decisions and then act on them. Additionally, you can display your aptitudes and skills for your family and friends to see. Here are some additional advantages of being an entrepreneur:

- **Making Your Own Rules.** When you own a business, you get to be your own boss. Depending on your business, you can decide what type of schedule you work, where you work, and how and when you get paid. You also have the final word on which products or services the business provides and how they are provided. For example, when you have a creative idea, you have the power to put that idea into action.

Figure 1-2 ▶

Making Your Own Rules
When you own a business, you are your own boss.

Applying Concepts. *What do you think the advantages of being your own boss would be? The disadvantages?*

- **Doing Work You Enjoy.** The majority of most peoples' lives is spent working. Why not spend that time doing something you enjoy? People tend to stay more focused and motivated when they are passionate about their work. This helps a business succeed.

- **Creating Greater Wealth.** Typically, employees can only make the salary a company is willing to pay. However, there's no limit to what an entrepreneur can make. Entrepreneurs can also do more than just make a living from their yearly business earnings. A successful business, particularly one that keeps growing, can often be sold for much more than the amount that was invested in it.

- **Helping Your Community.** Being an entrepreneur opens up opportunities that help make your community and world a better place in which to live. For example, entrepreneurs help others by providing products or services needed by the community. They also create jobs. Entrepreneurs often gain personal satisfaction and community recognition from the time and money they donate to worthy causes.

Risks of Being an Entrepreneur

Business ownership is not without risks. Here are some potentially stressful disadvantages that usually come with being an entrepreneur:

- **Potential Business Failure.** The flip side of getting to make all the business decisions is the possibility of making the wrong ones. Being fully responsible means the success or failure of your

Serial Entrepreneurship

Most people who find something they love want to keep doing it. Why should it be any different with entrepreneurs? A growing percentage of people who start successful businesses do it again. And again. This is called serial entrepreneurship. These serial entrepreneurs take the lessons learned from their first businesses and apply them to new businesses.

For several reasons, serial entrepreneurship is more common now than in the past. First, companies—particularly technology companies—develop and mature more quickly now and can be sold while the founders are still young. Second, resources for growing a company are more easily available because of the Internet and the concentration of new businesses in certain geographic areas, such as Silicon Valley in California. With customers only a click away, many new businesses can become wildly profitable in just a few years.

Serial entrepreneurs report that they are not driven by the desire for money so much as the impulse to innovate and to challenge themselves. There are resources specifically designed to help entrepreneurs who want to start not one, not two, but several successful businesses.

THINKING CRITICALLY

Comparing/Contrasting. Take some time to think about the differences and similarities between a serial entrepreneur and an entrepreneur who sticks to one business. Write down two similarities and two differences these people might have.

For more information on serial entrepreneurship, go to "Entrepreneurship Issues" on the Student Center at entrepreneurship.pearson.com.

business rests on you. The time and money you invest in starting and running a business just might not pay off.

- **Unexpected Obstacles.** Problems can happen that you don't expect. This can be discouraging and frustrating unless you choose to keep a positive attitude. Facing these challenges can get scary and lonely, especially if you don't have the emotional support of family and friends.

- **Financial Insecurity.** The amount of money you can pay yourself may go up or down, depending on how well your business is performing. Many new businesses don't make much money in the beginning, so you may not always be able to pay yourself. During rough times, you may even have to put more money into the business just to pay your employees.

- **Long Hours and Hard Work.** It's not unusual for entrepreneurs to work a lot of extra hours to make their businesses successful. This is especially true during the initial start-up process. These long hours can decrease the time you have available for your friends and family. Until you can afford to hire other people to help, you may have to perform many types of tasks. This will require discipline and a willingness to do whatever needs to be done.

 **READING CHECKPOINT** *What are the risks and the rewards of being an entrepreneur?*

Entrepreneurship in History

Entrepreneurship (on-trah-prih-NER-ship), the process of being an entrepreneur, is more than just learning how to run a business. It can affect the economy, your community, and ultimately the world in which we live. Here is a brief list of examples of entrepreneurs who have changed the world in one way or another.

The 1800s

- At 12, Thomas Edison already showed signs of being an entrepreneur. He was selling newspapers, candy, and snacks at the local railroad station. By 14 he had his own newspaper business. Gathering the daily news releases that were teletyped into the station, he pulled out the "scoops" and convinced over 300 commuters to subscribe to his paper, which he called the *Weekly Herald*. One of the most prolific inventors in history, he held over 1000 patents, Edison is credited with numerous inventions that contributed to mass communication. One of his inventions was the phonograph. Edison's greatest achievement, however, was creating a practical and economical system to generate and distribute electric light, heat, and power. He changed the world forever.

Early Edison phonograph

- P.T. Barnum was 60 years old when his circus staged its first show. The circus generated $400,000 in sales in the first year. Later, it became known as the "Greatest Show on Earth" and still tours all over the United States.

The 1900s

- In 1903, two friends—William Harley and Arthur Davidson—wanted to improve on the two-wheeled bicycle, and the motorcycle was born. Harley-Davidson was one of only two manufacturers to stay afloat during the Depression of the 1930s. Now it has out ridden its competition to become the world's largest manufacturer of motorcycles, with revenues of over $41 million annually.

- Maggie Lena Walker was a staunch advocate of human rights, humanitarian causes, self-sufficiency, and improving race relations. Through the philosophy of turning "nickels into dollars," she became the first woman to charter a bank in the United States. Her bank, the St. Luke Penny Savings Bank, opened in 1903 with receipts totaling $9,430.44. Today it has assets of over $116 million. Now known as the Consolidated Bank and Trust Company, Walker's bank is the oldest continuously operating minority-owned bank in the United States. Actively committed to its philosophy, Walker remained its chairperson until her death. Among her many honors, she was inducted into the U.S. Business Hall of Fame, a school was built in her honor, and her home has been designated as a historic site.

Present

- In Sweden, Ingvar Kamprad learned at an early age how to make money from available resources. By buying matches in bulk at a low price, he could sell them in smaller quantities at a higher one. He invested the money he made in this and other small business ventures. When Kamprad was 17, he founded IKEA, a furniture company. IKEA has expanded to 300 stores in over 35 countries—and Ingvar Kamprad has become one of the ten wealthiest people in the world.

- Who can imagine a world without computers? In 1976, Stephen Wozniak and Steve Jobs started a company with the goal of bringing personal computers to everyone. To help pay for their venture, they sold some of their personal possessions for a total of $1,300. Weeks later, the first Apple computers were sold. In 1980, Apple went public and made Wozniak and Jobs multi-millionaires. Today, Apple also sells such popular devices as the iPod and the iPhone.

- When Russell Simmons was a young man, he turned his passion for hip-hop into a venture that is now worth millions. His Def Jam Recordings launched a cultural revolution and his vision impacted music, fashion, film, television, and social action. Named one of the Top 25 Most Influential People of the Past 20 Years by USA Today, Simmons started a movement that not only created wealth but also changed America's understanding of African-American culture.

- In 1995, Dineh Mohajer wanted some light-blue nail polish to match her sandals. She decided to combine different polishes in her bathroom to get the color she wanted. When she wore her custom nail polish, lots of people noticed—and she began taking orders as a result. Within two years her company, called Hard Candy, had sales of $10 million and was producing dozens of unusual colors.

▲ *Apple's iPod*

Today's Entrepreneurs

As in the past, present-day entrepreneurs pay attention to social trends to attract customers. To be successful in today's business world, most entrepreneurs use the Internet in some way. In fact, more and more companies are making the Internet their primary business resource. Amazon.com is a good example, conducting its business entirely online. Typically, these companies use an electronic address that ends in ".com" and are sometimes referred to as dot-com companies.

Another contemporary trend is running a business in ways that are friendly to the environment. A **green company** is one that adopts business practices aimed at protecting or improving the environment. For instance, Excellent Packaging & Supply distributes products made from "green" resources. One of these products is SpudWare, utensils made from corn and potato starch that can withstand boiling water. Another example of a green company is SELCO-India. It provides solar-powered lighting to mostly rural areas in India and other developing countries.

Today, entrepreneurs operate all types of businesses. They are willing to take risks because they hope for great rewards. In the process, they help make life better for many people with the products, services, and jobs they provide.

 *What is a green company?*

 Your Business Plan. Begin developing your standard business plan. Go to "Section 1.1" of the *Business Plan Project* in your *Student Activity Workbook*, or "Section 1.1" of the BizTech Software.

ASSESSMENT 1.1

Reviewing Objectives

1. How do entrepreneurs and employees differ?
2. What are four rewards and four risks of being an entrepreneur?
3. Name three successful entrepreneurs and describe what they achieved.

Critical Thinking

4. **Applying Concepts.** Choose an entrepreneur from the past who is not discussed in this chapter, and describe the risks and rewards involved in starting his or her business. Discuss whether the entrepreneur made life better in some way with a product or service.
5. **Inferring.** Why do you think an entrepreneur might choose to keep a business small rather than expand it?

Working Together

Form a discussion panel to debate whether the rewards of entrepreneurship outweigh the risks. Half of the panel should focus on the rewards of entrepreneurship and the other half on the risks.

Science
Conserving Natural Resources

Some natural resources, such as oil and water, are becoming harder and harder to obtain in many parts of the world. Trees are being cut down faster than people can plant and grow new ones. Use the Internet to research ways that entrepreneurs, and the employees that work for them, can help conserve our natural resources. Present your findings in a report.

OBJECTIVES

- Describe who becomes an entrepreneur
- List the key characteristics of an entrepreneur
- Explore ways to build your business potential
- Explain the value of learning about entrepreneurship

VOCABULARY

- aptitude
- attitude
- intrapreneurship
- mentor
- self-assessment
- skill
- vision

? *Think about the following question:*

What kinds of abilities are needed to run a business?

List at least five. Be as specific as you can. Be prepared to discuss your answers in class.

Who Are Entrepreneurs?

Periodically, the United States Census Bureau conducts a survey of business owners, many of whom are entrepreneurs. The most recent survey received feedback from an estimated 16.7 million businesses nationwide. Here are some highlights:

- Sixty-four percent of the business owners had some college education when they started the business.

- More than 60 percent of the business owners used money of their own, or from their families, to start or buy the business.

- Slightly more than half of the business owners who had employees worked overtime (that is, the business owners worked more than 40 hours per week). About half of the businesses were home-based.

- About a third of the business owners were over 55 years old, 29 percent were between 45 and 54, 24 percent were between 35 and 44, 12 percent were between 25 and 34, and 2 percent were under 25.

Minority-Owned Businesses

1982
7%

2002
18%

According to research by the Small Business Administration, the number of women and minority entrepreneurs in the United States has steadily increased in recent years. Studies show that minority-owned businesses went from 7 percent of the total to 18 percent between 1982 and 2002. Businesses owned by women also increased, from 1.76 million to 3.75 million between 1976 and 2000.

Based on the survey, you can say this about American entrepreneurs: many work from home, invest their own money, are educated, and are men and women of all ages and nationalities—and they work hard.

READING CHECKPOINT *What does research show about the number of women and minority entrepreneurs in recent years?*

Characteristics of Successful Entrepreneurs

Self-assessment—evaluating your strengths and weaknesses—is an important part of becoming an entrepreneur. Self-assessment helps you maximize your strong points and strengthen your weaker ones. The key thing to remember is that everybody has strengths and weaknesses. It's what you do with what you have that counts. Also, entrepreneurs who are self-aware are able to focus on hiring employees with characteristics that complement their own.

Aptitudes and Attitudes

An **aptitude** is a natural ability to do a particular type of work or activity well. For example, you may find math very easy, or you may naturally be good at sports. Aptitudes can sometimes be developed through hard work.

An **attitude** is a way of viewing or thinking about something that affects how you feel about it. Entrepreneurs tend to be people with positive attitudes. Instead of seeing a situation as a problem, they look at it as an opportunity. This helps them find solutions more easily than people who think negatively.

Think about your own experience. Positive thinking and talking tends to make you feel happier and have more energy. You feel motivated to take steps toward accomplishing your goals. In contrast, negative thinking and talking tends to make you feel less happy and reduce your energy. You will be much less likely to take action to solve a problem.

Even though you didn't get to choose which aptitudes you'd inherit, you do have the power to choose your attitude. An entrepreneur needs to have self-esteem. Entrepreneurs need to view themselves in a positive way. A positive attitude can make the difference between failure and success. Someone with a strong aptitude but a negative attitude will probably achieve less than someone who has less natural ability but a positive attitude. Throughout history, entrepreneurs have proved that thoughts have power. But only you can ultimately decide who you will become.

Personal Characteristics

No one is born with all the characteristics needed to be a successful entrepreneur. But if you keep a positive attitude and believe in yourself, you can develop many of them. In the following list, notice the personality traits you already possess. Then focus on the ones you think you need to develop.

- **Courage:** A willingness to take risks in spite of possible losses.

- **Creativity:** Inventing new ways of doing things; thinking outside the box.

- **Curiosity:** The desire to learn and ask questions.

- **Determination:** Refusing to quit in spite of obstacles.

- **Discipline:** The ability to stay focused and follow a schedule to meet deadlines.

- **Empathy:** Being sensitive to the thoughts and feelings of others.

- **Enthusiasm:** Being passionate about something; the ability to see problems as opportunities.

> Watch your thoughts — they become words.
> Watch your words — they become actions.
> Watch your actions — they become habits.
> Watch your habits — they become character.
> Watch your character — it becomes your destiny.

▲ *Based on a Chinese proverb*

◀ **Figure 1-3**

Enthusiasm
Being enthusiastic is helpful in business.

Drawing Conclusions. *Which personality traits do you have? Which do you need to develop?*

- **Flexibility:** The ability to adapt to new situations; a willingness to change.

- **Honesty:** A commitment to being truthful and sincere with others.

- **Patience:** Recognizing that most goals are not reached overnight.

- **Responsibility:** Being accountable for your decisions and actions; not passing the buck.

Skills

A **skill** is an ability that's learned through training and practice. For example, you didn't know how to tie a shoe when you were born. You learned this skill through practice and the help of adults. Some of the basic skills entrepreneurs need are:

- **Business Skills:** Understanding how to create and manage a business.

- **Communication Skills:** The ability to listen well, write well, and speak well.

- **Computer Skills:** The ability to use technological tools effectively.

- **Decision-Making and Problem-Solving Skills:** Knowing how to apply logic, information, and past experiences to new decisions and problems.

- **Mathematical Skills:** Using math to create budgets, keep accurate records, and analyze financial statements.

- **Organizational Skills:** The knack of keeping tasks and information in order; the ability to plan well and manage your time.

- **People Skills:** The ability to persuade and motivate people; knowing both how to be a leader and work in a team.

 *What are some of the basic skills needed by an entrepreneur?*

Increasing Your Potential

Don't be discouraged from becoming an entrepreneur just because you don't yet have all the traits and skills you will need. You can increase your business and entrepreneurial potential by focusing on six specific areas. Even if you never become an entrepreneur, paying attention to these areas will help you be more successful in life.

Business Knowledge

Make a habit of reading magazine and newspaper articles on business topics. Use the Internet to research business subjects. Watch films or television programs about successful entrepreneurs. This can help you learn more about business. If you know someone who owns a business, discuss the business with that individual.

Financial Skills

Strengthen your math skills by taking a course in accounting, personal finance, or investing. If math is a difficult subject, ask a teacher to spend a little extra time with you before or after school. Team up with a friend who is good at math. Play math games or do math homework together.

Career Exploration

First, evaluate your strengths and weaknesses. Be as honest as you can about your characteristics without being too easy or too hard on yourself. Remember, nobody is perfect, but everyone has something to contribute to the world. Practice thinking and acting as if you already have the characteristics you want to develop. A positive attitude will keep you on the right track.

Next, explore career areas that interest you. Include fields that match with aptitudes and skills you have or are developing. There are many books, magazines, and Internet sites on careers. Ask a career or guidance counselor at your school for research suggestions.

Think about putting together a career portfolio that summarizes your achievements and lists your activities. Keep your résumé in your portfolio, along with any cover letters you've written and any letters of reference that you may have received. This way, everything related to your future career will be in one place. If you plan to go to college, your career portfolio would be an ideal location for keeping college scholarship information.

Finally, talk with people who have a career you think you'd like. Some companies have programs that allow employees to bring someone to work with them for a day. During that time, you get to observe what that particular job is like.

Community Awareness

Look for volunteering opportunities in your community. Also, find out if any companies in your area provide internships where you can get some practical, on-the-job experience. If you know of a particular problem in your community, consider how you can help improve the situation.

Education

Learning is a lifetime occupation, no matter what career you choose. Take advantage of chances to learn new things, ask lots of questions, and strive to do your best in whatever you do. Obtaining an educational certificate, diploma, or degree not only benefits you personally, it can also help open doors to more career opportunities. Whether in school or working in a job, remember that you are responsible for what you learn—and no one else.

Relationships

Spend time with people who believe in you and inspire you. Being around positive people will help you stay positive and accomplish more. People who are negative and complain all the time will influence you to be the same way. Some organizations have programs in which experienced people volunteer to share their knowledge. This **mentor** will provide free guidance, tutoring, and suggestions for achieving your goals.

What six main areas can you focus on to increase your business and entrepreneurial potential?

YOUR BUSINESS **CAREER**

Choosing to Attend College

Like most high school students, you probably regard the decisions about what you'll do after graduation to be among the most important ones you'll ever make. They certainly will influence the rest of your life. Perhaps the most important decision is whether to continue with your education or to enter the world of work immediately.

To make a good decision about continuing your education at a two- or four-year college or a trade school, you'll need to think about these questions:

- What are your ultimate career goals?

- Is a two- or four-year degree typically required for the type of work you want to do? If not, what education or skill is necessary (and how will you acquire it)?

- What are your feelings about school?

- Have you talked this decision over with your parents, other adult family members, teachers, or mentors?

- If you wish to continue your education, how will you fund it?

- Will you work while attending school?

- Where will you live while attending school?

THINKING CRITICALLY

Classifying. Working in teams of four, brainstorm a list of careers, appropriate colleges for those careers, and appropriate programs/majors (or job training) at that college. Be creative. Focus on careers that interest you.

For more help in thinking about whether to attend college, go to "Your Business Career" on the Student Center at entrepreneurship.pearson.com.

Why Study Entrepreneurship?

Owning a business isn't for everyone. But that's okay because both employees and entrepreneurs are needed in the world of work. Whether or not you choose to become an entrepreneur, the things you will learn in this book can benefit you in many ways. There are two primary reasons why studying entrepreneurship makes sense, even if you don't plan to be an entrepreneur: you learn to think like an entrepreneur and you develop a vision for your life.

Think Like an Entrepreneur

Thinking like an entrepreneur and being conscious of how to make a business run more successfully can help you be a better employee. In effect, you can treat someone else's business as if it were yours. Employers often promote these kinds of employees, the ones who think entrepreneurially. Here are three ways to think like an entrepreneur when you are working as an employee:

- **Observe.** Keep on the lookout for chances to learn new skills and accept new responsibilities. Staying aware of what goes on around you can help generate new ideas for business growth. This includes ideas for new products or services that customers may need or want.

- **Listen.** Pay attention to what others have to say. Challenges that other employees are facing may give you ideas for making business improvements.

- **Think.** Instead of complaining about a problem, analyze it. Then suggest possible solutions.

More and more businesses today encourage the practice of **intrapreneurship** (in-tra-prih-NER-ship). That is, they give employees opportunities to be creative and try out new ideas, almost like being an entrepreneur within the company.

Thinking like an entrepreneur can also help you make smarter decisions about managing the money you earn. This includes how to keep good personal records, make wise purchases, invest personal funds to earn more money, and plan for retirement.

Develop a Vision for Your Life

Learning about entrepreneurship often inspires people to develop a **vision** for their life. A vision is a "picture" of what you want the future to be. What kind of life do you want? What things are most important to you?

How can learning about entrepreneurship help you to be a better employee?

Figure 1-4 ▶

Vision
Entrepreneurship can help you form and fulfill your life's vision.

Applying Concepts. *After reading this chapter, what type of vision do you see for your life?*

 Your Business Plan. Continue developing your standard business plan. Go to "Section 1.2" of the *Business Plan Project* in your *Student Activity Workbook*, or "Section 1.2" of the BizTech Software.

ASSESSMENT 1.2

Reviewing Objectives

1. Based on U.S. Census Bureau data, name the top two things entrepreneurs tend to have in common.
2. Name at least five personal characteristics that an entrepreneur needs.
3. List the six main areas that will help improve your business and entrepreneurial potential.
4. Name two reasons, other than becoming an entrepreneur, for learning about entrepreneurship.

Critical Thinking

5. **Recognizing Patterns.** List several personal characteristics that might hinder someone from becoming an entrepreneur. In what ways could these characteristics also prevent someone from becoming a valued employee?
6. **Relating Concepts.** Develop a vision and mission for your life now, as a student. Then develop a vision and mission for your future life. Keep these simple.

Working Together

Working with a partner, identify two career areas that interest you both. Each of you will take one of the career topics and research it, using the Occupational Outlook Handbook in your library or online (www.bls.gov/oco). Then, together, prepare a report that compares and contrasts the information you found.

Language Arts
Mentor Role-Playing

Imagine that you've volunteered to be a mentor to a middle-school student who wants to start a business. Based on what you've learned so far, write a simple plan for teaching your student about the concept of entrepreneurship. Suggest activities that will help the student apply the newly learned knowledge.

Entrepreneurial Skills for Whatever You Do

When Robert Reffkin was 11 years old, he realized that his mother was struggling financially as a single parent. "I knew that I wanted to earn money to help her out. For the next three years I thought about how to do that." When he saw a DJ at work at a party, Robert thought being a DJ might be a good way for him to earn money so he could help his mother. "I learned from the DJ that he made good money, had fun, and had a lot of independence," said Robert. "I love music so I decided to become a DJ."

Becoming a DJ

For the next three years, Robert saved up every dollar he could. When he had enough money, he bought the minimal amount of equipment it took to be a DJ and started his business. "I created professional contracts, a music list, a request list, and some business cards. Finally, I bought the equipment, started to advertise, and I got my first job that summer. It was a small house party that only paid $50, but people liked my work and referred me to their friends. I was on my way!"

Robert worked at school dances, homecomings, bar mitzvahs, weddings, NAACP parties, and Black Student Union dances. He also organized his own events. Being a DJ was a physically and emotionally tiring job and combining it with school left him exhausted.

Learning How to Run a Business

In high school, Robert took an entrepreneurship course in which he learned some critical business and professional skills he didn't have. He developed a business plan, which won a $500 grant that he invested in his business. Robert's success in business gave him the confidence to pursue bigger dreams, even though many people discouraged him. For example, when his high school counselor said he wouldn't be admitted to Columbia University, Robert decided to apply.

Making His Skills Part of His Life

In the course of applying to Columbia, Robert used everything he had learned in his entrepreneurship course and from running his own business. He interacted with the university's admissions officers with the

▲ *Robert Reffkin*

same level of professionalism he employed with his clients. He gave them his business card, sent them his résumé, wrote them thank-you letters, and followed up on major developments in his life. Robert believes that "this lent credibility to my application" and led to being accepted at Columbia. He received a partial scholarship and was able to help pay for the rest of his college education with the money he had earned from his DJ business.

Robert's entrepreneurial skills and successful DJ business gave him the "extraordinary confidence and the entrepreneurial belief that anything is possible." He graduated from Columbia in 2½ years and went on to become a consultant at McKinsey & Co., get his MBA at Columbia, and become a White House Fellow and then a Wall Street investment banker.

Thinking Like an Entrepreneur

1. Robert picked a business that appealed to his love of music and also one that would pay well. How would you decide on a business opportunity?
2. What entrepreneurial skills do you think would be necessary to start a DJ business?
3. Robert believes that entrepreneurship will help you in other aspects of your life. What do you think?

CHAPTER SUMMARY

1.1 What Is Entrepreneurship?

An entrepreneur is someone who creates and runs his or her own business. In contrast, an employee is a person who works in a business owned by someone else. When an entrepreneur starts a new business, risk is involved. An entrepreneur is willing to risk an investment of money, time, and energy in the hope of gaining greater rewards, or benefits. Perhaps the biggest reward for an entrepreneur is empowerment. Other rewards are making your own rules, doing work you enjoy, helping your community, and creating wealth. Some of the risks of being an entrepreneur are potential business failure, unexpected obstacles, financial insecurity, and long hours and hard work. Entrepreneurs throughout history have demonstrated that entrepreneurship involves more than just learning how to run a business. It can affect the economy, the community, and ultimately the world. As a result, entrepreneurs help to improve life not only for themselves, but also for many others by providing products, services, and jobs.

1.2 Characteristics of an Entrepreneur

Entrepreneurs include people of all ages from all over the world. In the United States, more than half of the entrepreneurs have some college education, invest their own money in their businesses, and work over 40 hours per week. Before becoming an entrepreneur, self-assessment is important. Evaluating your aptitudes, attitudes, personal characteristics, and skills will help determine what areas you need to strengthen. Entrepreneurs tend to be people with positive attitudes. Instead of seeing problems, they see opportunities. Even if you choose not to become an entrepreneur, here are two good reasons for studying entrepreneurship: thinking and acting like an entrepreneur will help you become a more valued employee, and it can lead you to develop a vision for your life.

REVIEW VOCABULARY

Suppose your friend Mary tells you she is thinking about starting a business. However, she isn't sure if becoming an entrepreneur is right for her. Prepare a questionnaire that will help Mary evaluate her options and her entrepreneurial potential. Include at least half of the following terms somewhere in the questionnaire:

- apprenticeship (p. 7)
- aptitude (p. 14)
- attitude (p. 14)
- business (p. 5)
- employee (p. 5)
- entrepreneur (p. 5)
- entrepreneurial (p. 5)
- entrepreneurship (p. 10)
- green company (p. 11)
- internship (p. 7)
- intrapreneurship (p. 19)
- mentor (p. 18)
- self-assessment (p. 14)
- skill (p. 16)
- vision (p. 19)

CHECK YOUR UNDERSTANDING

Choose the letter that best answers the question or completes the statement.

1. An entrepreneur
   a. has the final say in business decisions
   b. may not employ anyone else
   c. is responsible for the success or failure of his or her business
   d. all of the above

2. Which of the following is *not* a risk for an entrepreneur?
   a. potential business failure
   b. financial stability
   c. financial insecurity
   d. long hours and hard work

3. How many business owners have home-based businesses?
   a. about 75 percent
   b. about 50 percent
   c. about 25 percent
   d. fewer than 10 percent

4. A natural ability to do a particular type of work or activity well is called
   a. a skill
   b. an attitude
   c. an aptitude
   d. self-esteem

5. When a business encourages employees to be creative within the company, the practice is called
   a. entrepreneurship
   b. creating a vision
   c. implementing a mission
   d. intrapreneurship

6. What is a dot-com company?
   a. a small company
   b. a company that runs most or all of its business from the Internet
   c. a company that adopts business practices aimed at protecting or improving the environment
   d. a foreign company

7. What is possibly the biggest reward of becoming an entrepreneur?
   a. empowerment
   b. fame
   c. money
   d. none of the above

8. A common standard that defines a non-manufacturing business as small is
   a. having fewer than 500 employees
   b. having fewer than 250 employees
   c. having fewer than 100 employees
   d. having fewer than 50 employees

9. As an entrepreneur, the amount of money you receive from your company
   a. is constant, like a paycheck for any other employee
   b. is typically less than for an employee
   c. is typically more than for an employee
   d. may go up or down, depending on the business

10. As an entrepreneur, the amount of time you spend working is typically
    a. constant—35 to 40 hours a week, just like an employee
    b. a little less than for an employee
    c. more than for an employee, particularly during initial start-up
    d. significantly less than for an employee— around 20 hours a week

11. What percentage of business owners use their own money to start the business?
    a. more than 75 percent
    b. more than 60 percent but less than 75 percent
    c. more than 40 percent but less than 60 percent
    d. less than 40 percent

12. An experienced person who volunteers to provide free guidance, tutoring, and suggestions to younger individuals is called a(n)
    a. mentor
    b. intrapreneur
    c. entrepreneur
    d. employee

Business Communication

13. Make a list of activities or tasks you've done in the past (hobbies, part-time jobs, Boy or Girl Scouts, science fairs, school activities, classes, and so on). Then create another list that identifies the kind of personal characteristics and skills needed to perform those activities. Based on the two lists, write an essay that describes how past experiences could help you as an entrepreneur.

14. Using a library and/or the Internet, research information about the use of the Internet by small businesses. Consider these questions: Do small businesses use the Internet more than large ones? How important is the Internet for a small business compared to a big business? Write a report on your findings.

15. Create a poster with a collage that illustrates the vision you currently have for your life.

Business Ethics

18. You are walking to work with one of your employees. On the way, you stop to get a newspaper at a self-pay newspaper box. You insert the required number of coins, open the door, and pick up a newspaper. Before closing the door, you ask your employee if he would like a newspaper too. "Two for the price of one," you say. First, resolve whether this is an ethical action. Then describe the impact it could have on your employee. Finally, consider whether this action could have a larger impact on your company.

Business Math

16. Studies show that about 18 percent of all businesses in the United States are minority-owned. Brian lives in Centerville, a town with a population of 25,000 and 200 businesses. Assuming that the national percentage holds true for the businesses in Centerville, how many of these are minority-owned?

17. Businesses owned by women increased from 1.76 million to 3.75 million between the years of 1976 and 2000. Calculate the percentage rate that women-owned businesses increased during this time period.

Business in Your Community

19. Working with another student, research businesses in your community who welcome volunteers. What kind of experience or training, if any, is needed by a volunteer? What type of entrepreneurial skills could you strengthen if you became a volunteer?

20. Interview an entrepreneur or small business owner in your community. Ask this individual to share stories of successes and failures. Ask which personal characteristics or skills have contributed most to business success. Then ask what the owner would do differently if starting the business today.

The Internet and the World Wide Web

The world changed in the 1990s. That was when the Internet expanded into popular use. Today nearly a billion-and-a-half people use the Internet. You probably use it yourself. But what is it, really? The **Internet** is a global system of interconnected networks. It is really a network of networks and includes all the hardware and software that allows computers on the network to be connected.

The World Wide Web

Perhaps the most important element of the Internet (and the one that people most often think of) is the **World Wide Web**. This is a huge set of documents (some with pictures, and other elements) that are linked together. One of these documents is called a **Web page**. A collection of Web pages is a **Website**. You can visit a Website and buy products, find information, or meet people, for example. **Web surfing** is a process of visiting one Website after another. One way to surf the Web is to click on the links in a Website. A **link** takes you to a related Web page or Website. Links are usually a different color from other text or underlined.

Websites are stored on a **server**. These are computers that contain all the information you see on the Website, including Web pages, other documents, videos, graphics, and sound files. When you visit a Website, the server is actually transferring all the required information to display on your computer. When a server isn't working, you can't visit the site. Because companies now invest so much in their Websites, many install multiple servers so that, if one goes down, the others pick up the slack. This way, the Website will always be "on line."

HTML

Web pages are created by using the **HTML** computer language. (HTML stands for Hypertext Markup Language.) Programmers use this language to identify how text is used on the Web page (as a link, as a paragraph, as a list, and so on). HTML also controls the appearance of a Web page. For example, when you see <b> and </b> around a word, it indicates that the word will appear in boldface. So <b>sample text</b> would make the words "sample text" appear bold on the Website.

Web Browsers

A **Web browser** is software that enables you to navigate the Web. It is located on your computer and works together with the Website's server to produce an image of a Web page on your computer. You can't view Web pages without a Web browser. A browser also allows you to "bookmark" your favorite Websites. This means you can add the Website location to a list of favorite sites. Then you can click on one of your favorite Websites and the browser will display the site immediately. Common Web browsers are Microsoft's Internet Explorer and Apple's Safari.

Today, no entrepreneur or businessperson should be unaware of the power of the Internet and the World Wide Web. They can help almost any business. In some cases, business would be impossible without them.

Tech Vocabulary

- HTML
- Internet
- link
- server
- Web browser
- Web page
- Web surfing
- Website
- World Wide Web

Check Yourself

1. What is the Internet and when did it expand into popular use?
2. What is the World Wide Web?
3. What is HTML?
4. What does a Web browser do?

What Do You Think?

Classifying. What are some examples of businesses that would be impossible without the Internet and the World Wide Web?

CHAPTER 2

ENTREPRENEURSHIP & THE ECONOMY

Importance of Entrepreneurship in the Economy

OBJECTIVES

- Describe an economic system
- Identify different economic systems
- Examine supply and demand relationships
- Explore the role of competition in a market economy
- Describe the profit motive
- Learn about nonprofit organizations

VOCABULARY

- capital
- capitalism
- command economy
- demand
- demand curve
- economic system
- economics
- economics of one unit
- economy
- enterprise
- equilibrium point
- equilibrium price
- equilibrium quantity
- free enterprise system
- market economy
- mixed economy
- nonprofit organization
- profit motive
- scarcity
- supply
- supply and demand curve
- supply curve
- voluntary exchange

Think about the following question:

Is making a profit a good thing?

Write your answer (yes or no) on a piece of paper. Be prepared to discuss your answer in class.

What Is an Economic System?

Economics is a social science concerned with how people satisfy their demands for goods (things you can buy) and services (things people do for a fee) when the supply of those goods and services is limited. This is a somewhat technical definition, so what does it really mean?

Economics is all about the flow of goods and services between people. This is measured in numbers, so economics always involves mathematics. However, economics is called a social science because *people* play the central role in it. It is people who decide which goods and services have value and what that value is. It is people who decide how goods and services should be used and how they will be distributed within a society. It is people who decide whether to buy or to sell goods and services. Ultimately, math may be the language of economics, but people are its soul.

Earth's population grows larger every day. More people means there will be a greater demand for food, clothing, housing, and all the other essentials of life. These essentials are what we *need*. But we also want things that are not necessary to survive. These are our *wants*. People try to satisfy their needs and wants by buying goods and services that have value to them. The demand for goods and services is often larger than the supply that can be provided. When there are not enough to meet the demand, the result is a **scarcity** of those goods and services.

An **economic system** (or **economy**) is a method used by a society to allocate goods and services among its people and to cope with scarcity. Political, moral, and cultural factors affect what kinds of economic systems develop and thrive in different societies.

Every economic system answers four basic questions. They are the fundamental questions of economics.

Fundamental Questions of Economics

- What goods and services are produced?

- What quantity of goods and services are produced?

- How are goods and services produced?

- For whom are goods and services produced?

What is an economic system?

Types of Economic Systems

Two very different types of economic systems are often used to compare how societies deal with the fundamental questions of economics. These two types of economic systems are the command economy and the market economy. In a **command economy**, the government controls the production, allocation, and prices of goods and services. In a **market economy**, suppliers and consumers control the production, allocation, and prices of goods and services.

In reality, no country has a pure command economy or a pure market economy. This leads to a third type of economic system, a **mixed economy**. This is an economic system that blends elements of the command economy and the market economy. All modern economies are actually mixed. However, most countries lean so strongly toward one model or the other that their systems are called command economies or market economies.

The Command Economy

In a command economy, the government owns or manages the nation's resources and businesses. The government controls what suppliers produce, how much is produced, and how it is produced. The government also regulates how goods and services are distributed throughout the country and the prices people pay for them. Ultimately, the government decides the answers to the fundamental questions of economics.

Command economies are associated with political systems in which the government has strict control over social and economic affairs. Socialism and communism are two political systems that are strongly associated with command economies. The former Soviet Union featured many elements of a pure command economy. Governments run by dictators, or controlled by one political party or one ruling family, also lean toward the command economy.

Although no country at present has a pure command economy, some nations come close to it. China, Russia, Syria, Iran, Haiti, Cuba, Vietnam, North Korea, Guyana, Venezuela, Zimbabwe, Angola, Republic of Congo, and the Central African Republic are said to have command economies. In these countries, government planners usually make economic decisions and long-term plans for the nation. The government controls most resources and businesses. Entrepreneurship may be allowed to a small degree, so long as it does not interfere with the overall government control of the economy.

The Market Economy

In a market economy, suppliers produce whatever goods and services they wish and set prices based on what consumers are willing to pay.

▼ **Figure 2-1**
Voluntary Exchange
Voluntary exchange is a transaction in which both suppliers and consumers believe they benefit.
Drawing Conclusions. *How does the consumer benefit in this transaction? The supplier?*

Prices are responsive to consumer demand. The government does not tell businesses what to produce nor does it tell consumers what to buy. This system is characterized by individual freedom of choice and voluntary exchange. **Voluntary exchange** is a transaction in which both suppliers and consumers believe they benefit.

Another name for the market economy is the **free enterprise system**. People are free to become entrepreneurs and own and operate an **enterprise** (business). There are also many investment opportunities in a market economy. Individuals can invest money in their own businesses or those of others. Another name for the cash and goods a business owns is **capital**. That's why the market economy or free enterprise system is also referred to as **capitalism**. Individuals and businesses are free to own and trade goods and invest cash in businesses.

The democratic political system is associated with the market economy. Democracies typically favor personal choice, voluntary exchange, and the right of individuals to own property, businesses, and capital. Although no country has a pure market economy, the United States, Canada, Australia, Hong Kong, Singapore, and many western European nations are said to have market economies, because they allow much economic freedom for individuals. This does not mean that their governments exert no control over economic decisions. The level of government intervention varies by country. So some free enterprise systems are actually "freer" than others.

The United States has one of the freest market economies in the world. Americans are free to become entrepreneurs and engage in whatever legal enterprise they choose. Suppliers and consumers largely determine which goods and services are offered for sale and at what prices. However, the U.S. government does exert some economic control. It regulates businesses, enforces labor and product safety laws, imposes taxes, and takes other actions that affect economic flow.

 *What are the three types of economic systems?*

Supply and Demand

In a market economy, businesses provide goods and services because consumers will pay money for them. Businesses typically want to get the most money possible for the goods and services they offer. Consumers typically want to pay the least amount of money possible for what they buy. These two opposing forces actually work together to make the market economy operate efficiently.

Supply is the quantity of goods and services a business is willing to sell at a specific price and a specific time. **Demand** is the quantity of goods and services consumers are willing to buy at a specific price and a specific time.

As you can see, both price and timing are important when considering supply and demand. For example, a garden store may have a supply of

Self-Awareness

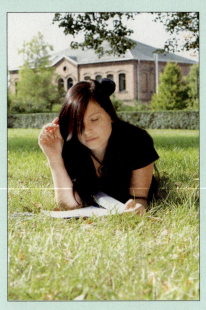

Do you really know what your capabilities are? Have you ever put together a list of your skills? Your interests? Your likes and dislikes? Your goals? If you have, you have demonstrated self-awareness. Being self-aware means knowing yourself and knowing your capabilities. This type of knowledge will be important as you go through life. But how can you increase your self-awareness?

Perhaps the best way to increase self-awareness is to retreat to a calm, quiet place when you have time to do so. Bring a new notebook you will use for only these self-awareness exercises and bring a pen or pencil you enjoy using. Clear your mind. Don't think about the events of the day or your current issues. Focus first on your goals. Ask yourself what goals you have, both for the short term and the long term. Write them down. Then think about what skills and capabilities you have. Think about what skills and capabilities you might need for the future. Write these down. Then focus on your likes and dislikes. Write these down. Make sure to date your entry in your notebook.

In the future, at regular intervals, repeat this self-awareness exercise. Look back at past entries in your notebook. Think about how you have changed. Describe these changes in each new entry. With increased self-awareness, you will be much more likely to set reasonable goals and, thus, to be more successful in your life and business.

THINKING CRITICALLY

Communicating. Individually perform the self-awareness exercise described in this feature. After you have made your entry, gather in small groups and discuss the experience. Was it helpful?

To read more about self-awareness, go to "Your Business Career" on the Student Center at entrepreneurship.pearson.com.

seeds and plants in the spring, when the demand would be high and the price would also be high. But there would be substantially less demand for seeds and plants in the fall, when prices would be low (if, in fact, consumers would be interested in seeds or plants at all).

In a market economy, the price of a particular good (product) or service is determined by supply and demand. Suppliers control the amount of supply; that is, they decide what quantity of a good or service they are willing to sell at a particular price. Consumers decide how much they are willing to pay for a given good or service.

Supply and Demand Curves

A **supply curve** on a graph shows the quantity of a product or service a supplier is willing to sell across a range of prices over a specified period of time. Quantity is shown on the x-axis, and price is shown on the y-axis. The supplier is willing to provide more as the price increases and less as it decreases.

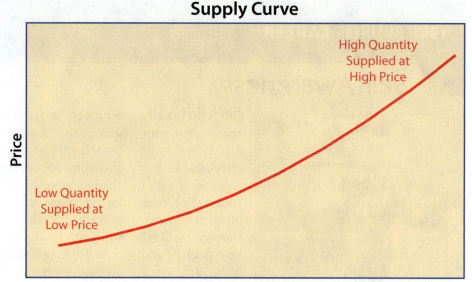

Supply Curve

High Quantity
Supplied at
High Price

Low Quantity
Supplied at
Low Price

Price

Supply (Quantity)

Figure 2-2 ▶

Supply Curve
A supply curve shows the quantity
and price relationship acceptable
to suppliers.

Inferring. *Why is a supplier willing
to provide greater quantities as the
selling price increases?*

A **demand curve** on a graph shows the quantity of a product or service consumers are willing to buy across a range of prices over a specified period of time. Once again, the quantity is shown on the x-axis, and the price on the y-axis. Consumers are willing to buy more of a product at a lower price than at a higher one.

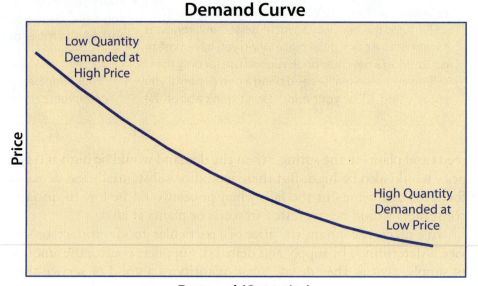

Demand Curve

Low Quantity
Demanded at
High Price

Price

High Quantity
Demanded at
Low Price

Demand (Quantity)

Figure 2-3 ▶

Demand Curve
A demand curve shows the quantity
and price relationship acceptable to
consumers.

Comparing/Contrasting. *Why
is the demand curve sloping in a
different direction from the supply
curve?*

A **supply and demand curve** is a graph that includes both a supply curve and a demand curve. It shows the relationship between price and the quantity of a product or service that is demanded and supplied. The **equilibrium point** is where the supply curve and the demand curve intersect. This is the point at which supply and demand are balanced.

The x-axis coordinate of the equilibrium point identifies the **equilibrium quantity**. This is the quantity at which the supply equals the demand. If a supplier produces more than the equilibrium quantity, there

Supply and Demand Curve

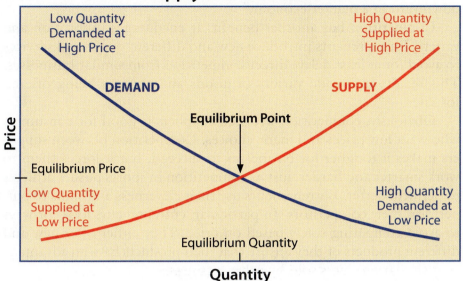

Low Quantity Demanded at High Price

High Quantity Supplied at High Price

DEMAND

SUPPLY

Equilibrium Point

Price

Equilibrium Price

Low Quantity Supplied at Low Price

High Quantity Demanded at Low Price

Equilibrium Quantity

Quantity

◀ **Figure 2-4**

Supply and Demand Curve
A supply and demand curve shows the price relationship between the quantity supplied and the quantity demanded.

Interpreting graphs. *Which portion of the supply curve indicates a surplus? What about a shortage?*

will be a surplus of the item. To sell the surplus items, the supplier will have to lower the price. If a supplier produces less than the equilibrium quantity, there will be a shortage of the item, and demand will not be satisfied. The supplier will miss out on sales that could have been made.

The y-axis coordinate of the equilibrium point identifies the ==**equilibrium price**==. This is the price at which supply equals demand. It is the price buyers are willing to pay and the supplier is willing to accept.

Supply and demand curves are one tool entrepreneurs use to determine the prices to charge for their goods or services. In fact, the curves can help an entrepreneur decide whether or not to go into a particular business. There must be sufficient demand for a product to make it worthwhile for a supplier to produce it.

What is a supply and demand curve?

Competition in a Market Economy

Competition is common in a market economy. People are free to start and operate businesses that compete against each other, so suppliers are often offering similar products or services. Buyers are free to compete against each other to buy products they need and want. Competition between suppliers pushes prices downward. Competition between buyers pushes prices upward.

Competition Between Suppliers

If a supplier lowers the price of a product or service, consumers typically buy from that supplier rather than from others. This assumes that only the price changes and all other aspects are equal. The supplier who lowers the price offers an incentive for consumers to change their buying habits. The other suppliers will probably have to lower their prices to keep their customers. This is how competition pushes prices downward in a market economy.

Competition has another benefit. It encourages innovation and variety. Entrepreneurs introduce new and different goods and services to avoid (or at least delay) direct competition from similar businesses. This results in a wide variety of goods and services being offered for sale.

Obviously, competition between suppliers is good for consumers who want low prices and many choices. Competition between suppliers makes it tougher for businesses to succeed, but it forces them to work smarter and harder, just as competition in sports pushes athletes to perform better. Entrepreneurs use their cleverness and skills to outperform their competitors. In particular, entrepreneurs look for ways to avoid competing solely based on price. They either offer new and different products or they ensure that their products have an advantage over similar products sold by other businesses.

Competition Between Consumers

In a market economy, there is not only competition between suppliers but also competition between consumers. When consumers compete against each other to buy a product, they push prices upward. For example, parents rush to stores in December to buy a popular toy as a holiday gift for their children. Consumers compete against each other to buy the limited supply of that toy. Suppliers can charge more for that toy in December than at other times of the year because demand is higher than usual.

Another example of this would be suppliers who charge more for flowers around Mother's Day or Valentine's Day than at other times. Customers are willing to pay more, so suppliers charge more. Competition among consumers for the same or similar products pushes prices upward in a market economy.

 *What role does competition play in a market economy?*

Profit Motive

In very simple terms, a business makes a profit when the amount of money coming in from sales is greater than the business's expenses. (You will learn more about calculating profit in later chapters.) Entrepreneurs choose how to use their profit. They can save it, spend it, invest it, or donate it to worthy causes (or any combination of these).

Businesses provide goods and services in an effort to satisfy consumers' demands. Profit is a business's reward for successfully making this effort. If the business is unsuccessful, it will make no profit and the business is likely to fail. Consumers understand that the prices they pay for goods and services include a profit for the suppliers. Otherwise, the suppliers would not be motivated to make the effort.

Profit is a strong incentive in a market economy. Starting a business is a risky thing to do. Many businesses fail. The opportunity to earn a profit encourages entrepreneurs to accept the risks of starting new enterprises. The **profit motive** is an incentive that encourages entrepreneurs to take business risks in the hope of making a profit.

Although profit is a strong incentive, it is not the only goal that motivates entrepreneurs. In recent years, in addition to profit, businesses have also begun focusing on the social and environmental impact they have. As you learned in Chapter 1, green companies adopt business practices aimed at protecting or improving the environment. Some entrepreneurs refer to this approach as the "people, planet, profit" style of business. Entrepreneurs who do business this way try to be economically successful by making a profit, but they also try to ensure that their businesses have a positive impact on people and the planet.

A New Approach to Business

People   Planet   Profit

Benefits of Profit

Entrepreneurs who consistently make a profit over time can build their own wealth and ensure financial independence. This means they do not have to depend on others—family, friends, employers, or the government—for money. Prosperity and financial independence are goals for many people. Entrepreneurs must work hard and make wise business decisions to earn a profit, but the personal financial benefits can be very rewarding.

Many entrepreneurs use profit to benefit their existing businesses, start new ones, or invest in the enterprises of others. Profit can be used to grow a business, for example, by offering more products or advertising to reach more customers. In addition, an entrepreneur can save profit for use when the business is not doing well financially.

Successful entrepreneurs also use profit to benefit society. Some businesses donate part or all of their profit to worthy causes. In 1982, actor Paul Newman established Newman's Own, Inc., to produce and sell grocery items, such as salad dressing, orange juice, and popcorn. All the profits from this business have gone to charities. As of 2008, the donations from Newman's Own totaled more than $200 million. This money has been used to help people around the world.

Economics of One Unit

It is always helpful for entrepreneurs to calculate the profit they make on each individual item or service sold. For instance, an entrepreneur could know that for every $20 T-shirt sold, $2.20 was profit. Another entrepreneur could know that of every $40 haircut, $3.80 was profit.

The **economics of one unit** is a calculation of the profit (or loss) for each unit of sale made by a business. Calculate the economics of one unit by subtracting the expenses for the unit of sale from its selling price.

In some cases, it's easy to figure out what a unit of sale is. Your business could make T-shirts, computers, or skateboards. A unit of sale would then be one T-shirt, one computer, or one skateboard. But what about a company that sells decorated toothpicks? Then a unit of sale might be a box of 50 toothpicks. A company that offers a service might figure a unit as one haircut or shoe shine. However, other service companies might think of a unit as an hour of babysitting, lawn mowing, or window washing. These are all examples of one unit of sale.

A unit of sale has a selling price to the consumer and an expense for the entrepreneur. The economics of one unit is the difference between the selling price and its expense. In other words:

$$\text{Selling Price} - \text{Expense} = \text{Profit (or Loss)}$$

If this equation results in a positive number, you've made a profit. If it's negative, you have taken a loss. For a business to be successful financially, the economics of one unit must result in a profit. A business that cannot make a profit from one unit of sale will not ever make a profit, no matter how many units it sells.

Another way to look at profit is as a percentage of the selling price. This calculation tells an entrepreneur the profit percentage based on sales. The formula per unit of sale is:

$$(\text{Profit/Selling Price}) \times 100 = \text{Profit \%}$$

If an entrepreneur made a profit of $2.20 on a $20 T-shirt, the profit would be 11%: (2.20/20) × 100 = 11%.

Figure 2-5

The Economics of One Unit

An entrepreneur buys plain backpacks and decorates them at home with handrawn art, stitching, buttons, and stickers before reselling them at the flea market for $25 each.

Because each backpack is different, the entrepreneur uses an average backpack as the unit of sale.

The expenses to the entrepreneur per unit of sale are:

Plain backpack	$11.00
Ink, thread, buttons, etc.	3.00
Labor	6.00
Expenses per unit of sale	**$20.00**

The economics of one unit of sale are:

Selling price per unit of sale	$25.00
Expenses per unit of sale	– 20.00
Profit per unit of sale	**$5.00**

The profit as a percentage of sales is:

$$\frac{\text{Profit per unit of sale}}{\text{Selling price per unit of sale}} \times 100 \qquad \frac{\$5.00}{\$25.00} \times 100 = \mathbf{20\%}$$

The Economics of One Unit
The economics of one unit is a calculation of the profit or loss from a unit of sale.

Analyzing Data. *How could the entrepreneur make a larger profit?*

What is the profit motive?

Nonprofit Organizations

A **nonprofit organization** (often called a nonprofit or not-for-profit) operates solely to serve the good of society. Nonprofits are not governmental organizations. They operate much like for-profit businesses. Money comes into the nonprofit from donations, government grants, or the sale of goods and services to consumers. Nonprofit companies also have expenses. If the money coming in is greater than the money going out, a nonprofit company will have a surplus (profit). Business owners can keep profit for themselves, for their own personal gain. However, any profit a nonprofit earns must, by law, be used to support the organization's social mission. It cannot be used for the financial gain of the people running the nonprofit.

Some people prefer to use their entrepreneurial skills to start a non-profit rather than a for-profit business. These entrepreneurs sacrifice the chance to build personal wealth and financial independence for the personal satisfaction they obtain through nonprofit work.

 *What is a nonprofit company?*

 Your Business Plan. Continue developing your standard business plan. Go to "Section 2.1" of the *Business Plan Project* in your *Student Activity Workbook*, or "Section 2.1" of the BizTech Software.

ASSESSMENT 2.1

Reviewing Objectives

1. What are the four fundamental questions of economics?
2. Name three types of economic systems.
3. What is an equilibrium price?
4. How does supplier competition benefit consumers?
5. What is the purpose of the profit motive?
6. How is profit used by a nonprofit organization?

Critical Thinking

7. **Applying Concepts.** Why does supplier competition make it harder for an entrepreneur to be successful?
8. **Relating Concepts.** Explain how supply and demand affect prices in the U.S. economy.

Working Together

Working in a team, pick two countries with different economic systems. Using the Internet and library resources, study the economies of these two countries and learn about the role played by entrepreneurs in each. Prepare a short presentation that describes the economic system used in each country and the role of entrepreneurship in each economic system.

Science
Treasuring Trees

Trees are a natural resource. Humans value trees for a variety of reasons. Write two paragraphs about the value of trees. In the first paragraph, talk about the economic value of trees. In the second paragraph, describe why trees are valuable for other reasons.

2.2 Thinking Globally, Acting Locally

OBJECTIVES

- Define the global economy
- Identify factors that affect entrepreneurs in international trade
- Describe relationships between the global economy and the local economy

VOCABULARY

- exporting
- fair trade
- foreign exchange rate
- global economy
- importing
- local economy
- quota
- sustainability
- sustainable economic development
- tariff
- trade barrier

? | *Consider the following question:*

Do you care if the clothes you buy are made in America?

Think carefully about your answer, and be prepared to explain your feelings to the class.

The Global Economy

The **global economy** is the flow of goods and services around the whole world. No nation's economic flow is confined within its own borders. Scarcity, among other factors, forces countries to buy goods and services from abroad. Most nations have developed specialties. They specialize in sending certain goods and services to the rest of the world. Specialization helps countries make the most efficient use of their natural and human resources.

In nations with more of a command economic system, the government conducts and controls global trade. Individuals may have little to no opportunity to engage in international buying and selling. Countries with more of a market economic system, such as the United States, allow individuals much more access to the global economy. This provides business opportunities for entrepreneurs who wish to trade with people in other nations.

Exporting and Importing

Exporting is the business activity in which goods or services are sent from a country and sold to foreign consumers. **Importing** is the business activity in which goods and services are brought into

Alumni Networks

Most of us want to stay in touch with the friends we made in high school and college. But what does this have to do with entrepreneurship? More than you think.

In this age of hyper-connection through Websites such as Facebook, LinkedIn, and MySpace, a person's group of friends and contacts from school is a great way to get the word out about a new business. Many schools offer formal alumni organizations just for this purpose. Although grads have usually maintained these connections through events and newsletters, today it is possible to keep a more active connection alive online. By posting to alumni forums, commenting on a former classmate's blog, or simply updating their Facebook status long after graduation, entrepreneurs have a built-in audience for their entrepreneurial efforts.

Maintaining connections between alumni can benefit entrepreneurs in many ways. School friends and contacts can help spread positive word of mouth for the launch of a new product or can refer good potential employees when it is time to hire someone. Maintaining these friendships is just one more way of "acting locally."

THINKING CRITICALLY

Applying Concepts. Working with a partner, come up with three or four ways your friends from school might help you succeed as an entrepreneur.

To read more about alumni networks, go to "Entrepreneurship Issues" on the Student Center at entrepreneurship.pearson.com.

a country from foreign suppliers. Goods are physical objects, so they are imported and exported by shipping—for example, by truck, train, plane, or ship. Services are not physical objects. They are actions provided by people for a fee. For example, an engineering firm located in one country exports its services when it provides engineering advice to customers in another country. Services can be exported and imported in various ways. People travel between countries to provide services. They can also use traditional delivery methods (such as the postal system), or modern telecommunications to provide services.

Technology and the Global Economy

Advancements in shipping, travel, and telecommunications permit much more international trade than in the past. Goods ship over water, land, and air routes and can circle the world in a matter of days or weeks. Passenger and freight airlines have added more foreign destinations to their routes, allowing goods and businesspeople greater access to international trading. Modern means of telecommunications—phone, fax, e-mail, and Internet—connect suppliers and consumers around the world. The Internet, in particular, has made international trade easier, faster, and more convenient than ever before.

 *What is the global economy?*

Entrepreneurs and International Trade

Entrepreneurs can benefit from international trade by exporting goods or services that are in demand in other countries. Entrepreneurs may also benefit from importing. For example, they could import foreign goods to resell in their own country or they might import foreign materials that they then use to produce goods. These exchanges will only be financially beneficial to entrepreneurs if the supply and demand factors result in prices consumers will be willing to pay.

Business risks can be associated with international trade. To properly assess these risks, entrepreneurs must learn about the economic and monetary systems of the foreign countries in which they wish to do business. They also must learn about government regulations relating to exporting and importing. In addition to financial and political challenges, there are also cultural factors to consider. Wise entrepreneurs examine all of the possible consequences (both good and bad) for their businesses before engaging in international trade.

Trade Barriers

Governments are often protective of the resources within their borders. Even nations with market economies typically put some restrictions on imports. There are two main reasons for this. First, most nations want to give domestic businesses a competitive advantage over foreign ones selling the same product or service. Second, governments want to protect their consumers from foreign goods that might be unsafe or of poor quality.

A **trade barrier** is a governmental restriction on international trade. The most common trade barriers are tariffs and quotas on imports. A **tariff** is a fee, similar to a tax, that importers must pay on the goods they import. A **quota** is a limit on the quantity of a product that can be imported into a country. Entrepreneurs must be aware of tariffs or quotas that apply to products they wish to import or export.

Foreign Exchange Rates

Many types of money are in use around the world. In general, each country or group of countries has its own currency. Examples include the U.S. dollar, the Japanese yen, the Chinese yuan, the Canadian dollar, the British pound, the Mexican peso, and the euro (the currency unit of the European Union, a group of European countries).

▼ *Foreign exchange rate board*

Exchange Rates	We Sell
AUSTRALIA	0.8264
BRAZIL	0.5263
CANADA	0.9677
CHINA	0.1417
Costa Rica	0.0023
Euro	1.4093
HONG KONG	0.1412
JAPAN	0.0094
MEXICO	0.1014
NEW ZEALAND	0.7284
S Korea	0.0012
SINGAPORE	0.6922
Sweden	0.1502
Switzerland	0.8837
TAHITI	0.0123
TAIWAN	0.0342
THAILAND	0.0303
UNITED KIN…	

International sellers and buyers have to be able to calculate the value of one currency in relation to another. To do this they need to know the **foreign exchange rate**. This is the value of one currency unit in relation to another. Imagine that 1 U.S. dollar has an exchange rate of 0.50 British pounds. This would mean that $1 has the same value as 0.50 British pounds. Foreign exchange rates change day to day and must be monitored closely by entrepreneurs engaged in international trade. American and British businesses trading with each other would need to use the most current exchange rate to convert prices between the two currencies.

Fair Trade

Fair trade is a policy of ensuring that small producers in developing nations earn sufficient profit on their exported goods to improve their working, environmental, and social conditions. Typical products include handmade crafts and farmed goods, such as coffee or bananas. Fair trade organizations help link small producers in developing countries with foreign merchants and consumers interested in encouraging fair trade. U.S. entrepreneurs interested in selling fair trade goods can coordinate with these organizations to import and resell goods to American consumers.

Respecting Other Cultures

Entrepreneurs who wish to engage in international trade need to show respect for the culture of the people with whom they want to do business. "Culture" includes language, beliefs, attitudes, customs, manners, and habits. Obviously, a nation can include people of many different cultures; however, many people within a country often share general characteristics. In addition, businesspeople in most societies follow particular social rules and customs called *etiquette*. Entrepreneurs should learn and follow the business etiquette practiced in foreign countries where they want to do business.

▼ **Figure 2-6**

Respecting Other Cultures
Entrepreneurs need to show respect for the culture of the people with whom they do business.

Predicting. *Would you be inclined to do business with someone who you felt did not show respect for your culture?*

Entrepreneurs who fail to respect the cultures of foreign trading partners will most likely be unable to take advantage of business opportunities.

 **READING CHECKPOINT** *What is a trade barrier?*

The Local Economy

Effects of Entrepreneurship on the Local Economy

A **local economy** covers a limited area, such as a community or town. Because many entrepreneurs operate small businesses that sell primarily to local consumers, entrepreneurship has a profound effect on local economies. Entrepreneurs can benefit their local economies in the following ways:

- Purchasing materials and supplies from local merchants

- Opening an account at a local bank, credit union, or other financial institution

- Joining a local business association, trade group, or civic organization that supports local economic development

- Paying local taxes that benefit schools and other public services

- Investing money in local businesses

- Donating money, time, or goods to local charities and organizations

- Hiring local employees (this produces multiple benefits for the local economy, because the employees will likely spend their wages in the area)

- Supplying goods and services to local consumers

Entrepreneurs engaged in international trade will provide these benefits to their own local economies but will also indirectly help the local economies of their foreign trading partners. For example, a U.S. entrepreneur who buys cloth from Africa is likely to affect a local economy there.

Importance of Sustainability

It is important that economic development does not harm society or the environment but ensures that human and natural resources are maintained for future generations. This is referred to as **sustainable economic development**, or **sustainability**. The goal of sustainability is to maintain and perhaps even to improve the quality of human life and the quality of the environment. Entrepreneurs who support sustainability consider the welfare of people and the environment in their business practices—for example, by using recyclable packaging.

Although sustainability is an idea of global importance, it is mainly practiced at the local level. When an entrepreneur's decisions and actions incorporate sustainability, the local economy benefits. And, as one local economy after another benefits from sustainability, the global economy will benefit as well. Entrepreneurs who focus on sustainability provide an excellent example of thinking globally but acting locally.

 READING CHECKPOINT *What is a local economy?*

 **Your Business Plan.** Continue developing your standard business plan. Go to "Section 2.2" of the *Business Plan Project* in your *Student Activity Workbook*, or "Section 2.2" of the BizTech Software.

ASSESSMENT 2.2

Reviewing Objectives

1. What roles do exporting and importing play in the global economy?
2. Name three challenges entrepreneurs face in international trade.
3. List four ways an entrepreneur can help his or her local economy.

Critical Thinking

4. **Predicting.** What likely effect will a new tariff have on the price of an imported product? Why?
5. **Drawing Conclusions.** The United States is a large and wealthy nation with many natural and human resources within its borders. So why does the United States import goods and services?

Working Together

Working with team members, research the primary exports and imports of the United States and the countries with which it trades. Write a short report that includes tables and charts summarizing the data. In the report, discuss the following points: What is America's supply specialization? Who are America's primary trading partners? Why?

Social Studies
Culture Smarts

Imagine you have a small business selling screen-printed T-shirts. You want to begin selling the T-shirts via an Internet Website to customers outside the United States. Pick a country and list five things you should research about its culture before you set up your Website.

Nonprofit versus Profit

Nadia Campbell has been an entrepreneur since she was 11. Back then she founded The Victorian Hands Foundation. It's a not-for-profit organization dedicated to enhancing awareness and respect among the younger generation for our elderly. "It has been an extremely gratifying 14 years," said Nadia. "Even those who were skeptical in the beginning were able to see the difference their time was making."

Starting a For-Profit Company

At 24, Nadia saw an opportunity to start a for-profit day spa in her community. Nadia had been to spas for facials and massages, but she didn't have any experience running one. She knew the basics of business from her foundation and from an online entrepreneurial course she had taken.

"I did a lot of research on the income levels and needs of my community, as well as on the spa industry's growth and latest trends," said Nadia. For her spa, called Jewel in the Crown, she rented two floors of a building. Then she put together a staff of experienced professionals. "We have a great pampering team of massage tharapists, aestheticians, and nail technicians. Our staff is passionate about their work, and providing quality customer service is our priority."

Making Mistakes

Like any businessperson, Nadia made some early mistakes. Against the advice of her family, she hired a receptionist, who didn't work out. "It was a waste of money," said Nadia, "money I should have been saving. I would have preferred to do it myself and go a little crazy for a couple of months until I could find a solution." Her solution ultimately was using interns who were willing to work without pay for the experience.

Managing interns is a skill Nadia had learned from her earlier experience in the nonprofit. There, she had no problem finding volunteers to help with everything from Web design to visiting seniors. But in the for-profit world, Nadia was surprised to find that "No one wanted to volunteer their time. You have to pay people to do work, even to pass out a brochure."

Learning on the Job

For Nadia, running a spa has given her the opportunity to learn about herself. "I didn't realize I knew

▲ *Nadia Campbell*

how to do certain things, like come up with creative marketing techniques," she said. "That is a skill that I don't have to use as often in the nonprofit sector."

She is now marketing her spa online, as well as advertising on the radio and in newspapers. "We've sponsored and hosted events, as well as rented space. We focus on all levels of marketing, especially word of mouth."

How does this all feel to Nadia? "I feel blessed to have the opportunity to run a nonprofit and open a for-profit business that encourages others to reduce stress."

Thinking Like an Entrepreneur

1. Nadia carried out research on her community to find out how to price the services in her spa. What other reasons are there to research a community?
2. Why didn't people want to volunteer their services to help Nadia with her spa? Would you have been surprised at this?
3. Would you be comfortable learning on the job, or would you prefer not to have any surprises and to have everything prepared for you?

CHAPTER SUMMARY

2.1 Importance of Entrepreneurship in the Economy

Economics is concerned with how people satisfy their demand for goods and services when the supply of those goods and services is limited. An economic system is used by society to allocate goods and services for its people and to cope with scarcity. Economic systems answer the four fundamental questions of economics. There are three main types of economic systems: command economy, market economy, and a mixed economy. The United States and many other democratic nations are generally market economies. They feature voluntary exchange and freedom of choice. Prices in a market economy are affected by supply and demand. Supply and demand can be graphed as curves, with the equilibrium point where the two curves intersect—indicating that supply and demand are balanced. Competition affects supply and demand. The profit motive is an incentive for entrepreneurs to take business risks in the hope of making a profit. The economics of one unit is a calculation of profit or loss from one unit of sale. Nonprofit organizations differ from for-profit businesses in how they can use profit.

2.2 Thinking Globally, Acting Locally

The global economy encompasses the world. International trade consists of exporting and importing. The risks and challenges of international trade include trade barriers (tariffs and quotas), shifting foreign exchange rates, and cultural differences between nations. Entrepreneurs should practice the rules and customs of business etiquette in countries where they wish to do business. Entrepreneurs can play vital roles in both local economies and the global economy as they work to achieve social and environmental goals. Increasingly, companies are becoming concerned with sustainable economic development that does not harm society or the environment, but ensures that human and natural resources are maintained for future generations.

REVIEW VOCABULARY

Imagine you are a journalist writing an article for an English-language magazine published in a foreign country. Use at least 15 of the following terms in an article describing the role of entrepreneurs in the U.S. economic system:

- capitalism (p. 30)
- command economy (p. 28)
- demand (p. 30)
- economic system (p. 28)
- economics (p. 27)
- economics of one unit (p. 36)
- economy (p. 28)
- equilibrium point (p. 32)
- equilibrium price (p. 33)
- equilibrium quantity (p. 32)
- exporting (p. 39)
- free enterprise system (p. 30)
- global economy (p. 39)
- importing (p. 39)
- local economy (p. 43)
- market economy (p. 28)
- mixed economy (p. 28)
- profit motive (p. 35)
- scarcity (p. 28)
- supply (p. 30)
- sustainable economic development (p. 43)
- tariff (p. 41)
- voluntary exchange (p. 30)

CHECK YOUR UNDERSTANDING

Choose the letter that best answers the question or completes the statement.

1. Which of the following is a problem a nation might attempt to solve through its economic system?
   a. limited supply of goods and services
   b. democracy
   c. entrepreneur's profit motive
   d. all of the above

2. The equilibrium price is
   a. the price set by the government
   b. the price at which supply equals demand
   c. the price at which exports equal imports
   d. the price set by the foreign exchange rate

3. Profit is beneficial to entrepreneurs because
   a. profit builds wealth and financial independence
   b. profit is the equilibrium quantity on a supply and demand curve
   c. profit is a barrier to international trade
   d. profit is the answer to one of the fundamental questions of economics

4. A market economy is also called
   a. socialism
   b. capitalism
   c. free enterprise system
   d. b and c

5. The profit motive is
   a. the money left over after expenses are subtracted from sales
   b. the economics of one unit
   c. a reason entrepreneurs take on business risks
   d. profit calculated as a percentage of expenses

6. Which of the following statements about competition is false?
   a. competition motivates entrepreneurs to introduce new products to consumers
   b. competition between suppliers drives prices upward
   c. competition between consumers benefits suppliers
   d. competition occurs between suppliers and between consumers

7. Importing and exporting are activities primarily associated with
   a. nonprofit organizations
   b. the profit motive
   c. the economics of one unit
   d. the global economy

8. The economics of one unit is a calculation of
   a. the equilibrium quantity on a supply curve
   b. how many items an entrepreneur has for sale
   c. the profit or loss associated with a unit of sale
   d. foreign demand for an entrepreneur's product

9. The United States economy is best described as
   a. a pure market economy in which the government plays no role in the economy
   b. a pure command economy in which the government controls the economy
   c. a mixed economy in which suppliers and consumers play the primary role
   d. a socialist economy in which suppliers and consumers play the primary role

10. Which of the following challenges poses a business risk to entrepreneurs who want to conduct international trade?
    a. tariffs that must be paid to import goods
    b. cultural differences between nations
    c. trade barriers
    d. all of the above

11. A nonprofit organization
    a. is not allowed to make a profit
    b. must use any profit it earns to further its social mission
    c. can use profit any way it sees fit
    d. uses profit for the financial gain of its operators

12. A local economy is best described as
    a. the flow of goods and services within a community
    b. the flow of goods and services in international trade
    c. an economic system based on foreign exchange rates
    d. an economic system dominated by nonprofit organizations

Business Communication

13. You want to do business in a foreign nation. Research business etiquette in that country and use a partner to demonstrate to the class at least three rules or customs an American entrepreneur should practice when meeting with business-people there.

14. You operate a nonprofit organization that benefits society. Imagine that your classmates are successful entrepreneurs gathered for a convention. Give a speech in which you try to convince them to donate some of their profits to your organization.

15. Imagine that you support fair trade and you import decorative fabric produced in a foreign village. You make jackets that you sell in your store. The U.S. government wants to put a high tariff on this type of fabric. Write a letter addressed to your congress-person about why you oppose this tariff.

Business Ethics

18. You buy glow sticks for 50 cents each and sell them for $1 each at park concerts. One night a citywide blackout occurs. People at the dark concert want desperately to buy your glow sticks. Should you raise the price? Why or why not?

Business Math

16. Use the following supply and demand data for a cake business to draw a supply and demand curve. Circle the equilibrium point. How many cakes should the entrepreneur supply each week? Why? What price should the entrepreneur charge for each cake? Why?

Supply						
Quantity per wk.	2	4	6	8	12	14
Price per cake	$5	$10	$15	$20	$30	$35

Demand						
Quantity per wk.	19	16	13	10	7	4
Price per cake	$10	$15	$20	$25	$30	$35

17. Here are the expenses for your silk-screened T-shirt business: $5 for each plain T-shirt and $3 per T-shirt for ink, other supplies, and the cost of silk screening. You sell the T-shirts for $10 each. Calculate the economics of one unit of sale. What is the percentage of profit based on price?

Business in Your Community

19. Working with several classmates, survey local businesses to compile a list of at least 20 products that are imported from foreign nations. Strive for variety in the products and countries. On a world map, draw an arrow from each foreign nation to your community. List the imported product above the line.

20. Interview a local entrepreneur or small-business owner whose enterprise involves producing goods and/or providing services. Determine the answers to the four fundamental questions of economics for that business. Write a one-page report summarizing the results.

Information Technology

When you combine computers with communications technology, you get information technology. Broadly defined, **information technology** (IT) is the study, design, development, implementation, support, and management of computer-based information systems. It is particularly focused on software applications and computer hardware.

Whenever you use a computer or computer software to convert, store, process, transmit, or retrieve information, you are using information technology. Think about it. A video game is an example of information technology. So is word processing software, such as Microsoft Office Word®. So is a spreadsheet program, such as Microsoft Office Excel®. So is a search engine, such as Google®. A program for manipulating any type of data is an example of information technology.

Data Storage

Data storage is one of the most important aspects of information technology. It's also an area in which vast improvements have been made over the last decade. There are two basic types of storage: primary storage and secondary storage. **Primary storage** is contained in the computer and is directly accessed by the **central processing unit (CPU)**. The CPU does all the actual computing. Primary storage is also referred to as **random access memory (RAM)**. When you turn off your computer, all the data stored in its primary storage, in RAM, is wiped clean.

Secondary storage isn't directly accessed by the CPU. It's a more permanent type of storage and doesn't lose data when the computer is turned off. The most common type of secondary storage is a computer's hard drive. Other common types of secondary storage are CDs, DVDs, USB sticks, floppy disks, and tape drives. Because these drives aren't directly accessed by the CPU, the time it takes for the CPU to access them is a bit slower than for primary storage. For example, the time it takes to access data in primary storage is measured in billionths of a second (**nanoseconds**), while the time it takes to access information on a hard drive is measured in thousandths of a second (**milliseconds**).

IT Professionals

Most businesses require the assistance of information technology professionals to install applications, design networks and information databases, and manage data and all aspects of that business's information technology. Large companies tend to have IT groups—employees within the company—who provide these services. Smaller companies often hire independent IT specialists. A small company may pay IT specialists by the hour or, as a way to budget for their IT needs, pay a set amount each month for the assistance of an independent IT group who then is on call.

As information systems become more complex and businesses require Websites and sell their products on the Internet, the day when business owners could take care of their own IT needs is fast disappearing.

Tech Vocabulary

- central processing unit (CPU)
- information technology (IT)
- milliseconds
- nanoseconds
- primary storage
- random access memory (RAM)
- secondary storage

Check Yourself

1. What is information technology?
2. What are the two types of storage?
3. What are some types of secondary storage?
4. What does an IT professional do?

What Do You Think?

Solving Problems. If you were a business owner who was experienced with information technology, would you choose to manage your company's IT? Explain your answer.

CHAPTER

3 TYPES OF BUSINESS & BUSINESS OWNERSHIP

3.1 Types of Business

OBJECTIVES

- Identify the four main types of business
- Examine trends in business startups in recent decades
- Explore growth expectations for business

VOCABULARY

- franchise
- manufacturer
- manufacturing business
- North American Industry Classification System
- reseller's permit
- retailer
- retailing business
- service business
- trade business
- wholesaler
- wholesaling business

Answer this question:

When I think of "business," what type of business do I think of first?

Write down the first type of business that comes into your head.

Types of Business

In general, businesses are divided into four broad categories, depending on their primary function and the kinds of products they sell.

Manufacturing Businesses

A **manufacturing business** (**manufacturer**) converts materials into goods suitable for use and then sells those goods to others. Manufactured products typically fall into two categories: industrial and consumer. Industrial goods are sold to other manufacturing businesses. Examples include metal and plastic parts, lumber, and heavy machinery. Consumer goods are products that are eventually bought by the public.

Small manufacturing businesses that produce consumer goods sometimes sell directly to the public. For example, entrepreneurs making baked goods, silk-screened T-shirts, or jewelry most often sell their products directly to consumers. Large manufacturing businesses usually do not sell directly to consumers. They may sell to wholesalers.

Wholesaling Businesses

A **wholesaling business** (**wholesaler**) buys goods in large quantities, typically from manufacturers, and resells them in smaller batches to retailers. Wholesalers are also known as middlemen, go-betweens, distributors, or intermediaries because they provide a link between manufacturers and retailers, who sell goods to consumers. Wholesalers do not generally sell directly to the public.

Retailing Businesses

A **retailing business** (**retailer**) buys goods, often from wholesalers, and resells them directly to consumers, who are the end buyers. Retailing businesses are stores, shops, and boutiques. They sell groceries, clothing, shoes, household goods, computers, CDs, sporting goods, cosmetics, jewelry, and thousands of other consumer items directly to the public. Retailing businesses include traditional stores that people visit in person and online stores that sell from the Internet. Some retailers also sell through catalogs. In most states retailers must have a special permit (often called a **reseller's permit**) to purchase goods tax-free from wholesalers and collect sales tax from the end buyers.

A business that is either a wholesale or retail business is commonly referred to as a **trade business**.

Service Businesses

A **service business** provides services to customers for a fee. Service businesses provide a wide variety of professional, technical, and everyday services that people need and want. Examples include engineering, legal, medical, accounting, garbage pick-up, package delivery, dry cleaning, auto repair, babysitting, pet sitting, music lessons, tutoring, house cleaning, and landscaping.

Most states and some local governments have licensing requirements for people who provide particular services. This applies to professionals (doctors, dentists, engineers, lawyers,

▼ **Figure 3-1**
Service Business
A service business sells services to customers.
Classifying. *This entrepreneur owns a barber shop. What other types of service businesses do you encounter on a regular basis?*

Career Orientation

Some high school students have a good idea about what type of work they want to do after graduation. Others may be undecided about their future plans. They need to know more about careers that suit their skills.

If you know the field you hope to work in, you can plan a career pathway while still in high school. If you intend to go on to college, you will need to think about what to study. Your college major may require you to take specific math, science, or foreign language courses in high school. If you haven't taken these courses, you will have to take them in college before you can actually begin taking the courses that interest you. If you want to follow a specific career, ask your guidance counselor for help in choosing courses that fit with your prospective plans.

If you are not sure about a career path, ask your guidance counselor about tests designed to match your interests and abilities to specific occupations. The results may lead you to some possibilities for which you are especially suited.

options suggested by the test and then describe your reaction to these options.

THINKING CRITICALLY

Analyzing Information. Take a career aptitude test online (at www.careerkey.org). List the career

To read more about career orientation, go to "Your Business Career" on the Student Center at entrepreneurship.pearson.com.

and so on) as well as other types of service providers, such as hairstylists, dog walkers, automobile mechanics, athletic trainers, and daycare providers. In addition, some states require service businesses selling taxable services to have a permit to collect sales tax from their customers.

Special Types of Businesses

Farming is a special type of business. Sometimes it is more like manufacturing (if the agricultural products are used to create new products, as when grain is used to make bread). Farming is a combination of manufacturing and retailing when fruits or vegetables are sold directly to the consumer.

Mining is another special type of business. Often referred to as an "extraction business," mining takes resources from the environment and converts them into a form that can typically be sold to manufacturers. Examples of extraction businesses are copper mining, oil drilling, and converting sea salt to table salt.

 *What are the four main types of business?*

Trends in Business Startups

Over the past fifty years the business make-up of the United States has changed significantly. In the 1950s, the country's dominant industry, in terms of national income and number of employees, was manufacturing. Wholesale and retail businesses were also important, but service businesses played a relatively minor role in the economy.

During the 1950s and 1960s, America experienced a boom in franchising. A **franchise** is an arrangement in which an established company sells the right for others to use the company's name and operating plan to sell products or services. Franchising became popular in the service and retail industries, particularly among fast food restaurants. McDonald's is one of the best-known franchise companies in the world.

After 1950, manufacturing began to be less important in the U.S. economy. By 1970, service, wholesale, and retail businesses accounted for the majority of America's economic production. The vast majority of businesses started in the 2000s have been service and trade businesses. According to the U.S. State Department, private companies in the service industry created nearly two-thirds of America's economic production in 2006.

 *Which types of business dominate the U.S. economy today?*

FASTEST-GROWING INDUSTRIES

Rank	Industry	NAICS #
1.	Management, scientific, and technical consulting services	5416
2.	Individual and family services	6241
3.	Home health-care services	6216
4.	Financial investments and related services	523
5.	Facilities support services	5612
6.	Residential care facilities and related services	6232, 6233, 6239
7.	Independent artists, writers, and performers	7115
8.	Computer-systems design and related services	5415
9.	Museums, historical sites, and similar institutions	712
10.	Child daycare services	6244

Businesses of the Future

The <mark>North American Industry Classification System</mark> (NAICS) assigns a numerical code to every industry in North America based on its primary business function. NAICS codes are useful for classifying particular types of businesses. The U.S. Department of Labor makes predictions on which industries will likely experience the largest growth in number of employees in the following decade. The top ten companies have one thing in common: they provide some type of service. This demonstrates that service businesses are expected to dominate the U.S. economy through 2020.

 *Which type of business is predicted to dominate the U.S. economy in the future?*

 Your Business Plan. Continue developing your standard business plan. Go to "Section 3.1" of the *Business Plan Project* in your *Student Activity Workbook*, or "Section 3.1" of the BizTech Software.

ASSESSMENT 3.1

Reviewing Objectives

1. What is the difference between wholesale and retail businesses?
2. What types of businesses have had the most startups in the past decade?
3. What type of business is expected to undergo the greatest growth over the coming decade?

Critical Thinking

4. **Classifying.** Using the four business types, how would you classify the following: (a) restaurants, (b) construction companies, (c) a company that produces music videos?
5. **Inferring.** Based on the examples given of service providers that must have state licenses, why do you think states have licensing requirements for certain occupations?

Working Together

Working with three classmates, use the Internet or other resources to learn exactly what kinds of businesses are included in each NAICS category under "Businesses of the Future." Choose three businesses within a category. Prepare a short presentation that analyzes why these three businesses can be expected to grow so strongly. Use statistics to support your presentation.

Social Studies
Dog Food

The dog food industry is not usually associated with entrepreneurship. However, in recent years, entrepreneurs have introduced new options for healthy dog food and dog treats. These innovations are revolutionary for a society that, despite spending millions on pet-related care, hasn't focused on healthy food. Write a short paper describing some of these innovations. Do you think they will be embraced by society at large? Explain why or why not.

SECTION 3.2 Types of Business Ownership

OBJECTIVES

- Define liability
- Examine sole proprietorships
- Learn about partnerships
- Examine corporations
- Understand cooperatives

VOCABULARY

- C corporation
- cooperative
- corporation
- dividend
- general partnership
- incorporate
- liability
- limited liability
- limited liability company
- limited partnership
- nonprofit corporation
- partnership
- partnership agreement
- share of stock
- shareholders
- sole proprietorship
- stockholders
- subchapter S corporation
- unlimited liability

? | *Consider this question:*

If a business fails, should the owner be responsible for paying its debts, even if it means selling a home or car?

Write your answer on a piece of paper and be prepared to discuss it in class.

Liability of Business Owners

When considering the types of business ownership, an important consideration is the owner's **liability**. This is the legal obligation of a business owner to use personal money and possessions to pay the debts of the business. These business debts could include loans that must be repaid, money owed to other businesses, and judgments resulting from lawsuits against the business.

Unlimited liability means that a business owner *can be legally forced* to use personal money and possessions to pay the debts of the business. **Limited liability** means that a business owner *cannot be legally forced* to use personal money and possessions to pay business debt. Business owners with limited liability only risk the money specifically invested in the business. The level of liability for a business owner depends on the type of ownership structure used by the business.

 *What is liability?*

Sole Proprietorships

A **sole proprietorship** (pruh-PRY-uh-tur-ship) is a legally defined type of business ownership in which a single individual owns the business, collects all profit from it, and has unlimited liability for its debt. In the eyes of the law, the owner and the business are one and the same. Most small businesses operate as sole proprietorships, particularly new ones. The vast majority of all businesses in the United States are sole proprietorships.

Advantages

The sole proprietorship is the simplest and least expensive option for business ownership. Because the owner and the business are one and the same, business income and costs are reported on the owner's personal income tax return. This means less paperwork and easier tax accounting for the sole proprietor. The sole proprietor is also the sole decision maker, with complete control over the management of the business.

Disadvantages

In a sole proprietorship, only one individual is responsible for the business. That person has to carry a heavy workload—raising the financial backing to set up, operate, and expand the business. The sole proprietor has *unlimited liability* for any business debts. As noted previously, this means that the owner's personal money and possessions (house, car, and so on) are at risk if they are needed to pay business debts.

Sole proprietors often find it difficult to borrow money or attract investors. If they are unable to work, or make poor decisions, the business could fail. Lenders and investors are reluctant to take that risk. Because of this lack of access to outside cash, sole proprietors often find it difficult to expand their businesses.

How to Set Up a Sole Proprietorship

For federal tax purposes, any business not specifically organized under a more complicated ownership structure is considered a sole proprietorship. Federal, state, and local government regulations must be considered when setting up a sole proprietorship. Most communities require a business license, at least. In addition, there are usually other requirements, such as:

- **Naming the Business.** An entrepreneur may choose to use his or her name as the business name. For example, John Washington provides pet sitting, using his own name. He could also choose Westside Pet Sitting, John's Pet Sitting, or Super Pets. Any business name other than the owner's name is called a trade name, or a D.B.A. ("Doing Business As") name. Some states require sole proprietorships to register their names with a state or local government agency.

▲ Figure 3-2

Sole Proprietorship
In a sole proprietorship, only one person is responsible for the business.

Comparing/Contrasting. *What do you think the advantages and disadvantages of this sole proprietorship would be?*

• **Tax I.D. Number.** The federal government and some state governments require every business to have a taxpayer identification number. Typically, sole proprietors can use their Social Security numbers for this purpose, as long as the business has no other employees. If employees are hired, the entrepreneur must obtain an Employer Identification Number (or EIN). There are other situations in which EINs are necessary, so entrepreneurs must research the requirements carefully.

READING CHECKPOINT ✓ *What is a sole proprietorship?*

Partnerships

A **partnership** is a legally defined type of business organization in which at least two individuals share the management, profit, and liability. The most common form of partnership is a general partnership. In a **general partnership**, all partners have unlimited liability. Like sole proprietors, general partners are personally responsible for business debt. Because they assume personal financial risk, general partners usually take an active role in a business.

A **limited partnership** is structured so that at least one partner (the general partner) has limited liability for the debts of the business.

The other partners have no say in the company's day-to-day operation but are only investors.

Advantages

A general partnership is much like a sole proprietorship as far as establishment and taxes are concerned. Setting up and maintaining a general partnership is relatively simple. It requires little paperwork compared to a corporate structure.

The primary advantage of a general partnership compared to a sole proprietorship is that a general partnership can rely on the entrepreneurial skills and financial backing of at least two individuals instead of just one. This makes it easier for a partnership to borrow money or appeal to outside investors. Also, general partnerships can attract and motivate employees with the incentive of becoming partners in the business at some point in the future.

Disadvantages

Because general partners have unlimited liability, they risk losing personal money and possessions to pay business debts. Partnerships have three main disadvantages compared to sole proprietorships. First, profit is split between the partners. Second, each partner is responsible for the business-related actions of all the others. And, third, partners may have trouble agreeing on how the business should be operated.

ENTREPRENEURSHIP ISSUES

Employee-Owned Corporations

When you think of a typical business owner, do you picture someone in a suit sitting in a fancy office? Well, these days business owners can be found everywhere, from the copy room to the factory floor. Several large businesses are employee-owned cooperatives, which means that the employees own the company's stock and make the decisions about how it is operated. As with other corporations, a share of company stock represents a portion of ownership. An ESOP (Employee Stock Ownership Plan) is a formal arrangement that allows employees to participate in the ownership of a firm.

There are several good reasons for corporations to pursue an employee ownership structure. Productivity and profitability increase when workers dedicate themselves to the business. The spirit of entrepreneurship filters through the whole organization. Employees directly elect the people who will lead the company, and everyone takes responsibility for the business's success. The Tribune Company and Woodman's Food Market are two examples of employee-owned corporations.

THINKING CRITICALLY

Relating Concepts. Employee-owned corporations are like democratic forms of government, in which representatives are elected to lead a nation. In small groups, talk about the similarities and differences between ESOPs and democracies. List two similarities and two differences.

To read more about employee-owned corporations, go to "Entrepreneurship Issues" on the Student Center at entrepreneurship.pearson.com.

Figure 3-3

Corporation
Most of the world's largest companies are corporations.

Drawing Conclusions.
How would you feel more comfortable—as an owner in a sole proprietorship or as an employee in a corporation?

Writing a Partnership Agreement

Entrepreneurs should write a partnership agreement before they go into business together. A **partnership agreement** is a legal document that clearly defines how the work, responsibilities, rewards, and liabilities of a partnership will be shared by the partners. It also specifies what will happen if a partner dies or decides to leave the business. A well-written partnership agreement can help partners avoid conflicts and concentrate on managing and growing the business.

 **READING CHECKPOINT** *What is a partnership?*

Corporations

A **corporation** is a legally defined type of business ownership in which the business itself is considered a "person" (an "entity") under the law, and limited liability is granted to the business owner(s). Although a corporation may have only one owner, most have more than one. The owners of a corporation are its **shareholders**, or **stockholders**. A **share of stock** is a unit of ownership in a corporation. Corporations sell shares to raise money. They may limit share ownership (within the founder's family, perhaps) or offer it to the general public. Shareholders are said to have equity (financial ownership) in the corporation. In other words, anyone who owns at least one share is an owner. Each share may earn its owner a **dividend**, which is a portion of the corporation's profit. Most corporations are **C corporations**, which are taxed as entities by the federal government.

The majority of states require a corporation to have a board of directors, consisting of one or more individuals responsible for making decisions about how the business should be operated.

Advantages

Shareholders have a limited liability. They risk only the money they invested in the corporation. Shareholders can end their ownership by selling their shares to someone else. Shares also change hands when shareholders die. The life span of a corporation is not tied to the life span of its owners. Many of America's largest corporations have been in business for decades. Management of a corporation is delegated to the board of directors, who typically hire the corporation's officers. All of this means corporations can raise money more easily than sole proprietorships and partnerships.

Disadvantages

The primary disadvantage of corporations is that they are more difficult and expensive to set up and maintain than other business structures. Corporations are regulated under state laws, so to **incorporate** means to set up a corporation in accordance with the laws of the particular state where the business is located. In general, corporations must follow very specific procedures for keeping records and selling shares. In addition, corporations are not taxed the same way as sole proprietorships and partnerships. Corporate profit is taxed twice. A corporation pays taxes on the profits it earns. Then the shareholders pay personal taxes on corporate dividends received.

Subchapter S Corporations

A **subchapter S corporation** differs from a C corporation in how it is taxed. It is not taxed as an entity, rather its income or loss is applied to each shareholder and appears on their tax returns. A subchapter S corporation is not taxed twice, so it may offer tax benefits to business owners. However, it also has more restrictions than a sole proprietorship or a partnership and is more complicated and expensive to set up.

Limited Liability Companies

A **limited liability company** is a legally defined type of business ownership similar to a C corporation, but with simpler operating requirements and tax procedures and greater liability protection for the business owners (who are called members). Like a corporation, it is possible for a limited liability company to be owned by only one individual. In recent years, the limited liability company has become a popular ownership option for professionals, such as doctors and lawyers, because it combines the liability benefits of a corporation with the tax benefits of a sole proprietorship or partnership.

Nonprofit Corporations

A **nonprofit corporation** is a legally defined type of business ownership in which the company operates not to provide profit for its shareholders but to serve the good of society. It uses any profit to further its mission. Nonprofit corporations exist through donations to raise money rather than selling shares of ownership. The owners of nonprofit corporations have limited liability regarding the company's debts.

Additionally, nonprofit corporations often receive special tax treatment from the Internal Revenue Service.

 **READING CHECKPOINT** *What is a corporation?*

Cooperatives

A **cooperative** is a business owned, controlled, and operated for the mutual benefit of its members—people who use its services, buy its goods, or are employed by it. For example, farmers form cooperatives to sell crops and buy farming equipment. In the U.S., cooperatives are not as common as other types of businesses and are often organized as corporations. Cooperatives often share their earnings with the membership as dividends.

▼ **Figure 3-4**
Cooperatives
Farmers often form cooperatives to buy farming equipment.
Inferring. *Why might it make sense for farmers to form cooperatives to buy farm equipment?*

 **READING CHECKPOINT** *What is a cooperative?*

TYPES OF BUSINESS OWNERSHIP

Ownership Issues	Sole	General or Limited Partnership	C Corporation	Subchapter S Corporation	Nonprofit Corporation	Limited Liability Company
Who owns?	Proprietor	Partners	Stockholders	Stockholders	No one	Members
What is liability?	Unlimited	Limited in most cases	Limited	Limited	Limited	Limited
How is it taxed?	Individual rate (lowest rate)	Individual rate (lowest rate)	Corporate rate ("double taxation")	Individual (lowest rate)	None	Individual (lowest rate)
How are profits distributed?	Proprietor receives all	Partners receive profits according to partnership agreement	Earnings paid to stockholders as dividends in proportion to the number of shares owned	Earnings paid to stockholders as dividends in proportion to the number of shares owned	Surplus cannot be distributed	Members receive profits per agreed-on operating procedure
Who votes on policy?	Not necessary	Partners	Common voting stockholders	Common voting stockholders	Board of directors/trustees agreement	Members per agreed-on operating procedure
How long can company exist?	Terminates on death of owner	Terminates on death of partner	Unlimited	Unlimited	Unlimited through trustees	Variable
How easy is it to capitalize?	Difficult	Easier than sole proprietorship	Very easy (ownership is sold as shares of stock)	Same as partnership	Difficult (there is no ownership to sell as stock)	Same as partnership

Your Business Plan. Continue developing your standard business plan. Go to "Section 3.2" of the *Business Plan Project* in your *Student Activity Workbook*, or "Section 3.2" of the BizTech Software.

Reviewing Objectives

1. What is the difference between limited and unlimited liability?
2. How is a sole proprietorship different from a general partnership?
3. What is a partnership agreement?
4. Name one advantage and one disadvantage of a corporation over a sole proprietorship.
5. Who owns a cooperative?

Critical Thinking

6. **Comparing/Contrasting.** A sole proprietor owns two businesses: a clock store and a skateboard outlet. Which business most needs limited liability? Why?
7. **Analyzing Information.** What aspects of a proposed business should an entrepreneur consider before choosing a type of business ownership?

Working Together

Working as a team, write a partnership agreement as if you were going into business together. Assume that some partners can work 40 hours per week and others can only work 20 hours. Also assume that some partners can contribute $5,000 each to setting up the business and others can contribute $1,000. Be certain to specify in the agreement how the profits will be divided among the partners.

Science
Cooperative Energy

Many electric companies around the country are organized as cooperatives. These cooperatives are active in providing energy from renewable sources (for example, wind or solar power). Research electric cooperatives in your state and their renewable energy projects. If your state does not have an electric cooperative, choose one that does. Prepare a brief report describing your findings.

Flying into Business

Joe Pascaretta and his friend Aaron Dowen had always been fascinated with computers. At the age of 11, they developed their first Website together, where Aaron put up pictures of airplanes that Joe had taken. With this experience and their knowledge of the Internet, they designed a Website for a local construction company. With the design in hand, they went to the construction company and got their first customer.

Alps: Providing Internet Solutions

In August 1999, Joe and Aaron formed Alps Technology, LLC, as a Website development firm. In the beginning, Joe sold the company's services to clients and Aaron built the Websites. They were very successful. Within two years, Alps Technology had 15 employees. They differentiated themselves from their competition by offering round-the-clock customer support every day of the week, complementary consulting services, and flexible financing options. They also narrowed their profit margin. Because they were young, they had a lawyer co-sign contracts with their customers.

Taking Advantage of Opportunities: Alps Lawn Care

When a client told Joe that keeping up the grounds of his business was expensive, Joe saw a new opportunity. In 2002, Alps Technology started the Alps Lawn Company. The Alps Lawn Company provided lawn cutting and landscape services and began with a single commercial lawnmower. As they added more customers, they hired managers and employees. In the first year, they grossed over $100,000. To attract even more business, Alps Lawn Company used software developed by Alps Technology to show customers what the finished landscaping would look like. Aerial photos of the landscaping were another selling tool. Because Joe had earned his pilot's license, he was able to take the pictures. Within a few years, Alps Lawn Company serviced over 60 residential and commercial properties and grossed over one million dollars annually.

In 2008, Joe and Aaron formed a new company, Alps International, combining Alps Lawn Company and Alps Holding Group.

Joe Pascaretta

Overcoming Obstacles

"If we would have listened to other people's advice, Alps and our successful joint ventures would have never been established," said Joe in an article in *Future CEO Stars Magazine*. The boys discovered that people sometimes didn't take them seriously because they were young. But they didn't let their youth stop them. "In fact," wrote Joe, "it motivated me to break through this age/image barrier and prove that, in fact, I know what I am talking about and can do what I claim. I never have let detractors slow me down. There will always be people who try to discourage risk taking. Of course, they don't think like entrepreneurs and can't see the benefit of facing the challenge. Facing fear head on is the only way I know to conquer it, so that's what I do."

Thinking Like an Entrepreneur

1. Doing things on spec, which is short for "on speculation" (as Alps did for their first job), means you may not get paid. Many people get their first account that way. What could you do on spec for your business to get customers?
2. What incentives would you offer customers to buy your product or service?
3. What would you do to have potential customers take you seriously?

CHAPTER SUMMARY

3.1 Types of Business

The four major types of business are manufacturing (manufacturers), whole-saling (wholesalers), retailing (retailers), and service. Manufacturing businesses convert materials into products for sale. Wholesalers purchase products in large quantities from manufacturers and resell them in smaller quantities to retail-ers. Retailing businesses sell products directly to consumers. Wholesale and retail businesses together are called trade businesses. Service businesses sell services (examples: doctors, babysitters, athletic trainers, and barbers). Over the past 50 years, service and trade businesses have replaced manufacturing as the primary industry in America. Service businesses are expected to dominate the U.S. economy for the forseeable future.

3.2 Types of Business Ownership

The major types of business ownership are sole proprietorship, partnership, corporation, and cooperative. Business structures differ primarily in terms of liability, taxes, who controls the business, and who shares its profits. Liability is the legal obligation of an owner to use personal money and possessions to pay business debt. There are significant legal restrictions and requirements associated with some types of ownership, particularly the corporation.

REVIEW VOCABULARY

Working with three or four classmates, develop a short presentation for the class, using at least half of the follow-ing terms. The rest of the class will play the role of potential entrepreneurs who need to be educated about types of business and types of business ownership.

- C corporation (p. 60)
- cooperative (p. 62)
- corporation (p. 60)
- dividend (p. 60)
- franchise (p. 54)
- general partnership (p. 58)
- incorporate (p. 61)
- liability (p. 56)
- limited liability (p. 56)
- limited liability company (p. 61)
- limited partnership (p. 58)

- manufacturer (p. 51)
- manufacturing business (p. 51)
- nonprofit corporation (p. 61)
- North American Industry Classification System (p. 55)
- partnership (p. 58)
- partnership agreement (p. 60)
- reseller's permit (p. 52)
- retailer (p. 52)
- retailing business (p. 52)
- service business (p. 52)

- share of stock (p. 60)
- shareholders (p. 60)
- sole proprietorship (p. 57)
- stockholders (p. 60)
- subchapter S corporation (p. 61)
- trade business (p. 52)
- unlimited liability (p. 56)
- wholesaler (p. 52)
- wholesaling business (p. 52)

CHECK YOUR UNDERSTANDING

Choose the letter that best answers the question or completes the statement.

1. Which type of business ownership provides limited liability for the owner(s)?
   a. corporation
   b. sole proprietorship
   c. general partnership
   d. all of the above

2. One advantage of a general partnership over a sole proprietorship is a general partnership
   a. provides limited liability
   b. is a corporation
   c. provides unlimited liability
   d. can rely on more than one person for financial backing

3. Which of the following phrases best describes a wholesaling business?
   a. a business that converts materials into products for sale
   b. a business that sells products to final buyers
   c. a business that performs services
   d. a business that sells products to retailers

4. Most businesses in the United States are
   a. corporations
   b. partnerships
   c. sole proprietorships
   d. cooperatives

5. Over the past fifty years the American economy has changed in what way?
   a. manufacturing has replaced retailing as the most dominant industry
   b. service businesses have become far less important to the economy
   c. wholesaling has become the dominant industry in the economy
   d. service and trade businesses have become the dominant industries

6. Which of the following statements about corporations is true?
   a. corporations are easier to set up than sole proprietorships
   b. a limited partnership is a type of corporation
   c. corporations sell stock to raise money
   d. a cooperative is a type of corporation

7. The businesses predicted to undergo the most growth in the coming decade are
   a. primarily service businesses
   b. primarily manufacturing businesses
   c. businesses that convert materials into products
   d. businesses that sell retail products to wholesalers

8. A business owner with unlimited liability
   a. could have to sacrifice personal money and possessions to pay business debt
   b. is not personally responsible for the debts of the business
   c. is a shareholder of a corporation
   d. would not have to sacrifice personal money and possessions to pay business debt

9. The purpose of a cooperative is
   a. to earn profits for management
   b. to benefit its members
   c. to provide unlimited liability to its members
   d. to pay dividends to investors

10. One advantage of a corporation as compared to a sole proprietorship is
    a. a corporation is easier to set up and requires less paperwork
    b. a corporation provides limited liability for its owners
    c. a corporation has fewer shareholders
    d. a corporation has a partnership agreement

11. A nonprofit corporation
    a. provides unlimited liability to its members
    b. provides limited liability to its members
    c. is set up to make profits for its investors
    d. is set up to pay dividends to its shareholders

12. The special permit that allows retailers to purchase goods tax-free from wholesalers and collect sales tax from final buyers is called a
    a. reseller's permit
    b. retailing permit
    c. tax permit
    d. wholesale permit

Business Communication

13. You own a service business that helps sole proprietorships become limited liability companies in your state. Create an advertising brochure that explains your services and the benefits of becoming a limited liability company.

14. You want to start a sole proprietorship retail business that employs several people. Research the steps necessary to comply with federal, state, and local government requirements for setting up your business. Summarize your research. Be creative. You can use a diagram, a flowchart, a 1-2-3 list, or any other method to summarize your research.

15. Imagine that your classmates are wealthy investors interested in putting money in a new business that could be franchised around the country. Prepare a short presentation in which you try to convince them that your business idea would be a great franchising opportunity.

Business Ethics

18. In a general partnership, do you think the partner who works the most hours is entitled to the largest share of the profits? Consider the partner who may have invested the most but doesn't put in nearly the same number of hours as the other partner. Also, consider how liability is shared. Come up with general rules that consider the amount each partner invests in the business and addresses how profit, liability, and work should be shared in a general partnership.

Business Math

16. A manufacturing company produces brushes and sells 500 for $300 to a wholesaler. The wholesaler sells a quantity of 20 for $15 to a retailer who sells each brush for $1.50. Calculate the percentage by which the price per brush increases at each step.

17. You own 1,260 shares in Corporation X that are worth $40 per share. Your cousin offers to trade you his 700 shares in Corporation Y that are worth $55 per share and will add $10,000 in cash. Should you make the trade?

Business in Your Community

19. Interview a local small-business owner who has set up a sole proprietorship or general partnership within the past year or two. Make a list of the permits, licenses, identification numbers, and fees that were required for the business to open.

20. Working with a group of classmates, find five local retail businesses (as diverse as possible) that also offer one or more services to consumers (for example, a gas station that also offers oil changes). Prepare a short presentation for the class in which you describe the retail businesses and explain why they provide services as well as products.

E-Commerce

Increasingly, people and businesses buy and sell goods online. This is referred to as **e-commerce**. You can typically recognize a Website that focuses on e-commerce because it has ".com" as part of its online address.

E-Commerce Technology

An e-commerce Website can be a stand-alone business or the Web-based counterpart of a traditional storefront business. Typically, running an e-commerce Website is less expensive than running a storefront business. That's because the cost of renting physical space is usually much more than the cost of renting space on the Web from a **Web host**—a business that stores all the information for a Website on its servers (computers with a large storage capacity that are connected to the Internet).

▲ *Placing items in a cart on an e-commerce site*

The site will also need a **commerce server**. This type of server runs commerce-based applications, such as credit card processing and inventory management. Credit card processing requires security measures, such as a **secure sockets layer (SSL)** that "locks" the site, making it secure so it cannot be read by outsiders. It is common to get a Web host, commerce server, and security program in one package.

Paying Online

E-commerce sites normally use credit or debit cards as the method of payment (although checks or cash can be used in some cases). E-commerce sites require a payment system to process orders. One of the most common is a **shopping cart.** This type of system asks shoppers to place selected items in a "cart." When finished shopping, customers pay for the selected goods.

Affiliate Marketing

Sometimes Website owners do not even store the products they are selling. What they sell is shipped from a location other than the Website owner's personal location. An example of this type of process is affiliate marketing. With **affiliate marketing**, a Website owner sells items from another store and takes a percentage of the profits.

Traffic and Conversion Rates

Website owners prize **Web traffic**, which is the number of visitors a site gets over a specific time period. However, a more important statistic is the Website's **conversion rate**. This is the percentage of Web traffic that translates into sales. It is a measure of how many potential customers actually buy something. An e-commerce Website owner uses a **Web analytics tool** to track daily traffic, length of stay on the site, sales, and conversion rates.

Tech Vocabulary

- affiliate marketing
- commerce server
- conversion rate
- e-commerce
- secure sockets layer (SSL)
- shopping cart
- Web analytics tool
- Web host
- Web traffic

Check Yourself

1. Why is running a Website typically less expensive than running a storefront business?

2. What is a commerce server?

3. What is affiliate marketing?

4. Why is Web traffic less important than its conversion rate?

What Do You Think?

Comparing/Contrasting. What are some ways a Website can stand out from other sites?

BECOMING AN ENTREPRENEUR

Although she didn't realize it at the time, Eva Tan became an entrepreneur when she was a high school student in Westerville, Ohio. Follow her story, beginning here and continuing at the end of each unit of the book.

Planning for Success

One summer, when Eva was in high school, she helped plan her older sister's wedding. There were so many issues! Invitations, flowers, clothing, and music were just a few of the things that had to be arranged.

Helping the entire process go smoothly was a big challenge, but one that Eva really liked. The reception menu planning was particularly interesting, because Eva's parents came from two very different backgrounds: Irish and Filipino.

The event was a success. After it was over, Eva said, "As my sister's wedding planner, I had to wear many hats. The whole experience helped me realize the importance of problem-solving, paying attention to details, being organized but flexible, and remaining cool under pressure. The wedding took a lot of time and effort, but the results were worth it. My sister was pleased, and I discovered I could do things I didn't know I could."

That fall, back in high school, Eva took an "Introduction to Business" class as one of her electives. The class, and her experience with her sister's wedding, made her think of creating an event-planning business. She wondered what she could do to develop her skills and gain experience.

Eva began looking for opportunities to volunteer for more event-planning. She helped plan her Junior Prom and organized fund-raising events to finance a senior class trip to Florida.

Her mother, a high school teacher who earned her degree at Ohio State University (OSU), introduced Eva to friends from the university who needed event planning. They began asking Eva to plan small events like birthday parties and baby showers.

Eva's grandmother was a widow who lived with Eva's family. Although Eva's grandmother had never done event planning, she had run a small restaurant with her husband. Eva had always found her grandmother's stories about the restaurant entertaining, but now Eva began asking her for advice about upcoming events.

Profiting from a Loss

During her senior year, Eva had difficulty deciding what career route to take after graduation. At the time, event planning seemed more like a hobby than a long-term career goal.

Eva decided to enroll in the two-year Business Management program at Columbus State Community College. She said, "I think the general business courses will be useful, no matter what career path I eventually decide to take." An agreement between Columbus State and OSU would also allow her to transfer her associate degree credits to OSU if she wanted to complete a four-year degree.

One of the first college courses Eva took was "Principles of Microeconomics." Topics such as supply and demand, the role of competition, and the profit motive made her think about the economy in and around Columbus. "With my professor's permission, I fulfilled one of my class requirements by researching how the city's current economy would impact a new event-planning business," she said. "I wanted to find out, economically speaking, what my chances for success were."

Eva continued to work part-time, planning events to help pay for college. Charging for her services by the hour, Eva researched vendor options, placed orders for goods and services, and coordinated their delivery. She began to wonder if she could increase her profits by making some of the food and party decorations herself.

To test this, Eva created samples of her food for customers. They loved them! As a result, she landed her first order that included her handmade food items. With her grandmother's help, she filled the order on time and to the customer's satisfaction. Later, after analyzing the cost of her materials, Eva discovered that she had lost money instead of making a profit. In her desire to get the order, she had set the price too low. Eva promised herself that, in the future, she would pay closer attention to her costs and be sure that she made a profit!

A Business Is Born!

In her college course, Eva learned about different business structures. She made a chart that compared the advantages and disadvantages of each. She decided to set up her part-time service business as a sole proprietorship. It seemed like the simplest and least expensive way to operate for the time being. She named her business "Eva's Entertainment Services," filled out the necessary forms, and obtained a tax I.D. number.

Eva's Entertainment Services was off and running!

What Would You Have Done?

1. **Applying Concepts.** How would you have increased your knowledge about event planning if you were in high school, like Eva?

2. **Analyzing Information.** It costs Eva $40 in materials to make a table centerpiece. It takes her half an hour to make the centerpiece. She charges her client $50 for it. What would you charge? Why?

3. **Drawing Conclusions.** If you were Eva, would you have set up the company as a sole proprietorship?

UNIT **2**

PREPARING FOR BUSINESS

In This Unit:

4. Business Communication
5. Ethics & Social Responsibility

YOUR BUSINESS PLAN

In this unit, you'll focus on the **Business Idea** section of the business plan and answer this question:

- How is my business socially responsible?

OBJECTIVES

- Understand how to communicate in business
- Use business letters, memos, e-mails, and faxes
- Understand when to use telephone calls, conference calls, and videoconferences
- Understand how to use instant messaging
- Demonstrate active listening

VOCABULARY

- active listening
- conference call
- emoticon
- fax (facsimile)
- instant messaging (IM)
- memo
- message thread
- salutation
- texting
- videoconference

Consider this question:

Is it dishonest to change the way you communicate in business compared to your everyday method?

Write your answer (yes or no) on a piece of paper. Be prepared to defend your answer in class.

Effective Business Communication

Calvin Coolidge, the 30th President of the United States, was known as a man of few words. Once, at a dinner party, a guest told him that she had bet she could get him to say more than two words that evening. Coolidge replied, "You lose."

As an entrepreneur, your approach must be different from President Coolidge's. Even if you are your business's only employee, you'll need to communicate—to share information, thoughts, or opinions—with suppliers, customers, family members, friends, business colleagues, and many others. Not only do you need to share information, you must also have the right tone when you share it. An informal tone is usually not appropriate, nor is one that is either too aggressive or too unassertive.

Although every type of work has its own special vocabulary, you don't need to learn technical terms to communicate in business. In fact, the less technical your writing is, the better. But you will need to communicate effectively. The six qualities of good communication are:

- **Briefness.** Professional writers have a rule abbreviated as KISS—"Keep it short and simple." In the business world, that means identifying yourself and the reason for the communication. Avoid using unnecessary words or getting side-tracked with personal information or other unrelated subjects.

> **KISS**
> Keep It Short and Simple.

- **Organization.** Give information in an easy-to-follow format. Some messages might need numbered steps or an outline. For a letter or speech, you should introduce your subject, add details in a logical order, and close by summarizing your main ideas.

- **Clarity.** Your audience may not know all the facts as you do. Include the details your audience needs to understand to act on your message.

- **Relevance.** Supply the right information to the right audience. Wading through unneeded facts can be confusing and time-consuming. Suppose you ask an employee to order pens to give away at a grand opening. That individual needs to know the color, quantity, and wording you want on the pens. She doesn't need to know how much you're spending on radio ads.

- **Courtesy.** Communicate respect and a positive attitude. Assume that the other party is interested in helping you solve your problem or meet your goal. Even if you have to point out someone else's mistake, avoid personal attacks and criticism.

- **Suitability.** As you'll learn in this chapter, different types of communication are required for different situations.

Once you've learned these qualities, you can apply them to different situations and purposes. Not surprisingly, achieving them takes preparation. To make a phone call brief, for example, might mean jotting down a few points you want to make beforehand. To be brief when writing a business proposal might mean making an outline and sticking to it.

 *What are the six qualities of good communication?*

Written Communication

With advances in electronic technology, some people predicted that writing skills would be less important in the business world. Instead, just the opposite has occurred. As electronic communication opens more doors, businesspeople need to express their ideas in writing more often. Can you imagine having to contact potential customers all over the world by telephone?

Writing is also important because some messages are best put in writing for legal reasons. If you have a complaint against a nonpaying client, or an idea for an invention, written communication creates a "paper trail" backing up your claim.

Writing gives you the chance to review and edit your message. You will always need to ask yourself such questions as: Are the ideas clearly stated? Is the tone friendly but professional? Are the grammar, spelling, and punctuation correct? Even if you use a word-processing program that checks your spelling, you will need to proofread for errors. The program won't know if you've misspelled the recipient's name. Or if you should have used "their" instead of "they're" or "there." Or that you meant to type "baked beans," not "naked beans"!

It is often a good idea to ask someone to review written communication before you send it. If that isn't possible, take a break before you send it and then re-read it to make sure the information is correct and the tone is right.

Business Letters

Business letters are used for longer or more official messages. For example, you would use a letter to answer a customer's inquiry or to ask for information about a product. A business letter should be typed in an easy-to-read font, not a fancy script. Following an accepted form shows professionalism and attention to detail.

The well-developed business letter includes the following elements:

- Include the date in the upper-left corner.

- Skip a line or two and key the recipient's name and address below the date. Use the same name and address you use on the envelope.

- Skip a line and key the **salutation**, or greeting, starting at the left margin. "Dear" is the accepted greeting, followed by the person's title (Mr., Ms., or Dr., for example), the last name, and then a colon. Use the first and last name without a title if you're not sure whether the recipient is a man or woman. Use a comma only if you are on a friendly basis with the recipient.

- For the body of the letter you can either indent the first line of each paragraph or skip a line between paragraphs.

- Start a new line at the left margin for the closing. "Sincerely," is the usual closing. If you use a phrase such as "Sincerely yours," capitalize only the first word. End every closing with a comma.

- Skip a few lines and key your name, position, and address (unless your address is shown on your stationery—your letterhead).

- Sign your name in the space you left above your keyed name. Sign your name as you keyed it unless you are on a friendly basis with the recipient—then sign only your first name.

In some cases, you might also include a reference line under the date. This would begin with the abbreviation "re:" (for "regarding") and summarize the subject of the letter, much like the subject line in an e-mail.

If you're sending a copy of the letter to others, skip a line below your address and key "cc:" (for "courtesy copy") at the left margin. Then add the names of the people who are receiving a courtesy copy.

If you are enclosing a document, such as an ad to be run in a newspaper, you would key "enc:" (for "enclosed") below your name and address (and below the cc: line, if there is one) at the left margin. Then you would add an abbreviated description of the material.

Once you establish a working relationship with someone, you might drop some formality. Remember the qualities of good communication, however, and always keep the letter brief and organized.

Word-processing software usually includes various templates to use for letters. You can pick the one you think most effectively conveys the "look" you want for your business.

▼ **Figure 4-1**

Parts of a Business Letter
A business letter should be typed and error-free.

Writing. *Would you use a template from a word-processing program that created a letterhead for you?*

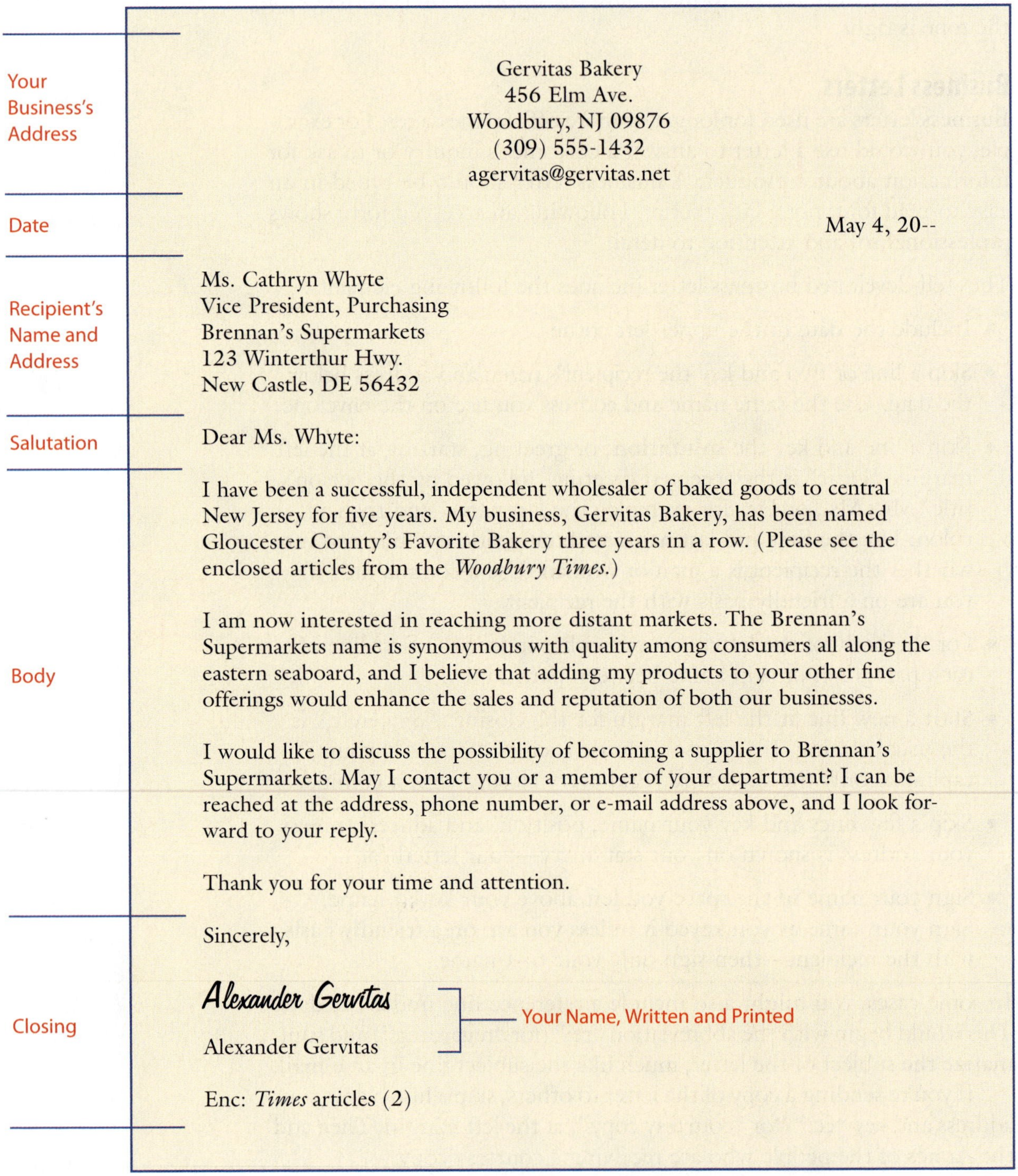

Your Business's Address	Gervitas Bakery 456 Elm Ave. Woodbury, NJ 09876 (309) 555-1432 agervitas@gervitas.net
Date	May 4, 20--
Recipient's Name and Address	Ms. Cathryn Whyte Vice President, Purchasing Brennan's Supermarkets 123 Winterthur Hwy. New Castle, DE 56432
Salutation	Dear Ms. Whyte:
Body	I have been a successful, independent wholesaler of baked goods to central New Jersey for five years. My business, Gervitas Bakery, has been named Gloucester County's Favorite Bakery three years in a row. (Please see the enclosed articles from the *Woodbury Times.*) I am now interested in reaching more distant markets. The Brennan's Supermarkets name is synonymous with quality among consumers all along the eastern seaboard, and I believe that adding my products to your other fine offerings would enhance the sales and reputation of both our businesses. I would like to discuss the possibility of becoming a supplier to Brennan's Supermarkets. May I contact you or a member of your department? I can be reached at the address, phone number, or e-mail address above, and I look forward to your reply. Thank you for your time and attention.
Closing	Sincerely, *Alexander Gervitas* — Your Name, Written and Printed Alexander Gervitas Enc: *Times* articles (2)

Addressing an envelope is easy. Put the recipient's address in the center of the envelope and put your address (referred to as the "return address") in the upper-left corner. Put the stamp in the upper-right corner.

Memos

A **memo** (short for memorandum) is a brief note that informs employees about a business-related matter. A letter is written to people outside the business, and a memo is written to people within it. Compared to business letters, memos are typically shorter and less formal. They share relevant news or information employees need to perform a task. The subject might range from a reminder of an office birthday party to a marketing trend that will affect a company's profits.

A memo has two main parts:

- **Heading.** The heading consists of the lines that identify the recipients, the sender, the date, and the subject of the memo. A precisely worded subject line lets recipients know how the message applies to them and how quickly they should respond. Be careful to match the message to the audience. Information meant for only a few should be sent in separate memos to those individuals. This is a matter of privacy as well as relevance.

- **Body.** The body contains the message. Memos tend to cover only one subject. However, you may still want to break down the topic with separate paragraphs or a list, for easier reading.

▼ **Figure 4-2**
Business Memo
Memos may be e-mailed or handwritten.
Solving Problems. *How do you think memos would be distributed in a small business?*

TO: Baxter's Bakery Sales Associates
FROM: Ginny Baxter
DATE: May 15, 20--
SUBJECT: Organic Chocolate Ingredients

As of June 15, Baxter's Bakery will be using only organic, sustainably grown chocolate in its baked goods. This includes baking cocoa, baking chocolate, and semi-sweet chocolate chips.

I've ordered promotional pamphlets. Please place one in every bag with customers' purchases. Also read a pamphlet yourself, so you can promote the cause of sustainable agriculture (and our tasty baked treats!) and help answer customers' questions.

Word-processing software usually includes memo templates. Often, word-processing software has "families" of templates. Each family has a common name and a similar look. For example, the software might have a "Professional" family of templates, with a "Professional" letter template and a "Professional" memo template. Another style might be designated "Classic" and would have a "Classic" letter template and a "Classic" memo template. If your software has families of templates, use the memo version from the same family as your letter template for a consistent look in communications.

E-Mail

As you know, an e-mail is a message that is sent and received electronically over a computer network. E-mails are a favorite type of communication for business because they are easy. You can read and respond to the message on your own schedule. You can forward it to others without paying postage. Also, if you do not print the message, it's environmentally friendly, with no paper or empty ink cartridges to be recycled.

Unfortunately, speed and ease of use also make e-mail a potential hazard. You may not take as much care writing e-mails as you would for a letter or a memo. It's easy to send an e-mail to the wrong person or to respond too quickly, without thinking. It's also easy to send an e-mail without the attachments you intended. Once you have sent an e-mail, you usually cannot retrieve it. In business, the consequences of a badly written, sloppy, or poorly conceived e-mail can be dramatic.

You should write an e-mail with the same care you would give to a business letter. Practicing the following guidelines will not only prevent potential trouble but will also help you slow down and give the e-mail proper consideration:

- Write a short, but useful, description in the subject line.

- Before sending attachments, ask the recipient if he or she can accept them. Many businesses automatically delete attachments to prevent viruses. Learn what format to use for your attachments and make sure they are a manageable size; anything over five megabytes (5MB) is likely to be rejected at some point as it travels over the Internet.

- Consider using a signature. This is information you have keyed that is added automatically by the word-processing software at the end of your e-mail. A signature often consists of your name, the company name, the company phone number, and, sometimes, a company slogan.

- To avoid sending an e-mail before you mean to, compose it off-line first. Fill in the "to" field last, just before sending.

- Get the sender's permission before forwarding an e-mail.

- If you send the e-mail to many people, hide their addresses by using the "bcc" (blind courtesy copy) feature. This respects their privacy and saves them from scrolling through a long list of names to get to the message.

- Using "reply" automatically creates a **message thread**, which shows every previous message in the correspondence. Over time, these may become unnecessary. You might want to start a fresh thread, summarizing the most recent, relevant messages.

- If the information is sensitive, write a business letter instead.

Faxes

Fax is short for **facsimile** (fak-SIM-uh-lee), an exact copy of something. A fax machine uses telephone lines to transmit a copy of a document. Each fax should be accompanied by a cover sheet that identifies the sender, the recipient, the subject, the date, a brief description of the items being sent, and the number of pages.

► Figure 4-3
Fax Cover Sheet
The sender fills in the cover sheet and includes it with the fax.
Applying Concepts. *What other information might a sender supply in the message area?*

904 West Meadows Place
Peoria, IL 61604
(309) 555-7857

Lady Best Apparel

Fax

To:	Tara Sedgewick	From:	K. Anne Smith
Fax:	(203) 555-6658	**Pages:**	5
Phone:	(203) 555-6665	**Date:**	11/10/20--
Re:	New Spring Line	**CC:**	Fran Aldasoki

☐ Urgent ☒ For Review ☐ Please Comment ☐ Please Reply ☐ Please Recycle

● **Comments:**

Please look over the suggestions for the new Spring line and let me know what you think. I'd like to finalize this by Thursday.

Make sure the recipient expects a fax before you send one. The recipient's machine must be turned on to receive the material, and many small businesses turn off their fax machines to avoid unwanted advertisements. Remember, many people may read a fax you send to a workplace. Prior notice helps ensure some degree of privacy; however, faxes are not the best way to send confidential information.

Word-processing software often includes a fax cover sheet in a family of templates. So, again, if you are using a certain type of template for your letters and memos, use a template from the same family for your fax cover sheets.

 READING CHECKPOINT

What is a message thread?

Spoken Communication

Have you heard the saying "Word of mouth is the best advertising"? That applies to the value of spoken (verbal) messages in other business situations as well. When you need an immediate reply or just want to know the person or people with whom you are working, your best choice is often to meet in person—or over the phone.

You probably know good speakers when you hear them. To be a good speaker yourself, remember these points:

- **Speak Clearly.** Having to repeat information can be disruptive, time consuming, and frustrating to your audience.

Web Conferencing

Meetings are a fact of life in business. Entrepreneurs must meet with customers, potential investors, and employees. It isn't always possible, or desirable, to fly across the country or drive to an in-person meeting. That's why many businesses regularly use Web conferencing. According to the Gartner Group, a technology research firm, Web conferencing will be a $1.37 billion industry in 2008.

Web conferencing has many advantages. Attendees take part in the virtual meeting through live video and audio by using Webcams and microphones. They can share PowerPoint slide presentations. They can take Web tours of specific sites or conduct polls. In many ways, Web conferencing can be more productive and cost-effective than in-person meetings.

There are many ways for a small business to enable Web conferencing. You must decide whether to purchase Web conferencing software and service from a vendor, such as WebEx, or use a Web-based service, such as GoToMeeting.com. Participants either download software on their computers or log in to a particular address on the Web. With the high cost of oil and gas—and the environmental impact of oil production, flying, and driving—Web conferences are one way a business can save expenses while helping the planet.

THINKING CRITICALLY

Predicting. In small groups, research ways businesses will use Web conferencing in the future. Do you think businesspeople will still drive or fly to in-person meetings? Why or why not?

To read more about Web conferencing, go to "Entrepreneurship Issues" on the Student Center at entrepreneurship.pearson.com.

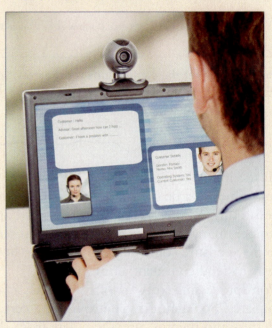

- **Draw in the Entire Audience.** Look and nod at people individually. Refer to individuals if possible, especially to give them praise or credit.

- **Encourage Participation.** Use pauses and careful word choices. Saying something like "I've heard this is a better approach, but I've never tried it—what do you think?" asks listeners to offer their own opinions.

- **Read the Mood of the Room.** If the audience seems relaxed and sociable, act the same. If they are in a hurry, indicate that you are aware of this and attempt to give them the information in the most efficient way possible.

- **Use Gestures.** Avoid distracting gestures. Use gestures for emphasis.

Telephone Calls

With wireless technology, making business calls is more convenient than ever. But receiving them is not always convenient. Here are five tips for making effective phone calls:

- Identify yourself immediately. Even people who know you might not recognize your voice at first.

- Ask if the person has time to talk.

- If you're put on hold, be patient.

- If asked to leave a message, be sure to include enough information to help the recipient prepare a response and return your call.

- When someone can take your call, give the conversation your full attention. Provide feedback by saying things like "Yes," "OK," or "Uh-huh" to indicate you are listening. Show the same courtesy when you receive calls. If you can't give the other person the attention needed, find a time that's more convenient for you both.

Remember to record a helpful, and professional-sounding, message on your answering machine or voice mail. For example, say, "I'm in the office from eight to five o'clock. In an emergency, I can be reached at home between seven and nine o'clock." Check your messages often and return calls promptly. With the increasing use of Caller ID, make your business calls from a phone number that is appropriate for a return caller to call.

Conference Calls

A **conference call** allows three or more parties in different locations to speak to each other over the same phone line. For example, someone at the home office in Chicago might arrange a conference call between a salesperson in Nashville and a writer in a satellite office in New York who is writing a brochure.

Scheduling is absolutely necessary to coordinate a conference call. If the callers are located in different time zones, everyone must be sure of the time. Three o'clock in Portland, Maine, for example, is noon in Portland, Oregon.

A quiet setting is important for focusing on several callers at the same time. Land phones are preferable to cell phones, which tend to pick up background noise. Using the "mute" button to silence the line when you are not speaking can also help the other participants hear each other if the lines are noisy.

If any charts, contracts, or other written materials will be required in the conference call, send copies to all parties in advance.

Videoconferences

A videoconference offers "the next best thing to being there." A **video-conference** is a meeting in which participants in different locations see and hear each other through monitors, cameras, microphones, and speakers. However, videoconferences cannot duplicate the experience of face-to-face meetings. A videoconference takes some getting used to and some special preparation.

A videoconference room usually has two monitors. The party you're talking to appears on one monitor. You and your party appear on the other. This helps you communicate effectively. If you hold up a chart, for instance, you can see whether it's legible on the receiving end—but seeing yourself on camera can be distracting.

Bright colors and detailed patterns in clothing can appear more vibrant on camera. White garments and glittery jewelry can reflect light and create a glare. Neutral colors and subtle patterns, such as solid tan or blue-gray pinstripes, are easier on the eyes.

You also need to be concerned about the audio aspect of videoconferencing. Microphones magnify any noise you make. Habits such as shuffling papers or tapping a pen on the table can quickly become irritating.

 **READING CHECKPOINT** *How does a conference call differ from a videoconference?*

▼ Figure 4-4
Videoconference Room
Videoconference rooms may be found in large hotels, civic centers, and corporate offices.

Relating Concepts. *How can videoconferencing lower a business's operating costs?*

Instant Messaging

More and more, advances in technology are creating forms of communication that combine writing and speaking. Instant messaging (IM) is one popular example. **Instant messaging** is immediate communication using typed text over the Internet. Like e-mail, instant messages are written. However, they are exchanged nearly as quickly as talking.

Instant messaging can be an asset to an entrepreneur. Suppose a carpenter is looking for a door for a house he is renovating. He spots a door that would be perfect and snaps some pictures with his digital camera. He then contacts the client via instant messaging, sending the photos as a video file. An hour later, the happy client has the door—and the carpenter is installing it.

Instant messaging has a downside. The software can be expensive. Some instant-messaging users feel their privacy is invaded every time they go online. People on your contact list will know when you're online. Signaling "busy" or "away" limits some intrusions, but not everyone respects these status messages. Instant messaging offers no guarantee of privacy, because messages can be saved, printed, and shared with others.

Instant messaging is quickly moving forward technologically. Software will soon offer both instant messaging and visual communication, so you can see, talk, and message all at the same time. Another new feature is the use of global positioning systems (GPS) to map the exact spot where you are **texting** (as using instant messaging is called). GPS can also show from where members of your contact list are texting.

Dealing with IM technology is a challenge for today's entrepreneurs. Here are some tips to help you manage instant messaging in a business context:

- Choose a user name that projects the image you want to convey to clients and colleagues. Determine whether a name is considered offensive by certain groups or cultures.

- Start a conversation by asking whether the other person would like or has time to communicate.

- Take care when using an **emoticon**—a symbol, such as those on the right, or a combination of punctuation marks used to convey emotions—such as a smiley face :-) or a wink ;-). Don't use abbreviations (such as JAM for "just a minute" or BTW for "by the way")—many businesspeople consider that unprofessional. Also, they can cause confusion or misunderstandings.

- As with phone calls, IM doesn't allow for visual or audible cues that let others know you're paying attention. Break the "silence" with short replies such as "Good point" or "Let me think for a second."

 *What is an emoticon?*

The Importance of Listening

A critical aspect of communication is listening: to be more specific, the ability to listen actively. **Active listening** is listening consciously, and responding in ways that improve communication. Active listening is a two-part process, and both parts take work:

▲ Emoticons

- **Focus on the Speaker.** The words and tone of voice will give clues to his or her frame of mind. Does the speaker sound unsure? Concerned? Enthusiastic? Don't be distracted by your surroundings. Encourage and support the speaker with useful responses, such as nodding your head or saying "I see"—even if you disagree. This is just showing that you are listening.

- **Give Feedback.** This tells the speaker that you understand what is being said. Feedback is typically phrased in a way that encourages the speaker to correct any misunderstandings. For example, a financial advisor might say to a client, "It sounds like saving for retirement is more important to you than a quick return on your investment. Is that right?"

Active listening can improve your speaking skills by making you more aware of how facial expression, tone of voice, and other aspects of verbal communication color your message. You can then better use these elements to communicate exactly what you mean.

 *What is meant by active listening?*

 Your Business Plan. Continue developing your standard business plan. Go to "Section 4.1" of the *Business Plan Project* in your *Student Activity Workbook*, or "Section 4.1" of the BizTech Software.

ASSESSMENT 4.1

Reviewing Objectives

1. List the six qualities of effective business communication.

2. How are memos similar to e-mails? How are they different?

3. Give five points to remember when making a business presentation.

4. What are some advantages and disadvantages of instant messaging in business?

5. Explain the purpose of feedback in active listening.

Critical Thinking

6. **Comparing/Contrasting.** Explain how effective business communication is a balance between qualities. For example, how does briefness need to be balanced with clarity? How does briefness need to be balanced with courtesy?

7. **Solving Problems.** Suppose you need to write a letter to a company's customer service department, but you don't know the name of the person to contact. How would you word the salutation?

Working Together

With a partner, write a dialog that shows how two classmates might discuss a class assignment outside of school. Then write a dialog showing how a classmate would discuss the assignment with a teacher in school. Perform your dialogs for the class.

> ### Science
> **Communication Technology**
> Research the history of communication technology. Choose one important invention for a class presentation. Explain the technology behind the invention and how it affected the business world.

4.2 Negotiating

OBJECTIVES

- Explain why negotiation is important in business
- Describe ways to prepare to negotiate
- Demonstrate positive techniques for conducting negotiations
- Discuss how to benefit from negotiated agreements
- Understand how values relate to negotiations
- Understand how to negotiate with people from other cultures

VOCABULARY

- bargaining in good faith
- compromise
- concession
- negotiation
- values

How would you answer this question?

In a negotiation, should someone win?

Write your answer (yes or no) on a piece of paper. Be prepared to talk about your answer in class.

What Is Negotiation?

What do these two scenarios have in common?

- A third grader swaps a peanut butter sandwich for a granola bar and fruit yogurt at lunch.

- World leaders work out the complicated details of a peace settlement.

Both situations involve negotiation. **Negotiation** is a process in which two or more parties reach an agreement or solve a problem through communication.

Negotiating is different from buying and selling. For a negotiation to succeed, the parties must be willing to adjust their expectations so they can come to an agreement. In business, that's called **bargaining in good faith**. This means that each party in a negotiation has an honest intention to resolve differences in a way that is acceptable to all. Each side sees the other as a partner in finding a solution, not an adversary. Together, they focus on their shared goal—making the deal—rather than on their individual demands.

Negotiation is essential to business—not only to *your* business but also to the economy as a whole. Here's an example: Shelly owned a dog-grooming business. She wanted to expand her business to include boarding, but a number of problems stood in her way. She found a property for the kennels but thought the rent was too high. She couldn't find employees for the wages she wanted to pay. And some prospective customers were unwilling or unable to pay the rates she planned to charge.

If Shelly can't find a way to negotiate these issues, she won't realize her dream. If she doesn't succeed in starting this business, there will be a "ripple effect." Other business owners could be hurt as well. The landlord will have to maintain an empty, unproductive property. Workers won't have jobs. Dog owners won't have a useful service. The local economy could suffer.

New entrepreneurs are sometimes surprised at how often people are willing to negotiate. You might expect that independent business owners, who have more control over their companies, would be willing to lower a price or add an extra service. If you've seen or heard of car buyers and auto dealers haggling over price, you're familiar with this concept. Large chains also give salespeople and managers leeway in making deals. The trend toward negotiating is expected to grow because of increased competition from Internet-based companies. Negotiating is always more popular in tight economic times.

 *What does it mean to bargain in good faith?*

Preparing to Negotiate

In a fast-food restaurant, has the counter clerk ever asked "Can I help you?" before you could look over the menu? You probably asked for more time: time to think about what you wanted, time to learn what was available, and, finally, time to decide whether you were willing to pay the price being asked. You need to consider these same issues when preparing to negotiate.

Ideally, you'll give yourself enough time to carefully consider the issues when you plan to negotiate. Suppose you decide that your delivery van will have to be replaced in a year. The sooner you start planning to buy a new van, the better your negotiating position will be. You can decide what features you need and compare the prices of different models. You can save more money and give yourself more choices.

Outlining the Issues

Before you can negotiate, you need to decide what you hope the outcome will be. Answering these four questions can help clarify your negotiating goals:

- **What do you need and what do you want?** Good negotiations involve give-and-take. Some offers can sound appealing and yet introduce side issues that complicate the discussion. To make the negotiation successful, focus on meeting your needs. Only after these are met should you consider your wants. Shelly, the dog groomer, faced this situation when she negotiated the rent.

The landlord wasn't able to reduce the rent but did offer to paint the fence around the property to make it more attractive. Shelly *wanted* the nicely painted fence, but she *needed* a lower rent, so she couldn't accept the offer.

- **What concessions can you make?** A **concession** is something you're willing to give up. Identifying points you are willing to concede relates to distinguishing needs from wants. You don't want to give up something that is essential to your business's survival. Shelly could concede on the nicely painted fence, but she couldn't concede when it came to paying the higher rent.

- **What concessions can you ask of the other party?** Good faith requires that all sides be ready to make sacrifices. Learning about the other party can help you decide what sacrifices they might be willing to make. Suppose Shelly's prospective landlord had many properties, with many of the tenants owning dogs and cats. Shelly might offer the landlord's tenants free boarding and grooming in exchange for a lower rent. The landlord would then be able to offer something special to entice prospective tenants.

- **What will you do if you can't reach an agreement?** If neither you nor the other party is willing to change a position, what other options do you have? Is the issue on which you disagree critical to the deal, or can you meet that need in some other way? If Shelly isn't able to get her prospective landlord to reduce the rent, she will have to locate another property for her business.

▼ **Figure 4-5**
Points for Negotiation
Researching your options puts you in a better position to bargain.
Interpreting Illustrations. *How does this list show that the entrepreneur has done some research?*

> **Colvin Young, Photographer**
> **123 Oak Alley**
> **(337) 555-0109**
>
> Negotiation with Triple A Courier
>
> Ask about:
>
> Discount for frequent/regular deliveries?
> (ACME Courier offers 10% off)
>
> Less-than-truckload rates?
>
> Minimum pick-up charges?
>
> Extra charge for weekend delivery?
> (Website says weekday rates plus 50%—why so much more?)

Planning to Negotiate

As you reflect on these ideas, it can be useful to put them in writing as notes for your negotiation. Pay close attention to your choice of words. Think about their impact. Otherwise, through pressure or frustration or simple forgetfulness, you might phrase them in ways that sound confrontational. Work on phrasing your position positively. For example, suppose Shelly said to a possible job applicant, "I hope we can come to terms on a salary. I think you would be a great addition to our team." Do you think the prospective employee would be more or less likely to want to work for her?

For major negotiations, you might rehearse your presentation with another person playing the role of the other party. Negotiating skills must be learned. You might also consider having a partner who is more skilled in negotiating help you in your actual negotiation. You can benefit by seeing how a more experienced individual handles various situations. Also, people have different negotiating styles. Yours might complement someone else's so you would work well together as a team.

 **What four questions can help you outline the issues to be negotiated?**

Guidelines for Productive Negotiations

Negotiations may take place in person, over the phone, by e-mail, or by instant messaging. Whatever the situation, these guidelines will help make the discussion productive:

1. **State your offer firmly.** As the saying goes, "You can't get what you don't ask for." Ask for what you hope to get, even if you don't expect it. Remember to focus first on your needs, not on your wants.

2. **Explain your position.** Do not simply state your position; explain it. Give reasons why you cannot meet the other party's demands, but suggest that your position could change in the future as a result of this negotiation. For example, suppose you can't afford a supplier's price. You might say, "Right now, that's not in my budget. But if you can help me by dropping your price now, we could renegotiate later when my business takes off." Remember the principle of good faith. Make only promises on which you can realistically act.

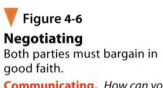

▼ **Figure 4-6**
Negotiating
Both parties must bargain in good faith.

Communicating. *How can your body language show that you are open to compromise?*

3. **Look for common ground.** If you can't resolve a primary issue, finding a less important point you can agree on will sometimes lead the way to a larger resolution.

4. **Be willing to make compromises.** A ==compromise== is an agreement arrived at when all sides have made concessions. Everyone gives up something but gets something in return. In fair negotiations, the trade-offs are roughly equal.

5. **Put the offer in writing.** Having the offers written out helps you compare your terms to theirs. It lets you see what concessions and compromises each of you has made. This will help you put the negotiation in perspective. Eventually, for negotiations involving significant issues, you'll probably sign a written contract indicating the terms on which you've agreed. (You will learn more about contracts in Chapter 16.)

6. **Weigh the short-term and long-term consequences.** Ask yourself whether you must get everything you need from this agreement. Sometimes, accepting less than what you hoped for will create goodwill that can help you in the long term. The opposite is also true: Getting ideal terms today can sometimes mean accepting terms that are not so good in the future.

7. **Take time off.** If possible, take a break and pick up negotiations later. You may get fresh ideas or see things in a new light. This could lead to a solution that would be better for everyone. Also, over time, the situation could change, which would alter the negotiations.

 *Why do negotiating parties make compromises?*

Managing the Agreement

Every successful negotiation has a follow-through, some action that is defined by the negotiated agreement. For instance, one party might buy a product or perform a service. Learn to see this stage not as an end but as a beginning. Even a single action, such as buying a business car or cleaning a house, is a way to strengthen relationships and improve your position for future negotiations. It's an opportunity to build a reputation for honesty and reliability.

This principle applies even more to longer-term agreements. Suppose you own a small greenhouse. You negotiate with the managers of an office building to supply every office with a variety of seasonal blooming plants. After the agreement, you might go beyond the negotiated deal to e-mail notices of new varieties of plants on the market or tips for plant care. You are going beyond the agreement to gain goodwill and, possibly, future business.

You also might encounter times when you can't meet your commitments. This could be due to inexperience, poor planning, or unforeseen

Expectations

Teachers may have specific expectations for each of their students. Parents have expectations for each of their children. Often these expectations are the same. For example, an expectation that parents and teachers share is that students will have academic success. However, "academic success" can have many meanings. What would be a success for one student may not be so for another.

Think about other people's expectations for you. These expectations may require a great deal of effort or they may be easily met, but they will always be someone else's. What matters more than these expectations? The expectations you have for yourself.

As you move from high school to college, other types of training, or a career, you will need to set reasonable expectations for yourself. Teachers and parents won't be as involved in your life as they once were. You will need to keep your own expectations relatively high to succeed. Always set them just a bit higher than is comfortable. Don't make them too easy to achieve. After all, if you don't expect much from yourself, you will probably get what you expect.

THINKING CRITICALLY

Writing. Write a paragraph describing why having high, but reasonable, expectations can increase a person's self-confidence.

To read more about expectations, go to "Your Business Career" on the Student Center at entrepreneurship.pearson.com.

events. In these cases, communication is especially important. The other party needs to know about the problem as soon as possible so they can try to make other arrangements. Not meeting your commitments can feel like failure, and it certainly can cost you financially. However, you can minimize the damage to your personal and professional reputation. Accept responsibility for the problem and try to correct any difficulty you may have caused.

What if you are disadvantaged because the other party isn't able to meet the agreed-on commitment? How you react can turn a bad situation into a better one. Accommodate the other party, if possible. People tend to remember those who helped them get through a difficult time and are likely to repay the favor.

Remember too that you had a reason to do business with the other party. You might still feel that way even if problems have occurred. For example, Brian, a jewelry maker, had a long-term contract with a metal supplier. Once, the supplier sent a shipment to the wrong address. This meant that Brian wasn't able to finish some jewelry for an important show. However, the supplier had impressed Brian with the company's overall reliability. Brian decided to let the supplier make up for the mistake by sending the next shipment at no charge.

Even if things are flowing smoothly, staying in touch with the other party is a good idea. A simple e-mail update can be reassuring, letting the other party know that you are following through and the project is on schedule. Then, too, situations can develop that might threaten the agreement: rising production costs, a workers' strike, and bad weather are just a few examples. It is only fair to let the other party know of your concerns in advance so action can be taken if needed. However, use good judgment in deciding how much and how often to communicate. Constant updates can be distracting. Mentioning small problems can cause unnecessary alarm and may lead to questions about your judgment.

Why should you tell the other party if you can't meet your commitments?

Importance of Values

Negotiated agreements tend to involve major issues, ones that may affect you on a very deep level. When negotiating these agreements, you need to consider your values. **Values** are intangible things that you believe are worthwhile and important. A value can be a quality or a way of doing something.

How can you recognize if something is part of your value system? Your actions are the truest measure of what you hold important. If, for example, you often put your needs on hold to help a friend, you can conclude that friends and loyalty are among your values.

Recognizing and acting on your values can make the difference between negotiating an agreement you feel good about and one you will regret. Staying true to your values may rule out certain options in a negotiation. On the other hand, if you try to act against your values, you may find that you can't fulfill your end of the agreement. In this case, the other party could even say that you had negotiated in bad faith. Ultimately, if you have serious doubts about your ability to carry out your negotiated commitment, you may be ignoring something important in your values.

What are values?

International Negotiations

Imagine that one of your classmates is an exchange student. She tells you about a traditional snack in her culture: raw fish. She explains that fish are high in protein and good for you. You don't find raw fish appealing, and some of your classmates would not eat them either. It is not a matter of right or wrong, but a cultural preference.

These preferences at the dinner table are also true of the negotiating table: what seems perfectly acceptable in one culture might be unthinkable in another. Rules of etiquette, the behavior that is accepted and expected in a situation (discussed in Chapter 2), can vary greatly in societies in general and for conducting business in particular.

Entrepreneurs who learn about these differences can find the effort rewarding. The Internet is breaking down geographic barriers. A business

Figure 4-7 ▶

Culture Clash
The spread and blending of cultural influences can lead to confusion about social and business etiquette.

Drawing Conclusions. *How have entrepreneurs contributed to this trend?*

with an online presence (that is, a Website) can contact potential customers, suppliers, and investors all over the world. Increased migration and travel (for work, pleasure, or education) also open doors to other countries and cultures. Some business owners even bypass markets at home if the opportunities for growth look better overseas. Although you could do business in a country without visiting it, understanding the culture is definitely an advantage when trying to conduct international negotiations.

A seasoned international businessperson is often the best source for advice on understanding the social and business etiquette of a different culture. Someone who has lived and worked in a particular country will have insights that no one else can offer.

Social Etiquette

In every culture, business negotiations take place in a broader social setting. Every nation has a unique culture, but cultural differences also exist within a nation. For example, culture varies from big city to small town, from north to south, from one neighborhood to the next.

General rules for proper behavior apply. For example, a businessperson should know how to dress. Because appearance is the first thing people notice, meeting this expectation is a way to make a good impression in a one-on-one negotiation.

Another important thing to know is how people address one another. Do they call each other by the first name or as "Mister," "Miss," or other title? In some cultures, business relationships are very formal and coworkers may know each other for years without learning each other's first names.

Topics for polite conversation may have a bearing on a negotiation. Political issues may be too sensitive. Discussions of sports and the arts, if they avoid strong personal opinions, are safer.

Outward signs of friendship and respect have a role in business negotiations as well. When people meet, do they bow, shake hands, or kiss on the cheek? Is giving gifts appreciated (or even expected)? If so, what gifts are appropriate?

The importance of family relationships can be a powerful influence on business negotiations. Several generations may be involved in running a business. This may make the business a part of the family identity. Negotiated agreements might have to meet the approval of family elders, as well as those directly involved. Family members might also be favored over outside parties, even if the deal offered by the nonrelatives makes more sense financially. On the other hand, family and work life may be kept completely separate, with work taking priority. To ask about a man's wife and family members, or to suggest that you meet in someone's home, could be considered rude in some cultures.

▲ Figure 4-8
Social Etiquette
What do people do when they meet?

Relating Concepts. *What do various cultures do when they meet people of the same culture? Different cultures?*

The role of religion in public life can also affect business negotiations. Businesses may be closed on certain days and for religious celebrations. Also, certain actions or attitudes contrary to the other party's religious beliefs could be extremely offensive. For example, you should not eat or drink in front of someone who is engaged in a religious fast.

Because business is often conducted over meals, you should learn the rules of the other party's dining etiquette. People who handle themselves with confidence during meals are more apt to be taken seriously.

Negotiation Etiquette

Different countries also have different attitudes about time, appointments, and schedules. In some countries, a business contact who is 15 minutes late is not being rude. He might be surprised, and even angry with you, if you are upset.

Attitudes toward written agreements also vary. In the United States, these agreements tend to be extremely detailed. Other cultures see this need to account for every possibility as a lack of trust. Instead, they view an agreement as an outline. Specific questions are decided as the need arises.

What's more, the agreement's strength relies on the character of the negotiators. Negotiations may be spread out for several days and include social activities, giving each side a chance to know the other personally as well as professionally. If both sides believe that the other bargained in good faith, they trust that the agreement will serve them both well. In this sense, the negotiations never close. They continue for the length of the agreement.

Decision-making authority is another question that varies with culture. The person you negotiate with may have the authority to accept or refuse the deal. In some countries, however, that power rests only at the very top of the company, with a president or board chairperson. This is especially true of cultures with well-defined social classes. Elsewhere, such decisions can be made by lower-level management or a board of directors.

Finally, cultures have different attitudes toward the negotiation process itself. In some countries, each point is a source of lively (and sometimes loud) debate. A forceful argument earns respect; it shows determination and commitment. In other cultures, the discussion is reasoned and to the point. Lengthy arguments are taken as stubbornness, and loudness is considered impolite. Both may lead to the end of a negotiation.

If you make a mistake, remember that the whole purpose of learning etiquette is to show respect. If your words and actions communicate appreciation and respect as you know it, others will be likely to tolerate your lack of specific understanding. Simply apologize for not being as familiar with the other party's culture as you would like. Don't expect explanations to excuse careless offenses. Instead, let your respectful attitude generate goodwill.

 **READING CHECKPOINT** *Why is learning the etiquette of other cultures an advantage to entrepreneurs?*

 Your Business Plan. Continue developing your standard business plan. Go to "Section 4.2" of the *Business Plan Project* in your *Student Activity Workbook*, or "Section 4.2" of the BizTech Software.

ASSESSMENT 4.2

Reviewing Objectives

1. What is negotiation?
2. What is a concession?
3. What is a compromise?
4. How can you use the result of a negotiation to benefit your business?
5. How can your values affect negotiating?
6. Identify some areas of business where different cultures have different attitudes or practices.

Critical Thinking

7. **Relating Concepts.** How is a concession related to a compromise?
8. **Analyzing Information.** A friend comes away from a negotiation very happy. "I was ready to make concessions," he reports, "but they agreed to everything I asked for." Would you call these negotiations successful? Why or why not?

Working Together

With a partner, write a dialog between two parties negotiating for a large purchase to be delivered by the end of the month. Specify other details of the negotiation to make it more realistic. One partner should repeatedly act uncooperative or confrontational, while the other tries to keep the process moving forward. Perform your dialog for the class.

Social Studies

SPAM and SPIM

Most people who communicate over the Internet eventually get SPAM, unwanted e-mail advertisements, or its IM equivalent, SPIM. Investigate SPAM and SPIM. Who is credited with "inventing" SPAM? What laws govern such electronic junk mail? What arguments are used for and against this practice?

Spreading the Word!

When Michael Simmons was 16 years old, he co-founded his first business, PrincetonWebSolutions, a Web development company. Although his company was very successful, Michael made one mistake that cost him and his partner several thousand dollars. The mistake? They didn't prepare and plan enough for what could go wrong. "Now," said Michael, "before I do anything, I do a pre-mortem by making a list of what could go wrong and how I could keep it from happening." At an early age, Michael learned one of the basic principles of running a business.

Michael met Sheena Lindahl on their third day of college at New York University. The two discovered they had a lot in common. Sheena had become financially independent of her parents when she was 17 and was paying for her own college tuition, which cost over $30,000 yearly. She used the same strategies Michael was using to run his business. Both had learned how to capitalize on limited resources, build a network, develop a personal brand, and step outside their comfort zone, even to the point of getting married.

▲ *Michael Simmons and Sheena Lindahl*

Putting It Together

In their junior year, Sheena and Michael launched the Extreme Entrepreneurship Education Corporation. They had spent months interviewing successful people and put their research as well as their life experiences into *The Student Success Manifesto*, which they self-published. *The Student Success Manifesto: How to Create a Life of Passion, Purpose, and Prosperity* by Michael Simmons became an Amazon bestseller.

After publishing the book, Sheena and Michael started receiving speaking requests. As they spoke to high school and college students, they recognized the need for students to hear about young entrepreneurs—about their peers who were taking action and starting businesses. They decided to spread the word to help college students plan, prioritize, and pursue their vision for life.

Going on the Road

Just after Sheena and Michael graduated, they launched the Extreme Entrepreneurship Tour. Traveling in a big red bus, they started visiting college campuses nationwide, conducting half-day workshops where students could hear all about entrepreneurship and how to follow their dreams. Sheena and Michael put together a network of young entrepreneurs who related their experiences at these events. As a follow-up to workshops, they developed an online anti-procrastination and coaching tool called JourneyPage.

Sheena and Michael believe the best time for students to start a business is while they're in college. A number of resources support youth entrepreneurs, including foundations and organizations. Many students don't necessarily have to worry about paying for health care or raising children, factors that may influence their decisions in later life. Often, students can receive financial support from their parents. Sheena and Michael feel that becoming entrepreneurs gives students a unique experience that will help them in the future and promote a maturity and personal growth that comes from launching a business.

Thinking Like an Entrepreneur

1. How can you prepare for things that might go wrong?
2. How would you get the information you might need for writing a book?
3. Why might starting a business while you're in school be a good idea? What are some of the pitfalls?

CHAPTER SUMMARY

4.1 Communicating in Business

Communication is an essential, everyday part of entrepreneurship. Effective communication is brief, organized, clear, relevant, courteous, and appropriate. Communication may be written, spoken, or electronic. Each type is best suited for certain situations and audiences. Written communication includes business letters, memos, e-mails, and faxes. Business letters have a specific format and are written to people outside of the company, while memos, which also have a specific format, are written to individuals within the company. E-mails require the same care in composing as a business letter. Spoken communication includes telephone calls, conference calls, and videoconferences. Instant messaging is electronic communication. Active listening is consciously paying attention and responding in ways that improve communication.

4.2 Negotiating

Negotiation is a process in which two or more parties reach an agreement or solve a problem through communication. It is essential to doing business. Negotiating requires that you bargain in good faith. Successful negotiations start with identifying needs and deciding where concessions can be made. All sides must be ready to make compromises. Following through on a negotiated agreement allows you to improve business relationships and build a reputation for honesty and reliability. Your values influence your negotiations and affect the success of an agreement. Entrepreneurs who respect and appreciate other cultures can benefit from global markets. Learning a country's business and social etiquette can help an entrepreneur in international negotiations.

REVIEW VOCABULARY

Write a short play in which a business owner and a few employees meet to share ideas on where and how to buy a particular needed product or service. Incorporate at least half the terms listed below in the conversation, the actions, or a description of the surroundings. The play can use humor, but be sure to use the terms correctly.

- active listening (p. 85)
- bargaining in good faith (p. 87)
- compromise (p. 91)
- concession (p. 89)
- conference call (p. 83)
- emoticon (p. 85)
- fax (facsimile) (p. 80)
- instant messaging (IM) (p. 84)
- memo (p. 79)
- message thread (p. 80)
- negotiation (p. 87)
- salutation (p. 77)
- texting (p. 85)
- values (p. 93)
- videoconference (p. 83)

CHECK YOUR UNDERSTANDING

Choose the letter that best answers the question or completes the statement.

1. One advantage of instant messaging is that it
   a. lets you see and hear the other party
   b. allows complete privacy
   c. gives you plenty of time to compose messages
   d. is almost as fast as a phone call

2. A good speaker
   a. avoids making eye contact with listeners
   b. encourages participation
   c. discourages listeners from asking questions
   d. uses gestures constantly

3. To get the most from a videoconference,
   a. wear bright clothing
   b. avoid making unnecessary noise
   c. use the mute button when talking
   d. none of the above

4. Entrepreneurs who learn the social etiquette of a different culture
   a. can't negotiate in good faith
   b. miss business opportunities in their own country
   c. can participate more effectively in an international negotiation
   d. none of the above

5. On an envelope, the return address is
   a. in the center
   b. in the upper-right corner
   c. on the back
   d. in the upper-left corner

6. If you can't meet your commitment after negotiating an agreement, you should
   a. avoid doing business with the other party again
   b. try to make up for any problems you caused
   c. avoid negotiating in the future
   d. point out ways that the other party contributed to the problem

7. A country's rules of business etiquette reflect
   a. the country's overall social customs and attitudes
   b. the country's level of economic development
   c. the country's openness to outside entrepreneurs
   d. all of the above

8. Memos don't include the recipient's address because
   a. they're used as notes in negotiation
   b. they're written as reminders to yourself
   c. they're usually sent to a business's own employees
   d. they're going to unknown recipients

9. A concession is
   a. all sides giving up something to reach an agreement
   b. communication so everyone wins
   c. neither side giving in
   d. one side giving up something to reach an agreement

10. In a negotiation, it is important to focus on
    a. what you need
    b. what you want
    c. winning
    d. making sure the other party concedes more than you do

11. In a letter today, "cc" stands for
    a. complete copy
    b. carbon copy
    c. courtesy copy
    d. complimentary copy

12. When preparing to negotiate, you should
    a. decide what concessions you can ask from the other party
    b. focus on your wants, not your needs
    c. develop an aggressive, confrontational style
    d. focus on getting the other party to give you everything you want

Business Communication

13. Write a business letter. Exchange it with a class-mate. You will each describe how you would respond to the other's letter if you were its intended recipient. Rewrite your letter based on your classmate's feedback.

14. Work in a small group to create an eight-page booklet giving pointers on how to negotiate. Use pictures as well as written text. The tone can be humorous, but the advice should be practical.

15. Choose a foreign country that interests you. Learn about one area of etiquette in that country that would be useful for an entrepreneur to know, such as dress, greetings, or eating in a restaurant. Demonstrate what you have learned for the class.

Business Ethics

18. You're a caterer negotiating to provide an outdoor picnic dinner for 150 people. The major item in your picnic will be fried chicken. The client agreed to your price yesterday and you shook hands on it. You know, however, that the price was higher than your client expected. You haven't signed a contract yet. Today your poultry supplier offers you a special price on chicken parts. This lowers your costs. You know you could pass on the savings to your client and still make the profit you planned. What would you do?

Business Math

16. Debra imports Irish lace for her wedding dress boutique. The Irish currency is the euro (symbol-ized as €). At the time of Debra's last order, the exchange rate was \$1.00/€0.65. Debra ordered €480 worth of lace. What did the lace cost in U.S. dollars? The lace maker added €87 to cover ship-ping. What was Debra's total cost in U.S. dollars?

17. You run an auto-detailing shop that specializes in custom paint jobs. You have agreed to repaint a classic Ford Mustang at no charge. In exchange, you will get 15 percent of the car's selling price when the owner auctions it on eBay. The paint and other supplies you need cost \$172. The job will total about 9 hours at \$38 an hour. The owner expects the Mustang to sell for about \$11,000. What would your share be? How much profit would you make?

Business in Your Community

19. Contact an architectural firm to learn about the design and planning of videoconference rooms. How are physical elements chosen to promote communication? For example, what colors reduce distractions? What materials improve sound qual-ity? Does the technology require special wiring or create other concerns? Report your findings to the class.

20. Locate businesses that could help entrepreneurs "go global." These companies might help with making travel plans, understanding the language, or learning the customs and laws of a country. Contact one business for details on their service or product. Develop a presentation about the busi-ness you researched.

Competing Online

What is your most important goal if you are an e-business owner? Easy! It's getting customers to visit your site. Just as with a traditional store, customers can't buy something without first walking through the door. An e-business owner has to think about **site traffic**, the number of visits a Website gets over a specified period.

But how do potential customers find your Website? Considering all the Websites on the Internet, how do they come to yours? You probably already know the answer. Many potential customers find Websites by using a search engine, such as Google. Because of this, an e-business owner is very interested in **search engine ranking**, the order of specific words or groups of words in a particular search engine. The goal is to be on the first page of search results. No business wants to be buried on the tenth page. Very few customers would have the patience to find the company.

Deciding to Compete

With a traditional store, it is relatively easy to determine whether you should open in a particular neighborhood. You need to determine if there are competing businesses in the area and whether the neighborhood needs the products or services you are offering. For an e-business, it's a bit more complicated. You need to know how many other Websites are offering similar products or services.

What Makes a Business Special?

Once you know how many Websites are selling a similar product or service, you need to figure out what will make your business stand out from the others. One way to do this is to check which of the competing online businesses is getting the most traffic. You can do this by visiting a **site-ranking portal,** which lists top-ranking sites. One site-ranking portal is Alexa.com.

Once you know which of your possible online competitors is getting the most traffic, you will need to figure out why. Some questions are: Is this site's design especially engaging? Is it easy to navigate? What about it sets it apart from competitors? What makes it special? Often, analyses of competing Websites are undertaken by an outside consultant.

Setting Goals

Once a Website is up and running, the e-business owner sets goals for daily Web traffic. Having researched the site traffic at competing Websites, you will likely have a realistic expectation for your Web traffic. Most new e-businesses take a while to begin to generate optimal Web traffic. You can typically plan for lower traffic for the first few months until the business begins to generate the amount of traffic it should. Even with extensive planning, a start-up business may not see a profit in the first year or more. Businesses that aren't well funded sometimes cannot make it through this initial period and are shut down when their traffic goals are not met.

Tech Vocabulary
- search engine ranking
- site traffic
- site-ranking portal

Check Yourself
1. Why is traffic important for any store?
2. Why is a high search engine ranking important for an e-business?
3. How would a prospective e-business owner use a site-ranking portal in the business planning process?

What Do You Think?
Solving Problems. What would you do if you did not meet your projected traffic goals for a new e-business?

Why Is Time Management Important?

Time management is a skill you will need throughout life. Adults need to manage the time they spend at work and at home. As a student, you need to manage the time you spend at school and the time you spend studying. You also need to manage the time you devote to other activities and family and friends.

Time Management

Time can be a valuable friend or your worst enemy. You can never recapture misused or lost time. Learn to use time as a valuable resource. The way you manage this resource can make the difference between success and failure.

Planning how to use your time is called time management. It will be a key element in your study habits. You are the only one who can plan and manage your time. Many people feel they don't have enough time, or they allow others to use it up. The key to success is to make the best use of your time.

If you are in the habit of wasting time, you can work to break the habit. Managing your time is not difficult. Much of your time is planned for you. For example, your school hours are determined by your teachers and school officials. Your work hours are determined by your employer. But it is your job to manage the rest of your time. You might plan for the following activities:

- Uninterrupted periods for study
- Personal duties and chores
- Relaxation and fun

Have you ever run out of time and then wondered, "Where did the time go?" Most people don't know how they spend their time. A good way to find out is to keep a daily time log for two weeks. A time log is a written record of a person's use of time. After keeping a time log for two weeks, you may be surprised to see how you use your time.

Time Tips

The earth's timetable is fixed at 365 days a year, 24 hours a day, 60 minutes an hour, and 60 seconds a minute. How can you stretch this time? How can you get more time to do everything you want to do? The answer is to take these steps to make the best use of your time:

1. **Write a To-Do List Each Day.** What you don't write down, you can easily forget.

2. **Prioritize.** Priorities are things you consider most important. Tasks that have the highest priority should be done first. Categorize your tasks in order of (A) most important, (B) next important, and (C) least important. Check off the tasks as you complete them. Do the "C" tasks only if you have time.

3. **Focus on One Task at a Time.** Stay with one task and give it your full attention. Resist the urge to be distracted.

4. **Don't Procrastinate.** Do not delay or put off decisions or activities. Don't leave things until the last minute. Do a little each day on long-term assignments.

5. **Reduce Interruptions.** Beware of time thieves—instant messaging and phone calls will steal precious time and prevent you from completing tasks. Tell friends when you can be reached and try not to let anyone or anything interrupt your schedule.

6. **Establish a Regular Time and Place for Study.** This will help to program your mind to stay on-task and discourage interruptions.

7. **Use Your Spare Time Wisely.** When you find yourself with some free time during the day, make it productive. Do some reading.

8. **Get a Good Night's Sleep.** You'll be better able to handle your tasks if you get the sleep your body and mind need.

9. **Make Time for Fun!**

TIME LOG

	Mon	Tue	Wed	Thu	Fri	Sat	Sun
School							
Study							
Socialize in Person							
Phone/ Texting							
Computer							
Exercise							
Chores							
TV							
Eat							
Sleep							
Other							

Time Log

A time log shows the number of hours used for various activities. It can help you see if you are wasting time.

PREDICTING *How much time during a week do you spend watching TV? Talking on the phone?*

Reviewing Concepts

1. How can keeping a time log assist you in managing your time?

2. Why is prioritizing tasks important?

3. List at least three of the time thieves in your life.

Manage Your Time

4. **Using Tables.** Create a time log that tracks how you spend your time in a week.

5. **Applying Concepts.** Based on your time log, describe how you could make the best use of your time (use the Time Tips on the previous page as a starting point).

5 ETHICS & SOCIAL RESPONSIBILITY

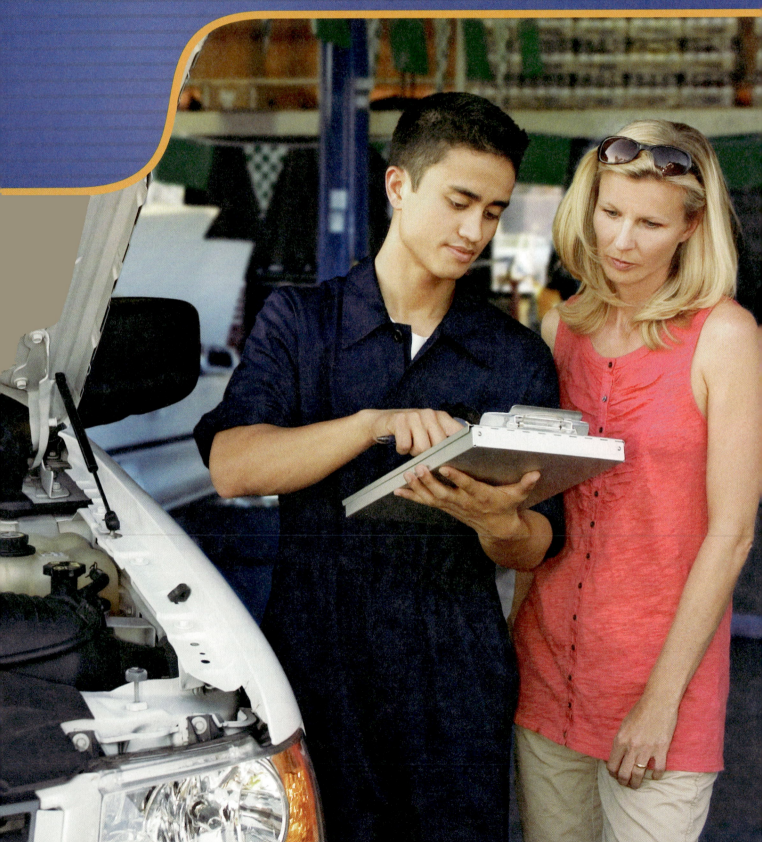

5.1

•
•
•

•

VOCABULARY

- business ethics
- conflict of interest
- copyright
- ethics
- fair use
- infringement
- intellectual property
- patent
- public domain
- social media
- trademark
- transparency
- universal values
- whistle-blower

?

How would you finish this statement?

One rule everyone should live by is . . .

Write your response on a piece of paper. Be prepared to explain your answer.

What Are Ethics?

In Chapter 4, you read about *values*, intangible things that you believe are important. Individual values are the foundation of **ethics**, a set of moral principles that govern decisions and actions. To act ethically is to act in ways that are in keeping with certain values.

Ethics and Culture

Suppose you ask three people if friendships are important. All three will probably say yes. You then ask if succeeding in school and volunteering for good causes are important. Again, everyone will likely agree. Now, suppose you ask: Which is more important: spending time with friends, studying, or volunteering? Here, disagreement may arise, with such answers as "Volunteering is always more important than just hanging out with friends" or "Spending time with friends is fine—unless you need to study to bring up your grades." People tend to agree on values but have different ideas about how to apply them.

That pattern is repeated throughout society. You could study cultures with vastly different foods, languages, and governments. Yet you'll find that they all value friendship, family, and helping others. They all nurture the young and care for the old or sick.

▼ **Figure 5-1**
Universal Value
Nurturing the young is a universal value.

Applying Concepts. *What would happen to a society that didn't nurture its young?*

These are examples of **universal values**, values shared by all cultures throughout history.

Universal values are recognized because they promote the conditions needed for individuals to survive, enjoy life, and get along with others. They start with the basics of life: food, water, shelter, and physical safety. Actions that further the common good are universally accepted as right: obeying the law, for example, and caring for the young and the old. Likewise, certain acts are seen as wrong: killing, stealing, and irresponsible behavior. Positive qualities such as generosity and fairness are encouraged everywhere, while greed and dishonesty are universally discouraged.

This agreement on values creates a similarity in ethics as well. However, just as individuals differ in their opinions on values, cultures differ in how they express and enforce ethical standards. For instance, all cultures have laws, written or unwritten, to punish dishonest actions. But what actions are considered dishonest and how they are punished varies with different cultures.

Business Ethics

If you follow the news, you may have learned of illegal deals involving large corporations. One company lied to employees about its financial health, encouraging workers to invest in company stock. Then the business declared bankruptcy, wiping out the savings the workers had counted on for retirement. Another company knowingly sold toys containing lead-based paint, which was banned years ago as a health hazard to children.

Stories like these, along with common complaints such as hidden fees and poor customer service, have tarnished the image of business. They've also brought attention to the topic of **business ethics**, moral principles applied to business issues and actions. Many people now wonder if such a thing as business ethics exists at all.

Entrepreneurs have considerable influence on their company's business ethics. Like operating a business itself, this is both an opportunity and a responsibility.

 *What are universal values?*

Why Practice Business Ethics?

The main reason for behaving ethically, in business or in any area of life, seems obvious: It's the *right* thing to do. It's what you *should* do.

It's what *anyone* would do. It's just following the golden rule: Do unto others as you would have them do unto you.

However, there are three *practical* reasons why you should practice business ethics:

- Customers are more confident when buying goods and services from an ethical company. As a consumer yourself, you may prefer buying from companies with a history of acting ethically. Consumer surveys show you're not alone. This makes sense—people don't trust a company to offer high-quality goods and services if it has a reputation for acting unethically.

- An ethical workplace motivates employees. Have you ever seen other students copy a paper or cheat on a test and not get caught? You may have wondered why you should play by the rules when people who break them seem to succeed just as well. Employees also feel discouraged and frustrated when that happens in the workplace. In contrast, people are proud to work for someone with high ethical standards. They feel more confident about their work and more loyal to a fair and ethical employer.

- Ethical behavior also prevents legal problems. Defending yourself in court can be expensive. Lawsuits obviously cost a company money for lawyers' fees, judgments, and penalties. They also damage your reputation, which can lead to lost customers for years to come. It may even be enough to cause your business to fail and ruin your career.

 *How does practicing business ethics help attract employees?*

Establishing an Ethical Workplace

Universal values establish a strong foundation for society. Universal values are also a good basis for running your business. Deciding how to apply these values will be as important as any other planning you do. This section describes issues and ideas that will help you foster an ethical atmosphere in your workplace. It points out opportunities to show that you take ethics seriously and expect others to do the same.

Creating Transparency

Have you heard the expression "The buck stops here"? It describes a management style that assumes it has the authority to make decisions and takes responsibility for those decisions. That's the idea behind **transparency,** or openness and accountability in business decisions and actions. Letting people see what a company is doing, and why, is a strong deterrent to unethical behavior. For example, when transparency is practiced, employees know how their retirement fund is being invested. Consumers know that wrongdoers are punished.

Figure 5-2

Harry Truman
Harry Truman is famous for the sign on his desk saying "The buck stops here."

Communicating. *What was Harry Truman saying to the American people through that sign?*

Communication is essential to transparency. Companies have traditionally communicated through memos to employees and press releases and press conferences for the public. More and more, they're using social media as well. **Social media** are interactive electronic forms of communication. Blogs and message boards, where people carry on public conversations, are two popular examples.

Although social media can be just another form of advertisement, they're also a means of demonstrating transparency. In one company, for example, employees routinely accessed files on the company computer from remote locations so they could work away from the office. This increased productivity but also posed a security risk because the information could have fallen into the wrong hands. So a company vice president discussed the subject in his blog at the firm's Website. Anyone with Internet access could see that the leadership recognized the threat and had a strategy to help prevent and deal with it.

Can you see how going public in this way with a potential problem enhanced the business's reputation? If the company had only circulated a memo or held meetings among employees, it would not have been quite such a positive (transparent) response.

Of course, not everyone has a need or even a right to know everything a company does. A business is justified in concealing a "trade secret" that is crucial to its success, such as a recipe for a food it sells or plans for a new product. Revealing personal information, even voluntarily, should be done with care. You need to ask whether the value of transparency outweighs the invasion of privacy and the possible harm that may result.

Responding to Whistle-Blowers

A **whistle-blower** is a term for someone who reports illegal or unethical conduct to superiors or to the public. In some cases, these actions are protected by law. For example, the Sarbanes-Oxley Act of 2002 makes it illegal to fire or punish employees who help authorities investigate stock market fraud. Other laws protect individuals who report workplace safety and environmental violations.

Management's response to whistle-blowing, beyond these legal requirements, sends a message about its commitment to business ethics. Does a company encourage employees to speak up when a job or situation troubles them? Does it discourage employees who pressure whistle-blowers to keep silent? Finally, does it take these reports seriously and act to correct unethical practices?

Writing a Code of Ethics

A code of ethics describes a business's moral philosophy and gives concrete guidelines for carrying it out. Writing a code and distributing a copy to every employee is a wise move for several reasons.

First, writing a code of ethics forces you to clarify your own values and principles. Before you can write such a code, you will have to ask yourself what you believe is important. Answering those questions helps you understand the concepts in more concrete terms. Everyone says they value honesty, for instance, but what does that word mean to you exactly?

Having a code will also help prevent and resolve problems. When a question arises about whether an action is ethical, you and others can see how it compares to the code.

Finally, a written code provides some protection against claims of unfairness. Employees know from their first day what behavior is encouraged and what could result in dismissal. Suppliers can see your reasons for choosing another business over their own. The code shows that you don't knowingly tolerate unethical behavior.

Because business ethics can be so complex, professional advice on writing and maintaining a code of ethics is a worthwhile investment. Many large companies hire a compliance officer to ensure that their practices comply with their written code and that the code follows state and federal law. Compliance officers also answer employees' questions about how the code is applied and investigate reports of possible unethical behavior.

Developing a useful code of ethics can be difficult. The challenge can be summed up in one word: balance. The code must balance contrasting qualities in an effective way. For example:

- The code must be general enough to apply to many situations, yet specific enough to offer practical help. Likewise, it should hold true to moral principles, yet be flexible enough to make allowances for the circumstances of the individual case. To strike this balance, codes are often divided into several parts: the first lays out the general values and ethical goals. Next are rules for behavior in particular situations.

- The code should reflect your values but also respect the beliefs of those who will be affected. Recall that people can hold the same values but act on them differently. Suppose one point in a code concerns the importance of giving back to the community. One employee might carry out this value by volunteering with a wildlife preservation group. Another might join the Chamber of Commerce, which promotes economic development. To bring in

Figure 5-3 ▶

Code of Ethics

This code of ethics would be used by the owner of a childcare center.

Relating Concepts. *Suggest a practical rule or guideline that could be based on these values and beliefs.*

Our Code of Ethics

I. *We value learning and will dedicate ourselves to giving each child the best education possible.*

We believe that education must encompass the whole child, both the body and the mind. We bring all of our skills and knowledge to promoting good physical health, fostering a full range of healthy emotions as well as social and relationship skills, and developing the mind to the fullest.

II. *We value equality and will attack barriers of prejudice and injustice.*

We believe that each child has untold potential that must not be hindered by unfair limitations of stereotypes or bias. Rather, each child deserves the opportunity to identify and develop all the talents and skills that he or she possesses.

III. *We value human dignity and will treat each child as a worthy, unique, and valued individual.*

We believe that dignity and worth are inborn qualities in every human being. Each child must be made to feel valued and loved unconditionally, regardless of abilities, social circumstance, behavior, personality traits, or any other interior or exterior condition.

a range of opinions, you may want to involve employees, trusted advisors, and experienced businesspeople in your efforts.

- The values can be idealistic, but the guidelines must be realistic. A code needs achievable language, such as "encourage" and "promote." Reserve absolutes and terms such as "always" and "never" for clear issues of right and wrong. Compare these two statements: "We prefer environmentally friendly products when available" and "We will use only recyclable products." Which statement is practical?

- A code of ethics should be continually evolving without drifting from its core beliefs. Universal values may stay the same over time, but your views on how to carry them out may change. You may need to adapt and revise your rules to meet new situations and developments in technology.

READING CHECKPOINT *What is transparency?*

Ethical Issues for Entrepreneurs

For a child, an ethical decision might be whether to share a graham cracker with a friend. A high school student faces more complicated choices with more serious potential consequences: writing an original essay for school versus "borrowing" material found on the Internet, for instance. An entrepreneur faces even more complex decisions. When faced with any ethical decision, it's usually best to rely on your own strong personal values to help determine your response.

Intellectual Property

When music downloads first became available, many music fans started filling their MP3 players and swapping songs with friends. They were stunned when record companies began prosecuting them for theft.

▲ *Copyright Symbol*

Can music be stolen? Yes. Music, paintings, literature, inventions, and architectural designs are types of intellectual property. **Intellectual property** is artistic and industrial creations of the mind. "Possession" of these creations is protected by law. The owners are entitled to credit and usually some form of payment when their works are used, especially when used for commercial gain.

Artistic creations are protected by copyright. **Copyright** is the exclusive right to perform, display, copy, or distribute an artistic work. Copyright applies automatically as soon as a work is created. It covers all forms of expression, whether words, music, images, or concrete objects. It includes works published on the Internet.

Another type of intellectual property—industrial invention—is protected by patent. A **patent** is the exclusive right to make, use, or sell a device or process. Many types of creations can be patented, from an improved design for a ketchup bottle, to a variety of tomato used to make the ketchup, to a process for bottling the ketchup.

A **trademark** is a symbol that indicates that the use of a brand or brand name is legally protected and cannot be used by other businesses. A trademarked brand or brand name is a type of intellectual property. Two symbols are associated with U.S. trademarks. The trademark symbol ™ is used to indicate that the brand is protected in a general way, but does not have formal legal protection.

Empathy

Can you see things from another person's point of view? If so, you have empathy for that person. *Empathy* is being aware of and identifying with another person's feelings. Think about Martin Luther King Jr. and Mother Teresa. They each devoted a large portion of their lives to showing empathy for the struggles of others.

Empathy plays a part in our everyday lives. Showing empathy when a friend or coworker has a particular problem or concern can be a comfort to them. Sometimes just spending time with and listening to a friend provides support. Your body language and facial expression can help the person see that you understand what he or she is going through. Offering comforting words may make them feel better. Often, you can show that you understand their issues and empathize with them by paraphrasing what they have said to you, using an appropriate tone of voice.

When you work with the public, you will probably run into people who have personal and emotional concerns that may make it difficult to conduct business with them. Being able to understand and accept another person's feelings and perceptions is important to good business interaction. Show empathy to those who may need it: friends, coworkers, and customers. A caring, empathetic response increases the likelihood that you will be able work together effectively.

Martin Luther King

THINKING CRITICALLY

Communicating. With a partner, discuss ways you may have shown empathy in the past to a person who needed it. Think about the strategies you may have used to show you understood what that person was going through. Share ways someone else may have shown empathy to you.

To read more about becoming an empathetic person, go to "Your Business Career" on the Student Center at entrepreneurship.pearson.com.

▲ *Trademark Symbol*

▲ *Registered Trademark Symbol*

The registered trademark symbol ® can only be used if the owner of the brand or brand name has registered it with the U.S. Patent and Trademark Office.

Violating a copyright, trademark, or patent holder's rights is called **infringement**. A shop owner who plays music for customers' enjoyment commits copyright infringement. A fashion designer who copies software that creates dress patterns commits patent infringement.

There are ways to avoid infringement. A doctrine called **fair use** provides for the limited quotation of a copyrighted work without permission from or payment to the copyright holder. Also, some creative works or inventions have the status of **public domain**, meaning that their copyright or patent has expired. Works produced by the United States government are included in public domain.

Patent infringement isn't an issue for most entrepreneurs. Almost every item you use, buy, or sell is patented, so the inventor has been compensated. However, imagine that you invented a new knee pad for athletes and that Velcro® fasteners were essential to the design. To sell the pads without patent infringement, you would have to compensate Velcro Industries B.V., which holds the patent for Velcro® products. Otherwise, you would have to redesign the new pad to close in some other way, using an unpatented method—perhaps laces (which would be a device in the public domain).

Conflict of Interest

Another ethical decision that entrepreneurs often face is related to conflicts of interest. A **conflict of interest** exists when personal considerations and professional obligations interfere with each other. It's wise to avoid such situations—or even the appearance of them—even if you think you can act fairly and objectively. For example, Dan has a lawn care business, specializing in commercial lawn maintenance. Often customers ask Dan to recommend full-year programs using lawn treatment products. Dan has been approached by salespeople representing these products. They have offered to pay Dan a percentage of the price of any products purchased by his customers. Recently, a customer asked Dan for a recommendation, and he had to choose between a product for which he would receive a percentage and a similar product for which he would not. If the two products were equally useful, and cost the same, Dan could be accused of having a conflict of interest if he recommended the product for which he received money.

A well-thought-out code of ethics can help identify and prevent such problems. Besides addressing specific scenarios, the code should also call for employees to report questionable situations so the owner can decide on the best way to handle them.

Confidentiality

As an entrepreneur, you will be gathering a good deal of information. You may run a background check and find that a job applicant has a criminal record, or discover sensative financial data through a credit check on potential investors or partners.

◀ **Figure 5-4**
Secret Recipe
If you were a business owner with a recipe for fried chicken, you would probably ask your employees to sign a confidentiality agreement.

Predicting. *How would you feel if one of your employees violated the confidentiality agreement and started a restaurant that served chicken made from your recipe?*

How you and others in your company use this information can be an ethical matter, and the decision isn't always clear-cut. On one hand, you have a duty to respect the confidentiality (privacy) of others. On the other hand, keeping silent could expose some people to harm. Someone may have a criminal conviction on record, for example, but you should ask yourself whether you have a reason, or a right, to make it known.

Confidentiality can also create conflict of interest. As an accountant with a large company, Angela knew the financial details of many clients' businesses. When she left to start working for herself, she could have used this knowledge and asked the clients if they would like to work with her. Instead, she chose to build up her own clientele through her talent and hard work and not to "steal" her old company's customers.

Confidentiality also has legal aspects. An employee who signs a nondisclosure agreement is legally barred from sharing some types of information with others, even after leaving the company. Health care professionals can lose their license for revealing facts about a patient's condition without permission. In some professions, taking advantage of "insider" information—facts about a business's dealings that aren't made public—can lead to a prison sentence!

 **READING CHECKPOINT** *What kinds of work do patents and copyright protect?*

 Your Business Plan. Continue developing your standard business plan. Go to "Section 5.1" of the *Business Plan Project* in your *Student Activity Workbook*, or "Section 5.1" of the BizTech Software.

ASSESSMENT 5.1

Reviewing Objectives

1. What are ethics?
2. Give three practical reasons for practicing business ethics.
3. What is transparency?
4. What is intellectual property?

Critical Thinking

5. **Inferring.** What do you think is the difference between a whistle-blower and a chronic complainer?
6. **Drawing Conclusions.** How do you think using social media can affect a business's image? With what audiences would blogs and other types of social media be especially effective?

Working Together

Working in small groups, write a scene concerning an entrepreneur who faces a conflict of interest. Don't resolve the conflict, however. Perform the scene for classmates and ask them to suggest ethical endings.

Social Studies
Studying Ethics

Research an aspect of ethics, such as how children learn ethics, the effects of peer pressure on ethical choices, or how ideas about ethics have changed over time. Write a short report on how this affects ethics in business.

Socially Responsible Business & Philanthropy

OBJECTIVES

- Define corporate social responsibility
- Explain entrepreneurs' responsibilities to individuals
- Describe entrepreneurs' environmental responsibilities
- Identify entrepreneurs' community responsibilities

VOCABULARY

- carbon footprint
- carbon offset
- cause-related marketing
- corporate social responsibility
- ethical sourcing
- facilitated giving
- greenwashing
- in-kind donation
- philanthropy
- purchase-triggered donation
- sponsorship
- sustainable

? | *Think carefully about this question:*

What three things would make the world a better place?

Write your answers on a piece of paper. Be prepared to discuss your list in class.

Corporate Social Responsibility

Barny Haughton is owner and executive chef at the upscale Bordeaux Quay Restaurant in Bristol, England. Katie VandenBerg owns Eli's Coffee Shop in the small town of Morton, Illinois. What do these two people, in very different circumstances and half a world apart, have in common?

They both are entrepreneurs. And they both demonstrate **corporate social responsibility**—their respective businesses act in ways that balance profit and growth with the good of society. Corporate social responsibility is based on the concept that the relationship between business and society ought to go deeper than economics. Barny designed Bordeaux Quay as a model of resource conservation, from its recycling program to its low-flush toilets (which are refilled by captured rainwater). At Eli's Coffee Shop, Katie serves only ethically sourced coffee. **Ethical sourcing** means buying from suppliers who provide safe working conditions and respect workers' rights.

The examples of Barny Haughton and Katie VandenBerg demonstrate that corporate social responsibility is an opportunity for entrepreneurs at every level. What's more, it's not just an afterthought, separate from daily operations. Increasingly, behaving in a way that is socially responsible is part of how a company does business. In some cases, it *is* a company's business.

Corporate social responsibility also makes good business sense. Whether it's a large corporation sponsoring a charity telethon or a local supermarket offering a refund for using canvas shopping bags, corporate social responsibility often translates into profits. This advantage for business is sometimes described as "doing well by doing good."

Corporate Social Responsibility	**=**	**Doing Well by Doing Good**

 *What is corporate social responsibility?*

Responsibility to Individuals

Corporate social responsibility builds from the ground up. It can affect all the individuals who are connected in some way to the business: the employees, customers, investors, and creditors.

In a way, your first responsibility to all these individuals, as well as to yourself, is to run the business to the best of your abilities. All of these people rely on your company for something. Your employees count on you for their incomes. Your customers trust you to supply a quality product or service. Your investors and creditors have trusted your business judgment and rely on you to fulfill your financial obligations. Treating a business seriously and making well-thought-out decisions shows that you take your responsibilities to heart.

Employees

Entrepreneurs have legal obligations to provide a safe workplace and fair employment policies. (You'll read more about these in Chapters 15 and 17.) If you've ever held a job yourself, however, you know that these conditions are only part of what employees need and want.

On a practical level, employees need the tools to do the jobs expected of them. Imagine the director of a preschool asking a teacher's aide to lead a class in an art activity without supplying the paper, crayons, paints, glue, or other necessary materials. Or suppose the director of the preschool asked the aide to plan a menu for a child with diabetes, without knowing whether the aide had any knowledge of nutrition or special diets. The results could be frustrating and even dangerous.

On the other hand, employees also need trust. They need respect for their skills and the freedom to use them. Trust may come easily when you have only a few employees and work with them closely. The test comes in giving them responsibilities without supervision. Yet that's a necessary step if a business is to grow.

Some employers are cautious about trusting workers, especially with jobs that encourage them to learn new skills. They don't want employees to outgrow the job and move on to another, possibly opening a competing business. In contrast, other entrepreneurs feel a responsibility for helping employees grow personally and professionally. They might practice job rotation, for instance, training workers for different jobs in the company. These business owners value employees' personal satisfaction—and enjoy the advantage of having a back-up to fill a position in an emergency.

Employees also deserve consideration for personal needs. If you're needed at home to care for a sick child, or if your car is in the shop, or if the bus was late, you can appreciate an understanding and considerate boss. Employers must recognize that an employee may have a spouse, children, and day-to-day responsibilities. Employers must respect and understand their employees' needs to meet these commitments. In fact, companies that are rated by employees as the best places to work usually help employees balance work and personal needs.

◀ **Figure 5-5**
Employers Value Employees
Employees would rather work for an employer who trusts and respects them.
Applying Concepts. *If you were an employer, how would you show that you respected and trusted your employees?*

Customers

As with employees, business owners are bound by law to treat customers fairly. A wise entrepreneur, however, understands that the ethical obligation goes beyond these legal minimums. As a practical consideration, attracting new customers also costs more than maintaining existing ones. The following four qualities, which cost nothing to put into practice, mark a responsible relationship with customers:

- **Honesty.** Be honest and transparent in all areas. Inform customers about your products, both the advantages and drawbacks. If you offer a service, describe your qualifications and abilities accurately. Carefully estimate the time and cost of completing a project. Admit to mistakes without offering excuses.

- **Respect.** Customers come to you hoping you can meet their needs or solve their problems. Their needs and problems are important to them, and they should be to you, as well. Take customer complaints seriously. These are opportunities to improve your business. Research suggests that only one of every fifty dissatisfied customers complains to the merchant. When you fix a situation that made one customer unhappy, you may be saving 49 other customers from the same frustration—and keeping them as customers.

- **Accessibility.** Be available when you promise to be. Keep to the business hours you advertise. Honor your appointments with clients and don't be late. Give customers contact information where they can reach you with questions. Take the initiative on keeping them updated about the status of an order or work in progress.

- **Attention.** Whether you're selling a single light bulb to a walk-in customer or installing solar panels on a university library, focus your attention on the customer with whom you are working at the moment. Be present for that customer. Don't be distracted by your cell phone or other obligations.

▼ **Figure 5-6**

Supplier
Acting responsibly toward suppliers or vendors carries its own reward.

Applying Concepts. *How can suppliers and vendors help a business owner?*

Suppliers

Acting responsibly toward suppliers or vendors carries its own reward. The people who sell the materials your business needs are also those who can advise you on making the best choices and using the materials wisely.

It should go without saying that you owe suppliers timely payment in the amount and method on which you agreed. You also need to respect their decisions on pricing. Although it is acceptable to attempt to negotiate with suppliers, you have the option of going elsewhere if you're not satisfied. Complaining or suggesting that the supplier is being unfair or dishonest is not appropriate.

If you mislead suppliers into thinking you might do business with them when you are really using them as "bargaining chips" to get another supplier to lower a price, you are not bargaining in good faith.

Suppliers appreciate cooperation in making a transaction as efficient as possible. Have a clear idea of what you want so you can help the supplier sell it to you. Have realistic expectations for the supplier's policies when it affects your satisfaction as a customer. For example, if you order a product, expect a reasonable amount of added time and money for shipping and handling.

Suppliers deserve to hear that you're a satisfied customer—or that you are not. They benefit from knowing when a product or service could be improved. Give a supplier the chance to keep you as a customer before you switch to another. Staying with the same suppliers builds helpful relationships that will serve you well over time.

Investors and Creditors

Investors and creditors provide the money to start and run a business and, along with it, an emotional boost. After all, people don't invest or loan money unless they believe in both the idea behind the business and the entrepreneur whose work will make it a success. Likewise, vendors who extend credit are showing faith that you'll be able to pay for your purchase.

Investors are not *guaranteed* a financial return, but they have a right to regular, and timely, communication. Understandably, they will want to know the status of their investments. Investors with experience in your field of business may be equally ready to offer advice and help. They might put you in touch with other contacts or suggest other resources. Often investors actually assume some control of the business in exchange for their financial support. (You'll read more about different types of investors in Chapter 13.)

Whatever the relationship, you need to give an investor's input the weight it deserves. A friend with little understanding of your business (but a lot of faith in you) who has made a modest investment and the professional investor who has bankrolled half of your business have both contributed to your potential success. Both deserve respect.

Unlike investors, creditors are owed a return on their money, usually with interest. They too need ongoing updates, especially if the business is struggling. Again, this is to your benefit. Creditors are as eager to be paid back as you are to get out of debt. If they see that you're working hard but still having trouble, they're sometimes willing to rework the terms to make repayment more manageable.

Communication with investors and creditors alike must be based on honesty and transparency. Taking money based on false expectations may be illegal and, in any case, can hurt you and your business.

 **READING CHECKPOINT** *What four qualities mark a responsible relationship with customers?*

Responsibility to the Environment

To an environmentalist, "green" means protecting natural resources. To an entrepreneur, "green" refers to another resource: money. Increasingly, these two meanings go hand-in-hand. Being environmentally green can be profitable. Surveys and sales figures show that consumers look favorably on businesses that show a commitment to protecting the environment. This, in turn, makes investors more willing to finance those businesses.

Environmentally Friendly Enterprises

Like other societal trends, concern for the environment is creating new industries and expanding older ones. Opportunities for the individual with imagination and initiative—in other words, the entrepreneur—seem to arise almost daily. What entrepreneurial ventures can you see in the following four fields?

- **Sustainable Design.** Traditionally, products were made and used without much thought for their long-term impact on people or the planet. In contrast, design that is **sustainable** meets the planet's current needs while preserving resources for future generations. Sustainable design ranges from planned, "walkable" cities that reduce the need for automobiles to fashions made from natural fabrics and dyes.

- **Alternative Energy.** Researchers are working to make alternatives to oil and coal—such as solar, wind, and hydrogen power—more efficient. They're testing newer forms of biofuels extracted from corn, sugar cane, and even vegetable oil left over from frying foods. Investors are particularly excited about the potential of these "clean" technologies and have sunk hundreds of millions of dollars into their development.

- **Organics.** Concerns about personal health, as well as the environment, have increased interest in organic products, those made from crops and animals that are raised without manufactured chemicals. Organic produce, grains, and meats make up a small but steadily growing segment of the food market. Independently owned producers and natural-food stores generate a large percentage of those sales. Organic personal-care items are also gaining popularity.

- **Fair Trade.** As you learned in Chapter 2, fair trade is a way of doing business that is based on principles of social and environmental responsibility and promoting sustainable growth. Most producers involved in fair trade are small farmers and skilled crafters in developing countries. These microentrepreneurs form cooperatives to set prices and product standards. Most fair trade items are then sold through a network of independent wholesalers and retailers. Sales of fair trade goods have risen worldwide

Figure 5-7 ▶

Fair Trade Products
Through fair trade, entrepreneurs help each other succeed.
Applying Concepts. *Why do you think entrepreneurs are especially important to the economies of small, developing nations?*

by double digits in the last decade as consumers grow more aware of the impact of their spending decisions.

The Energy-Efficient Workplace

Businesses that aren't specifically green can benefit from green practices. Creating an energy-efficient workplace saves money and can draw customers. The most efficient, money-saving appliances, equipment, and electrical-system components bear the "Energy Star®" label. To earn this designation, an item must meet strict specifications.

For example, suppose you own a copying service. Using Energy Star®-designated copiers can cut electrical costs by 25 percent. They also power down when not in use, saving even more money over standard models. You could post signs advertising these facts to customers, along with the hint that they could save money and reduce waste by printing on both sides of the paper. To add appeal, you might offer a low-cost or no-cost, environmentally helpful service—such as placing containers for customers to drop off ink cartridges for recycling.

What's more, workplaces that meet efficiency standards can themselves earn national recognition as Energy Star® Partners. This is another selling point for environmentally aware buyers.

Here are five ways that a business can lower its expenses, while also helping the environment:

▲ Energy Star® Label

- **Get into the recycling loop.** First, recycle everything your community has facilities for. Most localities have paper and plastic recycling programs. Your community also might have businesses that recondition older computers and other office equipment. Then use recycled and recyclable products when available. Look for the triangular arrow-chasing-arrow symbol on containers. Read product packaging, being alert for any indication that it is recyclable. Tell suppliers that you prefer these items.

- **Do business electronically.** Reduce paper as much as possible. Take advantage of vendors' toll-free telephone numbers and Websites to place orders. If you send out newsletters to regular customers, encourage them to take an e-mail version instead of paper.

- **Buy supplies in bulk.** Items sold in large quantities usually cost less per piece and may use less packaging.

- **Replace incandescent light bulbs with fluorescent ones.** Compact fluorescent light bulbs have a longer life and greater efficiency and will save money in the long run.

- **Use environmentally friendly transportation.** You might adjust schedules or business hours to take advantage of carpooling or public transportation. Offer employees low-cost incentives, such as a gift card from a bicycle shop for those who ride to work. Encourage the use of hybrids or other energy-efficient cars.

▲ Recycling Triangle

▲ Compact Fluorescent Light Bulb

Peace through Entrepreneurship

Entrepreneurship can create more than just new products and opportunities. It can also lead to peace in locations that need it most. Organizations such as the Business Council for Peace work to foster small-business growth in war-torn regions such as Afghanistan and Rwanda. In an effort to provide a path to security for citizens there, business leaders from around the world visit to offer training and find ways to export local products. Local entrepreneurs can then provide jobs, income, and a feeling of self-worth to the people of the region. A more sustainable economy allows for people to stay in the country and improve their communities, which can lead to long-term stability.

PeaceWorks is another venture designed to foster understanding through entrepreneurship. This global business has Arabs and Israelis working as partners to create a line of food products such as gourmet *tapenades* (savory spreads featuring olives, vegetables, and olive oil). United by profit, former foes create more than just a healthy bottom line. By making entrepreneurs out of enemies, PeaceWorks is doing its part to use the principles of business to foster peace.

THINKING CRITICALLY

Drawing Conclusions. In addition to creating a more stable society and providing opportunities for former enemies to work together on a common goal, entrepreneurship can lead to peace in other ways. Gather in groups of three or four. Discuss additional ways small businesses could create peace in a region.

To read more about creating peace through entrepreneurship, go to "Entrepreneurship Issues" on the Student Center at entrepreneurship.pearson.com.

You may have heard of the **carbon footprint**, which measures the amount of carbon you use and thus release into the atmosphere. Carbon is a byproduct of burning coal and oil-based fuels. A combination of factors—such as the type of car you drive, how much you drive, the method of heating your home—determine your personal carbon footprint. One recent development in environmental responsibility is the practice of buying carbon offsets. Through a **carbon offset** you "buy" a certain amount of carbon, usually at a per-ton price, to help offset your carbon footprint. Offsets are sold by both nonprofit groups and for-profit traders, who invest the money in renewable energy producers or resource-conservation projects.

Following the guidelines above for energy efficiency is the surest way to lighten a business's carbon footprint. If your company leaves a heavy footprint because you do a lot of automobile travel, for instance, you might want to look at carbon offsets as an option. Look closely, however. Regulation of carbon offset trading is uneven and the benefits can be hard to verify. You have the most assurance in buying carbon offsets through a company that has the resources to monitor how the money is used. You might find that a company you do business with has an innovative carbon offset program. For example, certain airlines allow fliers to buy offsets based on the number of miles they fly.

Some businesses try to appear environmentally responsible by over-stating their commitment; this is called **greenwashing**. Such businesses take small steps, more for appearance than for impact, or advertise a practice that's required by law anyway. For example, a lawn and garden shop may claim, "All our pesticides meet federal guidelines for environmental protection." In reality, it would be illegal to sell products that did *not* meet these standards. Greenwashing is unethical at the very least and can hurt a business's reputation.

READING CHECKPOINT *List five things a business can do to lower its expenses while helping the environment.*

Responsibility to the Community

Businesses are increasingly supporting the cause of disadvantaged and needy people. Sometimes financial gain is the motive. Sometimes they do it through outright gifts or by making donations to nonprofit groups chartered to help those in need.

Cause-Related Marketing

Cause-related marketing is a partnership between a business and a nonprofit group for the benefit of both. At its best, cause-related marketing accomplishes two goals: it increases sales for the business and raises money and awareness for the nonprofit group.

One form of cause-related marketing that you're probably familiar with is **sponsorship**, in which a business sponsors a community event or service in exchange for advertising. For example, a travel agency might want to sponsor the local Little League baseball team. The agency's financial support makes participating in Little League affordable for more children. In exchange, the business's name and logo appear on the ball-field fences and the back of team shirts. The team's Website has a link to the

◀ **Figure 5-8**
Sponsorship
Many local companies sponsor Little League teams.
Applying Concepts. *How does this type of sponsorship help a business?*

travel agency. The travel agency contributes to the community's quality of life while advertising to the community. The community and the business both benefit.

Other types of cause-related marketing are becoming popular. One is **facilitated giving**, in which a business makes it easier for customers to contribute to a cause. For example, a store might have canisters in checkout lanes for customers to drop in their change for a local charity. Another might sell packaged food baskets to be donated to food banks around the holidays. In a **purchase-triggered donation**, for every purchase of a particular item the business contributes an amount of money or a percentage of the purchase price. Restaurant owners used this technique to raise $12 million for victims of Hurricane Katrina. Some 17,000 restaurants took part in the one-day campaign, called Dine for America, donating the proceeds to the American Red Cross.

Cause-related marketing requires careful planning. The cause should be popular and the nonprofit group well known. Often a business partners with a nonprofit group to which the business (or the business owner) has a special connection. For example, Wendy's hamburger-restaurant chain had a cause-related marketing program that encouraged the adoption of foster children. The cause was undeniably a worthy one, but the fact that Dave Thomas, the founder of Wendy's, was himself an adopted child demonstrated the business's special connection to this cause.

Philanthropy

The energy and initiative that makes entrepreneurs leaders in business can also make them leaders in **philanthropy** when they donate money and other resources for socially beneficial causes. Although philanthropy is often associated with large corporations, owners of much smaller businesses are often actively involved in giving back to their communities. In fact, many local service groups couldn't survive without the contributions of local entrepreneurs and small businesses.

Ideally, philanthropy is "a help up, not a handout." That is, its aim is to give people the resources they need to improve their lives on their own, and to build something for future generations. This has been the philosophy of the most notable philanthropists, both past and present.

Money is the chief way of being philanthropic. Besides writing a check to support a nonprofit group's immediate needs, entrepreneurs can invest by creating or contributing to an endowment fund. The nonprofit group uses the income from the endowment for ongoing needs or for a specific project. Other business owners have established matching gift programs in which they match contributions made by employees or clients.

Some businesses find themselves in a position to donate property. A restaurant that's changing its decor could give its curtains, wall hangings, or dinnerware to a social service agency that helps clients transition from homelessness. A business that's switching to a new computer network might have old hardware and software that would be an upgrade for a nonprofit group. Charitable organizations need donations of products and services to make silent auctions a success, as well as snacks for volunteers who work at nonprofit-sponsored events.

A gift of a good or service is called an **in-kind donation**. Both monetary gifts and in-kind donations can be declared on an entrepreneur's income tax statement and may help lower his or her tax liability. Gifts that are used to help people in a particularly disadvantaged area are sometimes eligible for additional tax breaks.

A business's workforce can be an asset to a service group, as well. Volunteers from a local business who help with a community project are making a visible statement about that business's commitment. This sort of volunteering also helps the business. Experts on workplace relations recognize volunteer projects as an effective, low-cost way to foster unity and teamwork among employees.

Entrepreneurial skills translate well for volunteering efforts. For example, the organizational skill involved in scheduling employees is easily applied to scheduling volunteers. Because they are comfortable being in charge, many business owners serve on a nonprofit group's board of directors or help with management. This gives them more say in how their donations are spent and provides the nonprofit with capable leadership.

Other entrepreneurs have special talents related to their respective businesses. A photographer who takes wedding and family photos for a living can use those skills to lay out an attractive fundraising brochure.

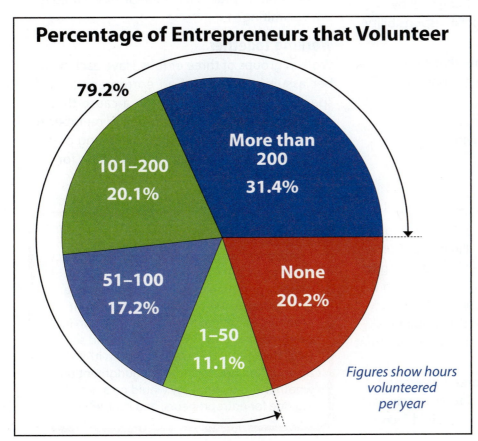

Percentage of Entrepreneurs that Volunteer

79.2%

101–200
20.1%

More than
200
31.4%

51–100
17.2%

None
20.2%

1–50
11.1%

Figures show hours volunteered per year

◀ **Figure 5-9**

Percentage of Entrepreneurs that Volunteer
Of the entrepreneurs surveyed, almost 80 percent said they and their families did volunteer work. This chart breaks down that figure by the number of hours volunteered annually.

Analyzing Data. *In which hour range did the largest percentage of entrepreneurs and their families fall? How do you explain this finding?*

This type of hands-on philanthropy takes time. Although time is a scarce resource for many entrepreneurs, they often see spending time on the community as a wise investment. Giving back to the community is a chance to build professional and personal relationships. Staying involved lets them know what people in their area need, which can help them make business decisions. Also, working in new situations can restore creativity and teach useful skills for the entrepreneur to use in business.

On the other hand, volunteering can be a mental and physical break from business, from the pressure to succeed and make a profit. *Philanthropy* comes from two Greek words that translate as "one who loves humankind." For many entrepreneurs, that definition sums up their reasons for giving.

 **READING CHECKPOINT** ✓ *What is cause-related marketing?*

 Your Business Plan. Continue developing your standard business plan. Go to "Section 5.2" of the *Business Plan Project* in your *Student Activity Workbook*, or "Section 5.2" of the BizTech Software.

ASSESSMENT 5.2

Reviewing Objectives

1. Explain how the phrase "doing well by doing good" relates to social responsibility for entrepreneurs.

2. What four qualities indicate that a business has a responsible relationship with customers?

3. List five ways a business can lower its expenses and help the environment.

4. What is philanthropy?

Critical Thinking

5. **Problem Solving.** Meredith owns an orchard. She is alarmed by the mysterious loss of honeybees that pollinate her fruit trees. She wants to use facilitated giving to support a nonprofit group investigating the situation. However, she's worried that very few people have heard of the problem so she won't be successful raising money. What should she do?

6. **Communication.** Entrepreneurs whose business is directly related to environmental responsibility are sometimes called "ecopre-neurs." How could being labeled an ecopreneur be helpful to a business? How could it be limiting?

Working Together

Work in groups of three or four. Have each member assume the role of an entrepreneur for a specific business. Then choose a cause that all members can support. Assign each member to use one form of cause-related marketing or philanthropy to raise money or awareness for the cause. Present your plans to the class.

Science
Green Technologies

Investigate one green technology or product of green technology, such as starch-based plastics, pest management, or a renewable energy source. What opportunities for entrepreneurs might the technology hold—in its production and use or in products and services that might be developed from it? Write up your findings. Include your judgment on whether this technology would be a promising one for entrepreneurs, and if so, why.

Giving Back: We Lend A Hand

When Terrence L. Hargrove was in high school, he started a candle-selling business called Passions. He bought candles wholesale and sold them retail. Several months later, he started Dynasty Cleaners, a cleaning service for schools and businesses. Both ventures were successful and Terry made money. He went on to college and also worked as an assistant teacher in a Connecticut high school.

▶ *Terry Hargrove*

Lending a Hand to Students

While attending college, Terry continued teaching in high school. "I saw a lot of kids that had potential," he said, "but they were repeat offenders and kept getting in trouble with discipline action—detention, in-school suspension, and out-of-school suspension." Terry met with the principal, trying to figure out what could be done to help these students and keep them from getting in trouble. His next business, called We Lend A Hand, was created from that meeting.

We Lend A Hand helps students who are at risk of being suspended or expelled by providing mentors and access to community action programs where they can channel their frustrations into a productive activity. The at-risk students are given their choice of serving detention or in-school suspension or completing a We Lend A Hand program. This could involve, for example, choosing a plot of land on school grounds, transforming it into a mini-garden or walkway, and then writing about the experience.

Raising Money

We Lend A Hand is a not-for-profit company, and everyone working for it, including Terry, is a volunteer. "We raise money through the community," said Terry. "We go to different small businesses and ask them to donate to We Lend A Hand to build up our treasury so that we're able to do different projects." Although raising money is typically the hardest job in a non-profit organization, We Lend A Hand has had a different experience. "The community has really jumped on to

help out. I guess they recognize the issue and see the problem and believe that We Lend A Hand has one of the solutions to the problem."

Keeping Books

One difference Terry has found between his for-profit companies and We Lend A Hand is in keeping financial records. Because the money is being donated from outside sources, "We pay very much more attention and detail to how we do our books. Our donors can see where their money is going . . . and how it's being spent. Our books always have to be correct and right at all times."

For Terry, We Lend A Hand reflects a certain philosophy. "No matter how successful you can be, you have to remember your community. You can't put yourself always first. You have to use everything that you have to go back and build the next generation, so they can have a better opportunity."

Thinking Like an Entrepreneur

1. What about the We Lend A Hand program do you think most helps at-risk students?
2. How would you go about raising money if you had a nonprofit organization like Terry's?
3. What's the difference between using your own money and someone else's to run your organization? Does this explain why Terry pays so much attention to his financial records?

CHAPTER SUMMARY

5.1 Ethical Business Behavior

Ethics are moral principles that govern decisions and actions. They are based on universal values that have been shared by all cultures throughout history. Cultures differ in how they express and enforce ethical values. Business ethics are moral principles applied to business issues and actions. Practicing business ethics benefits entrepreneurs. Businesses demonstrate ethics by practicing transparency, encouraging whistle-blowers, and writing a code of ethics. Transparency is openness and accountability in business decisions and actions. An important ethical concern for entrepreneurs is intellectual property, which is an artistic or industrial creation or invention. The protections for intellectual property are copyrights for artistic work, trademarks for brands and brand names, and patents for inventions. Other ethical concerns for entrepreneurs are conflicts of interest and confidentiality.

5.2 Socially Responsible Business and Philanthropy

Businesses demonstrate corporate social responsibility when they act in ways that balance profit and growth with the good of society. Businesses have a responsibility to treat employees, customers, suppliers, investors, and creditors ethically. Four qualities mark a responsible relationship with customers: honesty, respect, accessibility, and attention. Socially responsible entrepreneurs also try to preserve and protect the environment. Businesses and entrepreneurs give back to the community through cause-related marketing, which can include sponsorships, facilitated giving, and purchase-triggered donations.

REVIEW VOCABULARY

Imagine you are a reporter writing a story on ethics and business. Incorporate at least ten terms from the following list in your story.

- business ethics (p. 106)
- carbon footprint (p. 122)
- carbon offset (p. 122)
- cause-related marketing (p. 123)
- conflict of interest (p. 113)
- copyright (p. 111)
- corporate social responsibility (p. 115)
- ethical sourcing (p. 115)
- ethics (p. 105)

- facilitated giving (p. 124)
- fair use (p. 112)
- greenwashing (p. 123)
- infringement (p. 112)
- in-kind donation (p. 125)
- intellectual property (p. 111)
- patent (p. 111)
- philanthropy (p. 124)
- public domain (p. 112)

- purchase-triggered donation (p. 124)
- social media (p. 108)
- sponsorship (p. 123)
- sustainable (p. 120)
- trademark (p. 111)
- transparency (p. 107)
- universal values (p. 106)
- whistle-blower (p. 108)

CHECK YOUR UNDERSTANDING

Choose the letter that best answers the question or completes the statement.

1. Greenwashing is unethical because it
   a. infringes on copyright
   b. misleads consumers
   c. creates conflict of interest
   d. all of the above

2. Pauline's Pooch Palace gives $1 from every dog grooming to the local animal shelter. This is an example of
   a. sustainable design
   b. fair trade
   c. purchase-triggered donation
   d. philanthropy

3. A well-written code of ethics
   a. enhances a business's reputation
   b. helps attract quality employees
   c. helps prevent legal problems
   d. all of the above

4. The owner of a children's clothing store uses popular cartoon characters in her ads. This might be an example of
   a. copyright infringement
   b. social media
   c. cause-related marketing
   d. conflict of interest

5. By donating much of his fortune to building libraries, the American industrialist Andrew Carnegie demonstrated his belief in
   a. sponsorship
   b. philanthropy
   c. sustainability
   d. ethical sourcing

6. One way to reduce a business's carbon footprint is through
   a. greenwashing
   b. sponsorship
   c. communicating with investors
   d. sustainable design

7. When communicating with investors, an entrepreneur should
   a. give both good news and bad news about the business
   b. suggest ways that a larger investment would improve sales
   c. make confident predictions about the business's growth
   d. give only the information the investors specifically ask for

8. One challenge to writing a code of ethics is
   a. balancing contrasting qualities in an effective way
   b. avoiding controversial issues
   c. pleasing investors
   d. avoiding copyright infringement

9. A carbon footprint measures
   a. your sustainable energy
   b. the amount of carbon in the environment
   c. the amount of carbon you use
   d. the amount of carbon offsets you have purchased

10. A business promotes transparency through
    a. energy efficiency
    b. protecting whistle-blowers
    c. buying carbon offsets
    d. fair trade

11. Lila, a kitchen designer, helps clients choose appliances. An appliance dealer gives her gifts and tickets to shows. This situation has the potential for
    a. cause-related marketing
    b. patent infringement
    c. conflict of interest
    d. fair use

12. A code of ethics is most useful when it is based on
    a. philanthropy
    b. universal values
    c. fair use
    d. environmental responsibility

Business Communication

13. Working in small groups, choose a specific type of business. Write three items of a code of ethics that apply to that business. With each, explain how it relates to universal values.

14. Imagine that you made a mistake that inconvenienced and angered customers. Write a paragraph that will be posted on your company's Website. Keep in mind the importance of both transparency and confidentiality.

15. In small groups, write and perform a scene in which you give a financial report for your business at a meeting with investors. The business hasn't done well, and you need money. How will you answer investors' questions, accepting responsibility without causing them to lose confidence?

Business Ethics

18. Your business went through a slump last month, and you weren't sure you could pay your employees. You decided that, if needed, you would take the money from your own savings. Fortunately you didn't have to, but one employee found out and told the others. She said she thought they had the right to know when their jobs were in danger and that you had acted dishonestly in not telling them. She also said she would do the same thing in the future. How would you handle this situation?

Business Math

16. *See the table below.* For each unit, what percentage of the operating cost goes for electricity? How much money in water costs could be saved by replacing three conventional dishwashers with three Energy Star® models?

Commercial Dishwasher: Annual Costs		
Operating Costs	Energy Star® Unit	Conventional Unit
Electricity	$890	$1,556
Water	$112	$222
Total	$1,002	$1,778

17. In a survey of 809 small-business owners, eighty-five percent said they donated money to a charity the year before. Specifically, how many made charitable contributions?

Business in Your Community

19. Contact your local Better Business Bureau. Ask what ethical standards a company must uphold to be accredited by the Better Business Bureau. Does the Better Business Bureau feel that membership in the Bureau has an affect on profits, employees, or other aspects of business?

20. Working in a group, do a telephone or walking survey of area businesses to learn what steps they are taking to improve energy efficiency. Which steps do the people you talk to think are most useful? Why? Present your findings in a presentation to the class.

E-Mail

When the U.S. Postal Service was formed on July 26, 1775, letters were delivered by horse-drawn carriages. It could take weeks to receive a reply to a letter. A little over one hundred years later, the telephone was invented. Two people in different locations could talk to each other instantly—if they were connected by phone lines.

Today, e-mail combines features of both mail and telephone service. People can now receive messages instantly. They can also instantly send and receive many other types of information: videos, photographs, documents, music files, and links to Websites. They can do all this without having to be connected to phone lines.

Managing E-Mails

Electronic mail, or e-mail, is the most common type of computer-enabled communication. Because e-mail is so easy to use and can be sent to multiple recipients, businesspeople can receive hundreds of messages a day. Of course, not all of these are equally important. That's why there are e-mail management programs to help you. For example, you can sort e-mail into folders. Some e-mail programs have pre-set categories, such as "Waiting," "Hot Contacts," and "Time and Expenses." You can even establish rules that allow your computer to sort your e-mail automatically.

Another way to manage your incoming e-mails is to set up a system of "flags." For instance, all your red-flagged items might be important business e-mails that need immediate attention. Blue flags might indicate e-mails from an organization you belong to. Yellow flags might indicate e-mails from friends.

Sending E-Mail

People sending you e-mail can also help you organize it. They can use their e-mail management programs to tell you that the message you are receiving is confidential or of high importance.

Most e-mail programs will allow you to change the appearance of the messages you write. You can select various colors, backgrounds, and **fonts** (styles of typefaces). You may also be able to select the **stationery** to use for writing e-mails. This is a pre-set selection of fonts, font color, background color, and graphics that resemble printed stationery and make your e-mails look more finished and attractive. You can even have your e-mail management program add a signature to your letter automatically. A **signature** is text that is added to a letter along with your name. This could be a quote you like, your office phone numbers and hours, or anything else you would like to add automatically at the end of your messages.

The ease and speed of e-mail has changed business, as well as people's everyday lives. Any entrepreneur working today needs to know how to manage and send e-mails in the most efficient way possible.

Tech Vocabulary
- fonts
- stationery
- signature

Check Yourself

1. Would you organize e-mails by sorting into folders, by flagging messages, or by a combination of both methods?

2. How would you feel about a sender who sent a message that was labeled "high importance" when you didn't think it was?

3. Why would people want to use e-mail stationery?

What Do You Think?

Writing. If you used a quote in your signature, what would it be?

Why Is Goal Setting Important?

Most successful people say that the secret to their success is setting goals. When you set a goal, you decide what you want to accomplish. Goal setting enables you to focus on your dreams and turn them into reality. By setting goals, you create a path for your future success. Learning how to set goals is a valuable lesson you'll use throughout your life.

Start with a Dream

Everyone has wishes and dreams. This is the starting point for success. The idea is to convert a wish or dream into an achievable goal. Sometimes a wish or a dream is a **long-term goal**, something you'll make happen in a few years. You can also set **short-term goals** to achieve right now. For example, you might dream of being the owner of a successful company. To achieve this, you might set a series of short-term goals—each of which can take you a step closer to your final destination.

As with any journey to a specific destination, you need a roadmap. Setting goals lets you map out exactly where you're going and how you'll get there. Each goal becomes a manageable step along the way. And accomplishing each short-term goal helps you keep your focus on the long-term goal.

Where do you begin? You begin by identifying your dream. What do you desire? In what area do you want to be successful? What do you want to change, improve, or achieve in your life? Allow your imagination to dream big! Dare to dream!

Think Positively

When we identify a dream, we often come up with excuses that prevent us from reaching our goals. We think about the work involved and the challenges and before long we're using words like *no, can't, won't, never, maybe, impossible,* and *later.* To achieve a goal, you need to develop an "I will make it happen" attitude. Get out of your own way and start planning your future. Surround yourself with people who will support your dream and cheer you on. You may encounter roadblocks along the way, but a positive attitude will help you figure out how to overcome each challenge.

The Goal-Setting Process

When you begin the process of setting a goal, you need to make sure you are working with a SMART goal. A **SMART** goal is one that is:

Specific. Your goal statement spells out exactly what you want to achieve, in simple language.

Measurable. You must be able to measure your progress.

Action-Oriented. You must list the actions required for reaching your goal and commit to them.

Realistic. Your goal must be manageable. Do you have everything you need to achieve it?

Time-Specific. Goals need to have a target date for completion.

SMART goals are focused and achievable. You decide what you want, you agree to the steps involved, and you control the outcome. You are in the driver's seat.

Try it. Set a goal for yourself by following these steps:

1. **Goal Statement.** Decide what it is you want and then write a goal statement. Make sure it is a SMART goal. Write the goal in the form of a positive "I will" statement.

2. **Action Steps.** Below the goal statement, write a numbered list of the action steps required for completing the goal.

3. **Completion Date.** Below your list of action steps, write the date when you want to complete your goal.

Goal Setting

When you set goals, you are investing in yourself and your future. Stay positive, focus on your action steps, and keep your final destination in mind. A positive outlook helps you overcome challenges.

COMPARING/CONTRASTING *What are some of the negative statements that can get in the way of your success? How can you change those negatives into positive statements?*

Reviewing Concepts

1. Why is it important to think positively about goal setting?

2. What is the difference between a long-term goal and a short-term goal?

3. What is a SMART goal?

Goal Setting

4. **Writing.** List examples of goal statements, including personal goals (such as goals that relate to you physically, mentally, emotionally), school goals, and community goals.

5. **Applying Concepts.** Choose one school or community goal, and describe how it meets the SMART goal criteria.

COMMUNICATING EFFECTIVELY & RESPONSIBLY

Eva Tan, sole proprietor of Eva's Entertainment Services, is in college. She's using her home-based business to help reduce her education costs. As you read about her challenges, consider how the lessons Eva learns might help you.

Let's Make a Deal

Eva found that negotiating often helped her in her business. Here are two examples:

Always Get It In Writing

Eva always takes notes when talking to customers on the phone or face-to-face. She uses these notes to plan and carry out the events she was hired to handle.

One day, however, she realized that her notes just weren't enough. She had a miscommunication with a customer. As a result, there wasn't enough food for an event. Eva tried to figure out what happened.

Maybe she had written down the wrong number of attendees. Maybe her customer had given her the wrong figure. Either way, Eva had to scramble fast to supply more food for the hungry, waiting guests. Luckily, she was able to find a caterer who had something she could substitute and could delivery it quickly.

Eva needed to salvage her reputation. She negotiated a discounted price for her services. To avoid similar problems in the future, Eva created a form that each customer had to approve and sign. "Now I always follow up an order with a formal business letter, thanking the customer for hiring me and explaining the attached form. The customer has to verify and sign the agreement before sending it back to me in a self-addressed, postage-paid envelope that I provide."

Good Relationships

When Eva found a vendor who did a good job at a reasonable price, she went back to that vendor when she needed the same product or service. By doing this, Eva found that she began to develop a good relationship with several vendors.

She approached these business owners and asked them if they would be willing to give her a discount in exchange for a certain amount of repeat business. They agreed. In fact, some even said that they would recommend Eva to customers looking for an event planner. The negotiations ultimately benefited both Eva and her vendors.

An Ethical Problem

Eva had a customer named Tom who hired her to plan personal parties. One day, Tom asked Eva to plan a big event for the corporation where he worked. He asked her to order more supplies for the event than were actually needed. With a grin, he said, "I'm going to use the extra supplies for a party at my house. I'll ask you to handle it."

Eva was stunned. This was a real ethical problem!

She wanted Tom's corporation to continue using her event-planning services. She made a lot of money when they had big parties and she was a preferred vendor. Being a preferred vendor meant Eva's business received many orders from the corporation. She was worried that Tom might not use her company if she refused, and might even say bad things about her.

Eva thought about it. She decided she would rather risk losing Tom and his company as customers than be dishonest. Not only would Eva's conscience bother her, but also her reputation as a businessperson could be ruined if the fraudulent transaction were discovered.

Eva politely refused to fulfill Tom's request to inflate the order. Tom was angry, but it was too late for him to go to another event planner. Eva planned the corporation's party and it was successful. However, Tom never asked her to plan another event.

Another employee of the corporation who attended the event was very impressed by Eva's work. He asked her to plan an event for his department. Luckily he had no contact with Tom and was very pleased with his event. Other employees took notice and they asked Eva to plan their events.

Eva's experience led her to consider what types of ethical and social standards she would like her business to have. She wrote a code of ethics that reflected her values, and made sure to mention the respect she had for her customers and vendors.

One item in her code of ethics almost always drew comments. It stated that Eva's company would be as "green" as possible. In keeping with her own code of ethics, Eva worked on making her home office energy-efficient. She also made an effort to choose vendors who were environmentally and socially responsible.

She gave copies of her code of ethics to potential customers and vendors as a way of informing them what kind of standards her company had—and hoped never to have another experience like the one with Tom again!

What Would You Have Done?

1. **Writing.** When Eva miscommunicated with her customer, she gave a discounted price. What would you have done if this happened to you? Was a discount enough? Explain your answer.

2. **Communicating.** If you had been in Eva's shoes, what would you have said to Tom? Do you think Eva had a responsibility to act as a whistle-blower and report Tom's conduct to someone at his corporation?

UNIT **3**

OPPORTUNITY RECOGNITION & MARKET ANALYSIS

In This Unit:

6. Opportunity Recognition
7. Market Research

YOUR BUSINESS PLAN

In this unit, you'll focus on the **Opportunity & Market Analysis** section of the business plan and answer these questions:

- Is my idea for a business a real business opportunity?
- How should I conduct market research?
- Who are my competitors?
- What is my competitive advantage?

CHAPTER

6 OPPORTUNITY RECOGNITION

OBJECTIVES

- Explain the purpose of a business plan
- Describe the types of business plans
- Identify the parts of a business plan
- Understand how to put together a business plan

Think about this question:

If I were going to do something important, would I plan before I did it?

Write your answer (yes or no) on a piece of paper. Be prepared to discuss your answer in class.

Purpose of a Business Plan

Creating a business could be one of the most important things you do in your life. So it would only make sense to spend time planning it. Most entrepreneurs initially develop a business plan as a way of describing their business precisely. A **business plan** is a statement of your business goals, the reasons you think these goals can be met, and how you are going to achieve them.

If you start your business without a plan, you will soon be overwhelmed by questions you haven't answered. A business plan forces you to figure out how to make your business work. A well-written business plan will show investors that you have carefully thought through what you intend to do to make the business profitable. The more explanation you offer investors about how their money will be used, the more willing they will be to invest. Your plan should be so thoughtful and well written that the only question it raises in an investor's mind is "How much can I invest?"

A well-written plan will also guide you every step of the way as you develop your business. It becomes a decision-making tool. An entrepreneur uses the business plan to track whether the company is meeting its goals. From time-to-time, the business plan needs to be revised to keep up with the changing nature of the business.

Some business owners might do this on an annual basis; others, in well-established industries, might do it every three years. Still others, in newly developed or high-tech areas, may need to do it monthly or even weekly.

If your company is for-profit, your business plan will typically focus on your financial goals. If you are a nonprofit, your plan will typically focus on your mission and services in support of that mission. (As you know from previous chapters, a nonprofit company can make a profit, but the funds must remain in the company and be used in pursuing its mission.)

 **READING CHECKPOINT** *What is a business plan?*

Types of Business Plans

Business plans have no set format. A plan is developed based on the type of business that is intended. However, it is also based on the audience. Businesses need different types of plans for different audiences. There are four main types of plans for a start-up business:

- **Quick Summary.** This is a synopsis lasting from thirty seconds to three minutes. It's used to interest potential investors, customers, or strategic partners. It may seem strange to consider this a type of business plan, but it is. In some cases, the quick summary may be a necessary step toward presenting a more fully developed plan. (Examples of this type of summary are the elevator pitch and the twitpitch, described later in this section.)

Professional investors often receive hundreds of business plans a year

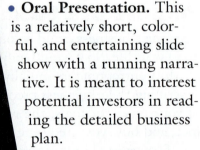

- **Oral Presentation.** This is a relatively short, colorful, and entertaining slide show with a running narrative. It is meant to interest potential investors in reading the detailed business plan.

- **Investor's Business Plan.** Anyone who plans to invest in your start-up business (banks, investors, and others) needs to know exactly what you are planning. They need a detailed business plan that is well written and formatted so all the information can

Figure 6-1 ▶

Oral Presentation
Be sure to maintain the interest of your audience when making an oral presentation.

Communicating. *What are some of the ways you could maintain the interest of an investor when presenting a business plan?*

be easily understood. When entrepreneurs talk about a business plan, this is typically the type of plan they mean.

- **Operational Business Plan.** Often a start-up business will develop an *operational* plan that is meant for use within the business only. This plan describes in greater detail than the investor's business plan how the company will meet its goals. It is also often less formal than an investor's business plan.

Although there is no set format for a business plan, each type of plan will address The Three C's.

The Three C's

- **Concept.** What is your product or service and how is it different from similar products or services?

- **Customer.** Who will be buying your product or service and why?

- **Capital.** How will you locate the money your business will need? What will be your costs and what kind of profit can you expect?

What are the four main types of business plans for a start-up?

Parts of a Business Plan

In this course you will be focusing on developing an investor's business plan. Bankers and other professional investors will need to see your business plan before they lend you money. You may have a brilliant idea, but if you do not explain it fully in a well-written business plan, no professional investor will be interested.

Professional investors typically see many business plans each year and make very few investments. They will immediately reject an incomplete or poorly written plan. Investors are busy people and don't have time to read an overly long business plan. Your plan, including the financials, should be no longer than 20 typed pages (and many are much shorter). It should require no more than an hour of reading time.

Most plans will include these seven parts (although the order may differ, depending on the type of business):

- **Business Idea.** Not only do you describe your product or service in this part of the business plan, but you also talk about the type of business you will start and the type of business ownership you will use. Recently, in this part of the business plan, entrepreneurs have begun to describe how their business is socially responsible.

- **Opportunity & Market Analysis.** Your description of the market should include an account of the market, its size, its trends and characteristics, and its growth rate. Describe your market research. List your competitors and describe your competitive advantage. Provide your marketing plan, your product and pricing strategies, and your plans for promotion.

- **Financial Strategies.** This section shows any historical financial data, as well as projected figures including estimated sales and expenses (typically extending for five years). This section also describes any financing required by the business.

- **Organizational Structures.** In this part of the business plan you discuss the organizational structure of the company. You can provide profiles of key managers and, if appropriate, information about your board of directors. You can also describe how you plan to train and motivate your employees, if appropriate.

- **Legal Structures.** In this part of the business plan you describe any intellectual property or contract issues. You also talk about how your business will be protected by insurance, the affect of taxes on your business, and any relevant government regulations that affect the business.

- **Business Management.** Describe how the business will be managed (focusing on production, distribution, operations, purchasing, and inventory).

- **Plan for Growth.** Here you describe your plans to grow the business and the challenges it may face. You may also describe your plans to franchise or license the business, if that is part of its plan for growth.

To ensure that investors understand the key points of your idea, the plan should include an <mark>executive summary</mark>, a one- or two-page summary of highlights, including the key selling points of the investment opportunity. (See the description of an executive summary on the following page.)

The Internet offers many sources of information about business plans. One of the best is the Website of the Small Business Administration (www.sba.gov), which has links to other organizations that provide business planning help. Another good source for help with business plans is www.entrepreneur.com.

 **READING CHECKPOINT** *What seven parts do most business plans include?*

Putting Your Plan Together

You will be putting together your own business plan for investors. In the process, you may discover that what you thought was a good

Executive Summary

- Mission Statement

- Business Name & Location

- Date Business Will Begin

- Owner's Name, Function, & Contact Information

- Opportunity

- Products or Services

- Economics of One Unit (EOU)

- Future Plans

business opportunity is not quite the opportunity you thought. You might need to abandon the idea or tweak it to make it more viable. It is better to discover that the business won't work on paper before you invest significant time and money.

Developing a business plan is not a simple, straightforward process. You don't start at the beginning and move to the end. Each new piece of information or financial calculation could cause you to reexamine, and possibly change, everything you have done up to that point.

You will need to consider two basic questions early in the process of developing your business plan (both were discussed in Chapter 3):

- What type of business will you form (manufacturing, wholesaling, retailing. or service)?

- What type of ownership will it have (sole proprietorship, partnership, corporation, or cooperative)?

The remainder of this book will provide what you need to know to put together a business plan. The first 14 chapters help you build a standard business plan. The reminder of the book helps you with more advanced topics. The table on the next page gives a summary of how the book relates to the business planning process.

 *What two questions do you need to consider early in the process of developing a business plan?*

STANDARD BUSINESS PLAN

Part of Business Plan	Section of Book	Key Question
Business Idea	1.2	What skills do I have to start this business?
	2.1	What factors will influence the demand for my product or service?
	3.1	What type of business will I start?
	3.2	What type of business ownership is right for me?
	5.2	How is my business socially responsible?
Opportunity & Market Analysis	6.2	Is my idea for a business a real business opportunity?
	7.1	How should I conduct market research?
	7.2	Who are my competitors?
	7.2	What is my competitive advantage?
	8.1	What is my marketing plan?
	8.1	What are my product and pricing strategies?
	8.2	How do I promote my product?
	9.1	How do I sell my product?
Financial Strategies	9.2	How do I estimate sales?
	10.1	What are my business costs?
	10.2	How do I measure the economics of one unit?
	11.1	How do I develop an income statement and track cash flow?
	11.2	How do I develop a balance sheet?
	12.1	Are my financial ratios good?
	12.2	What is my break-even point?
	13.1	What types of financing are available?
	13.2	Should I obtain financing?
	14.1	What records should I keep?
	14.2	What kind of accounting system should I use?

For a sample business plan, see pages 194–207.

Your Business Plan. Continue developing your standard business plan. Go to "Section 6.1" of the *Business Plan Project* in your *Student Activity Workbook*, or "Section 6.1" of the BizTech Software.

ADVANCED BUSINESS PLAN

Part of Business Plan	Section of Book	Key Question
Organizational Structures	15.1	What organizational structure is right for my business?
	15.1	How should I staff my business?
	15.1	Do I need the help of outside experts?
	15.2	How do I train and motivate employees?
Legal Structures	16.1	Does my product involve intellectual property rights?
	16.1	What contracts will my business require?
	16.2	How will I protect my business by using insurance?
	17.1	How will taxes affect my business?
	17.2	How will government regulations affect my business?
	17.2	How will government regulations affect employees?
Business Management	18.1	How will I manage my business?
	18.2	How do I manage expenses, credit and cash flow?
	19.1	How do I manage production and distribution?
	19.2	How will I manage my operations?
	20.1	How do I manage purchasing?
	20.2	How do I manage inventory?
Plan for Growth	21.1	How can I plan for business growth?
	21.2	What are the challenges of growth?
	22.1	Can I franchise or license my business?
	22.2	When and how should I leave my business?

Elevator Pitches

Entrepreneurs often need funds from outside sources to start their businesses. To obtain financing, entrepreneurs have to explain the idea for a new business to a bank loan officer, a venture capitalist, or other potential investor. This is called a "pitch."

Entrepreneurs often don't have much time to make their case. This has led to the "elevator pitch" (so named because the pitch has to be succinct enough to be delivered during an elevator ride). In an elevator pitch, an entrepreneur has only 30 seconds. He or she must communicate in fewer than 150 words what the product does and how the consumer will benefit. Venture capitalists may ask entrepreneurs for an elevator pitch to weed out bad ideas immediately.

Now, with the advent of micro-blogging Websites such as Twitter—in which readers post updates of 140 characters or less—the "twitpitch" is the newest type of elevator pitch. Entrepreneurs post two-sentence business ideas to their accounts, efficiently getting through to time-crunched consultants and venture capitalists.

THINKING CRITICALLY

Applying Concepts. Think of a new idea for a small business. Can you communicate that idea in 30 seconds? How about in 140 characters or less? Start by practicing an elevator pitch in a small group and then take turns writing your own twitpitches and sharing them with the class.

To read more about pitches, including elevator pitches and twitpitches, go to "Entrepreneurship Issues" on the Student Center at entrepreneurship.pearson.com.

ASSESSMENT 6.1

Reviewing Objectives

1. What is a business plan?
2. What are the four main types of business plans?
3. What are the seven parts of a business plan?
4. What two questions do you need to consider early in the process of developing a business plan?

Critical Thinking

5. **Comparing/Contrasting.** Why do the business plans for nonprofit organizations differ from those of for-profit businesses?
6. **Drawing Conclusions.** How would the business plan for a one-person service operation run from a home differ from that of a manufacturing business requiring 100 employees, equipment, and a building?

Working Together

Working in groups of four, use the Internet to research three business plan models. Record the parts of each plan and the order in which the parts are presented. Compare these business plans with the one outlined in this chapter. What are the differences between the plan in the text and the plans you researched? What are the similarities?

Language Arts

Summarizing a Business Plan

Select six existing businesses: two manufacturing, two retailing, and two service. For each business, identify the concept and the customer in one sentence.

6.2 What Is a Business Opportunity?

OBJECTIVES

- Identify ways to recognize business opportunities
- Explain how to use creative thinking to generate ideas
- Compare various types of business opportunities
- Describe methods used to evaluate business opportunities

- business broker
- business opportunity
- calculated risk
- cost/benefit analysis
- creative thinking
- critical thinking
- feasibility
- franchisee
- franchisor
- intangible
- need
- nondisclosure agreement
- opportunity cost
- prototype
- royalty fee
- SWOT analysis
- trade show
- want
- window of opportunity

Quickly consider this question:

If you started a business, what would it be?

Write your answer on a piece of paper. Think about your reasons for choosing this business.

Recognizing Opportunities

Usually you start a business because you see an opportunity. A **business opportunity** is a consumer need or want that can potentially be met by a new business. In economics, a **need** is defined as something that people must have to survive, such as water, food, clothing, or shelter. A **want** is a product or service that people desire.

Ideas versus Opportunities

Not every business idea is a good business opportunity. For example, you might have an idea for a neighborhood restaurant. But if that idea has no commercial potential, if it can't make a profit, it isn't an opportunity. If the public didn't like the type of food you planned to serve, for example, the business would be doomed to fail.

Your idea could be an opportunity in a different location, however. Let's say that the people in another town really wanted your potential restaurant's cuisine. In addition, no similar restaurant currently existed in the area. In this case, your idea *could* be a real opportunity.

Opportunity Recognition ● **147**

You can ask yourself five questions to begin the process of determining if a business idea might be a good business opportunity. If the answer to any of these questions is "no," there is a good chance that the idea is not a real business opportunity. (As you read this book, you'll discover practical ways of answering these questions.)

- Does the idea fill a need or want that's not currently being met?

- Will the idea work in the location or in the way that you plan to sell it?

- Can you put the idea into action within a reasonable amount of time—that is, before someone else does or while resources are still available? This concept is called the **window of opportunity**: the period of time you have to act before the opportunity is lost.

- Do you have the resources and skills to create the business (or know someone else who could help you do it)?

- Can you provide the product or service at a price that will attract customers but still earn a reasonable profit?

Sources of Opportunity

Staying aware of things going on around you can help you recognize potential business opportunities. Here are just a few sources of ideas:

- **Problems.** Many well-known companies were started because an entrepreneur wanted to solve a problem. A problem could be something you are experiencing personally. Or it could be a problem you observe others experiencing. What product or service would improve your life or the lives of others? What would you like to buy that is not available for purchase in your area?

- **Changes.** Our world is continually changing—changes in laws and regulations, social customs, local and national trends, even the weather. Change often produces needs or wants that no one is currently supplying. Consider climate change and the trend toward taking better care of the environment. Many new business opportunities have occurred because people are interested in purchasing "green" products and services.

- **New Discoveries.** The creation of totally new products and services can happen by accident. For example, someone who has an enjoyable hobby can discover something recognizable as a business opportunity. Inventions also come about because someone wanted to find a way to solve a problem. Other examples include changes in technology or medical and technological discoveries that entrepreneurs find ways to convert into products and services.

- **Existing Products and Services.** You can get ideas for opportunities from businesses that already exist. This is *not* the same

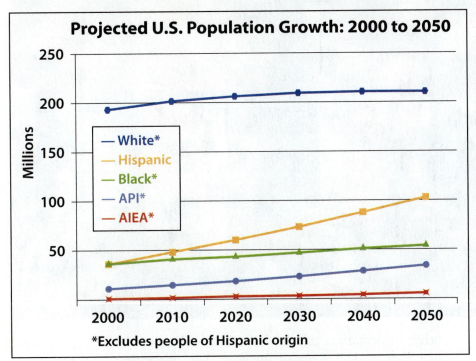

Projected U.S. Population Growth: 2000 to 2050

*Excludes people of Hispanic origin

Legend:
— White*
— Hispanic
— Black*
— API*
— AIEA*

Figure 6-2
Trends
This graph projects U.S. population growth from 2000 to 2050 based on U.S. Census Bureau estimates.
Interpreting Graphs. *What area suggests the greatest increase in business opportunity?*

API: *Asian or Pacific Islander*
AIEA: *American Indian, Eskimo, or Aleut*

thing as copying a product or service and then calling it by another name (which can be illegal). Instead, it means looking for ways to significantly improve a product, perhaps at a lower price. It could also involve improving the quality and manner in which customers are served—including such features as better locations, longer hours, or quicker service.

- **Unique Knowledge.** Entrepreneurs sometimes turn one-of-a-kind experiences or uncommon knowledge into a product or service that benefits others. Think about your own knowledge and experiences. Is there anything unique or unusual that you could use to create something new or to help others?

Where to Look for Opportunities

There are many ways to locate business opportunities. Your own community is a good place to begin. Here are some resources you might find useful:

- **Newspapers and Magazines.** Examine not only your local newspapers but also those from such metropolitan areas as New York, Miami, Chicago, Dallas/Fort Worth, and Los Angeles. Sampling the news from across the country may help you see a developing national trend. News magazines such as *Time* and *Newsweek* are other resources, as are magazines published about your particular city or region. In addition, take a look at specialized magazines that focus on a hobby or subject you are interested in.

- **Business and Governmental Agencies.** Some good examples of government agencies that provide useful statistical data and

Trade shows can help give you ideas for new businesses

other information are the U.S. Census Bureau, U.S. Department of Labor, and U.S. Small Business Administration. You can also contact your local Better Business Bureau or Chamber of Commerce for information on businesses in your area.

- **Trade Resources.** Various types of trade resources can help you get ideas for new businesses. A **trade show** is a convention where related businesses come to promote their products or services. Similarly, trade magazines are published for specific types of businesses. Trade associations exist for nearly every industry. A few examples of trade associations include the American Booksellers Association, Pet Sitters International, the Soap and Detergent Association, and the National Roofing Contractors Association.

- **World Wide Web.** Surfing the Web is a great way to explore just about any topic. By browsing, you might discover sites that you otherwise would not have known about.

READING CHECKPOINT ✓ *When is a business idea a business opportunity?*

Thinking Creatively

Entrepreneurs are constantly coming up with business ideas by thinking creatively. Training yourself to think like an entrepreneur may take some practice, but it is well worth the effort.

Types of Thinking

Creative thinking is a thought process that involves looking at a situation or object in new ways. It is also called *lateral* thinking. The phrases "Think outside the box" and "Use your imagination" refer to creative thinking. You can also define creative thinking as having an attitude that "plays" with many possibilities.

In contrast, **critical thinking** is also called *vertical* thinking, but it doesn't mean you are being negative. Critical thinking refers to a logical thought process that involves analyzing and evaluating a situation or object. Perhaps you've asked someone to help critique an essay or project on which you were working. They read or analyzed what you did. Then, they probably evaluated the project, suggesting things you could change.

Creative and critical thinking are both important, but they tend to produce different results. It is wise to learn when and how to apply them. For example, creative thinking works well for generating ideas and recognizing opportunities. Later in this chapter you will learn more about how to apply critical thinking when evaluating business opportunities.

Creative Thinking Techniques

You can help yourself think more creatively. Here are a few techniques:

- **Challenge the Usual.** Ask lots of "Why?" and "What if?" questions. Challenge what you believe about how products should work or how things are done.

- **Think Backward.** Sometimes solving a problem is easier when you start by imagining the end result you want. Then mentally trace imaginary steps backward to see how you could get there.

- **Be Flexible.** There is almost always more than one way to solve a problem. Force yourself to examine things from different angles. Problems can even become solutions. Take Post-it® Notes, for

---

YOUR BUSINESS CAREER

Respect

Respect is a vital component of all healthy relationships. Most high school students know that you have to give people respect to get it back.

The first step to gaining respect is to respect yourself. Think about the relationships you have in your life. The best ones are those where you can be yourself, express your opinions freely, and make decisions together. You never feel pressured to do something that you would not be comfortable doing.

As you join the workforce or move on to college after high school, you will encounter people with an assortment of ideas, temperaments, and beliefs. Don't forget that respect is shown both in actions and in words. When people are respectful, they don't put people down or make them feel uncomfortable. They accept the individual differences and beliefs of others.

THINKING CRITICALLY

Drawing Conclusions. Imagine that a coworker has asked you to do something with which you are not comfortable. How can turning that person down indicate that you respect yourself? How might this action actually command respect from others?

To read more about respect for yourself and others, go to "Your Business Career" on the Student Center at entrepreneurship.pearson.com.

---

example. A glue created by a 3M scientist was not very strong. Later, another 3M scientist thought about using the glue in a different way—and that produced a *very* successful product.

- **Judge Later.** When brainstorming ideas, don't worry about being practical. Also, try not to be negative or prejudiced. Those attitudes lower creativity. Not all ideas have to make sense in the beginning. You'll have time later to decide which ones are not useful. Sometimes ideas that seem silly at first inspire other, more useful, solutions later.

- **Draw Idea Maps.** Use whiteboards, chalkboards, and poster boards to sketch out ideas. For example, one thought might branch out into six directions, and some of those branches might generate additional ideas. Drawing possibilities in this way often helps you to see a bigger picture, with new possibilities that you might have otherwise missed. You might also try using sticky notes on a wall or poster board. This method allows you to move ideas around.

▲ Brainstorming can help you generate ideas

- **Brainstorm in a Group.** Ask your friends, family, and classmates to help you generate ideas. The old saying "two heads are better than one" is often true. All of these thinking techniques can be used when working in a group.

- **Daydream.** Letting your mind wander is okay; just make sure you pick an appropriate time. With your eyes closed, practice visualizing what your new product or service would be. What would it look like, smell like, taste like, feel like, sound like?

Whether thinking creatively on your own or in a group, keeping a positive attitude helps build creativity. Former First Lady Eleanor Roosevelt wrote: "The future belongs to those who believe in the beauty of their dreams."

 *What is the difference between critical thinking and creative thinking?*

Turning Ideas into Opportunities

After you've generated a number of business ideas, the next step is to compare options for applying them. Should you start a new business or buy one that already exists? Does the problem you've identified call for a new invention or the modification of an old product? Here are four common ways to turn ideas into opportunities:

- Start a new business
- Buy an independent business
- Buy a franchise
- Become an inventor

Starting a New Business

The beauty of starting a new business is that you can build it your own way. However, you must make many decisions and complete many tasks before your business can run effectively. This could initially be a real challenge if you don't have the necessary resources or skills. How much time and effort are you willing to invest? How will you obtain the knowledge and skills you need to start and operate a new business?

A potential disadvantage of starting a new business is the amount of risk or uncertainty involved. If your product or service is new, you may have difficulty predicting how well it will sell. There typically will be less information available on which you can base your decisions. How much are you willing to risk?

Although starting a new business may seem overwhelming, everything doesn't have to happen at once. As the saying goes, "Rome wasn't built in a day." With proper planning and strong motivation, you can succeed in building a new business, one step at a time.

Buying an Independent Business

When you start a business from the ground up, becoming successful can take a long time. That's one reason some entrepreneurs prefer to purchase a business that already exists. Finding a business for sale is similar to looking for a house to buy. You can start by reading advertisements in local newspapers and real estate magazines. You may also want to hire a **business broker**, someone who is licensed to sell businesses.

An existing business normally has much already in place: trained employees, operating equipment, merchandise and supplies on hand, established credit for making new purchases, and established procedures for running the company. Most important of all, an existing business already has customers. If current customers are happy with the products or services, their continued purchases will help to ensure your success.

Sometimes the previous owner of an independent business is willing to provide a period of training for the new owner. The business seller may also allow for a down payment, followed by monthly installments. This can reduce the amount of money you need to borrow from a bank, family, or friends.

Buying an independent business is still very much an entrepreneurial activity. You may not have initially created the business, but you will be responsible for its continued growth and success. For example, you can use your business skills and creativity to attract additional customers. You might also find new ways to improve the current processes and procedures of the business. You may even decide to add new products or services at some point.

Buying a business usually requires a large amount of money initially. In comparison, you may not have to invest much money at the beginning when you start a new business. When buying a business, you also risk inheriting problems—both visible and hidden ones.

▲ Figure 6-3
Franchises
Many fast-food restaurants are franchises.
Recognizing Patterns. *What are the names of some fast-food franchise businesses located in your community?*

Buying a Franchise

As you learned in an earlier chapter, a franchise is a way to buy a business in the name of another company. This legal agreement gives the **franchisee**, or franchise buyer, the right to sell the company's products or services in a particular location and for a specified length of time. The franchise seller is called a **franchisor**.

As you've already learned, buying a business has less risk than starting a new one. This is particularly true of franchises. Some sources estimate that a franchise has a 90% or better chance of success. Some of the reasons for this include:

- **Proven System.** Most franchises have a system in place that has already been tested. Following the proven processes and procedures created by the franchisor helps ensure the success of your business.

- **Customer Awareness.** People tend to buy from businesses they recognize and trust. When you buy a franchise that is well known and liked, you will benefit from the name and reputation already established.

- **Multiple Benefits Provided by the Franchisor.** A franchisor provides initial training on how to operate the business. In addition, the franchisor provides ongoing support in answering questions. An individual franchise also benefits from the national advertising purchased by the franchisor.

- **Exclusive Geographical Area.** A franchisor allows only a certain number of franchises to operate within a particular region. This keeps competition down.

- **Easier Financing.** Bankers are often more likely to lend money to an individual buying a franchise, because historically franchises have a high rate of success. From the bankers' point of view, a franchisee is less likely to default on a loan than owners of other types of businesses.

Owning a franchise may also give you additional opportunities to grow as an entrepreneur. Once you become a successful franchise owner, you may want to buy additional units of the same franchise. You will manage all the teams who work at the various sites.

There are also some downsides to consider before buying a franchise:

- **Initial and Ongoing Fees.** When you first buy a franchise, you pay a fairly high fee for the right to operate it. This cost can range from $5,000 to $100,000 or even higher. You need additional money to set up and operate a franchise. For example, you must purchase equipment. You need to set aside money to pay bills and employees until the business is making enough profit. A franchise owner also pays a **royalty fee** to the franchisor. This is a regular, ongoing payment that is based on a percentage of the sales a franchise earns.

- **Less Entrepreneurial Freedom.** Starting a new business or buying an independent business presents decision-making freedom. When you own a franchise, however, you must abide by the rules in the agreement. If you fail to meet the conditions of the franchise, the franchisor can cancel the agreement and put you out of business. There is also no guarantee that the franchisor will renew your agreement when it expires.

Becoming an Inventor

Some entrepreneurs invent new products, designs, or processes. They may choose to sell or license their inventions to someone else. Or they may create a business of their own that uses or manufactures the invention. Often inventors significantly change an existing product or process, rather than creating a totally new one, just as the following two companies did:

- **HurriQuake Nail.** The HurriQuake nail is designed to resist pulling out of wood during hurricanes and earthquakes. Because building a house with HurriQuake nails only costs about $15 more, a lot of builders are likely to purchase HurriQuakes instead of standard nails.

- **XO Laptop.** One Laptop Per Child (OLPC) is a nonprofit organization with the goal of providing laptops for children worldwide. OLPC found a way to create a low-cost laptop called the XO. They also reduced the laptop's energy use by 90 percent. This was achieved by inventing a new kind of screen display.

Whether you want to create a new invention or improve an existing one, here are some of the things you will need to do:

▲ *Inventors should keep a detailed logbook.*

- **Keep a Logbook.** Keep a detailed record, with dates, of everything related to your potential invention. Start with the date when you first thought of the idea. Use a type of notebook that is hardbound, not a loose-leaf binder. Your logbook can be used in the future to help prove the origin of your invention. In addition, a logbook is a good way to keep track of your sketches, notes, and research information.

- **Conduct a Search.** Find out whether somebody else has already patented an invention that's the same or similar to yours. A patent provides a legal means for protecting an invention. A patent gives the inventor the exclusive right to make, use, and sell the invention for a certain period of time. Patents are issued by the U.S. government's Patent and Trademark Office (www.uspto.gov). If no one has patented an invention like yours, you may want to consider applying for a patent.

- **Create a Prototype.** A <mark>prototype</mark> is a model on which future reproductions of an invention are based. Start by building a non-working model out of materials such as foam, wood, or cardboard. This step will help you determine the correct form and shape of the product. With CAD (computer-aided design) software, you can also make an electronic drawing of your invention. Later you will also need to create a working prototype. This is an exact sample of how the final product will look, move, and operate. Any manufacturer or designer with whom you discuss your product should be asked to sign a **nondisclosure agreement**. This is a legal document in which a person or group agrees to keep certain information confidential.

 *What are four common ways you can turn an idea into a business opportunity?*

Evaluating an Opportunity

Once you've gathered your ideas, tested them to see if they appeared to be opportunities, and compared various ways of activating them, you will need to make a more detailed evaluation. Start with the business ideas you like best. Then use critical thinking to logically evaluate the **feasibility** of each idea. Feasibility refers to how possible or worthwhile it is to pursue your idea, to see if it is actually an opportunity. You can use three practical methods for determining the feasibility of your business ideas:

- Cost/benefit analysis
- Opportunity-cost analysis
- SWOT analysis

Cost/Benefit Analysis

Even though it is necessary to take risks as an entrepreneur, successful people take a **calculated risk**. This means carefully considering the potential costs and benefits. One method used to determine a calculated risk is called **cost/benefit analysis**. It is the process of adding up all the expected benefits of an opportunity and subtracting all the expected costs. If the benefits outweigh the costs, the opportunity may be worthwhile.

Costs can be one-time payments or ongoing. Benefits are most often received over a period of time. For example, perhaps you want to buy a computer but you currently don't have the money to pay for it. The purchase price could be a one-time cost if you save up and pay cash for it in six months. But if you use a credit card to buy the computer today, you should calculate how much extra you will pay in interest charges over the next six months. If buying the computer now enables you to earn more money than the total interest, the benefit may outweigh the cost.

A difficulty in cost/benefit analysis is assigning a monetary value to **intangible** (nonmaterial) things. For example, what is the value of your time? In what ways can you use your time most profitably? Obviously, some costs and benefits have to be based on personal values and priorities. What you find important may not be the same as for someone else.

Another difficult part of doing a cost/benefit analysis is that you can't precisely assign numbers to the costs or the benefits at the beginning of your evaluation. You have to think only in general terms. Eventually, as you continue with the business planning process, you will need to calculate the actual costs and benefits as accurately as you can.

Opportunity-Cost Analysis

An important factor often overlooked when evaluating ideas is the **opportunity cost**. This is the value of what you will give up to get something. An opportunity-cost analysis examines the potential benefits that you forfeit when you choose one course of action over others.

Suppose you are offered a one-year internship at a company where you can gain valuable work experience. However, you will not receive wages. To make the best decision, you should compare the benefits the internship offers with the benefits of any opportunities you will be losing or postponing. These might include the chance to go to college immediately, earn money at a different job, or start a business.

Money can be invested to earn more money over a period of time. An opportunity cost is the benefit you don't receive by investing the money in one way versus another. For example, if you spend $500 to buy products you were going to sell, rather than depositing the money in a savings account, you won't get the interest you would have earned on the $500. But your calculated risk is that you will earn more from selling the products than you would have earned in interest on the $500.

SWOT Analysis

Another way to determine an idea's feasibility is to perform a **SWOT analysis**. A SWOT analysis is a business evaluation method that draws its name from the four areas it evaluates (**S**trengths, **W**eaknesses, **O**pportunities, and **T**hreats):

- **Strengths.** What skills do you have that would enable you to do well with this specific opportunity? What resources do you have available (time, money, and people who can help you)? Do you have any unique knowledge or experiences that could give you an edge?

- **Weaknesses.** In what skill or knowledge areas do you need to improve? What resources are you lacking? What might potential customers see as a weakness in your product or service?

- **Opportunities.** Does this business idea fill an unmet need or want? Are there any trends or changes happening in your community that you could use as an advantage? What could you do better than other companies already in the same type of business? Does the proposed business location give you any advantages?

- **Threats.** What obstacles stand in the way of pursuing this opportunity? What current trends could potentially harm your business? How fierce is the competition in this business area? Does this business idea have a short window of opportunity?

The following table shows an example of a simple SWOT analysis for starting a DJ business. Notice that strengths and opportunities are placed side by side in the chart. This helps you to see if you currently have the strengths you need to take advantage of existing opportunities. Ask yourself, "What can I do to build my strengths so I can make the most of my opportunities?"

Likewise, weaknesses and threats are placed side by side in a SWOT analysis. This allows you to evaluate whether your weaknesses make existing threats more serious. Ask yourself, "What can I do to address my weaknesses so I can minimize potential threats?"

SWOT ANALYSIS: STARTING A DJ BUSINESS

Strengths	Opportunities
I have experience working in a music store and know what type of music is bought most often.	Some friends have already asked me to DJ at upcoming parties.
Together, my potential partner and I have the necessary equipment and music resources.	My potential partner knows another DJ who says we can sub for him.
I have an older brother who was a DJ when he was younger. He can answer questions and provide helpful tips.	People in our area really like salsa music. Maybe we could add that to our play list.

Weaknesses	Threats
I'm not sure how dependable my potential partner will be. He is often late.	There are several good DJs already in the neighborhood.
We need money to continue building our music library and keep it current.	People planning parties don't know us and already know the established DJs.
We need a way to transport our equipment from place to place.	If times are hard economically, people won't pay for expensive parties with DJs.

Keep in mind that you can also use a SWOT analysis to evaluate a business after it is up and running. Many companies perform a SWOT analysis periodically to stay aware of changes that could help or harm their businesses.

 **READING CHECKPOINT** *What do we call the value of something given up to get something else?*

 Your Business Plan. Continue developing your standard business plan. Go to "Section 6.2" of the *Business Plan Project* in your *Student Activity Workbook*, or "Section 6.2" of the BizTech Software.

ASSESSMENT 6.2

Reviewing Objectives

1. What is the difference between a business idea and a business opportunity?

2. List at least three creative-thinking techniques used to generate ideas.

3. Name four common ways of turning business ideas into opportunities.

4. Describe three practical methods for determining the feasibility of a business idea.

Critical Thinking

5. **Comparing/Contrasting.** Compare the advantages and disadvantages of buying an independent business versus buying a franchise. How are these business opportunities alike? How are they different?

6. **Relating Concepts.** What type of business opportunities match well with your current goals, both financial and nonfinancial?

Working Together

Working in a team, create a poster that compares the opportunity cost of a high school diploma, an associate's degree, and a bachelor's degree. Assume that college tuition is $5,000 per school year. Select a specific career area and calculate the annual salary each type of degree would earn working in it. Does the cost of education outweigh the long-term earning potential?

Social Studies
Connecting to Your Community

List 10 major issues that have appeared in the local news over the past few months. Which of these could be solved or reduced by creating a business that doesn't yet exist in your community?

Challenges of Being a Student Entrepreneur

Tonya Groover has always been fascinated by computers. While she was in high school, she helped her family and friends learn how to use computers. And when she got to college, she started a company called WebElegance. WebElegance designed Websites for local companies and individuals.

Tonya ran WebElegance for her first two years at the University of Pittsburgh. But she found that she had underestimated how much work college would require. "I had jobs I actually had to turn down because I was here to go to school," said Tonya. "I wasn't here to make a Website." Tonya closed WebElegance and continued with her studies as a computer science major.

Opening the World of Computer Science to African Americans

As an African American herself, Tonya noticed that there were very few people of color studying computer science. She did some research and found that just 3% of the degrees in computer science went to African Americans. She also found that there wasn't much support to encourage them. Tonya decided to do something about that.

She submitted a proposal to the University of Pittsburgh after her sophomore year. With Pitt's funding and backing, Tonya started Technology Leadership Institute in 2006. It's a six-week summer program that encourages African American high school students to pursue careers in computer science. Tonya spends 10 to 15 hours a week working in the Institute during the school year. In the summer, it's her full-time job.

Wearing Multiple Hats

"The main challenge is being a student as well as running Technology Leadership Institute," said Tonya, now doing graduate work at the University of Pittsburgh. She is doing research in addition to taking a heavy course load. "I have to prioritize and make sure that I manage my time wisely."

Tonya develops curriculum, teaches, writes grants, and raises funds. She supervises a staff of seven students. "I let my staff members know that I'm very open

▶ *Tonya Groover*

and that's how we have to be because we're a team. It is different from working by yourself," said Tonya. "You have more help, but at the same time, you have to train your help."

Tonya is also networking the organization to take it to the next level. "I have to stay on top of everything so that I can be successful and the organization can be successful as well."

Tonya thinks she'll be an entrepreneur for the rest of her life. "It's about the independence, the flexibility, the reach, and impact that I have. I enjoy having this leadership role. There's always a new challenge to tackle. You're always making a change and a difference in whatever you're doing."

Thinking Like an Entrepreneur

1. What are your priorities? For Tonya, going to school was more important than running WebElegance. Would you make the same decision? Why?

2. Tonya submitted a proposal to her school to fund Technology Leadership Institute. What other ways could she have financed the organization?

3. What are the good and bad points of supervising a staff? Would you like to train other people?

CHAPTER 6

Review and Assessment

CHAPTER SUMMARY

6.1 What Is a Business Plan?

A business plan is a statement of your business goals, the reasons you think these goals can be met, and how you are going to achieve those goals. You need a complete, well-written plan before you start a business, and a good business plan will also guide you as you develop the company. The plan for a for-profit business is significantly different from that for a nonprofit organization. There are four main types of business plans, each intended for a different audience: the brief summary, the oral presentation, the investor's business plan, and the operational plan. Each type of plan addresses The Three C's: concept, customer, and capital. Most business plans include seven parts: product or service, market analysis, strategy, company description, organization and management, plan for growth, and financials. In addition, business plans include an executive summary.

6.2 What Is a Business Opportunity?

A business opportunity is a consumer need or want that can be met by a new business venture. However, not every idea is an opportunity. An idea with no commercial potential isn't an opportunity. Ideas for business opportunities can arise from problems, changes/trends, new discoveries and inventions, existing products and services that need improvement, and unique knowledge or experiences. Places to look for opportunities include newspapers, magazines, business and governmental agencies, trade resources, and the Internet. Once you've generated an idea, the next step is to compare options for applying it. Major choices include starting a new business, buying an independent business, buying a franchise, and becoming an inventor. Finally, you need to evaluate the feasibility of your ideas. Practical ways to do this include performing a cost/benefit analysis, an opportunity-cost analysis, and a SWOT analysis.

REVIEW VOCABULARY

Write a two-page article for the school newspaper. Describe what a business opportunity is and why you need to write a business plan before you start a business. Use at least ten of the following terms as you can in your article.

- business broker (p. 154)
- business opportunity (p. 147)
- business plan (p. 139)
- calculated risk (p. 157)
- cost/benefit analysis (p. 157)
- creative thinking (p. 150)
- critical thinking (p. 151)

- executive summary (p. 142)
- feasibility (p. 157)
- franchisee (p. 154)
- franchisor (p. 154)
- intangible (p. 157)
- need (p. 147)
- nondisclosure agreement (p. 157)

- opportunity cost (p. 158)
- prototype (p. 156)
- royalty fee (p. 155)
- SWOT analysis (p. 158)
- trade show (p. 150)
- want (p. 147)
- window of opportunity (p. 148)

CHECK YOUR UNDERSTANDING

Choose the letter that best answers the question or completes the statement.

1. Which of the following is *not* one of "The Three C's"?
   a. concept
   b. competition
   c. customer
   d. capital

2. A patent
   a. is issued by the U.S. government
   b. provides a legal means for protecting an invention
   c. involves research to avoid duplication
   d. all of the above

3. A brief summary business plan should take no more than
   a. 30 seconds to 3 minutes
   b. 3 to 5 minutes
   c. 5 to 10 minutes
   d. 10 to 15 minutes

4. The period of time you have to act on a business opportunity before it disappears is called the
   a. opportunity time limit
   b. window of opportunity
   c. reasonable time frame
   d. none of the above

5. The type of business that provides the greatest amount of entrepreneurial freedom is a(n)
   a. business you start from scratch
   b. independent business you purchase
   c. franchise
   d. family business

6. Which of the following types of business plans is meant for use within the business only?
   a. brief summary
   b. oral presentation
   c. investor's business plan
   d. operational business plan

7. Which of the following is *not* used to evaluate the feasibility of a business opportunity?
   a. invention analysis
   b. cost/benefit analysis
   c. opportunity-cost analysis
   d. SWOT analysis

8. Who is the intended audience for the oral presentation type of business plan?
   a. potential employees
   b. potential investors
   c. newspaper reporters
   d. a and c

9. Which of the following is *not* a characteristic of creative thinking?
   a. using your imagination
   b. lateral thinking
   c. looking at a situation in new ways
   d. vertical thinking

10. A royalty fee is a(n)
    a. single fee paid when a franchise agreement expires
    b. ongoing payment based on a percentage of sales
    c. single fee paid when the franchise agreement is signed
    d. ongoing payment based on the value of the business

11. The business plan of a for-profit company typically focuses on
    a. the business mission
    b. the products or services that support the mission
    c. financial goals
    d. a and b

12. Which of the following is true about a business plan?
    a. developing it is simple and straightforward
    b. once developed, it doesn't change
    c. it has a set format
    d. it will need to be changed from time to time

Business Communication

13. Research real-life stories of how entrepreneurs recognized the business opportunity that made them successful. Find an example for each of the following sources of business opportunities: problems, changes, new discoveries, existing products and services, and unique knowledge. Create a presentation about your findings (include pictures).

14. Working with a partner, select a local business with which you are both familiar. Construct a SWOT analysis of the business.

15. Identify a local business with which you are familiar. Write a 30-second brief summary describing the concept and customer to an investor. Present your summary to the class and ask them whether they would invest in the business.

Business Ethics

18. When choosing a business to start or to buy, evaluating and planning is important. One way of evaluating a business opportunity is to ask whether it agrees with your ethical values. Think of a service or product that is legal according to the law but may conflict with your beliefs. Write one or more paragraphs explaining your position. Then write at least one paragraph suggesting why others may view the service or product differently from the way you do.

Business Math

16. You've been told that a potential investor wants at least 22% of the business plan to focus on market analysis. If your business plan is 18 pages, about how many pages should be devoted to market analysis?

17. You own a franchise and need to pay an 11.25% monthly royalty fee to the franchisor. Your franchise had sales of $36,780 in August. What is your August royalty fee?

Business in Your Community

19. Imagine that you've been asked to help plan a mall to be built near your school. Working in a small group, brainstorm ideas for businesses. What types of businesses would do well in this location? Have each person pick a potential business and do a SWOT analysis, pretending to be the business owner. Share your results. Which ideas have the most potential? The least?

20. Interview a small-business owner, a franchisee, or an inventor in your community. Ask what types of planning he or she did before starting/buying the business or before marketing the invention. How did he or she determine whether the business/invention had a good chance of succeeding? What were the advantages and disadvantages of this type of entrepreneurship? Share your research results with the class.

Web Design

Web design is the process of manipulating graphics and text to create a unique and eye-catching Website. In an increasingly crowded Internet, Web owners hire independent **Web designers**—professionals who will design a Website that will stand out from others. Web design can be a big project, because a Website can have hundreds of individual pages.

HTML Language

As you learned in earlier chapters, Web pages are designed in HTML (Hypertext Markup Language), a unique type of computer language that uses a series of brackets and other commands that determine how the site is displayed online. For example, here's HTML code for creating color on a Website's background:

```
<body style="background:#0404B4">
```

The numbers and letters after "#" stand for a particular color. Changing #0404B4 to #FF0000 would change the background from blue to red. Each color has a unique number and letter combination. In fact, every font, border, and graphic has a unique HTML code. As you can imagine, HTML is a complicated language that can take a long time to master. Beginners can bypass this code by using a pre-made **Web template**. This is a Website that includes already-created graphics and an established layout. Web templates make quality Web design available to people who are new to it. Web design software is also available for both professional Web designers and beginning users.

Website Components

Web designers use a number of components to design a high-quality site. (These also are included on Web templates.) **Drop-down menus** are at the top of the page and allow users to navigate through the site. Web-sites are often broken up by adding a **sidebar** on the left or right of the page, where there are links to pages within the site or to other Websites. Some sites use **flash animation**. This is a software program used to create animated graphics. The goal in using these features is to make the site both interesting and easy to navigate.

Website Navigation

Creating a user-friendly site is an important component of Web design. Some Websites may work well with certain Web browsers (Firefox, Safari, or Internet Explorer) but not with others. A Website may have several sections. For instance, there may be individual pages within the site for a variety of products. A drop-down menu may include choices for different products, such as books, music, apparel, or whatever the Website sells. Because many Websites are designed to sell products, a Web designer needs to make it easy for visitors to the site to find and buy products.

Tech Vocabulary
- drop-down menu
- flash animation
- sidebar
- Web designer
- Web template

Check Yourself

1. What does HTML do?
2. What is a Web template and why would you use one?
3. What are some of the main components of Web design?
4. What is a drop-down menu?

What Do You Think?

Applying Concepts. What are the most effective forms of Web design and why?

CHAPTER 7

MARKET RESEARCH

7.1

·
·
·

? | *Think about this question:*
What are your three favorite ways to spend free time?

Quickly write down your list. You don't have to place them in any special order.

Why Is Market Research Important?

We live in a world that changes rapidly and frequently. Because of this, each business must stay informed about its <mark>market</mark>. A market is a group of potential customers—people or businesses—who are willing and able to purchase a particular product or service.

<mark>Market research</mark> is an organized way to gather and analyze information needed to make business decisions. For example, market research can help you decide to start a new business. But market research isn't just something you do when starting a business. To ensure a company's continued success, market research needs to be an ongoing activity.

Understanding Your Market

Market research tends to focus on three main areas. Just as each piece of a jigsaw puzzle is important to the whole picture, researching each of these areas is key to understanding your market.

- **Business Environment.** In its broadest sense, the <mark>business environment</mark> refers to any social, economic, or political factors that could impact your business. This includes global, national, and industry-related factors. ("Industry," here, means businesses that are connected to a category

VOCABULARY

- business environment
- business-to-business (B2B) company
- business-to-consumer (B2C) company
- carrying capacity
- customer profile
- demographics
- focus group
- geographics
- list-rental company
- market
- market research
- market segment
- mass market
- primary data
- psychographics
- secondary data
- target market

of products or services. For example, if you had a dry cleaning business, you would be concerned with the dry cleaning industry.) Gathering data related to the business environment will help you stay aware of trends and important events. In turn, this information may reveal new business opportunities or threats.

- **Customers.** Customers can be individual consumers or businesses. To be successful, businesses need to satisfy their customers while making a profit. You can't do this without knowing who your customers are and what they need or want. Market research helps you determine very specific information about potential customers. It also helps you precisely define their needs and wants.

- **Competition.** Running a business would be a lot easier if it were the only one of its kind. However, this doesn't happen very often. Usually, a number of competitors are already in the marketplace. They may offer a product or service similar to yours or one that fills the same customer need or want. Market research helps you identify who your competitors are and how they operate. This information will be helpful in planning for sales efforts related to your market.

▼ **Figure 7-1**

Market Awareness
Rising gasoline prices is a market trend that affects various businesses in different ways.

Inferring. *What negative and positive effects could rising gasoline prices potentially have on a travel agency?*

Avoiding Costly Mistakes

Making incorrect guesses about your market can lead to wrong decisions. If an incorrect decision has a major impact on your business, your business could fail. Market research helps ensure that you don't misjudge what your potential customers need or want. It helps you avoid spending time and money developing a product or service that won't sell.

For example, you may want to use market research to test a prototype so you can evaluate potential customer reactions to a new product. Or, you may want to find out the **carrying capacity** of the industry you want to enter. In the business world, carrying capacity refers to the maximum number of companies an industry can support based on its potential customer base. If a particular industry has little room for growth, there may not be room enough for your business to prosper.

Sometimes what you don't know *can* hurt you. Ignorance of your market, or failure to react to your market, can mean lost customers and lost opportunities. This means lost income and lost profit. Although it is true that everyone makes mistakes, entrepreneurs can avoid costly ones by doing their homework.

Obtaining Finances

Attracting people, banks, or companies to invest in your business or lend you money is easier if you've done thorough market research. Most potential investors and business partners aren't willing to risk their time or money without evidence that backs up your business concept. Market research may also provide you with information about people or companies who have invested in competing businesses. If you can learn more about the investors who already have a stake in the market, you can better understand the expectations of your potential investors.

 *What is market research?*

Targeting Your Market

You may be tempted to try to sell your product or service to as many customers as possible. This type of market is often called a **mass market**. For most small businesses, this approach isn't the best strategy. Selling to a mass market takes a great deal of resources. Instead, many entrepreneurs focus on identifying a **target market**, a limited number of customers who are most likely to buy the product or service.

Types of Customers

One of the goals of market research is to develop a **customer profile**. This is a detailed description of your target market's characteristics. To begin, consider the two main types of customers:

- **Consumers.** A company who sells to individuals is sometimes referred to as a **business-to-consumer (B2C) company**. The customer profile of a B2C company might include characteristics such as age, gender, occupation, and the neighborhoods where potential customers live. Consumers are somewhat difficult to profile because they are so varied. Most consumers' priorities also change as they get older or when major life events take place (such as getting married or having a baby).

- **Businesses.** A company who sells to other companies is sometimes called a **business-to-business (B2B) company**. In this case, the customer profile might include such details as company size, type of industry, and geographical location. Over time, businesses tend to be more consistent in their buying habits than consumers. They also have larger budgets to work with than most individuals would have.

You do not have to choose just one of these customer categories. Your market research may indicate that it makes sense to target both types. The product or service you provide to both consumers and businesses might be the same. However, you will probably need to approach each type of customer differently.

Market Segments

A **market segment** is a grouping of consumers or businesses within a particular market that has one or more things in common. By exploring various market segments, you can begin to form a clear picture of your target market. A target market often includes more than one market segment. Here are some ways you can group customers into market segments:

- **Demographics.** **Demographics** are objective social and economic facts about people. Demographics for consumers include age, gender, marital status, family size (number of children), ethnic background, education, occupation, annual income, and whether they own a home or rent. Demographics for businesses include industry type, number of employees, and annual sales.

- **Geographics.** Basing market segments on where consumers live or where businesses are located is called **geographics**. Groupings could include a nation, geographical region (such as the Northeast), individual state or province, county, city, neighborhood—and type of climate.

- **Psychographics.** Psychological characteristics of consumers, such as attitudes, opinions, beliefs, interests, personality, lifestyle, political affiliation, and personal preferences, are called **psychographics**. An example of psychographics for businesses is how much they are employee-oriented or customer-oriented.

Buying patterns are often influenced by a combination of market-segment characteristics. For example, you can objectively measure how many times a year people buy airplane tickets, but they may be most likely to travel around holidays to spend time with family members.

Segment Factors	Consumer Profile	Business Profile
Demographics	Single, professional women Age: 25–40 yrs. Annual income: $80,000+	100+ employees $3.5 million in revenue per year Variety of tourist service industries
Geographics	Work or live in Manhattan's financial district	Orange County, southern California
Psychographics	Liberal politics Fashion- and quality-conscious Read the *New York Times* daily	Customer-oriented Employee-oriented Focus on quality of service
Buying Patterns	Purchase airline tickets 7 to 9 times per year	Hire temporary contractors during summer months and holiday periods

The table above provides an example of how market segments are combined to produce customer profiles.

READING CHECKPOINT *What is a target market?*

Market Research Methods

The methods and data sources you choose for your market research largely depend on what type of information you need.

Types of Research

There are two basic types of market research:

- **Secondary Data.** Existing information that was previously gathered for a purpose other than the study at hand is ==secondary data.== Examples of secondary data are economic forecasts issued by financial organizations and demographic data collected by the U.S. government. Secondary data is relatively cheap and easy to obtain. However, it may not be specific enough to answer all your questions.

- **Primary Data.** New information that is collected for a particular purpose is ==primary data==. It is obtained directly from potential customers. Primary data can be very useful because it is up-to-date and aimed at your target market. But gathering primary data is more time consuming and expensive than obtaining secondary data.

Secondary Data Sources

When you first begin your market research and don't know much about your area of interest, it's a good idea to do some general, exploratory research. Examining existing secondary data is useful for this purpose. Some resources that provide a wide range of market information are:

- **Government.** Departments of the U.S. federal government, as well as state governments, collect a great deal of data. The Bureau of Economic Analysis (www.bea.gov), the Bureau of Labor Statistics (www.bls.gov), and the Census Bureau (www.census.gov) are several examples. Another excellent online resource is FedStats (www.fedstats.gov). It provides information on over a hundred agencies. You can search FedStats by state, by subject, and alphabetically.

- **Trade Groups and Journals.** Trade associations often conduct market research related to their respective industries. You may find some of this information on the Website of a particular association, or by reading trade journals that such associations publish. A good place to learn about associations for your industry is in the *Encyclopedia of Associations* (which many libraries have). The American Society of Association Executives has a database you can use to search for associations by name, industry area, or geographic location (www.asaecenter.org/directories/associationsearch.cfm).

- **Business Magazines and Reports.** Examples of companies that publish business data or business news include Forbes (www.forbes.com), *American City Business Journals* (www.bizjournals.com), *Entrepreneur* (entrepreneur.com), *Fast Company* (fastcompany.com) and Dun and Bradstreet (www.dnb.com/us). *BizStats*, owned by the Brandow Company, is a free online source of business data (www.bizstats.com). MarketResearch.com (www.marketresearch.com) is a huge collection of market research that is continually updated. However, they do charge a fee that varies in price depending on the specific report. Another source is the *Thomas Global Register®*, a directory of worldwide industrial suppliers and product information (www.thomasglobal.com).

- **Local Community Resources.** Most communities have a Chamber of Commerce or other business development agency. Examples of information and services provided by these organizations include demographic reports, business directories, and market-related seminars. A simple but effective print resource is your local Yellow Pages phone book. It provides a brief overview of potential local competitors. Don't overlook local business schools or colleges. They have libraries and career centers that you may find helpful.

U.S. Census Bureau

FAQs | Subjects A to Z | Help   SEARCH: GO

Data Finders

HALLOWEEN

New on the Site
Data Tools
American FactFinder
Jobs@Census
Catalog
Publications
Are You in a Survey?
About the Bureau
Regional Offices
Doing Business with Us
Related Sites

2006 County Business Patterns

United States Census 2010
2010 Census · News · Become a Census Taker
American Community Survey · Census 2000

People & Households
Estimates · Projections · Housing · Income |
State Median Income · Poverty · Health Insurance ·
International · Genealogy · More

Business & Industry
Economic Census · Get Help with Your Form ·
Economic Indicators · NAICS · Survey of Business Owners
· Government · E-Stats · Foreign Trade | Export Codes ·
Local Employment Dynamics · More

Geography
Maps · TIGER · Gazetteer · More

Newsroom
Releases · Facts For Features · Minority Links ·
Broadcast & Photo Services · Embargo/News Release
Subscription · More

Special Topics
Census Bureau Data and Emergency Preparedness ·
Census Calendar · Training · For Teachers & Students ·
Statistical Abstract · FedStats · USA.gov

✓ Good Pay
✓ Flexible Hours
✓ Close to Home
Apply now to be a census taker!

Population Clocks
U.S. 305,474,788
World 6,731,869,546
20:29 GMT (EST+5) Oct 22, 2008

Population Finder
city/ town, county, or zip
or state
Select a state   GO

Find An Area Profile with QuickFacts
Select a state to begin
Select a state

Latest Economic Indicators
• Housing Starts/Building Permits
• Manufacturing and Trade Inventories and Sales

Economic Indicators
Select an indicator
Select an indicator

USCENSUSBUREAU
Helping You Make Informed Decisions

Accessibility | Information Quality | FOIA | Data Protection & Privacy Policy | U.S. Dept of Commerce

Primary Research Techniques

Once you have a sense of who your target market may be, you can begin to gather data directly from that potential group of customers. Some common ways to obtain such primary data are:

- **Interviews/Surveys.** This technique uses a one-to-one approach. You can develop a questionnaire that you can use in person, by telephone, by regular mail, or by e-mail. If you are mailing out your survey, you can obtain names and contact information for specific groups of consumers or businesses from trade associations or from a **list-rental company**. This type of company provides lists of names and addresses for targeted markets, typically allowing you to use the list for a single mailing. Both trade associations and list-rental companies typically charge for their services.

- **Focus Groups.** A **focus group** is a small number of people who are brought together to discuss a particular problem, product, or service. (See "Entrepreneurship Issues" on pg. 174.) A focus group discussion is typically led by a moderator, who asks questions, directs the discussion, and makes sure the meeting agenda is covered in the specified amount of time. The results of a focus group are usually recorded so the feedback can be studied in detail later.

▲ Figure 7-2

Census Bureau Home Page
The Census Bureau is a very good source of demographic and geographic information.

Analyzing Information. *Why might information such as income, housing, or health insurance be important for a B2C company?*

Focus Groups

If you were launching a new product—no matter if it costs a million dollars to produce or one dollar—you'd want to try to guarantee its success, right? Entrepreneurs feel the same way. To ensure healthy sales for new products, businesses test them—from fast food to new cell phones—by using focus groups. These are individuals who are brought together to give feedback on the products so changes can be made before the products are launched. One example of an influential type of focus group is the movie test audience.

Test audiences for feature films are a type of focus group. Nielsen National Research Group (NRG) is the company many Hollywood producers turn to for audience testing. Such companies select test audience participants from movie lines. Once selected, a test audience participant gets to watch a new film

for free, long before it is actually released. Then he or she fills out a comment card or takes part in a discussion about the movie. Based on the opinions of these test audiences, a movie studio might change the film, even to the extent of reshooting the ending!

THINKING CRITICALLY

Applying Concepts. In small groups, select a movie that everyone has seen. Pretend you are a test audience and discuss the following: How could the film have been improved? Would you suggest a different ending? Was any part of the movie confusing?

To read more about focus groups, go to "Entrepreneurship Issues" on the Student Center at entrepreneurship.pearson.com.

- **Observations.** You can learn a lot about potential customers' reactions and behaviors without talking with them. Observation can sometimes be an advantage, because people may act differently when they are not being formally asked to participate in a study. For example, you can observe which stores attract the most customers in a shopping mall. Or you could offer a complimentary product sample such as food or perfume and watch how people react to it.

Evaluating Data

As you conduct market research, try to stay alert for potential problems. This doesn't necessarily mean the data you find is wrong. But some of it could be presented in a biased way. For example, a source might tend to emphasize negative results over positive ones, or vice versa. When evaluating data, ask yourself these questions:

- Is the source well known and reliable?
- How relevant is the data to my industry area and target market?
- Is this set of data collected and updated on a regular basis?
- Have I confirmed research results with more than one source or method?

You can develop your own market research survey.

Think of market research as a process. The data you collect may support your idea for a business, or it may not. It will most likely make you change your thinking in some way. Don't be discouraged if the data suggest that you should change your direction, or even start over with another idea. One of the purposes of market research is to help you avoid costly mistakes. Everything you learn from market research is valuable and will help you in the future.

 **READING CHECKPOINT** *What is the difference between primary and secondary data?*

 Your Business Plan. Continue developing your standard business plan. Go to "Section 7.1" of the *Business Plan Project* in your *Student Activity Workbook*, or "Section 7.1" of the BizTech Software.

Reviewing Objectives

1. Name the three main areas on which market research focuses.

2. Identify three ways you can group customers into market segments.

3. List four secondary data sources and three primary research techniques.

Critical Thinking

4. **Applying Concepts.** Suppose you've recently built a prototype for a new video game. Which primary research technique do you think would work best to test it in the marketplace? Why?

5. **Classifying.** Which of the following customer characteristics are considered demographics? Which are geographics? Which are psychographics? Characteristics: Likes to sew, three children in the family, married, earns $40,000 per year, works in Atlanta, 50+ employees, enjoys Chinese food, financially conservative, lives in Putnam County, 18 years old, customer-service focus, Spanish heritage, outgoing personality.

Working Together

Imagine that you are planning to survey students at your school about a potential bookstore to be located on school grounds. The proposed store will be run by students with teachers' guidance. Profits will go to a charitable group chosen by the students. Working in a small group, develop a questionnaire for the survey with no more than 20 questions. Make sure the questions focus on the *most* important issues involved in this startup.

Math
Statistics

Suppose there are 40 homes in your housing community. You survey each one to help determine the feasibility of opening a daycare center in the neighborhood. Following are the results. Each number (separated by a comma) represents the number of children who live in one of the houses.

1, 0, 0, 3, 0, 0, 0, 3, 0, 0, 0, 2, 0, 0, 3, 0, 0, 2, 3, 0
0, 4, 0, 0, 3, 0, 3, 0, 1, 0, 0, 3, 0, 0, 0 2, 0, 0, 1, 2

Use the survey results to answer the following questions: What is the average number of children per home in your community? What is the average number of children per home, in houses that have children? Which of these two averages do you think is a better statistic to use when deciding whether to open a daycare center? Why?

What Is Your Competitive Advantage?

OBJECTIVES

- Learn how to identify competitors
- Determine your competitive advantage
- Identify the steps in researching a market

VOCABULARY

- competitive advantage
- competitive intelligence
- competitive matrix
- differentiator
- direct competitor
- indirect competitor

Take a few minutes to think about the following question.

Is competition in business good?

Write your answer (yes or no) on a piece of paper, along with one reason for it. Be prepared to discuss your thinking in class.

Identifying Your Competition

In addition to your target market, another critical area of market research involves identifying your competitors. They are the rival businesses with whom you are competing for the dollars your target market spends. The data you collect about your competitors is called **competitive intelligence**.

Types of Competition

Your competitive intelligence will be of two types:

- **Direct competitors.** A business in your market that sells a product or service similar to yours is your **direct competitor**. McDonald's® and Burger King® are examples of direct competitors in the fast-food industry, because they sell a similar line of products. An ice cream shop that also sells hamburgers might also be considered direct competition for McDonald's and Burger King. However, the ice cream shop would not be considered a strong competitor, because its main focus is on ice cream products. Hamburgers are only a sideline.

- **Indirect competitors.** A business that sells a different product or service from yours but fills the same customer need or want is your **indirect competitor**. For example, Taco Bell® is in the fast-food industry, but it is an indirect competitor to McDonald's and Burger King. This is because Taco Bell sells fast-food products but not hamburgers. On a broader level, non-fast-food restaurants could also be considered indirect competition because the food they sell fills the same basic need.

Other Forms of Competition

Keep in mind that your target customers may choose options other than buying from your business, or even your direct and indirect competitors. For instance, potential customers may decide to cook a hamburger at home rather than buying it. Purchasing the ingredients of a meal at a local grocery store will likely be less expensive than buying a prepared version.

In tough economic times, consumers may choose to provide a particular service for themselves rather than pay someone else to do it. Women who give themselves manicures instead of going to a nail salon are examples of customers who become the competition. Another example is someone who changes the oil in the family car, rather than taking it to a service station.

Indirect competition may include businesses outside your industry if they provide a product or service that has the same benefit as yours. Competition can also vary depending on the time of year or a temporary situation. For example, suppose you own a candy store. Around Valentine's Day, florists become indirect competition even though they are not in the same business. This is because flowers and candy both fill a particular want: to present a gift to your valentine.

▲ **Figure 7-3**
Identifying Competition
Large department stores offer many types of products.
Applying Concepts. *What products do large department stores sell? What are some businesses that compete directly with large department stores?*

 **READING CHECKPOINT** *How does indirect competition differ from direct competition?*

Determining Your Competitive Advantage

Competitive intelligence enables you to compare your competitors' strengths and weaknesses with your potential business. During this process you will be looking for unique ways to provide your product or service to your target market. You will be looking for your **competitive advantage**: something that puts your business ahead of the competition.

Gather Competitive Intelligence

Many of the secondary data sources mentioned in Section 7.1 will help you gather competitive intelligence. Make sure to consider the various places where competitive products or services might be available to your target market. Some of your competition may be located nearby in physical stores, but they may also be on the Internet or in direct-mail catalogs.

One way to gather valuable competitive intelligence is to pose as a customer and gain a sense of what it's like to buy your competitor's product or service (provided you do not cause your competitor to exert a significant amount of effort if you don't intend to buy anything). Go at different times of the day and on different days of the week, and note which times were busiest and what kinds of customers were there. For example, you could visit a competing store posing as a potential customer. As you walk through, ask yourself these questions:

- What products do they carry? How are the products displayed? How much do they cost?

- What is their customer service like? Did the staff offer to assist me? Were they friendly and helpful?

- How many other potential customers are in the store? What do some of the customer demographics seem to be (age, gender, etc.)? What about customer psychographics, geographics, and buying patterns?

- Does the competitor offer any special purchasing terms, such as credit with no interest? Do they provide any other special services, such as free delivery? What is their policy for returning purchases?

Analyze the Competition

Just gathering market data is not enough. You must organize that data and then analyze it. Don't be surprised if your list of indirect competitors is much longer than your list of direct ones. Instead of listing indirect competitors individually, organize them into categories. For example, you could divide them by industry type or by the products or services they sell. After the indirect competitors are grouped, you can evaluate each category's level of competitiveness. That is, which groups will compete most often and most strongly with your business?

Analyzing direct competitors requires a more detailed and thorough approach. A helpful tool for doing this is a **competitive matrix**. This is a grid that compares characteristics of your business with those of your direct competitors. First, pick the chief direct competitors by reviewing the information you've been collecting. Next, plug selected data into the matrix. Finally, use the matrix to help pinpoint your potential competitive advantages.

A competitive matrix can be formatted in various ways. The following table provides a simple example. You can vary the factors you wish to compare depending on the business opportunity you are exploring.

COMPETITIVE MATRIX

Factors	Your Business	Competitor A	Competitor B	Competitor C
Price				
Quality of Product/Service				
Location				
Reputation/Brands				
Delivery Method				
Customer Service				
Unique Factors & Knowledge				

Identify Your Differentiators

There are several reasons for creating a competitive matrix. It will help you spot any holes or missing data in your research. It can also enable you to see patterns in the data. Most importantly, it can show where your business fits in the marketplace.

Your competitive advantage could consist of one or more differentiators. A **differentiator** is a unique characteristic that distinguishes your business from others. Ask yourself these four questions to help identify potential differentiators for your business:

- What product or service can your business provide that your competitors don't?

- What *mix* of products or services can your business provide that your competitors don't?

- What specialized selling or delivery method can give your business a competitive edge?

- In what unique ways can your business meet customers' wants or needs?

Answering these questions can help you differentiate your business, setting it apart from your competitors. When thinking about your business, resist the temptation to copy exactly what other successful companies have done. An approach that works well for one business may not work for another. You can, however, learn helpful lessons and gain inspiration from the experiences of other businesses. Here are a few examples of successful companies that used differentiators to create a competitive advantage that set them apart:

- Apple's Macintosh computer and 3M's Post-it® Notes are examples of ground-breaking products that were initially unique in their respective industries.

- FedEx Office℠ (formerly FedEx Kinko's) has become successful because it found a unique way to combine office products and business services (such as photocopying) with shipping.

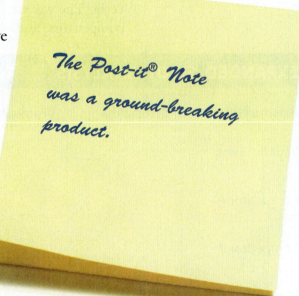

The Post-it® Note was a ground-breaking product.

- Amazon.com used an unusual mix of selling and delivery methods to set itself apart from competitors. It was one of the first businesses in its industry to use only the Internet to sell a huge selection of music, books, and movies. This enabled Amazon to sell products at lower prices. Customer options include overnight delivery and, under certain conditions, free shipping. Customers also have the choice of buying new or used products.

- When the cable channel Black Entertainment Television (BET) was launched, it filled the needs and wants of a target market that hadn't yet been met in the cable television industry.

Anticipate Future Competition

As you conduct market research on your competition, keep this in mind: Just because you have an advantage in your target market today doesn't mean it will last. One of your competitors could become aware of its weaknesses and find a way to improve. Once you start a business, all your current competitors could copy you, eliminating your differentiating characteristics. And new competitors could enter the market at any time.

As you've already learned, market research is an ongoing process. You need to continue to watch trends in your industry, and in the general economy as well. Stay alert to any customer needs and wants that may start to change. Continue to monitor what your current competition is doing. In particular, keep an eye out for any new direct competitors that begin selling to your target market.

Expand Your SWOT Analysis

You used a SWOT analysis in Section 6.2 to test the feasibility of a business idea. As you obtain new data through market research, you can update and expand the scenario. The Expanded SWOT Analysis shows a useful way to include competitor data. Basically, the table provides a method for translating the detailed data from your competitive matrix into strengths, weaknesses, opportunities, and threats. This information can help you further evaluate a business idea. The threats to your potential business are often opportunities for your competitors, and vice versa. The weaknesses of your business are often the strengths of your competitors, and vice versa.

EXPANDED SWOT ANALYSIS

Businesses	Strengths	Weaknesses	Opportunities	Threats
Your Business				
Competitor A				
Competitor B				
Competitor C				

 **READING CHECKPOINT** *What are two tools used to organize and analyze competitive data?*

Steps in Researching a Market

Here's a quick review of the six basic steps of market research. This is the way an entrepreneur would follow a market and make a preliminary "go/no-go" decision about pursuing a prospective business opportunity.

1. Identify Research Objectives

Before you actually start gathering data, list the objectives you want your research to accomplish. Determine the information you need. What problems are you trying to solve? What questions do you have?

Make a specific checklist of all the information you need to resolve the problems and questions you've identified. The information will probably include:

- **Industry Data.** This could be composed of industry size, potential room for the industry to grow, seasonal or economic trends in the industry, government policies that impact the industry, social and environmental trends that could affect the industry, and so on.

- **Customer Data.** This could include data about consumers, businesses, or both. Demographics, psychographics, geographics, customer spending habits or patterns, and factors that motivate customers are all types of data in this category.

- **Competitive Data.** This category of information includes data about direct and indirect competitors. Don't forget to consider potential future competitors. Details could consist of competitors' locations, annual sales, number of employees, products, services, prices, selling and delivery methods, any unique features or benefits provided, and so on.

2. Determine Methods and Sources

Based on your objectives, decide which research methods will best help you achieve your goals:

- Will you need secondary research, primary research, or a combination of both?

- If you are using secondary sources, which will you use (government, trade groups, business reports, or local community resources)?

- If you are using primary sources, which research techniques will work best (interviews, surveys, focus groups, or observation)?

If you are using primary research, you will need to design any questionnaires you may need for an interview or survey. If you are using a focus group, you will need to prepare questions for the person moderating it.

▼ **Figure 7-4**
Focus Groups
Focus groups can help you discover what customers think about your competitors and your business ideas.
Drawing Conclusions. *What advantage might a focus group have over a mailed survey?*

Teamwork

Think about any team you have ever been on. Did the team members work together to reach both personal and team goals? Effective and efficient teamwork always rises beyond individual accomplishments. It may be a personal triumph to hit a home run, for example, but it is also important that the *team* has scored a run.

Employers today often look for workers who enjoy being part of an efficient team and know what it means to be a team player. A team player cares deeply about his or her job but will do another task when needed. This may mean pitching in when another worker needs help or doing a job a more-skilled or less-skilled employee ordinarily does. A team player realizes that this work is important to the team

as a whole and enjoys the occasional challenge of additional duties.

A team is only as strong as its weakest member. Think about yourself. When you are on a team or in a group of any sort, do you give just enough or do you pitch in and get the job done?

THINKING CRITICALLY

Relating Concepts. Describe examples of being a team player that you have witnessed. How could someone work on becoming a better team player?

To read more about teamwork, go to "Your Business Career" on the Student Center at entrepreneurship.pearson.com.

Potential questions might include: What does the customer need or want to buy? Who makes this type of purchase? How often? In what quantity is it purchased? Where? Why is it purchased? Is the customer satisfied with the competitor's product or service? If not, what would make it better? What would the customer like that is currently not being provided?

3. Gather the Data

As you collect the data, you may discover additional things you need to find out. Market research is usually a process of discovery. You typically will have to make adjustments to your course of action depending on what you learn.

Make sure the secondary data you collect is relevant to your industry and target market. Also, don't forget to confirm research results with more than one secondary source, if possible. Use an adequate number of customers when doing primary research. Make sure they are in your target market.

4. Organize the Data

As you gather information, begin to organize it:

- Group indirect competitors into categories by industry, product, or service.
- Select the three or four direct competitors who appear to be your strongest competition. Then create a competitive matrix that

includes all the specific characteristics you wish to compare. You may also want to make a separate grid just to compare details of products or services that may compete with yours.

- Look for areas where important data may be missing. Go back and collect more information if necessary.

5. Analyze the Data

Analyze your data by:

- Comparing competitor's characteristics.

- Identifying potential differentiators. What could you potentially do or create to set your business apart from your competition?

- Creating an expanded SWOT analysis that compares the strengths and weaknesses of your business to those of your competitors.

6. Draw Conclusions

Using the information in Step 5, decide whether to proceed with your business idea or to stop. When making your decision, be as objective as you can. That is, try not to be overly positive or negative. The following focus areas may help you draw realistic conclusions:

- **Target Market.** Is there a definite market for your proposed product or service? Is there room for your company?

- **Market Size and Demand.** How large is the target market? How satisfied is the target market with the current competition? How often does the target market buy a product or service like yours? What do the answers to these three questions suggest about the current level of demand?

- **Carrying Capacity.** Based on the number and strength of your competitors, can the target market support your proposed business?

- **Expanded SWOT Analysis.** Do your strengths outweigh your weaknesses? Is your business potentially stronger, weaker, or about the same as those of your competitors? Are there any serious threats in the business environment that increase the risk of your business failing? What can you do to minimize threats and take advantage of opportunities?

Based on market research, you decide whether to proceed with your business idea, alter it, or stop completely.

▲ *Stop or go?*

What six steps are involved in researching a market and making a preliminary go/no-go decision about pursuing a prospective business opportunity?

Your Business Plan. Continue developing your standard business plan. Go to "Section 7.2" of the *Business Plan Project* in your *Student Activity Workbook*, or "Section 7.2" of the BizTech Software.

ASSESSMENT 7.2

Reviewing Objectives

1. Describe the two types of competitors.
2. What is a competitive advantage?
3. In order, list the six basic steps used in market research.

Critical Thinking

4. **Recognizing Patterns.** On the expanded SWOT analysis, why would your weaknesses often be a competitor's strengths and vice versa?

Working Together

With a partner, put together a list of ideas for competitive advantages that would enable a small clothing store to compete more effectively with a large department store.

Social Studies
Market Research History

Research the life of Arthur C. Nielsen, Sr., one of the founders of modern market research. Write a short report that summarizes his accomplishments. How did the methods developed by Nielsen revolutionize the market research industry?

It's All in the Details

When Marcus Craft was 15 years old, he wasn't legally old enough to drive a car. But, as he puts it, "I could certainly clean them." That's what detailing is. It involves everything from vacuuming the vehicle to buffing and compounding to make the car look as good as possible.

Marcus had always loved cars and anything that involved them. His father passed on his own love of cars to Marcus, as well as teaching him how to clean and preserve a vehicle to keep it in pristine condition. It was the perfect pick for a business for Marcus, and Mac's Auto Detail was born. "I absolutely love cleaning cars," said Marcus. "It really helps to have passion in your chosen field. It keeps you motivated toward always improving your performance and makes the work fun."

Competing for Business

Getting customers wasn't easy at the beginning. "I spent a lot of time making and printing business cards, flyers, and brochures to give to every person I saw or met," said Marcus. It's a time-proven way to increase business—and it worked for Marcus.

He also needed to find a way to make his business unique, to give it a competitive advantage. He relied on pricing (which he kept as low as possible) and his positive attitude. He would do whatever it took to make a sale, and he would go the extra mile to make the client satisfied: "Excellent customer service doesn't just mean providing a good product or service. It needs to be reflected in everything you do."

Planning His Time

Marcus started his business as he completed his sophomore year at William Boone High School, in Orlando, Florida. He was able to work full-time during the summers. However, during the school year, he was extremely busy with various activities. He was a member of a school music ensemble, played on the tennis team, and was an active member of his church. But he still had a business to run and phone calls to return from prospective customers and current clients.

▲ *Marcus Craft*

When he got his homework done, he would return the calls and schedule times for detailing. "I would also leave time in my schedule to clean cars for my neighbors," said Marcus, "because they would see me working and want theirs done too. I always made sure to leave a slot for them." For Marcus, having a workable plan and sticking to it was important for long-term success. But the bottom line in business, Marcus believes, is dealing with people. If customers see the value of your product or service, you will be successful.

Thinking Like an Entrepreneur

1. What is a competitive advantage?
2. What did Marcus use as a competitive advantage?
3. How would you show customers that your services or goods have value?

CHAPTER SUMMARY

7.1 What Is Market Research?

Market research is an organized way to gather and analyze information needed to make business decisions. It helps you avoid costly mistakes as well as obtain financial support for a new business. Market research tends to focus on three areas: the business environment, potential customers, and the competition. Identifying a target market, rather than selling to a mass market, is usually the best approach for small businesses. Exploring market segments such as demographics, geographics, and psychographics can help you create a customer profile. This profile will provide a detailed description of your target market's characteristics. Secondary data sources—existing information that was gathered previously—can be valuable and relatively easy to find. Primary data is new information that is collected for a particular purpose. It is obtained directly from consumers.

7.2 What Is Your Competitive Advantage?

The data you collect about your competitors is called competitive intelligence. There are two types of competitors, direct and indirect. Direct competitors are businesses in the same market that sell a similar product or service. Indirect competitors sell a different product or service but one that fills the same customer needs or wants. After you gather data, you can use a competitive matrix and an expanded SWOT analysis to organize and analyze the information. The goal is to find one or more differentiators that can set your business apart from others. Any unique way that your business can meet customers' needs or wants is a potential differentiator. In review, the general steps taken during market research are (1) identify research objectives, (2) determine methods and sources, (3) gather data, (4) organize data, (5) evaluate data, and (6) draw conclusions.

REVIEW VOCABULARY

Write an article for your school newspaper that summarizes the nature of market research and how to determine a competitive advantage. Use at least half of the following terms in your article:

- business environment (p. 167)
- business-to-business (B2B) company (p. 170)
- business-to-consumer (B2C) company (p. 169)
- carrying capacity (p. 169)
- competitive advantage (p. 179)
- competitive intelligence (p. 177)
- competitive matrix (p. 179)
- customer profile (p. 169)
- demographics (p. 170)
- differentiator (p. 180)
- direct competitor (p. 177)
- focus group (p. 173)
- geographics (p. 170)
- indirect competitor (p. 178)
- list-rental company (p. 173)
- market (p. 167)
- market research (p. 167)
- market segment (p. 170)
- mass market (p. 169)
- primary data (p. 171)
- psychographics (p. 170)
- secondary data (p. 171)
- target market (p. 169)

CHECK YOUR UNDERSTANDING

Choose the letter that best answers the question or completes the statement.

1. Carrying capacity refers to
   a. the number of differentiators a business can have
   b. how current your secondary data is
   c. the maximum number of companies an industry can support based on its potential customer base
   d. all of the above

2. Companies that sell to other companies are called
   a. C2C
   b. B2C
   c. B2B
   d. none of the above

3. Market research
   a. does not include global factors
   b. is used to help sales efforts
   c. is only needed when planning a new business venture
   d. all of the above

4. Before gathering data, the first thing you should do is
   a. determine research methods
   b. identify research objectives
   c. find research sources
   d. identify your target market

5. Which of the following is *not* a source for obtaining secondary data?
   a. interviews about your product
   b. government statistics
   c. annual business reports from other companies
   d. chamber of commerce

6. Psychographics refers to such things as
   a. objective social and economic facts about customers
   b. where customers live or where businesses are located
   c. attitudes, opinions, beliefs, interests, personalities, lifestyles
   d. none of the above

7. A competitive matrix is used to compare your business with
   a. direct competitors
   b. indirect competitors
   c. target markets
   d. a and b

8. Which of the following is *not* an example of data that would be included in a B2C customer profile?
   a. geographic location of customer
   b. number of employees
   c. age of customer
   d. education level of customer

9. Social, economic, and political factors that could impact your business are called
   a. industry dynamics
   b. carrying capacity
   c. mass market
   d. business environment

10. Competitors can
    a. sell different products from yours
    b. sell through direct-mail catalogs
    c. both a and b
    d. neither a nor b

11. All primary research
    a. involves talking directly to people
    b. requires a questionnaire
    c. involves a focus group
    d. is collected for a specific purpose

12. Which of the following is *least* important when collecting and evaluating data?
    a. finding data that supports your idea
    b. confirming research results with more than one source or method
    c. making sure data is relevant to the target market
    d. staying alert to biased sources

Business Communication

13. Pick three competitive food products (for example, breakfast cereal or barbeque sauce) for a focus group. Prepare questions for the group and then conduct the focus group, having members see, taste, touch, and smell the products. Create a presentation that describes the results.

14. Choose a business opportunity and do market research for it. Then create a poster of how you "see" the marketplace. For example, use shapes (such as circles or boxes) to represent potential customers, competitors, investors, or industry factors. Use lines and arrows to show relationships between shapes. Be creative.

15. Working in groups of three, imagine that you own your favorite local restaurant. Create a competitive matrix for this restaurant compared to three local direct competitors.

Business Ethics

18. Market research professionals operate by a code of ethics. Use the Internet to find several sets of rules. Print out at least two of these. Working in groups of three, analyze the rules you printed. What do they have in common? In what ways do they differ? Write a code of ethics to use when conducting research of your own. Exchange your set of rules with another group's. Analyze their rules compared to yours. As a way of determining how good their rules are, try to imagine scenarios that would present problems for them. After your analysis, return the rules to the group that wrote them, along with your suggestions for making them better. Each group should then revise its own set of rules based on the other group's suggestions.

Business Math

16. You live in a town with four bookstores and a population of 10,000 people. A recent survey showed that 50% of the population shops at bookstores. Assume that all factors (such as products, customer service, convenience of location, number of hours open) are the same for all four of the stores. What is the number of potential customers for each?

17. You are opening a dry-cleaning business in a town of 20,000 adults. There are two dry cleaners in town. The ABC bank is your source of funding. ABC considers the town's carrying capacity to be a minimum of 7,500 potential adult customers per dry cleaner. If every adult in town is a potential customer, what would the average number of potential customers be per dry-cleaning business if you started your business? Is this figure within the bank's requirement?

Business in Your Community

19. Contact a local market research firm in your area. Ask if you may have a few samples of old survey questionnaires. Or ask if you may observe a survey or focus group in progress. Later, make a list of ways you might adapt what you saw to research projects of your own.

20. Interview an officer at your local bank who lends money to new businesses. Ask what type and amount of market research the bank likes to see before considering a loan. Also, what advice would he or she give to someone who wants to attract financial investors?

Web Domains

The primary part of a Website's address is its **Web domain**. (So, for www.website.com, the domain would be "website.") The Web domain, often referred to as the **domain name**, may be the name of the site itself, as is the case with Google (which has a Web address of www.google.com). A site has a **main domain**, also referred to as a **homepage**, and then a series of **subdomains**, such as individual product pages. Choosing a good Web domain is important. The domain name can mean the difference between success and failure. A domain name that is hard to remember may not become popular. Because many Web addresses have already been taken, Web businesses use creative spelling or invent new words—such as MySpace, YouTube, or Facebook.

Domain Registration

To get a domain name, a Website owner must contact a **domain registrar**, such as GoDaddy.com, that manages domain names. Such sites provide a search engine where you can type in a name and see if it has been taken. For instance, you could type in the name "Joe Smith" and see if www.joesmith.com is available. Web addresses that have been bought but remain unused are called **parked domains**. The owner of the parked domain may be waiting to sell the name to the highest bidder. Purchasing a potentially popular Web name can cost thousands of dollars, which is why many businesspeople choose creative spelling over buying a parked domain.

Domain Suffixes

A **domain suffix** (such as .com) is the Website's **top-level domain (TLD)**, meaning that these are the largest groupings of domains. International Websites have domain suffixes based on the country of origin, such as .co.uk for the United Kingdom or .fr for France.

IP Addresses

In addition to a Web domain, each Website is given an individual **Internet protocol (IP) address**. This is a unique string of numbers that identify the domain. For instance, the IP address for MySpace.com is

Common Domain Suffixes	
Domain Suffix	Type of Website
.com	Commercial Website
.net	Network—for commercial and noncommercial Websites
.gov	Government Website
.org	Organization—often the Website of a nonprofit organization
.biz	Business—similar to .com

216.178.38.121. Typical users don't need to know the IP address, however. Think of it as the difference between a person's name and his or her Social Security number. When a computer accesses a Website, it is actually a conversation between two IP addresses. IP addresses are regulated by the Internet Corporation for Assigned Names and Numbers (ICANN). Without them, our computers wouldn't be talking at all!

Tech Vocabulary

- domain name
- domain registrar
- domain suffix
- homepage
- Internet Protocol (IP) address
- main domain
- parked domain
- subdomain
- top-level domain (TLD)
- Web domain

Check Yourself

1. What does a domain registrar do?
2. Why might Website-owning businesspeople choose creative spellings for Web domains?
3. What does .com indicate?
4. What is an IP address?

What Do You Think?

Communicating. Why do you think domain names such as MySpace, Facebook, or YouTube are so effective?

STARTING A NEW BUSINESS

Eva graduated from Columbus State Community College with an associate's degree in Business Management. She then worked full-time so she could pay back her college loans. But she kept on the lookout for an opportunity to start her own full-time business. Join Eva as she adds to her work experience and considers a new business opportunity.

Something's Cooking!

After graduating, Eva decided to work full-time. Her mother told her about an opening at Ohio State University. "It's an administrative assistant job with the Campus Dining Services," she said. "They manage ten restaurants and a catering service on campus. With your business degree and experience in event planning, it could be a good match."

Eva got the job. She worked for the Director of the Campus Dining Services. Eva's job allowed her to apply her business skills, while learning how various types of food service are managed.

Although she enjoyed her work, Eva missed running her own business. She realized that, of all the event-planning tasks, she had most of all enjoyed cooking.

One day Eva was talking with a friend who said, "After working all day, I wish I had someone to cook dinner for me!" "Wow," Eva thought, "what a great idea! People who work all day might appreciate having someone prepare their meals. That's an idea for a business. I could become a personal chef for working people." It seemed like a great way for Eva to combine her passion for cooking and her desire to start a full-time business.

Eva knew that some of her cooking skills were weak. She needed improvement in knife technique, cost-cutting, and efficiency. Eva also figured that people might be reluctant to hire a personal chef who had no formal culinary training. She decided to do some market research to help her decide if her idea was a viable business opportunity.

Making It Personal

Here's what Eva discovered through her market research:

- **Description of Service.** Eva would be responsible for planning, buying, and preparing five dinners for a household. Food is often prepared at customers' homes. The chef packages dinners family-style with heating instructions and stores them in the customer's refrigerator or freezer. Kitchen clean-up is the personal chef's responsibility.

- **Start-Up Expenditures.** A low financial investment is needed to start a personal chef business. Eva would have to purchase her own set of professional knives, and possibly some cooking utensils.

- **Training and Certification.** Both homestudy and on-site training courses were available through associations such as the American Personal and Private Chef Association (APPCA) and the U.S. Personal Chef Association (USPCA). A personal chef could become certified after meeting educational and work-experience guidelines. Eva figured that certification would help potential customers have more confidence in her.

- **Competition.** In the greater Columbus area, there were currently 15 personal chefs.

- **Market.** Columbus had a growing market segment of professionals. Eva thought households of professionals making a combined income of over $50,000 would be her most likely market. In the greater Columbus area this market was growing steadily. Like her friend, these professionals were often too busy to cook dinner.

- **Growth Potential.** Personal chef businesses made up one of the fastest growing segments in the food-service industry. According to the APPCA, about 9,000 personal chefs were currently serving about 72,000 clients nationwide. Those numbers were expected to double over the next five years.

Eva made a list of established competitors and visited their Websites. She also telephoned them to find out more about their services.

Eva created a customer survey, which she conducted at a local mall. She discovered that people didn't use personal chefs because they weren't aware they existed. They also assumed that the cost of a professional chef would be out of their price range.

Based on her love of cooking and market research, Eva decided to switch from being a part-time event-planner to a full-time personal chef. She created a new name for her company, Eva's Edibles. On a vacation from her job at the Campus Dining Services, Eva took a five-day personal-chef training course to prepare for certification tests.

When Eva returned from vacation, she prepared a business plan on evenings and weekends. When she was satisfied with it, she did something everyone had advised her not to do: she quit her day job (but with appropriate notice).

She was going to be a personal chef. She was about to start Eva's Edibles!

Eva Tan's business plan for Eva's Edibles begins on the next page.

What Would You Have Done?

1. **Applying Concepts.** After Eva's graduation from community college, she took a full-time job to pay for her college loans. What did Eva give up by beginning to work full-time? Would you have made the same choice?

2. **Analyzing Information.** Based on Eva's background, her personal skills, and her market research results, draw up a SWOT chart for Eva's Edibles. Do you think her business idea is a good opportunity?

BUSINESS PLAN
EVA'S EDIBLES
A Personal Chef Service

EXECUTIVE SUMMARY

One- or two-page summary of the highlights of the business plan. Completed after the Business Plan is put together. Described in Section 6.1, pages 139–146.

Mission Statement

Eva's Edibles, a personal chef service, will provide busy professionals with healthy and delicious dinners that are based on their preferences and prepared in their own kitchens.

Business Name & Location

Eva's Edibles, LLC, will be located in Columbus, Ohio.

Date Business Will Begin

Eva's Edibles will begin operation on April 1, 20--.

Owner's Name, Function, & Contact Information

Eva Tan, the president of the company, will solely own and operate the company.

Contact Information: Eva Tan, 303 Olentangy River Rd., Columbus, OH 43202, (614) 555-6208

Opportunity

Columbus has a growing population of professionals who have busy lifestyles, but want healthy, yet affordable, dinner options.

Services

Eva's Edibles will prepare healthy homemade dinners for busy professionals. Each dinner will be based on the client's personal preferences. Dinners will be cooked in the client's kitchen, with all clean-up performed by Eva. The dinners will be stored in the client's refrigerator or freezer. Clients can reheat the dinners at their convenience. It is estimated that this service will save a client nine to ten hours per week by reducing shopping, evening-meal preparation, and clean-up.

Economics of One Unit (EOU)

One Unit of Sale = a 5-Dinner Plan

Selling Price per Unit = $325

Contribution Margin per Unit = $71

Future Plans

Within the first month, the company anticipates locating enough clients for Eva to cook in one client's kitchen each day on five successive weekdays. By the end of the first year, Eva's Edibles expects to be cooking in clients' kitchens 22 days in every month. Within three years the company expects to change its primary location for food preparation from clients' homes to a full-size commercial kitchen.

BUSINESS PLAN
EVA'S EDIBLES
A Personal Chef Service

For more information about Business Plans, see the chart on pages 144 and 145.

1.   BUSINESS IDEA

1.1   Qualifications

See Section 1.2, pages 13–20.

Eva Tan has an associate's degree in Business Management from Columbus State Community College. As Assistant to the Director of the Campus Dining Services at Ohio State University, Eva acquired experience in the management of various types of food-service operations, including catering. She also ran her own event-planning business, Eva's Entertainment Services, for four years. Eva has completed an intensive training course offered by the U.S. Personal Chef Association (USPCA) and has received the federally recognized trademarked designation of Certified Personal Chef (CPC).

Eva has many personal characteristics and skills that are particularly valuable in the personal chef business, including a passion for cooking, attention to detail, organizational skills, flexibility, creativity, sociability, ability to multitask, high physical energy, and endurance.

1.2   Factors Influencing Demand

See Section 2.1, pages 27–38.

Three factors influence the demand for personal chef services: busy lifestyles, an increase in health consciousness, and a desire for nutritious dinners. Eva's Edibles will appeal to individuals who are too busy to shop or prepare dinners but yet want healthy, nutritious food.

1.3   Type of Business

See Section 3.1, pages 51–55.

Eva's Edibles will be a service business preparing healthy dinners that clients can easily reheat.

1.4   Type of Business Ownership

See Section 3.2, pages 56–64.

Eva's Edibles will be a Limited Liability Company (LLC), wholly owned and operated by Eva Tan. The LLC status will protect Eva Tan's personal assets and allows the company to enjoy some tax benefits.

1.5   Social Responsibility

See Section 5.2, pages 115–126.

Eva's Edibles will use natural, organic, and locally grown ingredients whenever possible. The company's code of ethics directs that the business be as "green" as possible. It will choose vendors who are environmentally and socially responsible.

Eva's Edibles will also provide internships for interested culinary students in the community. In the future, Eva Tan hopes to volunteer at local elementary schools to speak with students about healthy eating and lifestyle choices. After three years, Eva's Edibles plans to contribute 1% of yearly net profit to a local food bank.

2.   OPPORTUNITY & MARKET ANALYSIS

2.1   Business Opportunity

See Section 6.2, pages 147–160.

The personal chef business is a viable opportunity for the Columbus area. Columbus has a large population of professionals, primarily from the business and medical spheres, that is growing steadily. Of the 301,800 Columbus households having two or more people, 36.7% (110,760) have incomes of $50,000 or more.

Annual Combined Household Income

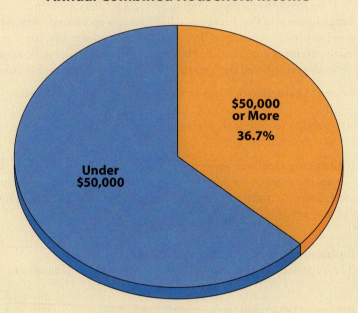

Total: 301,800 Columbus households
having two or more people.

People in this market have busy lifestyles and want healthy dinners. The target households go out to dinner or order in at least four days each week. Based on research conducted by Eva's Edibles, this market represents approximately 25% (27,690) of the households having combined household income of over $50,000. Eva's Edibles will provide people an opportunity to stay healthy without compromising a busy and productive lifestyle.

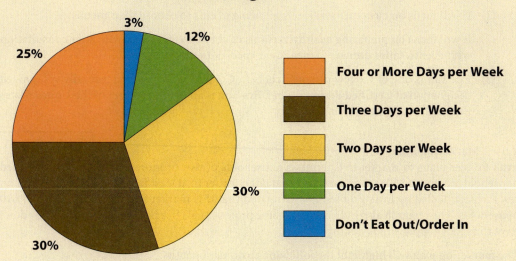

Households Eating Dinner Out or Ordering In

- 3%
- 12%
- 25%
- 30%
- 30%

Legend:
- Four or More Days per Week
- Three Days per Week
- Two Days per Week
- One Day per Week
- Don't Eat Out/Order In

Total: 110,760 Columbus households of two or more people with a combined income of $50,000 or more.

See Section 7.1, pages 167–176.

2.2 Market Research

The personal chef business is one of the fastest-growing segments in the food-service industry. According to the American Personal and Private Chef Association (APPCA), about 9,000 personal chefs are currently serving some 72,000 clients nationwide. Those numbers are expected to double over the next five years.

See Section 7.2, pages 177–186.

2.3 Competitors

Direct Competition: There are currently 15 personal chefs, or businesses performing some type of personal chef service, in the greater Columbus area. Of these, only seven advertise that they are members of one of the professional personal chef associations. Based on Website research, only one direct competitor is federally recognized as a Certified Personal Chef. Only two indicated specifically that they were focused on preparing healthy meals. On average, similar personal chefs in the Columbus area charge between $300 and $500 for their chef services. Groceries are an additional cost. Eva's Edibles will charge $325, including groceries, making its pricing very competitive.

Indirect Competition: Columbus area restaurants, including fast food and takeout establishments, will indirectly compete with Eva's Edibles. The upscale restaurants are generally expensive and not an everyday option. The majority of lower-priced family-style and fast food restaurants offer meals much lower in quality and nutrition than the dinners that Eva's Edibles will provide.

2.4   Competitive Advantage

See Section 7.2, pages 177–186.

Eva's Edibles has three major competitive advantages:

(1) It will focus on customer service by allowing clients to choose their menus.

(2) It will focus on preparing healthy versions of client favorites and will, after consultation with clients, tailor dinners to meet their special dietary needs.

(3) Eva Tan is one of the few personal chefs in Columbus to have the federally recognized designation of Certified Personal Chef. Eva Tan is an active member of the United States Personal Chef Association.

2.5   Marketing Plan

See Section 8.1, pages 211–222.

Eva's Edibles plans to market to Columbus households of two or more people with a combined household income of $50,000 or more, who eat out or order in at least four times a week. Based on research conducted by Eva's Edibles, it is estimated that this market segment amounts to 27,690 households. The research also indicates that these professionals live hectic lives and feel they don't have time for shopping and cooking.

The marketing plan will highlight the following customer benefits:

(1) Less time spent planning and shopping for dinners

(2) Less time spent in the kitchen cooking and cleaning up

(3) The convenience of eating dinner whenever the client wishes

(4) Delicious and healthy dinners tailored to the client's personal choices

(5) Less money spent eating out

(6) More time to spend with friends

(7) Dinner choices that can be tailored for diabetics, vegetarians, and those who need low-cholesterol or low-sodium meals

2.6   Pricing Strategy

See Section 8.1, pages 211–222.

Description of Service: Eva's Edibles will be based on a **5-Dinner Plan**, cooking five dinners for one household in one day. Households may range from 2 people to 5 people.

A dinner consists of:

- A main course
- A starch
- A vegetable
- A dessert

Clients can select dinners from a list of healthy home-style meals offered by Eva's Edibles or come up with others in consultation with Eva. The dinners will be stored family-style in the client's refrigerator or freezer in appropriate containers, with reheating instructions.

Pricing Strategy: Eva's Edibles will base prices on both demand and competition. As a member of USPCA, Eva has access to competitive prices and services. On average, similar personal chefs in the Columbus area charge between $300 and $500 for cooking dinners. Groceries are generally an additional cost. Eva's Edibles will charge $325, including groceries, making her service and prices very competitive. She is starting at a low price so she can create a reputation for Eva's Edibles and gain market share.

2.7   Promotion

See Section 8.2, pages 223–232.

Eva's Edibles will engage in five types of promotional activities:

(1)   Establishing a Website

(2)   Maintaining a referral listing on the USPCA Website

(3)   Hosting in-store promotions

(4)   Promotions at local events

(5)   Developing strategies for retaining current clients

Company Website: Eva's Edibles will construct its own Website, which will provide full information about services and display a selection of dinner menus. The Website will offer monthly catering promotions and offer a sign-up list for prospective clients. Sample dinners will be showcased. The Website will promote Eva Tan as one of the few personal chefs in the Columbus area who has the federally recognized designation of Certified Personal Chef. It will indicate that Eva Tan is an active member of the United States Personal Chef Association.

USPCA Referral Website: Eva's Edibles will use a referral listing provided by the USPCA. Because of her membership in the USPCA, Eva Tan can access its referral listing at www.hireachef.com. Eva's Edibles will be able to create and modify its listing and track listing statistics. According to the USPCA, this service "is the most effective, efficient method to put customers and personal chefs in touch with each other." Annually, hireachef.com logs over 500,000 listing views and 95,000 clicks for more information. These statistics represent more than simple Web-page hits, which can be deceiving. Clients on the hireachef.com system review personal chef pages and make contact. Inquiries from potential clients are sent directly to the chef's e-mail account.

In-Store Promotions: Eva's Edibles plans to offer in-store promotions at local cookware shops on a regular basis. One store, The Wire Whisk, has agreed to host an hour-long presentation by Eva Tan every other week. The presentation will be dedicated to healthy eating and feature the company's dinners. At each event the company will offer sample menus and a brochure describing its philosophy.

Promotions at Local Events: Eva's Edibles will also participate in local events at shopping malls, cultural fairs, environmental exhibits (Earth Day), and other appropriate venues. It will offer free samples, gift baskets, and discount raffles. Eva's will offer its brochure at each of these events as well.

Strategies for Retaining Current Clients: Eva's Edibles will provide current clients with extras for their loyalty—for example, free snacks and desserts after purchasing three 5-Dinner Plans. Another strategy will be to offer current customers a 10% discount when they refer Eva's Edibles to a potential client who signs a contract with the company.

2.8   Sales Methods See Section 9.1, pages 239–248.

Eva's Edibles will depend heavily on personal selling. This involves contacting past customers of the event-planning business and pursuing business contacts through Ohio State University.

Direct mail pieces and the brochure will have a mail-back card to capture a prospective client's e-mail address and telephone number. Eva Tan will follow up all mail-back cards personally by e-mail or phone.

Future selling strategies will include asking customers for referrals and recommendations of potential clients. Again, Eva will get in touch with each prospect personally.

3.   FINANCIAL STRATEGIES

3.1   Sales Estimates See Section 9.2, pages 249–258.

Sales estimates for the first two years are shown below. Each 5-Dinner Plan represents cooking five dinners for one household in the client's kitchen.

Eva's Edibles will be available to cook every weekday and on some weekends, when required.

Month	Year 1		Year 2	
	5-Dinner Plans	Monthly Sales	5-Dinner Plans	Monthly Sales
January	20	$6,500	22	$7,150
February	20	6,500	22	7,150
March	20	6,500	22	7,150
April	20	6,500	22	7,150
May	21	6,825	22	7,150
June	21	6,825	23	7,475
July	21	6,825	23	7,475
August	21	6,825	23	7,475
September	22	7,150	23	7,475
October	22	7,150	23	7,475
November	22	7,150	24	7,800
December	22	7,150	24	7,800
Annual Totals	252	$81,900	273	$88,725

Projected five-year sales estimates are shown on the next page. The projections assume that Eva's Edibles moves to a commercial kitchen in its third year. That will allow the company to deliver meals to clients, rather than to cook in their kitchens, thus significantly increasing the number of 5-Dinner Plans the company can provide.

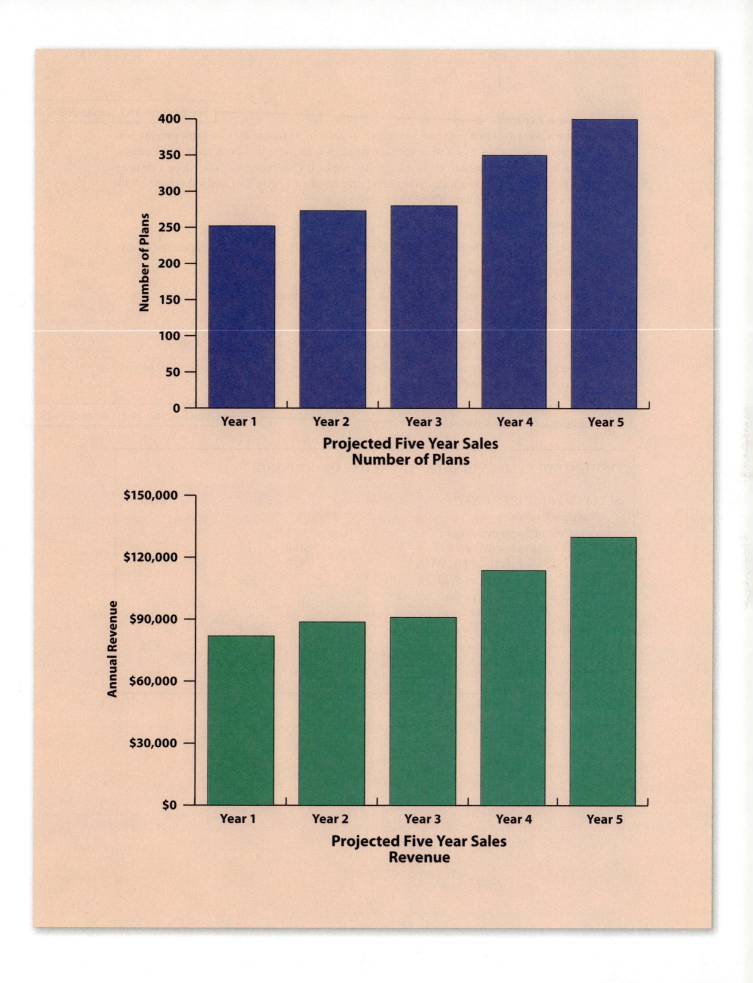

Projected Five Year Sales
Number of Plans

Projected Five Year Sales
Revenue

3.2 Business Expenses See Section 10.1, pages 269–274.

Eva's Edibles will keep its fixed expenses at a very low level in its first year. Eva Tan's parents will pay for her health insurance. Eva Tan is the sole employee, so there will be no salaries. Because Eva will cook at the clients' homes, there will be no rent or utility expenses other than a cellular telephone. The company will use an existing computer donated by Eva Tan and valued at $1,000. The computer will back up all data offsite every day.

Operating expenses for the first year of business will be:

- Advertising: Brochure ($600), cards ($50), postage ($300), Website development ($800)

- Depreciation: Computer ($200 per year)

- Insurance: Automobile ($800), USPCA Liability Insurance ($600)

- Utilities: Cellular telephone ($1,200)

- Other Operating Expenses: Automobile-related maintenance & gas ($1,300)

- Other Operating Expenses: Cooking-related—knife kit, equipment not supplied by customers, spices, oils, and so on ($1,000)

3.3 Economics of One Unit See Section 10.2, pages 275–282.

ONE UNIT OF SALE = 5-DINNER PLAN (1 DAY OF COOKING)

SELLING PRICE (PER UNIT):			**$325**
Variable Expenses			
Cost of Services Sold			
Materials (Groceries)	$100		
Labor ($25 per Hr., 6 Hrs.)	150		
Cost of Services Sold		250	
Other Variable Expenses			
Gas, $4 per Day	$4		
Total Other Variable Expenses		4	
Total Variable Expenses			254
CONTRIBUTION MARGIN (PER UNIT):			**$71**

3.4 Income Statement

See Section 11.1, pages 289–303.

Projected Annual Income Statement: End of Year 1
March 31, 20--

REVENUE

Sales (252 Days @ $325/Day)	$81,900	
Total Revenue		$81,900

COST OF SERVICES SOLD

Materials (Groceries @ $100/Plan)	$25,200	
Labor ($150/Plan)	37,800	
Cost of Services Sold		63,000

GROSS PROFIT $18,900

OPERATING EXPENSES

Advertising	$1,750	
Depreciation	200	
Insurance	1,400	
Telephone	1,200	
Other Operating Expenses (Auto-Related)	1,300	
Other Operating Expenses (Cooking-Related)	1,000	
Total Operating Expenses		6,850

PRE-TAX PROFIT $12,050

Taxes (15%) 1,808

NET PROFIT $10,242

3.5 Balance Sheet

See Section 11.2, pages 304–314.

Projected Balance Sheet: Start of Business
April 1, 20--

ASSETS

Current Assets

Cash	$5,000	
Total Current Assets		$5,000
Total Assets		**$5,000**

LIABILITIES & SHAREHOLDER'S EQUITY

Current Liabilities

Total Current Liabilities		$0
Total Liabilities		**$0**

Shareholder's Equity

Eva Tan, Shareholder's Equity (100 Shares)		$5,000
Total Liabilities & Owner's Equity		**$5,000**

3.6   Financial Ratios See Section 12.1, pages 321–332.

Return on Sales (ROS): Eva's Edibles projects a return on sales of approximately 12.5% (Net Profit ÷ Total Sales) x 100 = Return on Sales. Thus, ($10,242 ÷ $81,900) x 100 = 12.51% Return on Sales.

Return on Investment (ROI): Eva's beginning equity of $5,000 in the business (shown as Shareholder's Equity on the balance sheet) represents her initial investment in the company. Eva's Edibles projects a first year net profit of $10,242. So Eva's Edibles projects a return on investment of approximately 204.8%. (Net Profit ÷ Initial Investment) x 100 = Return on Investment. Thus, ($10,242 ÷ $5,000) x 100 = 204.84% Return on Investment.

3.7   Break-Even Point See Section 12.2, pages 333–336.

Eva's unit of sale is a 5-dinner plan (one day of cooking), for which the company charges $325. Eva's cost for labor and materials for a day of cooking is $250. Her other variable costs are $4 per unit, so her total variable costs per unit are $254. The resulting contribution margin per unit is $71 ($325 – $254 = $71).

Eva's Total Variable Expenses are $19,908 (COSS of $18,900 + Other Variable Costs of $1,008). (The other variable expense was gas at $4 per day for 252 days.) Fixed Operating Expenses, which don't include the variable expense for gas, are $5,842 ($6,850 - $1,008 = $5,842). This means that Eva's Edibles will break even after approximately 82 days of cooking ($5,842 ÷ $71 = 82.28 days to break even).

3.8   Financing Strategy See Section 13.1 & 13.2, pages 347–364.

Start-Up Investment: Eva Tan will invest $5,000 of her own money in the company. This is her beginning equity in the company.

Reserve for Fixed Expenses: The company will establish a reserve for fixed expenses of $2,012. This is enough to cover the company's operating expenses for three months (Total Operating Expenses ÷ 12) x 3. Thus, ($8,050 ÷ 12) x 3 = $2,012.

Start-Up Expenditures & Emergency Fund: The company will use the remaining portion of the start-up investment, $2,988, to cover start-up expenditures, which are expected to be approximately $2,000, and to establish an emergency fund of $1,000.

3.9   Recordkeeping & Accounting Systems See Section 14.1 & 14.2, pages 371–398.

Eva's Edibles will use the latest version of QuickBooks accounting software. Offsite backups of the business accounts and records will automatically be made every day.

4.   ORGANIZATIONAL STRUCTURES

4.1   Organizational Structure See Section 15.1, pages 405–415.

Eva's Edibles will be operated solely by Eva Tan, who will perform all shopping, cooking, and sales functions in the business. Her title will be President.

4.2   Staffing See Section 15.1, pages 405–415.

Eva Tan will be the only person employed full-time by Eva's Edibles during the first year. If sales increase as projected, it may become necessary to hire part-time assistance in the second year. As the business grows, Eva's Edibles anticipates offering internships to local culinary college students.

4.3 Outside Experts
See Section 15.1, pages 405–415.

Eva's Edibles will use outside services for legal and accounting/tax needs. In addition, Eva will seek the mentorship of colleagues who are also members of USPCA.

4.4 Training and Motivating Employees
See Section 15.2, pages 416–426.

Eva Tan plans to take a USPCA course on growing a personal chef business after the company's first year of operation. The first year will be very strenuous. The company plans to devote at least one day of every weekend to cooking for clients.

In case of illness, the company has entered into a reciprocal agreement with James Martin, a personal chef in Columbus, who will prepare dinners for Eva's Edibles clients on short notice.

5. LEGAL STRUCTURES

5.1 Intellectual Property
See Section 16.1, pages 433–442.

The company has started the process of trademarking "Eva's Edibles" as a brand name. Eva will also copyright her brochures and all printed materials.

5.2 Contracts
See Section 16.1, pages 433–442.

Eva's Edibles will have a written contract with each of its clients that will specify the dates on which the service will be performed, the menus chosen by the client, and any dietary requirements. The contract will also set out provisions for the cancellation of services by either party.

5.3 Insurance
See Section 16.2, pages 443–452.

USPCA liability insurance costs $600 annually for members. It is a standard general-liability policy with clauses that cover food products, personal injury, advertising injury, and property damage. The company will also pay for automobile insurance for Eva Tan.

5.4 Taxes
See Section 17.1, pages 459–470.

Eva's Edibles will pay self-employment tax and collect sales tax. Workers' Compensation will be made available should three or more full-time employees be hired.

5.5 Government Regulations
See Section 17.2, pages 471–480.

Currently, there are no government regulations concerning a personal chef cooking in a client's home. In the future, if the company leases a commercial kitchen, Eva Tan will investigate all appropriate license and inspection protocols.

6. BUSINESS MANAGEMENT

6.1   Expenses, Credit, and Cash Flow See Section 18.2, pages 499–504.

Because of the large volume of food shopping, Eva's Edibles will establish credit with local grocery stores and food-supply companies.

In its first year, Eva's will not accept credit cards. Payment will be received in cash or by check.

The following projected monthly cash budget for Eva's Edibles shows a typical month in the first year of business, in which Eva cooks for clients on 21 days of the month.

CASH INFLOWS		
Cash Sales (21 x $325)	$6,825	
Total Cash Inflows		$6,825
CASH OUTFLOWS		
Variable Expenses: Groceries (21 x $100)	$2,100	
Variable Expenses: Labor (21 x $150)	3,150	
Advertising	146	
Depreciation	17	
Insurance	117	
Telephone	100	
Other Fixed Expenses (Automobile-Related)	108	
Other Operating Expenses (Cooking-Related)	83	
Total Cash Outflows		$5,821
CASH AVAILABLE		$1,004

6.2   Production and Distribution See Section 19.1, pages 511–520.

In its first year of business, Eva's Edibles will prepare food at clients' homes. The only distribution involved will be the transportation of groceries to the clients' homes, which will be accomplished by using Eva Tan's automobile, for which the company will contribute gasoline and maintenance.

6.3   Operations See Section 19.2, pages 521–526.

Hours of Operation: Eva's Edibles will typically work at a client's home from 11:00 a.m. to 5:00 p.m. Eva Tan will shop for groceries in the morning, buying in bulk for multiple clients whenever possible.

Rework Requests: If a customer is unhappy with a dinner, Eva's will cook another dinner for the client. If a client is unhappy twice in a period of four months or less, Eva will work carefully with that client to establish the reason for the dissatisfaction, and the company will provide two additional dinners to the client free of charge.

Client Satisfaction: Eva's will depend on word-of-mouth referrals. Clients must be pleased at all costs. Customer service will be critical to the success of Eva's Edibles.

6.4 Purchasing

See Section 20.1, pages 533–540.

Eva's Edibles will purchase groceries on an as-needed basis in the mornings, according to client needs. Eva Tan will buy in bulk whenever possible, choosing vendors for both price and quality. Some ingredients, such as meat or produce, will be purchased as needed to avoid spoilage. Eva's Edibles will cook dinners with seasonal ingredients. In addition, the company will build relationships with local organic farmers to ensure the highest quality and best price.

6.5 Inventory

See Section 20.2, pages 541–548.

Eva's Edibles will keep a minimum inventory of frequently used ingredients, such as condiments and spices, in a cooler and a storage container in her car. The company will use a just-in-time inventory strategy. This means items will be purchased as needed, and long-term storage will not be necessary.

7. PLAN FOR GROWTH

7.1 Business Growth

See Section 21.1, pages 559–566.

Short-Term Business Goals: In its first year, Eva's Edibles plans to build a profitable customer base so that, by the end of the year, it will be cooking in clients' kitchens 22 days in every month. This will allow the company to reach its revenue goal of $81,900.

Long-Term Business Goals: Eva's Edibles anticipates that, after a profitable customer base has been built, the company will develop an intensive growth strategy. Eva's intends to increase its market penetration by leasing or buying a commercial kitchen. This will allow increased storage and allow the company to serve more clients, thereby increasing its revenues and profits. Dinners will then be delivered to customers.

7.2 Challenges

See Section 21.2, pages 567–570.

Short-Term Business Challenges: The biggest challenge facing Eva's Edibles in its early years will be its business model. Cooking dinners at clients' homes will limit the number of clients that the company can serve.

Long-Term Business Challenges: The biggest long-term challenge for the company is space. Eva's Edibles will need to change its business model and lease or buy a commercial kitchen to increase the number of clients. This, in turn, may require additional financing and will almost certainly require additional employees, particularly those with some degree of cooking skills.

7.3 Franchising and Licensing

See Section 22.1, pages 577–586.

Although premature to plan for, Eva's Edibles may represent a business that could be franchised in other cities with large upscale populations of professionals.

7.4 Exit Strategy

See Section 22.2, pages 587–598.

After establishing itself as a viable business with a stable roster of clients, it is likely that Eva's Edibles could be valued as a desirable business operation for a chef looking for a single-person business. However, Eva Tan has no plans to leave the business in the foreseeable future.

UNIT 4

MARKETING PLAN & SALES

In This Unit:

8. Marketing Your Product
9. Selling Your Product

YOUR BUSINESS PLAN

In this unit, you'll focus on the **Opportunity & Market Analysis** and **Financial Strategies** section of the business plan and answer these questions:

- What is my marketing plan?
- What are my product and pricing strategies?
- How do I promote my product?
- How do I sell my product?
- How do I estimate sales?

8 MARKETING YOUR PRODUCT

OBJECTIVES

- Identify the components of a marketing plan
- Describe various types of product strategies
- Specify ways to apply place (distribution) strategies
- Explain methods used in developing price strategies

VOCABULARY

- benefits
- brand
- brand mark
- bundling
- competition-based pricing
- cost-based pricing
- demand-based pricing
- direct channel
- distribution channels
- exclusive distribution
- features
- indirect channel
- intensive distribution
- intermediary
- markdown price
- marketing
- marketing mix
- marketing plan
- market share
- markup price
- mind share
- product mix
- product positioning
- promotion
- selective distribution

Think about a product you like, and then answer this question:

Is the brand of the product important?

On a piece of paper, identify the product and its brand (for example, Product: Athletic Shoes; Brand: Nike). Be prepared to discuss how this brand differs from other brands.

What Is a Marketing Plan?

As you've already learned, a market is a group of potential customers for a particular product or service. **Marketing** is a way of presenting your business to your customers. The main reason for marketing is to clearly communicate the value of your product or service. To do this successfully, you create a **marketing plan**. A marketing plan is a detailed guide with two primary parts:

- Marketing goals
- Strategies for reaching your goals (the marketing mix)

Marketing Goals

Every marketing plan is unique because each business has its own marketing goals. When you first begin creating a marketing plan, it's important to know what you want to accomplish. Write these goals down so you can refer to them as you develop marketing strategies. Later, as you work out the details of your strategies, you can make adjustments. You may also discover that you need to do some additional research.

Your marketing goals should agree with your business plan's overall objectives. However, marketing goals are usually more specific and action-oriented. You should be able to measure them in practical ways. For example, "I want to increase the number of customers that come to my store" is too general. Adding the words "by 25%" to the end of this statement makes it more specific and measurable. Another way to state goals in a measurable way is to specify the amount of sales or profit you wish to reach.

Marketing goals also require a time frame:

- **Short-Range Goals.** What do you want to accomplish in the next year? You may find it helpful to break one-year goals into smaller periods, such as quarters (three months).

- **Mid-Range Goals.** What do you want to achieve in the next two to five years?

- **Long-Range Goals.** Where do you see your business ten or twenty years from now?

Some additional things to keep in mind when considering goals:

- **Motive.** Think about *why* you want to reach each objective. What rewards do you hope to obtain? Also, consider the opportunity cost of setting one particular goal rather than another.

- **Consistency.** Be careful that your goals do not conflict with one another. That will only create frustration. It will also decrease your chances of accomplishing them.

- **Cost.** Eventually, you will need to work out a budget for your marketing plan, to check the feasibility of your goals. Cost includes not only money but also your personal energy and emotional investment. Try to be as realistic as you can when thinking about goals. At the same time, remember that many worthwhile aims will require you to step outside your comfort zone.

Another potential marketing goal can be defined in terms of market share. **Market share** is the percentage of a given market population that is buying a product or service from a particular business.

Determining a reasonable market share should be based on the level of competition in your target market. In most cases, you will be entering a market with many competitors. Or, your industry may have a few large competitors that currently hold most of the market share. Either way, don't expect to grab much market share, at least in the beginning. However, if your business has created a unique product with no direct competition, you will have a 100% market share for that product. That, of course, can change if competitors create a similar product in the future.

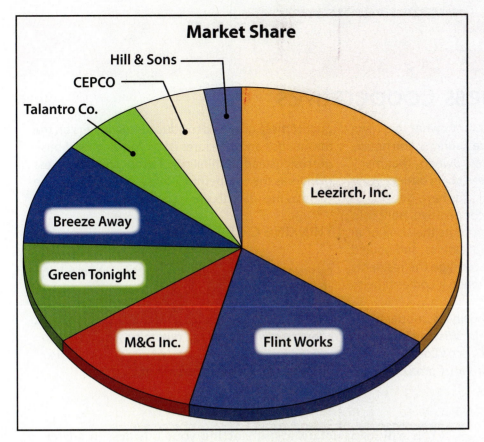

Market Share

Hill & Sons
CEPCO
Talantro Co.
Leezirch, Inc.
Breeze Away
Green Tonight
M&G Inc.
Flint Works

◀ Figure 8-1
Market Share
Pie charts are often used
to visualize market-share
percentages.
Communicating. *What would
be another way of illustrating
market share in graphic form?*

Let's say your goal is to sell $100,000 worth of product or service in the first year. Based on research, you know that your target market spends about $2 million per year on this type of product/service from your competitors. Use the following formula to determine your estimated market share:

(Total Sales ÷ Total Market Size) × 100 = Market Share %

$100,000 ÷ $2 Million   × 100 = 5% Market Share

Marketing Strategies (Marketing Mix)

Every marketing plan has five main strategy areas, sometimes referred to as the "Five Ps." How a company chooses to combine these areas is called its **marketing mix**. Think of it as creating a recipe for reaching and keeping customers:

- **People.** Without a doubt, your target customers are the key to defining all the other strategies in a marketing plan. Include a detailed customer profile to help keep your focus on the best prospects. You can also include a description of the people (employees) you will need to carry out the marketing plan.

Local Business Cooperatives

Imagine you are a local restaurant owner in a town with many well-known chain restaurants. You notice, along with other small-business owners, that many people seem to be visiting these chain outlets. What do you do? Some local businesses have decided to help each other by forming cooperative, nonprofit organizations. These groups promote their one-of-a-kind offerings with events, publications, and pooled marketing resources. They encourage the residents of their towns to "think local" when it comes time to decide where to shop or eat.

Examples of these local business cooperatives include Madison Originals in Wisconsin (madisonoriginals.org) and San Francisco's Locally Owned Merchants Alliance in California (sfloma.org). The goal of these groups is to educate consumers on the advantages and pleasures of patronizing local businesses. Instead of thinking of other small-business owners as the competition, these entrepreneurs see them as friends with similar goals.

THINKING CRITICALLY

Predicting. In pairs, describe three ways that small businesses could help one another when a large chain store or restaurant threatens to take away their customers.

To read more about local business cooperatives, go to "Entrepreneurship Issues" on the Student Center at entrepreneurship.pearson.com.

(You will learn details about staffing your business in a later chapter.)

- **Product.** What item(s) can your business provide that will *best* meet the needs of your target market? This is a description of the product(s) or service(s) your company plans to offer.

- **Place.** This strategy refers to selling and delivery methods. How and where will customers be able to buy or receive your product or service?

- **Price.** What price will your target market feel is reasonable, or perhaps even a good deal, for your product or service? Your pricing strategy may need to vary over time depending on various factors, about which you'll learn later.

- **Promotion.** The process you use to make potential customers aware of your product or service and to influence them to buy it is referred to as **promotion**.

The rest of this section will focus on how to develop strategies for the people, product, price, and place marketing elements. Section 8.2 will focus on promotional strategies.

What are the two main parts of a marketing plan?

Determining People and Product Strategies

Building a product image refers to creating a specific impression of it in the minds of your customers. In a marketing plan, your product is the physical item you plan to sell or the service you plan to provide. (In this section, we'll use the term "product" whether it is a physical item or a service you are selling.)

Attracting Customers to Your Product

To attract people in your target market, you need to choose a product that matches well with their needs or wants. When given a choice, consumers buy the product with the features and benefits that best meet their requirements.

The **features** of a product are what it does and how it appears to the senses (sight, sound, taste, smell, and touch). The **benefits** of a product are the reasons customers choose to buy it. Here are just a few examples of benefits: saving time, increasing social status, protecting the family, getting rid of a problem, improving a relationship, reducing worry, providing entertainment, and saving money.

Often you can get customers' attention by how you choose to package a product. The design and labeling of a bottle, box, bag, or other container is one way you can emphasize your product's features and benefits.

If you choose to sell more than one product, you need to consider how the products relate to each other. The combination of products a business sells is called its **product mix**. The mix you choose will largely depend on the product image you want to communicate. It will also depend on the number and type of markets you are targeting.

Maintaining Customer Loyalty

Successful businesses do more than attract new customers by marketing a product's features and benefits. Their ultimate goal is to keep customers coming back again and again. Your product may currently be superior to your competitors' products. But this alone may not be enough to maintain customer loyalty over a long period of time. Great ideas can be copied and modified by competitors. The competitors may even be able to make improvements. Or they may be able to sell a similar product at a lower price than you can.

What competitive edge can you create that cannot be easily copied? One answer is to build a brand. A **brand** is a marketing strategy that can create an emotional attachment to your product in the mind of the consumer. This is because a brand is perceived in a certain way. It may be seen as excellent quality or high status—a *premium* brand. The perception is not always reality. A premium brand may not be significantly different from a "lower-quality" one, but the consumer perceives it as on a higher level. This process of creating a strong image is called

▲ Figure 8-2
Branding
A brand mark is a way to associate a symbol with a product and its qualities.
Interpreting Illustrations. *What is an advantage of using a brand mark?*

product positioning. It is a way of influencing potential customers to distinguish your brand's characteristics from those of the competition.

Branding can cause customers to think of a particular company first. For example, what name do you think of when you want to buy a new pair of athletic shoes? Perhaps Nike, with its "Just Do It" image, comes to mind. Or when you need a tissue, maybe you ask for a "Kleenex." **Mind share** is the awareness or popularity a certain product has with consumers.

In addition to its name, you can use a symbol or other graphic design to identify a brand. This is often referred to as a logo, or **brand mark**. For example, the "golden arches" symbol is probably enough for you to recognize a McDonald's restaurant without ever seeing the name. Brand marks are usually included on store signs, packaging, Websites, and in print ads and television commercials.

Packaging

An important aspect of a product's strategy is how that product is packaged. Packaging contains and protects the product until the consumer uses it. The packaging needs to be suited to the method used for the product's distribution and sale. It should be cost-effective and also environmentally responsible.

Packaging should be designed for your target market and, if sold in a retail store, should be eye-catching. It should promote the image of the brand and be distinguishable from competitors' products. Packaging for certain types of products must meet legal requirements (for example, child-proof medicine bottles). Overall, your packaging can sometimes cause your product to be a success—or a failure.

READING CHECKPOINT *What is a brand?*

Determining Place (Distribution) Strategies

Distribution channels are the various ways that a product can reach the consumer. Place strategies (sometimes referred to as distribution strategies) are used to answer the following: How will you get your product into the hands of your customers? How can you ensure that your product will be available to customers where and when they want it?

If you can find an efficient distribution channel, you may be able to gain a competitive advantage. The more cost-efficient the channel is, the lower you can keep the product's price. The more time-efficient the channel is, the faster the product will reach customers (and the happier they will be).

What Channels Will You Use?

There are two kinds of distribution channels: direct and indirect. A **direct channel** is a pathway in which a product goes from the producer straight to the consumer. Think of it as a trip with no stops between the starting point and the destination.

An **indirect channel** is a pathway in which the product goes from the producer to one or more intermediaries before it reaches the consumer. An **intermediary** is the bridge between a producer and a consumer. Intermediaries include agents, brokers, wholesalers, distributors, and retailers. Following is an example of an indirect channel in a consumer market:

1. A manufacturer produces millions of cell phones.

2. A wholesaler buys thousands of cell phones from the manufacturer.

3. A retailer buys dozens of cell phones from the wholesaler.

4. A consumer goes to the retail store and buys one cell phone.

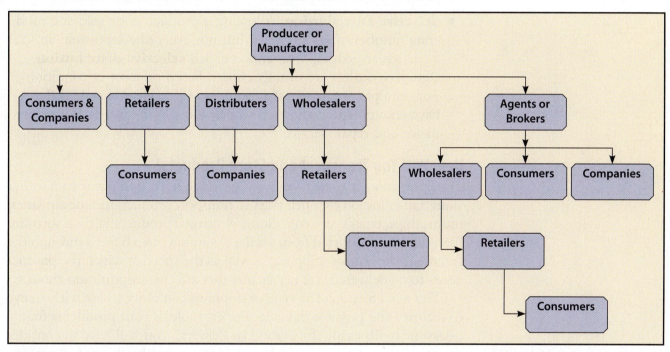

▲ Figure 8-3
Distribution Channels
The path from producer to consumer can take many routes, both direct and indirect.
Recognizing Patterns. *What is an example of an item you've bought that flowed directly to you?*

Where and When Will You Sell?

Place strategies need to include the selling location and the hours during which customers can buy the product. Examples of such strategies include the following:

• Choosing an excellent location for a physical store.

• Determining the days and hours when customers are most likely to shop.

• Providing an easy-to-use Website that customers can access any time, from any location.

• Taking orders via a toll-free telephone number, with operators standing by 24 hours a day.

When determining your strategies, be sure to consider how widely you want to distribute your product. For instance, do you want to use many sales outlets or only a few? Here are three basic options:

- **Exclusive Distribution.** This type of distribution is the most limited of the three. **Exclusive distribution** gives a specific retailer, or authorized dealer, the sole right to sell a product in a particular geographical area. An exclusive distribution agreement usually requires that the retailer or dealer cannot sell competing products.

- **Intensive Distribution.** The opposite of exclusive distribution is **intensive distribution**. The object of intensive distribution is to make a product available at as many sales outlets as possible. This means selling the product at a variety of stores, many of which may compete with each other. For example, you can buy toothpaste at drugstores, grocery stores, large outlets such as Kmart or Walmart, and convenience shops at gas stations.

- **Selective Distribution.** Allowing a product to be sold at a moderate number of sales outlets, but not everywhere possible, in a particular geographical area is called **selective distribution**. Retailers/dealers are usually chosen based on a set of conditions. For example, a car manufacturer may select dealers only if they have enough space and staff to provide a high level of maintenance and repair service.

How Will You Transport and Store Products?

Transportation is used to move a product from one point to another along a distribution channel. Ways to transport products include airplanes, trains, ships, trucks, or a mix. Some electronic products, such as software files, can be transported from a seller's computer to a buyer's through the Internet. The cost of shipping, as well as the speed at which the product needs to be delivered, are key factors that affect transportation choices.

You need to select the type of shipping container to use with an eye to security and possible damage. For example, if your product is fragile (glass) or spoils easily (fresh food or flowers), you will have to consider special transportation needs. If a product cannot be shipped directly to its final destination, you will need to decide where it will be temporarily stored along the way.

 *What is the difference between a direct distribution channel and an indirect one?*

Developing Price Strategies

There are many kinds of pricing strategies and techniques. However, you should base the price of your product on two things: your target market and the potential profits for your company. Your product's price should be low enough that customers want to buy from you rather than the competition. At the same time, your product's price must be high enough for your company to earn a profit.

Identifying Price Objectives

The first step toward setting a price is to identify what you want to achieve by it. For example, what do you want the price to "say" about your product? What do you want the price to accomplish for your business? When deciding price objectives, keep in mind your overall business plan goals, your marketing or brand goals, and what your target market can afford to pay. Following are a few samples of price objectives:

- **Build or Maintain an Image.** Prices can create or affect the image of a product in consumers' minds. For example, people may perceive lower-priced goods as having a lower quality than similar items sold at a higher price.

- **Increase Sales Volume (Quantity).** Higher prices may lower the number of sales, and lower prices may increase the number of sales. However, you can charge a slightly higher price than the competition if your product has more features or benefits.

- **Obtain or Expand a Market Share.** Sometimes an initial lower price can help a new business attract customers from competitors. After you obtain a market share, you can increase your prices slightly to improve profits.

- **Maximize Profits.** If you are introducing a new product into a market, you could charge a high price to maximize profits. Later on, if competitors imitate your product or find some other way to reduce its attraction, you could drop the price.

Selecting a Basic Pricing Strategy

After defining objectives, the next step is to pick a strategy for determining actual prices. There are three basic pricing strategies. Your decision about which one to use will depend on your product mix, your price objectives, and the market you are targeting.

- **Demand-Based Pricing.** A pricing method that focuses on consumer demand—how much customers are willing to pay for a product—is called **demand-based pricing**. A demand-based pricing strategy is most useful when customers perceive your product as unique or having greater value than similar products. You can determine a maximum price by surveying potential target customers. The price is basically the most that an actual customer would be willing to pay. For example, for a one-of-a-kind item, such as an antique or a painting, you would use demand-based pricing.

- **Competition-Based Pricing.** A pricing method that focuses on what the competition charges is called **competition-based pricing**. After you find out your competitors' prices, you can decide to charge the same price, slightly more, or slightly less. Because the focus of this strategy is staying competitive, you will need to regularly review what your competitors are doing. This will allow you to make price adjustments if needed.

- **Cost-Based Pricing.** Setting a product's price based on what it costs your business to provide it is called **cost-based pricing**. To use this strategy you must first know the economics of one unit, which was discussed in Chapter 2. After you figure out what the cost is for a single unit of your product, you then decide how much to add on to ensure a profit.

Allowing for Price Adjustments

If the distribution channel for a product is an indirect one, the price will get adjusted as it moves from the producer to the consumer. When a retail store buys a product from a wholesaler, they add an additional amount to the wholesale cost to make a profit. This results in a **markup price**. Frequently, a percentage is used to calculate the markup:

Wholesale Cost × Markup Percentage/100 = Markup Amount

Wholesale Cost + Markup Amount = Markup Price (Retail Price)

For example, if the wholesale price of a product was $10 and the markup percentage was 30%, the markup amount would be $3.

$$\$10 \times 30 \div 100 = \$3$$

The markup price (retail price) would be the wholesale cost ($10) plus the markup amount ($3), or $13. So you would buy this product wholesale at $10, mark it up by 30%, and sell it at $13.

A **markdown price** is set when a retailer wants to reduce the price of a product. Retailers often use markdown prices when they are overstocked (have too much of a product). Or perhaps the retailer needs to make room for new products. Another reason would be a change in customer demand. For example, a clothing store will probably set markdown prices at the end of the summer to get rid of warm-weather clothing. To calculate the markdown price, use the following formulas. Keep in mind that to avoid losing money, the markdown price should not be less than the wholesale cost.

Retail Price × Markdown Percentage/100 = Markdown Amount

Retail Price − Markdown Amount = Markdown Price ("Sale" Price)

For example, if the retail price of a product was $10 and the markdown percentage was 25%, the markdown amount would be $2.50.

$$\$10 \times 25 \div 100 = \$2.50$$

The markdown price ("Sale" price) would be the retail price ($10) minus the markdown amount ($2.50), or $7.50. So you would normally sell this product retail at $10, but mark it down by 25% and put it on sale at $7.50.

Price Factors for Services

When a "product" is a service, time is a primary factor used to determine price. Some services are charged simply by the hour, as a physical therapist, business consultant, or marriage counselor usually does.

Vendors such as car mechanics or electricians commonly add a separate fee for materials in addition to their hourly charge. This strategy provides flexibility for services that vary widely. For example, a job may require replacing expensive parts, inexpensive parts, or perhaps none at all.

Another way that businesses charge for services is based on a flat fee. Both material costs and time are built into one price for a particular service. Consider a business that performs oil changes in cars. The amount of time it takes to complete an oil change, as well as the new oil and oil filter that's put in the car, are factored into one price.

Bundling

Another technique to explore when setting prices is **bundling**. Bundling is the practice of combining the price of several services (and/or physical products) into one price. The travel industry commonly uses bundling to create vacation packages that include airline services, hotel accommodations, and a rental car for one price.

Bundling can be a convenience factor for customers. It also allows the business to sell services at a slightly lower price. This is because customers are buying a greater quantity of goods or services.

Bundling might also include optional services or product accessories with an item that's more in demand. Car dealers and appliance

Figure 8-4 ▶

Bundling

Bundling combines the price of several services and/or products into one price.

Applying Concepts. *How might computer stores use the technique of bundling?*

retailers often use this strategy. It helps them sell items that a customer might not buy if sold separately.

 **READING CHECKPOINT** *When are markup prices and markdown prices used?*

 Your Business Plan. Continue developing your standard business plan. Go to "Section 8.1" of the *Business Plan Project* in your *Student Activity Workbook*, or "Section 8.1" of the BizTech Software.

ASSESSMENT 8.1

Reviewing Objectives

1. What are the five main elements in a marketing mix?

2. Define branding and explain its potential advantages.

3. Describe the three basic distribution strategies.

4. Explain the three basic strategies used to determine prices.

Critical Thinking

5. **Comparing/Contrasting.** What would you say are the advantages and disadvantages of cost-based pricing versus demand-based pricing?

6. **Drawing Conclusions.** What do you think happens to the price of an object as it goes through a large number of intermediaries?

Working Together

Work with two partners. Each will focus on a distribution strategy (exclusive, intensive, or selective). Research the advantages and disadvantages of your strategy. When finished, assemble your research results into a PowerPoint presentation or other method of displaying information.

Science

Life Cycles

Every living creature has a life cycle. Think, for example, of an insect that begins as a caterpillar, changes into a chrysalis, and then transforms into a butterfly. Products have life cycles too. At each stage, market conditions can differ. Research some products' life cycles. Then, for a specific product, identify the stage of its life cycle. Support your view by assembling advertisements on a poster board and making a short presentation to the class.

OBJECTIVES

- Summarize the basic principles of promotion
- Define the elements in a promotional mix
- Examine what's included in a promotional plan
- Discuss ways to budget for promotion

VOCABULARY

- 360° marketing
- advertising
- AIDA
- cooperative advertising
- CPM (cost-per-thousand)
- direct mail
- infomercial
- media
- networking
- newsgroup
- personal selling
- pitch letter
- premium
- press release
- product placement
- promotional campaign
- promotional mix
- publicity
- public relations (PR)
- sales promotion
- telemarketing
- trade-out
- visual merchandising
- Web banner

Think about this question:

Do you always believe advertisements?

Write your answer (yes or no) on a piece of paper. Give examples of believable and not-so-believable ads.

Principles of Promotion

Promotion is a type of communication and persuasion we find throughout our daily lives. It is also one of the Five P's (people, product, place, price, and promotion) in your marketing plan. To use promotion effectively, you should understand the basic principles behind it.

Getting Customers

AIDA is a popular communication model used by companies to plan, create, and manage their promotions. The letters in AIDA stand for the following steps in any type of promotion:

1. **Attention.** The first step when introducing a new product to a market is to grab the attention of potential customers. For example, using a well-known celebrity to introduce a product may cause people to take notice.

2. **Interest.** After you get people's attention, you want to keep it. To hold consumer interest, you need to focus your message on the product's features and benefits. Clearly communicate to potential customers how these features and benefits will specifically relate to them.

3. **Desire.** What can you do to make your product desirable? One way might be to demonstrate how the product works. Another tactic would be proving in some way that your product is a bargain.

4. **Action.** Don't forget to ask consumers to take action, to buy. You may also want to give them a reason to act right away. For example, a limited-time offer might motivate them. Another important part of this stage is making sure that purchasing your product is easy and convenient.

Keeping Customers

Most experts agree that promotional messages have to be repeated many times to maximize their effectiveness. In other words, for customers to remember what you want them to know and keep them coming back to buy again, promotion must be an ongoing process. One way to retain customers is by rewarding them. Frequent-buyer programs, special price offers, and thank-you notes or e-mails are possibilities.

To help keep your customers, stay aware of how your competitors are promoting their products. Also, continue to listen to your customers about what's important to them. When they buy, offer them immediate ways to provide you with feedback. This could include sending a coupon after they fill out a short e-mail survey. Another example is the questionnaire cards that some restaurants provide at their tables.

 **READING CHECKPOINT**   *What does AIDA stand for?*

Choosing a Promotional Mix

You should consider many forms of promotion when developing your marketing plan. The combination of promotional elements that a business chooses is called a **promotional mix**.

Elements in a Promotional Mix

The elements in a promotional mix are varied but also interconnected. All of them have common goals: to build a favorable awareness about your product and business, and to influence people to buy your product. The six elements of a promotional mix are:

- **Advertising.** A public, promotional message paid for by an identified sponsor or company.

- **Visual merchandising.** Using artistic displays to attract customers into a store. It also refers to how products are visually promoted inside a store.

- **Public relations (PR).** Activities aimed at creating goodwill toward a product or company.

- **Publicity.** A form of promotion for which a company does not pay. It is sometimes referred to as "free advertising."

- **Personal selling.** Direct (one-to-one) efforts made by a company's sales representatives to get sales and build customer relationships.

- **Sales promotion.** A short-term activity or buying incentive, such as conducting product demonstrations or providing coupons or free samples. Think of sales promotions as temporary "specials" used to motivate potential customers.

Each element of the promotional mix has advantages and disadvantages. As you think about how to balance the various elements in your mix, try to visualize how each relates to the others. Look for ways that one type of promotion can be used to back up or support another. This will help make the most of your promotional efforts.

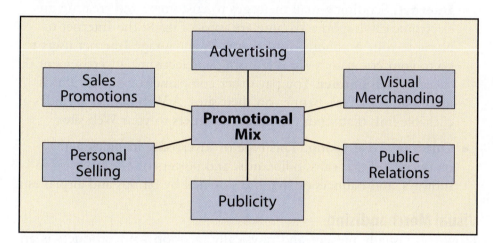

◀ **Figure 8-5**
Promotional Mix
To achieve your marketing goals, you should consider all forms of promotion.
Relating Concepts. *What factors determine the makeup of a promotional mix?*

Forms of Advertising

Advertising uses various **media**, or communication channels, to send promotional messages to potential customers. Advertising helps build a brand's image. Also, customers often perceive advertised products and services as being more valid or acceptable than nonadvertised items. However, because advertising can be expensive, you should focus on the types that will best reach your target market. Six of the most common types of advertising are:

- **Print Advertising.** Ads placed in newspapers, magazines, Yellow Pages, school yearbooks, and trade association directories are all examples of print advertising.

- **Direct Mail.** Another form of print advertising, **direct mail** is one-to-one communication. You can have it delivered specifically to individual customers in your target market. Brochures, print catalogs, fliers, postcards, sales letters, and newsletters are examples of direct mail.

- **Radio and Television.** This type of media has the advantage of reaching large numbers of people. It also has the added benefit of communicating with motion (in TV) and sound. However, creating the advertisements and purchasing the media time can be expensive. Most radio and television commercials are short: 15 to 30 seconds. **Infomercials**, usually produced as cable television shows, are product demonstrations that typically last from 30 minutes to an hour.

- **Product Placement.** This is a more subtle type of advertising. In **product placement**, a company pays a fee to have a product displayed during a movie or television show in a prominent or obvious manner. No mention is made of the product. The fact that a famous actor or other well-known personality is using it suggests to viewers that they, too, should buy it. When you see an actor drinking a bottle of Coca-Cola® in a television show, that's product placement.

- **Internet.** Sending e-mail messages to customers and creating an electronic catalog on a Website are ways of using the Internet to promote your product. Another way to encourage Internet users to go to your company's site is by using an electronic advertisement called a **Web banner**. You pay other companies or organizations to embed your Web banner on their sites. A Web banner includes a clickable link that sends potential customers to your Web site.

- **Outdoor Advertising.** This type of advertising includes signs on buses and taxi cabs, billboards, and posters on the street or in subways, and banners or streamers carried by blimps and airplanes.

Visual Merchandising

How you visually present and physically position your products is an important part of promotion. For example, how attractive are the displays in your storefront windows? Is there an eye-catching sign outside? Another example of visual merchandising is retailers positioning selected products at the ends of aisles or near checkout lines to draw customers' attention.

Companies that provide services should also consider the visual impact they make. A place of business that looks clean and well-organized sends a more positive message than one with dirty floors and windows. Even the arrangement of the furniture, and the comfort or pleasantness of a waiting room, can make a difference.

Public Relations and Publicity

Many companies have a public relations (PR) department to help build and maintain a positive image. As an alternative, a PR firm is sometimes hired to carry out the promotion. In either case, PR staff use publicity—non-paid advertising—to attract attention and create interest. Examples of activities and tools used to get publicity include the following:

- **News Articles and Announcements.** The PR staff works to develop good relationships with reporters in the local news media. They send a press release to the media whenever there is anything new or interesting involving the company. A **press release** is a written statement that typically consists of several paragraphs of factual information about a product or business. A reporter can use this information to create a printed news article or a feature story. Or it may become a news report read by radio and television announcers. A cover letter, called a **pitch letter**, is often sent with a press release to introduce it. One or more photos may also be included.

- **Community Events.** Sponsoring an event that promotes a good cause can create favorable publicity. For example, a business may plan a dinner, entertainment, or sports event in which all the money from ticket sales goes to a local charity group. A small amount of time during the program is sometimes used to provide information about the sponsoring company. Upcoming community events are also excellent reasons to send press releases.

- **Contests.** Contests help create excitement about your product or business by offering prizes to winners. They also provide opportunities to learn more about customers or to get their feedback. For example, ask customers who visit your store to drop a business card into a box for a contest drawing. Or, enter people into a contest after they complete a short survey. Like community events, contests provide an opportunity to send a press release.

FOR IMMEDIATE RELEASE
May 15, 20--
Contact: Maria Gonzales (555) 123-4567

Local High School Students to Teach Marketing Workshop for Community Teens

Anytown, NY — Wayne High School students Amy Chang, Tom O'Connor, and Brian Jones will be conducting a 5-day workshop for Anytown teenagers who want to learn how to market their own business.

The workshop will be held at the town hall June 16 to 20, from 7:00 to 9:00 PM. The workshop fee of $25 per person will include educational handouts. Participants will apply newly learned information in small-group activities.

According to Mrs. Anita Andretti, a teacher at Wayne High School, "These students want the opportunity to share some of what they learned in the Entrepreneurship course last semester. They feel it's important to contribute to the community."

For more information, please contact Maria Gonzales at (555) 123-4567.

▲ **Figure 8-6**
Press Releases
When writing a press release, be sure to answer these questions: Who? What? When? Where? Why?

Analyzing Information. *Using this press release, identify the answers to the five questions.*

Personal Selling and Sales Promotion

As mentioned earlier, sales staff meets and talks with customers person-to-person on a daily basis. This may occur on the phone, in the store, or at trade shows and conferences. Sometimes salespeople visit the places where customers work or do business. For example, a textbook salesperson may visit teachers at their schools, or a medical supplies salesperson may visit doctors' offices and medical clinics.

When salespeople meet with customers, they routinely leave a business card. They may also provide free samples of the company's product, or give them a **premium**. A premium is a giveaway item or free gift that usually has the company's name, address, and telephone number printed on it. T-shirts, pens, note pads, coffee cups, and calendars are all examples of premiums.

Networking

Networking is creating connections with people in the business world. A network is made up of like-minded businesspeople. Their goal is to exchange business ideas and information and to support each other. People who network share business skills and connections—usually in an attempt to increase revenue for their businesses. The relationships are mutually beneficial, meaning that people help each other and benefit from the give-and-take of the relationships. For that reason, the most successful networking relationships are long term.

Some types of businesses hold events where people can gather in a meeting place to network and build rapport. Later, these new connections will get together to assess whether there is a way they can work together. Some people network only in an attempt to find individuals who can help them. That is rarely the way to form a long-term relationship. Instead, the most successful people are those who spend their time listening as well as talking and thinking about how they can help others.

THINKING CRITICALLY

Inferring. How might a salesperson for copier machines and a caterer be able to help each other? Work with a partner to brainstorm mutual benefits each could derive from a networking relationship.

To read more about networking, go to "Your Business Career" on the Student Center at entrepreneurship.pearson.com.

Telemarketing, promoting or selling products or services one-to-one over the telephone, is another type of sales promotion. Telemarketing can be used in two different ways. Sales staff can talk directly with potential customers. Or, a recorded sales message can be played over the telephone by using an automated dialing system. You should take care when using telemarketing to avoid irritating potential customers. Calls made too frequently to the same numbers, or calling at the wrong times (such as dinner time), can annoy people.

Salespeople also use a technique called **networking** (see "Your Business Career," above.) to find new customers and promote products. Networking is meeting new people though current friends and business contacts. People you know refer you to people they know. In turn, these new people introduce you to more people. You can also meet new contacts at networking events. These are gatherings at which businesspeople meet and socialize with other entrepreneurs in their locality.

A form of electronic networking can be accomplished by using a **newsgroup**. A newsgroup is an online message board where people post information about a particular topic. These messages form an ongoing discussion. Although newsgroups are not used for advertising, they do help you "meet" new people and gain insights from potential customers.

360° Marketing

Some marketing professionals have recently come up with a new approach to marketing called **360° marketing**. This approach communicates with your prospects and customers from all directions; it blends low-tech and high-tech methods to deliver your message to customers in as many ways as possible. In some respects 360° marketing can be a cost-effective method of promoting your product. Its goal is to take advantage of every means possible to put your message in front of prospects and customers.

A 360° marketing mix might include a company Website, e-mails to existing customers, faxes, direct-mail postcards and catalogs, instant messaging, and telephone calls to customers alerting them to new promotions. It might mean becoming involved with the local community for networking possibilities and referrals. It could involve face-to-face meetings with prospects and customers in nonbusiness settings. Entrepreneurs who practice this sort of marketing take networking seriously. They join clubs, organizations, and online social networks. They offer free consultations and demonstrations.

An entrepreneur using 360° marketing might publish an online newsletter, write a blog, or host an online conference related to the company's product. In the future, more and more entrepreneurs will use the Internet and participate in the rich variety of channels and opportunities it offers to surround their prospects and customers with messages about their products.

 *What are six common types of advertising?*

Developing a Promotional Plan

A promotional plan for a new business must take into consideration three stages of a business start-up:

1. What promotions are needed *before* the business is opened?

2. What promotional adjustments will need to be made when the new business is launched?

3. What ongoing promotional strategies are needed?

Creating Campaign Strategies

Breaking down each stage of your promotional plan into one or more campaigns will help focus your efforts. A **promotional campaign** is a group of specific promotional activities built around a theme or goal. Each campaign provides descriptions of the media to be used, dates, quantities, costs, and other details. For example, in stage 1, your campaign could focus on:

- Establishing a favorable business image

- Educating your target market about the features and benefits of coming products

- Creating an awareness of where and when you will be opening

At stage 2, your campaign might include announcements that you are now open for business. Stage 2 also usually includes sales promotions to get people to try a product or service. As your customer base increases, your stage 3, or ongoing plan, should add strategies for keeping current customers loyal.

Keep in mind that you may need to vary your ongoing plan based on seasons or cycles in your industry. You may also need to make adjustments along the way if the target market, business environment, and competition change.

Measuring Promotion Effectiveness

In your promotional plan, don't forget to include ways to track responses that result from specific types of promotion. Setting up a computerized database will make it easier to record and analyze data. This information will help you decide what forms of promotion to use in the future. Here are some examples of tracking strategies:

- Ask customers where they first heard about your business.

- Create an ad with a coupon or other clip-out feature. Use the same ad for various print media sources, but include an individual code on each ad. When customers bring or send the clip-out to your business, you can identify which advertising source provided the best response.

- Compare sales results with the time and place that a particular promotion was offered. See if you can detect any correlation between the two.

- Pre-test potential advertisements before finalizing and submitting them to the media. For example, ask focus groups made up of your target market to view several versions of an advertisement. Their reactions and feedback can help you decide which ad would be most effective.

 *What three stages of a promotional plan must a new business take into consideration?*

Budgeting for Promotion

Your budget for promotion will be determined by four factors:

- Your business industry
- The strength of your competition
- Which media best reaches your target audience
- The funds you have available

Research Rates and Other Costs

After you have conducted a number of promotional campaigns, you will have historical data available to help estimate costs. In the meantime, if you're starting a new business, you'll need to do some research. Following are a few strategies you can use:

- Contact sales managers at radio and television stations, newspapers, and magazines to request a list of their rates. As an alternative, you can pay a subscription fee to access databases at SRDS® (Standard Rate and Data Service) Media Solutions® (www.srds.com).

- When you buy a TV or radio spot, you are purchasing the ability to reach the number of people who are watching or listening at that specific time. The Nielsen Company (www.nielsenmedia.com) and Arbitron, Inc. (www.arbitron.com) publish guides that provide audience delivery estimates for television and radio. Ask your media salesperson to help you calculate the **CPM (cost-per-thousand)** by using these guides. The CPM is the amount it will cost you to reach 1,000 potential customers with a particular advertising type and time slot.

- Factor in public relations and publicity costs. For example, if you plan to stage a community event, you may need to hire a catering service or other vendor.

- Research companies that produce promotional items and compare their prices. InkHead Promotional Products (www.inkhead.com), Superior™ Promos (www.superiorpromos.com), and Pinnacle Promotions (www.pinnaclepromotions.com) are just a few examples.

- Advertising agencies can help you create, plan, and manage advertising and other promotional activities. If you intend to hire such an agency, you will also need to include its fees in your budget.

Consider Low-Cost Promotion Strategies

If your promotional budget is low, here are some potential ways to keep costs down:

- **Swapping Services.** A **trade-out** is a bartering practice whereby you trade your company's products or services for air time on a radio station.

- **Cooperative Advertising.** When two companies share the cost of advertising, it is called **cooperative advertising** ("co-op" for short). For example, a wholesaler who distributes snack food and a convenience store retailer might work out an agreement to split advertising costs. Ask potential suppliers if they offer any co-op programs.

- **Testimonials and Endorsements.** If customers, news sources, or organizations praise your products or services, ask if you can quote them in brochures or catalogs or on your Website. If you join a trade organization or your local Better Business Bureau, this is a type of association you can mention in promotional materials. You can also use membership logos on business stationery.

After collecting all your research data, make a list of priorities. Outline a budget that includes the items at the top of your priority list. But keep in mind that you will probably need to adjust your budget over time.

 *What four factors determine your promotional budget?*

 Your Business Plan. Continue developing your standard business plan. Go to "Section 8.2" of the *Business Plan Project* in your *Student Activity Workbook*, or "Section 8.2" of the BizTech Software.

ASSESSMENT 8.2

Reviewing Objectives

1. Summarize the basic steps of the AIDA promotional model.

2. List the six elements of a promotional mix.

3. What are the three stages that you must take into consideration in the promotional plan for a new business?

4. What four factors will determine your promotional budget?

Critical Thinking

5. **Relating Concepts.** Describe an example of visual merchandising that recently attracted your attention. Did you buy the product you described in your example? Why or why not?

6. **Writing.** List two words or concepts you think would help persuade customers or grab their attention, if you were writing promotional material.

Working Together

Working in a group of three, create a newspaper or magazine advertisement. One member should write the text for the ad, and another should create art or take photos for it. The third member of the group should research media prices for different ad sizes and placements. Present a mockup of your ad to the rest of the class. Explain what you learned about the process of creating a print advertisement.

Social Studies
Advertising Timeline

Working in groups of four, use a word processing program, paper, or poster board to create a historical timeline showing key events and milestone ads in the advertising industry.

A New Spin on Biking

For Kelly Rapp, RAGBRAI®, which stands for the Des Moines **R**egister **A**nnual **G**reat **B**icycle **R**ace **A**cross **I**owa, was a fun-filled annual event. RAGBRAI began in 1973 as a challenge between two of the Des Moines paper's reporters, who were both avid cyclists. They wanted to find stories from a different perspective: riding a bike. From a few hundred riders that first year, the race has grown into the largest and longest bike tour in the world, with 10,000 riders (8,500 week-long riders and 1,500 daily riders). People can enter as individuals or as part of groups or teams. They can also enter as non-riders and travel along in a bus or other vehicle with their group. For many people, RAGBRAI is a tradition, where friends and families get together to enjoy a week of energizing riding, lots of delicious food, and some unique fun.

▲ *Kelly Rapp*

Turning Fun into Experience

After three years of riding alongside his father with their "Team White Bus," Kelly decided to work for one of the larger charter groups. He helped them with their tent service. "We had over 70 tents to set up and take down every day," he said. "The year I worked for them consisted of long hours, hard work, and low pay. Although this was not one of my most memorable experiences, I benefited by learning the business."

Along with this practical experience, Kelly had academic experience. He had taken many business classes in school, including Marketing and Sales, Introduction to Business, Accounting, Sports and Entertainment Marketing, Keyboarding, and Business Applications. "With help from these classes and my dad's business knowledge and experience," said Kelly, "I decided to end my employment with the charter company and start my own tent business." With his tent business, he could give ride participants a place to sleep at night while on the road.

Beginning a Business: Sleeping on the Road

Kelly's total target market was everyone who was a participant in the ride. He only needed a small group from that market to be successful. He had space for 15 people on his bus. If he could get more people on his bus, he could increase the number of customers and make more money. But the bus also carried supplies and paraphernalia. To allow more room on the bus for customers, Kelly added a support vehicle with a trailer behind it. This actually doubled Kelly's customer base from 15 to 30 people. To promote his business, he made flyers and sent them out.

Kelly works hard during the week of RAGBRAI. "We wake up at 5:30 and have tents down by 7:00. We load the trailer and drive to the next town. After finding a camp spot, we unpack and pitch the tents and then blow up air mattresses. By noon we are finished. After RAGBRAI is over, I check the tents and air mattresses and make sure they are ready for next year before storing them for the winter." Kelly's business has grown over the years, and he's hired two friends to help him. The income he makes during the summer provides his spending money for the entire year.

"I have made wonderful friends from all over the USA," said Kelly. "I love working for myself. I have more risk, but the profit and benefit have been much greater. I would tell anyone who wants to go into business to go for it!"

Thinking Like an Entrepreneur

1. Was Kelly's practical experience critical to starting his business? Why?
2. Are there events in your community that would serve as the basis for a business?
3. Which of Kelly's academic classes do you think were most relevant to his business?

CHAPTER SUMMARY

8.1 Developing Your Marketing Mix

A marketing plan is a detailed guide that includes marketing goals and strategies for meeting those goals. There are five main marketing strategy areas, called the Five P's: people, product, place, price, and promotion. How a company chooses to combine these elements defines the marketing mix. Your target market and employees make up the people element. Building a product image involves attracting new customers and keeping current ones loyal. Product strategies for doing this include branding and communicating product features and benefits. To determine place strategies, you should decide what distribution channels to use, where and when you will sell your products, and how you will transport and store them. Developing price strategies involves identifying objectives, selecting a basic price strategy (demand-based, competition-based, or cost-based), and making adjustments.

8.2 Promoting Your Product

You use promotion to build a favorable awareness about your product and influence people to buy it. A communication model for planning, creating, and managing promotion is abbreviated as AIDA: attention, interest, desire, and action. The many forms of promotion that make up a company's promotional mix can include advertising, visual merchandising, public relations (PR), publicity, personal selling, and sales promotions. When developing a promotional plan, you should consider what promotions you will need before opening a new business, when it is first opened, and as ongoing strategies. It's also important to include methods for measuring promotion effectiveness in your plan.

REVIEW VOCABULARY

Create an outline that could be used to develop a course that would teach high school entrepreneurs how to market products. Use only those terms from the following list that you think would be most important for them.

- 360° marketing (p. 228)
- advertising (p. 232)
- AIDA (p. 223)
- brand (p. 215)
- bundling (p. 221)
- cooperative advertising (p. 232)
- CPM (cost-per-thousand) (p. 231)
- direct channel (p. 216)
- direct mail (p. 225)
- distribution channel (p. 216)
- exclusive distribution (p. 218)
- indirect channel (p. 217)
- intermediary (p. 217)
- market share (p. 212)
- marketing (p. 211)
- marketing mix (p. 213)
- marketing plan (p. 211)
- media (p. 225)
- mind share (p. 216)
- networking (p. 228)
- personal selling (p. 225)
- pitch letter (p. 227)
- press release (p. 226)
- product mix (p. 215)
- product placement (p. 226)
- product positioning (p. 216)
- promotion (p. 214)
- promotional campaign (p. 229)
- promotional mix (p. 224)
- publicity (p. 224)
- public relations (p. 224)
- sales promotion (p. 225)
- telemarketing (p. 228)
- trade-out (p. 231)
- visual merchandising (p. 224)
- Web banner (p. 226)

CHECK YOUR UNDERSTANDING

Choose the letter that best answers the question or completes the statement.

1. Which of the following is *not* considered a one-to-one promotional strategy?
   a. telemarketing
   b. direct mail
   c. magazine advertisements
   d. personal selling

2. Which of the following is *not* considered a product "feature"?
   a. quiet
   b. colorful
   c. soft
   d. fun

3. Marketing plan goals should
   a. have a time frame
   b. be measurable
   c. be action-oriented
   d. all of the above

4. A group of specific promotional activities built around a particular theme or goal is called a
   a. promotional campaign
   b. community event
   c. contest
   d. none of the above

5. The percentage of a target market population that is buying a particular product or service from your business is called
   a. mind share
   b. market share
   c. market size
   d. markup percentage

6. Combining the price of several different items into one price is called
   a. a package
   b. a flat rate
   c. a unit rate
   d. bundling

7. What is the term used when two companies share advertising costs?
   a. co-op advertising
   b. trade-out advertising
   c. combination advertising
   d. dual advertising

8. Which of the following is *not* considered an intermediary?
   a. agent
   b. manufacturer
   c. retailer
   d. distributor

9. A communication model used by companies to plan, create, and manage promotion is
   a. ADIA
   b. AIDA
   c. IADA
   d. AAID

10. Which of the following is the *least* effective price strategy?
   a. Charge a slightly higher price than the competition when your product has more benefits.
   b. Set a high price when introducing a new, unique product into the market.
   c. After market share is gained, lower prices to improve profits.
   d. Lower prices to increase sales volume.

11. Which of the following is *not* a term related to radio or television advertising?
   a. trade-out
   b. premium
   c. infomercial
   d. CPM

12. The type of distribution that gives a retailer the sole right to sell a product is called
   a. intensive
   b. selective
   c. exclusive
   d. restrictive

Business Communication

13. Watch a popular recent movie or a successful sitcom. As you watch, keep a list of any product placement promotion that was used in the movie/show. Afterward, write a short essay about how the target market for the product placement tied to the audience.

14. Design and draw a brand mark for a real or imaginary product, service, or company. Then develop a short presentation explaining why you created this design.

15. Work in a group of four. Each member should research the advantages and disadvantages of a different type of advertisement (such as newspapers, magazines, television, radio, Web banners, and so on.). Together, create a chart on poster board that summarizes your combined research results.

Business Ethics

18. Work in groups of four. Research unethical advertising practices. Write a short presentation about these practices and how to avoid them. Develop ads that demonstrate these unethical practices. Ads can be on posters or magazine size. You can also create unethical television or radio ads that you would act out for the class. If your school has the capability, you could develop filmed or taped examples of unethical television or radio ads.

Business Math

16. Suppose you are calculating financial estimates for a new business. Based on research available to you, assume that the total sales your target market spends for your type of product is $500,000 per year. What annual sales amount will your company earn if it gains a 15% market share in its first year of business?

17. Imagine that you're a retailer who purchases a product at $2.50 per unit. Based on practices in your industry, you decide to use a 100% markup. What will the markup price (retail price) be for this item? Later in the year, you find that you are overstocked with this product. You decide to sell it "at cost" (the purchase, or wholesale, price) at a clearance sale. What will the markdown percentage be?

Business in Your Community

19. Working in a group, brainstorm an idea for a fundraising event at your school to benefit a local charity. Next, make a list of specific ways you may be able to get publicity for your event. What media resources should you contact? What local organizations might be willing to help spread the word? Then, write a press release about your upcoming event.

20. Interview someone who works at a local advertising agency, or an individual who designs advertisements for a living. Find out what's involved in running their businesses and how they got started in advertising. Also, ask about the creative processes they use to produce actual advertisements. Then, develop a short presentation describing what you learned.

Website Branding

Coca-Cola bottles, McDonald's Golden Arches, and the Nike "Swoosh" are ways companies have used to identify or *brand* their products. You know instantly which company it is and what it sells. Branding is a marketing strategy used to create an emotional attachment to a product or service. When it comes to Website branding, Google is at the top! To "Google" has become part of our language. Everyone immediately knows that Google provides a way to find information online—it is a **Web search engine**. Google's name is one part of its branding strategy. Its logo is another:

Names and logos as well as colors and **typefaces**—the design of printed characters (fonts)—are all elements in branding a company. Branding is important for Websites, as for other businesses; each must create a unique presence online.

Domain Name Branding

Google can be found at www.google.com. Usually, a Website's name is the same as its Web address. If the site's name and Web address are different, Website branding is more difficult. So users can find them easily, businesses want to have the same Web address and site name. **Domain name registration** provides a way to reserve a Web address. The company then uses this address in all marketing materials and as an e-mail address for the business. If the Website is www.goodstuff.com, for example, e-mail addresses for the business might be joe@goodstuff.com, jane@goodstuff.com, and so on. Web hosts—companies that rent out space online—can often set up both the Website and e-mail accounts, with a series of e-mail addresses, all listed at the same location.

Logos and Slogans

Creating a Website logo is an extremely important part of branding. People hire professional graphic designers to design an eye-catching logo. Logos need to be easy to read and distinct from logos that already exist online. A Website's logo says a lot about the site—a toy store will have a different style of logo from that of a law office. A **Website slogan** is a short phrase that describes what a company does. It, too, is an element of a company's brand. For example, the Website Ehow.com, which lists a series of how-to articles, has the slogan, "How to Do Just About Everything." The slogan appears just below the Website's logo. A slogan becomes a **catch phrase**, a phrase that is repeated so often that people use it without knowing its original context. Some with which you might be familiar are "We bring good things to life." (GE) and "Snap, crackle, and pop" (Rice Krispies).

Design Repetition

Design elements, such as the site logo, typeface, color, any unique graphics, and the company's slogan, should be repeated throughout the Website. Consistency—repeating the same thing—is an important element of branding and helps consumers recall the company, product, or service easily. Generally, businesses use the same logo and slogan in all their materials, from the Website to business cards, letterheads, printed brochures, and Web and TV advertisements. Another good place to put the company's logo and slogan is at the close of your e-mails, just after the signature. It's another opportunity to reinforce your branding.

Tech Vocabulary

- catch phrase
- domain name registration
- typeface
- Web search engine
- Website slogan

Check Yourself

1. Why is branding important?
2. What elements are included in branding?
3. What is a Website slogan?
4. Why is brand repetition important?

What Do You Think?

Comparing/Contrasting. Research five companies that you like. Do they have logos and Website slogans?

CHAPTER 9

SELLING YOUR PRODUCT

9.1 Principles of Successful Selling

OBJECTIVES

- Explain the importance of personal selling
- List the characteristics of successful salespeople
- Describe the main parts of the selling process
- Understand the key documents and forms used in selling

Most people have sold a product or service at some time. Based on your experience, answer this question:

Are you a good salesperson?

Write your answer (yes or no) on a piece of paper. Be prepared to discuss your answer.

The Importance of Personal Selling

As you learned in the previous chapter, personal selling is a promotional technique used by a company's **sales force**. Sales force is another term for salespeople or sales representatives. They are the company employees who are directly involved in the process of selling.

Personal selling has several advantages over other types of promotion:

- **Helps Build Personal Relationships.** Personal selling involves contact by means of face-to-face meetings and telephone calls. Videoconferences are another way to speak with customers. Many people appreciate the opportunity to provide feedback as well as receive information.

- **Allows for Customized Communication.** Because personal selling is an interactive form of communication, salespeople have the opportunity to adapt their message to each potential customer. When someone has questions or objections regarding a product or service, the salesperson can address them individually. **Objections** are the reasons that a customer may be reluctant or cautious about buying. Nonpersonal forms of promotion, such as media advertisements, cannot be easily adjusted, and making changes to them can be expensive.

- **Helps Reach Business Customers.** Personal selling's two-way method of communicating is especially effective for selling to business customers. Often several people at a company are involved in making purchasing decisions. By scheduling a group meeting, you can provide sales information to multiple individuals at one time.

 *Why is personal selling effective in dealing with customer objections?*

Characteristics of Successful Salespeople

Salespeople have various personalities and styles of selling. However, the most successful salespeople have the following characteristics:

- **Positive Attitude.** Successful salespeople focus on the positive, even when times are tough. When salespeople are genuinely excited about the product or service they are selling, their enthusiasm shines through in their conversation and actions. Choosing to keep an upbeat attitude makes work more productive, for the individual and for others in the sales force. It also has a positive effect on customers, which can lead to an increase in sales.

- **Good Listener.** Successful salespeople learn how to ask their customers quality questions and then listen closely without interrupting. The salesperson can then offer a solution for the specific situation. This flexible approach usually proves more effective than giving an identical sales pitch to everyone.

- **Persistent.** Selling is not as easy as some people make it look. Salespeople often make many contacts before making a sale. Patience and persistence are needed by all who wish to become successful. This is especially true for new salespeople with little experience. The good news is: the more you learn, the easier the selling process can become.

- **Hard Worker.** Salespeople who take responsibility for their own success make goals for themselves and then form strategies to reach them. They work hard to produce positive results, instead of blaming their company, the economy, or the competition for their problems.

- **Truthful.** Some salespeople tell customers only what they think they want to hear. This approach can lead to misunderstandings and deception. The result is often a breakdown in business/customer relationships. Reestablishing trust with a customer once it is broken can be difficult. In addition, customers who feel betrayed may tell others about their negative experiences. This can cause an even greater loss of sales and a bad reputation.

- **Consistent.** To become successful, you need to be dependable. That means you don't promise something you cannot deliver within a reasonable timeframe. The customer may get annoyed and decide to buy elsewhere. Another form of consistency is keeping in touch with your customers. This could include sending thank-you notes, birthday cards, newsletters, and such. Consistency builds trust, which leads to better customer relationships. In other words, it encourages customer loyalty to your brand or business.

▲ Figure 9-1
Customer Relationships
Interactive communication is a key part of personal selling.

Relating Concepts. *If you were interviewing a person for a sales position in your company, what characteristics would you look for?*

Remember, even though a salesperson is only one individual, he or she represents the company when dealing with customers. A customer often forms an opinion about an entire company based on the attitude and behavior of a single salesperson.

 *Why is being consistent important for a salesperson?*

The Selling Process

The phrase "selling process" is another way to refer to personal selling. This process is a cluster of activities used to obtain sales and build long-term relationships with customers. Although these activities are used for selling both products and services, the order in which they are performed may vary somewhat, depending on the particular situation.

The main steps in the selling process are:

- Finding and qualifying sales leads
- Preparing for a sales call
- Making the sales call
- Closing a sale and following up

Finding and Qualifying Sales Leads

The selling process starts by finding sales leads. A **sales lead** is a person or company that has some characteristics of your target market. Leads (as they are often called) are obtained in several ways:

- **Promotional Responses.** Some sales leads come directly from people who respond to various types of promotion. For example, information is obtained when people fill out surveys, information request cards at trade shows, Website forms, or mail-in postcards from magazines.

- **Referrals.** When a person provides contact information for someone else who may be interested in your product or service, it is called a **referral**. Referrals may be freely offered to a salesperson by a satisfied customer. They also may be obtained at networking events. In some cases, a fee is paid to a customer if the referral turns into a sale.

- **Data Mining.** The process of using a computer program to search large collections of electronic information (databases) and look for patterns or trends is called **data mining**. When applied to the selling process, data mining can be used to sort through huge amounts of material and pick out sales leads based on selected factors.

- **Cold Calls.** When a salesperson contacts someone he or she does not know, and without prior notice, it is called a **cold call**. Another name for cold calling is *canvassing*. Various types of mailing and telephone lists are available for purchase from companies that have made a business out of gathering information, organizing it, and selling it to others. Salespeople use these lists for cold calls.

Salespeople investigate a sales lead's characteristics. If a sales lead has many of the characteristics of the target market, including some key characteristics, the sales lead becomes a **prospect**, or potential customer. A key characteristic might be whether the customer has purchased a product similar to yours in the past or, for a business customer, if there is more than a certain number of employees. Keep in mind that not every sales lead turns into a prospect. To avoid wasting time in pursuing leads that have little chance of becoming prospects, you have to make an evaluation. This process is called "qualifying the lead." If the lead is a business, you may be able to qualify it as a prospect

Customer Word-of-Mouth

The things customers say to friends about a business often have a direct effect on its success. Imagine that you own a spa or an auto body shop. Both kinds of businesses usually get new customers from word-of-mouth. As an entrepreneur, what would you do to make sure your reviews and comments were positive?

Small-business owners everywhere know how important it is for customers to have a good experience. By going the extra mile to give good service and value, business owners are hoping their clients tell their friends. This kind of referral can be more effective than a television ad for increasing sales. Putting the customer first, with a policy of "the customer is always right," goes a long way toward building a positive reputation.

Customer word-of-mouth has now taken to the Web with review sites such as Yelp.com, giving people the opportunity to air their opinions of a business to a wide audience. Savvy small-business owners monitor these sites to see what their customers are saying. Some even adjust their operations based on the instant feedback.

THINKING CRITICALLY

Communicating. Think about three local businesses you heard about through word-of-mouth. Now, take a moment to consider which businesses you would like to promote in this way. What would you say to your friends about them?

To read more about word-of-mouth referrals, go to "Entrepreneurship Issues" on the Student Center at entrepreneurship.pearson.com.

by researching available public data on the business to see if there are certain key characteristics.

Many times, qualifying a sales lead requires making contact by telephone or in person. This is referred to as making a **sales call**.

Sales leads can lose their potential for becoming sales prospects for many reasons. For example, the person or business may no longer need your product or service due to having purchased something similar. Or, the sales lead may not be able to afford to buy at the current time. A sales lead may also lose its potential if the person you contacted has moved to a different locality or has left the company.

Preparing for a Sales Call

Before making a sales call, there are a number of things you should do to prepare:

- **Set Up an Appointment.** Many salespeople find that scheduling an appointment with a prospect is a successful approach to selling. It ensures that the person you want to see will be available when you visit. It also allows you to make sure you will be talking to the right person. For example, when making an appointment, ask if any other people need to be involved in the buying decision.

- **Learn About the Prospect.** During the process of setting up a meeting, the salesperson often has the opportunity to learn a little more about the prospect's current needs. Additional information may be gained by reading company reports and visiting the prospect's Website, if available. If the prospect was referred to you, you may also learn more by talking with the person who provided the contact information.

- **Know Your Product or Service.** A salesperson should make sure he or she knows as much as possible about the company and its products or services. The more knowledgeable you are about what you are selling, the more confident and relaxed you will likely be during sales calls.

- **Develop an Overall Selling Strategy.** Given what you know so far about the prospect, decide on the selling approach that will work best. Consider the aspects of your product or service that will appeal most to the prospect. Try to anticipate what questions or objections the prospect may have, and think about how you will answer. Keep in mind that you may need to change your strategy as you learn more about the prospect. In the meantime, it will help you plan and create the presentation for the scheduled sales call.

- **Write a Presentation Outline.** Plan what you want to say and what marketing materials you will show. If you are planning to demonstrate a product, practice those steps as well. If you are going to meet with a group of people, consider preparing an electronic presentation, such as PowerPoint slides. This is often an effective way of delivering a sales message. However, make sure you have all the necessary equipment and have practiced your presentation.

Making a Sales Call

Giving a sales presentation does not mean you will take center stage and do all the talking. The most effective presentations allow for plenty of give-and-take between the prospect and the salesperson. Here are some suggestions for making your sales calls more successful:

- **Be on Time.** Being punctual shows that you respect your potential customer and don't want to waste your customer's time. Plan carefully so you aren't late. If, for any reason, you are running late, call your customer to say so. If you are late, make sure to apologize to your customer.

- **Try to Build Rapport.** A word that comes from French, **rapport** (rah-POR) refers to an emotional connection between people, based on feelings of mutual trust and respect. To help build rapport, don't dive immediately into business talk when you arrive at a sales call. Take a little time to discover and talk about other things you may have in common. Sports, family, news events, and vacation plans are just a few possibilities. Pictures in the prospect's office may give you clues about possible subjects.

- **Ask Questions and Take Notes.** As you talk about the benefits of your product or service, ask the prospect questions. Try not to ask questions that only require a yes or no answer. Ask about things that will help reveal what needs, problems, feelings, and objections the prospect may have. During this process, take notes on key points the prospect makes. This will help you later to remember what is most important to the prospect. Taking notes also shows that you are listening and that you care about what the prospect has to say.

- **Answer Objections.** Often a prospect shows resistance to buying, either in words or by body language. When this happens, it is best to identify with the prospect and then ask for more details. For example, you might say, "I can understand why you feel that way." Then ask for more information, suggest options, and discuss other ways of solving the problem. If you don't know the answer to a question, be honest and say, "I don't know, but I'll find out for you as soon as possible."

▲ **Figure 9-2**
Sales Presentations
Sales presentations often include slides or a product display.
Inferring. *When making a sales presentation to a group, what can you do to make it more effective?*

- **Ask for a Commitment.** Asking for a commitment is an important part of closing the sale. Often, an indirect approach works well. For example, you might ask, "Now that I've addressed your concerns, is there anything else that might affect your decision to buy?" Or, you might ask about the product quantity, or delivery options. Another way of securing a commitment could be to offer an incentive. For example, you could provide a special discount if an order is placed immediately. In any case, never try to force a sale. If a prospect does not want to buy, it may be that the timing is not right but could be in the future.

Closing a Sale and Following Up

Technically, the final closing of a sale occurs after a product or service is delivered or provided, the prospect is satisfied, and the payment is received. So, after an order is taken, it is wise to follow up with the new customer to make sure that the entire process met his or her expectations. A happy customer will lead to a good relationship and additional sales.

Following up may also include asking a customer for referrals and written testimonials for use in promotional materials. Maintaining routine contact with a **sales account** (established customer) also helps a salesperson stay aware of possible changes in a customer's needs.

What's the difference between a sales lead and a prospect?

The Mechanics of Selling

Various documents and forms can help you organize, track, and process sales-related information. These are important for making sales operations run smoothly. Following are just a few examples of commonly used sales documents. Forms may be produced and used in a paper form. However, usually sales data is entered and tracked by using a computer.

- **Sales Call Logs.** You can use this form to record each telephone call you make to a prospect or to an established customer. Besides name and contact information, this form typically includes the date the call was made, the purpose, notes about the conversation (including objections and responses), and follow-up tasks (what and when). Many small entrepreneurs create their sales call logs by using an Excel spreadsheet.

Contact Name	Contact Information	Date of Call	Purpose	Notes	Follow-Up Tasks
John Simmons	Happy Pet 126 Alexandria Blvd. (415) 555-1236	11/30/--	Have Happy Pet carry our line of natural dog treats.	Was interested but concerned that he hadn't heard of us.	Send him sales kit, with video of Channel 12's feature on us. Check back in a week.

▲ *Sales Call Log*

- **Sales Proposals.** Prospects that are businesses often issue a **request for proposal (RFP)** when they are interested in buying a quantity of products or services or a customized order. An RFP is a formal way of asking a company to make a bid for a sale. It includes details about what the prospect wants. A business may send an RFP to three or four companies. Each interested company then prepares a sales proposal tailored to the RFP. The prospect then compares the proposals and makes a decision.

- **Order Forms.** Salespeople may use paper order forms to record orders when they do not have access to the company's computer. Order forms may vary in appearance, but most include the elements shown in Figure 9-3. Frequently, an order form is made up of multiple identical pages. When the salesperson fills out the form, duplicate or triplicate copies are automatically made. One of these copies is usually given to the customer.

Order Form

Date
Salesperson

Address

Sold To	Ship To
Phone	Ship By

Quantity	Item/Description	Price/Item	Subtotal

Total	
Sales Tax	
Shipping Charge	
Amount Due	

FORM FROM WWW.ENTREPRENEUR.COM/FORMNET/SALESFORMS.HTML

◀ **Figure 9-3**

Order Form
Most order forms include a place for sales tax, which is calculated by multiplying the purchase total by the tax rate.

Solving Problems. *If the purchase amount is $50 and the tax rate is 5%, how much is the sales tax?*

- **Sales Receipts.** Most retail and service businesses use electronic cash registers for sales transactions. A cash register totals the items being purchased, calculates sales tax, and produces a sales receipt for the customer. In addition to sales figures, this receipt often lists short descriptions of items purchased, the date, and how the items were paid for (cash or credit). Sales receipts are usually required by a business when a customer wants to return or exchange a product.

- **Sales Contracts.** The seller or the buyer may draw up a contract when a sale involves many details or is complex. Contracts are also used when a service or product is being delivered over a long period of time. A sales contract provides legal protection for both the seller and buyer. In most cases, contracts are reviewed by each party's attorney before they are signed.

 *How can an RFP be helpful to a salesperson?*

 Your Business Plan. Continue developing your standard business plan. Go to "Section 9.1" of the *Business Plan Project* in your *Student Activity Workbook*, or "Section 9.1" of the BizTech Software.

Reviewing Objectives

1. What are the main advantages that personal selling has over most other forms of promotion?

2. Name six characteristics of successful salespeople.

3. Describe the main steps in the selling process.

4. What are four types of documents or forms used in the selling process?

Critical Thinking

5. **Recognizing Patterns.** Thinking about your own buying experiences, what characteristics do you most appreciate in a salesperson? What selling behaviors have you witnessed that decreased your desire to buy? Why?

6. **Drawing Conclusions.** What could happen if you fail to follow up with a customer after a sale is made? What advantages might you gain from asking the customer for feedback?

Working Together

Working with a partner, choose a specific product or service. Pretend that you are a prospect for this item and write an imaginary profile of yourself. Then exchange profiles with your partner. Based on the information in the profile and what you know about the principles of successful selling, take turns role-playing as the prospect and as the salesperson. When finished, share with the class what you learned during the experience.

Language Arts
Persuasive Writing

Research the elements involved in persuasive writing. How could you apply the basic concepts you've learned to the process of writing a persuasive sales proposal?

9.2 Estimating Sales

OBJECTIVES

- Consider who may be needed in your sales force
- Identify costs related to a sales force
- Explore methods used to estimate sales

VOCABULARY

- commission
- direct sales force
- external sales
- internal sales
- order getting
- order taking
- salary
- sales forecast
- sales quota
- sales support
- sales territory

Think about this question:

Why would a company need to estimate its future sales?

Be prepared to explain your answer in class.

Sales Force Planning

You need to plan for your sales force as you develop and refine your marketing plan. Use your sales goals to shape your plans. If you discover that your goals are unrealistic at any point, you need to reevaluate them and make adjustments. Your sales force planning should answer such questions as:

- What selling methods do you plan to use? (External and internal selling methods are discussed later in the chapter.)

- Who do you need in your sales force?

- How much and what type of training do you need for your sales force?

- How large a sales budget do you need so you can pay your sales force?

- What estimated amount of sales can you expect the sales force to achieve over a specific time period?

External Selling Methods

External sales are obtained by hiring another company to do the selling for you. By using this approach, you can have a large sales force without hiring employees. Another advantage to external selling includes the potential to sell more of your products or services over a larger geographical area, even nationally. Also, you usually do not have to pay for the service until your customers actually pay you.

External selling can also involve hiring individuals who will remain independent of your company. These external salespeople, also called sales agents, are contracted by your business. Like sales companies, external salespeople typically are not paid for their work until after you receive payment from your customers. Because sales agents are not employees, they also normally pay for their own expenses. These could include travel, office, telephone, and office supplies.

A disadvantage of the external selling approach is that you have little control over the sales force. As a result, following up with your customers may be more difficult. It may also be harder to develop stable, long-lasting relationships with customers.

Sales agents and companies you hire to sell for you often are also selling products or services for someone else. As a result, they might promote other products more strongly than yours. Established products are usually easier to sell than new ones. They may focus more on selling products that offer a greater income potential than yours do.

Internal Selling Methods

Internal sales are obtained by you or your employees who sell your products or services exclusively. This method gives you the most control over all aspects of the sales process. Internal salespeople are often referred to as a **direct sales force**, because they work directly for you as full-time employees.

A disadvantage of internal sales is that your company has to pay the costs related to selling. This usually means paying your sales team for their work and expenses even if the customers have not yet paid you.

Initially, you may be the only one who does the selling. This solo approach may be sufficient when you first begin your business. Or, you may have to choose this option because you cannot afford to pay anyone else. However, it's a good idea to sketch out a plan for expanding your sales force in the future. Using the Internet is another potential way to successfully sell your products with fewer salespeople.

Types of Roles in a Sales Force

When determining how many salespeople you will need, think about the various roles you need to fill. Also keep in mind that sales roles are not exclusive. That is, one individual may perform more than one of the following:

- **Order Getting.** A sales role in which the primary responsibilities are finding prospects, presenting the product or service, and helping to close sales is called **order getting**. Larger companies may break down order getting into more specialized groupings. For example, they may divide salespeople into those who do consumer selling and those who do business-to-business selling. Order getters are salespeople who actively locate and contact sales leads, give presentations to prospects during sales calls, address customer objections, and ask for order commitments. In a service business (such as a promotion company, ad agency, Web design firm, lawn mowing company, baby sitter, disc jockey, hair cutter, and so on), order getting is referred to as new business development.

- **Order Taking.** A sales role in which the primary responsibility is recording and processing orders from customers who seek out your product or service is called **order taking**. For example, when a customer telephones a company to place an order from a catalog, the person who answers the call and takes down the information is an order taker. Retail clerks who stand behind store counters, assist customers, and process purchases through a cash register are also considered order takers.

- **Sales Support.** Positions that mostly involve assisting others with selling activities are sometimes called **sales support**. For example, trainers who teach and coach salespeople are often considered sales support. Office assistants to salespeople are another example. Sometimes sales support people are also assigned to do any follow-up needed after a sale is made.

What is the difference between an external sales method and an internal sales method?

Expenses Related to a Sales Force

After you have considered what selling methods you'd like to use and what kind of sales force you'll need, the next step is to estimate the costs related to your sales plan. There are three basic expenses related to a sales force:

- Compensation
- Training
- Miscellaneous Costs

How Salespeople Are Paid

There are three main options for compensating salespeople:

- **Salary Only.** A **salary** is a fixed amount of money that an employee is paid on a regular basis, such as weekly, biweekly, bimonthly, or monthly. A salary is paid regardless of the amount of sales the person makes. This payment method is sometimes referred to as a flat salary or straight salary because it does not include any selling incentives. Although a salary gives the salesperson a stable income, it does not provide motivation for selling a lot of product.

- **Commission Only.** A **commission** is an amount paid based on the volume of products or services that a salesperson sells. Usually, a commission is a percentage of the total amount sold. Because a salesperson on straight commission only gets paid if he or she sells something, this approach is directly tied to work performance and results. A disadvantage of paying straight commission is the difficulty in attracting and keeping experienced salespeople. They know that budgeting finances can be difficult when sales can vary widely from month to month. People who are paid this way may also have difficulty getting loans or credit cards from banks that look for stable incomes.

- **Base Salary Plus Commission.** Most often, salespeople are paid with a combination of salary and commission. The challenge is to find the proportional mix that works best for your company. The right balance will help motivate your sales staff to do their best and also encourage company loyalty.

In addition to salaries and commissions, some companies choose to include extra monetary incentives, such as a bonus for salespeople who sell more than their quota. A **sales quota** is a target amount of sales per month or quarter that a salesperson is expected to achieve.

Sales quotas are one way of evaluating a salesperson's work performance. If someone consistently misses a sales quota, and most of the other salespeople are meeting theirs, some type of action is usually taken. However, if few are making their sales quotas, it may mean you've set the quotas too high.

Dressing for Success

You probably dress a lot like other students in your high school. You probably think it is important to dress so you will fit in. In this respect, school isn't that much different from the work world. The first thing an employer or a prospective customer will notice about you is what you're wearing. Dressing in a certain way won't get you a job or make the sale, but first impressions are important. When you interview with a prospective employer, wear clothing that makes you fit in with those who work at the company. Don't overdress, but don't underdress either. You should want the employer to feel that you take the job seriously. Make sure you are well-groomed and that your hair is neat. Body piercings are often not part of the look of conservative businesses, so they should not be visible. Keep jewelry to a minimum. Regardless of what you are wearing, your clothing should be neat and clean.

If you don't know what to wear to an interview, don't be afraid to do some detective work. You may know someone who works at the company who can provide information, or you could check the company's Website for pictures of employees. You can also call the business's human resources department for tips. If you are serious about doing well in an interview, dressing for success is an important first step.

THINKING CRITICALLY

Comparing/Contrasting. Think about the local businesses you know. How do the people who work in a bank dress differently from those who work in, for example, your school? Think of other examples of local businesses and what their employees wear. Prepare a table comparing the attire worn by ten different types of businesspeople.

To read more about dressing for success, go to "Your Business Career" on the Student Center at entrepreneurship.pearson.com.

Sometimes a sales quota for a particular salesperson is based on the type and size of the **sales territory**. A sales territory is the specified geographical area for which a salesperson is responsible, such as a city, county, state, or region. The sales quota for a small area with a very high population density will probably be different from the quota for a larger area with a low population.

Sales Training

Most businesses that employ a sales force provide extensive training for new salespeople. Even newly hired individuals with lots of selling experience need a great deal of information. Some of the subjects taught in company training programs are:

- **Company Information.** Like other new employees, salespeople need to learn about the history of your company, its goals and business policies, how it is organized, and how it operates.

- **Product or Service Knowledge.** The more your sales force knows about what they are selling, the more successful they can be. This includes a product's physical features, how it works, and any service options available. Perhaps even more important are the personal benefits customers will get from buying your product or service.

- **Target Market Characteristics.** Salespeople will need to know the characteristics of your target market. They also need to understand the motives that most often cause your potential customers to buy your type of product or service. In other words, what are your target market's primary concerns? What is most important to them?

- **Information on the Competition.** Sales training would not be complete without knowing as much about the competition as possible: who they are, how their products or services compare to yours, what your business does better than other companies, and so on.

▼ Figure 9-4

Nonverbal Communication
Crossed arms may indicate that the person is feeling resistant or defensive.

Communicating. *What other nonverbal clues could you look for when meeting with a prospect?*

- **General Selling Techniques and Mechanics.** Knowing the fundamentals of selling and communication is key for all salespeople. This consists of sales approaches, speaking and presentation skills, good listening skills, how to interpret the nonverbal clues of prospects, and how best to handle prospects' objections to buying. The general forms, documents, and procedures used by your sales force should also be included.

- **Technology Skills.** Salespeople should also be taught how to use any special equipment and computer software programs they need to perform their jobs well. Technology can provide a number of tools to help your sales team work efficiently and stay organized.

Training does not end after a new salesperson has completed your company's initial training program. Most businesses provide periodic meetings or seminars that help their salespeople stay current with the latest information on the company, its products or services, and the competition. Because salespeople are often geographically widespread, there is a growing trend to provide more training electronically. This includes use of the Internet, downloadable files and programs, and CD-ROMs or DVDs.

Sales Expenses

As we have discussed, most companies pay salespeople for travel expenses related to their work. These expenses usually include airfare, rental cars, taxis, road and bridge tolls, hotels, and meals. Each salesperson must obtain receipts when these items are paid for and create a report that lists each item. Then they turn in this expense report with the receipts for repayment. Depending on the company, expense reports may be submitted weekly, monthly, or based on some other time period.

 *What are the three main options for compensating salespeople?*

Sales Forecasting

A **sales forecast** will be a key part of your company's financial planning process. A sales forecast is a prediction of the amount of future sales your company expects to achieve over a certain period of time. Think of a sales forecast as a tool to help evaluate the health of an established company or the feasibility of a new business venture.

Preparing a Sales Forecast

Sales forecasts for established companies are usually based on past sales performance. A forecast also takes into account such factors as the current economy, sales trends, company goals and capabilities, and what the competition is currently doing. There are four general steps in preparing a sales forecast:

1. Analyzing current conditions.

   Analyze the current company and market conditions. Do this through market research and by updating your SWOT analysis chart to analyze strengths, weaknesses, opportunities, and threats.

2. Reviewing past sales.

   Review your company's past sales figures. You can usually use past sales to project future sales. Sales often show seasonal variations. For example, you would sell more skis and sleds in the winter and more shorts and sandals in the summer. If you do not have past sales data because you are starting a new business, you will need to research general sales history for your industry. You can obtain this information from industry associations and by asking similar businesses outside your area.

3. **Making educated predications about the future.**

   Is there something in the future that could cause a change in your future sales? Will you need more or less promotion, or perhaps different types of promotion? Will you need more employees to accommodate these changes? Should you increase or decrease prices?

4. **Estimating your future sales for a specific time period.**

   Ask yourself if these sales will bring in more income than you expect to spend. Will these sales be enough to make a profit?

Sales Forecasting Techniques

There are many methods for estimating sales. Often, more than one technique is used to help make predictions as accurate as possible. This is because most techniques cannot take into account all of the factors that can impact sales.

If you plan to work with a bank to help finance your new business venture, you will probably want to make multiple sales forecasts. For example, make one that represents a best-case scenario, one for a worst-case scenario, and one in between. This will lend more credibility to your business plan.

Here are some common forecasting techniques:

- **Full Capacity.** This technique is pretty simple: you forecast selling as many products (or performing as many jobs) as you can. Often a young entrepreneur who is going to school has only so much time to devote to the business. For example, if you can spend 10 hours a week making candles, and you can make 20 candles an hour, your full capacity for a week would equal 200 candles. If it turns out that you can't sell all you can make, you'll need to adjust your forecast.

- **Observational Data.** One of the best ways to forecast sales is to observe your competitors' customers. For example, if you are opening a restaurant, you could sit in the restaurants your target customers frequent that are near your desired location. You could note such things as the number of customers who ate in the restaurant, how much they spent, and what they ate. This data would help you forecast your own sales.

- **Industry Standards.** To make a proper sales forecast, you will need to know how sales are estimated in your particular industry. For example, consultants, technicians, and designers are usually paid by the hour. In contrast, sales forecasts for retail stores are sometimes based on sales per square foot. (So, for a retail store's sales forecast, you would need to find out the annual sales per square foot for similar types and sizes of stores, in locations similar to yours. You would average the results, and then multiply that dollar figure by the estimated floor space of your business.)

- **Industry/Seasonal Cycles.** Keep in mind the particular buying phases that apply to your industry. For example, some retail businesses do about 50 percent of their annual sales from the end of October to the end of December. Fireworks companies, on the other hand, do almost all of their business around July 4th. So vary your monthly sales estimates based on appropriate market cycles.

◀ **Figure 9-5**

Sales Cycles
Florists are an example of an industry greatly affected by sales cycles.
Predicting. *In what months do you think florists sell the most? Why?*

- **Team Effort.** Many businesses find that getting multiple groups of people involved in the forecasting process is helpful. You get a broader perspective on issues when you ask customers, salespeople, sales support, and company executives to all provide feedback.

- **Number of Customers versus Distance.** This technique is used primarily by businesses in which the customer must visit a physical store to make purchases. Examples include a hair or nail salon, a dry-cleaning business, and a car-wash. You would determine the number of households living within one mile of your business location that use your product/service. Then estimate how much they will spend for these items per year. Estimate what percentage of money they will spend with you as compared with your competitors. You can use this technique with other distances, such as five miles and ten miles. Estimated sales figures usually get lower as the distance increases.

- **Market Share.** If the main portion of your goods is sold via the Internet or by catalog, you first estimate your market share in terms of customers in your shipping range. Then calculate how often and how much the people in your market share

Selling Your Product ● **257**

might buy from you per year. Your annual sales estimate could be calculated as:

Number of Customers	×	Number of Purchases per Year	×	Average Amount of Each Purchase

- **Proportional Scaling.** You should estimate sales separately for each product or service you sell. For each item, first estimate the quantity you think you will be selling six months from now. Then calculate the total of all sales per day. Next, multiply the sales per day by the number of days per month that you will be open for business. This determines the total sales per month. Using this as your goal for month 6, build up estimated monthly figures gradually, from little or no sales when the business first opens in month 1 to that monthly figure you calculated for month 6. Then gradually scale up your sales for months 7 through 12.

 **READING CHECKPOINT** *What are the four general steps taken in sales forecasting?*

 Your Business Plan. Continue developing your standard business plan. Go to "Section 9.2" of the *Business Plan Project* in your *Student Activity Workbook*, or "Section 9.2" of the BizTech Software.

ASSESSMENT 9.2

Reviewing Objectives

1. Define three roles you are likely to find in a sales force.
2. What cost-related factors do you need to include in your plan for a sales force?
3. Why is it important to make more than one type of sales forecast?

Critical Thinking

4. **Inferring.** Electronic training documents can be kept up-to-date more quickly and easily than printed ones. What other benefits might be gained by conducting training electronically? What disadvantages might there be?
5. **Applying Concepts.** Besides salary, commission, and bonuses, what other things do you think would motivate salespeople to do their very best work?

Working Together

Team up with a classmate to research computer software products that perform sales forecasting functions. Create a chart in Microsoft Word or Excel, or draw one on poster board, that compares major features and prices. Based on your research, make a recommendation to the rest of the class and explain the reasons behind your choice.

Science
Making Predictions

Like businesspeople, scientists make predictions based on a combination of current observations and historical data. Find out what methods scientists use to predict the strength and time or location for *one* of the following: earthquakes, volcano eruptions, tornados, or hurricanes. Then write an essay that compares how scientific methods compare with the methods businesspeople use to make forecasts. How are they alike? How are they different?

E-Media Mogul

When Timothy "Chip" Lowe was in middle school, two of his teachers wanted Websites. As Chip puts it, "They were willing to pay." He didn't know much about creating Websites, but he decided to take on the challenge. He did it successfully and his business began. He expanded his skills when the owner of a childcare facility needed a new technician to record her annual graduation ceremony. Chip did the recording and took it a step further by producing and selling DVDs to parents of the preschoolers.

Taking Advantage of New Technology

As a ninth-grade student at The Academy of Entrepreneurship at F.W. Buchholz High School in Gainesville, Florida, Chip won first place in the Sunkist Challenge Viral Advertising Campaign. Viral advertising is a form of marketing that takes advantage of technology. Chip's viral ad campaign used what he called five essential viral markets. They were the iPhone market, the TXT MSG (text messaging) market, the Internet market (using Facebook), the bottle market (using slogans on the back of the actual Sunkist bottles), and the music market (using QTrax to deliver digital music). For each component, Chip demonstrated a possible text message or other way that Sunkist could promote its products.

Chip has five active Websites and three in production. He produces graphic designs, Websites, CDs, and DVDs for two recording artists. He also does DVDs annually for two childcare graduation services. And he is launching a new hosting and e-mail service.

Pleasing the Customer

To Chip, being successful means making the customers feel important and providing them with good value for service and pricing. Although much of his business is done online, he also needs to provide physical media: paper, CDs, and DVDs. At the beginning, Chip was using a low-quality printer and sometimes had to make several copies before getting an acceptable copy. Later he acquired a new color laser printer that provides much better quality. He's also learned how to cut down the time it takes to make the CDs and DVDs.

▲ *Timothy Lowe*

"As you progress in any business," said Chip, "you learn tricks and simple ways to increase productivity."

Chip plans on growing his company to become a well-known brand. He wants to expand to consumer-friendly Web-based services. He has three secrets of success that have helped him so far and will be the foundation of his future growth. They are:

- Do only what you know how to do, and do it extremely well.
- Never sell a product or service you know is faulty or inadequate.
- Always aim higher than your customers' expectations so they become return customers.

Thinking like an entrepreneur

1. Have you ever used or seen viral marketing? Can you think of other components of viral marketing you would use?
2. How can you help customers become return customers?
3. Would you add anything to Chip's secrets of success, or do you think his three are enough to serve as the foundation for future growth?

CHAPTER SUMMARY

9.1 Principles of Successful Selling

Personal selling is a promotional technique used by a company's sales force to help build customer relationships, address customer questions and objections, and reach business customers more effectively. Some of the characteristics of successful salespeople include having a positive attitude, being a good listener, being persistent, working hard, and being truthful and consistent. You start the selling process by finding and qualifying sales leads through promotional responses, referrals, data mining, and cold calls. Next, you prepare for a sales call, which includes setting up an appointment, learning about the prospect, knowing your product or service, developing an overall selling strategy, and writing a presentation outline. When meeting with the prospect, you try to build rapport, ask questions, take notes, answer objections, and ask for a commitment. The last steps in the selling process are the closing of the sale and following up with the sales account.

9.2 Estimating Sales

Include sales planning as you develop your marketing plan. One part of sales planning is deciding whether to use external or internal selling methods. External sales are obtained by hiring another company to do the selling for you. Internal sales are obtained by you or your employees selling your products or services. A sales force includes the order getters, the order takers, and the sales support. The next step is to estimate costs related to your sales plan. You need to make decisions about compensation: salary, commission, or a combination of the two. Sales training and travel expenses are two other costs related to the sales force. Finally, you make a sales forecast that predicts the amount of future sales your company expects to achieve over a certain time period. It includes analyzing current company and market conditions, reviewing your company's past sales figures, making educated predictions about change and opportunity, and then estimating sales based on your research.

REVIEW VOCABULARY

Imagine that you have the sales support position of training a sales force. Create a PowerPoint presentation that introduces new salespeople to the basics of selling. Use at least 12 of the following terms in your presentation:

- cold call (p. 242)
- data mining (p. 242)
- direct sales force (p. 250)
- external sales (p. 249)
- internal sales (p. 250)
- objections (p. 239)
- order getting (p. 250)
- order taking (p. 251)
- prospect (p. 242)
- rapport (p. 244)
- referral (p. 242)
- sales account (p. 246)
- sales call (p. 243)
- sales force (p. 239)
- sales forecast (p. 255)
- sales lead (p. 242)
- sales quota (p. 252)
- sales support (p. 251)
- sales territory (p. 253)

CHECK YOUR UNDERSTANDING

Choose the letter that best answers the question or completes the statement.

1. The approach that gives you the most control over the selling process is
   a. external selling
   b. direct selling
   c. internal selling
   d. none of the above

2. A common term used to identify people who are directly involved in the selling process is
   a. sales callers
   b. sales force
   c. selling machine
   d. none of the above

3. All of the following are examples of sales support positions *except*
   a. trainers who teach and coach salespeople
   b. office assistants to salespeople
   c. retail clerks
   d. support people who perform follow-up after the sale

4. The number of sales per month or quarter that a salesperson is expected to achieve is called a
   a. commission
   b. bonus
   c. sales target
   d. sales quota

5. The most successful salespeople
   a. tell customers what they want to hear
   b. know how to listen and ask questions
   c. don't have to make many sales calls
   d. push until the prospect finally says yes

6. Sales forecasting can involve
   a. a team effort
   b. industry cycles
   c. sales history
   d. all of the above

7. In the selling process, prospecting involves all of the following *except*
   a. asking for a commitment
   b. asking for referrals
   c. data mining
   d. following up with trade show attendees

8. What legal document is often issued when a sale is complex, detailed, or occurs over an extended period of time?
   a. sales receipt
   b. sales contract
   c. order form
   d. none of the above

9. When making a sales forecast, it is a good idea to
   a. use only one forecasting technique
   b. focus on just the current month's sales
   c. update your SWOT analysis charts
   d. none of the above

10. A sale is closed when
    a. the salesperson asks for a commitment
    b. the product or service is delivered
    c. an order is placed
    d. the customer is satisfied and payment is made

11. What method of payment is most often used to compensate salespeople?
    a. base salary plus commission
    b. salary-only
    c. commission-only
    d. straight commission plus bonus

12. In the selling process, contacting someone you do not know, without prior notice, is called a
    a. sales call
    b. promotional call
    c. cold call
    d. prospect call

Business Communication

13. Working with a partner, research techniques for improving active listening skills. Practice these skills with each other, with one person taking the role of speaker and the other the role of listener. For three to five minutes, the speaker should talk about a topic such as "What I want to do with my life" or "What I most enjoy doing." Afterward, the speaker should give feedback to the listener on the listening skills demonstrated. Then switch roles and repeat the process.

14. Research design tips to create effective Power-Point slides. Create a slide show that demonstrates examples of "good" and "bad" design.

15. Research characteristics that help make a speaker successful. Then, listen to two talks by different speakers (on tape, television or in person). Take notes on how well you think each speaker communicates. Afterward, make a list of things you think each speaker could do to improve.

Business Ethics

18. Write an essay on the topic of "How Lying Impacts the Selling Process." Explore reasons that sales-people who lie increase customers' resistance to buying rather than lowering it. Then work with a group to act out a scene in which a salesperson lies in the selling process. Finally, with the same group, act out the same scene, but this time show a sales-person acting ethically, without lying. Try to have the salesperson demonstrate all six characteristics of successful salespeople.

Business Math

16. Suppose you want to open a retail drug store. You've already determined you will need sales of $250,000 by the end of the first year to make a profit. Your sales forecast predicts that you can capture 25% of the population within a two-mile radius of your store as customers. Your research indicates the following: (a) There are 5,000 people within two miles of your store; (b) Customers will visit your store fives times a year and spend an average of $35 per visit. Based on this data, will you meet your annual sales projection of $250,000?

17. Suppose the sales tax rate in your state is 4.75%. What is the sales tax amount on a $155.02 purchase? A $2,549.99 purchase?

Business in Your Community

19. Attend a sales demonstration or presentation in your local community. What selling techniques were used? From a prospect's perspective, what do you think could have been done to make the dem-onstration more effective?

20. Interview a salesperson in your community. Find out what the salesperson likes best and least about the work. Also, ask about the preparation for a sales call or other interaction with potential customers.

Web Hosts

Think of a traditional business renting a "brick-and-mortar" storefront. The business owner rents the space and pays a landlord every month. Web hosting works in a similar fashion. The owner of a Website rents space online from a Web host. A traditional storefront needs floor space, shelves for merchandise, and a cash register. A Website owner needs a place for Web graphics, such as pictures, video, and text. The Website owner can upload (transfer) new graphics, text, or video to the Web host. Just as the owner has a key to the store, the Website owner logs in to the Web host using a unique username and password so that no one else can access the site.

Web hosts commonly provide tools that help someone set up a site. These tools typically include Web design tools, e-mail accounts, and domain name registration. For e-commerce sites—sites that are selling a product—Web hosts also typically include shopping cart technology.

Keeping Web Servers Online

Web hosts use Web servers to store information for every site using that Web host. In a sense, a Web server is the Web host's brain. If a Web server stops working, due to a malfunction or other problem, no one can access the site. To prevent this, the Web host typically uses several Web servers at the same time, all containing the same information and often placed in different locations. If there's a problem at one Web server location, another server will make sure the site is still up and running. The amount of time a Website is online is called **uptime**. Web hosts generally promise that a Website will be online 99.9% of the time.

Types of Web Hosts

There are many opportunities to set up a Website by using a **free Web host**. Blogging software, such as Blogger, is free to use, as is setting up a page at MySpace.com. Most free Web hosts are limited in the types of Websites you can create. For instance, MySpace allows you to create a MySpace page, which is different from creating a unique, independent Website.

Shared Web hosting is the process of sharing server space with other Websites. Compare this to a **dedicated server**, which gives a Website its own server space. Very large, complex sites may need a dedicated server. Most personal and small-business Websites use shared Web hosting.

Web Hosting Costs

For a small Website, renting space on a Web host can cost as little as $5 a month. However, it can cost the Website owner more if the Website gets a lot of visitors. For example, a Web hosting package may allow for 5,000 visitors a day (these are also called **Web hits**). If the site goes over 5000 hits, the Website may go off-line so that it can't be accessed unless you pay an additional fee. This is similar to a cell phone plan that has a limited number of minutes, after which you incur extra charges. If a Website starts getting a lot of "traffic" (yet another word for visitors), the owner of the Website will need to upgrade to a different plan—usually with the same Web host.

Tech Vocabulary
- dedicated server
- free Web host
- shared Web hosting
- uptime
- Web hits

Check Yourself
1. How is a Web host similar to a landlord?
2. What is uptime and why is it important?
3. What are the three types of Web hosts?
4. What is one important factor influencing the cost of renting space on a Web host?

What Do You Think?
Solving Problems. What would happen if you had an e-commerce site on a Web server that stopped working?

MARKETING & SELLING

When Eva started her business, she built a marketing plan and projected her first year's sales. Then the hard work began! She actually had to go out and sell her services—but, in the first three months, things didn't quite work out as she had planned.

A Recipe for Success?

Eva's initial concept was to have five clients. She planned to cook one day during the week for each customer. She figured it would take her about six hours per day to make five family-style dinners that the customer could reheat later. She had included all of this in her business plan.

Eva thought she had done everything right. For instance, she thought about the Five P's when creating her marketing mix:

People

Eva believed that her primary target market were busy professionals who didn't have time to cook dinner, but still wanted a healthy, affordable evening meal.

Product

Eva's Edibles planned to sell family-style dinners that clients could heat up. Eva developed a large selection of high-quality menus from which customers could choose. She adapted them so she could increase the quantity based on the number of people in a client's family. Eva made everything from scratch. Nothing came out of a can or box. And the food was delicious!

Place (and Distribution)

Eva planned to cook in her clients' kitchens. Eventually she hoped she could rent a shared-space commercial kitchen.

Price

Eva planned to charge her customers $325 for five dinners. Based on her research, she thought her pricing was about right, and lower than that of many competitors. Her fee included the cost of ingredients, shopping, preparation, cooking, storage, and kitchen clean-up. She would consult with her clients to make sure they were happy with her menu choices. And she would focus on healthy food preparation using organic ingredients.

Promotion

Eva emphasized the convenience of her service. Her customers didn't have to cook or even shop for food. She figured this would allow them more time with family and friends and still provide the convenience and nutrition of home-cooked meals. Eva prepared a small but informative and colorful brochure. She also ordered business cards.

Then Eva began contacting satisfied customers of her event-planning business. She also contacted anyone recommended by her parents, other family members, or friends. She selectively mailed her brochure with a cover letter to local professionals, using a mailing list she purchased.

Eva planned to meet with potential clients to discuss her services. She figured that she would certainly have her five clients within one month. She even dreamed that there would be a waiting list.

Then reality set in.

Couples didn't seem to be that interested in her service. The biggest interest came from two-income families that had two or more children. And the kids wanted very different meals from those of their parents. This increased the amount of time cooking. She also didn't have many kid-friendly meal choices.

This wasn't at all what Eva was expecting. And it was taking her much longer to find clients than she had planned.

After three months, Eva knew she had to change her company's direction. She began marketing more specifically to double-income families with children. She changed her brochure and emphasized that she could prepare kid-friendly meals as well as "grown-up" food. The new approach seemed to work well and she had her first three clients.

Once she had satisfied customers, Eva asked them for referrals and recommendation letters. She also began to use other promotional methods to showcase her meals. This included giving out samples of her food at shopping malls, cultural fairs, and other family-oriented locations. By her fourth month, she had five clients and one on a waiting list.

Missing the Target

Eva expected her business to have sales of about $80,000 in its first year. She figured that she could supplement that by catering small parties on weekends. Due to her initial difficulty in identifying her target market, her first three months did not produce nearly as much revenue as she had expected.

Luckily, Eva had invested $5,000 in the business. This covered not only her start-up expenditures, but also her operating expenses for three months and gave her an emergency fund.

What Would You Have Done?

1. **Comparing/Contrasting.** Eva discovered that she had misjudged her target market. What would you have done if this had happened to you?
2. **Predicting.** What other types of promotion might Eva have used once she had identified her appropriate target market?

ANALYZING FINANCES

YOUR BUSINESS PLAN

In this unit, you'll focus on the **Financial Strategies** section of the business plan and answer these questions:

- What are my business costs?
- How do I measure the economics of one unit?
- How do I develop an income statement and track cash flow?
- How do I develop a balance sheet?
- Are my financial ratios good?
- What is my break-even point?

CHAPTER 10

BUSINESS DECISIONS & THE ECONOMICS OF ONE UNIT

OBJECTIVES

- Define and provide examples of fixed expenses
- Explain how variable expenses are calculated
- Define economies of scale

VOCABULARY

- cost of goods sold (COGS)
- depreciation
- depreciation expense
- disposal value
- economy of scale
- fixed expense
- salvage value
- straight-line method of depreciation
- variable expense
- volume discount

Think about this question:

Why do businesses need to control their expenses?

Write your answer on a separate piece of paper. Be prepared to explain your thinking in class.

Fixed Expenses

A business tries to earn a profit by selling products or providing services. Every sale has related expenses, so a business can only make a profit if the selling price for its product or service is greater than all of the expenses associated with that product or service.

For example, if you owned a business called Matt's Hats and you paid a wholesaler $6 for every hat you sold, you would have to charge more than $6 for a hat to make a profit. Besides paying for the hats, you would have other expenses—rent, utilities, and the other expenses of operating your business. In this chapter, you will examine how an entrepreneur can determine the actual cost of each product sold.

What Are Fixed Expenses?

After you start your business, you will have to pay certain expenses regularly. Monthly expenses typically include rent, Internet access, salaries, and utilities (gas and electricity). An expense of this type is called a **fixed expense**—an expense that isn't affected by the number of items a business produces. The business will incur fixed expenses no matter how many products it sells. For example, if the rent for your space at Matt's Hats is $500 per month, it will remain

▲ Figure 10-1

Rent
Rent is one of the most common fixed expenses.

Predicting. *If you were starting a small business, would you rent or buy? Why?*

$500 even if in September your business makes and sells twice as many items as it produced and sold in August.

Another way of looking at fixed expenses is that they are ongoing expenses a business must pay to be able to operate. The important thing to remember is that fixed expenses don't include expenses directly related to the products the business sells.

An easy way to remember eight of the most common fixed expenses is to remember the phrase:

I SAID U ROX

This stands for:

> ### Common Fixed Expenses
> #### "I SAID U ROX"
>
> **I**nsurance
> **S**alaries
> **A**dvertising
> **I**nterest
> **D**epreciation
> **U**tilities (Gas, Electric, Telephone)
> **R**ent
> **O**ther Fixed E**X**penses

Depreciation

Depreciation is an accounting method of spreading the total cost of the equipment a business buys over the number of years it will be used. There are several depreciation methods a company can use. One of the most common ways of determining depreciation is the **straight-line method of depreciation**. The entrepreneur estimates how long the equipment will last and then figures what it could be sold for at the end of its business life (this is often referred to as the equipment's **disposal value** or **salvage value**). Next, to find the total depreciation, the entrepreneur subtracts the disposal value of the equipment from its actual cost. Then he or she divides that number by the estimated number of years during which the equipment will be used. The amount calculated per year is the **depreciation expense**.

For example, suppose a manufacturer buys a $25,000 machine. The manufacturer estimates that the business will use the machine for five years and then will sell it for an estimated $4,000 (this would be the disposal value). The total depreciation is $21,000 (the cost of the machine minus the disposal value). Using the straight-line method of depreciation, you would divide the total depreciation by the number of years the machine was used:

Cost	–	Disposal Value	=	Total Depreciation	÷	Years Used	=	Depreciation Expense
$25,000	–	$4,000	=	$21,000	÷	5 years	=	$4,200

Self-Esteem

You probably know that having self-esteem means feeling good about yourself. Most adults would agree that the older a person gets, the more important self-esteem is to their overall well-being and happiness.

People who have high self-esteem are content to be themselves. They are sometimes said to be "comfortable in their own skin." Because of this quality, they are able to maintain personal standards. They don't discard their principles for the approval of someone else or just to become part of a group. They feel good about themselves as individuals.

Self-esteem will serve you well in the work world. No matter what a coworker or customer or anyone else may say to you, you will be able to maintain a positive view of yourself. Sometimes people will try to make you feel uncomfortable. Then you need to remind yourself that those people don't know you well at all. Stand tall and be proud that you feel good about yourself. Keep your self-esteem strong.

THINKING CRITICALLY

Applying Concepts. Talk with a partner about how a person can boost self-esteem. List ways for moving away from a negative self-image.

To read more about self-esteem, go to "Your Business Career" on the Student Center at entrepreneurship.pearson.com.

You can think of the $4,200 as the cost per year to the business of having the use of the machine. If you want to calculate the cost per month, you would divide the annual total ($4,200) by 12, to arrive at a monthly total of $350.

Here's another, more common, example: A company has computers, desks, chairs, tables that it values at $20,000. However, when the company finishes using these items in four years, the items won't really have any significant value. There will be no disposal value. So the straight-line method of depreciation would look like this:

Cost	−	Disposal Value	=	Total Depreciation	÷	Years Used	=	Depreciation Expense
$20,000	−	0	=	$20,000	÷	4 years	=	$5,000

The depreciation expense per month would be $5,000 ÷ 12 or $416.67.

Fixed Expenses Can Change

The word "fixed" doesn't mean the expense will never change. It means *only* that an expense doesn't change in response to sales. For example, if Matt's Hats needs air conditioning, its electric bills will likely be higher in the summer than they are in the winter. The electric bills will fluctuate based on the season. However, they will not change according to sales. The business might even have *more* sales in the winter, when the electric bills are lower.

Here's another example. Suppose you are an automobile dealer. If you pay your sales manager $5,000 per month in salary, you will have

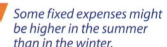

Some fixed expenses might be higher in the summer than in the winter.

Carbon Credits

A carbon footprint is a measure of how much greenhouse gas daily activities emit into the atmosphere. It includes everything from the amount of power you use to dry your hair to the gas needed to drive you to school. But should a small-business owner be concerned about the business's carbon footprint? For an environmentally conscious entrepreneur, reducing the carbon footprint of the business might be an important goal. Purchasing carbon credits (also called carbon offsets) is one option for meeting this goal.

A carbon offset is a tool designed to reduce our greenhouse gas emissions. A business owner purchases the offset. The money for the offset goes toward projects such as reforestation or the development of alternative energy sources, such as solar power. On a larger scale, corporations that are subject to emissions caps trade carbon credits in an international market. A monetary value is assigned to a unit of carbon, and companies can trade these units to comply with the cap. A company that emits a lot of greenhouse gas can purchase a credit from a company that emits little.

THINKING CRITICALLY

Relating Concepts. Think about three other ways a small business could "go green" in its operations by reducing energy usage or waste products. Working in small groups, write up a list of suggestions for one local business.

To read more about carbon credits, go to "Entrepreneurship Issues" on the Student Center at entrepreneurship.pearson.com.

to pay that same amount whether the business sells one automobile or a thousand. This is a fixed expense. Now let's say that you decide to give the manager a raise to $6,000. Your business's fixed expenses will increase by $1,000 per month, but this figure has no direct bearing on the number of automobiles your business will sell.

 READING CHECKPOINT *What are some common fixed expenses of a business?*

Variable Expenses

As you now know, fixed expenses don't vary with the amount of product sold. Most businesses have another type of expense, referred to as a **variable expense**. This is an expense that changes based on the amount of product or service a business sells.

For example, if Matt's Hats pays its hat supplier $6 per hat, the $6 is a variable expense. If Matt's Hats sells 500 hats in November, the total variable expense is $3,000 (500 × $6). If, in December, it sells 600 hats, the total variable expense will be $3,600 (600 × $6). Although the variable expense per hat remained at $6, the total of the variable expense changed due to the difference in the number of sales.

The two types of variable expenses are:

- **Cost of Goods Sold (COGS).** For manufacturing and merchandising (retailing and wholesaling) businesses, the variable expense that is associated with each unit of sale is called the **cost**

of goods sold. This includes the cost of materials and labor used to make the product or provide the service.

- **Other Variable Expenses.** These can include such expenses as commissions for salespeople, shipping and handling charges, or packaging.

Returning to the example of Matt's Hats: Suppose you have purchased hats from a wholesaler for $6 per hat. Because you are buying a finished product (the hats), no labor or other materials are involved. Your cost of goods sold per unit is $6.

Let's say Matt's Hats prints interesting designs on hats you buy from a wholesaler. You would still have a variable expense for each hat of $6, but you also have printing expenses—labor and materials (ink). The cost of labor and materials is other variable expenses added to your cost of goods sold. In this case they add another $2.50 per hat. You also have to pay shipping ($1) and handling ($0.25).

Cost of Each Hat

Cost of Goods Sold

Cost of Hat	$ 6.00	
Labor & Materials	2.50	
Total Cost of Goods Sold		$ 8.50

Other Variable Expenses

Shipping	$ 1.00	
Handling	.25	
Total Other Variable Expenses		1.25
Total Variable Expenses		**$ 9.75**

Knowing the variable expenses, you can calculate how much profit your business makes on each unit sold. Your goal would be to sell enough units each month to pay your variable and fixed expenses and have profit left over.

 *What is a variable expense?*

Economies of Scale

Check the prices of paper towels at your local supermarket. The price of three single rolls will be greater than the price of a three-pack of the same brand. The supermarket is offering you a lower price if you purchase a larger quantity of product. Typically in business the price per unit declines as you buy larger amounts.

Figure 10-2
Economy of Scale
Stores offer you lower prices when you purchase larger quantities.

Predicting. *Can you name some other products for which you pay lower prices when you purchase more?*

Similarly, as a business grows, it may be able to negotiate better prices from suppliers because it is purchasing larger quantities of goods. The cost reduction made possible by spreading costs over a larger volume is called an **economy of scale**. Two of the most common ways to gain an economy of scale are:

- **Spreading fixed expenses over as much output as possible.** If you have a monthly rent of $500 and you have $10,000 in monthly sales, 5% of your sales is being used for rent ($500 ÷ $10,000). If you can increase sales to $20,000, you will be paying only 2.5% of your monthly sales in rent ($500 ÷ $20,000). Typically, as your fixed expenses per unit decrease, your profit increases.

- **Getting better deals from suppliers.** You can get discounts from suppliers if you buy in quantity. (A discount for buying greater quantities is called a **volume discount**.) Typically, as your cost of goods sold per unit decreases, your profit increases. For example, normally Matt's Hats purchases 100 hats at a time at a price of $6.00 per hat. If Matt's Hats purchased 200 hats at a time, the price per hat would be reduced to $5.75 because of the volume discount.

 *What is an economy of scale?*

 Your Business Plan. Continue developing your standard business plan. Go to "Section 10.1" of the *Business Plan Project* in your *Student Activity Workbook*, or "Section 10.1" of the BizTech Software.

ASSESSMENT 10.1

Reviewing Objectives

1. What is a fixed expense? Provide at least three examples.
2. What is a variable expense?
3. What is an economy of scale?

Critical Thinking

4. **Applying Concepts.** What are some methods a business can use to minimize its fixed expenses?
5. **Analyzing Data.** How can a business decrease its cost of goods sold?

Working Together

Form two teams. Together, choose a retail business. The first team will create a list of fixed expenses for the business. The second team will create a list of variable expenses for it. Each team will present its list to the class. The rest of the class will evaluate the lists and make suggestions for additional items.

Math
Percentages
Often, businesses convert their fixed and variable expenses to percentages of the total sales. Convert the individual variable expenses for Matt's Hats in this chapter to a percentage of the Total Variable Expenses. For example, the cost of a hat would be $6.00 ÷ $9.75 × 100. Also show the Total Cost of Goods Sold and the Total Other Variable Expenses as percentages of the Total Variable Expenses.

OBJECTIVES

- Define a unit of sale
- Explain how to calculate the economics of one unit of sale

Imagine you are an entrepreneur selling athletic shoes. Consider this question:

Would you want to know how much profit you made every time you sold a pair of shoes?

Write your answer (yes or no) on a piece of paper. Be prepared to discuss it in class.

What Is a Unit of Sale?

Entrepreneurs need to know their businesses are profitable. One important way to examine profitability is to look at how much profit the business makes every time it sells one item. But what exactly is the business selling? In some cases, this is easy to figure out. If you sell shoes, you would figure your profit from each pair of shoes. But what happens if you make buttons? Would it make sense to figure your profit based on a single button?

This is where the concept of one unit of sale comes in. A **unit of sale** is what a customer actually buys from you. It's the amount of product (or service) you use to figure your operations and profit. The unit of sale is really the basic building block of your business.

If you were a retailer who sold athletic shoes, your unit of sale would be a single pair of shoes. But if you were a wholesaler and only sold a minimum of five pairs at a time, your unit of sale would be five pairs of shoes. The smallest unit a customer can actually buy from you isn't a single pair of shoes—it's a carton containing five pairs. So your unit of sale would be five pairs of shoes packed in a carton. (However, it would still be useful for you to know the cost of a single pair of shoes.)

If you were a manufacturer of buttons and sold them to other manufacturers, wholesalers, or large retail chain stores in cartons containing 1,000 boxes of 100 buttons each, your unit of sale would be one carton containing the 1,000 boxes. That's what your customer is actually purchasing.

Figuring out a unit of sale for a service business is usually based on how a customer is charged. For example, if you run a hair salon, a unit of sale might be one haircut. If you run a lawn-mowing company, your unit of sale might be mowing one lawn. But, because lawns are different sizes, you might have different rates for different sizes of lawns or you might charge by the hour.

The easiest way to think about a unit of sale is to ask yourself this question: What is it your customer is actually buying from you? *That* is your unit of sale.

 *What is a unit of sale?*

The Economics of One Unit of Sale

Entrepreneurs use their profits to pay themselves, to expand their businesses, and to start other businesses. Entrepreneurs want to know how much the business earns on the products it sells. To do this, they study the economics of one unit of sale (EOU). You learned a little about the economics of one unit in Chapter 2. You learned the general formula:

Selling Price – Expenses = Profit (or Loss)

Now you will get into more detail. In particular, you will analyze the expenses involved in the economics of one unit of sale in more detail. This will enable you to see the profitability of your company more accurately.

To calculate the economics of one unit of sale, subtract the variable expenses for a unit from the selling price for the unit. Remember from the previous section that the variable expenses vary directly as a result of sales. The result is the **contribution margin**. This is the amount per unit that a product contributes toward the company's profitability before the fixed expenses are subtracted.

Selling Price – Variable Expenses = Contribution Margin

Remember: The contribution margin for one unit does not take into consideration the business's fixed expenses. (Using both the variable and fixed expenses to calculate how much product needs to be sold to make a profit will be covered in Chapter 12.) In this chapter, you will examine the economics of one unit of sale and the contribution margin in more detail. You will see how EOUs are calculated for the four types of businesses.

EOU for a Manufacturing Business

Suppose a manufacturing business makes high school class rings and sells them wholesale for $40 each. We want to look at the economics of one unit based on a single ring. The materials used to produce a ring cost $3. Each requires one hour of labor at $15 per hour. So the cost of goods sold per unit would be $18 ($3 + $15). There are no commissions, and the expense of shipping and handling a single ring is $1.

Economics of One Unit: Manufacturing Business

One Unit of Sale = 1 Ring

Selling Price (per Unit):			**$ 40**
Variable Expenses			
Cost of Goods Manufactured & Sold			
Materials	$ 3		
Labor ($15 per Hour)	15		
Cost of Goods Sold		$ 18	
Other Variable Expenses			
Commissions	$ 0		
Shipping & Handling	1		
Other Variable Expenses		1	
Total Variable Expenses			19
Contribution Margin (per Unit):			**$ 21**

In this example, the contribution margin per unit is $21. The manufacturer uses this information to make business decisions. One possibility would be to see if a new, less expensive supplier could be found. This would decrease the cost of the materials per unit from $3.

Often manufacturers look at a single item as if that were the unit of sale. It can be a useful exercise, but they sell *very* large quantities of product. A manufacturer could then look at the unit of sale as 12 rings or 120 rings or even a larger number. If they do this, they are like wholesale businesses, which are described next.

EOU for a Wholesale Business

The method used to calculate the EOU for a wholesaler is similar to that of a manufacturing business. The difference is that the wholesale business buys finished products from a manufacturer, so its cost of goods sold per unit doesn't include labor.

In this example, the wholesaler buys rings from a manufacturer at $40 each. The wholesaler packages the rings in quantities of 12 per shipping carton. Shipping and handling for the carton is $16. Each carton with 12 rings is sold to a retailer for $1,200.

Economics of One Unit: Wholesale Business

One Unit of Sale = 12 Rings in a Carton

Selling Price (per Unit):			**$ 1,200**
Variable Expenses			
Cost of Goods Sold			
Rings (12)	$ 480		
Cost of Goods Sold		$ 480	
Other Variable Expenses			
Commissions	$ 0		
Shipping & Handling	16		
Other Variable Expenses		16	
Total Variable Expenses			496
Contribution Margin (per Unit):			**$ 704**

The contribution margin per unit for the wholesaler is $704. This might seem high in comparison with the $21 contribution margin per unit for the manufacturer, but remember that the wholesaler's unit of sale is a *carton of 12 rings*, while the manufacturer's unit of sale is a *single ring*. The wholesaler's contribution margin for a single ring would be $58.66 ($704 ÷ 12). The wholesaler's contribution margin per ring is still more than twice that of the manufacturer.

EOU for a Retail Business

Using the same ring example, let's look at a retail business. The retailer purchases the rings for $1,200 for a carton of 12 rings and then sells the rings one at a time. The unit of sale therefore is one ring.

The retailer sells each ring for $200.

The retailer's cost of goods sold per unit is $100 ($1,200 ÷ 12 rings). Like the wholesaler, the retailer buys finished products, so there is no labor expense. The retailer pays his salesperson a 15% commission based on the selling price of the ring ($30). The ring is sold to high schools from a catalog and then shipped to each student purchaser. The price of shipping and handling is $7.

Economics of One Unit: Retail Business

One Unit of Sale = 1 Ring

Selling Price (per Unit):			**$ 200**
Variable Expenses			
Cost of Goods Sold			
Rings (1)	$ 100		
Cost of Goods Sold		$ 100	
Other Variable Expenses			
Commissions	$ 30		
Shipping & Handling	7		
Other Variable Expenses		37	
Total Variable Expenses			137
Contribution Margin (per Unit):			**$ 63**

These examples using class rings show a typical method of distribution. A product is made by a manufacturer and sold to a wholesaler, who then sells it to a retailer. The retailer then sells it to the ultimate user, the consumer.

EOU for a Business Selling More Than One Product

A business selling a variety of products has to create a separate EOU for each product to determine whether it is profitable. However, when there are many similar products, you can develop a "typical EOU."

For example, David sells four brands of candy bars at his booth at the local food market. The cost for each bar is similar.

COSTS FOR CANDY BARS

Number	Brand	Cost
1	Chocolate Dee-Light	$0.36
2	Almond Happiness	$0.38
3	Fruit 'n' Joy	$0.42
4	Junior Chocolate Roll	$0.44

Rather than calculating EOUs for each of these similar products, David uses the average contribution margin of each transaction as his EOU. First, he adds up the cost of the four candy bars. Then he divides that total by four to get the average cost. The average cost is $0.40.

Chocolate Dee-Light	$ 0.36
Almond Happiness	0.38
Fruit 'n' Joy	0.42
Junior Chocolate Roll	0.44
Total	**$ 1.60**

$1.60 ÷ 4 = $0.40 (Average Cost)

There are other ways that David could calculate the cost of the candy bars. He could:

- Use the cost of the most expensive one. That way he would slightly overestimate the average cost. This method would work best if he sold about the same number of each bar.

- Use the cost of the best-selling candy bar. This method would work best if he sold significantly more of the best-selling bar.

- Use the average cost weighted by volume. This way, the cost of the best-selling bar would be given more weight in calculating the average cost; the next-best-selling bar would be given less weight, and so on.

Economics of One Unit:
Business with More Than One Product

One Unit of Sale =
1 Candy Bar (Average Cost)

Selling Price (per Unit):			$ 1.00
Variable Expenses			
Cost of Goods Sold			
Candy Bar (Average Cost)	$ 0.40		
Cost of Goods Sold		$ 0.40	
Other Variable Expenses			
Commissions	$ 0		
Shipping & Handling	0		
Other Variable Expenses		0	
Total Variable Expenses			0.40
Contribution Margin (per Unit):			**$ 0.60**

David sells the candy bars for $1.00 each. The economics of one unit of sale (EOU) for David's business is developed by using the average of $.40 per candy bar. David doesn't pay a commission and he sells directly to the consumer, so there is no shipping or handling.

EOU for a Service Business

Manufacturing, wholesale, and retail businesses have one thing in common: they sell products. A service business typically doesn't sell products. Because of this, a different method of determining an EOU must be used.

Sometimes figuring out what a unit of sale is for a service business is difficult. It might be one tutorial lesson, one lawn-mowing job, or one income-tax preparation. It could also be one hour of consulting, or a three-hour block of time.

Cost of Goods Sold (COGS) does not apply, because no goods are actually being sold. Instead, you would use Cost of Services Sold (COSS) when calculating an EOU. In the typical service business, you would calculate the cost of services sold by multiplying the number of hours the service takes to perform by the hourly wage of the person providing it.

Sometimes, to perform the service, you must use supplies. For example, if you were cutting hair, you might need hair gel, shampoo, conditioners, or other products. These would be variable expenses because they are directly related to the services being sold.

For example, Joan Barry has her own hair-styling business. She calculates an EOU based on each haircut. She estimates it takes her one hour to complete a hair-styling job. She values her time at $30 per hour. She estimates that each job requires about $5 worth of supplies (shampoo, conditioner, gel, and so on). She charges $55 to style a customer's hair.

Economics of One Unit: Service Business

One Unit of Sale = 1 Hair-Styling Job

Selling Price (per Unit):		**$ 55**
Variable Expenses		
Cost of Services Sold		
Materials (Shampoo, etc.)	$ 5	
Labor ($30 per Hour)	30	
Cost of Services Sold		$ 35
Other Variable Expenses		
Commissions	$ 0	
Shipping & Handling	0	
Other Variable Expenses		0
Total Variable Expenses		35
Contribution Margin (per Unit):		**$ 20**

In this case, Joan is both the person providing the hair styling and the owner of the business. She will earn $30 as the hair stylist and $20 as the entrepreneur. If she could hire someone else to do the hair styling for $30 per hour, she would still receive the contribution margin of $20.

Even better, if she could hire a stylist at $20 per hour, she would then have a contribution margin of $30 per styling job. Her cost of services sold per unit would be $25 and her contribution margin would be $30 ($55 − $25 = $30). By hiring additional stylists she would be able to increase the business's volume and also increase her profits. This is how you grow a business, which you'll learn more about in Chapter 22.

Figure 10-3

Service Business
A service business also needs to keep track of the expenses involved in a unit of sale.

Drawing Conclusions. *How would you keep track of the supplies required for individual styling jobs?*

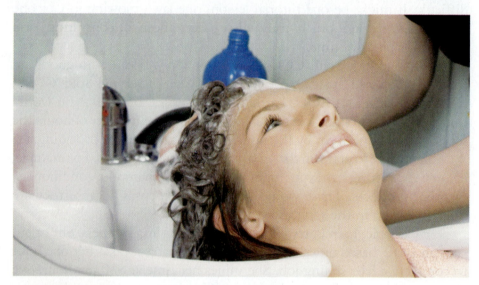

 READING CHECKPOINT ✓   *How do you calculate the contribution margin for a manufacturing business?*

Your Business Plan. Continue developing your standard business plan. Go to "Section 10.2" of the *Business Plan Project* in your *Student Activity Workbook*, or "Section 10.2" of the BizTech Software.

ASSESSMENT 10.2

Reviewing Objectives

1. What is a unit of sale?
2. How is the contribution margin for a typical manufacturing business calculated?

Critical Thinking

3. **Applying Concepts.** Imagine you have a company that offered a dog-walking service. What would you use as your unit of sale?
4. **Comparing/Contrasting.** How does the method of calculating the contribution margin for a manufacturing business differ from that used for a service business?

Working Together

Working with a partner, contact the owner of a service business you use. Interview that owner to develop an EOU for one unit of sale. Write the EOU on a poster and discuss it with the class.

Math
EOUs
For each of the EOU examples described earlier in the chapter, convert the Total Variable Expenses and the Contribution Margin to percentages of the Selling Price.

The "Write" Business

When Dave Pantoja was thinking about a business to start after taking an entrepreneurship course, his high school woodshop teacher suggested that he make pens. "It was something I knew how to do and it would give me some money right away," said Dave. "And I could use the money I gained from this business to launch other ventures in the future."

Starting Dave's Pens

Dave started Dave's Pens at the beginning of his junior year in high school. He made pens out of wood, plastic, and such exotic materials as onyx, deer antler, buffalo horn, and snakeskin. The pens were twist ballpoints that took commonly available refills.

Dave figured it cost him approximately $12 to make each pen, and he sold them for $15 to $25, depending on the material. "But as time went on, my own clients were telling me to raise my prices to match my competition," he said. "They felt I was ripping myself off with the prices. So I started studying my market and my competition a lot more to see where I stood with everything, and that's how my prices slowly increased."

Underpricing His Labor

One area where Dave underpriced his pens was his own labor. "I didn't have a good understanding of it when I first started." At the beginning, he was charging himself out at minimum wage. Now he's increased his prices to account for the time and effort he spends. It can take Dave between 10 and 15 minutes to make a wooden pen, and up to an hour and a half for a specialty pen requiring detailed work.

Dave keeps careful records for his business. "When someone orders materials or places an order with me, I keep records of the date they did it, what they ordered, how much it cost me to make it, the time it took me to make it, and what they paid."

Learning the Hard Way

Dave has made about 1,000 pens in two years of operation. When he goes to college, he plans to continue

▶ *Dave Pantoja*

Dave's Pens as a side business. Dave has learned how to operate a business. And he has learned some things that are even more important: "Before I started this business, I was huge on procrastinating. I learned the hard way—but I definitely learned not to procrastinate. The entire experience has been a huge maturing process of how to prioritize and set my priorities straight."

"I appreciate entrepreneurship," said Dave, "because it's such a general area to enter into. No matter what you want to do in the future, you can start a business."

Thinking Like an Entrepreneur

1. How would you calculate a price for your labor?
2. Dave waited for his customers to tell him he was undercharging. How would you find out if you were charging a competitive price?
3. How can being a procrastinator hurt you in business?

CHAPTER SUMMARY

10.1 The Cost of Doing Business

Entrepreneurs have two types of business expenses to consider: fixed expenses and variable expenses. The fixed expenses of a business are expenses that are not affected by increases or decreases in the number of products a business sells. Common examples of fixed expenses are insurance, salaries, advertising, interest payments, depreciation, utilities, and rent. Depreciation is an accounting method of spreading the total cost of the equipment a business buys over the number of years it will be used. Despite being called "fixed," fixed expenses may vary from month to month. Variable expenses vary based on the amount of product or services a business sells in a given time period. Variable expenses are divided into two categories: cost of goods sold per unit (COGS) and other variable expenses. The cost of goods sold per unit includes the cost of the labor and materials used to make a product. Other variable expenses could include commissions, shipping and handling charges, and packaging.

10.2 The Economics of One Unit of Sale

A unit of sale is what a customer actually buys from a business. It is the amount of product or service a business uses to figure out its operations and profit. The equation for the economics of one unit of sale is selling price minus expenses equals profits. To find the contribution margin per unit, subtract all variable expenses for the unit from the selling price.

REVIEW VOCABULARY

You are going to become a consultant for teen entrepreneurs. You want to write a series of questions and answers about fixed expenses, variable expenses, and EOUs to help you answer their questions. Use at least half of the following terms in your questions and answers.

- contribution margin (p. 276)
- cost of goods sold (p. 272)
- depreciation (p. 270)
- depreciation expense (p. 270)
- disposal value (p. 270)
- economy of scale (p. 274)
- fixed expense (p. 269)
- straight-line method of depreciation (p. 270)
- unit of sale (p. 275)
- variable expense (p. 272)
- volume discount (p. 274)

CHECK YOUR UNDERSTANDING

Choose the letter that best answers the question or completes the statement.

1. Which of the following is not a common fixed expense?
    a. rent
    b. labor
    c. salaries
    d. utilities

2. Expenses that are not affected by the number of products a business sells are called
    a. variable expenses
    b. fixed expenses
    c. contribution margin
    d. selling expenses

3. Using the straight-line method of depreciation, what is the annual depreciation expense for an automobile that costs $30,000, has a five-year life for the business, and can then be sold for $10,000?
    a. $7,000
    b. $6,000
    c. $5,000
    d. $4,000

4. Fixed expenses
    a. can never change
    b. change every year
    c. can change from time to time
    d. change in relation to products sold

5. One example of other variable expenses would be
    a. commissions
    b. labor
    c. materials
    d. supplies

6. Expenses that change based on the quantity of goods a business sells in a given period of time are called
    a. fixed expenses
    b. variable expenses
    c. fluctuating expenses
    d. selling expenses

7. Which of the following four types of business does not typically sell products?
    a. manufacturing
    b. retail
    c. service
    d. wholesale

8. Which of the following is *not* used in determining the contribution margin?
    a. variable expenses
    b. fixed expenses
    c. cost of goods sold
    d. other variable expenses

9. In a service business, an entrepreneur charges $500 for the job, pays a commission of 10% of sales, and has a cost of services sold per unit of $100. What is the entrepreneur's contribution margin per unit?
    a. $350
    b. $300
    c. $395
    d. $400

10. In a wholesale business, which of the following would you *not* expect to see in an EOU?
    a. materials
    b. other variable expenses
    c. total variable expenses
    d. contribution margin

11. In figuring straight-line depreciation, the disposal value is the value of the item when
    a. you buy it
    b. you finish using it
    c. you average out its cost over 5 years
    d. none of the above

12. The cost reduction made possible by spreading costs over a larger volume is called a (an)
    a. cost of goods sold
    b. variable expense
    c. contribution margin
    d. economy of scale

Business Communication

13. You want to start a business selling pretzels from a booth at the annual community festival. Prepare a written report that briefly summarizes your concept, provides a list of your fixed expenses, and includes an EOU that shows your contribution margin per unit.

14. Working in teams, prepare a presentation that traces a manufactured item through a wholesale business to a retail business. Prepare an EOU for the unit of sale for each of the three businesses in the chain.

15. Work with a partner. Imagine you operate a retail business selling disposable cell phones. First, decide on a selling price for the phones and prepare a list of the estimated fixed and variable expenses. You both want the business to increase its profit. One partner should suggest ways to lower the variable expenses; the other should suggest ways to lower the fixed expenses.

Business Ethics

18. You own a retail business that sells clocks, which you purchase from a local wholesaler. Your typical order is for 12 dozen clocks at a cost of $100 per dozen. The salesperson for the wholesaler offers you a special deal. She says that if you double your order to 24 dozen, she will give you one-half her commission on the extra clocks. This deal would lower your contribution margin per unit and you think you would be able to sell the extra clocks. However, you feel uneasy about the offer. Write a short report describing what you would do in this situation. Include an EOU for the current ordering amount and the special deal.

Business Math

16. A wholesale business sells pen and pencil sets to retailers for $12 per dozen. The wholesaler pays the manufacturer $0.50 for each individual pen and pencil set. The wholesaler pays its salespeople a commission of 10% of sales. The wholesaler has packaging expenses of $0.30 for each unit of 12 sets. What is the wholesaler's contribution margin per unit?

17. Dana Wright operates an airport limousine service. He owns the limo and does his own driving. He values his driving time at $25 per hour. He pays a commission fee of $10 to the person who brings him the business. A trip to the airport takes three hours and uses $25 worth of gasoline. If Dana charges each customer $200, what is his contribution margin per unit of sale? How much does Dana make on each trip as a driver? As the owner of the business?

Business in Your Community

19. Working with three or four classmates, prepare a survey to be completed by two owners of retail businesses in the community. The survey should ask the owners to identify their major fixed and variable expenses. Collect and tabulate the surveys. Write a report comparing the results and present them to the class.

20. Interview two service business owners in your community. Ask them how they calculate their fixed and variable expenses. Write a short report summarizing the results of your interviews and present your findings to the class.

Web Content

Simply put, Web content is the information you see on a Website. It can be presented in the form of pictures, video, audio, or copy (the words that describe a product, provide information, or make up the messages). A Website's content is key to the purpose of the site. Is it a site for information? For advertising? For public relations? For selling a specific product? A newspaper's Website, for example, will have mainly articles, while a Website for a fashion business will probably have photos and descriptions of clothing. Website owners often hire professionals to write, edit, and produce the content for their site.

The type and amount of content can help attract more traffic (visitors) to a site. Web content that stays the same over time is called **static content**. Generally, Website owners want to update their sites regularly so the content will reflect new products or changes in their companies. By adding new content, owners can increase the number of repeat visitors. New content can also raise the ranking on Web search engines, which in turn will attract new visitors who may be surfing the Web looking for something specific.

Web Pages

Websites may contain one page or many. Amazon and eBay, for example, have hundreds, if not thousands, of pages. The first page you see when visiting a Website is called the homepage. The homepage has **hyperlinks** that can take you to other pages on the site. These pages may also have hyperlinks that will take you to still other pages or outside Websites, or return you to the homepage.

Content Management System

To put content on a site, a Web designer might use a **Content Management System (CMS)**. A CMS provides the software or programs needed to set up a shopping cart, a **blog** (a personal journal, short for "weB LOG"), a chat room, or a newspaper, as well as many other applications. With a blog CMS, for example, a user can write a blog, add new posts, edit old ones, and even change the blog's template. (As you may remember from Chapter 6, templates are predesigned pages where certain features,

such as the color of the text, the placement of links, and the size of the type can be changed.) Content management systems that control each type of application let Website owners change Web content in a similar way.

Embedding Content

Early on, Web pages could only have static content in HTML text. Each successive revision of HTML has provided users with more capabilities, including the options of pictures, **active content** (information that changes frequently, such as the time and temperature), audio, and video. Sometimes audio and video are presented through links. In other instances, they are available through a process called **embedding**, which uses HTML to insert them into the Website. YouTube, for example, uses embedding throughout its site to display videos. Users can share content and even place it on their own Websites. New forms of content, such as video, are making the Web more exciting and giving site owners even more design options to attract traffic.

Tech Vocabulary

- active content
- blog
- Content Management System (CMS)
- embedding
- hyperlinks
- static content

Check Yourself

1. What are some different types of Web content?
2. What is static content?
3. What can you do with a content management system?
4. What is active content?

What Do You Think?

Writing. What do you think makes interesting Web content?

Income Statements & Cash Flow

OBJECTIVES

- Explain the importance of an income statement
- Identify the parts of an income statement
- Prepare income statements
- Understand how cash flow affects entrepreneurs
- Demonstrate a burn-rate calculation

VOCABULARY

- burn rate
- calendar year
- cash flow
- cash flow statement
- cyclical
- fiscal year
- income statement
- profit and loss statement

Think about this question:

Is it important for an entrepreneur to know basic accounting principles?

Write your answer (yes or no) on a piece of paper. Be prepared to discuss your answer.

Income Statements

One of the most important documents for a business is an income statement. An **income statement** is a financial document that summarizes a business's income and expenses over a given time period and shows whether the business made a profit or took a loss. That's why it's also called a **profit and loss statement**.

If a business's sales are greater than its expenses, the income statement will show a profit. If a business's sales are less than its expenses, the income statement will show a negative number, a loss.

When to Prepare an Income Statement

Because income statements show how a business is performing, they are prepared periodically.

- **Monthly.** Most small-business owners should create a monthly income statement.

- **Quarterly.** Most companies generate an income statement showing income and expenses for the quarter. If you prepare statements monthly, it will be easy to put together quarterly statements.

Many retail companies have a fiscal year that ends January 31 to reflect the holiday season.

- **Annually.** Most companies also prepare income statements on an annual basis that show how the company performed during the year. Preparing statements on a quarterly basis will make it easier to prepare an annual statement.

A **calendar year** is January 1 through December 31. However, your income statement might be based on what is called a fiscal year. A **fiscal year** is any 12-month period you choose to treat as a year for accounting purposes. This would be the period you would use when figuring your taxes. Once you make a choice, you cannot change it, so give it some thought. For example, many retail companies have a fiscal year that starts February 1 and ends January 31 to reflect the holiday season.

Differences in Income Statements

Income statements can vary in wording, but they all include the same basic information: revenue, expenses, and net income or loss. However, a significant difference in income statements is how businesses show their variable expenses. Based on the type of business, variable expenses will appear under these headings:

- **Cost of Goods Sold.** Merchandising businesses (wholesale and retail companies) keep track of the cost of their beginning inventory, the cost of any additional inventory they purchase, and the cost of their ending inventory. This allows them to calculate the cost of inventory sold during this period.

- **Cost of Goods Manufactured and Sold.** Manufacturing companies track the cost of both labor and materials. The two are added to arrive at the cost of the products they are selling.

- **Cost of Services Sold.** Service companies track materials involved in providing their services. Sometimes they include the cost of labor if the service can be easily broken down into segments. For example, a haircut could be separated into the cost of materials (shampoo, conditioner, etc.) and the time it takes to accomplish (say, 45 minutes). When labor is paid by the hour (for example, in a bike repair shop) or costs are based on projects (for example, with an event planner), the income statement wouldn't include this section.

What is an income statement?

Nonprofits

Entrepreneurs can have a variety of goals. Some start businesses because they've invented something new and want to sell it. Some want to share a unique talent—such as baking or computer programming—with others. Most hope to make money pursuing a personal passion. But not all entrepreneurs are motivated by making money. Some individuals with entrepreneurial spirit choose to start nonprofit organizations (NPOs) or work for those that already exist. A nonprofit could be a group whose goal is to support the arts, give humanitarian aid, or protect the environment. No matter what the goal, the nonprofit is not focused on earning money.

A group operating as a nonprofit may qualify for tax-exempt status from the IRS. Then it becomes a 501(c)(3) corporation and covers its operating expenses through donations that are tax-deductible to the donors. Examples of well-known nonprofit organizations include Amnesty International, the Red Cross, United Way, the YMCA, the Boys and Girls Clubs, and the Bill and Melinda Gates Foundation. Your town may have nonprofits that run museums, put on cultural events, feed homeless people, or shelter abandoned animals. There are thousands of nonprofit organizations around the world. To continue their work, they need entrepreneurs who can effectively manage funds, organize and inspire people, and promote the group's goals and initiatives.

THINKING CRITICALLY

Communicating. In small groups, research NPOs. Develop a list of nonprofits where you think you would enjoy working or volunteering. Explain to your classmates why you want to support these particular organizations.

To read more about nonprofits, go to "Entrepreneurship Issues" on the Student Center at entrepreneurship.pearson.com.

WEALTHIEST CHARITABLE NONPROFIT FOUNDATIONS

Rank	Organization	Location	Endowment
1	Bill & Melinda Gates Foundation	Seattle, Washington	$35.1 billion
2	Wellcome Trust	London	$26.4 billion
3	Howard Hughes Medical Institute	Chevy Chase, Maryland	$18.6 billion
4	Ford Foundation	New York, New York	$13.7 billion
5	The Church Commissioners for England	London	$10.5 billion
6	J. Paul Getty Trust	Los Angeles, California	$10.1 billion
6	Li Ka Shing Foundation	Hong Kong	$10.1 billion
7	Robert Wood Johnson Foundation	Princeton, New Jersey	$10.0 billion
7	Mohammed bin Rashid Al Maktoum Foundation	Dubai	$10.0 billion
8	William and Flora Hewlett Foundation	Menlo Park, California	$8.5 billion
9	W. K. Kellogg Foundation	Battle Creek, Michigan	$8.4 billion
10	Lilly Endowment	Indianapolis, Indiana	$7.6 billion

As of March 4, 2008

Parts of a Typical Income Statement

Matt Washington has a summertime business. He sells hats on the boardwalk near the beach. He stores his hats in a large locker he rents from a local merchant. He runs the business from his parents' home and makes a contribution toward their utilities.

Matt needs to prepare an income statement for August. Because he has a retail business (selling hats purchased from a wholesaler), Matt uses Cost of Goods Sold to categorize his variable expenses. Figure 11-1 uses Matt's Hats to identify the six parts of a typical income statement.

If you have a merchandising business (wholesaling or retailing), your income statement will be similar to Matt's.

- **Revenue.** This is the money Matt's Hat's receives from selling its products. The revenue section includes gross sales (the total revenue from all the hats sold), return sales (the total dollar amount of the hats that were returned), and net sales (gross sales – return sales). Matt sells hats for $20 each. So, with gross sales of $4,800, Matt sold 240 hats ($4,800 ÷ 20 = 240).

- **Cost of Goods Sold.** This is the cost of all the hats Matt sold. It's calculated by subtracting the value of the ending inventory from the value of the beginning inventory (and any additional purchases of goods). The beginning inventory was $1,200 (Matt pays a wholesaler $6 a hat, so this means 200 hats: $1,200 ÷ 6 = 200). He paid $600 for an additional 100 hats in August (600 ÷ $6 = 100). At the end of the month, he had 80 hats left in inventory. Because each hat cost $6, this meant that his inventory had a value of $480 (80 × $6 = $480).

- **Gross Profit.** Gross profit is calculated by subtracting the cost of goods sold from the net sales.

- **Operating Expenses.** All of Matt's expenses in running his business are included in the operating expenses section. Only the expenses that apply are listed. Because Matt doesn't pay salaries or interest, for example, those aren't on the list. Often, accountants organize operating expenses alphabetically.

- **Pre-Tax Profit.** The pre-tax profit is calculated by subtracting the operating expenses from the gross profit ($3,080 – $650 = $2,430).

- **Net Profit (Loss).** The net profit, also called net income, is calculated by subtracting taxes from the pre-tax profit. Taxes in this example are estimated at 15% of the pre-tax profit and are rounded off to the nearest dollar ($2,430 × 15% = $364.50, rounded to $365). The net profit is Matt's profit as an entrepreneur.

RETAIL BUSINESS

Matt's Hats
Income Statement
Month Ended August 31, 20--

REVENUE

Gross Sales	$ 4,800	
Sales Returns	400	
Net Sales		$ 4,400

COST OF GOODS SOLD

Beginning Inventory	$ 1,200	
Add: Purchases	600	
Total	$ 1,800	
Less: Inventory, August 31	480	
Cost of Goods Sold		1,320

GROSS PROFIT — $ 3,080

OPERATING EXPENSES

Advertising	$ 100	
Insurance	200	
Rent	150	
Telephone	100	
Utilities	100	
Total Expenses		650

PRE-TAX PROFIT — $ 2,430

Taxes (15%) — 365

NET PROFIT — $ 2,065

Figure 11-1

Matt's Hats: Income Statement

This shows the income statement for Matt's Hats as of August 31.

Predicting. *If hats sell at $20 each, how many hats did Matt's Hats actually sell in August? (Hint: Use the Net Sales in your calculation.)*

What are the six parts of a typical income statement?

Two Formats for Income Statements

There are two formats for income statements:

- The traditional format
- The contribution-margin format

Income Statement
Lola's Custom Drapery
Month Ended March 31, 20--

REVENUE		
Gross Sales	$ 85,456	
Sales Returns	1,200	
Net Sales		$ 84,256
COST OF GOODS SOLD		
Materials	$ 11,550	
Labor	17,810	
Total Cost of Goods Sold		29,360
GROSS PROFIT		$ 54,896
OPERATING EXPENSES		
Advertising	$ 1,100	
Commissions	8,000	
Depreciation	2,000	
Insurance	2,200	
Rent	4,000	
Salaries	12,000	
Utilities	4,000	
Total Expenses		33,300
PRE-TAX PROFIT		$ 21,596
Taxes (15%)		3,239
NET PROFIT		$ 18,357

Traditional-Format Income Statement

The traditional-format income statement subtracts the Cost of Goods Sold from the Net Sales to determine the Gross Profit. This format is used by banks and financial institutions. It is more commonly included in a business plan than the contribution-margin-format income statement.

Income Statement
Lola's Custom Drapery
Month Ended March 31, 20--

REVENUE

Gross Sales	$ 85,456	
Sales Returns	1,200	
Net Sales		$ 84,256

VARIABLE EXPENSES

Cost of Goods Sold

Materials	$ 11,550		
Labor	17,810		
Total Cost of Goods Sold		$ 29,360	

Other Variable Expenses

Commissions	$ 8,000		
Total Other Variable Expenses		$ 8,000	
Total Variable Expenses			37,360

CONTRIBUTION MARGIN $ 46,896

FIXED OPERATING EXPENSES

Advertising	$ 1,100	
Depreciation	2,000	
Insurance	2,200	
Rent	4,000	
Salaries	12,000	
Utilities	4,000	
Total Expenses		25,300

PRE-TAX PROFIT	$ 21,596
Taxes (15%)	3,239
NET PROFIT	$ 18,357

Contribution-Margin-Format Income Statement

The contribution-margin-format income statement subtracts all the variable expenses from the Net Sales to determine the Contribution Margin. This format is more commonly used by managers interested in tracking variable and fixed expenses. It is less commonly included in a business plan than the traditional-format income statement.

Preparing Income Statements

The following examples explain the structure of income statements for a manufacturing business (Ann's T-Shirts) and for a service business (Joan Barry Hair Styles).

Income Statement for a Manufacturer

Ann Waverly sells T-shirts that she prints with her own designs and messages. Ann's is a manufacturing business because she buys supplies and, through her labor, converts those supplies into a new product.

Ann needs to prepare an income statement for March. As a manufacturing business, Ann will use Cost of Goods Manufactured and Sold in her income statement. Her statement is shown in Figure 11-2.

If you have a manufacturing business, your income statement will be similar to Ann's.

- **Revenue.** Ann had gross sales of $7,500 in March, selling 500 T-shirts at $15 apiece. Her customers were very satisfied, as only 2 shirts were returned. So Ann sold 498 shirts.

- **Cost of Goods Manufactured and Sold.** Ann buys T-shirts from a wholesaler for $3 each. The total cost for T-shirts in March was $1,494 (498 × $3 = $1,494). In addition, Ann estimates that she spends $0.50 per shirt on inks and paints. The cost of these supplies in March was $249 (498 × $0.50 = $249). The total cost for materials was $1,743 ($1,494 for the T-shirts and $249 for the inks and paints). Ann spends 15 minutes printing each shirt. Because she wants to make $20 an hour, she estimates her labor at $5 for each shirt ($20 ÷ 4 = $5). So the total cost of labor in March was $2,490 (498 × $5 = $2,490). The cost of goods manufactured and sold is $4,233, the cost of materials plus the cost of (Ann's) labor ($1,743 + 2,490).

- **Gross Profit.** The gross profit is calculated by subtracting the cost of goods manufactured and sold ($4,233) from net sales ($7,470). Ann's T-Shirts had a gross profit of $3,237 in March ($7,470 – $4,233 = $3,237).

- **Operating Expenses.** Ann sells her T-shirts to local specialty clothing stores who are long-time customers, so she doesn't need to do much advertising. She is paying interest on a loan her parents gave her to help get her business started. She rents a small room in the back of a customer's store. Her rent includes utilities. She pays a salary to a part-time employee who cleans her office and helps pack her T-shirts for delivery to customers.

- **Pre-Tax Profit.** The pre-tax profit is calculated by subtracting Ann's operating expenses from her gross profit ($3,237 – $1,600 = $1,637).

- **Net Profit (Loss).** Again, taxes are estimated at 15% of the pre-tax profit and are rounded off to the nearest dollar

($1,637 × 15% = $245.55, rounded to $246). Ann had already paid herself $2,490 for her labor in printing the T-shirts. The net profit is Ann's revenue earned as an entrepreneur.

MANUFACTURING BUSINESS

Ann's T-Shirts
Income Statement
Month Ended March 31, 20--

REVENUE

Gross Sales	$ 7,500	
Sales Returns	30	
Net Sales		$ 7,470

COST OF GOODS MANUFACTURED AND SOLD

Materials		
T-Shirts	$ 1,494	
Inks/Paints	249	
Total Materials	$ 1,743	
Labor	2,490	
Cost of Goods Manufactured and Sold		4,233

GROSS PROFIT $ 3,237

OPERATING EXPENSES

Advertising	$ 100	
Insurance	200	
Interest	300	
Rent	400	
Salaries	400	
Telephone	200	
Total Expenses		1,600

PRE-TAX PROFIT $ 1,637

Taxes (15%)   246

NET PROFIT $ 1,391

 Figure 11-2

Ann's T-Shirts: Income Statement
This shows the income statement for Ann's T-Shirts as of March 31.
Analyzing. *How much did Ann make in March? (Hint: Include her labor and her profit as an entrepreneur.)*

Income Statement for a Service Business

Joan Barry styles clients' hair in their homes. She brings all her equipment on appointments and styles hair for both men and women. She also cuts children's hair. Many of her customers work during the day and appreciate Joan's willingness to come in the evening or on weekends. Often she styles an entire family's hair in one appointment.

Joan needs to prepare an income statement. She had 160 jobs. Joan will use a cost of services sold section in her income statement, with an average price of $25 per job and an average cost of $1 for supplies. She has a variety of prices for different types of jobs. Hair coloring or fancy styling costs more, but children's haircuts are less. Joan's income statement is shown in Figure 11-3.

If you have a service business, your income statement may be similar to Joan's. However, many service companies, particularly those that don't use materials in their service, won't use a cost of services sold section. The net profit in an income statement like this would represent the profit for the entrepreneur's labor.

- **Revenue.** Joan had sales of $6,900 in September. In a service business, customers can't "return" the service. If a customer is disappointed, the business owner needs to find a way to provide satisfaction. This may include refunding the money the customer paid. Joan is an accomplished hair stylist. She didn't have to make any refunds in September.

- **Cost of Services Sold.** Joan worked hard in September, going to 160 appointments and charging a variety of prices. Because she estimates the average job at $1 for materials and $25 for labor, her price for materials is $160 (160 × $1 = $160) and her price for labor is $4,000 (160 × $25 = $4,000). The cost of services sold is $4,160 ($160 + 4,000 = $4,160).

- **Gross Profit.** Joan's gross profit is the revenue minus the cost of services sold ($6,900 − $4,160 = $2,740).

- **Operating Expenses.** Joan advertises her business by sending out flyers. Because she visits clients in their homes, she doesn't need a hair salon. However, Joan rents a room from her parents, where she keeps her hair-styling equipment. She also contributes to her parents' utility bills. Joan purchased a car because she needs to travel to her clients and bring heavy equipment and supplies. She is paying interest on the car loan.

- **Pre-Tax Profit.** The pre-tax profit is calculated by subtracting Joan's operating expenses from her gross profit ($2,740 − $1,400 = $1,340).

- **Net Profit (Loss).** Taxes again are estimated at 15% of the pre-tax profit ($1,340 × 15% = $201). The net profit is $1,139 ($1,340 − $201 = $1,139). Joan already paid herself $4,000 in September as a hair stylist. The net profit is what she has earned as an entrepreneur.

Figure 11-3

SERVICE BUSINESS

Joan Barry Hair Styles
Income Statement
Month Ended September 30, 20--

REVENUE		
Sales		$ 6,900
COST OF SERVICES SOLD		
Materials (Hair-Styling Supplies)	$ 160	
Labor (160 Jobs)	4,000	
Cost of Goods Sold		4,160
GROSS PROFIT		$ 2,740
OPERATING EXPENSES		
Advertising	$ 400	
Insurance	200	
Interest	300	
Rent	200	
Telephone	200	
Utilities	100	
Total Expenses		1,400
PRE-TAX PROFIT		$ 1,340
Taxes (15%)		201
NET PROFIT		$ 1,139

Joan's Hair Styles: Income Statement
This shows the income statement for Joan Barry Hair Styles as of September 30.

Analyzing. *Is it likely that Joan would make money in a month when her business showed a loss in net profit? (Hint: Remember that Joan pays herself for her labor and makes a profit as an entrepreneur.)*

How do the income statements for a manufacturing business and a service business differ?

Cash Flow

An income statement provides a good picture of how well, or poorly, your business is doing. It shows your sales and your expenses. What it does *not* show is the amount of cash you have on hand.

Cash for a business is like gasoline for an automobile—without it, the business does not have the necessary fuel to operate. Size doesn't matter. A compact car, a luxury sedan, or an 18-wheel semi-tractor cannot go anywhere on an empty tank. Similarly, it doesn't matter if a business is small or large—if it doesn't have enough cash to pay its bills as they come due, the creditors can force the business to close its doors.

For example, the income statement for September might show a net income of $3,000, but that's not necessarily the amount of cash you received. If some of your sales were made on credit, you may not get the money from those customers until October, or even later.

A company must have sufficient cash on hand to continue to do business. You must also continue to pay your suppliers, to pay for items you have purchased on credit, and to repay any loans you may have. If you are constantly short of cash, you could lose your business.

To ensure that you have enough money to operate, you must track your business's cash flow. **Cash flow** is the money received minus what is spent over a specified period of time. The cash flow equation is:

$$\text{Cash Inflow} - \text{Cash Outflow} = \text{Net Cash}$$

To monitor cash flow, a business prepares a **cash flow statement**. This is a financial document that records inflows and outflows of cash when they actually occur. Besides preparing an income statement every month, a successful entrepreneur also prepares a cash flow statement.

Reading a Cash Flow Statement

Like income statements and other financial statements, the format and headings for a cash flow statement may vary. Figure 11-4 shows a typical cash flow statement prepared for Matt's Hats for August.

- **Beginning Cash Balance.** Matt started the month with $430 in cash.

- **Cash Inflow.** Matt received $4,400. Matt sells his hats on the boardwalk and only accepts cash payment. If Matt extended credit to his customers, he would show their payments as cash inflow. If Matt had any investments that increased in value, that would also be shown in this section.

- **Total Available Cash.** The beginning cash balance and the cash inflow for the month show the company's total available cash. In Matt's case, this is $4,830 ($430 + $4,400 = $4,830).

- **Cash Outflow.** This section notes the cash spent on purchases of additional inventory of hats ($600). The cash outflow section also includes money Matt spent on operating expenses. The total cash spent in August was $1,575.

- **Net Cash.** The last section shows the net change in cash flow. This tells the entrepreneur whether the business had a positive or negative cash flow that month. As you can see in Figure 11-4, Matt's Hats had a positive net cash flow of $3,255 for the month of August.

Matt's Hats
Cash Flow Statement
Month Ended August 31, 20--

BEGINNING CASH BALANCE	$ 430	
CASH INFLOW		
Sales	4,400	
AVAILABLE CASH		$ 4,830
CASH OUTFLOW		
Cash Purchases of Inventory	$ 600	
Insurance Paid	200	
Interest Paid	300	
Rent Paid	200	
Telephone Paid	200	
Utilities Paid	75	
Total Cash Outflow		1,575
NET CASH		$ 3,255

◀ Figure 11-4
Matt's Hats:
Cash Flow Statement
This shows the cash flow statement for Matt's Hats for August.
Analyzing. *What would happen if Matt didn't have enough cash on hand to pay for new inventory?*

Ways to Keep Cash Flowing

Here are five ways to avoid being caught without enough cash to pay your bills:

- **Collect Cash as Soon as Possible.** When making a sale, try to convince the customer to use cash rather than credit.

- **Pay Bills Close to the Due Date.** Always note the due date on your bills. Plan your payment to reach the creditor just before or on the due date. However, be careful not to send the payment so that it arrives after the due date.

- **Keep Track of Your Cash.** Check the cash balance every day. Always know how much you have. Keep track of the money your business earns and spends each day. Make sure you get and keep receipts for every purchase you make. You don't want to be surprised by a lack of cash.

- **Lease Equipment.** Often, a large down payment is required when you buy equipment. The down payment reduces your cash on hand. When feasible, don't buy equipment; lease it.

- **Keep Inventory to a Minimum.** Minimize the amount of inventory you stock unless it's part of your competitive advantage to offer customers a wide selection. Avoid large purchases of slow-moving inventory. Inventory ties up cash in two ways: the cash you use to purchase the inventory and the cash you spend in storing it.

Cash Flow Is Cyclical

Many businesses have sales that are based on the time of year. For example, Matt sells hats in the summertime on the boardwalk and beach. Matt closes his business in the winter. If you were operating an ice cream stand, your sales during the summer months would be higher than in the winter. If you were selling scarves and gloves, your sales would almost certainly be higher in the cold weather. Cash flow is **cyclical** (SIK-lih-kul) for many businesses, meaning that it varies according to the time of year.

Other examples of businesses with cyclical cash flow are flower shops, bridal shops, and college book stores. Each of these businesses must carefully monitor cash flow in the months of low sales.

Remember, you will have monthly expenses (fixed expenses) regardless of whether the month is typically high-sales or low-sales.

 *What is the cash flow equation?*

The Burn Rate

Most new businesses try to start with a surplus of cash. (You'll read more about the need for cash reserves in Chapter 13.) However, most new businesses also spend more money than they earn while getting off the ground. The question most beginning entrepreneurs need to know is: How long can I afford to lose money?

The rate at which a company spends cash to cover overhead costs without generating a positive cash flow is called the **burn rate**. It is typically expressed in terms of cash spent per month. A burn rate of $10,000 monthly means that the business is spending that sum every month to cover rent and other operating expenses.

Use the burn rate to calculate how long a company can go without revenue. If a business has, say $20,000 in cash and a burn rate of $2,000 a month, it can stay "in business" for 10 months without making any sales.

Cash on Hand ÷ Burn Rate = Number of Months before Cash Runs Out

$20,000 ÷ $2,000 = 10 months

 **READING CHECKPOINT** *How is the burn rate calculated?*

 Your Business Plan. Continue developing your standard business plan. Go to "Section 11.1" of the *Business Plan Project* in your *Student Activity Workbook*, or "Section 11.1" of the BizTech Software.

ASSESSMENT 11.1

Reviewing Objectives

1. What is the purpose of an income statement?

2. What are the six parts of the typical income statement?

3. How do the income statements for a manufacturing business and a service business differ?

4. What are five ways entrepreneurs can ensure that their businesses have sufficient cash?

5. How is a burn rate calculated?

Critical Thinking

6. **Applying Concepts.** Calculate the net profit for Joan Barry Hair Styles in a month when she had 70 fewer jobs. (Use Figure 11-3.)

7. **Analyzing Data.** What would be the effect on net profit for Matt's Hats if the price from his wholesaler had been $7 per hat? (Use Figure 11-1.)

Working Together

Work with a partner. Pick one of the sample income statements in this chapter. Rename the business and adjust the income statement to reflect the way you would operate it in your area. Make sure you make a profit.

Social Studies

Small Businesses

Many people believe that America's past economic success has been due to the ability of entrepreneurs to start and grow small businesses. Research the number of new business startups in your area. Write a brief report based on your findings.

11.2 The Balance Sheet

OBJECTIVES

- Identify the purpose and components of a balance sheet
- Explain how balance sheets are prepared
- Provide two methods used to analyze balance sheets

VOCABULARY

- accounts payable
- accounts receivable
- asset
- balance sheet
- current assets
- current liabilities
- liability
- long-term assets
- long-term liabilities
- owner's equity

? *Consider this question:*

If you owned a business, would you want to know its value?

Write your answer (yes or no) on a piece of paper. Be prepared to discuss your answer.

What Is a Balance Sheet?

The previous section of this chapter included two important financial statements: the income statement and the cash flow statement. This section will introduce another very important financial statement: the balance sheet.

A **balance sheet** is a financial statement that summarizes the assets and liabilities (debts) of a business. It shows how much a business is worth at a particular time. A balance sheet is like a snapshot of a business on a specific date. An income statement is more like a movie, reflecting changes in the business over a period of time.

A balance sheet answers the questions: What does the company own? To whom does it owe money? How much is the business worth?

The balance sheet focuses on the fundamental accounting equation:

Assets – Liabilities = Owner's Equity

Another way to show this equation is:

$$\text{Assets} = \text{Liabilities} + \text{Owner's Equity}$$

Let's examine each of the terms in this equation:

- **Assets.** Everything owned by the business that has a monetary value is an <mark>asset</mark>. This could include such things as cash, inventory, equipment, and supplies.

- **Liabilities.** Any outstanding bill or loan that must be repaid is a <mark>liability</mark>.

- **Owner's Equity.** The value of the business on a specific date is referred to as the <mark>owner's equity</mark>. It's the value of the business if all the assets were sold and all the liabilities were paid.

A balance sheet shows that assets are always balanced by liabilities and owner's equity.

The balance sheet shows you the value of your business on a specific date. For example, if you decided to close down your business, your first step would be to sell all your assets. The next step would be to pay off all your liabilities (debts). Any money remaining would be yours to keep. It's the value of your business, your owner's equity.

Fiscal Year

Businesses often prepare a balance sheet monthly and most prepare one annually. As discussed in the previous section, a business can choose to use a calendar year accounting period (January 1–December 31) or a fiscal year accounting period. A fiscal year is the 12-month period chosen by the business (for example, July 1–June 30).

Assets Are Owned

Assets are the items of value *owned* by a business: cash, inventory, furniture, machinery, and so on. On a typical balance sheet, assets are usually classified as either current assets or long-term assets.

- **Current Assets.** Short-term assets that can be converted into cash within one year are <mark>current assets</mark>. These include cash, inventory, marketable securities, and money owed the business by its customers (called accounts receivable). <mark>Accounts receivable</mark> is the amount of money owed to a business by its customers for credit sales.

- **Long-Term Assets.** Assets that usually take longer than one year to turn into cash are <mark>long-term assets</mark>. Examples of long-term assets are equipment, computers, furniture, machinery, buildings, and long-term investments.

Liabilities Are Owed

Liabilities are all sums of money *owed* by the business. One of the most common types of liability is **accounts payable**, which represents the amount of money a business owes to its suppliers for purchases made on credit. Other liabilities include bills owed for telephone, utilities, insurance, and taxes. Liabilities include such debts as short-term bank loans, mortgages, and loans from families or friends. On a typical balance sheet, liabilities are classified as either current liabilities or long-term liabilities.

- **Current Liabilities.** Short-term debts that must be repaid within one year are **current liabilities**. These include debts to suppliers for credit purchases (accounts payable), bank loans, and state sales taxes collected from customers and owed to the state.

- **Long-Term Liabilities.** Debts that usually take longer than one year to repay are **long-term liabilities**. The money owed on a mortgage, for example, is a long-term liability.

 *How do you calculate owner's equity?*

Preparing Balance Sheets

Balance sheets are divided into two sections. All the assets of the business are in the first section and the liabilities of the business and the owner's equity are included in the second section. Think of this second section as the creditors of the business, those to whom the business owes money, having the first claim on the assets. The owner receives any money remaining after all of the debts have been paid.

There are two formats for a balance sheet: one-column and two-column. Most large companies use the one-column format.

Matt Washington has been very successful over the past eight years. Matt's Hats now has a store that is famous for its large selection. Matt is preparing the annual balance sheet. The accounting period for Matt's Hats is the calendar year.

- **Current Assets.** The first step in preparing the income statement is to determine the value of the company's assets. Matt's Hats has cash on hand of $25,000 and the value of the inventory is $100,000. Inventory is the value of the goods a business has available for sale. Matt's Hats, for example, has a wide variety of hats available for sale. Customers owe the business $20,000 for sales made to them on credit (this is Matt's accounts receivable). Cash, inventory, and accounts receivable are classified as current asset accounts.

Matt's Hats
Balance Sheet
December 31, 20--

ASSETS

Current Assets

Cash	$ 25,000	
Inventory	100,000	
Accounts Receivable	20,000	
Total Current Assets		$ 145,000

Long-Term Assets

Building	$ 135,000	
Equipment	20,000	
Total Long-Term Assets		$ 155,000
Total Assets		**$ 300,000**

LIABILITIES & OWNER'S EQUITY

Current Liabilities

Bank Loans	$ 25,000	
Accounts Payable	40,000	
Sales Tax Payable	5,000	
Total Current Liabilities		$ 70,000

Long-Term Liabilities

Mortgage Payable	70,000	
Total Long-Term Liabilities		$ 70,000
Total Liabilities		**$ 140,000**

Owner's Equity

Matt Washington, Capital		$ 160,000
Total Liabilities & Owner's Equity		**$ 300,000**

Figure 11-5

Matt's Hats: Balance Sheet

This shows the balance sheet for Matt's Hats at the end of the year.

Analyzing Data. *What would be the owner's equity if Matt's Hats increased its inventory to $150,000?*

- **Long-Term Assets.** Matt's Hats owns its own building, which is worth $135,000. The company also has equipment for printing designs on baseball caps. The equipment is valued at $20,000. The building and the equipment are the only long-term assets owned by Matt's Hats.

- **Current Liabilities.** Next, Matt Washington has to determine the company's total liabilities. It has short-term bank loans of $25,000. The company also owes $40,000 to its merchandise suppliers for the inventory items purchased on credit, so the accounts payable total on the balance sheet is $40,000. The company also owes the state $5,000 for sales taxes it collected. So the company's sales tax payable is $5,000. These are the company's current liabilities.

- **Long-Term Liabilities.** Matt's Hats has a mortgage loan on its building. The company owes the mortgage company $70,000 on the loan, so its mortgage payable is $70,000. This is Matt's only long-term liability.

- **Owner's Equity.** The final step is to determine the owner's equity. Owner's equity is calculated by subtracting the total liabilities from the total assets. The owner's equity account for Matt's Hats, shown on the balance sheet as Matt Washington, Capital, has a balance of $160,000. The word "capital" in accounting refers to the investment or ownership value of the business. Because Matt is the sole owner of the business, this account reflects the value of the business to Matt.

> **Total Assets – Total Liabilities = Owner's Equity**
>
> **$300,000 – $140,000   = $160,000**

Not all businesses have all these accounts; however, the procedure for preparing the balance sheet (starting with assets and moving through liabilities to determine the owner's equity) will be similar to the procedure just outlined.

 *What are some typical accounts in a balance sheet?*

Analyzing Balance Sheets

A business usually prepares one balance sheet at the beginning of its fiscal year and another at the end. Comparing the beginning balance sheet to the ending one is an excellent way to determine whether the business is succeeding. For example, if the ending balance sheet shows that the owner's equity account has increased, it means that the business has gained value.

Another method used to analyze balance sheets is often called a same-size balance sheet analysis. A percentage change column is added to a comparative balance sheet. This column provides a quick method of analyzing all the changes in the two balance sheets (as in Figure 11-7).

Comparative Balance Sheet

Figure 11-6 shows a comparative balance sheet for Matt's Hats. The balance sheet on the right side was prepared on December 31 last year. The balance sheet on the left side was prepared December 31, one year later.

Compare the two balance sheets to see what has changed after one year.

Current Assets

- **Cash.** Cash has decreased from $25,000 to $20,000. Businesses have cash coming in and going out all the time, so the decrease isn't necessarily bad—as long as there is sufficient cash for daily operations. Remember, a successful entrepreneur prepares and uses cash flow statements to assure that the business has enough cash on hand.

YOUR BUSINESS CAREER

Responsibility

As a person grows in age and maturity, the level of responsibility should grow too. A responsible individual sees what needs to be done, does it, and doesn't expect anything in return. By this time in your life, you probably think of yourself as a fairly responsible person.

Some high school students may acknowledge that they aren't as responsible as they could be. Although they may want to be treated as adults, some still rely on their parents to do things they could be doing themselves. For example, they ask a parent to bring a textbook or an important paper to school when it was forgotten at home. They don't help clean the house or do the dishes at home. They expect their parents to give them spending money rather than finding ways to earn it.

Think of areas in your own life where you can strive to be more responsible. Then try to incorporate positive strategies into your life. No one expects you to become responsible overnight, but the more you try, the more you and those around you will notice the results.

THINKING CRITICALLY

Recognizing Patterns. Have you ever felt that you were irresponsible in a situation? What could you have done differently? In what ways could you be more responsible in your life?

To read more about responsibility, go to "Your Business Career" on the Student Center at entrepreneurship.pearson.com.

Matt's Hats
Comparative Balance Sheet

	December 31, This Year	December 31, Last Year
ASSETS		
Current Assets		
Cash	$ 20,000	$ 25,000
Inventory	125,000	100,000
Accounts Receivable	25,000	20,000
Total Current Assets	$ 170,000	$ 145,000
Long-Term Assets		
Building	$ 135,00	$ 135,000
Equipment	25,000	20,000
Total Long-Term Assets	$ 160,000	$ 155,000
Total Assets	**$ 330,000**	**$ 300,000**
LIABILITIES & OWNER'S EQUITY		
Current Liabilities		
Bank Loans	$ 20,000	$ 25,000
Accounts Payable	30,000	40,000
Sales Tax Payable	2,000	5,000
Total Current Liabilities	$ 52,000	$ 70,000
Long-Term Liabilities		
Mortgage Payable	70,000	70,000
Total Long-Term Liabilities	$ 70,000	$ 70,000
Total Liabilities	**$ 122,000**	**$ 140,000**
Owner's Equity		
Matt Washington, Capital	$ 208,000	$ 160,000
Total Liabilities & Owner's Equity	**$ 330,000**	**$ 300,000**

 Figure 11-6

Matt's Hats: Comparative Balance Sheet

This shows the comparative balance sheet for Matt's Hats on December 31, last year, and December 31, this year.

Predicting. *Based on this comparative balance sheet, how do you think Matt's Hats will do next year?*

- **Inventory.** The inventory has risen from $100,000 to $125,000. Matt's Hats has purchased more hats, which it hopes to sell. Because inventory has value, this asset account has increased.

- **Accounts Receivable.** This asset has increased from $20,000 to $25,000. This means the amount owed by customers to Matt's Hats from sales on credit has increased.

Long-Term Assets

- **Building.** The building account has not changed.

- **Equipment.** Matt purchased more equipment for customizing baseball caps during the year, so equipment has risen from $20,000 to $25,000.

Total Assets

- **Total Assets.** The total assets for Matt's Hats have risen from $300,000 to $330,000. The company has increased its assets, but does that mean that Matt's Hats has had a successful year? Let's look at the liabilities.

Current Liabilities

- **Bank Loans.** The amount owed to the banks for the loans taken out by Matt's Hats was reduced from $25,000 to $20,000. Decreasing the amount a business owes to its creditors is a good business strategy.

- **Accounts Payable.** The amount owed to the various whole-salers and manufacturers of hats decreased from $40,000 to $30,000. Despite adding inventory during the year, the amount owed to suppliers decreased. This shows that Matt made a deliberate business decision to reduce his liabilities.

- **Sales Tax Payable.** Matt's Hats collects sales tax for the state from its customers on every sale. It then makes payments to the state. Matt's Hats decreased the amount it owed the state from $5,000 to $2,000.

Long-Term Liabilities

- **Mortgage Payable.** The amount owed on the mortgage remained the same. This isn't unusual, because mortgages are structured so that payments in the early years are applied to the interest owed on the mortgage rather than to the principal. (The principal of a mortgage, or any loan, is the original amount borrowed, before interest is added.)

Owner's Equity

- **Matt Washington, Capital.** The owner's equity account of the business, written as "Matt Washington, Capital," increased from $160,000 to $208,000. That's good news for Matt, because it means that the business increased in value during that time period.

Despite having less cash at the end of the period, the comparative balance sheet shows very favorable financial information for Matt's Hats. The company has increased the amount of inventory it has available for sale, and it is owed more money from credit sales.

The company has reduced all its current liabilities. Amounts owed for bank loans, accounts payable, and sales tax payable all decreased. Remember:

$$\text{Assets} - \text{Liabilities} = \text{Owner's Equity}$$

By reducing liabilities, Matt Washington has increased his owner's equity, the value of his business. He reduced his liabilities by paying off some of the company's debt. Paying off debt is one of the smartest things a business can do with extra cash.

Same-Size Balance Sheet Analysis

Figure 11-7 shows the comparative balance sheet for Elton's Electronics, with an added column. This column shows all the changes from last year to this year as a percentage of last year's amounts.

For example, accounts receivable grew from $20,000 last year to $25,000 this year. That's a 25% growth.

$$\underset{\textit{(This Year)}}{\$25,000} - \underset{\textit{(Last Year)}}{\$20,000} = \underset{\textit{(Difference)}}{\$5,000}$$

$$(\$5,000 \div \$20,000) \times 100 = 25\%$$

The same-size balance sheet analysis statement provides a quick way to see how the business is performing. (Note that any value written in red and set in parentheses is a negative percentage.)

A quick look at the percentages shows that Matt's Hats has increased both its inventory and its accounts receivable by 25%. This reflects favorably on the business. Reducing all the current liabilities, especially the accounts payable, by 25% is another example of a good business strategy. The wise business decisions made by Matt are reflected in the 30% increase in his owner's equity.

Matt's Hats
Same-Size Balance Sheet

	December 31, This Year		December 31, Last Year		% Change
ASSETS					
Current Assets					
Cash	$ 20,000		$ 25,000		(20)
Inventory	125,000		100,000		25
Accounts Receivable	25,000		20,000		25
Total Current Assets		$ 170,000		$ 145,000	17.2
Long-Term Assets					
Building	$ 135,00		$ 135,000		0
Equipment	25,000		20,000		25
Total Long-Term Assets		$ 160,000		$ 155,000	3.2
Total Assets		$ 330,000		$ 300,000	10
LIABILITIES & OWNER'S EQUITY					
Current Liabilities					
Bank Loans	$ 20,000		$ 25,000		(20)
Accounts Payable	30,000		40,000		(25)
Sales Tax Payable	2,000		5,000		(60)
Total Current Liabilities		$ 52,000		$ 70,000	(25.7)
Long-Term Liabilities					
Mortgage Payable	70,000		70,000		0
Total Long-Term Liabilities		$ 70,000		$ 70,000	0
Total Liabilities		$ 122,000		$ 140,000	(12.8)
Owner's Equity					
Matt Washington, Capital		$ 208,000		$ 160,000	30
Total Liabilities & Owner's Equity		$ 330,000		$ 300,000	10

 Figure 11-7

Matt's Hats: Same-Size Balance Sheet Analysis

The same-size balance sheet analysis statement for Matt's Hats on December 31, last year, and December 31, this year, shows the percentage changes from one year to the next.

Drawing Conclusions. *Based on this statement, do you think Matt Washington made good business decisions during the year?*

 **READING CHECKPOINT** *What two types of balance sheets are used to analyze how a business is performing?*

 Your Business Plan. Continue developing your standard business plan. Go to "Section 11.2" of the *Business Plan Project* in your *Student Activity Workbook*, or "Section 11.2" of the BizTech Software.

ASSESSMENT 11.2

Reviewing Objectives

1. How do you calculate owner's equity?

2. What are some typical accounts in a balance sheet?

3. Describe the comparative balance sheet and the same-size balance sheet analysis statements.

Critical Thinking

4. **Applying Concepts.** Describe the relationship between liabilities and owner's equity in a balance sheet.

5. **Relating Concepts.** Why is inventory an asset?

Working Together

Working with a partner, use a spreadsheet program such as Microsoft Excel to create a same-size analysis for Matt's Hats based on the totals shown in Figure 11-7. Use a formula to calculate the percentages.

Math
Percentages

Using the same-size analysis in Figure 11-7, calculate the effect of reducing the current liabilities this year by 17%. Then calculate the effect of increasing liabilities by 17%. Make sure to adjust the % Change column.

Konspiracy Studios: Cash In, Cash Out

When Mike Greenberg of Damascus, Maryland, was in the eighth grade, he discovered he loved working with images. He became the go-to guy for video and graphic design throughout high school. During his junior year, he took an internship at a post-production facility. He was told that it would be several years before his manager would allow him to work directly with clients. That convinced Mike to focus on his own business. Within six months he was working full time for himself.

Mike's company, Konspiracy Studios, provides print, Web, and video services, with about 70% of the business video, 20% graphics, and 10% Web consulting. "We create videos that ultimately end up on TV, the Web, or DVDs," said Mike. "We've cut several promos for clients to present to networks for funding. We also create corporate identity packages and marketing materials for several firms."

Funding His Business

Mike bought his initial equipment by saving money he earned as a busboy. His parents helped him by matching 50% of what he earned at work. Now he's supporting himself completely through his business. He's managed to keep his overhead extremely low by negotiating and bartering. (Bartering is trading goods or services with another person or company for goods or services in return.)

Mike pays for all his expenses through his debit card and uses a free online service that allows him to track his card usage. "You can see what categories you're spending in," he said, "and it actually generates ways for you to save."

Spending for Profit

When it comes to spending money, Mike feels that "you have to look at what you're buying and see how that fits into the business." He only buys additional equipment when he needs it for a project. "I didn't

▲ *Mike Greenberg*

make any frivolous expenditures," he said. "I kept looking at the fundamentals of what worked and what didn't." He constantly reviews his progress in terms of both money and his morale—how he felt and how his customers felt.

At times, he's made some purchases that didn't pan out because he hadn't done enough research. A video converter, for example, wasn't compatible with his computer. On the other hand, he's also made some minor purchases that have proven to be extremely successful. An e-mail marketing service has enabled him to stay in touch with a number of clients.

Mike charges an hourly rate or, with established customers, uses a long-term fixed contract that includes a monthly retainer. "I reward people for booking long periods of time by giving them lower rates," said Mike. His Website highlights his services. It shows off his reel, displays his awards, and provides case studies of how he's solved client requests.

Thinking Like an Entrepreneur

1. How would you use bartering in your business?
2. Why is researching your buying decisions important?
3. Why should you look at the emotional as well as the financial results of your work?

CHAPTER SUMMARY

11.1 Income Statements & Cash Flow

An income statement includes sales and expense data as well as the net income or loss of a business. Income statements differ based on the type of business. Retailing and wholesaling use the category Cost of Goods Sold. Manufacturing companies use Cost of Goods Manufactured and Sold. Service businesses use Cost of Services Sold. A business must have sufficient cash to pay its bills and debts. To assure that enough cash is on hand, entrepreneurs prepare cash flow statements. These statements record cash inflows and cash outflows when they occur. Because of their importance, cash flow statements should be prepared monthly. In the beginning months of a new business, it is common that more money is spent than earned. The rate at which a company spends cash to cover overhead costs without generating a positive cash flow is called the burn rate.

11.2 Balance Sheet

A balance sheet is a financial statement that summarizes the assets and liabilities (debts) of a business. The balance sheet also shows the value of the business to the entrepreneur (owner's equity). The owner's equity is calculated by subtracting the total liabilities from the total assets. Entrepreneurs analyze balance sheets to help them determine how their businesses are performing. Comparative balance sheets and same-size balance sheet analysis statements are used by entrepreneurs to identify the changes in assets, liabilities, and owner's equity from one accounting period to another.

REVIEW VOCABULARY

Working in teams of three prepare an oral presentation, to be presented to a group of parents, explaining the role of income statements, cash flow statements, and balance sheets in operating a successful business. Use at least half the following terms in your presentation:

- accounts payable (p. 306)
- accounts receivable (p. 305)
- asset (p. 305)
- balance sheet (p. 304)
- burn rate (p. 303)
- calendar year (p. 290)
- cash flow (p. 300)
- cash flow statement (p. 300)
- current assets (p. 305)
- current liabilities (p. 306)
- cyclical (p. 302)
- fiscal year (p. 290)
- income statement (p. 289)
- liability (p. 305)
- long-term assets (p. 305)
- long-term liabilities (p. 306)
- owner's equity (p. 305)
- profit and loss statement (p. 289)

CHECK YOUR UNDERSTANDING

Choose the letter that best answers the question or completes the statement.

1. Entrepreneurs should prepare income statements
    a. daily
    b. monthly
    c. quarterly
    d. yearly

2. In an income statement, subtracting the cost of goods sold from the net sales provides the
    a. revenue
    b. net operating income
    c. gross profit
    d. net income

3. A cost of goods sold section is included in a
    a. merchandising business income statement
    b. service business income statement
    c. cash flow statement
    d. balance sheet

4. An entrepreneur should prepare a cash flow statement
    a. daily
    b. monthly
    c. quarterly
    d. yearly

5. The rate at which the business needs to spend cash to cover overhead costs before beginning to generate a positive cash flow is called the
    a. start-up rate
    b. overhead rate
    c. cash flow rate
    d. burn rate

6. The cash flow equation is
    a. Cash Outflow – Cash Inflow = Net Profit
    b. Cash Outflow – Cash Inflow = Gross Profit
    c. Cash Inflow – Cash Outflow = Net Cash
    d. Cash Inflow – Cash Outflow = Net Profit

7. A balance sheet includes
    a. assets
    b. liabilities
    c. owner's equity
    d. all of the above

8. The amount owed by a business to its suppliers for credit purchases is called
    a. accounts receivable
    b. accounts payable
    c. merchandise payable
    d. purchases on account

9. Owner's equity is calculated by
    a. subtracting total liabilities from total assets
    b. dividing total liabilities by total assets
    c. subtracting total assets from total liabilities
    d. dividing total assets by total liabilities

10. Which of the following is not a current liability?
    a. accounts payable
    b. mortgage
    c. bank loan
    d. collected state sales taxes

11. A statement that includes a column showing the changes in percentages from the first period to the ending period is called a
    a. balance sheet
    b. comparative balance sheet
    c. same-size balance sheet analysis
    d. competitive balance sheet

12. Which of the following is not a long-term asset?
    a. building
    b. equipment
    c. machinery
    d. accounts receivable

Business Communication

13. You want to start a dog-walking business. Prepare an income statement that shows this is a workable idea.

14. Partner with a classmate. You have an idea for a new energy drink. You need to raise capital to finance a test market in your area. Prepare an income statement that shows your plan. Role-play a presentation to a bank official, with a classmate playing the bank official. Then reverse roles.

15. Partner with a classmate. You own a sports equipment store with two partners. You've been in business for two years. You and another partner want to expand your product line. Prepare a presentation of your ideas. Use income statements, balance sheets, and cash flow statements to help you prove that the business will be financially capable of taking on the added risk. Make your presentation to the class, who will represent your third partner.

Business Ethics

18. You own an electronics store. While taking inventory, you notice that five cell phones are missing. Last month you hired a part-time worker who has access to the cell phones. You aren't absolutely sure that the new employee stole the phones, but you can't think of any other explanation. You can't afford to continue losing inventory. Do you confront the employee with your suspicions? How would you resolve your problem? With a partner, role-play the situation. Then reverse roles.

Business Math

16. Last year's balance sheet showed an owner's equity of $400,000 and this year's balance sheet showed owner's equity as $500,000. What is the percentage increase?

17. In a monthly income statement, if the gross profit is $10,000, the total operating expenses are $4,000, and the taxes are 15%, what is the net profit? If the total operating expenses double next month, what is the percentage change in net profit from this month to next month?

Business in Your Community

19. Working with three classmates, brainstorm a business you might like to start in your community. Write a short description of the business, including how much money you would need to start the business and what equipment would be required. Prepare a balance sheet for your new business.

20. Interview two entrepreneurs or small-business owners in your community. Ask them what financial statements have proven to be the most beneficial. Write a short report comparing the results of your interviews.

Networks

Technically speaking, a network is a connection of two or more computers working together. Networks can be quite small, such as in a home office where two computers are connected so they can use the same printer. But networks can also be very large, as in the case of the Internet—which is a worldwide interconnection of government, academic, private, and public networks.

Types of Networks

Some networks are defined by the method of connection. Computers and peripherals—printers, scanners, fax machines—can be connected through a wireless network or by actual wires and cables. A **wireless network** operates on a radio frequency, much the same way that cell phones work. Often networks contain both wireless and wired capabilities. **Hubs** are the devices that connect the computers both to each other and to the Internet.

Other networks are defined by their scale. A **Local Area Network** (LAN) is used in a limited area, such as an office, school, or other building. A **Wide Area Network** (WAN) connects large geographic areas, such as one city to another or one country to another, through the Internet. Most small-business networks run on a wired/wireless network, with all computers and peripherals connecting to a network server. A **network server** is a computer that stores files used by the networked computers. It may also store programs.

Resource Sharing

Networks began as a way for computers to share files so everyone involved could look at the same files without having to store copies on their individual computers. This is called **file sharing**, and it led to greater efficiency within companies. Networks also let businesses share resources, such as printers and scanners, which helps reduce costs. By using servers, networks allow program sharing, permitting several computers to use the same program at the same time. This further reduces costs because companies don't need to buy as many copies of a program. Networks also provide high-speed Internet access to all networked computers.

Network Security

Security is extremely important in business. With almost every computer connected to the Internet, the possibility exists that damage could be done to the network and to individual computers. By installing a firewall, you can protect both the network and the individual computers. A **firewall** is a software program or hardware device designed to prevent unauthorized electronic access to a networked computer system.

A computer network is about simplicity. It's important for businesses to be efficient—to do the most work in as little time as possible. Using a network helps businesses be cost-effective and be successful.

Tech Vocabulary
- file sharing
- firewall
- hubs
- local area network (LAN)
- network server
- wide area network (WAN)
- wireless network

Check Yourself
1. What is a wireless network?
2. Name two types of networks.
3. What is the advantage of resource sharing?
4. What is a firewall?

What Do You Think?
Classifying. How would you classify the various types of computer networks?

12 FINANCIAL RATIOS &
BREAK-EVEN ANALYSIS

OBJECTIVES

- Explain what a financial ratio is
- Describe how income statements are used for financial analysis
- Compare operating ratios and return-on-sales ratios
- Describe the ratios developed by using balance sheets
- Explain the importance of return on investment

VOCABULARY

- current ratio
- debt ratio
- debt-to-equity ratio
- financial ratio
- liquidity
- marketable securities
- operating ratio
- quick ratio
- return on investment (ROI)
- return on sales (ROS)
- same-size analysis

Think about how you would answer these questions:

How much profit should a company make? How much debt should a company have?

Partner with another student and discuss these questions. Be prepared to present your answers to the class.

What Are Financial Ratios?

How do entrepreneurs know if a company is healthy? They often rely on information from financial records. But it's not always easy to analyze these records, to see the relationships, patterns, and the trends they show.

One of the most effective ways for entrepreneurs to analyze their financial statements is to use **financial ratios**. These are relationships between important financial data that are expressed as fractions or as percentages. Entrepreneurs calculate financial ratios by using the data from the financial statements. All financial ratios are calculated by dividing one number by another.

An entrepreneur should *not* rely on just one or two ratios. Ratios are only indicators and each will shed light on a different aspect of the business.

Another way entrepreneurs can see relationships, patterns, and trends is by using charts. Pie charts and bar graphs are very helpful in illustrating financial ratios. You can create either one in a computer software program such as Microsoft Excel. An entrepreneur often makes presentations on the financial status of the business. Showing financial data—including financial ratios—visually can be an effective way to help others understand the significance of your information.

Pie Charts

A pie chart has "slices" that represent portions of the whole. You could create a pie chart by using the information on the income statement for Matt's Hats (Fig. 12-1).

Figure 12-1 ►

Income Statement and Pie Chart

This pie chart shows the relationship of the COGS, operating expenses, and pre-tax profit.

Interpreting Graphs. *How would you know if this is a good split of costs and operating expenses to sales?*

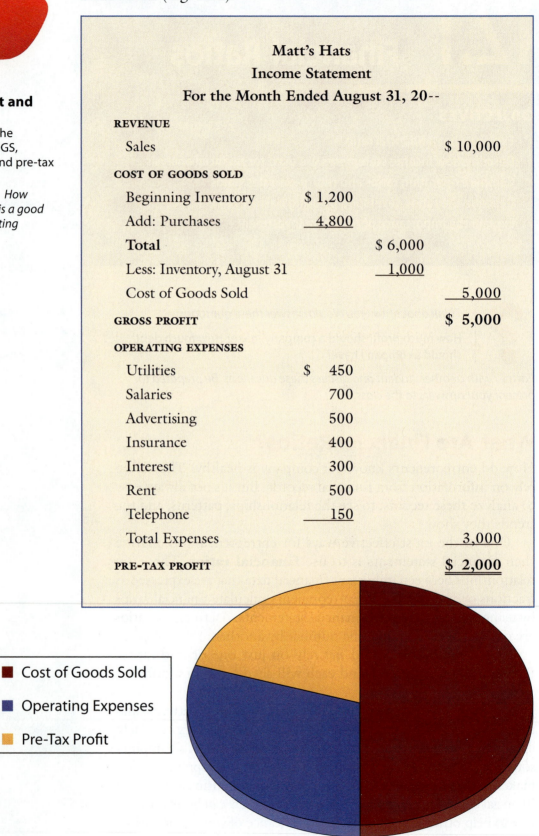

Matt's Hats

Income Statement

For the Month Ended August 31, 20--

REVENUE			
Sales			$ 10,000
COST OF GOODS SOLD			
Beginning Inventory	$ 1,200		
Add: Purchases	4,800		
Total		$ 6,000	
Less: Inventory, August 31		1,000	
Cost of Goods Sold			5,000
GROSS PROFIT			$ 5,000
OPERATING EXPENSES			
Utilities	$ 450		
Salaries	700		
Advertising	500		
Insurance	400		
Interest	300		
Rent	500		
Telephone	150		
Total Expenses			3,000
PRE-TAX PROFIT			$ 2,000

■ Cost of Goods Sold

■ Operating Expenses

■ Pre-Tax Profit

The pie chart shows the cost of goods sold, operating expenses, and net income. The entire pie represents 100% of Matt's Hats sales in August—$10,000. Costs, operating expenses, and pre-tax profit are shown as percentages of this total. For example, because Matt's Hats had expenses of $3,000 in August, the percentage of expenses to sales is 30%.

(Expenses ÷ Revenue) × 100 = **Expenses as a Percentage of Sales**

($3,000 ÷ $10,000) × 100 = 30%

Do you find it easier to review the status of Matt's Hats by using the pie chart or the income statement? They both give you the same information. In the future, Matt's Hats can use this percentage to evaluate whether its monthly operating expenses are in an acceptable range. Matt will know that, for his particular business, these expenses are about 30% of sales—at least for this current month. (The monthly percentage will probably vary—and every business will be different.)

Bar Graphs

A bar graph uses vertical or horizontal bars to show data. Bar graphs are good for demonstrating trends. For example, let's look at five monthly income statements for Matt's Hats. In January, the business had very little revenue ($300) because it was just getting started and didn't have many sales. Wisely, Matt had put aside some money that would take care of expenses for several months. (How much you should put aside when starting a business will be discussed in Chapter 13.)

After the slow start, sales picked up. In February, they were $1,500; in March, $2,000. In April, sales reached $2,500, and they increased again in May to $3,000. Do you see a trend? Sales for Matt's Hats increased every month. This same information would have been found in Matt's income statements, but the bar graph made the trend easy to see at a glance. Matt can use this information to make predictions about future sales.

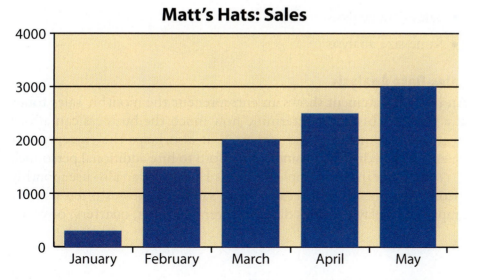

Matt's Hats: Sales

◀ **Figure 12-2**

Matt's Hats Bar Graph
This bar graph makes the sales trend from January through May easy to see.

Predicting. *Based on the trend shown, what do you estimate sales for Matt's Hats will be in June?*

Entrepreneurship Blogs

Small-business owners have to stay informed about trends in their industry. In addition, they need to be aware of tools and data that make running a company easier. A good way for an entrepreneur to do this is to follow a sampling of entrepreneurship blogs.

A blog is usually maintained by one person. It features regular entries of text, photos, and links. Most blogs have a specific topic. Entrepreneurship blogs focus on the concerns of small businesses and can be a great resource for the latest information about how to run a company efficiently and navigate changing market conditions. Most blogs also have comment sections where readers can interact with the blogger, as well as the entire readership.

Some notable entrepreneurship blogs that are updated frequently and feature timely, useful information and tips are:

www.smallbiztrends.com,
www.smallbusinessarena.com,
www.youngentrepreneur.com/blog,
bizzbangbuzz.blogspot.com,
www.ducttapemarketing.com/blog, and
www.entrepreneurs-journey.com.

Each blog has its own tone and focus, so you should look them over and choose the blog best suited to your needs.

THINKING CRITICALLY

Applying Concepts. Think about what makes a blog useful to an entrepreneur. Do any of these blogs, or any other entrepreneurial blogs, meet your criteria?

To read more about entrepreneurship blogs, go to "Entrepreneurship Issues" on the Student Center at entrepreneurship.pearson.com.

 *What is a financial ratio?*

Analysis Based on an Income Statement

As you've seen, entrepreneurs use income statements to show how their businesses are performing. The information contained in an income statement may sometimes need to be analyzed by using financial ratios or dramatized in charts and graphs. Two important types of analysis based on income statements are

- Sales-data analysis
- Same-size analysis

Sales-Data Analysis

An income statement shows an entrepreneur the monthly sales totals at a glance. This helps determine how much the business can afford to spend on purchases and expenses. It also helps the entrepreneur determine whether the business can afford to hire additional personnel.

As you saw in the example of Matt's Hats, you can also use monthly income statements to forecast future sales. Businesses often use bar graphs to display the sales data for several months, quarters, or years.

You can analyze the trends shown in bar graphs and use them to estimate future sales, just as Matt did. Combining income statement analysis and a knowledge of the industry (for example, slow periods, new competitors, or other factors that influence sales) will be very helpful in forecasting sales. An accurate forecast is an important factor in business success.

Same-Size Analysis

Besides using income statements for sales-data analysis, entrepreneurs also use income statements to measure how their cost of goods sold and operating expenses affect profits. They do this by using **same-size analysis**, which is a comparison of total revenue or other financial data against that same data converted into percentages (in much the same way as the pie chart and the balance sheet earlier in this chapter).

You create a same-size analysis of an income statement by dividing a line item by the sales and then multiplying by 100. This shows the line item as a percentage of sales. When calculating same-size analysis, many entrepreneurs just include the major items from the income statement.

SAME-SIZE ANALYSIS

Income Statement	Amount	Calculation	% of Sales
Revenue (Sales)	$10,000	($10,000 ÷ $10,000) × 100	100%
COGS	$4,000	($4,000 ÷ $10,000) × 100	40%
Gross Profit	$6,000	($6,000 ÷ $10,000) × 100	60%
Expenses	$3,500	($3,500 ÷ $10,000) × 100	35%
Pre-Tax Profit	$2,500	($2,500 ÷ $10,000) × 100	25%

Same-size analysis makes it clear how each item affects the business's pre-tax profit. Entrepreneurs review the percentages and make changes to improve their profits. An entrepreneur might know that the percentage for the average cost of goods sold in the industry is 30%. If the business has a cost of goods sold of 40%, any competing businesses will have an advantage. Other things being equal, they will be

10% more profitable. The entrepreneur should attempt to lower the percentage to at least the industry average.

Same-size analysis also allows you to easily compare income statements from different months, quarters, or years. Even if the sales are different from month to month or quarter to quarter, a same-size analysis will show you patterns and trends. Look at this example from Matt's Hats, showing the major items in the income statement for January and February.

JANUARY			FEBRUARY		
Income Statement	Amount	% of Sales	Income Statement	Amount	% of Sales
Revenue (Sales)	$50,000	100%	Revenue (Sales)	$40,000	100%
COGS	$19,000	38%	COGS	$10,400	26%
Gross Profit	$31,000	62%	Gross Profit	$29,600	74%
Expenses	$17,000	34%	Expenses	$15,200	38%
Pre-Tax Profit	$14,000	28%	Pre-Tax Profit	$14,400	36%

The comparison of sales for Matt's Hats shows that they dropped from $50,000 in January to $40,000 in February. However, in February the business was able to reduce its cost of goods sold from 38% to 26%. As a result, the company had an increase in pre-tax profit over January, despite having a drop in sales. So which month do you think was better for Matt's Hats?

 *What is same-size analysis?*

Income Statement Ratios

Sales-data analysis and same-size analysis are both based on the income statement. They are especially helpful for understanding how a business is doing over time. Some financial ratios that are based on the income statement are helpful for providing a "snapshot" of a specific aspect of a business. These ratios provide information you can use to monitor expenses, to compare the performance of the company with competitors in the industry, and to measure profitability.

The two most important financial ratios based on the income statement are:

- The operating ratio
- Return on sales (ROS)

Operating Ratio

One of the most significant ratios used by entrepreneurs is the **operating ratio**. It is the percentage of each dollar of revenue, or sales, needed to cover expenses. For example, if an income statement for Matt's Hats shows sales of $20,000 and an insurance expense of $1,000, Matt's operating ratio for insurance is 5%.

(Expenses ÷ Sales)	× 100 = Operating Ratio (%)
($1,000 ÷ $20,000) × 100 =	5%

Operating ratios are typically used to compare an entrepreneur's company with other businesses in the industry. For example, if Matt's Hats is paying $2,000 a month in rent and has sales of $10,000, its operating ratio for rent is 20%.

$$(\$2,000 \div \$10,000) \times 100 = 20\%$$

Matt could compare this 20% ratio with others in the industry. If 20% is higher than the industry average, Matt needs to make a decision: Should he remain in the present location or move to a less expensive one, where the rent would be lower? (Of course, there are usually many elements to consider before moving a business. For example, Matt's current location could be generating additional sales.)

Return on Sales (ROS)

Return on sales (ROS) is the financial ratio calculated by dividing net profit by sales. To convert that to a percentage, multiply the result by 100. ROS is an important measure of how profitable a business is, because it shows how much of each dollar of sales the company keeps as profit. ROS may also be called net margin, net profit ratio, net profit on sales ratio, or—most frequently—profit margin.

Here's an example of calculating return on sales. If the income statement for Matt's Hats shows sales of $30,000 and a net profit of $6,000, the ROS percentage for the business is 20%.

$$(\text{Net Profit} \div \text{Sales}) \quad \times \ 100 \ = \ \text{Return on Sales (\%)}$$

$$(\$6{,}000 \div \$30{,}000) \times 100 \ = \qquad 20\%$$

A high ROS ratio is usually a good indicator of success for a business. However, the ROS percentage alone doesn't provide a total picture. A business selling high-priced items, such as luxury automobiles, can be very profitable with a 5% ROS, while a retailer like Matt's Hats who sells inexpensive items may need a 25% ROS or more.

The ROS (Profit Margin) table below shows ROS ranges for various types of products.

ROS (PROFIT MARGIN)

ROS	Margin Range	Typical Product
Very low	2–5%	Very high volume OR very high price
Low	6–10%	High volume OR high price
Moderate	11–20%	Moderate volume AND moderate price
High	20–30%	Low volume OR low price
Very high	30% and up	Very low volume OR very low price

Ratios from Balance Sheets

In addition to the financial ratios calculated by using the data on income statements, entrepreneurs also create ratios from the data on the balance sheets for their businesses. They then use these ratios to monitor debt, to compare debt with equity, and to make sure the business has sufficient cash to pay its debts.

The four most important financial ratios based on the balance sheet are:

- The debt ratio
- The debt-to-equity ratio
- The quick ratio
- The current ratio

Debt Ratio and Debt-to-Equity Ratio

A business needs to control its debts. If the business is unable to make the interest payments on its debt, it can be forced into bankruptcy. A ratio used to monitor the debts of a business is the **debt ratio**. This is the ratio of a business's total debt divided by its total assets. For example, if Matt's Hats has $100,000 in total debts (also referred to as its total liabilities) and total assets of $500,000, its debt ratio is 20%.

(Total Debts ÷ Total Assets) × 100 = Debt Ratio (%)

($100,000 ÷ $500,000) × 100 = 20%

A debt ratio of 20% means that the debts for Matt's Hats equal 20% of its total assets. A high debt ratio indicates that a business has made the decision to use creditors and suppliers for financing, rather than its own money. This can be a good strategy, because it may help the owners achieve a higher return on their investment. The risk, however, is that the more debt a business has, the higher its interest payments will be. And, of course, if the business fails to pay its debts, it could be forced into bankruptcy.

Bankers don't like to lend money to businesses with high debt ratios. A high ratio may also make it difficult for a company to establish credit with suppliers. An ideal debt ratio is determined by the ability of the company to meet its loan payments, at an amount of debt considered acceptable in the industry. So when starting or operating your business, you will need to determine an ideal debt ratio based on your industry.

Another useful tool is the **debt-to-equity ratio**. This is the ratio of the total debts (liabilities) of the business divided by its owner's equity. For example, if Matt's Hats had debts of $100,000 and an owner's equity of $400,000, the debt-to-equity ratio would be 25%.

$$\left(\text{Total Debts} \div \text{Owner's Equity}\right) \times 100 = \text{Debt-to-Equity Ratio (\%)}$$

$$\left(\$100,000 \div \$400,000\right) \times 100 = 25\%$$

This means that, for every dollar of debt the business has, it has $4 of equity. *Because the value of a business is the owner's equity, you need to monitor the debt-to-equity ratio carefully.*

Quick Ratio and Current Ratio

The balance sheet also tells you about a business's liquidity. **Liquidity** is the ability to convert assets into cash. Two ratios that help you keep an eye on liquidity are the quick ratio and the current ratio.

The **quick ratio** is the comparison of cash to debt, based on the concept that a business should have at least enough money on hand to pay its current debts. The quick ratio is calculated by adding the value of its marketable securities to the cash on hand. **Marketable securities** are investments, such as stocks or bonds, that could be converted to cash quickly. Then, that sum is divided by the current liabilities of the business.

For example, if a company has $50,000 in marketable securities, $150,000 in cash, and $100,000 in current liabilities, its quick ratio is 2 to 1 (which can also be shown as 2:1). Both quick and current ratios are calculated as ratios rather than as percentages.

$$\left(\text{Cash} + \text{Marketable Securities}\right) \div \text{Current Liabilities} = \text{Quick Ratio}$$

$$\left(\$150,000 + \$50,000\right) \div \$100,000 = 2 \text{ to } 1$$

The quick ratio tells an entrepreneur whether the business has enough cash to cover its current debts. Because a business should be able to pay its debts, the quick ratio should always be greater than 1 to 1.

A similar formula is the **current ratio**. This is current assets divided by current liabilities. For example, if Matt's Hats has current assets of $250,000 and current liabilities of $100,000, its current ratio would be 2.5 to 1.

Current Assets	÷	Current Liabilities	=	Current Ratio
$250,000	÷	$100,000	=	2.5 to 1

Like the quick ratio, the current ratio provides information about the liquidity of the business. The current ratio indicates whether a business would be capable of selling its assets to pay its debts. Most businesses try to maintain a current ratio of 2 to 1.

 *What are four ratios calculated from a balance sheet?*

Return on Investment (ROI)

An entrepreneur starts a new business at least partially as an investment. One of the financial ratios used to determine how well the business is doing in relation to the amount of money invested in it is called **return on investment (ROI)**. This shows the profit on the initial investment expressed as a percentage of that investment. It is calculated by dividing the net profit by the initial investment and multiplying by 100. For example, if the net profit is $1,500 and the initial investment was $10,000, the ROI is 15%.

$$\left(\begin{array}{c}\text{Net} \\ \text{Profit}\end{array} \div \begin{array}{c}\text{Initial} \\ \text{Investment}\end{array}\right) \times 100 = \begin{array}{c}\text{Return on} \\ \text{Investment (\%)}\end{array}$$

$$(\$1,500 \div \$10,000) \times 100 = 15\%$$

 *How is a return-on-investment (ROI) ratio calculated and what will the results tell you?*

 Your Business Plan. Continue developing your standard business plan. Go to "Section 12.1" of the *Business Plan Project* in your *Student Activity Workbook*, or "Section 12.1" of the BizTech Software.

Reviewing Objectives

1. What is a financial ratio?

2. What is same-size analysis?

3. What are two ratios that are calculated with data from an income statement?

4. What are four ratios that are calculated with data from a balance sheet?

5. How is a return-on-investment (ROI) ratio calculated?

Critical Thinking

6. **Comparing.** Which do you think is more important to a business and why: the operating ratio or the return on sales?

7. **Drawing Conclusions.** If you were running your own business, would you prefer to maintain a low debt ratio or a high one? Why?

Working Together

Choose an imaginary business. Form two teams. The first team will create an income statement for the business and prepare an operating ratio and a return-on-sales (ROS) calculation. Using the same business and the first team's income statement, the second team will prepare a balance sheet for a business and prepare a debt ratio, a debt-to-equity ratio, and a quick ratio.

Math

Financial Ratios

Calculate the following:

Current Ratio—with total assets of $400,000 and total liabilities of $100,000.

Debt-to-Equity Ratio (%)—with total liabilities of $200,000 and owner's equity of $800,000.

Operating Ratio (%)—with expenses of $2,000 and sales of $40,000.

Return on Sales (%)—with net profit of $3,000 and sales of $10,000.

OBJECTIVES

- Explain the importance of the break-even point
- Perform a break-even analysis

VOCABULARY

- break-even analysis
- break-even point
- break-even units

? | *Quickly think about this question:*

How do you know if a business is profitable?

Write a short answer on a piece of paper. Be prepared to discuss your answer in class.

What Is a Break-Even Point?

In Chapter 11 and in the first section of this chapter, you learned a great deal about income statements and financial ratios—and why they are important to entrepreneurs. You learned that an income statement shows whether a business has made a profit or suffered a loss.

Now think about this: On an income statement, what would happen if the expenses were exactly equal to the sales? There would be neither a profit nor a loss. The net income at the bottom would be zero. That is what's called the **break-even point**, because the business has sold *exactly* enough units to cover expenses.

A **break-even analysis** is an examination of the income statement that identifies the break-even point for a business. A break-even analysis examines how many units of a product (or hours of a service) a business must sell to pay all its expenses.

For example, Matt would have a problem if Matt's Hats had sales of 500 hats and needed to sell 1,000 to break even (and pay his costs). Matt would have to make some decisions, because he wasn't selling enough hats to cover his expenses (let

Positive Attitude

Not everybody has a positive attitude. It just may not seem natural to you. It may be something you will have to work at. But regardless of how you attain it, you should work on having a positive attitude in everything you do.

Here's one way you can help develop a positive attitude: Don't compare yourself to those around you. Your peers may appear to be faster, smarter, or more knowledgeable than you are in some areas, but you will outshine them in others. Think about your individual strengths and what you like most about yourself. Concentrate on those things. Set short- and long-term goals. Work toward those goals by saying "I can." If you expect success, it will come to you.

To maintain your positive attitude, don't hang around with people who put themselves or others down. When you recognize that you are someone with a positive attitude, others will too.

THINKING CRITICALLY

Forming a Model. Do you have short-term goals for the rest of the school year? Have you set long-term goals? Write down three short-term and three long-term goals you would like to achieve. Think about how you will strive to reach each of these and how a positive attitude will help you.

To read more about positive attitude, go to "Your Business Career" on the Student Center at entrepreneurship.pearson.com.

alone make a profit!). He might decide to review his expenses to see if any could be reduced or eliminated. Or, he might find ways to increase sales. Frequently, business owners need to come up with combinations of methods to solve problems like this. The problems must be solved or the company will go out of business very quickly.

 **READING CHECKPOINT** *What is a break-even point?*

Break-Even Analysis

You use break-even analysis to determine how many units of a product a business must sell to pay all its expenses. Let's use Matt's Hats as an example of how to carry out a break-even analysis.

Matt's Hats bought 1,000 hats at $6 each. It sold the hats at $10 each. So the total sales revenue was $10,000.

> **Total Sales Revenue: 1,000 hats × $10 per hat = $10,000**

In this example:

- The unit of sale for Matt's Hats is one hat.
- The selling price per hat is $10.
- The cost of goods sold is $6.

This means that Matt's Hats had a gross profit of $4 per hat.

$$\begin{array}{ccc} \text{Selling Price} & \text{Cost of Goods Sold} & \text{Gross Profit} \\ \text{per Unit} & \text{per Unit} & \text{per Unit} \end{array}$$

$$\$10 - \$6 \qquad = \qquad \$4$$

The gross profit of the business is used to pay operating expenses. Matt's Hats didn't have any variable expenses other than the cost of goods sold. If the company had other variable expenses, it would have used the equation:

$$\begin{array}{ccc} \text{Selling Price} & \text{Total Variable} & \text{Contribution} \\ \text{per Unit} & \text{Expenses per Unit} & \text{Margin per Unit} \end{array}$$

The brief traditional-format income statement in Fig. 12-3 shows that Matt's Hats has operating expenses of $3,000.

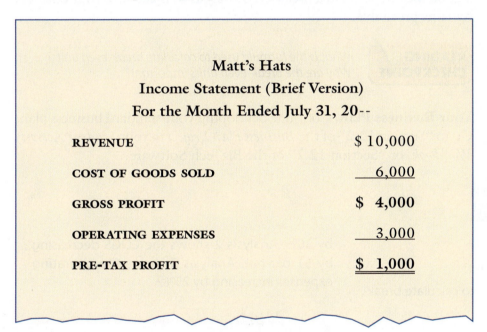

Matt's Hats

Income Statement (Brief Version)

For the Month Ended July 31, 20--

REVENUE	$ 10,000
COST OF GOODS SOLD	6,000
GROSS PROFIT	$ 4,000
OPERATING EXPENSES	3,000
PRE-TAX PROFIT	$ 1,000

Figure 12-3

Matt's Hats: Income Statement

This shows a brief income statement for Matt's Hats for the month of July, 20--.

Analyzing Data. *If the selling price per hat is $10, how many hats did Matt's Hats sell in the month of July?*

Using the information from the income statement, Matt can calculate how many hats Matt's Hats has to sell each month to cover operating expenses. These are its **break-even units**—the number of units of sale a business needs to sell to arrive at the break-even point (where the bottom line is zero). Matt's Hats needs to sell 600 hats per month to pay its operating expenses and break even. Here's how to calculate break-even units:

$$\begin{array}{ccc} \text{Operating} & \text{Gross Profit} & \text{Break-Even} \\ \text{Expenses} \div & \text{per Unit} = & \text{Units} \end{array}$$

$$\$3,000 \div \$4 \qquad = 750 \text{ Hats}$$

If Matt's Hats had used a contribution-margin-format income statement, the equation would have been:

$$\text{Fixed Operating Expenses} \div \text{Contribution Margin per Unit} = \text{Break-Even Units}$$

If Matt's Hats sells fewer than 750 hats, it will lose money. If it sells more than 750, it will earn a profit. If it sells exactly 750, the company will cover its expenses and will have neither profit nor loss.

It usually takes time for a new business to increase sales enough to make a profit. Until then, it has to have enough cash to cover its losses as the business grows. A break-even analysis and realistic sales forecast can help a business estimate how long it will take to make a profit. When planning a business, you should use break-even analysis to find how much product or service must be sold before the business becomes profitable. Sales and expenses can change frequently. When they do, it's a good idea to perform a break-even analysis to make sure your business remains profitable.

 **READING CHECKPOINT** *What is the formula used to calculate break-even units? Why are the break-even units important?*

 Your Business Plan. Continue developing your standard business plan. Go to "Section 12.2" of the *Business Plan Project* in your *Student Activity Workbook*, or "Section 12.2" of the BizTech Software.

ASSESSMENT 12.2

Reviewing Objectives

1. What is a break-even point?
2. What is the formula used to calculate break-even units?

Critical Thinking

3. **Analyzing Information.** Why is a same-size analysis helpful to a business owner?
4. **Applying Concepts.** Why would finding your business's break-even point help you operate the business?

Working Together

Work with a partner. Prepare three break-even analyses for Matt's Hats based on the information from the chapter. Analysis 1 shows sales increasing by 30%. Analysis 2 shows the COGS decreasing by $1 per hat. Analysis 3 shows the operating expenses increasing by 25%.

Math
Percentages

Using the brief version of the July income statement for Matt's Hats in this chapter as a base, project income statements for the remaining months of the year. Assume a month-to-month increase in sales and variable expenses of 12%, except in December, when sales and variable expenses rose by 20%. Assume that Operating Expenses don't change. Also calculate the break-even units for each of these months.

Relationship Building: The Art of Success

When Julene Fleurmond was in the tenth grade, she entered a Web design contest at her South Miami high school. "I began teaching myself how to use different Web-design programs," she said. "I didn't think I would win, and I won first place."

Relationships Lead to Business

Along with being awarded a scholarship, Julene also impressed one of the judges, who asked her to work with his organization, the National Urban League, on other projects. Julene began doing community service projects. She researched how to operate a creative graphic design business, took on internships at other firms, networked with professors and mentors, and made sure her work was on a professional level.

After two years of freelancing, Julene started Envibrance Studios, a media and promotional company that creates Websites, multimedia, creative content, and publications. Envibrance's motto is "Envision the possibilities; we'll bring them to life." Julene was confident about providing her services, but she didn't feel confident about pricing them.

Relationships Lead to the Right Pricing

"A lot of my first clients were friends of mine," said Julene, "and I wanted to give them discounts. But when I began working with other designers, I was told I was underpricing myself by hundreds of dollars." Julene researched how similar businesses priced their services. "I still gave discounts to service organizations," she said, "but I learned that underpricing yourself makes your service less worthy in people's eyes, and people might not take you seriously if you underprice."

▲ *Julene Fleurmond*

Julene discovered something else important about pricing: "Don't sell yourself short. Just because someone's your friend, you don't have to do everything for free for them."

Relationships That Count

In the beginning, Julene tried to do everything herself. Eventually she found that "Asking for help is not something you should be afraid of. Sometimes I would ask other designers I knew to do part of a project. Or we would collaborate if I didn't know how to do something. They would do one part of it and I would do the other."

Julene also learned how to take on projects that she's passionate about. "My genre now is mostly youth-oriented organizations or organizations that cater to youths. Having a genre or an audience that I'm very passionate about really helps me to be more passionate about my work." Her advice to other entrepreneurs is to make sure they're passionate about whatever they do, even if others say it won't be profitable.

"I think that if you pursue what you're truly passionate about and what you were made to do, financial benefits and everything else will follow naturally."

Thinking Like an Entrepreneur

1. How do relationships lead to business?
2. How can you be sure you're not underpricing your services?
3. What are you passionate about? Can you think of a way you could make it into a business?

CHAPTER SUMMARY

12.1 Financial Ratios

Analyzing a company's records to see relationships, patterns, or trends isn't always easy. That's why entrepreneurs use financial ratios and charts. Two important types of analysis based on the income statement are sales-data analysis and same-size analysis. Two important financial ratios based on the income statement are the operating ratio and return on sales (ROS). Four ratios are based on the balance sheet: the debt ratio, the debt-to-equity ratio, the quick ratio, and the current ratio. A ratio that is used to determine how well the business is doing in relation to the amount of money that has been invested in it is return on investment (ROI).

12.2 Break-Even Analysis

The break-even point is reached when costs and expenses are exactly equal to sales. At the break-even point, there is neither profit nor loss—the total at the bottom of the income statement is zero. To determine the break-even point perform a break-even analysis. This shows exactly how many units a business must sell to pay all its expenses. A start-up business needs to determine its break-even point to make sure it has enough money reserved to cover its losses early in the life of the company. When sales or expenses change, an entrepreneur should do a break-even analysis to make sure the company will remain profitable.

REVIEW VOCABULARY

Working with a partner, prepare an oral presentation explaining the roles of financial ratios and break-even analysis in operating a successful business. Use at least half of the following terms in your presentation:

- break-even analysis (p. 333)
- break-even point (p. 333)
- break-even units (p. 335)
- current ratio (p. 331)
- debt ratio (p. 329)
- debt-to-equity ratio (p. 330)
- financial ratio (p. 321)
- liquidity (p. 330)
- marketable securities (p. 330)
- operating ratio (p. 327)
- quick ratio (p. 330)
- return on investment (ROI) (p. 331)
- return on sales (ROS) (p. 327)
- same-size analysis (p. 325)

CHECK YOUR UNDERSTANDING

Choose the letter that best answers the question or completes the statement.

1. The financial ratios used by entrepreneurs to help manage their businesses come from
   a. bar graphs
   b. industry newsletters
   c. financial statements
   d. pie charts

2. One of the two most popular types of visual displays used by entrepreneurs is the
   a. line graph
   b. picture graph
   c. pie chart
   d. histogram

3. A type of analysis based on income-statement data and used to measure how a business's cost of goods sold and operating expenses affect its profits is called
   a. risk analysis
   b. return-on-investment analysis
   c. profit-based analysis
   d. same-size analysis

4. One of the most significant ratios calculated from data on an income statement is the
   a. operating ratio
   b. debt ratio
   c. return-on-investment ratio
   d. current ratio

5. Return on sales (ROS) has also been called
   a. net profit ratio
   b. net margin
   c. profit margin
   d. all of the above

6. Besides knowing the amount of sales, what other information is required to calculate a return on sales (ROS)?
   a. total assets
   b. total liabilities
   c. net income
   d. owner's equity

7. Total liabilities divided by total assets is the formula used to calculate the
   a. debt ratio
   b. current ratio
   c. quick ratio
   d. debt-to-equity ratio

8. Most businesses try to maintain a current ratio of
   a. 1 to 1
   b. 2 to 1
   c. 3 to 1
   d. 4 to 1

9. The total of cash plus marketable securities divided by current liabilities is the formula used to calculate the
   a. current ratio
   b. liquidity ratio
   c. debt ratio
   d. quick ratio

10. If the net income of a business is $3,000 and the owner's investment is $10,000, the return-on-investment (ROI) percentage is
    a. 300%
    b. 30%
    c. 3%
    d. 0.3%

11. When the bottom line on an income statement is zero because the business has sold exactly enough units to cover expenses, the business has reached the
    a. break-even point
    b. operating point
    c. income-to-expenses point
    d. risk-analysis point

12. If the operating expenses are $5,000 and the gross profit per unit is $5, the number of break-even units is
    a. 10
    b. 100
    c. 1,000
    d. 10,000

Business Communication

13. Working with a partner, prepare an income statement for a fictional business. The business should have at least five types of expenses. Prepare a pie chart that shows the company's sales, cost of goods sold, and net income. Then prepare a bar graph showing the business's expenses.

14. Working with a partner, prepare a balance sheet for a fictional business. From the data on the balance sheet, prepare the following ratios: debt ratio, debt-to-equity ratio, quick ratio, and current ratio.

15. Imagine you have recently started a new business of your choice. It has been in operation for several months. Create an income statement for your business. Then perform a break-even analysis. Present your income statement and break-even analysis to the class. Ask for evaluations of the business's potential for success.

Business Ethics

18. You and your partner own an electronics store. The two of you have decided to expand the business by adding silent partners. Your partner has created a bar graph to use in a presentation to potential investors. You notice that the graph has errors in the totals of two of the expenses. They are both listed as much lower than you know they really are. Your partner says it is too late to make the required changes and the errors aren't significant. You really believe that new partners would be making a sound business decision by investing in the business. What should you do?

Business Math

16. The income statement for your business shows sales of $50,000 in June. The operating expenses for the month totaled $20,000. What is the operating ratio percentage for June?

17. Your skateboard-painting business has operating expenses of $3,600 per month. The gross profit for each skateboard you paint is $12. How many skateboards do you need to paint to reach the break-even point?

Business in Your Community

19. Working in groups of three, brainstorm ideas for a new business that is needed in your community. Write a short description of the business. Then prepare an income statement and balance sheet for it. Calculate financial ratios based on the income statements and balance sheets. Prepare a presentation to potential investors. Use pie charts and bar graphs.

20. Interview two entrepreneurs or small-business owners in your community. Ask them if they use break-even analysis in their financial planning. Also ask each of them how long it took the business to become profitable. Write a short report comparing the results of your interviews.

ENTREPRENEURS & TECHNOLOGY

Internet Security

The Internet is a two-way street. By investigating the Web, you can access many thousands of sites. At the same time, hackers and malware can cause harm to your computer. **Hackers** write and often use programs that enable access to computers and networks by unauthorized users. For example, hackers can read the information on someone's computer, steal that information, or even erase it. **Malware** includes various types of malicious software and is discussed in the following paragraphs.

Computer Viruses and Trojan Horses

A **computer virus** is a software program that can cause damage to the data on your computer by erasing files, creating new ones, changing files, or moving them. It is a type of malware. A computer virus appears on your computer when you download a file that contains it. This can happen if you click on a link directing your computer to an infected Website or open e-mail that contains the virus. Computer viruses can spread from computer to computer just the way human viruses go from person to person. If a virus ends up on one computer in a network, it can infect other computers by attaching itself to files sent through the network. CDs and memory sticks can also carry viruses.

Another type of malware, a **Trojan horse**, is a program that takes control of your computer without your knowledge. Like computer viruses, you can receive a Trojan horse in e-mail. It can send data from your computer to a hacker's server over the Internet. It can also send out **spam** (junk e-mail) and attach itself to the spam to infect the computers of people in your address book. The Trojan horse is named after the legendary wooden horse that contained hidden Greek soldiers who emerged from it and conquered Troy after the Trojans had taken the horse through its gates.

Spyware

Spyware, another type of malware, lets computer users spy on other users. The spyware ends up on a computer in the same way as a virus—when you click on a link or download a malicious program. **Keyloggers** are programs that are used for surveillance by companies to make sure their employees are only using their computers for business. Keyloggers are also used to spy on unsuspecting users. The program records the letters and numbers (keystrokes) you make on a keyboard. Although you might think you're protected by typing in a password on a Website (which is often displayed as *******), the keylogger program can actually read what letters or numbers you keyed and send the information to a hacker who may use it for illegal activities. Another type of spyware is called a **screen recorder**. It takes a picture of your screen and could potentially record sensitive information.

Tech Vocabulary

- computer virus
- hackers
- keyloggers
- malware
- screen recorder
- spam
- spyware
- Trojan horse

Check Yourself

1. What is a hacker?
2. What is malware?
3. What is a computer virus?
4. What is spyware?

What Do You Think?

Solving Problems. What should you do to avoid computer viruses?

ANALYZING THE FIRST YEAR

It's the end of the first year. Things hadn't worked out quite as Eva Tan had projected. But she adapted and made adjustments. Sometimes doing that can be as important as having a good business plan. Eva took some time to reflect on her first year in business as she generated her first annual income statement.

The Best-Made Plans

Eva hadn't been able to locate any clients in her first month of business. It had taken her four months to gain five clients. The market for her service wasn't at all what she had expected. It turned out that single professionals and two-income couples weren't that interested. However, two-income families were very interested.

Her advertising budget was affected when she had to redo her brochure, her cards, and her Website to promote her new kid-friendly focus. And her car had also needed new tires.

Over the year she bought many more cooking supplies than she had expected. Among other things, she bought portable coolers that plugged into her car and some small, portable cooking equipment.

She also had to increase the variety of meals she cooked. The kids didn't want the same things as the grownups. This increased the overall cost of groceries by $10 but didn't increase her time cooking. After realizing this, Eva increased the price of a 5-dinner plan from $325 to $350, beginning in June.

You Can't Please Everyone

Eva even had one client she just couldn't please. After providing three free meals, Eva decided she needed to establish a policy about when to cancel an agreement with a client. She cancelled the client but wasn't able to sign up a replacement for two months.

After one year in business, Eva has put together the first annual income statement for Eva's Edibles.

New Economics of One Unit (End of Year 1)

One Unit of Sale = 5-Dinner Plan	
Selling Price (per Unit)	$ 350
Variable Costs	264
Contribution Margin	$ 86

Eva's Edibles
Annual Income Statement: Year 1
March 31, 20--

REVENUE		
Sales		
(186 Days Cooking; 56 @ $325/Plan, 130 @ $350/Plan)	$ 62,400	
Total Revenue		$ 62,400
COST OF SERVICES SOLD		
Materials (Groceries @ $110/Plan)	$ 20,460	
Labor (@ $150/Plan)	27,900	
Cost of Services Sold		48,360
GROSS PROFIT		$ 14,040
OPERATING EXPENSES		
Advertising	$ 2,550	
Depreciation	200	
Insurance	1,400	
Telephone	1,200	
Other Operating Expenses (Auto-Related)	2,100	
Other Operating Expenses (Cooking-Related)	1,900	
Total Expenses		9,350
PRE-TAX PROFIT		$ 4,690
Taxes (15%)		704
NET PROFIT		$ 3,986

What Would You Have Done?

1. **Comparing/Contrasting.** Prepare a comparative income statement for Eva's Edibles, using her projected income statement (p. 203). How did Eva do in her first year?

2. **Analyzing Information.** How do the ROS and ROI after the first year compare to those in her projected business plan (pg. 203).

STARTING YOUR BUSINESS

YOUR BUSINESS PLAN

In this unit, you'll focus on the **Financial Strategies, Organizational Structures, and Legal Structures** sections of the business plan and answer such questions as:

- What types of financing are available?
- What records should I keep?
- What kind of accounting system should I use?
- How should I staff my business?
- How will I protect my business by using insurance?
- How will taxes affect my business?

CHAPTER 13

FINANCING YOUR BUSINESS

13.1 Start-Up Investment

OBJECTIVES

- Describe start-up investment and explain how payback is calculated
- Explain bootstrapping strategies

VOCABULARY

- bootstrapping
- emergency fund
- financing
- payback
- reserve for fixed expenses
- seed money
- start-up capital
- start-up investment

? *Think about this question:*

Can you start a business without borrowing money?

Write your answer (yes or no) on a piece of paper. Be prepared to explain your answer.

Start-Up Investment

Raising money for a business is called **financing**. Sometimes entrepreneurs can raise all the money they need to start and operate their businesses by themselves, through their earnings and savings. However, you may find that, to start your business, you need more money than you have. Or, after your business is up and running, you may need additional cash to expand it. You might want to add new products, or enlarge or remodel your store. At some point, most entrepreneurs are likely to need some type of financing.

How much money will you need to get your business going? **Start-up investment** is the one-time sum required to start a business and cover the start-up expenditures. The start-up investment is also called **seed money** or **start-up capital**.

The start-up investment for a new company has two components:

- Start-up expenditures
- Cash reserves (for emergency fund and reserve for fixed expenses)

Start-Up Expenditures

The start-up expenditures for opening a restaurant would be purchasing stoves, food processors, tables, chairs, dishes, silverware, and other start-up supplies. The start-up expenditures might also include land on which to have the restaurant built or paying for the renovations needed for an existing space.

Here's an example on a smaller scale. Caesar wants to start a new business called "Caesar's Smoothies." He plans on selling his smoothies from a cart. The start-up expenditures for Caesar's Smoothies might look something like this:

Start-Up Expenditures—Caesar's Smoothies	
Cart (plug-in, with refrigeration bins)	$ 3,000
License from the city	500
Starting supplies of fruits, yogurt, nuts, etc.	700
Business cards and flyers (advertising)	400
Commercial refrigerator, cabinets (to store food)	800
Total start-up expenditures	$ 5,400

Cash Reserves

When starting a business, an entrepreneur needs to set aside extra money for two purposes:

- **Emergency Fund.** The ==emergency fund== is the amount of money a business should have available in the first three to six months for situations that often arise when a company is just beginning. Some experts say it should be half the amount of the start-up expenditures. After the initial start-up period is over and things have settled down, an entrepreneur can decide how much money to keep in an emergency fund.

- **Reserve for Fixed Expenses.** Businesses usually set aside a ==reserve for fixed expenses==. This is enough money to cover their fixed expenses for at least three months. The reserve for fixed expenses is maintained for the life of the business and is intended to be used to cover such costs as rent, insurance, etc., if the company should experience a downturn in sales.

If you were going to the bank for financing, you would usually include your emergency fund and the reserve for fixed expenses as part of your start-up investment.

> **Start-Up Expenditures**
>
> **+ Emergency Fund (½ Start-Up Expenditures)**
>
> **+ Reserve for Fixed Expenses**
> **(Covers 3 Months of Fixed Expenses)**
> _____
>
> **Start-Up Investment**

If the total start-up expenditures for Caesar's Smoothies was $5,400, his emergency fund would be half of that amount, or $2,700. Let's say that the fixed expenses for Caesar's for one month is $1,300, and Caesar wants to establish a 3-month reserve for fixed expenses, or $3,900. The total start-up investment for Caesar's Smoothies would be:

> *Start-Up Expenditures* = $ 5,400
>
> *Emergency Fund* =   2,700
>
> *Reserve for Fixed Expenses* =   3,900
> _____
>
> *Start-Up Investment* = $ 12,000

Many small entrepreneurs aren't able to afford to set aside an emergency fund or a reserve for fixed expenses that follows the experts' recommendations. Nevertheless, it is important to consider both of these concerns in your business planning. It is also important to make a record of your complete start-up investment (and not just your start-up expenditures).

Payback

Naturally, most entrepreneurs would like to know when their initial investment will begin to pay off in profit. That's the **payback**, the amount of time, measured in months, that it takes a business to earn enough in profit to cover the start-up investment.

To calculate payback, you will need to know your business's net profit per month. As you learned in Chapter 11, the net profit per month can be found on the income statement. (Remember: To find net profit, subtract the operating expenses from the gross profit.)

Figure 13-1

Start-Up Investment
Most start-up businesses, even one operating from a cart, require a start-up investment.

Applying Concepts. *Aside from the items mentioned previously, what are some things you might include in your start-up expenditures if you were selling food from a cart?*

Once you know the net profit per month, you can calculate the payback by using this formula:

$$\text{Start-Up Investment} \div \text{Net Profit per Month} = \text{Payback (in Months)}$$

Let's continue with the example of Caesar's Smoothies. Let's say that Caesar obtained financing for $6,000 and was able to contribute an additional $4,000 of his own money. This wasn't the $12,000 he had hoped for, but it was enough to cover his start-up expenditures and he thought he would divide the remainder between an emergency fund and a reserve for fixed expenses.

So Caesar's start-up investment was $10,000. Suppose he was projecting a net profit per month of $2,000.

Start-Up Investment	÷	Net Profit per Month	= Payback
$10,000	÷	$2,000	= 5 Months

It will take Caesar approximately five months to pay back the start-up investment.

READING CHECKPOINT *How is payback calculated?*

YOUR BUSINESS CAREER

Resiliency

A resilient person is able to cope with and learn from stressful and difficult circumstances. Think of Helen

▲ *Helen Keller*

Keller. Her blindness and deafness might have been insurmountable to a less determined person. Helen was able to rise above her disabilities and make a contribution to the world, as a speaker and author. Her positive outlook on life is a perfect example of how a resilient person can recover from almost any difficult—even tragic—situation.

A resilient person knows he or she doesn't have to handle things alone. When a particularly stressful situation occurs, someone with resilience is resourceful. If a problem or event seems to be too big to handle, a resilient person knows where to go for help. Some teens may first turn to their parents or other family members. They may talk with individuals at social or church groups. At work, they may talk with their boss or with coworkers.

Resilient people know that, from time to time, things won't go as they planned. They are able to see these experiences as opportunities to strengthen their resilience. They are able to bounce back and learn from each problem they successfully leave behind.

THINKING CRITICALLY

Drawing Conclusions. Why must people working in retail, service, and other businesses be resilient? What would happen if businesspeople did not bounce back from work situations, even from failures?

To read more about resiliency, go to "Your Business Career" on the Student Center at entrepreneurship.pearson.com.

Using your savings or credit cards for start-up capital can lead to problems.

Bootstrapping

Have you ever heard of the phrase "pulling yourself up by the bootstraps?" Basically, it means doing something completely on your own. As an entrepreneur, **bootstrapping** means starting a business by yourself, without any outside investment. This would typically be the most desirable way to start a business. However, unless you have a great deal of money, you would need to keep your start-up investment as low as possible. It often means starting your business with less money than you would like (as Caesar did).

Every business needs a different start-up investment, and some are lower than others. If your start-up investment is higher than the amount you have to invest, bootstrapping wouldn't be possible.

Many successful entrepreneurs began their businesses by bootstrapping, or with very little borrowed money, through such strategies as:

- Using personal savings
- Using credit cards

Using Personal Savings

Using your personal savings to finance your business is an ideal scenario. If you have enough money in your savings account for your start-up investment, you can be the sole owner of your business. All the profits will belong to you. However, this strategy has a major disadvantage. If your business fails, you will have lost *all of the money you invested*.

Also, by taking your money out of the savings account, you will have lost the interest the money would have earned. You lose the ability to draw money from the savings account that you could have used for other purposes. For example, perhaps you could have used part of your savings to buy an automobile. Using your personal savings to start a business is a very serious undertaking. Weigh the advantages and disadvantages carefully.

Using Credit Cards

Another strategy for funding the costs of starting a business is through your credit cards. Charging business items on your credit cards allows you to use the items while you are still paying for them. Although this certainly is an advantage, the strategy can also have some *very* significant disadvantages.

The major disadvantage is the interest rate charged by the credit card companies, which is often 20% or more on the outstanding balance. Unless your business is able make enough profit to pay the total amount you owe each month, the interest payments will add up very quickly. Also, if you reach the credit limits, you will not be able to use the cards for emergencies or for other opportunities. Keeping high balances on your credit cards also affects your credit rating. With a low credit rating, you may not be able to purchase merchandise from your suppliers on account. Other than in unusual circumstances, where you will very quickly earn back the money you borrow, using credit cards in your start-up investment is *not* a good idea.

Some entrepreneurs try to use credit cards with 0% introductory rates and 0% transfer fees to finance their business. However, such a strategy requires vigilance in locating and transferring balances to new credit cards when the introductory rate expires on the old ones.

 *What is bootstrapping?*

 Your Business Plan. Continue developing your standard business plan. Go to "Section 13.1" of the *Business Plan Project* in your *Student Activity Workbook*, or "Section 13.1" of the BizTech Software.

Reviewing Objectives

1. What are the components of a start-up investment?

2. What does bootstrapping mean in regard to entrepreneurship?

Critical Thinking

3. **Comparing/Contrasting.** When would it be appropriate to use your personal savings or credit cards for your start-up investment?

4. **Analyzing Information.** Name five businesses you could start with little start-up investment. What do they have in common?

Working Together

Form two teams. The first will plan for a new business that sells donuts (made at another location and purchased wholesale). The second team will plan for a new business that sells umbrellas (made at another location and purchased wholesale). Each team will determine the business's required start-up investment. Research costs on the Internet. Each team will present its analysis to the class.

Language Arts

Bootstrapping

Prepare a short report on the term "bootstrapping." Start with the historic origin of the term, and then discuss present-day meanings in areas such as business, computers, and biology.

13.2 Obtaining Financing

OBJECTIVES

- Identify the advantages and disadvantages of debt financing
- Identify the advantages and disadvantages of equity financing
- Describe some specialized sources of financing
- Describe how debt and equity financing affect the balance sheet

VOCABULARY

- angel
- bank debt ratio
- barter financing
- collateral
- co-signer
- credit union
- customer financing
- debt financing
- equity financing
- venture capital

? *Carefully consider this question, thinking about the risks and the rewards involved:*

Would you borrow money from friends or family members to start a business?

Write your answer (yes or no) on a piece of paper. Be prepared to discuss why you answered the way you did.

Debt Financing

You may be able to start a business with little or no start-up investment. You may also be able to fund the start-up investment yourself. However, if you need more money, you will have to find additional sources of capital. One method of obtaining more money is to borrow what you need. When you do that, you will increase your company's debt. This is called **debt financing**.

There are three main sources of debt financing:

- Banks
- Credit unions
- Relatives and friends

Banks

The major source of debt financing for an entrepreneur is a bank. The money the bank lends you can be used to start or to grow your business. Naturally, the bank expects to be repaid. You will be required to make regular payments. Banks are very careful with their loans—they want to be as certain as possible that they will get their money back, with interest. One of the things a bank or other source of funding looks at when considering loaning money is the entrepreneur's credit score. It's hard to get approved without a credit score in the high 600s. The bank will also look for some sort of track record of success.

To determine how much it might be willing to loan you, the bank will review your business's debt-to-equity ratio (discussed in Chapter 12).

The bank may also use a bank debt ratio. A **bank debt ratio** shows your monthly income compared to your debts.

$$\left(\frac{\text{Monthly Debt}}{\text{Payments}} \div \frac{\text{Monthly}}{\text{Income}}\right) \times 100 = \frac{\text{Bank Debt Ratio}}{(\%)}$$

A good ratio is typically 40% or less. Banks have found that customers with debt ratios over 40% often become unable to repay their loans. Here's an example: Suppose Caesar's Smoothies has a monthly income of $5,000 and debt payments of $2,500.

$$(\$2,500 \div \$5,000) \times 100 = 50\%$$

In this example, Caesar's bank debt ratio would be 50%. The bank would probably not give Caesar a loan.

Banks also use the bank debt ratio to determine how much they will loan you. Let's say Caesar has a monthly income of $5,000 and debts of only $1,500. How much would they loan Caesar then?

$$(\$1,500 \div \$5,000) \times 100 = 30\%$$

Because Caesar is already using 30% of his income to pay his existing debt, the bank might be willing to loan him about 10% of his monthly income. This is $500 ($5,000 × 0.1 = $500). Caesar could probably borrow an amount that would be repaid at $500 per month. This would allow him to spend 40% of his monthly income for debt payments, a percentage that is probably acceptable to the bank.

$$(\$2,000 \div \$5,000) \times 100 = 40\%$$

The actual dollar amount of the loan would vary based on the length of time and the interest rate. But the bank would make sure that Caesar's monthly payment would not exceed $500. The bank debt ratio is sometimes used to determine affordable monthly payments for customers seeking mortgage loans.

The bank may ask Caesar for collateral against a loan. **Collateral** is property or assets that you pledge to a bank to secure a loan. If you

Requesting a Loan
The major source of debt financing is in the form of bank loans.

Inferring. *Other than the bank debt ratio, what do you think a bank looks for when making a loan to an entrepreneur?*

fail to repay the loan, the bank will own your collateral and will resell it to get all or some of its money back. For example, if Caesar owned a truck that he used to pull his cart, the bank might ask him to use the truck as collateral. If he failed to repay the loan, the bank would take possession of the truck and sell it.

The bank may also ask Caesar to provide a co-signer for a loan. A **co-signer** is an individual who will sign a loan agreement to guarantee the loan payments in case Caesar, the first signer, is unable to make them. If Caesar asks relatives or friends to co-sign his loan and then isn't able to make the payments, they—the co-signers—will have to make them.

The biggest disadvantage of a bank loan for Caesar is what happens if he fails to repay it. The bank will probably bring a lawsuit against him. He is likely to lose his business and his credit rating could be ruined.

Entrepreneurs often use bank loans to start a business, but you need to be careful when assuming debt. Make sure you can make the payments.

Credit Unions

Another source of debt financing is the credit union. A **credit union** is a nonprofit cooperative organization that offers low-interest loans to members. Many entrepreneurs have financed their businesses through credit-union loans. Credit unions, like banks, will loan you money for growing your business. However, credit unions may offer you lower interest rates than banks. Because most credit unions will only make loans to members, you must first join the credit union. If you do not meet the membership requirements, you cannot get the loan.

A credit union, just like a bank, may ask for collateral or ask you to provide a co-signer. And, like a bank, if you fail to repay a loan, a credit union can bring a lawsuit against you.

Relatives and Friends

The start-up capital for many businesses has come as a loan from the entrepreneur's relatives or friends. A large number of successful small businesses have begun this way. However, the major concern for you, as a new business owner, will be to earn enough revenue to pay back the loans—the hard-earned money of your friends or relatives. What happens if your business does not generate sufficient sales to make a profit, or it fails entirely? How would you feel if you had to tell your friends or relatives that you were unable to repay them? It would certainly be a stressful situation.

On the other hand, the advantage to borrowing from relatives or friends is that you have a willing source of capital for your new business. The pride and confidence they would have in you and your business venture is often worth the risk. You are offering them an opportunity to receive a return on their investment—if your business is successful. Of course, if things don't go well, that's another story.

If you are planning to borrow money from friends or relatives for start-up capital, you must thoroughly explain the risks and the opportunities of the business. Finally, everyone must agree to the interest rate that will be paid and when payments are expected. With proper communication on the parts of all parties involved, this strategy can be very effective.

 *What is debt financing?*

Equity Financing

The other primary method of financing a start-up business is to sell shares of ownership in the business. If you use this method, called **equity financing**, you will be giving up some of your company and perhaps some control.

There are three main sources of equity financing:

- Relatives and friends
- Angels and venture capitalists
- Partners

Relatives and Friends

Sometimes start-up capital for a new business is obtained from relatives and friends as equity financing, in which they take a share of the company in payment for their investment. This is much the same as borrowing money from relatives and friends—with the same advantages and disadvantages—but with one big difference. Your friends and relatives now own part of the business. If they feel you are running it badly, or if they want to question a business decision, they have a right to tell you.

Angels and Venture Capital Companies

Some equity investors are referred to as "angels." An **angel** is an investor who is interested in financing start-up ventures. Like any investor, an angel wants to make a profit but may have additional reasons for investing. An angel investor might be interested in a specific type of business, or might want to support entrepreneurship in a certain community. Sometimes an angel takes an interest in an individual entrepreneur or might just want to be involved in something interesting. Because of a particular interest, an angel will often accept a lower return on an investment than other sources of equity capital. Typically, angel investors invest only on an equity basis; they don't make loans. Angels receive many requests for their capital but fund only a small percentage. Finding an angel willing to invest in your business may be difficult.

Another source of equity financing, similar to angel investment, is venture capital. **Venture capital** is money that is invested in a potentially profitable business by a specialized company whose purpose is to invest in start-ups. Venture capitalists are only interested in equity financing. Unlike angel investors, venture capital companies create funds in which many people have invested. Because of this, venture capital companies are more structured and more heavily focused on high returns on investment than the typical angel investor. For this reason, venture capital companies want to invest in businesses that expect to return large profits. Venture capitalists invest in less than one percent of the businesses they consider. Because venture capital

◄ **Figure 13-3**
Venture Capital Company
Typically a venture capital company wants to own a share of the business in which it invests.

Comparing/Contrasting. *How would sharing ownership with a venture capitalist be different from sharing it with a partner?*

investment is a high-risk business, these investors typically seek to earn five to ten times their original investment over five years. Because they see so many business plans, venture capitalists are typically difficult to interest in anything but very promising business start-ups.

You can use the Internet to research venture capital firms and angels who might be interested in investing in your business. Even though the odds are against you, there may be a specialized type of angel willing to take a chance. Although it is even less likely, you might find a venture capitalist willing to fund your idea.

Partners

The most common source of equity financing is giving a percentage of the ownership of a business to a partner. When seeking a partner, you should do as much research as possible to be assured that the two of you will have the same basic principles and goals for the business. You will be co-owners of the company. As with other forms of equity financing, adding a partner requires an entrepreneur to give up some ownership. Make sure you have a lawyer draw up a Partnership Agreement that carefully defines all aspects of the relationship.

Partners can bring new ideas and valuable expertise. But many partnerships fail because the partners disagree on how the business should be run.

Additionally, partners are typically personally liable for the actions taken in the business, and they are personally liable for paying debts or damages. If your partner incurs a debt on behalf of the partnership, you will be jointly responsible for paying it.

Unlike friends, family, angels, and some venture capitalists, a partner typically wants to play an active role in the operation of the business. For example, he or she may insist on approving all important business decisions. (See Chapter 3 for a review of the advantages and disadvantages of a partnership.)

 *What is equity financing?*

Specialized Sources of Financing

There are four specialized sources that may provide either debt or equity financing:

- **Small Business Investment Companies (SBICs) provide equity financing, as well as loans, for small businesses.** SBICs are partially financed through guaranteed loans from the government. SBICs often accept lower interest rates than other sources of debt financing. There are hundreds of SBICs that specialize in equity investments and loans for small businesses. You can use the Internet to search for up-to-date information on SBICs.

Micro-Loans

In the past, small-business owners had to go to a bank for a loan. Today, there is another option: the micro-loan. "Micro" means "small," and that's just what a micro-loan is: a small loan.

A micro-loan is ideal for a small start-up company that doesn't need much capital and has a limited credit history. (Credit history is a record of the ability of an individual or business to pay back a loan.) This history is what lenders consider when they decide whether to make a loan. Often, the entrepreneur applying for a micro-loan doesn't have enough collateral to qualify for a regular bank loan. A micro-loan is a relatively small amount of money, perhaps in the range of $10,000, and generally carries a higher rate of interest than a bank would charge.

Micro-loans are usually extended to small-business owners by nonprofit organizations through the Small Business Administration (SBA). There is also a new movement linking borrowers around the world to private lenders through Websites such as kiva.org.

THINKING CRITICALLY

Drawing Conclusions. Research several Websites offering micro-loans to entrepreneurs and list the requirements for applying for these loans.

To read more about micro-loans, go to "Entrepreneurship Issues" on the Student Center at entrepreneurship.pearson.com.

- **Minority Enterprise Small Business Investment Companies (MESBICs).** African Americans, Hispanics, Asians, and other minority groups—as well as women—can apply to Minority Enterprise Small Business Investment Companies (MESBICs) for start-up capital. MESBICs are private investment firms, chartered by the Small Business Administration, that provide both debt and equity financing for new small businesses. Just as with SBICs, MESBICs often accept lower interest rates than other sources of debt financing. You can use the Internet to search for updated information on MESBICs and other minority-financing opportunities.

- **Customer Financing.** Your customers will get to know and appreciate your products or services. With this first-hand knowledge, they are often willing to provide capital for a business. **Customer financing** can be either debt or equity. Your customers might be more willing to make a loan to you than a bank would, and they might be willing to accept a lower interest rate. It all depends on your relationship with your customers and the profitability of your company. A customer who offers you equity financing will become a co-owner of the business. The customer will have information about your operations that once was private. This could cause problems.

- **Barter Financing. Barter financing** is the trading of items or services between businesses. For example, your hardware store may sell lawn mowers while a landscaping business provides a

lawn-mowing service. As the owner of the hardware store, you need to have your property properly landscaped, so you make a deal with the owner of the landscaping business. You trade two of your lawn mowers to the landscaper for three months of landscaping services. The advantage of a barter system is that both parties get what they want without spending any money. Of course, the major problem is finding a suitable trading partner.

 *What are four specialized sources of financing?*

Effects of Financing on Your Balance Sheet

What are the economic consequences of using some form of financing for your business?

Effects of Debt Financing

Borrowing money for a business increases its debt (liabilities). You must repay the loans or you risk losing the business. The balance sheet (discussed in Chapter 11) provides a good example of the effect on the value of your business of increasing your debt. The balance sheet equation is:

$$\text{Assets} = \text{Liabilities} + \text{Owner's Equity}$$

Let's consider Caesar's Smoothies again. The business has assets of $10,000 and debts (liabilities) of $5,000. The owner's equity is therefore $5,000. (The calculation is Assets – Liabilities = Owner's Equity, or $10,000 – $5,000 = $5,000). For Caesar, the owner's equity and liabilities are equal; each is 50% of the total assets.

$$\text{Assets} = \text{Liabilities} + \text{Owner's Equity}$$
$$\$10,000 = \$5,000 + \$5,000$$

Now let's look at the balance sheet. If Caesar decides to borrow $5,000 for his business, his assets will increase to $15,000. However, his liabilities also increase by $5,000, to a total of $10,000. Now his balance sheet looks like this:

$$\text{Assets} = \text{Liabilities} + \text{Owner's Equity}$$
$$\$15,000 = \$10,000 + \$5,000$$

Caesar's liabilities increased in dollar amount (from $5,000 to $10,000). But they also increased in percentage, from 50% to 66.7% of his total assets.

$$(\$10,000 \div \$15,000) \times 100 = \text{Liabilities (as a Percentage of Assets)}$$

It is important to remember that a business with a high percentage of debt will have difficulty obtaining additional loans and credit. The interest payments on the loans will also increase Caesar's operating expenses. If he were planning to use debt financing to obtain start-up capital, he would need to keep these considerations in mind.

Effects of Equity Financing

Using Caesar's Smoothies again as an example, say that Caesar's owner's equity is $5,000. That amount did not change when his business obtained the loan. However, if he decided to use equity financing, the owner's equity would change. In the first example, the original balance sheet information was:

$$\text{Assets} = \text{Liabilities} + \text{Owner's Equity}$$
$$\$10,000 = \$5,000 \; (50\%) + \$5,000 \; (50\%)$$

Let's say Caesar decided to obtain additional capital by adding a partner, Ann. He accepted $5,000 from Ann in return for 40% of the business. The balance sheet now looks like this:

$$\text{Assets} = \text{Liabilities} + \text{Owner's Equity}$$
$$\$15,000 = \$5,000 \; (33.3\%) + \$6,000 \; (60\%) \; Caesar$$
$$+ \$4,000 \; (40\%) \; Ann$$

The business now has an additional $5,000 to use for expansion, to add new products, or for other changes. Looking at Owner's Equity on the balance sheet, however, you can see that the $5,000 has only increased the value of the business to Caesar by $1,000 (from $5,000 to $6,000). Caesar also now has a partner who will not only share in the success of his business but also has a voice in how it is being operated. Considering all of the consequences of equity financing as a means of obtaining capital is extremely important.

READING CHECKPOINT *How do debt financing and equity financing respectively affect a balance sheet?*

Your Business Plan. Continue developing your standard business plan. Go to "Section 13.2" of the *Business Plan Project* in your *Student Activity Workbook*, or "Section 13.2" of the BizTech Software.

ASSESSMENT 13.2

Reviewing Objectives

1. What is debt financing?
2. What is equity financing?
3. What are four specialized sources of financing that may provide either debt or equity funding?
4. How do debt financing and equity financing affect the balance sheet differently?

Critical Thinking

5. **Comparing/Contrasting.** If you had a business and needed money, which would you choose: equity financing or debt financing? Why?
6. **Drawing Conclusions.** Under what conditions do you think adding a partner would be in the best interest of your business?

Working Together

Form groups of three. Each group will investigate a different SBIC or MESBIC. Each will present a short presentation describing the selected company. Make sure to indicate the types of businesses in which the company invests and whether most of the investments are debt or equity financing.

Math

Bank Debt Ratio

Calculate the bank debt ratio of a business, based on the following data:

Monthly Income: $20,000

Monthly Debt Payments: $4,000

Would this company be a likely prospect for a loan?

All Aboard!

Every weekend, from Memorial Day through October, the Arcade and Attica Railroad in upstate New York runs a historic steam engine trip that travels for an hour and a half through farmlands and countryside that basically haven't changed in over a century.

John Thomas Robertson, nicknamed "JT," had always loved trains. His grandfather had given him a toy train set when he was a toddler. So taking the Arcade and Attica Railroad for the first time was a wonderful experience. After the trip, JT told his school class that he wanted to take them all on the train.

Getting Tickets: A Nickel a Can

JT lives in one of the poorest counties in New York State, and many of the kids couldn't afford the tickets. JT decided he was going to raise the money to buy the tickets and take the other children on the train. But how could he do it? His solution: collecting cans.

In New York, empty cans can be returned for a five-cent deposit. JT was eight years old when he started collecting cans in his little red wagon. With the help of his family and several businesses in town donating cans, JT took hundreds of cans to the recycling center, getting enough money to buy tickets for his 22 classmates. The next year, JT and his even younger friend Josh Tujimoto, collected 14,000 cans, enough to send 84 kids and their chaperones on the trip.

What JT did received national publicity, and he was profiled in *USA Weekend Magazine*'s "Make a Difference Day." He received a National Make a Difference Day Award along with nine other people. Paul Newman, the late actor and philanthropist, donated $100,000 for grant awards to charities chosen by the national award recipients. JT's $10,000 went to create volunteer opportunities for young people via the United Way of Cattaraugus County, in Olean, New York.

Helping the Handicapped Get On Board

Part of the appeal of the train trip is the old train cars. But old railroad cars aren't handicapped-accessible. When a group of children in wheelchairs couldn't get on the train, JT found a new mission: to make the cars wheelchair-friendly. JT began raising money online.

▶ *John Thomas Robertson*

He also wrote to the people at the TV show, *Extreme Makeover*, to see if they could help. *Extreme Makeover* works with volunteers to help rebuild people's homes. He hadn't heard anything from them when another television show contacted him.

JT was invited to appear on ABC's *Good Morning America* in Buffalo in recognition of his work in "Make a Difference Day." The show happened to be traveling across the country on an antique train. It was a total surprise to JT when the host of *Extreme Makeover*, Ty Pennington, also appeared on *Good Morning America*. It turned out that the *Extreme Makeover* crew, along with local volunteers, had fulfilled JT's wish. They had made one of the Arcade and Attica railroad cars wheelchair-accessible. For JT Robertson, the dream of providing a ride on the Arcade and Attica Train to hundreds of children continued to chug along.

Thinking Like an Entrepreneur

1. Is there a group of people you would like to help? Why?
2. How can publicity help in promoting a business or a cause?
3. What do you think the odds are of attracting a national television show to help a cause?

CHAPTER SUMMARY

13.1 Start-Up Investment

Raising money for a business is called financing. Entrepreneurs need to figure out how much money they need to get the business going. This is the start-up investment, made up of the start-up expenditures and the cash reserves. Typically, the cash reserves consist of an emergency fund and a reserve for fixed expenses. Entrepreneurs need to figure out when their initial investment will begin to pay off in profits. This is referred to as payback. When an entrepreneur starts a business alone, without any outside investment, it's called bootstrapping. Entrepreneurs can bootstrap a business by using personal savings and credit cards. Both are dangerous as sources of funding, however. If the company isn't able to pay these loans back, the entrepreneur will lose the money and, if credit cards are involved, could permanently damage his/her credit rating.

13.2 Obtaining Financing

Debt financing means borrowing the money needed for a business. The three main sources for debt financing are banks, credit unions, and relatives or friends. Banks use the bank debt ratio to determine whether a business is capable of borrowing additional funds. Typically, a good ratio is 40% or less. Banks almost always ask for collateral and sometimes a co-signer for a loan. Credit unions are nonprofit cooperatives that offer low-interest loans to members. A disadvantage to borrowing from relatives and friends is that, if the business is not successful, they could lose their investment. Equity financing is the selling of shares of ownership in a business to raise money. When an entrepreneur does this, he or she gives up some control of the company. The three main sources of equity financing are relatives and friends, angels and venture capitalists, and partners. Both debt and equity financing are available from specialized sources. Debt financing increases liabilities on the balance sheet and reduces owner's equity as a percentage of assets. Equity financing increases overall equity but also decreases the owner's equity as a percentage of assets.

REVIEW VOCABULARY

Write an e-mail to a friend who is an entrepreneur and considering financing a business. Give advice on the options. Use at least half of the following key terms from the chapter:

- angel (p. 359)
- bank debt ratio (p. 356)
- barter financing (p. 361)
- bootstrapping (p. 352)
- collateral (p. 356)
- co-signer (p. 357)
- credit union (p. 357)
- customer financing (p. 361)
- debt financing (p. 355)
- emergency fund (p. 348)
- equity financing (p. 358)
- financing (p. 347)
- payback (p. 349)
- reserve for fixed expenses (p. 348)
- seed money (p. 347)
- start-up capital (p. 347)
- start-up investment (p. 347)
- venture capital (p. 359)

CHECK YOUR UNDERSTANDING

Choose the letter that best answers the question or completes the statement.

1. The one-time investment of starting a business is called
   a. financing
   b. start-up investment
   c. venture capital
   d. working capital

2. Which of the following is the mathematical formula for payback?
   a. start-up investment + net profit per month
   b. net profit per month ÷ start-up investment
   c. start-up investment ÷ net profit per month
   d. net profit per month − start-up investment

3. Starting a business by yourself, without any outside investment, is called
   a. start-up investment
   b. payback
   c. capital control
   d. bootstrapping

4. Which of the following would not be considered a bootstrapping strategy?
   a. borrowing money from a bank
   b. using personal savings
   c. using credit cards
   d. getting by without any start-up costs at all

5. Venture capital is typically a source of which type of financing?
   a. debt financing
   b. equity financing
   c. bootstrapping
   d. government-sponsored financing

6. The major source of debt financing is a(n)
   a. credit union
   b. angel
   c. customer
   d. bank

7. If a business borrows money, the effect on the accounts in its balance sheet will show a(n)
   a. assets and owner's equity increase
   b. assets and liabilities increase
   c. assets increase and owner's equity decrease
   d. liabilities and owner's equity increase

8. If an owner of a business sells a share of the business to a partner, the effect on the balance sheet of the business will be that
   a. the total of assets and liabilities will increase
   b. the total of assets and liabilities will decrease
   c. the total of owner's equity will increase
   d. the total of owner's equity will decrease

9. Which one of the following is not a source of equity financing?
   a. an angel
   b. a venture capitalist
   c. a new partner
   d. a credit union

10. Which one of the following sources of equity capital makes investments mainly to receive a high return on investment?
    a. venture capitalists
    b. angels
    c. banks
    d. MESBICs

11. The bank debt ratio maximum is typically about what percentage?
    a. 10%
    b. 20%
    c. 30%
    d. 40%

12. Banks determine the bank debt ratio by using which of the following formulas?
    a. monthly debt ÷ monthly income
    b. monthly income − monthly debt
    c. monthly income ÷ monthly debt
    d. monthly assets ÷ monthly debt

Business Communication

13. Split into two teams. Each team will be starting a new business. Each will develop a list of what is necessary to begin the business. Then the team members will determine the start-up capital required. One team will be using equity financing to obtain the start-up capital; the other will be using debt financing. Each team will prepare a short presentation to convince their sources of financing to provide start-up capital. While one team presents, the other will play the role of the source of funding.

14. Prepare a list of potential sources of equity financing for an imaginary start-up business. For each source, provide the advantages and disadvantages in relation to that business.

15. Prepare a list of potential sources of debt financing for an imaginary start-up business. For each source, provide the advantages and disadvantages in relation to that business.

Business Ethics

18. You badly need a bank loan to be able to pay your operating costs. But you are aware that the bank requires a bank debt ratio of less than 40% before it will grant a loan. By your calculation, your ratio will be 42%. One of your friends loaned you some start-up money. Knowing that the total amount of debt will make your bank debt ratio too high, he makes a suggestion. He recommends that you do not include your payments to him in the bank loan application. He says he has confidence in you and your business and that the bank should be willing to loan you the money because your bank debt ratio is just slightly over the 40% limit. What should you do?

Business Math

16. The start-up investment for your business is $36,000. Your net income per month is $6,000. What is the payback period for your investment?

17. Your local bank requires its customers to have a bank debt ratio of 40% or less before approving a loan. Your entrepreneurial business provides you with an income of $4,200 per month. Your business has monthly debts of $1,500. Will you qualify for a loan at that bank?

Business in Your Community

19. Working in teams of three or four, prepare a questionnaire on how local small businesses financed their start-ups. It should include questions on sources of start-up investment, types of debt financing, equity financing, and any other types of funding the businesses use or have used. Present the questionnaire to the owners of small businesses in your community. As a team, prepare a short presentation based on the results of the questionnaire.

20. Interview individuals from at least two sources of debt financing (banks, credit unions, etc.) in your community. Ask them what criteria they use to determine whether to grant a loan. Ask how they calculate the maximum amount of money they will loan an applicant. Write a short report summarizing the results of your interviews.

Search Engine Optimization

Search engines, such as Google and Yahoo, are often the first place people look for information. After you type in a **query**—a question or phrase—the search engine comes up with a list of sites that relate to your search terms. A search engine can list thousands of pages of results, and the order in which they are listed is called the ranking. If you're offering a service or product on your Website, you want it to be at the top of the ranking. You want to have a high ranking because many Web surfers only click on links in the first few pages. **Search engine optimization**, or **SEO**, is composed of a variety of techniques that improve a site's ranking.

How Search Engines Rank Sites

Search engines use computer robots, called **spiders**, to scan Web pages on the Internet. The spiders read the information on the pages, see what links the pages connect to, and read the information on all the linked pages. Some search engine spiders also look at **metatags**, HTML tags that provide information about the page, including the **keywords**, which are words or phrases that represent the page's content. Keywords are usually one to six words in length. Although spiders can see metatags, ordinary site visitors do not.

All this information comes back to the search engine, where it is then indexed. How this data is indexed depends on the individual search engine. Google, for example, may use different criteria from Yahoo, which is why you get different lists of sites when using different search engines. Generally, though, a search engine ranks a site based on several factors, including content, keywords, and Web links to and from other sites. If a Website has more links coming in from other Websites, it means the site is popular, which can help ranking. Website owners try to get new links by engaging in **link trades** with other site owners, meaning each owner agrees to link to the other person's site. Before linking with another site, however, ask yourself if the link will be beneficial for visitors to your page. If the answer is no, don't link.

SEO Tips

Keyword placement can be crucial. If you have an e-commerce site that sells urban clothing, you'll want to put "urban clothing" or "selling urban clothes" in your site's title and also in **headers** throughout the site. A header is a line of text, sometimes only one or two words, that appears at the beginning of paragraphs or at the head of sections of your Website copy.

Some Websites use a number of techniques to increase links, such as selling them to raise its ranking. But if a search engine discovers this is going on, it lowers every page's ranking or even bans from its indexes all the sites involved. Search engine optimization is a brand new form of marketing and it is always changing. To find out what is permissible and what isn't, go to the search engines you're most interested in and check them out. They will provide optimization tips and techniques, as well as guidelines for the **Webmaster**—the person who manages the Website.

Tech Vocabulary

- headers
- keywords
- link trades
- metatags
- query
- search engine optimization (SEO)
- spiders (search engine robots)
- Webmaster

Check Yourself

1. What is a search engine ranking?
2. What is a query?
3. What are spiders?
4. What is search engine optimization?

What Do You Think?

Analyzing Information. How would you improve a Website's search engine ranking?

CHAPTER 14

RECORDKEEPING & ACCOUNTING

SECTION **14.1**

Recordkeeping

OBJECTIVES

- Understand financial records
- Differentiate between receipts, purchase orders, and sales invoices
- Know the basic principles of double-entry accounting
- Discuss the advantages and disadvantages of computerized accounting systems
- Describe the issues associated with the use of accountants and bookkeepers

VOCABULARY

- accounting
- accounting controls
- auditor
- bank reconciliation
- chart of accounts
- checking account
- double-entry accounting
- duality
- embezzlement
- Federal Deposit Insurance Corporation (FDIC)
- general journal
- internal audit
- payee
- purchase order
- receipt
- sales invoice
- savings account
- source document
- T-account
- transaction

Think about this question:

Do you keep records of your purchases?

Write your answer (yes or no) on a piece of paper. Be prepared to explain to the class why you do or do not keep records.

Financial Records

Entrepreneurs need to know exactly how much money is coming in to and going out of the business. In fact, one of the major reasons that businesses fail is the owner's lack of financial management skill. This includes not keeping good financial records. The more you know about recordkeeping, the more you increase your odds of being a successful entrepreneur.

Having business accounts at a local bank is important for an entrepreneur. You'll be able to discuss your savings and checking accounts directly with a bank representative. As a bank customer, when you apply for a loan, your application will typically receive preferential treatment over a non-customer's application.

One concern for your money is safety. Your money is obviously much safer in a bank than in your purse or wallet. Money in a bank account is insured, in case the bank goes out of business. The **Federal Deposit Insurance Corporation (FDIC)**, created in 1933, is an independent agency of the federal government that insures savings, checking, and other types of deposit accounts.

As an entrepreneur you'll certainly need a checking account soon after your start your business.

Savings Accounts

A **savings account** is a bank account in which you deposit money. The bank pays interest on the amount in your account. Typically, the rate of interest a bank pays on a savings account is low. However, because the FDIC insures savings accounts, you have virtually no risk of losing your money. Banks earn their profits by using the money in the savings account as a basis for making loans. The interest rate they charge on their loans is higher than the interest rate they pay you on your savings account.

Checking Accounts

A **checking account** is a bank account against which you can write checks. You can also remove money from your account by using a debit card. When you write a check, you authorize the bank to pay the holder of the check from the money in your account.

When you pay someone with a check, that person (the **payee**) goes to their bank and either cashes your check or deposits it in their own account. The payee's bank sends the check back to your bank, at which point your bank takes the money out of your checking account and pays the other bank.

Once your bank has paid the check, the check is cancelled. The bank may send the cancelled checks back to you. They provide proof that the payees received their money. To save on expenses, many banks now keep your cancelled checks instead of mailing them to you. You have access to them in person at the bank or through the bank's Website.

Banks have taken good advantage of modern technology. Online banking allows a bank's customers to use a secure Website for transacting their banking business. It is available 24 hours a day. You can monitor your accounts, transfer money from one account to another, pay monthly bills online, and even input information from your online bank statement directly into recordkeeping software on your computer.

You can use an ATM (automatic teller machine) card to access your money at many locations at any time of day. With a debit card, you can withdraw money directly from your checking account without having to write a check. When you use a debit card to make a purchase, the amount is automatically deducted from your checking account. Don't forget to subtract the amount of the debit card purchase from your checkbook.

Once a month, your bank sends you a checking account statement. The statement includes a list of all the deposits and checks

▼ Figure 14-1

ATMs
Automatic teller machines (ATMs) allow you to access your money at many locations at any time of the day.

Predicting. *What method would you use to make sure you kept receipts from ATM withdrawals?*

you've written that have cleared. It also shows the ending balance in the account.

The ending balance on the bank statement may not match the balance shown in your checkbook, however. The two main causes for this are outstanding checks and outstanding deposits. Outstanding checks are checks that haven't been cashed. Outstanding deposits are funds you have put in the bank but the bank hasn't yet recorded. Other differences between your account balance and the bank balance could include bank service charges and fees.

Bank Reconciliation

One of the best ways to maintain good control over cash is to reconcile your business checking account with the bank statement each month. A **bank reconciliation** is the process of verifying that your checkbook balance is in agreement with the ending balance in your checking account statement from the bank.

Here's an example of bank reconciliation.

Assume that the end-of-month balance in your business checkbook is $2,500. Your bank statement, however, shows a balance of $3,180. Follow these steps to reconcile your checkbook with your bank statement:

1. Compare your checkbook activity with the transactions listed in the bank statement to see if there are any outstanding checks. In our example, let's assume Checks #327 and #330 haven't yet cleared the bank. The total amount of these checks is $1,700.

2. Compare your checkbook with the deposits shown in the bank statement to see if you made any deposits that aren't listed on the bank statement. Let's say you made a deposit on the last day of the month for $1,000. It wasn't recorded by the bank until the next day and isn't shown on the statement.

3. Finally, check to see if the bank statement shows any bank charges or fees. You notice that the bank charged your account $20 to have new business checks printed.

Here's how your bank reconciliation would look:

▼ **Figure 14-2**
Bank Reconciliation
A bank reconciliation is the process of verifying that your checkbook balance is in agreement with the ending balance in your checking account statement from the bank.
Analyzing Information.
What kinds of fees might be shown on a bank statement?

Explanation	Checkbook Balance	Bank Statement Balance
Balance on October 31	$ 2,500	$ 3,180
Less Outstanding Checks		−1,700
Plus Unlisted Deposits		+1,000
Less Bank Service Charges/Fees	−20	
Actual Cash Balance	**$ 2,480**	**$ 2,480**

If the totals still don't agree:

1. Look for items on the bank statement that you haven't entered in your checkbook, such as other service charges, interest earned on your account or ATM withdrawals.

2. Check the amount written on each check against the amounts shown in your checkbook. A common mistake is a transposition error, which is reversing two numbers. For example, you might have written a check for $73 and written $37 as the amount in your checkbook.

 **READING CHECKPOINT** *What are the steps in reconciling a bank statement?*

Business Documents

When you start a business, you need to establish recordkeeping procedures. These procedures will typically involve receipts, purchase orders, and invoices.

Receipts

A **receipt** is the detailed written proof of a purchase. When you make a sale, always give the customer a receipt and always keep a copy for yourself. Write down the date, customer name, what the customer purchased, and how the customer paid.

Be sure to get a receipt when your business pays for goods or services. When merchandise is shipped to you, the receipt, or packing slip, is usually in one of the packages. Check to see that the shipment includes all the items on the receipt. The receipt will be helpful if you have a problem with the order or need to return merchandise. Save all receipts. Your purchases might qualify for a tax deduction. These deductions will save you money in taxes, but you need to save the receipts as proof of the expenses.

Various styles of receipt booklets are available at local office supply stores or discount retailers.

Purchase Orders

A **purchase order** (often referred to as a PO) is a detailed written record of a business's request for supplies or inventory. When purchasing supplies, write up a purchase order that contains a description of what you are ordering, from whom, at what price, and who is taking the order. Also, be sure to date and number the purchase order. Give the supplier the purchase order number when you place the order.

The purchase order system is highly reliable. A purchase order clearly states what you want to buy. The seller has a document that clearly states what you want. There is no confusion. Another advantage of this system is that it helps you record your business's purchases. Employees who make purchases from suppliers know that they must prepare a

Paperless Offices

Every company must keep records. Inventory order forms, receipts, customer contact information, bills, and invoices can all pile up in files around the office. Until recently, small business owners accepted the fact that good recordkeeping meant retaining hard copies of everything. A "hard copy" is an actual piece of paper, traditionally stored in metal filing cabinets.

Today, many entrepreneurs are looking at other options for data storage. With personal computers now as common as telephones, there is a more efficient and environmentally friendly way to stay organized. Computers and online data-archiving tools have made the paperless office a reality for millions of small businesses. A paperless office is one in which all documents are stored digitally. No filed hard copy of a document is necessary.

There are many reasons for a business to go paperless. In addition to the saved space, digital files make retrieval of information quicker and reduce paper waste. Many hospitals are now keeping patient records in digital formats by using advanced software systems. But for the average small business, simple tools like a scanner and a data storage service, such as www.xdrive.com, are enough to begin a significant reduction in paper use.

THINKING CRITICALLY

Applying Concepts. In small groups, discuss ways in which your classroom could reduce paper usage. What are the advantages and disadvantages to a "paperless school"?

To read more about the paperless office, go to "Entrepreneurship Issues" on the Student Center at entrepreneurship.pearson.com.

purchase order. They also know that the owner must sign the purchase order before it is sent to the supplier. The PO system helps prevent unauthorized purchases.

Purchase order forms are available in office supply stores or from discount retailers. You can also download purchase order templates and adapt them for your business.

Sales Invoices

You use a purchase order when you buy supplies or inventory. But what should you use when you sell goods or services? A **sales invoice** is an itemized list of goods delivered or services rendered and the amount due.

If your business offers credit terms, you are agreeing to let the customer pay you later. When payment is due, you will need to send the customer an invoice. The invoice contains much of the same information included on a receipt. It also includes the date when the payment should be made, to whom the check should be made out (for example, your business name), and your business mailing address. Depending on your business, the invoice may include additional information, such as the amount the customer will be charged for a late payment.

Once you receive the customer's payment, write or stamp "Paid" on the invoice. File all invoices, either by invoice number (in numerical order) or by customer name (in alphabetical order).

As with other receipts and purchase orders, invoice forms are available at many office supply stores and discount retailers. Invoice

templates are also available online and can be downloaded and adapted for your business.

 *What is a purchase order?*

Accounting Principles

Keeping good records is a crucial part of any business. Without accurate records, business owners can't be confident that their income statements, cash flow documents, and balance sheet are correct. The IRS also insists that you keep accurate records for tax purposes.

Accounting is the system of recording and summarizing business and financial transactions and analyzing, verifying, and reporting the results. Fortunately, as an entrepreneur, you aren't expected to perform all these accounting tasks personally.

When you start your business, you will probably pay an accountant to prepare the required financial statements. However, you should have a basic understanding of accounting so you know what information to collect for your accountant. Your accountant will need certain information to prepare monthly and annual financial statements, as well as for filing your taxes properly.

Before choosing an accounting system, you should know the various types available and how they differ. Accounting systems are categorized as either manual or computerized, but with today's technology, most small businesses use some type of computerized system.

Both manual and computerized accounting systems have basic similarities. All use some method of recording *every* business transaction. Any payment made or any income received is a **transaction**.

A journal or an accounting database is used to record each transaction as it occurs. The information that's recorded comes from source documents. A **source document** is the original record (source) of a transaction. Source documents include receipts, cancelled checks, invoices, bank deposit slips, and other records.

At a minimum, an entrepreneur must carefully track:

- All cash inflows (receipts)
- All cash outflows (payments)

The accounting requirements usually become more complex as a business grows. However, most small businesses can rely on a relatively simple system that requires only a journal or an accounting database.

All accounting systems make use of what is called **double-entry accounting,** which basically means that every business transaction affects at least two accounts.

Chart of Accounts

The first step in double-entry accounting is to create a chart of accounts. A **chart of accounts** shows all the accounts used in the business. For example, it includes all assets, liabilities, owner's equity, income, and expense accounts. Each account is numbered. Figure 14-3 shows an example of a chart of accounts for Matt's Hats.

Figure 14-3

Chart of Accounts
This is an example of a chart of accounts for Matt's Hats.
Analyzing Data. *When might Matt Washington use account C302?*

Matt's Hats
Chart of Accounts

ACCOUNTS	ACCOUNT CODES
ASSETS	
Cash	A101
Inventory	A102
Accounts Receivable	A103
LIABILITIES	
Bank Loans	L201
Accounts Payable	L202
Sales Tax Payable	L203
OWNER'S EQUITY	
Matt Washington, Capital	C301
Sales Revenue	R401
Utilities Expense	E501
Insurance Expense	E502
Interest Expense	E503
Rent Expense	E504
Internet Service Expense	E505
Matt Washington, Withdrawal	C302

The next step in double-entry accounting is to record transactions. All transactions must be recorded and must affect at least two accounts. There are two approaches to recording transactions:

- **Single-Column, Database Approach.** This is a simple method. Most computerized systems use it.

- **Double-Column Approach.** This method uses a left-hand (debit) column and a right-hand (credit) column for each account. Most manual accounting systems use a double-column method.

No matter which of the two you use, it depends on the same basic principle:

Assets = Liabilities + Owner's Equity

You first encountered this basic accounting equation in Chapter 11 when you were introduced to the balance sheet. The most important thing to remember about recording transactions is that, just as with a balance sheet, any change on the left side of the equation *must* equal a change on the right side.

Single-Column, Database Approach

Suppose Matt Washington buys a new computer for Matt's Hats, using $4,000 cash. The asset Cash would be reduced by $4,000, and the asset Office Equipment would be increased by $4,000. Each transaction in this example happened on the left side of the equation, dealing with assets. Therefore, there's no need to make an entry in the liabilities/owner's equity side of the equation.

This transaction can be shown as:

Cash	Office Equipment
−$4,000	+$4,000

What would happen if, instead of paying cash, Matt's Hats bought the new computer on account? Here, Cash wouldn't be affected. Instead, Office Equipment would go up by $4,000 on the assets side of the equation. And on the other side, a liability (Accounts Payable) would also go up by $4,000. The equation would balance.

A single-column accounting database, which is especially suited to computerized systems, shows the equation this way:

Office Equipment	=	Accounts Payable
+$4,000		−$4,000

Double-Column Approach

Manual accounting systems use the double columns of debits and credits. Each account has a left-hand and a right-hand column. The left-hand column is the debit side, and the right-hand column is the credit side.

Here's the key to understanding this approach:

- Increases in assets are recorded on the debit side.
- Increases in liabilities and owner's equity are recorded on the credit side.
- Decreases in assets are recorded on the credit side.
- Decreases in liabilities and owner's equity are recorded on the debit side.

This is a summary of the earlier transaction in which Matt's Hats purchased office equipment for $4,000 cash.

Cash		Office Equipment	
Debit	Credit	Debit	Credit
+	–	+	–
	$4,000	$4,000	

This sort of double-sided presentation is called a **T-account**. Here, we can see that Cash, an asset account, is credited because it decreased, and Office Equipment, another asset account, is debited because it increased.

Most transactions can be entered formally in what is called a **general journal**, an accounting record that shows all the transactions of the business. The purchase of the office equipment for cash would look like this as an entry in the general journal:

General Journal				Page:	1
Date	Explanation		Ref.	Debit	Credit
Aug. 2	Office Equipment			$4,000	
	Cash				$4,000
	Bought new computer				

What would a T-account look like if Matt's Hats bought the computer for cash?

Office Equipment		Accts Payable	
+	–	–	+
$4,000			$4,000

Rather than using T-accounts, you could make this entry in the general journal:

General Journal				Page:	1
Date	Explanation		Ref.	Debit	Credit
Aug. 2	Office Equipment			$4,000	
	Accounts Payable				$4,000
	Bought new computer				

Here, office equipment increased, so you debit that account. Accounts payable, a liability, also went up, so you credit that account. Remember that debits must *always* equal credits when you record a transaction.

Duality

No matter which approach you use, you are employing a key accounting concept called **duality**. In the single-column method, duality means that, for any transaction, all changes on the asset side minus all changes on the liability/owner's equity side must equal zero. In a computerized system, a transaction is entered only once and all journals and ledgers are updated automatically. At the end of each reporting period, the account balances are totaled and transferred to the financial statements.

In the double-column method, duality means that for any transaction posted to the general journal (and any special journals), all debits must equal all credits. At the end of each day, the general journal entries are posted to each respective account in what is called a general ledger. At the end of the accounting period, the general ledger balances are used to prepare financial statements.

Basic Process

No matter which approach you use, the end result produces the same set of financial statements. Although the number and types of accounts may increase and the approach may vary, the process used in a simple double-entry accounting system has five basic steps.

Five Steps in Simple Double-Entry Accounting Systems

1. Prepare a chart of accounts.

2. Record all business transactions in an accounting database or journal, using source documents.

3. Total each account in the database or journal at the end of the accounting period.

4. Prepare an income statement and statement of cash flow.

5. Prepare a balance sheet using the ending balances in each asset, liability, and owner's equity accounts.

The last two steps can be reversed. The order for preparing the balance sheet, income statement, and statement of cash flow doesn't matter.

 **READING CHECKPOINT** *What is double-entry accounting?*

Computerized Accounting

In the remainder of this section you'll learn the advantages and disadvantages of computerized accounting systems. Many accounting software programs are available. Some programs are meant to be used by entrepreneurs who have no knowledge of accounting, while others require the user to have a strong accounting background.

There are several accounting software packages for small businesses. Among the more popular products are QuickBooks, Peachtree, Business Works, and Mind Your Own Business. Entrepreneurs with only a basic understanding of accounting can use these software programs. They are often called general ledger programs and are similar in operation.

The programs all provide simple instructions, and most provide templates. They provide accounts common to most businesses, such as sales revenue and accounts payable. You can change the names of the accounts on the templates to match the actual names of the accounts in your business. You can also easily add additional accounts to the chart of accounts.

▲ **Figure 14-4**

Assets = Liabilities + Owner's Equity
Whether you use a computerized accounting system or a manual system, any change on the left side of the equation *must* equal any change on the right side.

Recognizing Patterns. *If Matt's Hats bought more inventory on credit, what would happen to Matt's assets and his liabilities?*

Although the method of entering transactions in these software programs may vary somewhat, they are basically similar. Most provide examples of how to enter typical business transactions. In some programs you would simply enter a transaction by using the name of the account involved. With this type of program, you don't have to be familiar with spreadsheet software or terms such as debit and credit that are needed with manual systems.

The tremendous advantage of this type of computer accounting system compared to a manual one is that a computerized system prepares financial statements automatically. In a manual system, the user must do the calculations by hand. Computerized accounting systems automatically prepare income statements, balance sheets, and other financial statements. This feature saves time and prevents mathematical errors. Furthermore, computer accounting systems don't generally require the user to have extensive knowledge of accounting procedures.

The major disadvantage of an accounting software program, like many computer programs, is the amount of time it takes to learn how to use it. Also, although accounting software programs are fine for inputting typical transactions, they often lack clear instructions for inputting unusual (atypical) transactions. For example, if you have to change a transaction because of an error, often called a correcting

Sense of Purpose

Do you have a sense of purpose? Having a sense of purpose means that you are working toward a personal long-term goal, often one that contributes to the world. Those with a purposeful life have a feeling of achievement and accomplishment with everything they do. They believe their life has value and that they are making a meaningful contribution to society.

A sense of purpose is individual. It varies with each person. One person's purpose may be to become a concert pianist. Another's may be to help those less fortunate. Someone else may take care of a sick family member. People with a sense of purpose tend to be happy and confident as they work toward their long-term goals.

Although it is important to be driven in this way, you may not yet have found your sense of purpose.

If you haven't, don't worry. Set small goals. Have a purpose for each day. Eventually you will see a larger purpose—something that will give you greater, longer-term satisfaction. Ultimately, a sense of purpose will benefit your health, enhance your self-esteem, and provide happiness.

THINKING CRITICALLY

Solving Problems. Do you have a clear sense of purpose? Jot down some long-term goals you have set for yourself in your own life. Think about how you are working toward those goals now and how they may guide you in your life.

To read more about sense of purpose, go to "Your Business Career" on the Student Center at entrepreneurship.pearson.com.

entry, the program may not have clear instructions on how to input the change.

Accounting software programs are available in a range of prices. Some are free and others can cost hundreds of dollars. Many entrepreneurs contract with accounting firms to prepare their financial reports. The employees of these firms use professional software programs, like those mentioned earlier, to keep the books and prepare reports.

What is one of the major advantages of a computerized accounting system as compared to a manual accounting system?

Using Accountants and Bookkeepers

Many entrepreneurs don't keep their own records. They feel their time is better spent managing the business rather than doing recordkeeping work. This is especially true if the entrepreneur has little or no background in accounting.

Some entrepreneurs pay a part-time accountant or bookkeeper to maintain their books. This of course is an additional business expense.

Having someone else keep the records for your business presents another potential problem. If the accountant has the authority to write checks and also does the bank reconciliation, there is the possibility of embezzlement. **Embezzlement** is the crime of stealing money from an employer. To avoid this, entrepreneurs need to have proper accounting controls in place. **Accounting controls** are checks and balances established so that accounting personnel follow procedures that will avoid potential problems. These procedures allow the owner to have better control of the financial operation of the business and also help prevent embezzlement. An example of an accounting control would be to require that all checks, purchase orders, and invoices have the owner's signature.

Some entrepreneurs pay an auditor to check their books. An **auditor** is an accountant who examines a company's financial records and verifies that they have been kept properly. This type of audit is often called an **internal audit**. It shouldn't be confused with the kind of audit performed by the Internal Revenue Service (to check an individual's or a business's income tax declarations).

 *What is one of the disadvantages of using an accountant or bookkeeper to maintain your books?*

 Your Business Plan. Continue developing your standard business plan. Go to "Section 14.1" of the *Business Plan Project* in your *Student Activity Workbook*, or "Section 14.1" of the BizTech Software.

ASSESSMENT 14.1

Reviewing Objectives

1. What are the steps in reconciling a bank statement?
2. What is a purchase order?
3. What is a chart of accounts?
4. What is one of the major advantages of a computerized accounting system compared to a manual accounting system?
5. What are accounting controls?

Critical Thinking

6. **Comparing.** Which do you think you would prefer, a manual accounting system or a computerized accounting system? Why?
7. **Analyzing Information.** Using a double-column approach to accounting, where would you record an increase in the asset Cash—on the debit side or the credit side?

Working Together

Form two teams, each with three students. One team will investigate computerized accounting systems for small businesses. The other team will investigate manual accounting systems for small businesses. Each team will present their findings to the class, which will then vote to determine which system is best suited for a small business.

Math
Bank Reconciliation

Calculate what your checkbook balance should be, based on the following information from your latest bank statement and your checkbook entries.

Bank statement ending balance:	$6,400
Outstanding Checks:	
# 106	$330
# 107	$275
# 111	$151
Outstanding Deposits:	
Sept. 15	$1,500
Sept. 22	$1,000

14.2 Accounting Systems

OBJECTIVES

- Describe how to use a single-column accounting worksheet
- Create financial statements based on a single-column accounting worksheet

VOCABULARY

- financing activities
- investing activities
- operating activities
- Pacioli check column
- posted

Consider this question:

As an entrepreneur, would you use a manual accounting system or a computerized accounting system for your business?

Write your answer (manual or computerized) on a piece of paper. Be prepared to explain you choice in class.

Using an Accounting Worksheet

You have learned the basics of recording accounting transactions using a single-column approach and a double-column approach. In this section, you will use the single-column approach, which can be done manually or with a computer spreadsheet program like Microsoft Excel.

The Accounting Worksheet

A simple accounting system is especially helpful to entrepreneurs starting their businesses. Often beginning entrepreneurs will use a single-column accounting worksheet. An accounting worksheet relies on one main database. After each transaction is **posted** (written in the accounting worksheet) in an accounting period (such as a month), an entrepreneur can immediately determine the effect the transaction has on the financial statements. In other words, an accounting worksheet is "real-time." It allows a business owner to make immediate decisions regarding the financial health of the enterprise. At the end of the accounting period, it is easy to prepare an income statement, statement of cash flows, and balance sheet.

An accounting worksheet is primarily a cash-only accounting system. The only time you will make entries that don't affect cash is when you remove inventory upon a sale of goods, or when you estimate your tax expense based on the current period income before taxes. All other worksheet entries will increase cash when it's collected or decrease cash when it's paid.

If you keep an accounting worksheet by hand, the entries should be made in pencil so you can erase mistakes. Use a mechanical pencil because it can make very thin lines, allowing you to write more in the limited space available. Write neatly. Since an accounting worksheet has many rows and columns, you can use a long ruler when inputting numbers to assure that you are placing the numbers on the correct line.

Preferably, however, you will use an accounting worksheet constructed with spreadsheet software (such as Excel) to record your transactions. The accounting worksheet template supplied with this text is shown in Figure 14-5 on the following page.

If You Aren't Familiar with Spreadsheet Software

- Search for "Free Excel Spreadsheet Tutorial" on Google or Yahoo.
- Find a tutorial that looks helpful and invest about an hour in learning Excel basics.

This will allow you to use the accounting worksheet template in a more informed way. It will also help with such activities as preparing budgets, preparing financial statements, and projecting cash flows.

Parts of the Accounting Worksheet

At the top of the accounting worksheet template is a heading for you to key such information as Company Name, Student Name, Class/Section, and Teacher, along with the relevant accounting period.

Cell References

Like any spreadsheet, the accounting worksheet has many columns and rows. An easy way to refer to a cell is to list the column of the cell first, and then the row of the cell. For example, the first cell in a spreadsheet is cell A1 (column A, row 1).

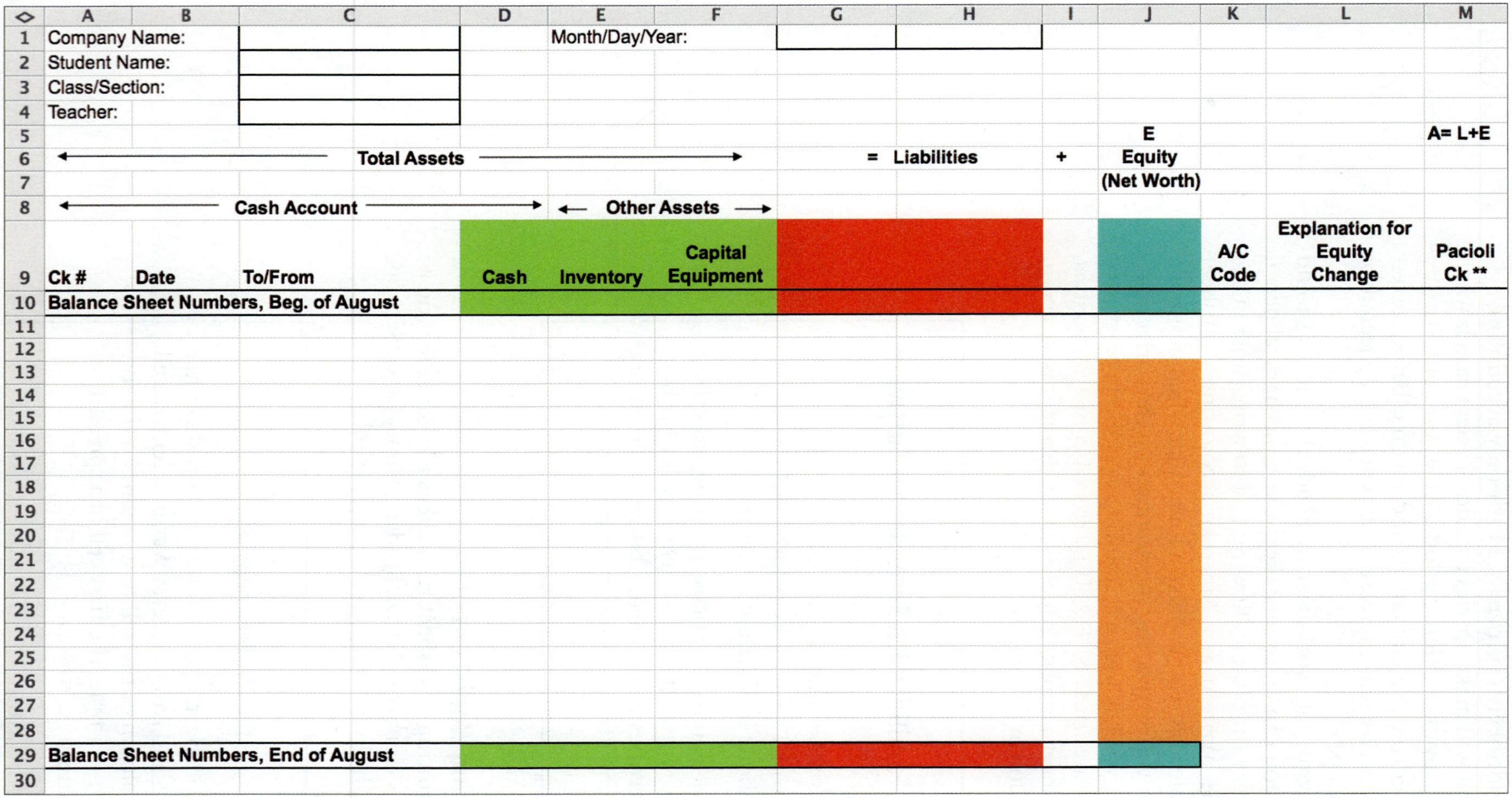

	A	B	C	D	E	F	G	H	I	J	K	L	M
1	Company Name:				Month/Day/Year:								
2	Student Name:												
3	Class/Section:												
4	Teacher:												A= L+E
5				Total Assets				= Liabilities	+	E Equity (Net Worth)			
6													
7				← Cash Account →	← Other Assets →								
8													
9	Ck #	Date	To/From	Cash	Inventory	Capital Equipment					A/C Code	Explanation for Equity Change	Pacioli Ck **
10	Balance Sheet Numbers, Beg. of August												
11													
12													
13													
14													
15													
16													
17													
18													
19													
20													
21													
22													
23													
24													
25													
26													
27													
28													
29	Balance Sheet Numbers, End of August												
30													

▲ Figure 14-5

Transaction Portion of the Accounting Worksheet

The accounting worksheet is organized according to the accounting equation: Assets = Liabilities + Owner's Equity.

Applying Concepts. *Can you explain the concept in row 6 as it applies to the accounts in rows 9 and 10?*

Here's an explanation of some of the important parts of the accounting worksheet template:

- **Check or Deposit Number, Date, and To/From Columns.** Beginning in cell A11, and running across the first three columns, are the columns for the Cash account. These are very much like the columns you would see in a checkbook.

- **Accounts.** The business accounts, beginning with Cash, in cell D10, run across columns D through J. Columns D through F show the Other Assets accounts. Columns G and H show the Liabilities accounts. And column J shows the Equity account. The Other Assets account titles have a green background. The Liabilities account titles (such as Loans Payable and Income Tax Payable) have a red background. The Equity account title has a blue background.

- **Equity.** Take a close look at the cells in column J under Equity (most are colored orange). As you will see a bit later, most changes in Owner's Equity (otherwise known as Net Worth) are due to revenues and expenses. Revenues increase Owner's Equity, and expenses decrease Owner's Equity.

- **A/C Code.** In column K, beginning in cell K10, the appropriate Chart of Account Code is shown for each transaction. The code is taken from the Chart of Accounts (which begins in cell A32.) The Chart of Account Code is a convenient way of labeling all revenues and expenses. This makes it easier to prepare your income statement.

- **Explanation for Equity Change.** In column L, beginning in cell L10, you can provide an explanation for the change in equity. This serves as a handy reminder of the type of each revenue and expense item.

- **Pacioli Check.** Column M, beginning with cell M10, is the **Pacioli check column**. The column is named after the father of modern-day bookkeeping, Luca Pacioli (pa-CHO-lee). Pacioli was a Franciscan monk from Sansepolcro, Italy. In 1494 he wrote the first textbook describing the duality aspect of accounting. This column will ensure that the accounting equation always balances after each transaction.

Entering Transactions

The following example shows you how to use the accounting worksheet for a merchandising business called Jean Waverly's T-Shirts. It's a sole proprietorship selling T-shirts.

Let's start with Transaction 1. Jean started her business on August 2, 20-- by contributing $2,000 of her personal savings to open a business checking account. When she deposited this money in the business account, she would make the following entry in the accounting worksheet.

Ck #	Date	To/From	Cash	Inventory	Jean Waverly, Capital	Pacioli Ck **
Balance Sheet Numbers, Beg. of August			0	0	0	0
Deposit	8/2/20--	Jean Waverly	2,000		2,000	0

Only the affected accounts are shown.

To get a bit more practice, let's look at Transaction 2. Here, the business purchased 200 blank T-shirts for $3 each from ACME T-Shirt Supply. The total cost of $600 is subtracted from Cash and added to Inventory (Check 101).

Ck #	Date	To/From	Cash	Inventory	Jean Waverly, Capital	Pacioli Ck **
Balance Sheet Numbers, Beg. of August			0	0	0	0
Deposit	8/2/20--	Jean Waverly	2,000		2,000	0
101	8/2/20--	ACME T-Shirt Supply	-600	600		0

Only the affected accounts are shown.

Note that Jean's current balance in Cash is $1,400, and her balance in Inventory is $600. You can determine the account balance for *any* account by adding up the numbers from the beginning of the period to the current date. This is what makes the accounting worksheet real-time.

 In an accounting worksheet, what role does the Pacioli check column perform?

Using the Accounting Worksheet

Let's start from the beginning for Jean Waverly's business. After she wrote a business plan and studied the market, Jean decided to open a merchandising business selling T-shirts. She began her business on August 2, 20--.

The first thing she did was to prepare a Chart of Accounts for her business and open a business checking account at a local bank. Jean pays the supplier of her T-shirts $3 for each shirt. She sells the shirts for $10 apiece.

The first step in using the accounting worksheet is to enter all the transactions. As an example, here are the business transactions for Jean's T-Shirts in August, 20--:

August 2	Jean Waverly invested $2,000 from her personal savings account to provide start-up financing for the business. She opened up a business checking account at her local bank.
August 2	The business purchased 200 T-shirts from ACME T-Shirt Supply (200 × $3 = $600). This is Check 101.
August 8	The business sold 50 T-shirts at $10 each (50 × $10 = $500). This transaction requires two entries. First, she records the sales revenue, adding $500 to Cash and $500 to Jean Waverly, Capital (as Revenue). Second, she records the Cost of Goods Sold (COGS) expense. The cost per shirt is $3. Thus, the COGS Expense is $3 × 50 shirts = $150.

> Each sale of inventory requires two entries: one to record the sales revenue and one to record the COGS expense.

August 9	The business paid $100 for advertising flyers. (Check 102)
August 10	The business paid $500 for a new Office Machine, a cash register. (Check 103)
August 11	The business paid its monthly rent of $300 to Ron's Real Estate. (Check 104)
August 15	The business sold 100 T-shirts at $10 each for the week (100 × $10 each = $1,000). The cost of each T-shirt is $3. Thus, COGS expense is 100 shirts × $3 = $300.
August 15	The business purchased 400 more T-shirts from ACME T-Shirt Supply (400 × $3 = $1,200). (Check 105).
August 16	The business paid its utility bill to Atlantic Electric Co. for $225. (Check 106).
August 22	The business sold 150 T-shirts for the week (150 × $10 = $1,500). The cost of each T-shirt is still $3. So COGS expense is 150 shirts × $3 = $450.
August 24	The business paid a salary of $125 to a part-time worker, Mary Smith. (Check 107)
August 25	The business paid its $200 insurance bill for the month to ABC Insurance Co. (Check 108)
August 26	The business sold 200 T-shirts for the week (200 × $10 = $2,000). The cost of each T-shirt is $3. So COGS expense is 200 shirts × $3 = $600.
August 31	The business calculated pre-tax net income for the period by adding all revenues and subtracting all expenses. Pre-tax net income is $2,550. At a 15% income tax rate (a tax liability) tax expense is calculated to be .15 × $2,550 = $382.50.

Figure 14-6

Transactions for Jean Waverly's T-Shirts

All the transactions for August have been entered in the accounting worksheet.

Predicting. *From the data in this accounting worksheet, do you think that Jean's T-Shirts was profitable in August?*

		Company Name:	Jean Waverly's T-Shirts	Month/Day/Year:							
		Student Name:	John Doe								
		Class/Section:	NFTE Ent 101/01								
		Teacher:	Mr. Killebrew	4/8/20---							

			Total Assets			= Liabilities		+	E Equity (Net Worth)		A= L+E

Ck #	Date	To/From	Cash	Inventory	Capital Equipment	Loans Payable	Income Tax Payable	Jean Waverly, Capital	A/C Code	Explanation for Equity Change	Pacioli Ck **
Balance Sheet Numbers, Beg. of August			0	0	0	0	0	0			0
Deposit	8/2/20---	Jean Waverly	2,000					2,000			0
101	8/2/20---	ACME T-Shirt Supply	-600	600							0
Deposit	8/8/20---	Dep. Cks. from Sales	500					500	R1	Sales Revenue	0
				-150				-150	VE1	COGS Expense	0
102	8/9/20---	Corner Print Shop	-100					-100	FE1	Adv. Expense	0
103	8/10/20---	Otto's Office Machines	-500		500						0
104	8/11/20---	Ron's Real Estate	-300					-300	FE2	Rent Expense	0
Deposit	8/15/20---	Dep. Cks. from Sales	1,000					1,000	R1	Sales Revenue	0
				-300				-300	VE1	COGS Expense	0
105	8/15/20---	ACME T-Shirt Supply	-1,200	1,200							0
106	8/16/20---	Atlantic Electric Co.	-225					-225	FE3	Utilities Expense	0
Deposit	8/22/20---	Dep. Cks. from Sales	1,500					1,500	R1	Sales Revenue	0
				-450				-450	VE1	COGS Expense	0
107	8/24/20---	Mary Smith	-125					-125	FE4	Salary Expense	0
108	8/25/20---	ABC Insurance Co.	-200					-200	FE5	Insurance Expense	0
Deposit	8/26/20---	Dep. Cks. from Sales	2,000					2,000	R1	Sales Revenue	0
				-600				-600	VE1	COGS Expense	0
	8/31/20---						638	-638	VE5	Income Tax Expense	0
Balance Sheet Numbers, End of August			3,750	300	500	0	638	3,913			0

Figure 14-6 on the opposite page shows the completed accounting worksheet for Jean's T-Shirts after all the transactions have been entered for August.

READING CHECKPOINT *What is the first step in completing an accounting worksheet?*

Creating Financial Statements

After the transactions for a period are correctly entered into the accounting worksheet, you can prepare the balance sheet, income statement, and statement of cash flows. It doesn't matter which financial statement you start with. See Figure 14-7 on next page.

Balance Sheet

First, look at row 34. These are the ending balances in each of the accounts in the Assets, Liability and Owner's Equity portions of the balance sheet. They are the basis for preparing the balance sheet in the accounting worksheet.

Look at the Owner's Equity part of the balance sheet. Compare it to the Balance Sheet at the beginning of the month. Jean Waverly, Capital had a zero balance on August 1 because the business was just beginning.

On August 2, Jean financed the business by contributing $2,000 of her personal money to the business. Jean's T-Shirts earned a net income of $1,913 during August. So, the August 31 ending balance for Jean Waverly, Capital is $3,913 (Aug. 1 balance $0 + $2,000 equity financing on Aug. 2 + $1,913 net income for August).

As is the case in every balance sheet, the Assets must equal the total of the Liabilities and Owner's Equity. In this balance sheet on August 31, 20--, they do.

Income Statement

For the income statement, begin by looking at cell K9, labeled "A/C Code" (which stands for Account Code). This code allows you to classify revenues, variable expenses, and fixed expenses.

Using the Account Code, you can add all the accounts for the month to the Income Statement portion of the accounting

◇	O	P	Q	R	S
34	**BALANCE SHEET 8/31/--**				
35	**ASSETS**				
36	Cash				$3,750
37	Inventory				300
38	Office Machines				500
39	TOTAL ASSETS				$4,550
40	**LIABILITIES**				
41	Bank Loan				$0
42	Income Tax Payable				638
43	**OWNER'S EQUITY**				
44	Jean Waverly, Capital, Beg. Bal.				$0
45	Plus: Owner's Personal Investment				2,000
46	Plus: Net Profit				1,913
47	TOTAL LIABILITIES & OWNER'S EQUITY				$4,550

▲ *Balance Sheet*

◇	K	L
9	**A/C Code**	**Explanation for Equity Change**
10		
11		
12		
13	R1	Sales Revenue
14	VE1	COGS Expense
15	FE1	Adv. Expense
16		
17	FE2	Rent Expense
18	R1	Sales Revenue
19	VE1	COGS Expense
20		
21	FE3	Utilities Expense
22	R1	Sales Revenue
23	VE1	COGS Expense
24	FE4	Salary Expense
25	FE5	Insurance Expense
26	R1	Sales Revenue
27	VE1	COGS Expense
28	VE5	Income Tax Expense

▲ *Chart of Accounts*

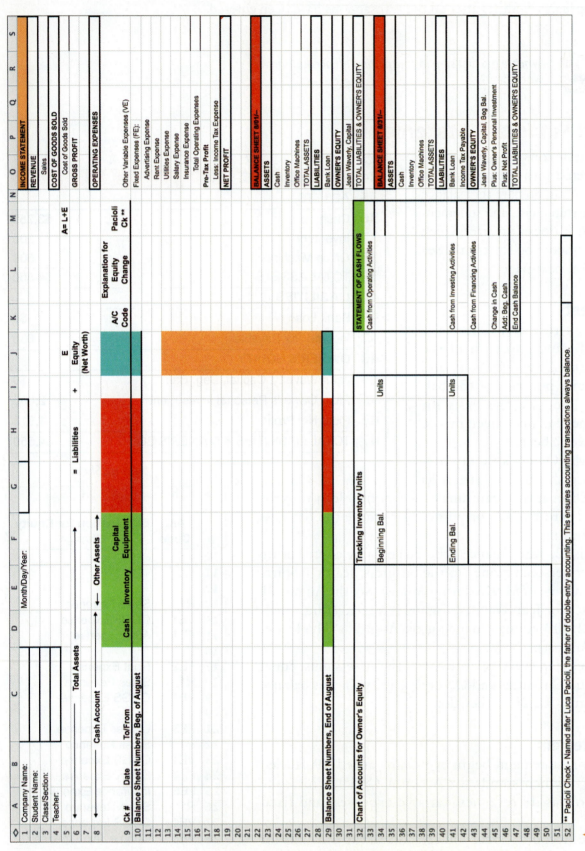

The complete worksheet shows an income statement, a beginning and ending balance sheet, a statement of cash flows, and an inventory report.

Predicting. *Which financial document would you prepare first?*

▲ **Figure 14-7**

Blank Accounting Worksheet

worksheet. For example, for your Sales (account R1), add all the R1 transactions:

- From 8/8, add $500
- From 8/15, add $1,000
- From 8/22, add $1,500
- From 8/26, add $2,000

So Jean Waverly's total sales revenue for the month of August is $5,000. Add that amount to the Income Statement under Revenue, Sales in cell S3.

Here's another example: For Cost of Goods Sold (account VE1), add all VE1 transactions:

- From 8/8, add $150
- From 8/15, add $300
- From 8/22, add $450
- From 8/26, add $600

Jean Waverly's total COGS for the month of August is $1,400. Add that amount to the Income Statement under Cost of Goods Sold in cell S5.

Continue in this way for all the accounts with entries in August. Some, such as Office Equipment, will only have one entry (on 8/10, when Jean bought a cash register). Others, like Jean Waverly, Capital, will have multiple entries that you'll need to add up.

Here, to the right, is the final income statement.

The Net Profit of $1,913 in the income statement is also reported on the balance sheet as an increase in Owner's Equity.

 Income Statement

◇	O	P	Q	R	S
1	**INCOME STATEMENT**				
2	**REVENUE**				
3	Sales				$5,000
4	**COST OF GOODS SOLD**				
5	Cost of Goods Sold				-1,500
6	**GROSS PROFIT**				$3,500
7					
8	**OPERATING EXPENSES**				
9	Other Variable Expenses (VE)				$0
10	Fixed Expenses (FE):				
11	Advertising Expense				-100
12	Rent Expense				-300
13	Utilities Expense				-225
14	Salary Expense				-125
15	Insurance Expense				-200
16	Total Operating Expenses				-950
17	**Pre-Tax Profit**				2,550
18	Less: Income-Tax Expense				-638
19	**NET PROFIT**				$1,913

Statement of Cash Flows

In relation to the statement of cash flows, there are three basic types of business activities:

- **Operating activities.** Day-to-day activities are called <mark>operating activities</mark>. Most cash changes fall into this category.

- **Investing Activities.** When a business buys assets that will last more than one year, they are called <mark>investing activities</mark>. Jean's only investing activity is the purchase of a cash register for $500 on August 10.

- **Financing Activities.** The third category is <mark>financing activities</mark>. It consists primarily of debt and equity financing. Jean's only financing activity in August is the $2,000 she personally invested to provide start-up equity financing for her business.

Jean can now prepare the statement of cash flows by adding all the changes in the Cash column (Column D) under the appropriate head, as shown here.

Statement of Cash Flows

◇	K	L	M
32	**STATEMENT OF CASH FLOWS**		
33	Cash from Operating Activities		
34		Cash Sales	$5,000
35		Cash Pd. Supplies	-1800
36		Cash Pd. Advert.	-100
37		Cash Pd. Rent	-300
38		Cash Pd. Utilit.	-225
39		Cash Pd. Salary	-125
40		Cash Pd. Insur.	-200
41	Cash from Investing Activities		
42		Purch. of Equip.	-$500
43	Cash from Financing Activities		
44		Jean's Pers. Contr.	2000
45	Change in Cash		$3,750
46	Add: Beg. Cash		0
47	Cash Balance, 8/31/--		$3,750

The ending cash balance of $3,750 is the same number as the cash balance reported on the balance sheet.

For businesses that are more complicated than Jean's, it is often a good idea to create a separate Chart of Accounts for all changes in cash (just as with changes in Owner's Equity). You could create a code column next to cash with three labels: "O" for operating activities, "I" for investing activities, and "F" for financing activities.

Figure 14-8

Completed Accounting Worksheet

A completed accounting worksheet includes a completed Income statement, a beginning and ending balance sheet, a statement of cash flows, and an inventory report.

Predicting. *In your opinion, how useful would this accounting worksheet be to you if you were a beginning entrepreneur?*

Company Name:	Jean Waverly's T-Shirts	Month/Day/Year: 4/8/20--
Student Name:	John Doe	
Class/Section:	NFTE Ent 101/01	
Teacher:	Mr. Killebrew	

Total Assets = Liabilities + Equity (Net Worth)   A = L + E

Cash Account / Other Assets

Ck #	Date	To/From	Cash	Inventory	Capital Equipment	Loans Payable	Income Tax Payable	Jean Waverly, Capital (Equity)	A/C Code	Explanation for Equity Change	Pacioli Ck**
		Balance Sheet Numbers, Beg. of August	0	0	0	0	0	0			0
Deposit	8/2/20--	Jean Waverly	2,000					2,000			
101	8/2/20--	ACME T-Shirt Supply	-600	600							0
Deposit	8/8/20--	Dep. Cks. from Sales	500					500	R1	Sales Revenue	0
				-150				-150	VE1	COGS Expense	0
102	8/9/20--	Corner Print Shop	-100					-100	FE1	Adv. Expense	0
103	8/10/20--	Otto's Office Machines	-500		500						0
104	8/11/20--	Ron's Real Estate	-300					-300	FE2	Rent Expense	0
Deposit	8/15/20--	Dep. Cks. from Sales	1,000					1,000	R1	Sales Revenue	0
				-300				-300	VE1	COGS Expense	0
105	8/15/20--	ACME T-Shirt Supply	-1,200	1,200							0
106	8/16/20--	Atlantic Electric Co.	-225					-225	FE3	Utilities Expense	0
Deposit	8/22/20--	Dep. Cks. from Sales	1,500					1,500	R1	Sales Revenue	0
				-450				-450	VE1	COGS Expense	0
107	8/24/20--	Mary Smith	-125					-125	FE4	Salary Expense	0
108	8/25/20--	ABC Insurance Co.	-200					-200	FE5	Insurance Exp.	0
Deposit	8/26/20--	Dep. Cks. from Sales	2,000					2,000	R1	Sales Revenue	0
				-600				-600	VE1	COGS Expense	0
	8/31/20--						638	-638	VE5	Income Tax Expense	
		Balance Sheet Numbers, End of August	3,750	300	500	500	638	3,913			0

Chart of Accounts

- R1 = Revenue Source #1
- VE1 = Cost of Goods Sold (a Variable Expense)
- VE2 = Sales Commission (a Variable Expense)
- VE3 = Utilities
- VE4 = Salary
- VE5 = Income-Tax Expense (also a Variable Expense)
- FE1 = Advertising Expense (Flyers)
- FE2 = Rent Expense
- FE3 = Utilities Expense
- FE4 = Salary Expense
- FE5 = Insurance Expense
- FE6 = Registration Fee for Market Booth
- FE7 = Business Cards
- FE8 = Flyers
- FE9 = Rent

Tracking Inventory Units

August 1 Beginning Bal.	0 Units
August 2 Purchase	200 Units
August 8 Sale	-50 Units
August 15 Sale	-100 Units
August 15 Purchase	400 Units
August 22 Sale	-150 Units
August 26 Sale	-200 Units
August 31 Ending Bal.	100 Units

Statement of Cash Flows

Cash from Operating Activities	
Cash Sales	$5,000
Cash Pd. Supplies	-1800
Cash Pd. Advert.	-100
Cash Pd. Rent	-300
Cash Pd. Utilit.	-225
Cash Pd. Salary	-125
Cash Pd. Insur.	-200
Cash from Investing Activities	
Purch. of Equip.	-$500
Cash from Financing Activities	
Jean's Pers. Contr.	2,000
Change in Cash	$3,750
Add: Beg. Cash	
Cash Balance, 8/31/--	$3,750

Income Statement

REVENUE	
Sales	$5,000
COST OF GOODS SOLD	
Cost of Goods Sold	-1,500
GROSS PROFIT	$3,500
OPERATING EXPENSES	
Other Variable Expenses (VE)	$0
Fixed Expenses (FE):	
Advertising Expense	-100
Rent Expense	-300
Utilities Expense	-225
Salary Expense	-125
Insurance Expense	-200
Total Operating Expenses	-950
Pre-Tax Profit	2,550
Less: Income-Tax Expense	-638
NET PROFIT	$1,913

Balance Sheet 8/01/--

ASSETS	
Cash	0
Inventory	0
Office Machines	0
TOTAL ASSETS	0
LIABILITIES	
Bank Loan	0
OWNER'S EQUITY	
Jean Waverly, Capital	0
TOTAL LIABILITIES & OWNER'S EQUITY	0

Balance Sheet 8/31/--

ASSETS	
Cash	$3,750
Inventory	300
Office Machines	500
TOTAL ASSETS	$4,550
LIABILITIES	
Bank Loan	$0
Income Tax Payable	638
OWNER'S EQUITY	
Jean Waverly, Capital, Beg. Bal.	$0
Plus: Owner's Personal Investment	2,000
Plus: Net Profit	1,913
TOTAL LIABILITIES & OWNER'S EQUITY	$4,550

** Pacioli Check - Named after Luca Pacioli, the father of double-entry accounting. This ensures accounting transactions always balance.

Tracking Inventory

Every time inventory is purchased, you should record the type of inventory, number of units purchased, and its cost. Also, every time inventory is sold, you should make a note of the type of inventory and number of units sold. At any one time, your accounting records should agree with the number of units on hand. This is a crucial accounting control to make sure customers or employees aren't stealing merchandise from your business.

Thus, in the accounting worksheet, you see that there should be 100 T-Shirts on hand at the end of August. If there are fewer than that, you have a problem. Customers or employees may have stolen T-shirts, or there may be an accounting error.

The inventory of T-shirts has a dollar value. At the end of the month, the balance in Inventory is $300 (100 T-shirts × $3). See Figure 14-8 on the previous page.

Using a Computerized Spreadsheet

If you use an electronic spreadsheet, such as Excel, you can easily keep track of transactions and prepare financial statements. There are three major features of a spreadsheet program that are particularly useful when using a spreadsheet accounting worksheet:

- **Linking Numbers from One Part of the Worksheet to Another.** One of the main advantages of a computer spreadsheet is that you can link numbers from one part of a spreadsheet directly to another part of the spreadsheet. For example, the amount in cell D29 for Cash is $3,750. This amount will also be shown on the balance sheet in cell S36 ("Cash"). To have the spreadsheet software place the amount in cell D29 into the cell at S36, you can click in cell S36, and then in the Formula Bar key "=d29". This tells the computer to take the amount in cell D29 and put it in cell S36.

- **Adding Columns of Numbers.** You can also have the spreadsheet software total columns of numbers for you. For example, you could add the Cash totals shown in column D. To do this, place the cursor in the cell where you want to place the sum of the column, in this case cell D29. Then, in the Formula Bar, key "=sum(d11:d28)" and press Enter. The software will place the sum for cells D11 through D28 into cell D29.

- **Adding Comments to Cells.** You can add comments for specific cells. You can easily remind yourself about a number in any cell by inserting a comment using the Insert/Comment command from the main menu of the spreadsheet program. See Figure 14-9 on the next page.

#	Ck #	Date	To/From	Cash	Inventory	Capital Equipment	Loans Payable
9							
10			Balance Sheet Numbers, Beg. of August	0	0	0	0
11	Deposit	8/2/20--	Jean Waverly	2,000			
12	101	8/2/20--	ACME T-Shirt Supply	-600	600		
13	Deposit	8/8/20--	Dep. Cks. from Sales	500			
14					-150		
15	102	8/9/20--	Corner Print Shop	-100			
16	103	8/10/20--	Otto's Office Machines	-500		500	
17	104	8/11/20--	Ron's Real Estate	-300			
18	Deposit	8/15/20--	Dep. Cks. from Sales	1,000			
19					-300		
20	105	8/15/20--	ACME T-Shirt Supply	-1,200	1,200		
21	106	8/16/20--	Atlantic Electric Co.	-225			
22	Deposit	8/22/20--	Dep. Cks. from Sales	1,500			
23					-450		
24	107	8/24/20--	Mary Smith	-125			
25	108	8/25/20--	ABC Insurance Co.	-200			
26	Deposit	8/26/20--	Dep. Cks. from Sales	2,000			
27					-600		
28		8/31/20--					
29			Balance Sheet Numbers, End of August	3,750	300	0	0
30							Units
31							
32			Chart of Accounts				
33							

Note that the formula bar reads: =sum(D11:D28), which adds up all numbers in this range of cells. The total is $3,750.

▲ Figure 14-9

Adding Comments to an Accounting Worksheet
You can add comments to specific cells.

Inferring. *Why might you add comments to specific cells?*

 **READING CHECKPOINT** ✓ *What are the three main types of business activities?*

 Your Business Plan. Continue developing your standard business plan. Go to "Section 14.2" of the *Business Plan Project* in your *Student Activity Workbook*, or "Section 14.2" of the BizTech Software.

ASSESSMENT 14.2

Reviewing Objectives

1. How do the rows where you post transactions in the accounting worksheet reflect the basic accounting equation?

2. In regard to the statement of cash flow, what are the three basic types of business activities?

Critical Thinking

3. **Applying Concepts.** How would you record the following transaction using the accounting worksheet template shown in this section? Your business purchased $200 of advertising brochures using the business's debit card.

4. **Analyzing Information.** Looking at Figure 14-7, what would the beginning inventory for Jean's T-Shirts be at the beginning of the next month?

Working Together

Form two teams. Using the accounting worksheet template as the model, one team will create an accounting worksheet for a service business of their choosing. The second team will create an accounting worksheet for a new merchandising business of their choosing. The teams will present their worksheets to the class.

Social Studies

Early Accounting

Research Luca Pacioli, the father of modern-day bookkeeping. Report on any of the following: Pacioli's life, the early history of bookkeeping, the development of the concept of duality, Pacioli's early texts on accounting, or how business was conducted in Pacioli's time. Present your report to the class.

Do, Re, Mi:
Piano Lessons with a Twist

When Danni Zhang was five years old and living in China, she took piano lessons from a famous teacher. "She was really strict and she would always hit my fingers with fly swatters and chopsticks," said Danni, remembering her fear every time she had to go to a lesson. But Danni continued taking lessons and practicing—with one two-year break while she was in boarding school—until she came to the United States when she was thirteen.

When Danni started giving her seven-year-old step-brother piano lessons, his friends' parents asked her to teach their kids as well. While the parents were willing to pay, the kids weren't willing to play. "They may be interested for two weeks," said Danni, "and then they stop because they hate it. It's boring for them. So I decided to do something different from the traditional way of learning piano."

▲ *Danni Zhang*

A Technical Twist

"Kids love iPods, the computer, and MP3 players," said Danni, "but they don't really like classical piano. I wanted to motivate them to practice and learn by using something that they really like." Her solution: using a MobiBLU—an MP3 player—to record the whole lesson. The MP3 recording has Danni playing the same piece as the student. It also includes Danni's instructions on what to do. Students take the recording home so they can review the lesson whenever they want.

Danni named her company "Dr. Mi." The "Dr." represents the doctor who cures people of their fear of piano playing. It also stands for the first notes of the scale—do and re. Danni's motto is "Dr. Mi teaches do, re, mi and cures piano fear."

Communicating

After her first year in business, several of her students moved away and Danni advertised in the Chinatown newspaper. She found new students who were willing to come to her house for lessons. Her only problem was one of language. Danni spoke Mandarin and Cantonese, and her pupils spoke English. "At first, if you can't talk to them, they say, 'I don't understand what you're saying. I'm not going to play.' But in the end,

they actually start to accept you," said Danni, noting that her English also improved.

Danni gave approximately 20 lessons a week to children from ages 5 to 9. She would spend a half-hour preparing for each hour-long lesson. Danni charged $25 a lesson. Because her piano belonged to her parents and because all her students came to her family's home, Danni gave 10% of her revenue to her parents for rent. She also set up a bank account and funded it with $50 per month for depreciation of the piano and for piano tuning, which needed to be done every six months. She kept accounts on her income and her expenses, which included soft drinks and snacks for her students.

Danni put Dr. Mi on hold when she started college, but she plans to continue the lessons after she graduates. "Right now, I just play for fun," she says.

Thinking Like an Entrepreneur

1. What hobbies or skills do you have that can be turned into a business?
2. Can you think of a way to incorporate technology into a hobby or skill so it becomes a business idea?
3. How important is communication in a service business?

CHAPTER SUMMARY

14.1 Recordkeeping

Entrepreneurs must keep accurate financial records. The first step a new business owner should take is to go to a bank and open both a business checking account and a savings account. Every month you should reconcile the bank's checking account statement with your checkbook balance. The next step in setting up a business is to install a recordkeeping system using business documents such as receipts, invoices, and purchase orders. All accounting systems make use of double-entry accounting which means that every business transaction affects at least two accounts. There are two approaches to recording transactions: the single-column, database approach and the double-column approach. Both approaches use the concept of duality—all changes on one side of the accounting equation must equal all changes on the other side.

14.2 Accounting Systems

An accounting workbook relies on one main database. After each transaction is posted, an entrepreneur can determine the effect the transaction has on the financial statements. An accounting worksheet includes a balance sheet, an income statement, a statement of cash flows, and an inventory report. Using a computerized spreadsheet makes preparing an accounting worksheet simpler.

REVIEW VOCABULARY

Working in teams of two or three, prepare an oral presentation explaining how the use of business documents and accounting systems helps a business become more successful. Use at least half the following terms in your presentation:

- accounting (p. 376)
- accounting controls (p. 382)
- auditor (p. 383)
- bank reconciliation (p. 373)
- chart of accounts (p. 376)
- checking account (p. 372)
- double-entry accounting (p. 376)
- duality (p. 380)
- embezzlement (p. 382)

- Federal Deposit Insurance Corporation (FDIC) (p. 371)
- financing activities (p. 394)
- general journal (p. 379)
- internal audit (p. 383)
- investing activities (p. 394)
- operating activities (p. 394)
- Pacioli check column (p. 387)
- payee (p. 372)

- posted (p. 384)
- purchase order (p. 374)
- receipt (p. 374)
- sales invoice (p. 375)
- savings account (p. 372)
- source document (p. 376)
- T-account (p. 379)
- transaction (p. 376)

CHECK YOUR UNDERSTANDING

Choose the letter that best answers the question or completes the statement.

1. The independent agency that insures savings and checking accounts is the
   - a. FHA
   - b. FDIC
   - c. FASB
   - d. FOMC

2. The most common reason that the ending balance on a bank's checking account statement doesn't match the balance you show in your checkbook is
   - a. a bank math error
   - b. banker fraud
   - c. employee embezzlement
   - d. outstanding checks

3. When you pay someone with a check, that person is the
   - a. payer
   - b. payee
   - c. debtor
   - d. depositor

4. A detailed written proof of a purchase is called a(n)
   - a. receipt
   - b. purchase order
   - c. invoice
   - d. purchase slip

5. An itemized list of goods delivered, or services rendered, and the amount due is called a(n)
   - a. receipt
   - b. invoice
   - c. purchase order
   - d. packing slip

6. An accounting term used to describe where all the transactions of a business are recorded is an accounting database or an accounting
   - a. ledger
   - b. journal
   - c. chart of accounts
   - d. entry book

7. The process of entering data into a database or journal is called
   - a. deducting
   - b. capitalizing
   - c. transferring
   - d. posting

8. The first step in creating a bookkeeping system for a business is to create a
   - a. general journal
   - b. general ledger
   - c. chart of accounts
   - d. transaction summary account

9. All accounting systems use
   - a. double-entry accounting
   - b. single–entry accounting
   - c. smallest sum postings
   - d. averaged sum postings

10. Checks and balances established by a business to provide employees with mandatory procedures are called
    - a. accounting controls
    - b. auditing controls
    - c. management controls
    - d. recording controls

11. Which one of the following columns in an accounting worksheet would not be needed by a service business?
    - a. Computer Equipment
    - b. COGS Expense
    - c. Revenue
    - d. Operating Expenses

12. Which one of the following is not prepared when using an accounting worksheet?
    - a. income tax return
    - b. balance sheet
    - c. income statement
    - d. statement of cash flows

Business Communication

13. You want to start a dog-walking business. Using a piece of paper, prepare a simulated accounting worksheet for your first month of business, assuming you invest $500 in the business. The worksheet should include column titles you would need for your business.

14. Using Internet search engines, prepare a list of some potential accounting programs. Make a chart showing the advantages and disadvantages of each program. Rank each program based on its usefulness for a small business. Report your results to the class.

15. Partner with a classmate. You and your partner own a sporting goods store. You need an accounting system. One of you wants to use a manual system; the other, a computerized system. Each of you should prepare a list of the advantages of your respective choices and the disadvantages of the other one. Then you will debate in front of the class.

Business Ethics

18. You work at a hardware store. You have become friends with the accounting clerk. After a few months, she tells you that she wants to "alter" the accounting system to create a fictitious vendor to whom the hardware store owes money. She plans to write checks to this vendor, who is really her sister-in-law. She asks you to submit fake invoices to the hardware store in order for her to "pay" the bill. She promises that you'll get 15% of what she "makes." What should you do?

Business Math

16. The owner of a costume shop pays the supplier $5 for each mask purchased. In turn, the owner sells the masks for $15 each. In the month of October, the business had mask sales revenue of $2,250. What was the cost of goods sold (COGS) for October?

17. An accounting worksheet showed the beginning inventory for December as $30,000. During the month, the business made two additional purchases—one for $6,000 and the other for $5,000. The COGS for the month was $20,000. What is the value of the ending inventory?

Business in Your Community

19. Working with three classmates, brainstorm how to start a business in your community that would provide accounting services to entrepreneurs. Investigate companies in your community that perform accounting services. What kinds of services do they perform and how do they charge for them? What services would your company perform and how would you charge for them? Write a description of your services and pricing policies, and share it with the class.

20. Interview two small-business owners in your community. Ask them what kind of accounting system they use in their businesses and why they chose to use that specific system. What do they feel are the advantages and disadvantages of the system? Write a short report with the results of your interviews.

ENTREPRENEURS & TECHNOLOGY

Online Finance

The Internet has made a huge difference in the way people and businesses conduct their financial affairs. For example, instead of going to a bank in person to deposit checks and transfer money, many individuals and small businesses do most of their banking transactions online. It's become even more important to keep track of both your business and your personal finances—and technology can help.

Accounting Programs

Accounting software gives business owners a fast and accurate way to see where their money is going. There are a number of different brands of accounting software, such as Intuit QuickBooks and Microsoft Office Small Business Accounting. An entrepreneur needs to make sure the program he or she chooses has features that are right for the business. For example, if you have a service-related business, you'll want a time-and-billing module within the program.

If you want to install it on more than one computer, you will need to investigate how the software is licensed to users. Most software is sold in two different versions: one for stand-alone computers, the other for networks. A **one-user license** gives one individual the right to use the program and is sold with the stand-alone version of the software. A **multi-user license** allows multiple users to use the software in a networked hardware environment. The cost of a multi-user user license is usually less expensive per user than a one-user license.

Another consideration is whether the software will integrate your credit card transactions, both incoming and outgoing.

Ways to Pay Online

There are three ways to pay online:
- You can pay directly, by using your credit or debit card.
- You can buy online and then pay by sending a check or money order to the seller before the item is shipped to you.
- You can use **third party transactions**.

Third party transactions are those in which someone collects the money from the buyer and then pays the seller. For example, third party transactions are often used when purchasing from Amazon. If you buy a used book on Amazon's Website, you pay Amazon, who in turn pays the original seller the stated amount less Amazon's commission.

Online payment services, such as PayPal, are another type of third party transaction. Here, users can deposit money into an online account, or use a credit card or bank account debit card. Online payment services are common with bidding sites like eBay (also called online auction sites), where the individual who bids the highest amount for an item buys it, and then instructs PayPal to send the money to the seller. Shoppers like online payment services because they offer an additional layer of security to using a credit card online. Online payment services are also a way for individuals and small businesses to accept payment without having to set up an e-commerce site.

Tech Vocabulary
- multi-user license
- one-user license
- third party transaction

Check Yourself

1. How does a one-user license differ from a multi-user license?

2. How many ways are there to pay online?

3. What is a third party transaction?

What Do You Think?

Analyzing. What would be important to you when deciding among various accounting programs?

CHAPTER

15

STAFFING YOUR BUSINESS

15.1 Hiring Decisions

OBJECTIVES

- Understand factors to consider when hiring employees
- Compare types of organizational structures
- Describe the process of recruiting employees
- Identify professionals whose services entrepreneurs might use

VOCABULARY

- benefits
- compensation
- human resources
- job description
- line organization
- line-and-staff organization
- organizational structure
- project organization
- recruit
- résumé
- salary
- wage

Think about this question in relation to your everyday life:

What task would you pay someone else to do for you?

Write your answer on a piece of paper. Think about how much it would be worth to you.

Is It Time to Hire?

You've probably heard the expression "Entrepreneurs wear many hats," which means they take on a lot of roles when running a business. Often they're involved with producing a product or supplying a service, whether it's T-shirts or home security software. They may also act as their own store manager, advertising agent, sales representative, bookkeeper, tax advisor, and more. Balancing all these roles can take considerable effort.

One solution is to hire people to wear some of those hats. However, sometimes being a boss means taking on yet another role: human resources manager. **Human resources** are the people who work in a business. Bringing new people into a company can be like adding new members to a family—it can change everything.

Therefore, it's wise to consider simpler solutions first. Perhaps better time-management skills are needed. Improved organization and newer technology might streamline tasks, saving time and energy. If these strategies are not enough, it may be time to take a closer look at expanding your workforce.

Advantages of Hiring Employees

The most obvious advantage of hiring employees is having others to share the work. This choice is easier if an employee's job duplicates the entrepreneur's own. For example, if your one-person limousine service is overwhelmed with calls, you can hire another driver who will be doing exactly what you do. If your gourmet pizza business can't keep up with demand, you hire another pizza maker.

An employee can also be a valuable second-in-command when a business owner is called away from work. Caitlyn Impinto runs a garden shop from her rural home. Previously, taking a day off meant closing the shop and losing sales. Now she puts her two assistants in charge, and the receipts for that one day almost equal their wages for the week. Knowing the shop is in trusted hands also helps her enjoy the time she takes off for family, hobbies, or volunteering.

Employees can supply skills and qualities the entrepreneur lacks. A logical thinker who designs hacker-proof business software may not have the persuasive skills to *sell* the software. One way to consider what kinds of help you might need is to look at your SWOT analysis for the business. Are there areas you have shown as weaknesses that might be filled if you hire employees with specific skills? Also, new ideas may emerge when people of different backgrounds and personalities work together on a project.

How do you run a garden shop and take a day off?

Some entrepreneurs leave the nuts and bolts of daily operation to employees so they can focus on the more challenging, rewarding aspects of their work. Hiring an assistant to schedule appointments and take care of day-to-day tasks, for example, allows more time to research the market for a new service, tinker with improving a product design, or promote the company to potential investors. Some entrepreneurs are in demand for unique talents. A music producer may hire dozens of people to operate studio equipment and record a musical number, but it's the producer's artistic and commercial insight that makes the music a hit.

Finally, many entrepreneurs take satisfaction in hiring entrepreneurially minded people. These employees may someday go on to become entrepreneurs themselves.

Disadvantages of Hiring Employees

In any area of life, benefits often come with responsibilities. The responsibilities of becoming a boss include the added expenses: not only employees' wages, but also taxes on those wages and insurance premiums to cover on-the-job injuries.

Dealing with these issues also entails a large amount of paperwork, beginning with the hiring process. For example, in the United States, an employer must first send in Form SS-4 ("Application for Employer Identification Number") to the Internal Revenue Service (IRS) to obtain an employer identification number (EIN). Most employers ask job applicants to fill out a form and submit a **résumé**, a written summary of work experience, education, and skills. Once an applicant is hired, the employer may need to fill out a form declaring that the employee has presented documents (photo ID, Social Security card, etc.) showing that he or she can legally work in the U.S. To deduct taxes from the worker's wages, the employer must file Forms W-2 ("Wage and Tax Statement") and W-4 ("Employee's Withholding Allowance Certificate") with the IRS. Records must be kept of the employee's hours worked, wages paid, and taxes withheld. If the worker is injured on the job or files a complaint, the government requires that this too must be documented.

Hiring employees may mean establishing more detailed workplace rules and policies. If you have many employees, you may need to develop an employee handbook. As with a code of ethics (discussed in Chapter 5), these guidelines must be carefully written to be reasonable, understandable, and enforceable. That requires staying current on laws regarding fair treatment, employee rights, and workplace safety.

Coworker relations are another concern. Problems between employees are problems for the employer. Personal or professional conflicts can slow the workflow and sour the workplace atmosphere. If the problem involves illegal conduct or unfair treatment, the employer can be held responsible.

Looking at Yourself

In the course of weighing the decision to hire employees, you will need to answer these basic questions:

- Can you afford employees?
- Are you ready to be a boss?
- Can you share control?
- Are you willing to delegate authority or responsibility to someone else?
- Do you have the people skills required to manage employees?
- Do you know how to act with authority?

Your employees will share credit for your business's success, but you must accept the ultimate responsibility if things go wrong.

▼ **Figure 15-1**

Documents for Establishing Identity
An employer usually must see a Social Security card or a driver's license to check an employee's identity and eligibility to work.
Solving Problems. *Where would be the best place to keep a Social Security card?*

READING CHECKPOINT *What are some of the advantages of hiring employees? Disadvantages?*

Organizational Structures

Do you remember your first day of school? You may have had no idea what was expected of you or who all those adults were. Gradually you learned you were expected to be in class at a certain time and do the work assigned. The adults were the principal, teachers, maintenance crews, and cafeteria workers.

You also figured out the relationships between authority figures. You were answerable to all adults, but especially to your teachers concerning your assignments. Your teachers answered to the principal but not to the maintenance crew, although they wisely heeded the maintenance chief's warnings about a leak in the hallway.

These elements—groups of people, responsibility, and authority—are found in a business as well. They are part of its **organizational structure**, a system for dividing work, authority, and responsibility within a company. When you hire employees, you will need to develop an organizational structure that suits the business.

Traditional Structures

The simplest structure is **line organization**, a direct chain of command through levels of personnel who are directly involved in a business's main activity. To use the school comparison, line organization describes the relationship between principal, teacher, and student.

An expanded version of a line organization is the **line-and-staff organization**. In this type of structure, staff members advise, assist,

Line Organization

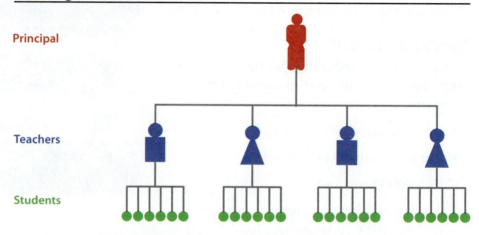

Line-and-Staff Organization

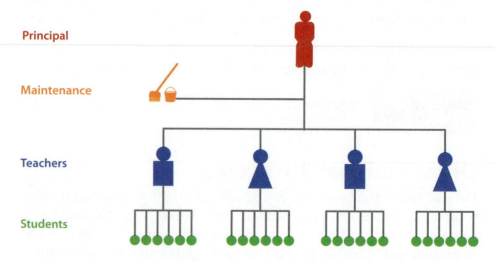

or support the work of line personnel. In the school example, that's where the maintenance crew fits in.

A business's organization often changes as the business grows or the market changes. For example, consider Nelson Ortega's independent bookstore. Nelson opened it with two employees, Mitchell Folse and Dinah Madrigal. All three were responsible for waiting on customers, ordering books, taking deliveries, and stocking the shelves. So the basic structure when the store opened was a line organization, with both Mitchell and Dinah reporting to Nelson.

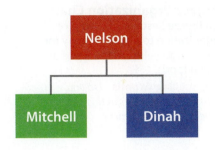

Five years later, the business has moved to a larger space and grown considerably. Nelson has hired six salespeople to work in the store. These employees became part of the line. As the business grew, Mitchell and Dinah took on more specialized tasks. Mitchell became the sales manager, with all salespeople reporting to him. Dinah became the marketing manager. She looks for ways to publicize the store and analyzes trends in publishing and book buying.

▲ *Organization of Nelson Ortega's Bookstore at opening*

Dinah is now staff. She doesn't take part in the business's revenue-producing work. Instead, she provides input that is needed to make the revenue-producing work more profitable. The final authority to make decisions, however, remains with Nelson.

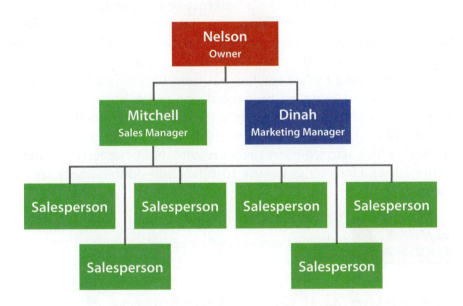

◄ *Nelson Ortega's Bookstore five years later*

At certain times, a business may use a **project organization**, in which employees from more than one department work as a team on a specific goal. Project organization ends once the project goal is reached. For example, at Sea Breeze Restaurant, Tim, the owner, wanted to develop a line of healthy frozen meals. He asked the executive chef and the marketing manager to work with an outside dietician on this project. Tim also participated and took on the responsibility of trying to finance the initiative through loans and investors.

Figure 15-2

Project Organization Chart
Sea Breeze Restaurant used project organization to plan a strategy for marketing healthy menu items as frozen foods.

Interpreting Graphs. *Do you think all participants in this project have equal importance?*

Trends in Structures

Although they are useful, traditional organizational structures don't always fit today's rapidly changing, global economy. To stay competitive, entrepreneurs are stretching traditional structures and inventing new ones. Clearly defined roles and responsibilities are giving way to interdepartmental teams and networks that can be put together as the need arises. Larger companies especially need this flexibility.

New communication technology is playing a role in this evolution. Electronic communication has created a virtual workplace, where project members meet by using only the Internet or cell phones.

These trends can open doors to small entrepreneurs such as Darren Novak. The owner of a small chemical analysis lab in Nevada, Darren was contacted by a fertilizer manufacturer in Texas. The fertilizer company was concerned when its chemists found unusually high amounts of pollutants in the water discharged as a result of the manufacturing process. Through teleconferences with other experts the company had assembled, Darren was able to track down a flaw in the sampling method, which had led to incorrect results. Now the fertilizer manufacturer uses Darren's company to randomly double-check its own chemists' findings.

What is the role of staff members?

Recruiting and Hiring Employees

To **recruit** means to find and hire qualified candidates for a job. Recruiting is an investment: the thought and preparation put into the process is repaid by the quality of the workers you hire. In small businesses especially, the impact of a single hiring decision can be felt throughout the company. Experts calculate that replacing an employee can ultimately cost three or four times that person's salary. This is a result of lost productivity, customer loyalty, company morale, down time without a replacement, hiring a replacement, training the new employee, and many other factors. So choosing employees wisely is critical to a small business.

Writing a Job Description

You can't fill a position until you can tell applicants what it entails. That's the purpose of writing a **job description**, an explanation of a position's purpose, tasks, and responsibilities and the qualifications needed to perform it.

To attract only qualified applicants, a job description should list specific activities and qualifications and rank their importance. A description for an assistant might read: "Answers phones, schedules appointments, and maintains office equipment. Must have experience with database and Internet research; familiarity with accounting software preferred."

Any required training or credentials should also be included. A child-care provider may need training in CPR and other emergency procedures, for instance.

The description should also reflect how responsibilities might grow in the future. If you hope the assistant hired today will advance to become the office manager of tomorrow, you might note: "Experience in personnel management desirable."

Figure 15-3
Job Description
A job description provides the basis of an ad when the position needs to be filled.

Inferring. *This description doesn't mention personal qualities; however, based on the requirements, what qualities do think this employer is looking for?*

ROUTE DELIVERY DRIVER

RESPONSIBILITIES:

- Deliver products in good condition to customer.
- Merchandise, display, and rotate products according to company standards.
- Invoice and collect monies due.
- Pick up company property.
- Ensure compliance with regulatory and company policies and procedures.
- Settle all accounts daily.

QUALIFICATIONS:

- Valid Class A Driver's License.
- MVR in accordance with company policy.
- Familiarity with DOT regulations.
- 1-3 years of general work experience.
- 1+ years of commercial driving experience preferred.
- Local delivery experience preferred.
- Prior grocery store and/or consumer products experience a plus.

Determining Compensation

Compensation refers to the money and benefits an employee receives in exchange for working. For employers, it's a balancing act between three main factors:

- What workers need and deserve based on their qualifications

- What the business can afford

- What other, similar-sized businesses in the same field are paying

How employers pay depends partly on the type of job. Work that requires a set number of hours or items produced is generally paid as a **wage**, payment to employees per hour worked or piece of work completed. A **salary**—a weekly, bimonthly, or monthly payment—is more typical for jobs where the hours and schedules vary. Some employers offer stock in the company as partial payment. This option adds an incentive to

Staffing

It is usually good news when a small business needs to hire employees. Imagine you're an entrepreneur and you have been doing everything either on your own or with a partner. After a while, you might want to cut back on your hours a bit. When the business gets strong enough, you feel you could pay someone to grow and improve your operation. But how can you make sure you get the best possible candidate?

Entrepreneurs have many tools available to them for hiring new people. Many small-business owners rely on word-of-mouth or hire someone they already know. But if very specialized or unusual skills are required, you might need to look in other places. Some companies turn to online classified advertisements through their local newspapers or craigslist.com. These companies then interview potential new hires on their own. Other companies use staffing agencies, such as Kelly Services or Adecco. Having someone else do your hiring will save significant time but may not ultimately result in the best fit for a small business.

THINKING CRITICALLY

Predicting. In groups, discuss how you would go about hiring an employee if you owned a small business. List two advantages and two disadvantages of having an outside staffing service hire someone for you.

To read more about staffing, go to "Entrepreneurship Issues" on the Student Center at entrepreneurship.pearson.com.

employees by making them owners as well—their income rises or falls based on the company's success.

Benefits are types of compensation other than salary or wages. Some benefits, such as family and medical leave, are required by law. Many more have become standard, especially health insurance, paid vacation, sick days, and investment plans for retirement saving.

New entrepreneurs often worry that they can't match the compensation offered by larger established firms. However, compensation isn't the only benefit of working for a business. Location, scheduling flexibility, on-site day care, the company's culture, and possibilities for advancement are just some of the factors that may increase a company's desirability to a prospective employee.

Locating Job Candidates

Ideally, you'll create a list of potential candidates before the need to hire becomes pressing. Take note of people you meet whose talents or work ethic you admire, including current employees of customers and the competition. When Mimi was recruiting a sales representative for her organic pet foods, she offered the job to the assistant manager of a pet store that carried her products. Mimi knew he was knowledgeable about animal nutrition and experienced at selling.

College and university placement offices connect employers to job-seeking students and graduates. College counselors keep up with the area job scene, using input from employers to help students prepare for the local market. They often coordinate with teachers to send students to companies as unpaid interns to gain experience and credit for coursework. At the placement office's Website, employers can post job openings and read student résumés at no charge. They can register to recruit on campus at job fairs or at information sessions with interested students. Employment agencies run by a state's Department of Labor or Commerce offer similar services.

Other useful sources are trade association Websites and publications. Some have online job banks or resources for employers. Leads might be found through association members' forums and blogs. Linda Joseph is a member of the American Saddle Makers Association. When she wanted to hire a skilled leather worker, she phoned a master saddle maker who was listed on the group's Website. Sometimes it is useful to advertise your job on general "help-wanted" type Websites. The problem with these more general sites is that you could receive many applications, which would increase the work you would need to do to locate an appropriate employee. Consider using the most specific online job listing you can.

Employers can eliminate some of the work of recruiting by hiring a personnel agency to locate and recommend candidates for them. The hefty fee—often a percentage of the employee's first year's wages, which can come to several thousand dollars—makes this an option of last resort for most small-business owners.

▲ *How would you locate a skilled leather worker?*

Screening Candidates

Taking applications or résumés is the most practical and legally safest way to evaluate job candidates. Those documents, along with the job description, provide a fair, fixed standard for comparing potential employees.

What can applications and résumés tell you about a job seeker? Correct spelling and grammar show basic language skills and attention to detail. Applicants who stress their recent experience and training in relevant skills show an understanding of the position. A job description for a sales associate in a clothing store might not include a background in fashion, for example. A candidate who highlights her degree from design school shows an understanding that leads her to mention that added qualification. It also suggests initiative.

Applications and résumés can also raise "red flags" that warn against hiring someone: unexplained gaps in the work or education history, for example, or holding a series of unrelated jobs without advancement.

You should contact the most promising applicants for interviews. Be sure to prepare for each interview. Make a list of questions you plan to ask. Focus on relevant information that expands on the facts given in the application or résumé. Remember, you cannot legally ask questions about age, race, sexual orientation, marital status, religion, or other personal matters.

Try to put candidates at ease during the interview. Give them time to answer questions and explain statements or information in their résumés. At the same time, notice how they handle stress or difficult questions.

▲ *Watch out for red flags!*

For example, a common question is, "What do you see as your biggest weakness?" A response such as "Sometimes I talk without thinking, so I'm working at listening better" shows not only honesty but also problem-solving skills. Other questions that focus on the applicant's behavior might be "Tell me how you solved a problem at work." Or, "Describe a situation where you resolved a customer complaint."

> ## Useful Questions for Revealing Facts about Background and Character
>
> - How did you get interested in this line of work?
> - What achievements are you most proud of?
> - What would you like to learn from this job?
> - What are your career goals for the next five years?

Get a feel for overall personality, as well. An employee should be enjoyable to work with and have traits that fit the workplace atmosphere. Recall, however, that diversity in philosophy and thinking style can be an asset for problem solving and creativity. Make written notes of all these impressions; don't rely on your memory.

Also realize that while you are judging the applicant, the applicant is also judging you as an employer. It will benefit both of you if you encourage questions about the job and the company. Be positive—but honest—about what you can offer and what you expect. Communicate respect for what a new employee can bring to the workplace.

If an applicant seems like a good match, check his or her references before offering the position. Learning about the candidate's relationship with former coworkers, teachers, or classmates can provide added insight. Also, more and more employers are taking the precaution of checking an individual's background for financial problems or criminal activity. This is required for certain positions, especially in health care, child care, and security services.

 *List four sources of potential job candidates.*

Hiring Outside Professionals

Some very important services are needed only occasionally. A growing business may require advice on financial planning or legal help. In these situations, bringing in professionals, consultants, or skilled workers as needed is more cost effective than retaining their services full time. The expense associated with these specialists will usually be more than the hourly wages of your employees. Their payment will usually be established by a contract that spells out what is expected and the compensation.

Choosing an outside expert requires the same type of research as hiring a regular employee. Get recommendations from other business owners, especially those with needs like your own.

Ask candidates for references from other clients. Check for consumer complaints through the Better Business Bureau. Check their credentials through a professional organization or state licensing or regulating agency.

For professionals whose services will be used on an ongoing basis, such as tax advisors or legal experts, look for someone with whom you can establish a long-term relationship. As with a doctor or dentist, you may see them only once or twice a year, but you're entrusting them with a valuable possession: your business's future.

 *Why do businesses hire outside experts?*

 Your Business Plan. Continue developing your standard business plan. Go to "Section 15.1" of the *Business Plan Project* in your *Student Activity Workbook*, or "Section 15.1" of the BizTech Software.

ASSESSMENT 15.1

Reviewing Objectives

1. Give two advantages and two disadvantages to hiring employees.

2. How does the work of a staff employee differ from that of a line employee?

3. What are the qualities of an effective job description?

4. Give three tips for choosing an outside expert.

Critical Thinking

5. **Comparing/Contrasting.** Some businesses take applications online. For what kind of jobs might this be an especially effective recruiting tool?

6. **Drawing Conclusions.** Why does hiring employees involve giving up some control of your business?

Working Together

With a partner, role-play a job interview. Outline the situation, including the type of business and the candidate's work and educational background. Don't write a script, however, or rehearse lines. Take a few minutes to prepare individually for your roles, and then perform the scenario for the class.

Social Studies
Apprenticeship Programs

Apprenticeships are a time-honored way to connect employers and employees. Learn more about the employer's role in these programs. Write a brief report that answers these questions: In what fields are apprenticeships most common? What are the qualifications for taking on an apprentice? What are the employer's responsibilities regarding pay, insurance, and other expenses?

OBJECTIVES

- Compare various methods of employee training and development
- Explain various techniques for motivating employees
- Describe the processes involved in evaluating, promoting, and dismissing employees

VOCABULARY

- accreditation
- flextime
- job enlargement
- job enrichment
- job shadowing
- orientation
- protégé
- telecommuting

Think about this question:

Are you motivated by school?

Write your answer (yes or no) on a piece of paper. Be prepared to discuss why you answered the question in the way you did.

Employee Training and Development

By successfully completing grade school, you were qualified to start high school. However, you still had some things to learn on your way to becoming a capable high school student—how to handle new freedoms and responsibilities, perhaps, or which foods to avoid in the cafeteria.

The same is true of employees. Qualified candidates may have the necessary skills but need to learn how to apply them. A new job might involve different responsibilities from the last one, or follow a different routine. In a growing number of fields, rapid advances in technology make updating skills an ongoing necessity. Training builds employee enthusiasm and eases the normal concerns of starting a job or assuming new duties.

Not all training is skill related. Workplace safety, business ethics, and coworker relations are a few areas where employers need to explain their rules and policies.

A company focuses on specific training and development needs and then figures out the best way to fill them. It marks progress by using definite, measurable goals. Such a program saves time, money, and other resources.

◄ **Figure 15-4**

Workplace Safety
A company needs to train employees about workplace safety.

Predicting. *What would happen if a company didn't train employees in necessary workplace safety?*

Learning relevant skills makes employees feel that they—and their employer—have spent their time well. Ideally, employees come away with a sense that their value as individuals has increased. They also feel they've learned something that makes them more valuable in the job market. For example, some training confers **accreditation**, certification by a professional group that an individual possesses certain skills or a specific level of expertise. Having accredited employees enhances a company's reputation as well as the employees' professional status.

In-House Programs

Some training and development takes place within the firm, involving only its own employees. These are referred to as in-house programs. In a smaller company, the owner and a few key employees might take care of the training. A large corporation might dedicate an entire division of the human resources department to this need.

Whatever the size of the business, training for a new employee starts with orientation. **Orientation** is the process of gradually integrating an employee into a workplace. During this stage, employees might tour the facilities, learn the company's policies and procedures, and meet the people with whom they'll be working. Equally important, they start on-the-job training. In a two- or three-person business, this may be as simple as learning how to access files on the company's computers. It also may involve **job shadowing**, a process of learning a job by watching an employee perform the job over a period of time. In a larger business, a new manager might spend several weeks learning to perform jobs in each department.

A business with many employees might offer a mentoring program. As you may remember from Chapter 1, a mentor is a person of greater experience or knowledge who guides and supports another person in developing as a professional. A mentoring relationship is typically a long-term relationship. Besides practical knowledge about the job and career, a mentor can impart lessons on life management—setting and reaching goals, for example, or the rewards of giving back to the community.

Informal mentoring is common in a workplace. If employees are interested in starting a formal mentoring program, business owners can show support by providing time, facilities, training, and a budget. Employees can set program goals that promote the company's values. Encourage all employees to take part in the program, with mentors chosen based on a set of objective requirements.

Mentors should be:

- **Interested in a Mentoring Relationship.** The individual must be willing to take on the responsibilities of mentoring. He or she makes time to meet with the **protégé** (PRO-tuh-zhay), the person who receives guidance in a mentoring relationship. Mentors offer useful ideas and find resources for resolving a protégé's questions.

- **Enthusiastic about Their Careers.** They genuinely care about the work they do and believe in its importance.

- **Positive and Constructive Communicators.** Good mentors recognize and encourage a protégé's strengths and explain any improvement needs.

Figure 15-5 ▶

Mentoring Program Application Form
In addition to their areas of professional expertise, mentor and protégé are matched according to personal qualities, background, and career goals.
Applying Concepts. *In what ways can diversity also benefit a mentoring relationship?*

Mentor Program Application Form

Company Name:	Mentor Application Name: Title:	
Street Address:		
City:	State:	Zip Code:
Telephone:	Fax:	
E-Mail:		
Number of years with business:		

Please check each of the boxes where you and your company are able to provide mentor assistance:

☐ Accounting	☐ Business Plan	☐ Contract Negotiations
☐ Finance	☐ Government Contracting	☐ HR/Benefits
☐ IT Technology	☐ Legal	☐ Loan Applications
☐ Management Consulting	☐ Marketing/Sales	☐ Proposal Writing
☐ Strategic Planning	☐ Other Resources (Please List):	

- **Respected Role Models.** They exhibit the traits of professionalism, especially a strong sense of ethics.
- **Trusted by Their Protégés.** Mentor and protégé should share qualities that allow the mentor to appreciate the protégé's situation and help the protégé feel comfortable and understood.

Training and Development Providers

Although in-house programs can help new employees adapt to the workplace, an entrepreneur might sometimes need outside advice for special training and development issues. Suppose, for example, you're a landscaper who needs to know how to accommodate workers with disabilities at a job site. You could talk to individual experts or read magazine articles, but this advice and information might not be complete. Instead, the solution may be a professional training and development provider.

There are many types of training and development providers. A large consulting company might address a range of public relations skills, from leadership to telephone etiquette. An individual expert may specialize in time management. Programs can range from simple to sophisticated. Sales staff might attend a daylong multi-media presentation, using role-playing activities to improve selling skills. A catering crew might spend an hour with a local florist learning how to arrange flowers for banquet tables.

Training and development providers educate employees, as well as employers, in a variety of settings:

- **Classes.** Classes may be offered individually or in a series, at the workplace or elsewhere. Online and videotape classes are popular because of their convenience and economy.

- **Workshops.** In a workshop, a small group of people gathers to learn through discussion, demonstration, and practice. A workshop may be a single session lasting a few hours or several sessions on related topics spread out over a few days.

- **Seminars.** At a seminar, participants in small groups exchange information and discuss topics in a selected field. If you attend a seminar, you will be expected to actively contribute to the discussion. Seminars often have an audience, which usually has an opportunity to ask questions of seminar participants.

- **Conferences and Expos.** A conference or an expo (short for "exposition") can be a "one-stop shopping" learning experience. These events, which usually run several days, may offer classes, workshops, or seminars at one site, along with panel discussions, vendors' booths, and representatives from professional associations. Attending a conference or expo can be costly in travel, lodging, and time taken off from work. Yet the expense can pay dividends in learning new techniques and keeping up with the latest developments—to stay ahead of the competition.

▲ **Figure 15-6**

Seminars
If you attend a seminar, you will be expected to participate actively in the discussion.

Relating Concepts. *How can participation in a seminar help you gain greater understanding of the topic you are discussing?*

What are five qualities of good mentors?

Motivating Employees

Milton Hershey, founder of the Hershey Chocolate Company, was a progressive-minded entrepreneur who believed in taking care of the people whose work helped build his fortune. He was also a shrewd businessman who understood that people are motivated to work harder when they feel appreciated. In the early 1900s, he developed the town of Hershey, Pennsylvania, as a model community for his employees. It included good housing, quality schools, parks and recreation facilities, and a trolley for transportation.

Most entrepreneurs couldn't match Hershey's scale of employee appreciation. Yet all entrepreneurs can follow his example of employee motivation. They can recognize employees' value and importance to the business and encourage them to realize their potential. Not all motivational techniques are expensive. In fact, some of the best forms of motivation cost nothing at all.

Performance-Based Rewards

Imagine that your teacher gave everyone in the class $25 for being a "good student." At first you might be delighted. Then you might start to wonder: What made you a good student? Was it something you could do again? If you were an even better student, would you get more money? Could your teacher afford to be that generous?

Performance-based rewards, when carefully thought out, avoid such confusion. First, the reward is linked to a specific, achievable goal and is related to the work involved—in other words, the greater the achievement, the greater the reward. An employer must also be able to afford it. A small reward employees can be sure of receiving will motivate them better than a large one that is doubtful. Withdrawing rewards that have been promised can be demoralizing. Also, the reward should be something the employees would value.

These guidelines allow a lot of possibilities. Suppose you own a trucking firm. You could award points for every mile driven without an accident or ticket. The points could be redeemed as a gift card from a business of the driver's choice.

Or imagine you own a home cleaning service. You might offer a finder's fee to workers who bring in new customers—or if you're hiring, for new employees. When a customer reports a cleaning crew's outstanding service, you could give the crew credit points that they could exchange for rewards.

Membership in professional groups is another valued reward. A sales associate in Gemma Gottlieb's quilt shop is also the store's Webmaster. When the site recorded its one millionth hit, Gemma bought the associate a year's membership in the American Webmasters Association, which entitled him to discounts on online Web design courses and other benefits.

▲ Figure 15-7
A Useful Reward
This watch might be appreciated by a sales executive.

Solving Problems. *What would you do if only a few employees were earning your business's performance-based rewards?*

Flexible Work Arrangements

When employees are asked what they value most in a job, it isn't always pay or benefits. It's often flexibility. Having more choices about when and how to work helps them find a time (or place) for focusing on the job. One way to take advantage of this is to offer **flextime**, or flexible work schedules. Some employees might start and finish work one hour earlier or later than others, or alternate between working four days and five days a week. Or employees could split duties through job sharing.

Another possibility is **telecommuting**, working from a location other than the business site, linked by telecommunication technology. Through telecommuting, a company can profit from the talents of people who otherwise would not be available—people with disabilities, parents of young children, and those who live far from the workplace.

Workplace flexibility isn't an option for all businesses or all employees, of course, but it may be practical for small operations. For instance, beginning entrepreneurs may not be able to pay high wages, so flextime allows employees to hold other jobs. A business may start out with only basic supplies and equipment. Through flextime and telecommuting, schedules can be arranged so workers share, rather than compete for, its limited resources.

Policies on flextime and other arrangements should be clearly described in an employee handbook. For example, a store may need a certain number of workers at certain hours. Telecommuters might be required to work on-site one or two days a week.

Delegating Responsibility

One trait entrepreneurs can appreciate in employees is the desire to take on more responsibilities. Two practices capitalize on this quality: job enlargement and job enrichment. Both practices motivate by delegating (assigning) more responsibility to workers.

Job enlargement means adding responsibilities to a position. For example, one restaurant worker's duties typically included cleaning and preparing fruits and vegetables, preparing salad dressings, and assembling these ingredients into salads. Job enlargement might involve adding new salads to the menu, requiring the salad maker to learn new recipes—and possibly new techniques. The basic tasks are the same, but additional responsibilities have been added.

Related to this technique is **job enrichment**, which means increasing the depth or involvement of a job. Here the restaurant worker might have to order the salad ingredients, based on cost, local availability, and the other items on the menu. She would gain new knowledge, develop new skills, and work in new relationships to play a greater role in the business. With job enrichment, the basic position changes.

Of course, job enlargement and enrichment should not simply mean more work for the employee. Instead, lesser tasks can be reassigned— ideally, to expand or enlarge another employee's job.

A Positive Environment

Did you know that enjoying yourself is a recognized psychological need? It's associated with learning, laughter, and a sense of belonging—all of which have proven emotional benefits. It's no surprise then that people are motivated by an atmosphere that meets their need for enjoyment and value recognition. Creating such a workplace makes good business sense.

First, work is more enjoyable when the physical environment is designed for efficiency and safety. Employees should have ready access to needed tools, such as insulated gloves or graphic arts software.

Employees also need to feel confident that they're doing their job well. A good training program and job description help provide this assurance. Giving employees reasonable, yet challenging, goals and deadlines will help them decide where to direct their efforts. Providing the opportunity for frequent, informal feedback helps employees feel confident.

Equally important is personal recognition, especially for unexpected or little-noticed contributions to the workplace (or to the community). Think of the motivational impact of giving a Good Egg award to an employee who handles a difficult situation in an ethical way—complete with a plastic egg filled with something useful, such as tokens for a car wash. Think of a workplace where recognition is given to the employee who was named Scoutmaster to the National Boy Scout Jamboree or who donated 50 pints of blood to the American Red Cross.

Also, don't forget the motivational value of employer-sponsored fun, tailored to employees' tastes and your resources. This could mean something as simple as having a pizza party at the end of work on a Friday or providing tickets to a local event. Showing that you value your employees in such a way will increase their loyalty and enthusiasm.

 *How is job enlargement different from job enrichment?*

▲ *A pizza party can be motivational!*

Evaluating Employees

Students are sometimes asked to review each other's work. For example, classmates might give their opinions of your essay. You might check a classmate's solution to a math problem. Giving and accepting this kind of feedback may be difficult. However, both parties can benefit when the judgment is formed with care and expressed with consideration.

The same applies to evaluating employees. Judging employees' work can help improve both their performance and your workplace, if handled with objectivity and respect.

Performance Evaluations

Performance evaluations are regular employee reviews, usually given at least annually. Some companies give formal quarterly or semiannual reviews to reinforce good performance and alert employees to improvement needs in a timely fashion. The review process is handled by the business owner, the employee's supervisor, or a human resources specialist. Performance evaluations have two goals:

- **To point out how well the employee is meeting the job requirements and expectations.** This is done by filling out an evaluation form. A well-written job description is valuable because it provides an objective standard for judgment.

- **To improve not only the employee's performance, but also the employer's.** Usually the employee and evaluator meet one-to-one to discuss the evaluation.

Suppose you notice that a sales representative is just barely reaching his sales quota each month. In discussing the problem, you find that his sales area overlaps that of a well-established competitor. Perhaps the employee could learn effective tactics by working with a more experienced representative. Maybe revising your training to include better education on your products and the competitor's would help your salespeople sway

Figure 15-8

Performance-Evaluation Form

Some evaluation forms break down and rate job duties in detail. Others describe and grade duties broadly as either acceptable or unacceptable.

Recognizing Patterns. *Why can comparing performance evaluations from one year to the next be helpful?*

Performance Evaluation Form

Reviewer: _____ Employee: _____

Criteria	Not Applicable	Excellent	Good	Fair	Unsatisfactory	Comments
Meets work quality standards						
Completes assignments reliably						
Shows initiative in problem solving and decision making						
Adapts well to changing circumstances						
Shows willingness and ability to learn new skills						
Arrives on time and prepared to work						
Effectively gets desired results from subordinates						

General comments on employee's performance:

potential customers. If many salespeople have the same problem, it might point out a flaw in your hiring practices.

Both the reviewer and employee sign the performance-evaluation form, indicating that they've had the discussion. They may write out and sign a list of goals and a plan for improving employee performance and job satisfaction. Some employers have employees fill out a form that asks what tools, training, or changes in the work environment would help them do the job better.

Promoting Employees

When a higher-level, better-paying job becomes available, promoting an existing employee has advantages. It shows recognition and respect for the people whose work and commitment helped build the company. It means the company's philosophy and values will be carried out in the higher position. It also saves resources spent on training someone from outside. For these reasons, publicizing a job opening within your own company makes sense.

However, employees should be promoted for the same reason they are hired: for being the best candidate for the job. It's a mistake to assume that success at one position automatically translates into success at a higher level. One important difference is that a promotion usually involves greater responsibility for managing people and other resources. Relationship skills become especially important. Employers need to ask whether the employee has shown these skills or shown an interest and aptitude in developing them. Can the employee see beyond his or her department in relation to issues that affect the entire business? Does he or she have the sense of initiative needed in a leader?

If you think an existing employee who would be a good prospect hasn't applied for a position, you might urge that person to do so. You might see skills and qualities in someone that could be successfully developed in a higher position. On the other hand, people may know themselves and their priorities better than you do. For example, they may not want to miss family time if the job involves travel. The decision ultimately must be theirs.

Once the job has been filled, make sure other employees understand why they weren't chosen. This will allow them to work toward preparing for the next opening, if they wish. Or they may decide their future lies with another company. That decision, too, is theirs to make.

▲ Figure 15-9
Promoting an Employee
Employees should be promoted because they are the best people for the job.
Predicting. *Why might an employee be uninterested in applying for a higher position?*

Dismissing Employees

Dismissing an employee may be the entrepreneur's most difficult responsibility. Firing an unproductive or troublesome worker may be necessary for the business's survival. Good employees deserve competent coworkers. However, losing a job can be devastating to an individual's self-image. For the employer, it means added time and expense to hire and train a replacement. It could also open the company to legal action. Dismissals due to financial troubles in the business can shake workplace morale. Thus, the decision to fire should be made only after other options have been tried.

Before considering dismissal, tell the employee how he or she is failing to meet your expectations. The conversation might yield a solution.

YOUR BUSINESS CAREER

Comfort with Diversity

You probably know that "diversity" means variety. When you look around your community, you typically see a variety of people. They may be young or old, tall or short, dark-skinned or light-skinned. People can be diverse in their religion, their sexual orientation, and their country of origin. Think about it: We're all humans, all the same in that regard, but different in many ways.

Being comfortable with this diversity means accepting the differences of others. As you move into the working world, you will likely encounter people from all walks of life. Some may be considerably older than you are, some may have disabilities you're not familiar with, and some may be of a race, sexual orientation, or religion different from yours. In the working world you will need to identify your own attitudes and behaviors that might stand in the way of teamwork and congeniality with all of your colleagues. Put aside any preconceived ideas and generalizations about certain groups of people. Remember that your goal is to work well with everyone in the organization.

THINKING CRITICALLY

Inferring. How comfortable are you with diversity? In what ways might it be difficult to work with others who may not be comfortable with diversity, even if you are fine with it?

To read more about being comfortable with diversity, go to "Your Business Career" on the Student Center at entrepreneurship.pearson.com.

The job's duties may have changed, for example, and the employee might need retraining or other support to adjust. Perhaps those duties could be reassigned, to develop and better use the employee's strengths. Or the worker's skills might be better utilized, and the worker might be happier, in a different position.

Make sure employees who are dismissed for economic reasons know that losing the job was not their fault. Make sure their former coworkers know this as well. The dismissal should be planned to give the employee a fair amount of time to make the transition and find another job. In this situation, you can also help by writing a recommendation or using business and personal connections to generate employment leads.

Whatever the reasons for the firing, be sure they are legally justified. Double-check your policy and employees' handbook—the grounds for dismissal should be clearly stated and enforceable. All discussions and actions should be documented and retained in the employee's file. To dismiss an employee who has the potential to help your business is your loss—and possibly the competition's gain.

 **READING CHECKPOINT** *What are the two goals of performance evaluations?*

 Your Business Plan. Continue developing your standard business plan. Go to "Section 15.2" of the *Business Plan Project* in your *Student Activity Workbook*, or "Section 15.2" of the BizTech Software.

ASSESSMENT 15.2

Reviewing Objectives

1. In a business, how does training for a new employee begin?
2. Give two examples of flextime.
3. What are the goals of a performance evaluation?

Critical Thinking

4. **Solving Problems.** A new employee in your business, a single father of two small children, is looking for a mentor. Only two employees are available in your mentoring program: an older woman with children in high school, and a young, single man with no children. How would you handle the new employee's request?

5. **Comparing/Contrasting.** How are benefits different from performance-based rewards?

Working Together

Working in a small group, develop an orientation program for new students at your school. Cover the formal aspects of student life, such as the location of classrooms. Also include insider tips about courses, the food in the cafeteria, sports, extracurricular activities, and so on.

Science
Psychology of Motivation
Research one aspect of the psychology of motivation and develop a short presentation on it. Consider such questions as: How did psychologists discover the human need for motivation? How did early theories explain it? How is it studied today? Consider including examples of motivational techniques, past and present, in business, sports, and education.

The Tattoo Team: Henoo

When five 14- and 15-year-old girls at the Skinners' Company's School, in London, were asked to come up with some concepts for starting a business, their first step was testing ideas to see which would attract more customers. They did a feasibility study as part of their market research, asking other girls in the school, teachers, family, and friends which product they would be most interested in purchasing. The answer: henna tattoos that could be applied in a matter of hours and would wear off within a few weeks. Their company, Henoo, was born.

The girls knew each other before they started Henoo, but they were classmates rather than friends. How were they able to form a successful team without the problems that usually occur when working with partners?

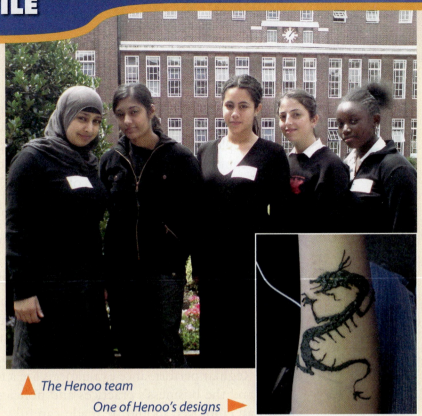

▲ *The Henoo team*

One of Henoo's designs ▶

Team Building: Communication

According to the girls, communication was vital. "We had to listen to each other's ideas and make sure everyone had a chance to express her thoughts and opinions on the business ideas. We learned how to work together as a team, making important decisions, problem solving, and taking risks."

All the girls took a Belbin® Team Role Test, which is widely used in Great Britain, to find out their skills and strengths in various areas. The developer, Meredith Belbin, discovered that the most successful teams are those that are balanced in Team Roles. With the results of the tests, the girls divided up the responsibilities according to individual strengths.

Each Team Member Has a Role

Arooj Akhtar was in charge of the expenses, profits, and revenue, and Duygu Atas was responsible for customer service—making sure customers were satisfied and handling any complaints.

Karess Laidley handled human resources, training, and stock control. She made sure there was enough henna and that the working area was clean and safe. She also took responsibility for dividing the profits equally.

Maimoonah Teladia did the marketing and advertising. Henoo had business cards, posters, a catalog showing all their designs, and an informational magazine containing everything a customer would need to know about henna. Kasanah Shalders-Gayley became the team manager, ensuring that everything ran smoothly.

Even though the girls had different responsibilities, they helped each other. Three of the girls were expert at applying the henna. While they worked, the other two made sure the customers were satisfied and that they paid for the designs.

The Henoo Team was remarkable, according to their advisor, Ms. Selda Kurtuldu. "There were no problems at all. They worked really well as a team."

Thinking Like an Entrepreneur

1. What are the differences between working by yourself and working with partners?
2. What's the most important thing when working with partners?
3. Which of the jobs at Henoo would you prefer?

15.1 Hiring Decisions

Employees can bring needed help and new ideas to running a business. They can free entrepreneurs to focus on business expansion and development. Hiring employees, however, means added expenses and paperwork and new legal requirements. Entrepreneurs can recruit potential employees from professional contacts and competitors, colleges, and Websites of professional organizations. Through taking applications and résumés and conducting interviews, they can choose the best candidate for the job. Entrepreneurs also hire outside experts for services that are needed only occasionally.

15.2 Training and Motivating Employees

Entrepreneurs train and develop employees in-house through orientation and mentoring. Outside providers include classes, seminars, workshops, and conferences. Entrepreneurs can motivate employees by offering flexible work arrangements, performance-based rewards, and a positive work environment. Regular performance evaluations are a tool to improve employee performance and the business's practices and policies. The decision to promote or dismiss an employee should be made carefully and objectively, based on what's best for the business.

REVIEW VOCABULARY

Imagine you're out to hire employees from a group of graduating college students. Outline a speech that you would give this group, describing the advantages of working for your company. Incorporate at least 10 of the following terms in your speech.

- accreditation (p. 417)
- benefits (p. 412)
- compensation (p. 411)
- flextime (p. 421)
- human resources (p. 405)
- job description (p. 411)
- job enlargement (p. 422)
- job enrichment (p. 422)
- job shadowing (p. 417)
- line organization (p. 408)
- line-and-staff organization (p. 408)
- organizational structure (p. 408)
- orientation (p. 417)
- project organization (p. 409)
- protégé (p. 418)
- recruit (p. 410)
- résumé (p. 407)
- salary (p. 411)
- telecommuting (p. 421)
- wage (p. 411)

CHECK YOUR UNDERSTANDING

Choose the letter that best answers the question or completes the statement.

1. The recruiting process includes
   a. résumés and interviews
   b. promotions and dismissals
   c. mentors and protégés
   d. seminars and workshops

2. The purpose of orientation is to
   a. assess a worker's performance over the past year
   b. locate potential job candidates
   c. acquaint a new employee with coworkers and job duties
   d. determine whether a worker should be dismissed

3. Accreditation is
   a. giving credit to employees for good work
   b. a type of job enlargement
   c. a type of job enrichment
   d. certification by a professional group that a person possesses a certain skill or level of expertise

4. Changes in the technology have led more entrepreneurs to use
   a. line organization
   b. line-and-staff organization
   c. project organization
   d. nontraditional, flexible organization

5. An employee is most likely to be an asset to a business if he or she is
   a. similar to the employer in every way
   b. younger than the employer
   c. more skilled at certain tasks than the employer
   d. none of the above

6. A payroll clerk who makes out employee paychecks by accessing the business's computer from home demonstrates
   a. mentoring
   b. flexible work arrangements
   c. an advantage of using outside experts
   d. a performance-based reward

7. A business owner is most likely to hire an outside professional to
   a. work part-time as an assistant manager
   b. prepare the firm's taxes once a year
   c. handle human-resource issues
   d. choose performance awards for employees

8. One possible argument against dismissing a particular employee is that he or she
   a. has worked for the company a long time
   b. supports a large family
   c. has skills that could be useful in another position in the company
   d. may not be able to find another job

9. To be effective, a performance-based reward should be
   a. withheld occasionally
   b. shared by all employees
   c. linked to a specific, achievable goal
   d. fairly expensive

10. Telecommuting is
    a. work involving talking on the telephone
    b. commuting a long distance to work
    c. working from outside the place of business, linked by telecommunication technology
    d. work involving significant air travel

11. The most important question to ask when deciding whether to promote an employee is
    a. Does the employee have potential as a leader and manager?
    b. How long has the employee been with the company?
    c. What are the possible legal consequences of promoting the employee?
    d. How successful is the employee in his or her current job?

12. An employee's compensation includes
    a. only wages or salaries
    b. wages or salaries and benefits
    c. wages or salaries and performance-based rewards
    d. only wages; salaries are not considered compensation

Business Communication

13. Write a "help wanted" ad for the "job" of being a high school student. Include at least six points detailing the position's purpose, tasks, and responsibilities; the education needed; and the qualities of an ideal candidate.

14. Create an organizational chart for an organization you're familiar with, such as a sports team, school committee, or service group. Use color coding or another key to show which positions are line and which are staff.

15. Working with a partner, role-play a meeting in which an employer and employee talk about the employee's unfavorable job evaluation. Choose a few points to discuss, but don't write a script or rehearse lines. Perform the scene for the class.

Business Ethics

18. You have a business credit card that gives mileage points that can be used toward airfare or other travel expenses. You have 10 employees. You announced that the company would award these points to the employee who missed the fewest days during the year, to help pay for a well-earned vacation. Now you find employees are coming in sick when they should, perhaps, have stayed at home. You have also been told that some employees are coming to work and missing family engagements or community responsibilities. Your performance-based reward doesn't seem to have worked out the way you wanted. How would you respond to this situation?

Business Math

16. In 1960, employers in the United States spent $36 billion on employees' health insurance premiums. In 1980, they spent $201 billion. How does the later figure compare to the earlier one as a percentage? In 2006, health insurance premiums cost employers $465 billion. How does that amount compare, as a percentage, to the 1980 figure? During which time period was the rate of increase faster?

17. Major League Baseball imposes a competitive-balance tax on teams whose players' salaries and benefits in a year exceed the maximum allowed. The tax equals 40 percent of the sum over the limit. In 2007, the maximum was $148 million. The New York Yankees' payroll was $207.7 million. How much did the Yankees pay in competitive balance tax? The Yankees averaged $24.32 million in taxes each year. How does the 2007 payment compare to that average?

Business in Your Community

19. With three or four other students, survey three area businesses of different types and sizes on their organizational structure. Are they traditional or modified? Has their organizational structure changed since the business began? Make a short presentation of your findings to the class.

20. Survey at least three business owners on cost-effective ways to motivate employees. How do they determine whether a method is successful? For example, do they see increased productivity? Fewer sick days taken? Happier customers? Describe the results of your survey to the class orally.

Internet Promotion

As you've learned, promotion is used to build a favorable awareness about your product and influence people to buy it. There are many forms of promotion—including advertising, public relations, publicity, and word-of-mouth.

Every business, whether e-commerce or brick-and-mortar (or some combination of these), needs to advertise its products. E-commerce companies use Web ads as well as traditional means of advertising—such as print, television, and radio—to help find new customers and boost sales. Brick-and-mortar firms use traditional means along with business Websites and Web advertising. There's a great deal of crossover. For example, although mcdonalds.com sells apparel and accessories online as an e-commerce business, the main purpose of the Website is to promote the McDonald's restaurant chain.

Internet Advertising

Banner ads are probably the most common type of Internet ad. A **banner ad** is typically a horizontal ad at the top of a Web page; however, banner ads can also appear as vertical ads at the side of the page. Banner ads can have multiple pages and include animation. When a banner ad appears in a vertical format at the side of a Web page, it is often called a **sidebar ad.** A **pop-up** is an ad that appears, or "pops up," in its own window on top of a Web page. An **interstitial ad** appears in its own window before a Web page loads. "Interstitial" means in between, and these ads often have a link that says "Skip to Website" to bypass the ad. A **floating ad** floats or flies over the Web page for 5 to 30 seconds. A **unicast ad** is a TV/Web commercial that appears in its own window.

By clicking on a Web ad, you're automatically taken to a page on the advertiser's Website. The **click-through rate** shows how many customers have clicked on a Web ad. The more people who click on the ad, the more effectively it sells a company's product or brands the business. Each type of ad has a different level of click-through. Generally, according to research done by DoubleClick, a provider of digital marketing technology and services, interstitial ads had more than 10 times the click rate of plain banner ads, while floating and pop-up ads had close to 50 times the click rates of banner ads.

Viral Marketing

Word-of-mouth promotion on the Internet has become known as **viral marketing.** Companies use e-mails, blogs, and social networks to promote a product and pass along brand awareness. Some things, such as a news clip or a YouTube video, can "go viral" on their own, without any forethought. This means that, for example, the same video will pop up on hundreds of sites within hours or days. Advertisers try to create buzz with viral campaigns. One company e-mailed existing customers an offer to join its consumer panel where they would get free products to review. But to join the panel, the customers had to get the most nominations from their friends. Customers used their own online social networks, such as MySpace or Facebook, to spread the word and get nominations. The advertiser found that this approach produced a response rate three times higher than banner ads or standard e-mail campaigns.

Tech Vocabulary

- banner ad
- click-through rate
- floating ad
- interstitial ad
- pop-up
- sidebar ad
- unicast ad
- viral marketing

Check Yourself

1. Name three types of Web advertisements.
2. What is the difference between a pop-up and an interstitial ad?
3. What is a click-through rate?
4. What is viral marketing?

What Do You Think?

Analyzing Concepts. Which type of ad do you find most appealing when you use the Internet?

OBJECTIVES

- Explain the value to entrepreneurs of intellectual property law
- Distinguish the types of work covered by each form of intellectual property protection
- Describe the conditions needed for valid business contracts
- Explain legal remedies for contract and intellectual property law violations

VOCABULARY

- breach of contract
- competent
- conditions
- confidentiality agreement
- consideration
- contract
- damages
- derivative
- express contract
- implied contract
- infringement
- injunctive relief
- intangibles
- lease
- license
- nondisclosure agreement
- sales contract
- service contract
- service mark
- trade secret

Consider this question:

Have you ever considered copying songs from a CD onto a computer?

Write your answer (yes or no) on a piece of paper.

Benefits of Intellectual Property Law

In Chapter 5, you looked at the ethics and legality of using other people's intellectual property—artistic or industrial creations of the mind. As an entrepreneur, however, you may need protection for your own creations: an invention, a song, a slogan, or a name that you give a product or process. You'll want to know what protections the law provides and how to secure these protections.

First, it helps to understand the thinking behind these laws. For hundreds of years, people have seen how granting legal ownership to creators of **intangibles**—things that have value but are not material goods—could benefit both the individual and society. The U.S. Constitution describes the goal "to promote the progress of science and useful arts," which would be achieved by "securing for limited times to authors and inventors the exclusive right to their respective writings and discoveries." The authors of the Constitution understood that creators would be more motivated if they were guaranteed some control over their work and could profit from it. However, society also deserves to enjoy and benefit from that work. Thus, creators were given an exclusive right, but for limited times. The doctrine of fair use—allowing other people restricted use of protected works—balanced the rights of both the individual and the public.

Figure 16-1 ▶

The U.S. Constitution Protects Copyrights and Patents
The framers of the U.S. Constitution understood that creators are more highly motivated if they are guaranteed control over their work and can profit from it.

Drawing Conclusions. *Do you think inventors or artists would create if they couldn't receive a profit from their work?*

The wisdom of that reasoning is proven every day. The chance for personal and financial reward still drives entrepreneurs—and the economy. Their success benefits society in other ways, too. Think of the songs and books that have become treasures of our national culture. Think of the progress in medicine, food production, and other technological advances that have taken place just in your lifetime. Inventors were willing to spend their time and money because they knew their creations and discoveries might someday be profitable, and also beneficial to others.

This understanding has had a global impact. In some countries, weak intellectual property laws drive talented entrepreneurs to leave for places that offer more protection for their ideas. Foreign businesses sometimes avoid these markets. Some governments have recently taken note and passed tighter restrictions. Safeguards for intellectual property have begun to be written into trade agreements.

The law is also stretching to accommodate advances in technology and societal trends. For instance, the Internet search engine Google was sued over its practice of saving electronic copies of Web pages in its archives for users to view. One author whose work was saved claimed copyright infringement; he argued that Google was making money by distributing copies of his work. The court ultimately ruled against the author, deciding that he should have indicated the material was not to be archived.

 *Why are intellectual property laws important for entrepreneurs?*

Protecting Your Works

In 1988, the Los Angeles Lakers of the National Basketball Association had won two straight championships. One of the players described winning a third title as a "three-peat." Lakers coach Pat Riley saw the earnings potential of the term and registered it as a trademark for his company. The Lakers lost the championship that year, but Coach Riley did cash in on the trademark—five years later. In 1993, after the Chicago Bulls had won their third straight title, Riley's company got a percentage on the sale of every item bearing the word, from key chains to collectible plates.

As that story shows, intellectual property law covers almost any kind of creation. Depending on the nature of the idea, you might take out a copyright, patent, trademark, or service mark. You might even protect a trade secret.

Copyright

As you read in Chapter 5, a copyright is the exclusive right to perform, display, copy, or distribute an artistic work. A copyright exists as soon as a work appears in a fixed, concrete form. A songwriter may play an original song on a guitar, for example, but holds the copyright only after recording it or writing it down. A copyright extends to a **derivative**, a work based on one or more existing works, such as a movie sequel or a translation into another language.

A copyright can be transferred to anyone the creator wishes. An illustrator might sign away a copyright as part of a contract with a book publisher, for instance. Certain rights may be sold with conditions. As an example, magazines typically require exclusive rights to an article for a limited time, after which the author is free to resell it. Any transfer of exclusive rights must be in writing. You can also provide nonexclusive rights to use your copyright.

Although a copyright is automatic, many creators identify their works by using the traditional notice: COPYRIGHT © [YEAR] BY [COPYRIGHT HOLDER]. This informs others that they can reproduce the work only by permission and with possibly a payment. Some creators take the official step of registering the work with the Library of Congress's Copyright Office. Registering establishes a public record, which is evidence of ownership in cases of infringement (violation). In fact, infringing on a registered copyright is a federal offense. Additionally, two international treaties, the Berne Convention and the Universal Copyright Convention, provide some kind of protection for a work in many other countries in the world.

In keeping with the goal of intellectual property law, a copyright does have limits. Generally, a copyright owned by the individual who created the work is held for the lifetime of the creator plus 70 years. (Different terms apply to copyrights that are owned by companies.)

Patents

Patent protection can be obtained for the invention or discovery of any new and useful process or the improvement to existing products and processes. A patent grants the exclusive right to make, use, or sell the work for 20 years from the date on which the patent is filed.

The U.S. Patent and Trademark Office (USPTO) grants three general types of patents: plant, design, and utility. Plant patents protect some kinds of agricultural and horticultural products. Design patents provide limited protection to new, original, or ornamental designs of products or processes.

By far the most numerous patents issued are utility patents, which protect how an article works and is used. Utility patents cover five categories of inventions:

- **Articles of Manufacture.** This category includes any material item.

▲ Figure 16-2
When Do You Hold a Copyright?
You only hold a copyright on a song when you record it or write it down.
Predicting. *If you were a musician and still working on a song, when would you write down or record it? Would you play the song to others?*

▲ *Copyright Symbol*

- **Machines.** A machine's distinguishing feature is moving parts that perform some kind of task. The typewriter and the telephone were patented machines.

- **Processes.** The process must lead to some tangible result. It may be a way to apply dye to fabric, or a series of exercises and drills to improve basketball-shooting skills. Since 1998, the definition has been expanded to encompass business methods that a company uses to carry out its operations. An example is the system that online stores use to save a customer's information and automatically print an order form. The patent on this "one-click shopping" is held by the Internet retailer Amazon.com.

- **Compositions.** Compositions are combinations of two or more substances. You might patent a mixture of clay, gravel, and sand for a new cement, or an original blend of plant oils and synthetic aromas for a perfume.

- **Improvements on, or New Uses for, Existing Inventions.** A patented invention can be the basis of another patent if the improvement substantially changes the function of the original. For example, a halogen light bulb is an improvement on an incandescent light bulb. A skin lotion for people that is found to be effective as a flea repellent in pets might get an improvement patent as a new use for an existing invention. A shampoo for horses that can also be used by people might not.

Not everything that fits into one of these categories can be patented. Unlike copyright, a patent must be earned. To qualify, the invention must meet all the following conditions:

- **Novel.** It must be unique in some important way, significantly different from anything that already exists.

- **Non-obvious.** Some relevant feature must be unexpected or out of the ordinary, given the trends and techniques at the time at which the inventor applied for the patent. The USPTO must conclude that a person "having ordinary skill in the art" related to the invention would be surprised by its purpose or construction.

- **Useful.** The purpose may be as practical as the arrangement of rivets securing the blade and handle of a kitchen knife or as playful as a singing hairbrush. This condition doesn't apply to plant or design patents because they are based on existing plant life or inventions that have already been judged useful.

How do inventors know if their useful creation is also novel and non-obvious—that no one has made something similar and is using it in the present? They can search for information that is publicly available in any form that relates to their invention. The place to start is the USPTO online database, where you can search for registered patents, and published patent applications by keyword, at no charge. Many fee-based services will search patent registries worldwide. You might also look for references to similar inventions in relevant scientific or historical literature, such as early cookbooks or agricultural journals.

Finding prior information about a similar invention isn't necessarily a dead end. Examining the records may suggest a way to refine or adapt your own idea. You may see a problem in the original creation that your design will correct. The difference could be enough to qualify for a patent.

The next step is to file a patent application, which requires a painstaking description of the proposed invention. The title must identify the work explicitly. Detailed drawings, showing pertinent sections from several angles, are required to indicate the appearance, design, and function. Drawings of the steps in a process patent may run a dozen pages.

The written description that explains the drawings must be equally precise—so complete, in fact, that a person of ordinary knowledge in the field could make or use the invention by reading the application. For example, consider this partial description from Patent #11,023, titled Design for a Statue: "A female figure standing erect... the body being thrown slightly over to the left, so as to gravitate upon the left leg, the whole figure being thus in equilibrium, and symmetrically arranged with respect to a perpendicular line or axis passing through the head and left foot." Pages of details written in such language may not paint a clear picture to most people, but an engineer might recognize this description. It's the Statue of Liberty.

At the USPTO, the application is thoroughly reviewed by a patent examiner, an authority in the area the invention pertains to. He or she conducts a more exhaustive search for prior information and analyzes whether the invention is new, useful, and nonobvious and satisfies the

ENTREPRENEURSHIP ISSUES

Federal Funding for Start-Ups

The federal government recognizes that entrepreneurs have the potential to make the world a better place. It is so sure of this, in fact, that funding for technology start-ups has risen to a total of 2.3 billion dollars annually. Grants coordinated by the Small Business Administration go to tech companies with 500 or fewer employees. These grants fund research on everything from energy independence to the best ways to transcribe medical records.

Entrepreneurs who are interested in this grant money can apply twice a year. Federal agencies such as NASA publish which specific new technologies they are looking for at www.fedbizopps.gov. If a small-business owner feels he or she has a potential technological solution to one of NASA's problems, the company could receive funding. In 2008, Congress voted to increase these grants through the Small

Business Innovation Research (SBIR) program and Small Business Technology Transfer Research (STTR) program. Government leaders have done this because they believe in the power of small business to tackle and solve real problems.

THINKING CRITICALLY

Applying Concepts. In small groups, name one problem the government would probably like to solve. Next, consider ways in which a small business could help, and write a one-page mock proposal to get funding.

To read more about federal funding for startups, go to "Entrepreneurship Issues" on the Student Center at entrepreneurship.pearson.com.

claims that the inventor has made in the application. The examiner may contact the applicant several times to clarify details or get more information. Most applications are rejected on the first submission. The reasons range from design flaws to using an improper format. The applicant is free to correct the problem and resubmit.

This process can be expensive. Filing fees will add up to several thousand dollars. Also, given the technicalities involved, most inventors hire a patent attorney or agent and a professional draftsperson who specializes in patent applications.

Trademarks and Service Marks

As an entrepreneur, you would try to deliver a quality product or service that you're proud of. You would not want a competitor to confuse or deceive consumers with a similar but inferior item. To guard against this, you might use a trademark or service mark. As you know from Chapter 5, a trademark is a word, phrase, or symbol that a manufacturer uses to identify the company's products. Likewise, a **service mark** is a word, phrase, or symbol a service provider uses to identify its services. When people refer to a product by its brand name, they are mentioning its trademark or service mark. Both marks are types of source indicators; they show where an item or service came from.

Although you don't need to register your mark to have trademark or service mark rights, you can obtain additional protections by obtaining a registration from the USPTO. The application process is useful to reduce the risk that you are using a trademark that is owned by someone else, which would cause legal problems, and provides you with additional legal rights to limit the use of your trademark by others. It can also bolster your claim if you want to register the mark in another country.

Registering for a mark is similar to applying for a patent, but much easier. You can start by searching the USPTO's database of registered and pending marks (those that have been submitted but not yet accepted). You might also look through state trademark registries, as well as other business listings, such as the *Yellow Pages*, or industry directories.

For its records, the USPTO requires a specimen of the mark—an actual sample as well as a drawing—as proof that it will be used in business or is being used already. The mark must meet certain conditions. It must be original, it may not use offensive or stereotypical images, and it may not include national flags or emblems. The mark cannot make false or confusing claims about the item and should not be descriptive of the goods or services the mark is being used in connection with. Using the name or likeness of a well-known person requires written permission. Not all marks will receive trademark protection.

Patent #11,023

Trade Secrets

A **trade secret** is information that a business or individual keeps confidential to gain advantage over competitors. A business or individual may take adequate precautions to keep this information secret, because it may have significant value. Some examples of trade secrets are Kentucky Fried Chicken and Bush Beans. The best way to protect trade secrets is with a nondisclosure agreement signed by employees and any others who have a need to have the information.

In most states, trade secrets are protected under that state's version of the Uniform Trade Secrets Act. The Act weighs certain factors in deciding whether the information qualifies as a trade secret. These include:

- **The Information's Value to the Business.** The economic advantage, either actual or potential, must be real and significant.

- **The Actual Difficulty in Obtaining the Information.** The information must be something others could not learn through ordinary means.

- **The Intention to Keep the Information Secret.** Those who have the knowledge must make an effort to keep it a secret.

- **The Business's Role in Developing the Information.** The more the business contributed, the stronger its claim.

 *What three conditions qualify an invention for a utility patent?*

▲ *Registered Trademark Symbol*

▲ *Trademark Symbol*

▲ *Service Mark Symbol*

Contracts & Intellectual Property Licenses

From this discussion on intellectual property law, it may sound like creating an invention or a song for public use is actually making a deal with society—you share your work with the public and your right to personal profit is ensured. But a **contract** (an agreement between competent parties in which each promises to take or avoid a specified action) and a **license** (providing rights to use intellectual property) also play a significant role in business ownership. Understanding how contracts and licenses (many of which are forms of contracts) operate is essential to succeeding as an entrepreneur.

What Makes a Contract Valid?

For a contract to be valid, or legally enforceable, all the conditions mentioned in the definition must be met. Let's take a look at these conditions one by one:

- **Agreement between the Parties.** The parties must agree on the **conditions**, or the events or circumstances that must occur for the contract to be binding. One party starts by making an offer. The other party may make a counteroffer, agreeing to some but not all of the conditions. Agreement is reached when one party makes an offer that the other one accepts.

- **Competence.** In the legal sense, **competent** means capable of understanding the terms of a contract and the consequences of entering it. Mental illness, the influence of drugs, or being underage are conditions that render an individual legally incompetent.

- **Mutual Exchange.** This is termed the **consideration**, the benefit that each party provides for the other. This exchange of one thing for another is what distinguishes an enforceable contract from an unenforceable promise.

To illustrate these terms, imagine that the owner of an antique shop tells a carpenter that she wants a display case made for her showroom. The carpenter offers to build a case made of walnut for $2,500. The shop owner makes a counteroffer of $2,000. The carpenter says that $2,000 isn't enough for a walnut case. For that amount, however, he will build one of cherry wood. The shop owner accepts the offer. These two people now have a valid contract.

Now suppose that the carpenter says he needs $300 to buy the cherry wood, and the shop owner gives him the money. The two would have an implied contract. An **implied contract** is made when the parties' actions demonstrate their agreement. However, the two still have other conditions to work out (such as size, design, and finish). They create an **express contract**, a contract in which the terms are explicitly stated either orally or in writing.

Notice that sometimes a verbal contract can constitute a valid contract. However, putting things in writing is safer for both parties. Certain types of contracts—such as the sale of land or the transfer of ownership of a copyright—must be in writing.

Types of Contracts

As the above example shows, a business owner will be at times either a buyer or a seller of goods or services. Thus the need for **sales contracts** and **service contracts**. These are agreements that include the service provided or items sold, the selling price and how it will be paid, and the date and location of the transaction. They also describe each party's rights and obligations. A landscaper's service contract may state that the company will replace any plants that die within 30 days, or that the customer will be charged a fee for canceling on less than 48 hours notice. Sales contracts typically give the buyer the right to inspect the goods and to refuse them if there is sufficient reason.

Leases are also common in business. A **lease** is a written contract in which a property owner gives temporary use of that property to another party. Terms of leases include the length of the contract, the amount of rent, and how often it's to be paid. Limitations may be placed on the use of the property, and penalties imposed for damages or late payments. Leases are usually associated with real estate but can apply to any type of tangible item. Equipment may be needed only occasionally, for instance, or may be so expensive that it can wear out or become outdated

▼ **Figure 16-3**

Implied Contract
The carpenter and shop owner agree that a bookcase made from cherry wood rather than walnut will be constructed.

Applying Concepts. *What kinds of things might you include on an express contract for the bookcase?*

before it's paid off. In these cases, leasing may make better sense than purchasing, especially for a small business.

A **confidentiality agreement** (also called a **nondisclosure agreement**) binds parties to secrecy and usually concerns employees, investors, or others with whom a business owner needs to share a trade secret or other sensitive information. A firm's marketing team may develop plans for a new product, for example, while potential investors will need to know a business's financial soundness. Confidentiality agreements describe the specific information that is considered confidential and how the parties may and may not use this information.

 **READING CHECKPOINT** *What three conditions make a contract valid?*

Seeking Remedy

Entering into a business contract usually gives the right to take action against the other party or parties to the contract if they breach the agreement. This applies to both written documents and oral agreements. Remedies are also available if another party violates your intellectual property rights. Violating the rights provided by a copyright or patent is called **infringement** of those rights. Failure to carry out the conditions of a contract is referred to as **breach of contract**.

The law allows different types of remedies, depending on the violation. In cases of infringement the common remedy is **injunctive relief**, an order for the violator to stop the illegal activity, such as selling purses printed with a company's trademark without that company's permission. In a breach of contract, the violator must agree to carry out the agreed-upon terms. In either situation, the guilty party may be forced to pay **damages**, a payment to reimburse the injured party for loss. The amount of damages may equal the money the guilty party earned, or the money the injured party lost, from the illegal activity. Under contract law, damages are often based on compensating the other party for the benefits they would have received had the contract been performed. Under patent law, damages are typically based on reasonable royalties and/or lost profits caused by the infringement. The violator may also be ordered to pay the injured party's attorney's fees.

Seeking remedy can be a lengthy and complicated process. It should be undertaken only with an attorney's advice. Accusing parties themselves can be sued and severely fined for knowingly or carelessly making false charges.

 **READING CHECKPOINT** *What is injunctive relief?*

 Your Business Plan. Continue developing your standard business plan. Go to "Section 16.1" of the *Business Plan Project* in your *Student Activity Workbook*, or "Section 16.1" of the BizTech Software.

Figure 16-4

Notice and Takedown Policy

Some Internet service providers explain on their Websites how copyright holders can request removal of material that has been used on a client's site without permission.

Solving Problems. *Removal requires only a "good faith belief" that infringement has occurred. What responsibility does this put on copyright holders who make this charge?*

Peacock Portal
Official County Government Website

Living in Peacock County   Employment   Doing Business   Government   Education   Learning   Visit
County Websites   Agency Contacts   Services A-Z   County Facts

How to Report Copyright Infringement

Digital Millennium Copyright Act (DMCA)
Anyone who believes their copyrighted work is being infringed upon through Peacock Portal should notify the following DMCA agent in writing at:

Address:
ABC Technologies
Attention: Designated DMCA Agent
PO Box 4445
Featherstown, WA 78504-4445

Fax:
(360)555-0109

DMCA Notification of Alleged Infringement
Notices of copyright infringement must be **mailed** or **faxed**. Please provide the following information in your written notice:

1. A description and location of the material that you believe is infringing. (For example, "The copyrighted work in question is the article that appears on the home page at www.nosite.com.")
2. The search term that you used and the URL for each search result that was allegedly infringing. (For example, the search query "Swiss cheese" returned the following infringing Web page(s).)
3. Your contact information, including your name, address, telephone number, and e-mail address if you have one.

   Please read the following statements carefully. If both are true, include them in your written notice:

   1. I have a good faith belief that use of the copyrighted materials described above is not authorized by the copyright owner.
   2. I swear, under penalty of perjury, that the information in the notification is accurate and that I am the copyright owner or am authorized to act on behalf of the owner of an exclusive right that is allegedly infringed.
4. Your signature.

ASSESSMENT 16.1

Reviewing Objectives

1. What are some of the purposes of intellectual property laws?
2. What are the five types of utility patents?
3. What three things make a contract valid?
4. What are damages?

Critical Thinking

5. **Classifying.** Suppose you take a statue of a cat and use it as the base of a lamp. What type of intellectual property protection might your new creation qualify for? Why?
6. **Comparing/Contrasting.** If you were a business owner and thought you had a trade secret, would you seek protection for it under the Uniform Trade Secrets Act? Why or why not?

Working Together

Pair with a classmate to create a contract for some service or item that students typically trade, such as foods at lunch or help in studying. Keep notes on the process, including each party's offers and counteroffers and reasons for accepting or rejecting each condition. Then write your final contract.

Science
Patenting Products of Technology

Learn about a patented product of scientific research. Some possible topics include genetically engineered plants or animals, artificial body parts, automotive innovations, or advances in cosmetics—but feel free to investigate any area that interests you. Who developed the invention? When and how? What issues had to be resolved before it was granted a patent?

OBJECTIVES

- Relate insurance to risk management
- Describe different business insurance needs and options
- Distinguish the qualities of a good insurance agent and good policies
- Create a plan for reducing business risk

VOCABULARY

- business interruption insurance
- cash value
- catastrophic risk
- coverage
- deductible
- ergonomics
- law of large numbers
- liability insurance
- policy
- premium
- property insurance
- pure risk
- replacement cost
- rider
- risk
- risk transfer
- speculative risk
- workers' compensation insurance

Think about this question:

Can you tolerate risk?

Write your answer (yes or no) on a piece of paper. Then think about how much risk you can handle. Think of specific examples.

Understanding Insurance

Insurance agents have a saying: "Don't think you can't afford insurance. You can't afford *not* to have insurance." Those words aren't just a sales pitch. What threatens a business, threatens everyone—owner, employees, customers, and community. Even if it were not required in some cases, buying insurance would still be a smart move—and a responsible one as well.

Another saying explains why a business needs insurance: "Hope for the best, but prepare for the worst." An entrepreneur wouldn't get far without both high hopes and realistic expectations. Insurance fits into that picture.

> ### Insurance
> **Don't think you can't afford insurance.**
> **You can't afford *not* to have insurance.**

Managing Risk

Many entrepreneurs will tell you that the element of **risk**, the possibility of loss, is part of the attraction of starting a business. It might be closer to the truth to say that *managing* risk is the attraction—in particular, managing **speculative risk**, or risk that holds the possibility of either gain or loss. Speculative risk is undertaken freely. It can be partly controlled to improve the chance for gain and lessen the chance for loss. When an ice cream manufacturer offers a new flavor, it is taking a speculative risk: the new flavor could be a bestseller, or it could be a flop. The company can increase the chances of success by first carrying out market research and taste tests. Then they hope for the best.

Running a business has other, less appealing risks. **Pure risk**, as the name suggests, is the chance of loss with no chance of gain. Managing pure risk consists of avoiding or reducing it. For example, kitchen fires are a pure risk in running a restaurant. Restaurant owners could avoid the risk by serving only cold foods, probably an unprofitable scenario. But they can reduce the risk by enforcing safety rules for using the stove. Knowing that fire is possible, they keep fire extinguishers on the premises. They prepare for the worst.

Insurance as Risk Management

There is another option for managing pure risk: **risk transfer**, which means shifting risk to another party. For business owners, that means purchasing business insurance. An insurance company takes on a client's risk.

Insurance companies are experts in risk management. They predict the likelihood of a pure risk, such as a kitchen fire, by using the **law of large numbers**. This theory says that if you want to predict how likely an event is to occur, you will get the most accurate answer by looking at the largest number of cases where it might.

For example, suppose a grocer wants to know how well the sauerkraut is selling. Over the course of one month, the grocer has 1,500 customers and sells 150 cans of sauerkraut. That averages to one can for every 10 customers. After three months, the customer count is 5,250, who buy 420 cans. The average has dropped to one can for every 12.5 customers. After six months, the totals are 10,400 customers and 1,095 cans of sauerkraut, for an average of one can per every 9.3 customers.

Which average is most accurate? According to the law of large numbers, it's the six-month figure, when the event—the sale of sauerkraut—has had the most chances to occur. Thus, that's the pattern that is most likely to hold true. Each customer represents one chance for occurrence. The annual average is likely to be more accurate still.

Insurance companies use the same principle. When they insure against a restaurant fire, they don't look at how often fires have occurred at a few restaurants over a few years, but at hundreds of thousands of restaurants over long stretches of time. They can predict how certain

A fire extinguisher helps manage risk.

factors—such as safety training and keeping fire extinguishers—affect the risk and the extent of the loss.

Using this information, the company puts together its insurance policies. A **policy** is a written contract between the insurer and the policyholder. The policy details the **coverage**, the protection provided, and lists the **premium**, the amount of money the person or business that is insured by the policy pays for coverage. It also shows the **deductible**, which is the amount the insured must first pay before the insurance company is required to chip in.

 **READING CHECKPOINT** *What is speculative risk?*

Types of Business Insurance

What does a business owner need to insure? Everything! At least that's how it may seem to the new entrepreneur. From a company's inventory to its reputation to the health of its employees—there's a special sort of policy for each. The business owner's job is to choose the coverage the operation should have from among the many types available. The three most common insurance needs are:

- Property insurance
- Liability insurance
- Workers' compensation

▼ *Personal auto policies don't apply to commercial use.*

Property Insurance

Property insurance protects a business's possessions in the event of fire, theft, or damage from the weather. A basic policy could cover the building, its furnishings, and the equipment, supplies, cash, and inventory stored there or offsite. Construction firms and home remodelers often leave equipment at the work site or in clients' homes, for instance. Property can be insured for its actual worth, called **cash value**. However, experts recommend insuring property for its **replacement cost**, the cost of replacing it at current prices, which is usually higher. Property insurance also covers electronic data and software lost to physical damage or computer malfunction.

Vehicles owned by or used for business are insured under a separate policy. These policies provide additional coverage for damage and injury caused to, or by, the vehicle or driver. Personal auto policies don't apply to commercial uses.

Business owners who rent property need to protect themselves with renter's insurance. It's sometimes a condition of a lease or a loan. A landlord may require a renter to be insured against fire damage, for example. Business owners can also protect improvements they make to the

▲ Figure 16-5

Catastrophic Risk
To stay profitable, insurers charge higher premiums for disaster insurance.

Predicting. *Some people want the government to guarantee disaster insurance bought from private insurers. The government would promise to pay claims if the private insurers could not. What might be some advantages and drawbacks of this plan?*

premises that can't be removed, such as new roofing or an addition to the space.

Yet another option in a property insurance policy is **business interruption insurance**. This covers losses if a business can't operate due to a covered event, such as a storm or fire. The insurer uses company records to determine what the business would have earned during the shutdown, and covers ongoing expenses that must be paid despite the closure, such as utility bills. Some policies cover the expense of running the business from a different location. A hair stylist, for example, might rent space in another salon while her shop is closed to repair a broken water main.

Like other types of insurance, property insurance is limited in one important respect: basic policies protect only against events where the occurrence and loss are predictable. This is in keeping with the law of large numbers. A disaster such as a hurricane or wildfire is classified as a **catastrophic risk**, an unpredictable event that causes severe loss to many people at the same time. In regions where a particular disaster is most likely, coverage is often extremely expensive (flood insurance for a restaurant on a river, for instance). As a result, business owners who most need the protection will have to assess the risk of not purchasing insurance against the possibility of catastrophic risk.

It is unlikely that an insurance policy will cover the entire amount of a loss. Insurance companies typically require the insured to bear a certain amount of the loss before the policy will make a payment. Generally speaking, the more of the loss that the insured agrees to bear, the less expensive the policy.

Liability Insurance

Of all the risks entrepreneurs face, the chance that their inexperience or negligence could hurt someone physically or financially is one of the scariest. **Liability insurance** eases some of those concerns by providing protection when a business's action, or lack of action, injures another party. As with property insurance, different policies cover different risks. The three main types of policies are described here.

- **General Liability.** This type of policy covers expenses related to injuries sustained on the business premises. It also covers injuries or damage due to employee carelessness at work. Suppose a lumberyard worker is using a hoist to load planks into a customer's truck. The worker misjudges the truck's position and drops the load on its roof. General liability insurance will pay for repairs to the roof. If the truck is the customer's business vehicle, the insurer may pay for lost income while the truck is unusable. If one of the planks falls on the customer's foot, the policy will pay the medical expenses and any legal liability.

- **Product Liability.** A product liability policy protects a business from losses caused by a product it produced or developed. This coverage is particularly important to manufacturers and food producers and processors.

- **Professional Liability.** This policy differs from product liability in that it covers harm done by a business's actions, or failure to act. A well-known example is malpractice insurance, taken out by medical professionals. Another example is error and omission (E&O) insurance—which would pay for stolen property if a self-storage business failed to hire enough security or used inferior locks.

Two other types of liability policies are becoming more common. One is identity theft insurance, which protects a business against damage done by the theft of sensitive information. It's recommended for companies that store a great deal of data electronically, which increases the opportunities for theft. A second type is called employment practices liability insurance. This policy covers claims of discrimination, sexual harassment, and other unfair treatment by employees and others a company does business with. This is a special risk for new businesses, where a code of ethics and hiring and firing procedures may not be fully in force.

Workers' Compensation

Workers' compensation insurance covers losses to employees due to job-related injury or illness. It's no-fault insurance, meaning it pays regardless of who is responsible. Workers' compensation is required in every state, and every state has its own coverage requirements. Generally, the policy pays employees' medical bills and reimburses them for lost wages. It pays for physical therapy or job training if the injury makes returning to the old job impossible. In case of death, the insurance covers funeral expenses and survivors' benefits to a spouse and dependents.

Requirements for employers vary also. In some states, very small businesses—those with five or fewer employees, for example—are exempt. In other states, it's needed for even one part-time employee. Business owners may be required to carry workers' compensation

▼ Figure 16-6

Workers' Compensation
Some states require that business owners carry workers' compensation for seasonal or contract workers.

Drawing Conclusions. *Why might states differ in their requirements for carrying this insurance?*

Honesty

Trusting people is probably important to you. Most of us like to believe we can take people at their word and that they will also trust what we say. At this stage of life, you probably know that being honest is not always easy. Some people feel that it is simpler to tell a quick lie rather than hurt a coworker, friend, or loved one. If you're concerned about how a person will interpret the truth, you may feel you can't be completely honest.

In business, words and actions that are less than completely honest can't be tolerated. Lying is often grounds for dismissal from a job, regardless of the reason for the dishonesty. Most people, employers included, would rather hear the truth and have it told in a way that is both respectful and caring, than have someone be less than honest.

Strive to be a person who can be trusted. Don't compromise your honesty to protect anyone. People may sometimes be upset, but truthfulness builds trust in others while it strengthens your personal integrity. Developing a reputation for honesty is helpful both personally and professionally.

THINKING CRITICALLY

Classifying. Do you have friends you trust completely and others you are not always sure about? Think about how important honesty is to you. Where do you fit in: Are you an honest and trustworthy person, or do you sometimes tell small lies? Are you comfortable with your reputation?

To read more about honesty, go to "Your Business Career" on the Student Center at entrepreneurship.pearson.com.

for seasonal or contract workers, such as a store owner who hires a company to patch and restripe a parking lot. Within a state, different rules may apply to different industries, such as agricultural and construction. Employers may carry workers' compensation insurance regardless of their legal obligation because, in most cases, it will protect them from lawsuits filed by employees injured at work.

 **READING CHECKPOINT** *What protection does general liability insurance give?*

Buying Insurance

Deciding on an insurance package should be an integral part of a business's start-up plan. The policies must be in effect before the doors open.

Choosing an Agent

Choosing an insurance agent is like hiring an important employee. You want someone who is familiar with your type of business. You might first check with trade or professional associations. They sometimes have agreements with certain insurers to provide coverage that targets group members' needs. For example, antique dealers can get insurance through the Antiques and Collectibles National Association. Property insurance policies cover items they are selling for private owners, whether in the shop or from a booth at a trade show.

Alternatively, you can ask advice from other businesspeople in your field. They might recommend both exclusive and independent agents.

Exclusive agents work for a single insurance company. They can usually get lower premiums by offering a package called a business owner's policy (BOP). Of course, their choices are limited to the policies their company sells. An independent agent represents several insurers and can offer a wider range of policies. Whoever you choose, look at the agent's professional affiliations and credentials. For example, agents who specialize in business insurance and financial planning can be identified by the designation CPCU—for Chartered Property and Casualty Underwriter.

Find someone who inspires personal trust as well. Like medical doctors, insurance agents ask for confidential information to assess a client's needs. They need to know about a business's assets and income, potential for growth, and ultimate goals to help the client make the most informed choice. They must be able to understand complex and important issues so they can give their best, most professional advice. Trustworthiness is especially valuable in independent agents, who may represent companies whose reputation and financial soundness are unknown to you. You should ask about the insurance provider's financial ratings by outside regulators such as A. M. Best and Standard and Poor's.

Choosing Policies

The best insurance package is the one that most closely fits your needs. A newspaper owner (publisher) requires liability protection against lawsuits due to inaccurate or prejudiced reporting. The supervisor of the press that prints the newspaper is more concerned with worker disability or injury from the noise or machinery.

Some standard policies can be modified by adding riders. A **rider** is an amendment to a policy that changes the benefits or conditions of coverage. The owner of a storage company might need a rider to cover antiques, paintings, or other items with a high value.

Many owners of home-based businesses believe their personal home and auto insurance protects their business operation as well. They are mistaken. A one-person company that has no customer traffic, such as a greeting card designer, might be protected by a rider that simply increases the coverage in the homeowner's policy. A carpentry shop with three employees and expensive, potentially dangerous, equipment would require a separate, in-home business policy.

▼ **Figure 16-7**

Special Insurance Situations
Vendors at fairs and organizers of sports tournaments need short-term insurance policies tailored to their unusual situations.

Applying Concepts. *How might the insurance priorities of a food vendor who travels to fairs differ from those of a restaurant owner?*

Some occupations have complete insurance packages designed just for them. Livestock producers, for example, need farm and ranch insurance that covers such risks as vehicle collision with animals, or milk loss from contamination or spoilage.

READING CHECKPOINT *Why might a policyholder want a rider?*

Reducing Business Risk

Insurance manages risk by transferring it from the business owner to the insurance provider. Another form of risk management is risk reduction. This involves limiting the chances that a policy-covered event will occur. Practicing risk reduction has three major benefits:

- It avoids property repairs, legal fees, and other expenses resulting from an accident, legal incident, or other misfortune.

- Practicing prevention tends to lower insurance premiums.

- Reducing risk saves the emotional and financial drain of filing a claim when something bad happens and then waiting to collect from an insurance company.

Securing Physical Property

Keeping buildings, supplies, and merchandise safe is an obvious place to start. A small workplace, such as a graphics designer's at-home studio, might need locks and alarms on doors and windows and possibly a surveillance camera. Workplaces that have a large number of visitors often have sign-in policies or a requirement for identification badges. Wireless systems let business owners monitor sensors by using the Internet. Alerts are sent as e-mails or text messages. A professional security provider brings a physical presence of regular patrols and instant communication with an offsite monitoring station.

Good lighting, inside and out, also discourages crime. Spotlights protect vulnerable areas, such as parking lots, back doors, stairwells, and loading or receiving bays.

Personnel can be assets in security as well. Screen and hire your employees carefully and then give them a code of ethics to work by. Train your employees well. The better they understand their own and others' jobs, the better they can recognize possible signs of theft or fraud. Also teach them effective legal ways to act when they suspect stealing by customers or clients. False accusations or attempts to stop

▼ *Security system*

a theft in progress can lead to lawsuits, injury, and ill will that can cost much more than the price of the merchandise.

Safeguarding Information

If sensitive information gets into the wrong hands, the consequences can be just as devastating as having a showroom ransacked. A business's own security is threatened, and it may be held liable for customers' losses as well. Yet many business owners use information and telecommunication technology without fully protecting against the risks that come with the efficiency and convenience.

One critical component of any computer system or network is technical support to explain how to use security features and handle security issues. Owners and employees alike should know how to use encryption software when sending electronic files. Web pages that register clients' personal and financial information need the same protection. Disks and other data storage units should be guarded like any other tangible property.

Businesses also need to guard information shared among employees. For example, suppose a manufacturer and a sales representative are keeping a paper or electronic file of memos about a merchant whom they suspect is underreporting sales and keeping the profits. That file is discovered and made public by an unthinking employee, starting rumors about the merchant's dishonesty. The merchant's reputation and sales suffer. Those memos might then become evidence in the merchant's lawsuit against the manufacturer and salesperson.

Promoting Health and Safety

It may be true that you can't put a price on good health. However, the price on bad health may be figured at around $87 billion. That's how much more U.S. employers paid beyond workers' compensation insurance and employee benefits in 2004. Keeping workers safe and healthy is sound financial preventive medicine.

Providing a safe workplace is an employer's legal and ethical responsibility. Safety training is required for certain high-risk jobs, from lab work to cutting trees. Every workplace should be equipped with first-aid and emergency supplies, and employees trained to use them. More and more workplaces now have defibrillators, devices that restore normal heartbeat during a heart attack. Companies should also practice fire drills and other emergency response routines.

▲ *Every workplace should be equipped with first-aid supplies*

Safety practices that prevent crime also prevent injuries. Many businesses require at least two people to work at night. Bank deposits are made at irregular times, with the money carried in a variety of unobtrusive containers. Some employers sponsor anger management and

▲ **Figure 16-8**
Healthy Food
Vending machines that offer healthy food can be part of a company's effort to promote healthy eating.

Relating Concepts. *If healthy food or these vending machines cost more than the traditional vending machines or unhealthy snacks, how would a company justify the expense?*

communication classes to counter the growing problem of workplace violence.

Business owners can go beyond preventing accidents and injury to promoting wellness. One step is to do an ergonomics assessment. **Ergonomics** is the study of designing environments to fit the people who use them. An assessment shows whether lighting, workstations, use of storage space, and scheduling of tasks help maintain physical and emotional health. Some insurance companies offer wellness consultation to help business owners develop health and fitness programs. More and more employers are offering lower health insurance premiums to workers who complete wellness programs.

Less expensive measures can be useful as well. Vending machines could offer fresh fruit and juice. Health department workers could offer flu shots onsite. Owners of health-related businesses, from organic grocers to physical therapists, are often happy to give talks on their respective areas of expertise.

 **READING CHECKPOINT** *What is ergonomics?*

 Your Business Plan. Continue developing your standard business plan. Go to "Section 16.2" of the *Business Plan Project* in your *Student Activity Workbook*, or "Section 16.2" of the BizTech Software.

ASSESSMENT 16.2

Reviewing Objectives

1. How is speculative risk different from pure risk?
2. What coverage does workers' compensation provide?
3. What is a rider on an insurance policy?
4. What are the three major benefits of risk reduction?

Critical Thinking

5. **Analyzing Information.** Based on the information in this chapter, suggest two businesses that might need more property insurance coverage than liability coverage, and vice versa. Give reasons for your choices.

6. **Comparing/Contrasting.** Which type of theft deterrence do you think is more

effective: visible, such as uniformed security guards; or invisible, such as two-way mirrors?

Working Together

With a partner, write and perform a scene between an entrepreneur and an insurance agent. The entrepreneur describes his or her business and priorities, and the insurance agent suggests policies. Use humor if you like.

Social Studies
Trends in Insurance
Research the history of one aspect of the insurance industry, such as training of agents, types of policies offered, alternative forms of insurance, size and growth of companies, insurance regulations, and methods of selling. Present your findings in a brief report or chart them on a timeline.

Singing Like a Pro!

Ashleigh Cole of Estill Springs, Tennessee, began singing with a Fisher-Price® tape recorder at the age of three. As she grew up, she continued singing, practicing every day, singing with her high school's show choir, with her church choir, and with the contemporary gospel group Won by One. Her dream? To be a professional singer.

▲ *Ashleigh Cole*

Learning How to Market Herself

One of the most important steps in becoming a professional in the entertainment field is knowing how to market oneself. Ashleigh signed with an online casting company, StarSearchCasting.com, that offers exposure to industry professionals. The basic level, which is free, provides a personal profile with one photo that can be seen by visitors to the site, such as casting agents and directors. Going further requires a certain amount of financial investment. In return, an actor, model, or singer can get more exposure through additional sites and assemble more photos and materials in a personal profile.

Ashleigh was contacted by a producer through the site and flew to Los Angeles with her mother. While in L.A., she and her mother attended an entrepreneurship program run by CEO Space. "This experience generated a lot of useful ideas," said Ashleigh. "One of the ideas was to go to Nashville and record a three-song demo and have promotional pictures taken. With my demo and pictures, I wrote a one-page overview and put them all together to create a basic promotional package for the newly formed Ashleigh Cole Music."

At the entrepreneurship program, Ashleigh also learned the importance of networking. She met people who were willing to donate their time to act as her business advisory board. One of her advisors introduced her to an entertainment attorney—a necessity in the world of professional music. She also met several songwriters, including Eric Haines.

Ashleigh loved a song that Eric had written, called "Cry," and recorded it. She used the song to enter a contest in Nashville sponsored by CATZ Radio. The winner would get a three-month spot on the play list. Ashleigh won. She was ecstatic! She signed up for a music site on MySpace.com to feature her recording.

Moving Ahead

To keep her business going, Ashleigh relies on her business advisory board, which includes people with expertise both in the music industry and in non-music businesses. She plans to raise seed capital to set up her business as an LLC. Her mother is her manager and is continually on the lookout for songs for Ashleigh. Her mother also helps Ashleigh expand her network. "I think it's cool that when she introduces me to people in the industry, she steps away and lets me do the talking," said Ashleigh, "but I know she's close by if I need her guidance."

Thinking Like an Entrepreneur

1. How does having a dream help you start a business?
2. What's important about having a business advisory board?
3. How could you locate members of an advisory board?

CHAPTER SUMMARY

16.1 Legal Issues

Intellectual property law gives artists and inventors exclusive rights to their works for a specified length of time. Copyright, patents, trademarks, and service marks protect artistic work, invented items or processes, or proprietary business interests. A valid business contract is an agreement for an exchange between competent parties. Violators of intellectual property rights and contracts face legal consequences.

16.2 Insurance

Insurance is a form of risk management that pays clients for losses due to unforeseen events. Business owners need to insure against property loss, liability, and work-related injury to employees. They should buy policies that meet their needs from a trusted agent. Businesses can also reduce risk by preventing theft and accidents and by promoting wellness.

REVIEW VOCABULARY

Write two paragraphs on the protection provided by intellectual property laws and by insurance. In the first paragraph, describe their similarities; in the second, their differences. Points of comparison and contrast might include how they are obtained, the process and fees required, the parts of each, and the specific protection provided. Use at least ten of the terms listed below.

- breach of contract (p. 441)
- business interruption insurance (p. 446)
- cash value (p. 445)
- catastrophic risk (p. 446)
- competent (p. 440)
- conditions (p. 439)
- confidentiality agreement (p. 441)
- consideration (p. 440)
- contract (p. 439)
- coverage (p. 445)
- damages (p. 441)
- deductible (p. 445)
- derivative (p. 435)
- ergonomics (p. 452)
- express contract (p. 440)
- implied contract (p. 440)
- infringement (p. 441)
- injunctive relief (p. 441)
- intangibles (p. 433)
- law of large numbers (p. 444)
- lease (p. 440)
- liability insurance (p. 446)
- license (p. 439)
- nondisclosure agreement (p. 441)
- policy (p. 445)
- premium (p. 445)
- property insurance (p. 445)
- pure risk (p. 444)
- replacement cost (p. 445)
- rider (p. 449)
- risk (p. 444)
- risk transfer (p. 444)
- sales contract (p. 440)
- service contract (p. 440)
- service mark (p. 438)
- speculative risk (p. 444)
- trade secret (p. 439)
- workers' compensation insurance (p. 447)

CHECK YOUR UNDERSTANDING

Choose the letter that best answers the question or completes the statement.

1. A restaurant owner offers to pay employees by giving them free meals. By eating a meal, an employee enters into
   a. a breach of contract
   b. an express contract
   c. an implied contract
   d. injunctive relief

2. An application to register the phrase "tasty corn" as a trademark for a seller of canned corn would be rejected because that phrase
   a. is not competent
   b. is not original
   c. can't be legally proven
   d. all of the above

3. Requiring food service workers to wash their hands before serving meals is a form of
   a. ergonomics
   b. risk reduction
   c. risk transfer
   d. infringement

4. A condition that will help earn a patent is
   a. non-obviousness
   b. speculative risk
   c. the law of large numbers
   d. none of the above

5. The most important quality in an insurance package is that it
   a. is inexpensive
   b. meets the policyholder's needs
   c. is sold by an exclusive agent
   d. covers catastrophic risk

6. A poem is in the public domain if
   a. the author has died
   b. it has not been published
   c. 70 years have passed since the author's death
   d. it wasn't registered with the Copyright Office

7. A lease is a type of
   a. contract
   b. derivative
   c. intangible
   d. rider

8. If a goat bites a visitor at a petting zoo, the zoo's owner would be covered by
   a. workers' compensation
   b. property insurance
   c. renter's insurance
   d. none of the above

9. One advantage of using an independent insurance agent is
   a. lower premiums
   b. a wider choice of policies
   c. superior credentials
   d. familiarity with the company the agent represents

10. Ergonomics reduces risk by
    a. preventing crime
    b. promoting health
    c. securing property
    d. protecting information

11. Liability insurance provides protection when
    a. a business's action or lack of action injures someone
    b. a business's vehicles are damaged
    c. electronic data or software is lost due to a computer malfunction
    d. a business has a fire or damage from the weather

12. An implied contract becomes valid when it is
    a. signed
    b. registered
    c. acted on
    d. copyrighted

Business Communication

13. Write a patent description for a product feature or a process that you're familiar with—for example, the pull-tab top on a soda can, the design of a computer mouse, lacing up and tying a shoe, or the way a coffeemaker brews coffee. Describe the subject precisely and thoroughly so that someone who has never seen the subject could re-create it.

14. Carefully worded directions for use included with a product can save a business from a product liability lawsuit. Choose an item that you're familiar with, such as a backpack or shampoo. Write at least three directions for use that would protect the manufacturer from claims of selling an unsafe product.

15. Give a presentation on simple safety practices for a particular workplace, such as an office, warehouse, factory, or bakery. Use props and demonstrations as needed.

Business Ethics

18. You own a catering business. The baker who supplies your bread has been teaching food service classes as part of a work-release program for low-risk offenders at a detention center. He urges you to hire some of his graduates. You support the program and you need the help, but your insurance agent warns you that the premiums on your property and liability insurance will go up if you hire these individuals. How would you respond to the baker's request?

Business Math

16. In 2002, the U.S. government spent $40,896,000 on processing copyright applications. That averaged out to $78.48 per application. How many applications did the government process that year? Each applicant paid a $30 application fee. How much did the government collect in fees?

17. Income exposure is the money lost due to business interruption. It's used to decide how much coverage is needed. A simple formula to estimate income exposure is Income Exposure = (Monthly Income + Operating Expenses) x Number of Months needed for recovery. A dry cleaner does $17,500 worth of business each month. Its operating expenses are $5,250. What would be the business's income exposure if it took seven months to reopen after a fire? If it needed an additional $1,580 per month to keep operating during that time, what would be the total amount of necessary coverage?

Business in Your Community

19. Survey three local business owners about the types of insurance they purchase, the premiums, and the coverage. Make a chart of your findings.

20. Interview a local musician, painter, graphic artist, writer, or other individual involved in the arts about his or her experience with copyrights. Has the artist registered works with the Copyright Office? Has the artist had trouble with copyright infringement? If so, how was the problem resolved? If not, why do you think there hasn't been trouble?

Internet Networking

Networking—meeting new people through various events—has taken place informally for generations. However, before Web 2.0, there wasn't any interaction between Websites and Web surfers on the Internet. **Web 2.0** changed the way software developers looked at the Web and the **applications** (end-user programs) they wrote. This made online networking possible. Now, people can share information online through blogs, **wikis** (which are collaborative Websites where anyone can edit, delete, or modify content), and **social networking sites**. This last category includes online discussion forums, chatrooms, social networks (such as MySpace and Facebook), business networks (such as LinkedIn), and other types of sites set up for groups to share information.

Social Networking Profiles

Social networking sites and business networks allow users to create their own Web page, called a **profile**. On social networks, profiles are where members can express their individual personalities, thoughts and feelings, and likes and dislikes, post photographs, and show off their network of friends. At MySpace or Facebook, for example, members can invite friends who are also members to join their personal networks, and the profile page lists all of the member's friends. Some social networks allow you to place music selections and video uploads on a profile page.

On business networks, profiles summarize members' professional accomplishments and help them find potential contacts and clients. Business networks help you search for jobs and they also allow potential clients or employers to locate you. A popular business-based social networking site is LinkedIn, which is described as a place for people to network on a professional level.

Although most social and business networks are free, users must join to take full advantage of them. Networks often have restrictions for people who are not members. For instance, a nonmember cannot add comments or become a "friend" to a member.

Spreading Information

Some social networking Websites, such as Digg.com and StumbleUpon.com, are mainly for sharing content from elsewhere on the Web or recommending other Websites. On Digg.com, members submit an article, video, or image they've seen online, which is then voted on by other Digg members. If enough members "digg" the content, it moves to Digg's homepage. Members can also create their own profile pages.

Uses for Social Networking Sites

People use social networking sites to communicate online with friends, for online dating, and to form and participate in online communities. Social networking sites can also be used for business purposes—mainly for low-key advertising that might be of interest to members of the site.

Tech Vocabulary
- applications
- profile
- social networking sites
- Web 2.0
- wikis

Check Yourself
1. What did Web 2.0 make possible?
2. What are wikis?
3. What is a social networking profile?
4. What is Digg?

What Do You Think?
Communicating. How would you use a social networking site as a business owner? Should you advertise to your friends?

17

TAXES & GOVERNMENT REGULATIONS

OBJECTIVES

- Explain how the government uses tax money
- Describe the purposes of business taxes
- Suggest ways that businesses can reduce their taxes

VOCABULARY

- deduction
- enterprise zone
- excise tax
- FICA
- infrastructure
- intrastate sales
- pass-through businesses
- sales tax
- subsidy
- tax avoidance
- tax credit
- tax evasion
- taxes
- tax-increment financing

Answer this question:

Do you personally pay taxes?

Write your answer (yes or no) on a piece of paper.

Why Do Businesses Pay Taxes?

Oliver Wendell Holmes, Jr., a Supreme Court Justice in the early 1900s, is credited with the statement, "I like to pay taxes. With them I buy civilization." Few people can claim they like paying **taxes**, money required by the government to support its various functions. Yet taxation is so important to the nation that it was authorized in the Constitution.

Article I of the Constitution states, "The Congress shall have Power To lay and collect Taxes, Duties, Imposts and Excises, to pay the Debts and provide for the common Defence and general Welfare of the United States." Some 220 years later, taxes—and the reasons for paying them—remain. Taxes may not "buy civilization," but they do buy government services, from trash pick-up to medical care.

The U.S. government raises money by taxation or by borrowing. It can be a problem when the government borrows money. Future generations must pay back this debt—and the interest on it.

Public Services

Life in the United States is built on the public services that taxes provide. Tax dollars support the **infrastructure**, the system of organizations, public systems, structures, and services that a society needs to function and be productive. For example, did you have

"I like to pay taxes. With them I buy civilization."
–Oliver Wendell Holmes

clean water to wash your face this morning? A regional sanitary district probably maintains the pipeline and water treatment plants and the health department tests the water quality. Further up the governmental ladder, human and environmental health is protected by state and federal agencies, ranging from the Centers for Disease Control to the National Weather Service.

Local and federal taxes also help you get across town and across the country. Workers who lay the roads are hired through government contracts. City buses, commuter rail services, and Amtrak (the national rail passenger carrier) are given subsidies by the government to keep fares low and encourage ridership. A **subsidy** is financial aid from the government to support an industry or public service. Other agencies oversee travelers' safety. Cities install traffic lights. State departments of motor vehicles test drivers and issue licenses. Local and state police enforce the laws.

Your education, too, is at least partly funded by the government. Public schools depend wholly on taxes for salaries, maintenance, and other expenses. You may use books and other resources from public libraries or attend programs at publicly supported museums. Later you may get a government loan or grant to help pay for college, where you may take part in research or other programs that receive government money.

Taxes support the life of the community through public parks and recreation areas. You might swim at a community pool, skate in a local park, or meet the local wildlife at a nature center.

Some tax money goes to maintaining the money supply. Taxes fund the work of the United States Treasury, which includes regulating national banks, printing money—and collecting taxes through the Internal Revenue Service.

Social Programs

Starting with the Great Depression in the 1930s, the government has taken an ever greater role in weaving a social safety net for people who can't meet their basic needs. Today, social services account for almost half of all federal government spending. Some programs are carried out by state or regional offices with funds from a federal agency. Others are supported by matching funds at each level of government.

The largest and oldest of all social programs is Social Security. The program's full name—Old Age, Survivors, and Disability Insurance

▲ Figure 17-1
Tax Dollars Support the Infrastructure
Local and federal taxes are used to build roads.

Relating Concepts. *Without adequate funding, roads and bridges fall into disrepair. How would this hurt our business and personal life?*

Program—gives a clue to its scope. Social Security provides benefits for retired workers, dependents of deceased workers, and workers who have disabilities and their dependents.

Another agency dependent on taxes is the Department of Health and Human Services (HHS). The HHS fills a range of needs that include early childhood education, immunizations, and programs to combat domestic violence and drug dependency. Through Medicare and Medicaid, it provides health insurance for one-quarter of all Americans.

The Department of Agriculture (USDA) offers similarly varied assistance through its Cooperative State Research and Education Extension Service at state universities and colleges. The USDA further works to ensure healthful diets with its Fresh Fruit and Vegetable Program for low-income school districts and the Senior Farmers' Market Nutrition Program, which provides vouchers to buy food from local producers at recognized markets.

Defense

The Department of Defense (DOD) is a prime recipient of tax money. Providing for the armed forces takes about 20 percent of the federal budget.

For their money, taxpayers get more than national security. The armed services also provide education and career training. Many commercial airline pilots, for example, learned their skills in the military. The armed forces assist in nonmilitary actions. The National Guard and the Coast Guard aid in disaster relief, drug enforcement, rescue operations, and environmental protection. To care for wounded service personnel, the DOD has funded medical research, from surgeon training to developing artificial limbs. The Global Positioning System (GPS) that helps drivers find their way in traffic uses DOD satellites.

Business

Some tax money returns to business as resources for growth and development. The Small Business Administration (SBA) is a federal agency that provides information, advice, government contracts, and loan guarantees for operations that fall within its size restrictions. It emphasizes underserved business owners, such as women, teens, military veterans, Native Americans, and other minority groups.

Subsidies for public transportation make it more affordable and available, help lower-income citizens, and reduce stress on the roads and the environment. The owner of a commercial property may qualify for a low-interest construction loan by including energy-efficient features in the new building.

Cities and states subsidize entrepreneurs, too, by creating enterprise zones. An **enterprise zone** is a geographic area in which businesses receive economic incentives to encourage development there. Entrepreneurs might be awarded grants to improve a property, or tax credits for hiring employees.

Another way business taxes are used to influence the economic climate is through tax-increment financing. **Tax-increment financing (TIF)** is the strategy of spending taxpayer money to encourage businesses to locate to an area or improve their property there, with the goal of starting a cycle of growth and prosperity. TIF designation is saved for areas in serious decline. It is somewhat riskier than establishing an enterprise zone, and the benefits take longer to realize. The designation usually lasts around 20 years.

For a TIF designation, the local government first raises money by selling bonds, just as a company can. The money may be used to upgrade the infrastructure, buy rundown properties, or reimburse entrepreneurs for their expenses.

▼ **Figure 17-2**
Tax Dollars at Work
Providing for the armed forces accounts for about 20 percent of the federal budget.
Classifying. *What other services does the armed services provide beyond fighting in wars?*

Businesses move into the TIF district and generate sales and property taxes. The taxes go to pay off the bonds, with interest, and also to fund public services. Potentially the city looks more attractive to other businesses, which promotes continued growth.

Business also benefits indirectly from government programs. Good roads make ground transportation more efficient. Sports arenas, museums, and tourist attractions bring customers to area merchants. Telecommunication networks use satellites built by the space agency NASA. And think how many businesses owe their existence to the Internet, which was created in the 1960s by the Department of Defense.

 *What kinds of social services are paid for by taxes?*

▲ **Figure 17-3**
Subsidized Agriculture
The USDA subsidizes loans for producers of grains, dairy foods, and other basic agricultural goods.

Inferring. *What are the pros and cons of subsidized loans for agricultural goods?*

What Taxes Do Businesses Pay?

As many parents will tell you, having a child changes life in ways they never could have imagined. Parents must meet all of a child's many needs, every day, including some they didn't expect. For instance, did you know that even a one-year-old needs to see a dentist?

It's fitting then that entrepreneurs often feel like parents to their businesses, especially when it comes to taxes. Paying taxes is a daily reality. They must be included in every sale that is made and paycheck signed. There are many business taxes, some of which many people don't know about. For example, did you know that some limited liability corporations have to file a tax return even if they never open their doors for business?

There is another important similarity between parents and entrepreneurs: Just as parents are responsible for their children's actions in the eyes of the law, entrepreneurs are responsible for their business's taxes before the IRS. Trying to avoid paying taxes through illegal or deceptive means is called **tax evasion** and is a federal crime. It's punishable by fine, seizure of property, or even imprisonment.

Payroll Taxes

As you learned earlier, retirement and disability insurance is one of the biggest items in the federal government's budget. The government pays for these by using Payroll taxes, also referred to as FICA. **FICA** is the acronym for the Federal Insurance Contributions Act, the law that requires employers and employees to share the cost of the federal government's insurance and retirement program through deductions from wages and income.

Although both employers and workers contribute to the tax, the employer is responsible for calculating and sending the payments to the IRS. FICA tax is composed of two separate deductions: a larger one for Social Security and a smaller one for Medicare. They are figured as a percentage of the employee's wages or salary and withheld from each paycheck. The employer's own contribution equals the contribution of the employee.

Most states also require employers to deduct state income taxes from an employee's paycheck. This amount is sent to the state government.

Here's an example of how to calculate the FICA for an employee making $20,000 a year, with a Social Security amount of 6.2%, and a Medicare amount of 1.45%.

Employee's Gross Salary	**$ 20,000**
Social Security ($20,000 × .062)	**– 1,240**
Medicare ($20,000 × .0145)	**– 290**
Employee's Net Salary	**$ 18,470**

This example shows two important things:

- As an employee, your gross salary is always reduced by your Social Security and Medicare payments.

- As an employee, you paid $1,530 in taxes. Your employer will deduct this from your paycheck in each pay period and send it to the government. Your employer will also pay an *additional* $1,530 in taxes to the government to match the amount you paid.

Federal Unemployment Tax

Just as payments to Social Security are technically called FICA taxes, payments to fund unemployment insurance are called FUTA, for the Federal Unemployment Tax Act. As the name tells you, the FUTA tax aids workers who have lost a job. It is also a percentage of employee wages; however, unlike FICA taxes, the FUTA tax is paid solely by the employer. Also, it's paid only on the first few thousand dollars an employee earns each year.

The FUTA fund is run jointly by the federal and state governments. Depending on individual state law, employers may or may not be required to make payments to the state, as well. If they are, the tax is divided, with the state's portion applied as a credit toward the federal government's share. Payments are typically sent in quarterly.

Consumption Taxes

As a consumer, you're probably well aware that most of the goods and services you buy are taxed. Because these things are used, or *consumed*, such taxes are called consumption taxes.

Lawmakers decide which goods and services are taxed, and at what rate. Business owners who sell these items decide who pays the tax. They either absorb the entire amount themselves or pass some or all of it on to the customer.

The most common consumption tax is a **sales tax**. Some local and state governments require this, so entrepreneurs may need to calculate taxes for a variety of situations. For example, a state may impose a sales tax on merchandise, such as a frying pan. However, merchandise that is bought to be resold later may be tax-free. So, if a restaurant equipment wholesaler sells a shipment of frying pans to a department store, the wholesaler wouldn't be liable for sales tax—the department store would be. However, the store would probably not collect a sales tax if it sold the pans to a church for use in its soup kitchen, because sales to nonprofit organizations are usually tax-exempt.

Even figuring the tax on a single product can be complicated. In some states, food products are tax-free. However, a bakery owner might have to collect a tax on a birthday cake based on candles, decorations, and other inedible elements if they make up over half of the cake's retail value.

▼ *A baker may have to pay taxes on the decorations, but not on the cake.*

Additionally, certain items are subject to excise taxes. An **excise tax** is a tax on a specific product or commercial activity. Federal, state, and local governments often impose excise taxes to control consumption or raise money for a project. A city may have a tax on restaurant sales to pay for a civic center, for instance. Excise taxes on large commercial trucks, diesel fuel, and truck tires help pay for highway maintenance. Taxes on alcohol help fund state programs to treat alcoholism.

Laws on taxing goods sold via the Internet are still evolving. Generally, these sales are exempt from sales tax. The main exception is **intrastate sales**—that is, sales made within the state where the company is physically located.

Goods that are traded internationally may be subject to tariffs. Some governments impose tariffs on imported goods to protect or strengthen a domestic industry by discouraging foreign competition. Exports may be taxed to encourage producers to satisfy the market at home rather than sell overseas. These taxes are sometimes controversial because they can restrict trade.

Business Income Tax

In many cases, income earned as a business owner is taxed in the same way as income earned as an employee. The business's income is the owner's personal income as well. This is true for sole proprietorships, partnerships, S corporations, and limited liability corporations (LLCs). For this reason, these types of businesses are called **pass-through businesses**.

The main difference, once again, is that the business owner is responsible for calculating and sending in these payments—not once a year, as an employee does, but throughout the year, even as they are earning income.

This is described as paying estimated taxes. Entrepreneurs predict what they will owe in income and payroll taxes and send in their payments each April, June, September, and January. Many business owners estimate conservatively, sending in the smallest amount necessary, to keep more money available for their business. They can also skip a payment if they believe they have no liability for that period. However, they need to be cautious or they may be penalized for underpaying. At year's end, they file a tax return, like any employee, to receive a refund or pay the balance of what they owe on their actual earnings.

For corporations other than S corporations and LLCs, taxation is more complex (and some believe less fair). C corporations are, in effect, taxed twice. First, a corporate income tax is assessed on the business's earnings. Then shareholders pay personal income tax on any corporate dividends received.

Property Tax

Entrepreneurs who own the land or building where their business operates are also subject to an annual commercial property tax. As with personal property, the tax rate for commercial property is set by the local government. Each government sets rates according to its own formula. In some areas, taxes are based on both the property's actual and potential value. Values rise in areas where homebuyers are building and the infrastructure is being improved, for example.

In addition, some states assess a tax on personal property used in business, including furniture, fixtures, supplies used for daily operations, and inventory held for sale.

U.S. Federal Revenue

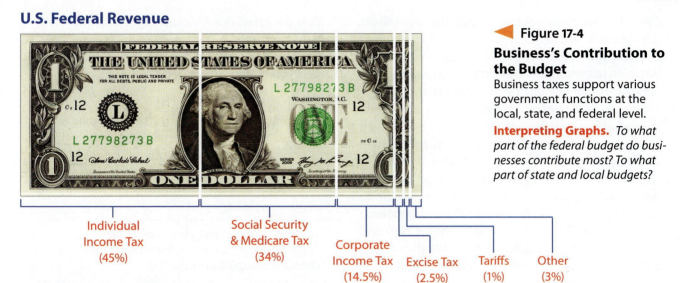

Individual Income Tax (45%)

Social Security & Medicare Tax (34%)

Corporate Income Tax (14.5%)

Excise Tax (2.5%)

Tariffs (1%)

Other (3%)

State & Local Revenues

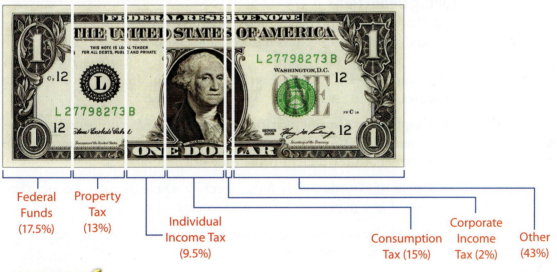

Federal Funds (17.5%)

Property Tax (13%)

Individual Income Tax (9.5%)

Consumption Tax (15%)

Corporate Income Tax (2%)

Other (43%)

◀ **Figure 17-4**

Business's Contribution to the Budget
Business taxes support various government functions at the local, state, and federal level.
Interpreting Graphs. *To what part of the federal budget do businesses contribute most? To what part of state and local budgets?*

READING CHECKPOINT *How does the government use payroll taxes?*

Tax-Saving Strategies

So far in this section, you've seen examples of how governments write tax laws to promote or discourage certain behaviors—by creating enterprise zones or taxing imports, for instance. When a government does this, it creates opportunities for **tax avoidance**, which amounts to using legal strategies to reduce one's tax liability. Unlike tax evasion, tax avoidance is taking advantage of what the law offers, and the law offers a lot to entrepreneurs who know where to look.

Self-Control

Every day, you make decisions about what you will do, who you will talk to, what you will eat, how you will conduct yourself, what you will read, what you will watch on television, and many other things. Most days are made up of one decision after another.

Having self-control means making conscious choices about how you will act in any situation, even in one you didn't expect. Having personal control over your emotions means not overreacting at school or work when something surprising—good or bad—happens. People with good self-control are able to keep a level head despite what may be happening around them. Those people may go home later and let it all out, but in a public environment, they stay in control of themselves and are even-tempered.

Most days at work will include highs and lows—and perhaps be extremely pressured. Keeping a level head and remaining in control of yourself will show those around you that you have good self-management.

THINKING CRITICALLY

Applying Concepts. How do you act in public when something exciting happens? When something upsetting happens? What is your typical reaction to news you did not expect? Do you think you exhibit good self-control? Do you think there are ways in which you could improve?

To read more about personal control, go to "Your Business Career" on the Student Center at entrepreneurship.pearson.com.

Taking Deductions

A **deduction** is an item or expense subtracted from your gross income in a tax return. Deductions reduce your taxes. Expenses that are considered "ordinary and necessary" for operating a business are typically tax-deductible. Utilities and rent, for example, are common business expenses. Others include:

- **Employees' Compensation.** You'll recall that compensation includes pay and benefits. Employers can deduct the wages and payments to retirement plans they offer employees.

- **Costs of Goods Sold.** A producer or wholesaler can deduct the cost of raw materials, labor, and storage of items sold.

- **Travel.** Reasonable deductions for transportation, meals, and lodging are all permitted.

- **Vehicle Use.** This includes the expense of maintenance, repairs, and mileage for business vehicles, and for personal vehicles when used for business purposes.

- **Taxes.** Business taxes, including consumption and property taxes, are themselves tax deductible.

- **Insurance.** Premiums for business insurance can be deducted. This includes, for example, policies that are associated with certain types of businesses, such as special insurance for employees who work in clients' homes.

- **Depreciation.** As you learned in Chapter 10, depreciation is a tax deduction that allows business owners to recover the cost of property used in the business. Any property that is used for over one year and loses value through wear or because it becomes outdated can be depreciated. A computer can be depreciated, for example, as can computer software.

In addition, new entrepreneurs can deduct start-up expenditures for up to five years after opening the business. That includes money spent on market research and scouting locations. Also, sole proprietors who aren't covered by an employer's insurance plan can deduct 100 percent of the premiums of private insurance. If you use part of your home to carry out any or all of your business activities, you can deduct a percentage of utilities and certain home-maintenance expenses.

Entrepreneurs who understand how deductions work can time spending and receipts to their advantage. For example, suppose your business is having a very profitable year and you expect a large tax liability. You could lighten the load by increasing the number of deductions. You might buy a needed copier this year rather than next, or put more money in a retirement plan. You could also reduce income by asking customers who owe money late in the year to delay payments until January.

Using Tax Credits

A **tax credit** is a dollar-for-dollar reduction in taxes owed. While a deduction lowers taxable income, a credit lowers the tax itself. Tax credits can be taken for a variety of business activities, from using green energy sources, to donating goods to a charitable group, to hiring those who are reentering society after serving time in prison. A small business may take a credit for making the workplace accessible to disabled workers, as required by the Americans with Disabilities Act.

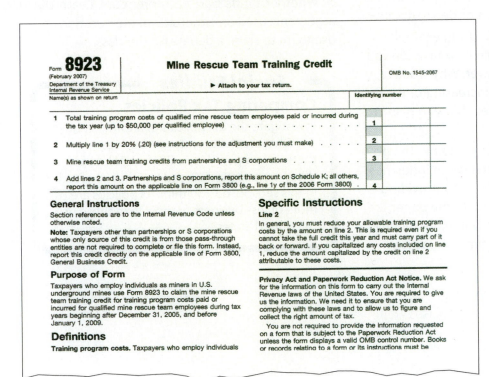

◄ **Figure 17-5**

Mine Rescue Team Training Credit
Staying current on tax credits that are useful only to a specific industry can pay off for an entrepreneur.

Solving Problems. *Some business activities are eligible for either a deduction or a credit. How would you go about making a decision about which to use?*

Tax credits tend to be less permanent than deductions. Standard deductions may remain the same from year to year. Credits are subject to phasing out, depending on how popular they are with taxpayers or how valuable they are to an industry.

 **READING CHECKPOINT** *What is a deduction?*

 Your Business Plan. Continue developing your standard business plan. Go to "Section 17.1" of the *Business Plan Project* in your *Student Activity Workbook*, or "Section 17.1" of the BizTech Software.

ASSESSMENT 17.1

Reviewing Objectives

1. List four general types of public services that taxes help pay for.

2. How do entrepreneurs pay estimated taxes?

3. What is the difference between tax evasion and tax avoidance?

Critical Thinking

4. **Comparing/Contrasting.** Many people believe that some services provided by government could be better handled by the private sector (for-profit businesses). Give arguments for and against this position, discussing specific agencies or departments.

5. **Recognizing Patterns.** Using examples from the chapter, explain how taxation can be used for political power. Why would a politician's position on increasing or decreasing taxes affect his or her ability to gain votes?

6. Write a short paper about whether the government should intervene when industries are not economically viable by providing them "stimulus packages." In the paper, address the question of where the money comes from for such a stimulus package.

7. Using the Internet, find out the total estimated national debt. Then determine the latest estimate for the U.S. population. Based on these two figures, calculate the amount of the national debt that that each citizen would pay, if individual citizens were responsible for the national debt.

Working Together

Taxes are a contentious topic on many fronts. Work with a partner to choose a tax-related issue, such as whether subsidies undermine the free market system, whether Social Security should be reformed, or whether tariffs hurt entrepreneurs. Learn the arguments used on either side of the question and use them to stage a debate for the class.

Social Studies
Comparing Tax Policies

Investigate the tax policies of another country. What are the tax rates on businesses there as compared to individuals? How are these monies used? Based on what you read in this section, do you think its policies are more or less business friendly than those of the United States?

SECTION 17.2 Government Regulations

OBJECTIVES

- Understand the role of government regulation
- Describe how laws require business owners to protect employees
- Recognize unfair business practices related to customers
- Describe requirements to protect the environment
- Describe government resources that help small business comply with regulations

VOCABULARY

- adulterated
- antitrust laws
- Fair Labor Standards Act
- license
- monopoly
- Occupational Safety and Health Administration (OSHA)
- permit
- price discrimination
- price fixing
- recall
- severance pay

Consider this question:

Would you be able to play a sport that had no rules?

Write your answer (yes or no) on a piece of paper. Be prepared to discuss your thinking in class.

The Role of Regulation

Entrepreneurs and government share a history in the United States that goes back to colonial times. If you wanted to start a company in the British colonies, you needed a charter from the British monarch. A charter was similar to today's articles of incorporation. It granted legal permission to carry out specified business activities. For example, the Hudson's Bay Company was founded in 1670. Its charter gave it "the whole, entire and only… Privilege of Trading and Trafficking to and from the Territories, Limits, and Places"—in other words, exclusive trading rights—with "all the Natives and Peoples inhabiting… within the Territories."

The charter also described the composition of the board of governors—whose head was also governor of the colony—and their duties. It spelled out members' voting rights and how they were to elect successors. It also forbade the Hudson's Bay Company from doing business in territories granted to another company without that governor's written permission, and authorized punishments for breaking the charter's rules.

In the newly independent United States, business was largely free from government oversight. No one wanted to stifle active trade and production. This freedom formed the basis of America's

▲ Figure 17-6

Industrialization
Industrialization in the mid-1800s brought rapid growth in industry—and in wealth.

Relating Concepts. *Why might rapid growth and the possibility of great wealth lead to unsafe workplaces and worker abuse?*

economic strength. In the 19th century, rapid growth through industrialization brought wealth. It was the mid-1800s version of today's technological revolution.

However, with this growth came abuses. Starting in the late 1800s, the U.S. government began to exert some control over industry. The argument for this was to protect smaller businesses from larger ones, to protect workers from unsafe work sites, to protect the health of the public, and to protect the environment. The process continues to this day.

Not only has the federal government attempted to control industry. But states have often passed their own laws, some of which have been stricter than the federal laws on which they were based.

Some entrepreneurs feel that regulation is an obstacle to growth. Some argue that the laws that seem to hinder the entrepreneur's dream are the same as those that promote the rights of the individual and thus make the realization of entrepreneurial dreams possible.

 READING CHECKPOINT ✓

What did a company's being "chartered" mean?

Employee Protection

Hazards in the workplace have always existed. However, they became more common, and more serious, as the United States went from a farming economy to one that was factory-based. The workforce has also grown more diverse, and employers have not always welcomed this diversity. Subsequently, laws were passed in an effort to ensure both workers' physical health and their career-advancement opportunities.

Workplace Safety

The **Occupational Safety and Health Administration (OSHA)** is the federal agency responsible for setting and enforcing standards of safety in the workplace. OSHA sets general standards that employers are expected to adjust to their own situations.

Some regulations that apply to many businesses include:

- Providing needed tools and equipment in good working order, and the training to use them.

- Supplying appropriate safety gear and garments.

- Documenting serious work-related illnesses, injuries, or accidents, their causes, and the number of workdays missed.

- Displaying posters telling employees of their right to work in a safe, healthful environment and to report possible violations.

- Giving workers access to records related to illness, injuries, or possible exposure to harmful substances in the workplace.

OSHA enforces its rules through workplace inspections. An inspection may be part of routine oversight or triggered by a complaint. Minor violations might bring only a warning. Serious offenses can easily result in thousands of dollars in fines, with follow-up inspections to ensure the problems have been corrected.

Employers have certain rights that go along with their responsibilities. They can contest inspectors' reports or ask to be exempted from certain standards. OSHA also has a nonretaliation policy, which states that employers who ask about health or safety policies are neither more nor less likely to be inspected for violations.

Fair Treatment

In 1840, President Martin Van Buren made a sweeping proclamation that, without any reduction in their current pay, federal employees could be made to work no more than ten hours a day.

The concept of fair treatment has grown considerably since then. The Equal Employment Opportunity Commission (EEOC) enforces

▼ **Figure 17-7**

Promoting Workplace Safety

OSHA provides posters like the one shown here to help employers comply with agency regulations.

Communicating. *Besides using posters, how can employers communicate safe procedures to employees?*

laws that promote a level playing field in the workplace. Fittingly, one of the first laws concerned hours and wages. The **Fair Labor Standards Act**, a federal law, guarantees most hourly workers a minimum hourly wage, a maximum number of hours worked, and extra pay for working overtime. Some states have a minimum wage that is higher than the national level and add requirements for lunch and rest breaks, pay periods, and severance pay. **Severance pay** is an amount of money given to employees when they are terminated for reasons other than performance.

Employees are also due time off. The Family Medical Leave Act gives them up to 12 weeks of unpaid leave a year after the birth or adoption of a child or the placement of a foster child. In cases of serious illness, they can take the same amount of time to care for a spouse, child, or parent—or themselves.

▼ **Figure 17-8**
Exceptions to the Rules
Some federal protections don't extend to employees in very small businesses or in certain agricultural jobs.

Drawing Conclusions. *Why might an employer offer these protections even if not legally required to do so?*

Employee protection against discrimination has grown as well. Landmark legislation, including the Civil Rights Act of 1964 and the Age Discrimination in Employment Act of 1967, outlaws discrimination based on age, gender, religion, race or ethnicity, or national origin. The Americans with Disabilities Act (ADA) of 1990 requires employers to provide reasonable accommodations to make the workplace and job duties more accessible for qualified workers with disabilities.

Antidiscrimination laws have had a far-reaching impact. For example, the Civil Rights Act forbids employers from making hiring decisions based on the assumption that married candidates are more responsible than unmarried ones. They cannot pass over an individual from a minority group for promotion. Employers are also responsible for creating an atmosphere of tolerance and respect in the workplace. Job ads that imply that older workers are not qualified for a position violate the Age Discrimination in Employment Act. The ADA also prevents employers from

Socially Responsible Investing

When you start planning for your retirement, you'll be investing some of your money. Investing is acquiring an asset with the expectation that it will rise in value over time. An asset could be land, art, or a share in a company. But where will you invest? Some people hire a financial advisor to help make choices. Others want to see not just a future profit but a social benefit. This sort of choice is called *socially responsible investing*, or SRI. Those who do this sort of investing generally look for companies with good records on the environment, human rights, diversity, and consumer protection.

In the 1960s and 1970s, SRI became increasingly widespread. Socially responsible investors sought to avoid companies that profited from war or human misfortune. Now the practice also focuses on avoiding companies that harm the environment, manufacture weapons, sell tobacco products, or conduct experiments on animals.

Some financial tools have developed in response to SRI. For example, some mutual funds consist only of socially responsible companies. About 11% of all assets that are professionally managed are considered socially responsible.

THINKING CRITICALLY

Predicting. In pairs, discuss what sort of investor you are. What kind of companies would you invest in? Is SRI important to you? Why?

To read more about socially responsible investing, go to "Entrepreneurship Issues" on the Student Center at entrepreneurship.pearson.com.

asking, during a job interview, how a candidate became disabled. They can't make taking a medical exam a condition of being hired unless it's required of all employees.

What qualities may not be used as a basis for hiring or firing decisions?

Customer Issues

Treating customers fairly is not only good business sense—it's the law. As a business owner, you are bound by laws regulating how you sell your goods or services, whether the customer is an international corporation or an individual consumer.

Labeling

Many people cannot remember when product labels were not covered with information. Some of this is legally required as a way to help customers make informed choices. The Fair Packaging and Labeling Act requires that all product packaging identify the item, its manufacturer, and the quantity, either in weight or number. The Food, Drug, and Cosmetic Act and its various amendments forbid any false or deceptive labeling. A product is also considered mislabeled if it leaves out essential information.

Other requirements vary depending on the product. Most packaged foods require an ingredients list and nutrition facts. Any health-related claims must meet the definition set by the Food and Drug

Administration (FDA) and the U.S. Department of Agriculture (USDA). The label must warn if the product contains, or may have had contact with, foods that are major allergens (allergy-causing ingredients).

Products that contain hazardous substances, from laundry detergent to pesticides, must be labeled with safety-related information. Manufacturers must describe the dangers associated with the product, its proper use and precautions, and first-aid or emergency treatment if it's misused or mishandled.

Product Safety

The FDA and the USDA are also concerned with food and drug safety. They forbid the sale of **adulterated** products—those containing harmful substances, processed in ways that may be harmful to health, or modified to mask poor quality. Some cases of adulteration that you may have heard of are meats or vegetables contaminated with the *E. coli* bacteria and pet foods containing the poisonous chemical melamine.

The task of regulating most other products falls mainly to the U.S. Consumer Product Safety Commission (CPSC), which sets standards for about 15,000 consumer goods. (Along with food products and drugs, major exceptions are motor vehicles, alcohol, and medical devices.) For example, CPSC requires that infants' toys must have no small parts that could pose a choking hazard. Fabrics must be flame-resistant. Packaging for drugs must be child-resistant.

If a manufacturer learns that one of its products does not meet these standards, whether by design or from some defect or flaw, it should issue a recall. A **recall** is a notice for customers to return a product that poses a risk of injury or illness. Recalls are not required, but businesses that learn of problems and don't act to correct them face serious consequences. The CPSC may ban the item from the market and the business can be held liable for the harm it causes. The damage to the firm's reputation may be beyond repair.

Fair Competition

A free market needs competition, and fair competition needs honest, accurate advertising. The Federal Trade Commission (FTC) enforces detailed truth-in-advertising laws that cover promotion in all of its forms, including endorsements, testimonials, sales, and special pricing. The FTC requires ads to be:

- **Truthful and Nondeceptive.** An ad must not mislead customers on any significant point that would affect their buying decision. For example, an item shown must be available for sale.

- **Supported by Evidence.** Business must have proof of any stated or implied claims. Health claims must be backed by scientific research. Letters from "satisfied customers" must be made available to confirm that the writers actually exist.

The FDA and USDA are concerned with food safety.

- **Fair.** An ad must not lead customers to "substantial injury," as by not mentioning possible dangers, conditions or requirements, or unwanted outcomes that customers could not have foreseen. Customers must be told about any added fees that increase the advertised price.

Price fixing is another anticompetitive practice. **Price fixing** refers to competing companies agreeing to set the price of goods or services or the terms of business deals. All of the growers at a farmers market might decide to charge the same price for their produce, for instance, or to give the same discount to restaurant buyers.

A similar practice is price discrimination. **Price discrimination** is charging competing buyers different prices for the same product. This is illegal only when used intentionally, to favor one customer over another. It would not be illegal to charge different prices to buyers in different parts of the state to stay competitive with the market in each area.

A monopoly is another illegal obstacle to fair competition. A **monopoly** describes the situation where a single supplier becomes a market's only provider of a certain product. This is sometimes called "cornering the market."

To combat monopolies and similar schemes, the FTC uses **antitrust laws**, which forbid anticompetitive mergers and business practices. (A trust is a type of business ownership that used a legal technicality to evade laws against monopolies.) The oldest is the Sherman Act of 1890, which outlaws "every contract, combination, or conspiracy in restraint of trade or commerce." The Clayton Act of 1914, and several later laws, have reinforced those restrictions.

Although antitrust laws are not used often, the penalties can be severe. Fines start at a million dollars for an individual, with prison sentences up to ten years.

Licenses and Permits

Many business owners need some kind of license. A **license** is a legal document issued by a state or local government that allows a business to provide a regulated product or service. It gives consumers assurance that a business or individual meets standards of professionalism and reliability, such as a beauty salon or a physician. Certain highly regulated industries require national (federal) licenses. These include broadcasting, investment consulting, and meats preparation.

▲ **Figure 17-9**

Price Fixing
Vendors cannot agree to charge the same price for the same product.

Predicting. *If you knew that a competitor priced a similar product at a specific price, how would you price your product?*

Licensing usually requires some type of certification, either from the state or a professional group. For example, some states require athletic trainers to be accredited by a Board of Certification for the Athletic Trainer. To become a licensed building contractor, you may need to pass a state exam testing your knowledge of engineering, electrical systems, and carpentry.

A **permit** is a legal document that allows a business to take a specific action. As a homebuilder, you might need several permits for a house: one for putting in a driveway, perhaps, and another to close street lanes in the construction area. Permits are generally issued by local governments.

Zoning Laws

Zoning laws, also called ordinances, are designed to help ensure that businesses are good neighbors in the community. Some laws determine the areas where a business can locate and the activities it can carry out there. A sheep farm would be located in an agricultural zone, while a textile factory that turns the wool into fabric operates in an industrial zone. A shop that sells the fabric would be sited in a commercial zone. A seamstress who makes clothing from the fabric for individual clients might run the business from home, in a residential zone. Other laws relate to a property's physical appearance, including the building's size, the number of parking spaces, and the type of signage allowed.

A recent trend in city planning is the creation of "walkable" cities, where small businesses are placed within walking distance of private

▼ **Figure 17-10**
Zoning Laws
Zoning laws determine where certain types of businesses can be located.

Drawing Conclusions. *How might zoning laws help businesses? Consumers? Neighbors? The locality?*

homes. The goal is to strengthen the residents' sense of community, reduce the need and impact of motor traffic, and increase opportunities for physical exercise.

 *What three qualities does the FTC require of advertisements?*

Environmental Protection

Business owners must be aware of laws designed to reduce the harmful impact they may have on the environment. Many of these regulations are set by the U.S. Environmental Protection Agency (EPA). These cover a wide range of business activities in almost every field.

- Under the Clean Air Act, for example, factories with smokestacks are limited in the types and amounts of chemicals they are permitted to release into the atmosphere.

- Farmers must learn whether they can burn crop stubble in their fields without damaging air quality.

- The owner of a road-construction firm has to avoid causing traffic delays that increase pollutants over the legal level.

- The Clean Water Act may require a business to get a permit to discharge wastewater (water left over from almost any human activity, including washing hands). Receiving permission depends on the amount of water released and the substances it contains.

- Builders who want to develop land near a wildlife preserve may need to submit plans to lessen the impact on the plant and animal life, in accordance with the Endangered Species Act.

Punishment for violating EPA laws can be costly. A business can be fined thousands of dollars each day until it meets standards.

 *What is the EPA?*

Help for Small Businesses

Following all these regulations could be an overwhelming task for many new entrepreneurs. Fortunately, some exceptions exist for small businesses. For instance, employers with fewer than 10 employees are not required to document minor workplace accidents. Businesses with fewer than 15 workers are exempt from some provisions of the Americans with Disabilities Act. Food sellers with less than $50,000 a year in sales don't need to include all nutrition information on labels.

As mentioned earlier, tax credits are available for businesses that follow sustainable practices, which help them meet EPA standards. Other tax credits offset some of the expenses of complying with the Americans with Disabilities Act.

The conditions for these and other types of aid can be complex. It's wise to consult the enforcing agency for exact details. Small business owners may also find these agencies their best resources for learning how to meet particular regulations.

Regulating agencies sometimes look to small businesses to assist them in developing rules and guidelines. OSHA, for example, has set up Small Business Advisory Review Panels to hear business owners' input on developing safety standards. The Equal Employment Opportunity Commission recognizes that small businesses are often the best setting for disabled workers, especially those looking for their first job. The agency can suggest affordable ways to make the workplace accessible.

 *What three general types of aid help small businesses comply with government regulations?*

 Your Business Plan. Continue developing your standard business plan. Go to "Section 17.2" of the *Business Plan Project* in your *Student Activity Workbook*, or "Section 17.2" of the BizTech Software.

ASSESSMENT 17.2

Reviewing Objectives

1. Name four industry abuses that the government began to try to control in the late 1800s.
2. List five employer duties mandated by OSHA.
3. What is the difference between price fixing and price discrimination?
4. Identify three business activities that are regulated by the EPA.
5. What kinds of help in meeting government regulations do agencies offer small business?

Critical Thinking

6. **Applying Information.** Based on what you read in this section about monopolies and the FTC, explain why communication companies are limited in the number of media outlets (such as radio stations and newspapers) they can own in one community.
7. **Recognizing Patterns.** Given the purpose of licensing, explain why each of the following should have a license: a teacher, a lawyer, a restaurant owner, an auto mechanic.

Working Together

With a partner, identify some concerns that a homeowner might have about a small business opening in the neighborhood—for example, noise and traffic. First identify the type of business that would be opening. Then devise a plan that a business owner could carry out to address the potential problem areas.

Science
Assistive Technology

Assistive technology involves products that help people with disabilities function in mainstream society. Research these developments and choose a product that would be helpful in accommodating disabled employees. Examples might include eye-controlled communication devices and keyboard-modification software. Present your findings to the class, including a brief explanation of how the product works and your reasons for choosing it.

Bling-Bling Discount Fashion Jewelry

"When I was 14, I got my working papers, and I wanted to work right away," said Natasha Spedalle. She went to some retail stores in her Queens, NY, neighborhood, but found that no one would hire her because she was too young. "I thought if nobody was going to hire me, I was going to start something myself."

To decide what to do, Natasha looked around—literally. At the time, she was taking a summer class at the Fashion Institute of Technology in Manhattan. To get to school, she had to walk through the city's wholesale district. Buying wholesale and selling retail looked like the answer!

To buy wholesale merchandise, Natasha needed a tax ID number. Once she had it, she was able to begin her career as an entrepreneur. Her first venture was selling make-up at flea markets, but the make-up melted in the sun. She then turned to jewelry.

Natasha's company, Bling-Bling DFJ, offers trendy jewelry at discounted prices. "I'm all about making a collection," said Natasha. It's her selection of pieces—necklaces, bracelets, earrings, and rings—that makes her jewelry attractive to buyers. Natasha reads 20 fashion magazines a month to discover the latest trends. "I carry a very low inventory so I can keep the new trends rolling in."

How Young Is Too Young?

Natasha started by selling her jewelry in church basement flea markets. "Then I decided I wanted more traffic," she said. "I wasn't getting enough people, so I branched out into street fairs." With her mother's help, she found out what she needed to do. At 15, Natasha became the youngest person in New York City to receive a street fair vending license.

Although entering entrepreneurship contests led to recognition and publicity, Natasha's youth was a drawback. "My age was a big issue when it came to getting ahead. It's hard to be taken seriously when you're so young," Natasha remembers. "I had to show that I was mature enough, that I actually meant business and that my age wasn't a factor in my business dealings. I just went in there with confidence and I

Natasha Spedalle

did what I had to do. You have to be determined and not really let anything get you down."

Expanding Her Business

After selling at street fairs for a year, Natasha found a new venue to sell her jewelry—college campuses. "It's a great market because college women are very interested in the jewelry I have to offer." Along with colleges, Natasha has also expanded to selling in stores on consignment. With consignment, she makes money only if the jewelry sells. So far, it's been successful. "I like the connection that you have when you sell at colleges and get to meet your customers, but right now, while I'm in college, I don't always have the time to do that. So, it's really great to have my stuff in stores where they're selling it for me while I'm concentrating on my school work."

Thinking Like an Entrepreneur

1. Natasha keeps abreast of trends by reading fashion magazines. What other ways could she use to know what's going to be popular?
2. How would you overcome the drawbacks of being a young entrepreneur?
3. Natasha has sold her jewelry in several locations: flea markets, street fairs, college campuses, and stores. What do you think might be the good and bad points about each type of location?

CHAPTER SUMMARY

17.1 Taxes and Your Business

Businesses pays taxes for government services. These include public transportation and highways, social programs, national defense, and assistance for business itself. Business payroll taxes fund workers' insurance and retirement; unemployment taxes aid workers who have lost their jobs; sales taxes are collected on products and services sold and sent to state governments. Businesses pay income tax on their profits and property tax on buildings and inventory. Businesses can reduce their tax payments by taking deductions and using tax credits.

17.2 Government Regulations

Governments regulate business to make the free market more open and fair and to protect workers, customers, and the environment. Business owners are legally bound to create a workplace that is free of physical hazards and discriminatory practices. They must give customers accurate information to make informed choices and safe products. They cannot use tactics that prevent free and fair competition or act in ways that threaten the environment.

REVIEW VOCABULARY

Working in a small group, write a scene showing a session from the fictitious Court of Bad Business Owners. Include the roles of a judge and owners of various businesses, who are appearing to argue their cases. Incorporate at least 12 of the following terms in the script, illustrating their meaning in the dialog and in the sentence that the judge passes on the violators.

- adulterated (p. 476)
- antitrust laws (p. 477)
- deduction (p. 468)
- enterprise zone (p. 462)
- excise tax (p. 466)
- Fair Labor Standards Act (p. 474)
- infrastructure (p. 459)
- intrastate sales (p. 466)
- license (p. 477)
- monopoly (p. 477)
- Occupational Safety and Health Administration (OSHA) (p. 473)
- pass-through business (p. 466)
- permit (p. 478)
- price discrimination (p. 477)
- price fixing (p. 477)
- recall (p. 476)
- sales tax (p. 465)
- severance pay (p. 474)
- subsidy (p. 460)
- tax avoidance (p. 467)
- tax credit (p. 469)
- tax evasion (p. 464)
- taxes (p. 459)
- tax-increment financing (p. 462)

CHECK YOUR UNDERSTANDING

Choose the letter that best answers the question or completes the statement.

1. Enterprise zones are created to
   a. accommodate workers with disabilities
   b. protect the environment
   c. encourage business development
   d. avoid paying taxes

2. Lawful tax deductions for entrepreneurs include
   a. cost of goods sold
   b. your personal car
   c. your children's education expenses
   d. a spouse's retirement fund

3. Taxes pay for
   a. roads
   b. the National Guard
   c. Social Security
   d. all of the above

4. One free source of information on worker safety guidelines is
   a. the FTC
   b. a business attorney
   c. OSHA
   d. the state licensing agency

5. Consumption taxes are paid on
   a. business property
   b. goods and services sold
   c. imported goods
   d. employees' wages

6. OSHA regulations require a business owner to
   a. eliminate discrimination
   b. provide severance pay
   c. give employees paid vacations
   d. train employees to use equipment properly

7. The goal of government regulation is to
   a. control business development
   b. balance the rights of different groups in society
   c. favor certain industries over others
   d. discourage competition by foreign companies

8. To avoid fines from the EPA, a business owner should
   a. pay required sales taxes
   b. rearrange work areas to accommodate workers with disabilities
   c. use green business practices when possible
   d. randomly check product labels for accuracy

9. FICA taxes are paid by
   a. sole proprietors
   b. corporations
   c. employees
   d. all of the above

10. Subsidies are used to
    a. limit competition
    b. make services more affordable
    c. lower income taxes
    d. none of the above

11. An auto dealer charges higher interest rates on car loans to large companies in the belief that they have more money than smaller ones. This could be an example of
    a. deceptive advertising
    b. a subsidy
    c. price fixing
    d. price discrimination

12. Entrepreneurs estimate taxes so they can
    a. pay what they owe over the course of the year
    b. reduce their overall tax liability
    c. avoid paying taxes on dividends
    d. all of the above

Business Communication

13. Working with a partner, obtain a copy of an IRS tax form for business and the instructions for filling it out (available online at irs.gov). Examples are Form 1120S (U.S. Income Tax for an S Corporation) and Form 1040, Schedule F (Profit or Loss from Farming). In a brief report, explain the purpose of the form and any problems you would have if you were a business owner filling it out. Then write suggestions for making the form easier to use.

14. OSHA requires employers to eliminate recognized hazards, which it describes as "causing or likely to cause death or serious physical harm." Look around school. Do you find any hazards? List and rank these in order of dangerousness.

15. Read print ads or take notes while watching television advertising. Evaluate them on the three criteria set forth by the FTC. Are the ads truthful? Fair? Are the claims supported? Choose one written and one televised ad and write a critique of each.

Business Ethics

18. Imagine that you are a restaurant owner. The city council is weighing a proposal to increase the excise tax on alcohol, with the added money going for a program to educate teens on underage drinking. Alcohol sales account for a large portion of your income. Paying the tax will cut significantly into profits. You could raise your prices to help pay the increased tax, but you're afraid this may hurt your business. You're torn! You strongly believe that teens must make educated choices about drinking. The president of the local restaurant association asks you to speak against the proposal at the next city council meeting. What is your position on the proposal? What would you tell her?

Business Math

16. The current FICA tax rate is 6.2 percent for Social Security and 1.45 percent for Medicare. If you employ one worker at an $18,000 annual salary, what amount is deducted from your employee's salary and sent to Social Security? To Medicare? How much will your company pay for each of these? What is the total amount you will be sending to the government?

17. In one state, the annual fee for a business license is $65 plus $1 for every $800 in gross receipts. Imagine that you own an apiary (a honeybee colony). You earned $26,000 in honey sales last year. Sales of bee-themed merchandise brought in another $1,700. Beeswax candles added another $1,100. What were your gross receipts? What was your annual license fee?

Business in Your Community

19. Interview area business owners about the impact of local, state, and federal laws on their business decisions. For example, have property taxes or sales taxes affected their choice of location? Has complying with safety and ADA requirements influenced workplace design and daily routines? Have labeling and safety laws influenced their choices about what products and services they offer?

20. Ask a local business owner for a cost analysis of complying with one of the laws described in the chapter. For example, how much time does he or she spend calculating and sending in payroll taxes? What costs are involved in maintaining safety standards? What are the business's productivity costs of granting family and medical leave?

Generating Leads

As you've learned, a lead is a potential customer, and every business, whether operated from a home, a store, or online, is interested in gathering leads. Businesses try to get **contact information,** such as names, street and e-mail addresses, and phone numbers, to let people know about offers on products and services. The Web offers new opportunities for **lead-generation**—the process of obtaining leads—and all types of businesses are using the Internet to find new customers.

Site Registration

Typically, businesses want leads from their target market: those consumers most likely to buy their goods and services. For example, there's no sense getting a list of leads for hair dye if the men on the list are bald.

One good way to generate leads is through **site registration**, because Web surfers visiting a site are more likely to be interested in the products and services it offers. Site registration usually involves signing up by providing an e-mail address. After registering, the user can take full advantage of the site and look over everything it has to offer. The Website owner now has the surfer's e-mail address for contacting that individual again.

An online registration form may include a message such as *Click here if you would like to receive additional offers*. This allows the Website owner to contact the person more often. An **opt-out** denies permission for the business to make future contact. Opt-out statements often appear at the bottom of promotional e-mails, like this: *Click here if you do not want to receive these messages*. Never keep someone on your mailing list who asks to be taken off.

Providing Free Information to Generate Leads

Webinars, short for Web-based seminars or lectures where there is interaction between the presenters and the audience, and **Webcasts**, presentations where there is no interaction, are frequently used by large companies to provide free information to interested parties. They are also great places for the companies to get leads, as each attendee needs to register. Another way to find

leads is by talking about your product or service at an online blogging site, such as Blogger.com. At the end of your entry, you can put in a link to your Website.

Lead-Generation Services

Building up a large number of leads can be time consuming, so some business owners go to lead-generation services. These businesses sell **lead lists**—contact information for potential customers—to Website owners. These lead-generation services offer various kinds of lists, some based on geographical data, others on whether the individual has previously purchased the same kind of product. The conversion rate (getting sales from the leads) often depends on the *quality* of the list. Bad lead lists include out-of-date information or consumers who simply would not be interested.

No matter how you find your leads, you will need to follow up. If a lead has requested more information from your Website, send out an automatic e-mail immediately, letting the person know that the information is on the way and thanking them for visiting the site. Generating leads is the first step in making a sale.

Tech Vocabulary
- contact information
- lead generation
- lead lists
- opt-out
- site registration
- Webcasts
- Webinars

Check Yourself
1. Name two ways to get leads.
2. What is an opt-out?
3. What is the difference between a Webinar and a Webcast?
4. What are lead lists?

What Do You Think?
Analyzing. Which method would you use to generate leads?

BUILDING THE BUSINESS

Eva's Edibles is now in its third year of business. After a slow start, Eva's company is a success! Now she's making adjustments that she thinks will make her even more successful. Find out how Eva is changing her business.

Growing and Changing

The start-up investment for Eva's Edibles was low compared to many new businesses. Because Eva initially used personal savings, she was able to bootstrap her business. She did the cooking in her clients' kitchens. She used her own car for making trips to the grocery store. She had only needed to purchase small kitchen appliances, some utensils and basic supplies, and business cards and brochures.

But Eva wanted to grow her business. She wanted more clients. To do this so it would be cost-effective, she would have to lease a commercial kitchen. She could then deliver prepared dinners to her clients.

To shop for groceries and to make deliveries, Eva would also need a van that was outfitted with shelves and refrigerated storage compartments.

Eva realized that she would need additional financing to expand her operations. She applied for a loan from the teacher's credit union to which her mother belonged. Her parents were proud of Eva's success and agreed to co-sign the loan.

There was another aspect to building her business—Sylvia Watson joined Eva's Edibles. Sylvia was a chef who specialized in pastries and desserts (an area where Eva was not strong). Sylvia had skills and experience and also some cash savings that she could immediately invest. She was interested in joining an existing business rather than starting her own.

When Sylvia and Eva discovered they had similar philosophies, they decided to become business partners. with Eva having sixty percent of the shares and Sylvia forty percent. They also agreed to continue doing business as Eva's Edibles.

Improving Record Keeping

Eva noticed how often she became bogged down with paperwork. Using her generic spreadsheet software just wasn't working anymore. Sylvia, who had worked for a catering company at one time, was familiar with a specialized software package that could help Eva's Edibles be more efficient.

This software made figuring out the cost of a meal's ingredients much easier. Eva and Sylvia could calculate the cost of a meal by entering the price of each ingredient directly into the computerized recipes. They could also use the software to draw up contracts, track customer prospects, create invoices, and run customized reports.

Hiring Help

Eva and Sylvia felt they needed two part-time employees—one would help with prep work in the kitchen and the other with deliveries. Prepping the food took a significant amount of time and involved a great deal of trimming, cutting, peeling, chopping, weighing, and measuring. So Eva and Sylvia decided they would advertise for a cook who had excellent knife skills and was good with details. They also advertised for a part-time driver. They created job descriptions and agreed on the type and amount of compensation. Then they placed advertisements online and in the local newspapers. Eventually they found the right employees.

Protecting the Business

When Eva started the business, she had a small insurance policy to cover her few pieces of equipment and product liability in case a client became ill from the food. Now, with the leased commercial kitchen and employees, she needed additional liability and property insurance. Sylvia pointed out that Eva's Edibles might also need workers' compensation insurance if they kept growing.

Keeping the Government Happy

Eva and Sylvia hired an accountant with business expertise to review their financial records regularly and make sure their taxes were paid on time. They wanted to take advantage of all the tax deductions for which their business was eligible. Eva wanted to buy a hybrid van for the business, not just because it was "greener" but also because she heard they could get a special tax credit.

What Would You Have Done?

1. **Inferring.** If you were Sylvia, would you have wanted to change the name of the company? Explain your answer.
2. **Comparing/Contrasting.** Compare specialized software programs for catering, such as CaterEdge (www.cateredgesoftware.com), CaterEase (www.caterease.com), and Visual Synergy (www.synergy-intl.com). Which would you recommend?
3. **Writing.** How would you write an ad for the prep-cook position that Eva and Sylvia wanted to fill?
4. **Applying Concepts.** Research product liability for a company like Eva's Edibles. What level of insurance would you choose? What might the annual premium be?
5. **Analyzing Information.** Would you buy a hybrid van because it was "green" and to get a special tax credit? Explain your answer.

UNIT **7**

MANAGING YOUR BUSINESS

YOUR BUSINESS PLAN

In this unit, you'll focus on the **Business Management** section of the business plan and answer these questions:

- How will I manage my business?
- How do I manage expenses, credit and cash flow?
- How do I manage production and distribution?
- How will I manage my operations?
- How do I manage purchasing?
- How do I manage inventory?

CHAPTER

18

WHAT IS MANAGEMENT?

OBJECTIVES

- Learn about management functions
- Study the management function of planning
- Examine the management function of organizing
- Investigate the management function of directing
- Explore the management function of controlling
- Understand the importance of a healthy business environment

VOCABULARY

- authoritarian leadership style
- company image
- controlling
- delegating leadership style
- democratic leadership style
- directing
- interpersonal skills
- management
- operational plan
- organizing
- planning
- quality control program
- strategic plan
- tactical plan
- team building
- workplace climate

Consider the following question:

Are you a leader?

Write your answer (yes or no) on a piece of paper. Be prepared to discuss your answer in class.

What Is Management?

Once an entrepreneur creates a business and gets it running, he or she takes over management of the business. **Management** is the skillful use and coordination of all the business's resources—money, facilities, equipment, technologies, materials, employees—in a systematic and effective way to achieve particular goals.

A manager has authority over employees and is ultimately responsible for their work. He or she must use many skills in this role but, mostly, a manager is a creative problem solver. The purpose of management is not just to achieve business goals but to achieve them with the greatest efficiency. This means maximizing production while minimizing expenses. Experts break down the job of a manager into four general functions.

Management Functions
- Planning
- Organizing
- Directing
- Controlling

READING CHECKPOINT *What is management?*

Planning

Planning is an ongoing process of setting goals, deciding when and how to accomplish them, and determining how best to accomplish them. A *plan* is a systematic process for achieving a specific goal.

Three types of plans are used in business management:

- **Strategic Plan.** A **strategic plan** lays out a broad course of action to achieve a long-term goal, typically three to five years in the future. These plans are usually created by top-level managers with a big-picture view of what needs to be done and the general way in which it will be accomplished.

- **Tactical Plan.** A **tactical plan** outlines specific major steps for carrying out the strategic plan. Tactical plans typically cover a time period of less than a year and include target dates for accomplishing goals. Tactical plans are usually laid out by mid-level managers who analyze the big picture of the strategic plan and choose the major steps needed to achieve it.

- **Operational Plan.** An **operational plan** details the everyday activities that will achieve the goals of the tactical plan (and thus, ultimately, the strategic plan). Operational plans are short-range, covering days, weeks, or at most, months. These plans are typically drawn up by low-level managers—usually supervisors—who are very familiar with the actual day-to-day workings of the business. Supervisors know the capabilities of their employees and the exact tasks that will be required to accomplish the goals of the tactical plan.

READING CHECKPOINT *What is planning?*

Organizing

Organizing is an ongoing process of arranging and coordinating resources and tasks to achieve specific goals. Organizing creates structure. It puts the people and other resources of a business in the right places and in the right combinations to maximize production and minimize expenses.

One of the most important aspects of organizing is choosing and hiring the best employees, training them properly, and assigning them authority and responsibilities. Managers create organization charts that outline the chains of command within the business and the working

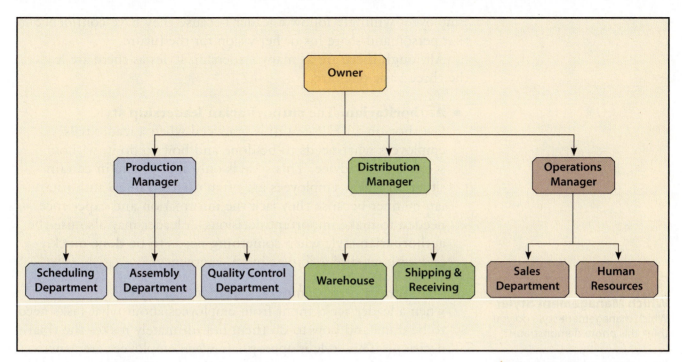

▲ Figure 18-1
Organization Chart
Organizing creates structure. An organization chart shows the chain of command and the relationships between departments.
Interpreting Illustrations.
Which manager is directly responsible for the warehouse?

relationships between different groups of people. Physical resources must also be organized. These include raw materials, machinery and other equipment, and inventory. Lastly, managers organize all the processes, duties, activities, and everyday operations that make a business successful.

Planning and organizing are interrelated. Planning a project is pointless if you cannot obtain and organize the people and materials needed to make it work. On the other hand, you cannot organize people and materials effectively without proper planning.

 *What is organizing?*

Directing

Directing is an ongoing process of leading, influencing, and motivating employees so they will work together to achieve specific goals. Leaders must have good **interpersonal skills**. These are skills used by people as they interact with others, particularly in a one-on-one setting. They include communicating clearly, listening, having a positive attitude, and behaving politely. Communication skills are particularly important. Leaders who communicate well with their employees build connections that help ensure the success of the business.

The ultimate goal of directing is **team building**, which is motivating individuals in a group to work together to achieve a shared goal. Leaders build teams. A good manager is not necessarily a good leader. Employees may obey a manager because he or she has authority.

Employees willingly follow a leader because they have confidence in that person and share his or her vision for the future.

Although there are as many leadership styles as there are leaders, the three basic ones are:

- **Authoritarian.** The <mark>authoritarian leadership style</mark> (aw-thor-uh-TEHR-ee-un) is practiced when a leader tells employees what needs to be done and how to do it, without seeking their advice. This style is only appropriate in certain situations. New employees are often directed in an authoritarian manner because they lack the information and experience needed to make important decisions. A leader may also use the authoritarian style when something needs to be done quickly and without discussion (as in an emergency).

- **Democratic.** The <mark>democratic leadership style</mark> is practiced when a leader seeks input from employees about what tasks need to be done and how to do them but ultimately makes the final decisions. This style is appropriate when employees are experienced and knowledgeable about their jobs. Their input may be valuable to the leader, but the leader, as the manager, bears final responsibility for the success of their performance.

▼ **Figure 18-2**

Which Management Style?
Which management style do you think this photo demonstrates?

Interpreting Illustrations.
Imagine the background story behind this photo. There are no right or wrong answers. Just explain your interpretation of the situation.

- **Delegating.** The <mark>delegating leadership style</mark> is practiced when a leader gives employees complete freedom to decide what tasks need to be done and how to do them. Obviously this style will only prove successful with experienced and knowledgeable employees who have demonstrated their ability to think and work independently. A leader who delegates responsibilities to trusted employees is able to tackle other, more pressing matters. This can be a very effective time-management tool.

In reality, good leaders choose and adjust their leadership styles depending on the situation. For example, they might lead a new employee in an authoritarian manner to ensure that he or she learns a task properly. They might use a democratic style and ask more experienced employees for suggestions about how to complete a task more efficiently. And they might delegate a task to the most skilled and trusted employees and ask them to accomplish it as they see fit.

Planning, organizing, and directing are all interrelated. A group of well-organized people with a solid plan will not be successful without good leadership. They must become a team with a shared goal and have a leader they want to follow.

READING CHECKPOINT ✓ *What is directing?*

ENTREPRENEURSHIP ISSUES

Think Fridays

When does innovation happen? We can never really know when a new idea will strike. Even entrepreneurs, who are known for their inventiveness, need to make time to sit and simply *think*. At IBM, a new business practice has been instituted to let all employees do just that. "Think Fridays" consist of a block of time in which meetings, e-mails, phone calls, and instant messaging stop. This time is set aside for problem solving and idea building. The company wants to give its employees the freedom to work on projects that might otherwise get pushed to the weekends, or never worked on at all.

Think Fridays give employees the time to talk to mentors or experiment with a new product. Cutting down on distraction is an important way for business leaders to foster not only a productive workplace but

also one in which their employees are happier. Intel has introduced a similar concept called Zero E-Mail Fridays, and engineers at 3M are encouraged to devote 15 percent of their time to freethinking. In this age of multitasking, mandates to set time aside to focus will lead to the one thing entrepreneurship cannot live without—new ideas.

THINKING CRITICALLY

Relating concepts. In small groups, discuss times in which a good idea has come to you. What were you doing then? Do you believe it's necessary to make time to sit and think?

To read more about Think Fridays, go to "Entrepreneurial Issues" on the Student Center at entrepreneurship.pearson.com.

Controlling

Controlling is an ongoing process of setting performance standards, measuring actual performance, comparing it to the standards, and taking corrective action if actual performance does not meet the standards.

A business has many components for which performance standards can be set: production, expenses, customer service, employee actions, equipment, finances, inventory levels, product quality, profits, and sales. In all cases, the standards and the components to which they apply should be quantifiable and specific, as with, say, the number of sales per day per employee. That way, actual performance can be easily compared to a standard.

Many businesses use the controlling management function to monitor the quality of the goods or services they sell. A **quality control program** is used by a business to ensure that its products or services meet specific quality standards. For example, a clothing manufacturer might set a quality standard for the number of straight seams sewn in a garment.

The most difficult component of controlling is usually implementing the appropriate corrective action. Equipment that is not meeting standards may be easy to fix. But most business tasks are accomplished by people, not machines. This explains why controlling is closely related to the other three management functions. Effective leadership of an organized team with a sound plan helps ensure that corrective action is applied successfully.

 *What is controlling?*

Maintaining a Healthy Business Environment

Workplace climate refers to the general feeling in a business, and is shaped by the psychological states and attitudes of the people who work there. Workplace climate is affected by many circumstances, including such things as interpersonal relationships, job security, and pay levels. Managers play a major role in shaping the workplace climate. Businesses that successfully implement the four management functions—planning, organizing, directing, and controlling—are much more likely to create a healthy environment.

A **company image** is the perception (thoughts, attitudes, opinions, and beliefs) that the public holds about a company. Companies build image every time they interact with the public. Logos, signs, Websites, store layout, business cards and letterhead, product choices and packaging, advertising, publicity, customer relations—even the way employees dress—contribute to a company's image. Companies try to create and foster images that fit the vision of how they want to be identified in

BEST COMPANIES TO WORK FOR

Rank	Company	Job Growth	U.S. Employees
1.	NetApp	12%	5,014
2.	Edward Jones	9%	34,496
3.	Boston Consulting Group	10%	16,80
4.	Google	40%	12,580
5.	Wegmans Food Markets	6%	37,195
6.	Cisco Systems	7%	37,123
7.	Genentech	5%	10,969
8.	Methodist Hospital System	1%	10,535
9.	Goldman Sachs	2%	14,088
10.	Nugget Market	22%	1,536
11.	Adobe Systems	9%	4,255
12.	Recreational Equipment (REI)	11%	9,780
13.	Devon Energy	11%	3,752
14.	Robert W. Baird	4%	2,184
15.	W. L. Gore & Associates	5%	5,481
16.	Qualcomm	19%	11,932
17.	Principal Financial Group	−1%	13,343
18.	Shared Technologies	12%	1,568
19.	OhioHealth	7%	11,858
20.	SAS	5%	5,381

Rankings from *Fortune,* February 2009

▲ **Figure 18-3**

Best Companies to Work For
Being identified as one of the best companies to work for enhances a company's image.

Predicting. *If you were a person choosing a company to work for, and you were choosing between one of these companies and one that didn't make the list, which would you prefer?*

the marketplace. A good company image is not only good for business; it also makes employees proud to be associated with the company and contributes to a positive workplace climate.

 **READING CHECKPOINT**   *What is workplace climate?*

Your Business Plan. Continue developing your standard business plan. Go to "Section 18.1" of the *Business Plan Project* in your *Student Activity Workbook*, or "Section 18.1" of the BizTech Software.

ASSESSMENT 18.1

Reviewing Objectives

1. What are the four management functions?
2. What are three types of plans used by businesses?
3. What does organizing create?
4. What is the ultimate goal of directing?
5. What is a quality control program?
6. Define workplace climate.

Critical Thinking

7. **Classifying.** Scheduling tasks would be classified as part of which management function?
8. **Applying Concepts.** What is the public image of your school in the community?

Working Together

Working in a group, use each leadership style to role-play each of the following situations: (a) assigning an employee a task, (b) discovery of a warehouse fire, (c) addressing a conflict between two employees.

Social Studies

Motivation

Research what motivates people to follow a leader. Prepare a presentation to the class about various theories about leadership and motivation. Make sure you discuss how this would apply to business, to normal social interactions, and to politics.

18.2 Managing Expenses, Credit, & Cash Flow

OBJECTIVES

- Learn about managing expenses
- Explore the role of credit in business
- Investigate cash-flow forecasting
- Examine ways to improve cash flow

VOCABULARY

- cash budget
- consumer credit
- credit
- credit bureau
- credit history
- credit terms
- creditor
- trade credit

Consider this question:

Which is better: "Buy now, pay now" or "Buy now, pay later"?

Writer your answer ("Buy now, pay now" or "Buy now, pay later") on a piece of paper. Be prepared to discuss the consequences of each choice in class.

Managing Expenses

As you learned in Chapter 10, a business can have many types of expenses, including payments for materials, equipment, merchandise for resale (inventory), rent, insurance, employee salaries and wages, sales commissions, and shipping and delivery. Managing expenses is a two-step process that involves:

- **Knowledge.** A manager must be knowledgeable about the expenses the business incurs. Expenses are listed on the income statement, which is typically prepared on a monthly basis.

- **Action.** Once a manager knows the extent of existing expenses, he or she can act to reduce future expenses. Cost-cutting measures include buying used equipment instead of new equipment; leasing buildings or company vehicles, as opposed to buying them; reducing energy usage (electricity, gas, oil); and hiring part-time or temporary workers instead of full-time permanent employees.

The Role of Credit

Credit is the granting of extended time to pay off a debt. To buy on credit means buying now, paying later. A person or business that grants credit is called a **creditor**. Creditors set particular conditions, called **credit terms**, when they grant credit. These terms typically state the time limit when the debt must be paid and any finance (interest) charges that will apply.

Types of Credit

Although there are many types of credit, two types are of particular interest to business owners.

- **Trade Credit.** When one business gives another business an extended payment time for purchased goods or services, it is called a **trade credit**. Business owners take advantage of trade credit to postpone payment of their expenses. Trade credit is a useful tool for managing cash flow. Consider a retail store that buys merchandise by using trade credit from a wholesaler who allows 30 days for payment. The retail store sells enough of the merchandise within the 30-day period to pay the debt on time. In other words, the cash inflow is sufficient to pay the debt. Suppose the store has poor sales and does not earn enough cash in 30 days to pay the money back. This situation is known informally as a credit squeeze. The store will have to dip into cash reserves to pay the debt.

- **Consumer Credit.** When a business gives consumers an extended payment time for purchased goods or services, it is referred to as **consumer credit**. Businesses choose to offer consumer credit to the public to generate sales. For example, a furniture store might allow consumers up to 12 months to pay for a purchase. Although credit cards are a form of consumer credit, they are issued by banks. A business that wants to accept credit cards from its customers must set up a merchant account with a bank. That bank works with the bank that issued the credit card to process transactions. Merchants pay fees for this service and typically receive cash payments from the bank within a few days.

Granting Credit and Collecting Payments

A sale made on credit is based on trust that the person or business will pay the debt in the future. Every person or business that has ever used credit has a **credit history**, which is a record of credit transactions and includes information about whether or not they were repaid in

Consumer Credit
Businesses choose to offer
consumer credit to the public
to generate sales.
Relating Concepts. *Why do you
think consumer credit generates
sales?*

accordance with the credit terms set by the creditor. A **credit bureau**
is a business that collects and maintains credit history records and sells
the information under certain circumstances. Businesses can access
credit records to help them determine if a credit applicant is likely to
repay a future debt.

Many businesses follow specific procedures when deciding whether
or not to grant credit to an applicant. The first step is to collect personal
and financial information from the applicant—for example, employment and income histories. Next, the business can check the credit
history of the applicant through a credit bureau. If credit is granted,
the federal Truth in Lending Act requires creditors to inform customers about the credit terms, including any finance charges.

Once credit has been extended to a customer, the creditor takes specific actions to make sure the debt is paid. The creditor starts by sending a routine bill to the customer when the debt is due. Unfortunately,
some businesses and individuals who are granted credit will not pay
as agreed. The creditor usually makes several attempts to contact the
customer by letter or phone to remedy the problem. If these measures
are not successful, the creditor may hire a business that specializes in
collecting so-called uncollectible accounts. Debt-collection businesses
charge a fee, often a percentage of the amount collected, for providing
this service.

What is credit?

Forecasting Cash Flow

Cash is often called the life blood of a business. The cash that is coming into a business must be sufficient to cover the cash that is flowing from it. A **cash budget** is a record on which a business owner forecasts (predicts) incoming and outgoing cash flows for an upcoming period (typically a month) and later compares actual cash inflows and outflows to the forecasted amounts. Making predictions about the future is difficult. However, business owners can use historical data and other records to make educated guesses about future cash flow.

Forecasting cash flow is a three-step process:

1. **List and Total Any Expected Incoming Cash Payments over the Next Month.** Orders from new, unknown, or unreliable customers that have been placed but not paid for yet should not be included in the cash forecast. There is an old saying, "Don't count your chickens before they hatch." Only

Figure 18-5

Cash Budget
A cash budget shows forecasted and actual cash inflows and outflows.

Classifying. *Most of the fixed expenses are shown as possible cash outflows. Why wouldn't depreciation be a cash outflow?*

Cash Budget for the Month of _____

Cash Inflows	Forecast	Actual	Difference
Cash Sales			
Credit Collections			
Bank Loans			
Other Income			
Total Cash Inflows			
Cash Outflows			
Estimated Variable Expenses			
Insurance			
Salaries			
Advertising			
Interest			
Utilities			
Rent/Mortgage			
Other Fixed Expenses			
_____			
Total Cash Outflows			
Cash Available			

cash receipts you really expect in the month should be counted. This includes, for example, checks from trusted customers or expected credit card payments.

2. **List and Total Expected Outgoing Cash Payments for the Next Month.** These include rent and any other expenses that will be paid in cash.

3. **Subtract Expected Cash Outflows from Expected Cash Inflows.** The resulting sum will provide an estimate of the surplus (or shortage) of cash expected for the next month.

 *What are the three steps involved in forecasting cash flow?*

Improving Cash Flow

Businesses use many methods to improve the flow of cash. New businesses often spend more cash than they earn during their early months. To avoid cash shortages during this time, start-up businesses should make sure they begin with sufficient capital from their own cash savings, loans, or investors. If cash falls short during the start-up period, they may have to find sources of additional capital.

In general, all businesses should continuously work to reduce cash outflows and increase cash inflows. Here are some methods they can use:

- Take advantage of trade credit offered by other businesses.

- Collect payments from customers as soon as possible.

- Offer discounts to customers who pay in cash.

- Do not allow customers to buy on credit if they have overdue bills. Insist they pay in cash.

- Be insistent on collecting overdue payments.

- Shorten the payment time for customers using credit—for example, from 60 days to 30 days.

- Do not tie up cash in excess inventory.

- Make sure inventory is not lost, damaged, or stolen.

- Reduce cash paid out in salaries and wages. If practical, eliminate positions that are not needed and reduce the hours worked by part-time employees.

 *List at least three methods for improving cash flow.*

Decision Making

Many decisions, both large and small, have probably been made for you throughout your life. Your parents were probably the ones to choose where you live, where you go to school, and even what you will have for dinner most nights. In the near future, you will be making those decisions yourself.

Making everyday decisions is easy. You will think, and then act, without too much effort. However, you must be prepared to make life-altering business decisions too. For example, your employer may ask you to transfer to an out-of-state or international location. You may receive offers for two very different jobs in different locations, and perhaps different industries. Your spouse may receive a job offer in another city but your job demands you stay where you are.

To make an important decision, you first need to identify exactly what you are deciding. List each option and think about it carefully as you write. Some people find it helpful to write out the positives and negatives associated with each choice, but just thinking about them can also be a help. In either case, use the information to make your decision. Choose one option. Then do it. Give it your full effort and attention. Don't look back.

Decision making is a big part of being independent. Take each decision seriously.

THINKING CRITICALLY

Analyzing Information. How would you rate your decision-making skills? What is the biggest decision you have ever made on your own? How did you make that decision?

To read more about decision making, go to "Your Business Career" on the Student Center at entrepreneurship.pearson.com.*

 Your Business Plan. Continue developing your standard business plan. Go to "Section 18.2" of the *Business Plan Project* in your *Student Activity Workbook*, or "Section 18.2" of the BizTech Software.

ASSESSMENT 18.2

Reviewing Objectives

1. What are the two steps involved in managing expenses?
2. Describe the two types of credit that are of particular interest to business owners.
3. What is a cash budget?
4. Identify three methods a business could use to improve its cash flow.

Critical Thinking

5. **Predicting.** What is one possible negative consequence of eliminating employee positions or reducing employee hours to reduce cash outflow?
6. **Inferring.** Why should orders that have been placed by new customers but not paid yet be excluded from a cash-flow forecast?

Working Together

Work with three or four other students to research the steps and fees required for a small business to set up a merchant account and accept credit cards from customers. Report your findings to the class.

Social Studies
Bankruptcy

Individuals and businesses that fail to properly manage their expenses and cash flow can wind up in bankruptcy. Use the Internet to research types of bankruptcy and identify those most often filed by individuals and businesses. Present your findings to the class orally. Discuss with the class how individuals who are forced into bankruptcy might feel.

Planning for the Future: One Cut at a Time

"My dad's really big on managing your own money and especially going out there and trying to survive for yourself," said Milan Alexander. "When I was 10, I had a lawn care service and when I was 11, I had a car wash service. My parents' friends would come over and I would wash their cars."

When Milan was 15, he found a new venture. "My friend was cutting hair and I noticed how he was making a lot of money with this." Milan wanted a way to help pay for college, and barbering seemed like the perfect solution. It could provide Milan with money while he was in high school, and he could continue doing it when he got to college. But first, he needed to learn how.

Using an old pair of clippers, Milan practiced on his little cousins and other family members. When he turned 16, he bought a professional set. It took Milan two years to become an expert. "If you're not practicing every day, it's very hard."

Pleasing the Customer: Honesty is the Best Policy

At the beginning, Milan tried to please all his customers, even when he wasn't sure what he was doing. When a client asked Milan to cut his hair in an unfamiliar style, Milan said yes, even though he didn't know how to do it. Although the client was satisfied, Milan wasn't. "I knew that I didn't perform to the best of my ability on that haircut," said Milan. He ended up not charging the client. Milan learned that he needed to be honest with his customers at all times. "You should let people know that you are inexperienced in a certain area and be truthful to them. After that situation, I was very experienced in that haircut because I kept practicing."

Milan's company, Exclusive Cuts Barber Service, is a mobile haircutting business. Milan will cut his clients' hair at their homes or offices at whatever time is convenient for them. "My competitive advantage is that I come to you," said Milan, "and that I'm open beyond local barbershop hours." Milan will go to clients at 9 or 10 o'clock at night if he needs to.

● NFTE
Teaching Youth to Build Businesses

2008 Global Young Entrepreneur of the Year

Milan Alexander
Chicago, IL
Exclusive Cuts Barber Service

▲ *Milan Alexander*

Pricing His Services

Milan has raised his prices in the three years he's been in business. Because he travels to his clients, his expenses include car maintenance, such as oil changes and gas, and supplies that he needs for the job, including hair spray and razor blades.

He gets new customers mainly through word-of-mouth and brings along a poster board showing most of the styles he does. Milan does approximately 30 cuts a month, with 15 regular biweekly customers. "I'm not trying to cut the whole of the Chicago area," he says. A graduate of the Chicago High School for Agricultural Science, Milan is studying agricultural business at the University of Illinois and plans on owning his own barbershop one day. As Milan says, "With the economy now, you want to have multiple incomes."

Thinking Like an Entrepreneur

1. Milan started earning money at an early age. How did that experience help him?
2. Milan regretted not telling a customer he was inexperienced with a certain type of haircut. He didn't charge the customer for the cut, even though the customer was satisfied. How would you have acted in that situation?
3. Is Milan's idea of having multiple methods of earning an income a good one? If you were to take this approach, what do you think your sources of income might be?

CHAPTER SUMMARY

18.1 How to Manage a Business

Business managers skillfully use and coordinate resources, such as money, facilities, equipment, technologies, materials, and employees, in a systematic manner to achieve particular goals. Managers have authority over their employees and are ultimately responsible for their work. Managers must be creative problem solvers to achieve business goals while minimizing costs. A good manager exercises the four management functions of planning, organizing, directing, and controlling and also works to build a positive company image and workplace climate.

18.2 Managing Expenses, Credit, and Cash Flow

Business owners manage their expenses, credit, and cash flow because these components are important to a business's financial health. Managing expenses requires knowledge of what they are and actions that should be taken to reduce them wherever feasible. Some businesses use trade credit to buy goods or services from other businesses and offer consumer credit to their own customers. There are specific procedures for granting credit and collecting payments when credit is extended. Cash is the life blood of a business. In a cash budget, owners forecast cash inflows and outflows on a monthly basis and then compare the forecasted amounts to the actual amounts. Many methods are used to improve cash flow by reducing cash outflows and increasing cash inflows.

REVIEW VOCABULARY

Imagine you have become a successful entrepreneur and have been asked to speak to a class of high school students on two subjects: management functions and managing expenses, credit, and cash flow. Use at least 12 of the following terms in your presentation:

- authoritarian leadership style (p. 494)
- cash budget (p. 502)
- company image (p. 496)
- consumer credit (p. 500)
- controlling (p. 496)
- credit (p. 500)
- credit bureau (p. 501)
- credit history (p. 500)
- credit terms (p. 500)
- creditor (p. 500)
- delegating leadership style (p. 495)
- democratic leadership style (p. 494)
- directing (p. 493)
- interpersonal skills (p. 493)
- management (p. 491)
- operational plan (p. 492)
- organizing (p. 492)
- planning (p. 492)
- quality control program (p. 496)
- strategic plan (p. 492)
- tactical plan (p. 492)
- team building (p. 493)
- trade credit (p. 500)
- workplace climate (p. 496)

CHECK YOUR UNDERSTANDING

Choose the letter that best answers the question or completes the statement.

1. Good interpersonal skills are most important to a manager who is
   a. planning a project
   b. directing employees
   c. controlling equipment
   d. improving cash flow

2. Which of the following is a planning activity?
   a. setting goals
   b. granting credit
   c. directing employees
   d. using interpersonal skills

3. Controlling is an ongoing process of
   a. using the authoritarian management style
   b. avoiding the democratic delegating style
   c. setting and measuring performance standards
   d. delegating to experienced employees

4. A positive workplace climate is associated with
   a. high pay for managers
   b. a poor company image
   c. happy employees
   d. credit bureaus

5. A method for reducing expenses is
   a. renting equipment instead of buying it
   b. allowing customers to buy merchandise on credit
   c. preparing daily operational plans for every department
   d. using the authoritarian leadership style on most employees

6. A cash budget includes
   a. a tactical plan and an operational plan
   b. forecasted and actual strategic plan charts
   c. forecasted and actual cash inflows and outflows
   d. a quality control program for reducing cash flows

7. Setting performance standards is closely associated with which management function?
   a. planning
   b. directing
   c. organizing
   d. controlling

8. Which of the following options might be selected to improve cash flow?
   a. offer discounts to customers who use credit
   b. offer discounts to customers who pay with cash
   c. extend consumer credit to customers with good credit histories
   d. lengthen the payment time from 30 days to 60 days for customers using credit

9. Motivation is associated with which management function?
   a. planning
   b. directing
   c. measuring
   d. forecasting

10. A manager who asks for employee input before making a decision is demonstrating
    a. the use of cash budget forecasting to lead employees
    b. the use of a strategic plan to lead employees
    c. the delegating leadership style
    d. the democratic leadership style

11. Which plan includes day-to-day activities?
    a. credit plan
    b. tactical plan
    c. strategic plan
    d. operational plan

12. A creditor is best defined as someone who
    a. owes money
    b. buys products or services
    c. lends money
    d. monitors and reports on credit histories

Business Communication

13. Many leadership styles are used besides the three described in this chapter. Using the Internet or other source, study other leadership styles and describe five of them to the class, using examples of famous people to demonstrate each one.

14. Some companies pay their employees to participate in team-building games. Use the Internet to investigate this type of activity. As a role play, imagine you are the owner of a small business and your classmates are your employees. Tell them what team-building exercise you have selected for them and why.

15. There are three major national credit bureaus in the United States. Research them and the types of services they offer to businesses and the general public. Write a brief report describing what you have learned.

Business Ethics

18. Your retail bookstore is having a serious cash-flow problem and you feel you must eliminate a part-time position. Your two part-time employees are Jill and John. They both work 20 hours per week and are equally good employees. Jill is working her way through college and makes $10 per hour. John makes $14 per hour. He is also working a second job because he has children and needs money for their medical bills. What would you do if you were the bookstore owner?

Business Math

16. A retail store buys 500 shirts for $11 each, using trade credit granted by the supplier. The total payment is due in 30 days. If the store sells the shirts for $20 each, how many shirts will it have to sell to have the cash to pay the trade credit debt?

17. A business owner forecasted $1,250, $1,000, and $1,150 as cash inflows for three months. Her actual cash inflows were 110%, 85%, and 90% of the forecasted amounts. What was the actual cash inflow amount for each month? How much over or under was she in her forecast after the three months?

Business in Your Community

19. Interview a local business owner in your community who uses performance standards as a control measure. Find out which components of the business are subject to performance standards and how their actual performance is measured in comparison to the standards. Report your findings in a brief paper.

20. Locate a small business in your community that sells products or services that interest you. Imagine that the business hires you to enhance its public image and gives you a large budget to do so. Explain to the class the type of image you would try to build for the company. Include the specific measures you would take.

Website Data

Imagine how useful it would be if an e-commerce owner could know exactly who visits the Website, how much time is spent there, what pages are viewed, and other important information. All of that is possible through **Web analytics software**—various programs that measure and monitor the traffic on a Website. Website owners can use this information to increase traffic and make sure that the visitors who come are finding what they want. It's like doing market research in **cyberspace**, which is the virtual world of computers. And acting on this information can mean the difference between a successful e-commerce site and an unsuccessful one.

Analyzing Web Traffic

One of the most important tools a Website owner can use is a **site traffic analyzer**. A traffic analyzer shows the number of visitors who came to the site on an hourly, daily, and monthly basis, as well as each visitor's location and type of browser. A traffic analyzer also shows how visitors came to the site—did they use a search engine or key in the Website's URL? If the visitor used a search engine, a traffic analyzer tells the site owner what keywords were used. This can help with search engine optimization, which can mean moving the Website higher in a search engine's ranking. It will also let the site owner know if the Website's content is successfully attracting visitors.

In addition, an analyzer tool shows how long the visitor remained on the site. It can show the **bounce rate,** the percentage of visitors who visit the landing page and exit without visiting another page. The **landing page** is the page that appears when the visitor clicks on an advertisement or search engine link. If the bounce rate is high, the landing page may need to be improved. Finally, a traffic analyzer shows which visitors actually bought something. All this information can help the site owner create additional content or change current content to get more sales and visitors.

Some site-analysis software works by analyzing the **traffic log,** the record of the raw traffic data that your server collects. Log analyzers are often included when you have a Web host.

Cookies

Cookies are short messages given to a Web browser (such as Internet Explorer) by a Web server when you visit that site. As you've learned, every Website either has its own server or shares Web hosting. There are various types of cookies: a **session cookie** is erased when you close your browser, while a **permanent** or **persistent cookie** is stored on your hard drive. Cookies store information about you and your browser that can make it easier for you when you visit the site again. The cookie may store your password for a site so you don't have to key it in every time.

A cookie can also store your past visiting habits, so that every time you go to that site, it will welcome you. If you have a cookie for Amazon, for example, you'll get a welcome back by name every time you return to the Amazon site. You'll see a list of new books that you may be interested in, based on your past purchasing history.

Tech Vocabulary

- bounce rate
- cookies
- cyberspace
- landing page
- permanent cookie
- persistent cookie
- session cookie
- site traffic analyzer
- traffic log
- Web analytics software

Check Yourself

1. What is Web analytics software?
2. What can site traffic analysis show?
3. What is a traffic log?
4. What is a session cookie?

What Do You Think?

Communicating. Describe how you feel when a site you have visited welcomes you back and makes recommendations based on your past purchasing history.

CHAPTER 19

MANAGING PRODUCTION, DISTRIBUTION, & OPERATIONS

19.1

-
-
-

? | *Think about this question:*

Would you like to run a business from your home?

Write your answer (yes or no) on a piece of paper. Be prepared to discuss it in class.

VOCABULARY

- automation
- distribution chain
- distribution channel
- distribution management
- free on board
- Gantt chart
- layout
- logistics
- maintenance
- markup
- milestone
- PERT chart
- production management
- productivity
- quality circle
- zoning laws

Site Selection and Layout Planning

One of the first actions entrepreneurs must take is to choose a site (location) for the business. Then, once the site is chosen, they must decide how to use the space.

Site Selection

The choice of location depends partly on the type of business. Retail and service businesses that expect walk-in customers need locations that are easily accessible and have adequate parking. A manufacturing firm that uses machinery or other kinds of equipment will likely require a large space. The same is true for wholesaling businesses that carry extensive product inventories.

Some entrepreneurs choose to operate their businesses from home. This choice has some advantages. It is convenient and saves the expense of buying or renting another location and commuting. In addition, certain expenses associated with operating a home business can be deducted from personal income tax. However, some entrepreneurs prefer to locate their businesses away from home so they can keep their personal and business lives separate.

Most cities and communities have **zoning laws**. These are local statues that specify the types of development and activities—residential,

▲ **Figure 19-1**

Zoning Laws
Some zoning laws forbid businesses, even home businesses, in residential areas.

Drawing Conclusions. *Why might some communities restrict home businesses in residential areas? How would you feel if you had a home business?*

commercial, industrial, or recreational—that can take place on a particular property. Some zoning laws forbid businesses in residential areas. If home businesses are allowed, there may be restrictions on the types of businesses that can be operated, the number of employees, the use of streets for customer parking, and the hours it can be open to the public. A business that cannot be located at home needs a space in an area that is appropriately zoned. As mentioned earlier this introduces additional expenses, such as rent, utilities, and commuting.

Layout Planning

A **layout** is a physical arrangement of objects in a given space. Layout considerations differ by type of business. A manufacturing business needs to arrange machines and processes so production proceeds as efficiently as possible. Having adequate storage space for incoming materials and outgoing products is also important. Wholesaling businesses are very concerned with storage layout, as they often have large inventories of products that must be well organized and readily accessible. Retail and service businesses that have walk-in customers need an appealing, customer-friendly layout.

Layouts must be custom designed to meet specific needs. Entrepreneurs may choose to do their own layout planning. If the business is complex, hiring a consultant can make sense. Using a consultant will certainly add to the cost of business set-up but could pay for itself by saving money through efficiency of floor plan or attracting customers to a well-laid-out showroom.

Production Management

Production management is the oversight of the processes that produce goods and services. The goal of production management is to use materials and resources efficiently to produce the desired quantity and quality of goods and services, while meeting cost and schedule requirements. Large companies, particularly manufacturing companies, often employ a production manager to perform this function. In small companies, the business owner typically oversees production management.

Production managers typically focus on three issues:

- Scheduling
- Productivity
- Quality

Scheduling

Scheduling is a key activity in every business. Manufacturers make schedules for their production processes. Wholesalers and retailers make schedules for their orders and deliveries. Service businesses make schedules of the actions they intend to perform for customers. However, making a schedule and keeping it are two different things. It is the responsibility of the production manager to ensure that schedules are followed.

A schedule is not a wish list; it is a plan for achieving goals. Like any good plan, a schedule should reflect reasonable expectations. Production managers need to know how long it will take to make a product, perform a task, get an order from a supplier, or serve a customer. Established businesses rely on past data to make these predictions. New businesses have to make sensible estimates, using the best information available.

Production managers use tools to create schedules. One tool is a **Gantt chart**, a bar chart that shows schedule goals for a list of tasks and the duration (length of time) of each task. A Gantt chart may also show the progress made at achieving each task. Although Gantt charts have many variations, a typical example includes a timeline across the top and a list of tasks on the far left. Bars indicate the start and end dates of each task. The timeline may list actual dates or chunks of time (for example, "Week 1"). A diamond shape is used to indicate a **milestone**—a significant point of progress. Bars and diamonds are outlined on a proposed schedule and then darkened as tasks are completed. If a particular task is finished late (or early), the start and end dates of future tasks and milestones may have to be adjusted.

This Gantt chart shows the schedule for opening a retail book store. Week 3 has just ended.

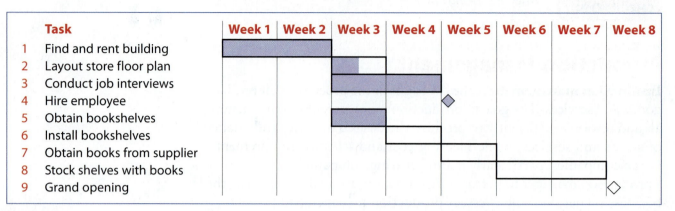

Task		Week 1	Week 2	Week 3	Week 4	Week 5	Week 6	Week 7	Week 8
1	Find and rent building								
2	Layout store floor plan								
3	Conduct job interviews								
4	Hire employee								
5	Obtain bookshelves								
6	Install bookshelves								
7	Obtain books from supplier								
8	Stock shelves with books								
9	Grand opening								

 Figure 19-2

Gantt Chart

A Gantt chart shows the schedule of goals for a list of tasks.

Interpreting Graphs. *Which task is behind schedule? Which task is ahead of schedule?*

Another scheduling tool is the Program Evaluation and Review Technique (PERT) chart. A **PERT chart** is a scheduling diagram that shows tasks as a sequence of steps and illustrates how those steps are dependent on each other. In other words, PERT charts show which tasks must be completed before others can be started. A basic PERT chart uses circles to represent completed tasks. Arrows between the circles illustrate the order in which tasks should be completed.

The illustrated PERT chart covers the same nine tasks that were included in the Gantt chart. The PERT chart makes it obvious that the building should be rented (task 1) before any other tasks take place. Store layout (task 2), job interviews (task 3), and obtaining bookshelves (task 5) can proceed at the same time. They are not dependent on one another. However, hiring an employee (task 4) should be completed before the bookshelves are stocked with books (task 8), so the employee can help with the stocking.

Figure 19-3

PERT Chart

A PERT chart shows tasks as steps in a sequence and illustrates how they are dependent on each other.

Interpreting Graphs. *Task 6 is dependent on which other tasks? Why?*

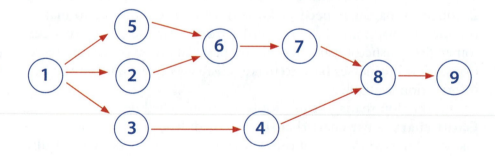

Productivity

Productivity is a measure of business output compared to business input. An example of productivity is the number of items produced per employee or the number of customers served per day. Productivity is a ratio of one numerical value to another numerical value. It can be measured in time intervals (hours, days, or weeks) or labor increments (employee, department, or division). The most common measures of productivity for a small business are: output per employee, output per unit of time, and output per dollar of cost.

Production managers use productivity data to monitor the performance of processes and people. Imagine that employee A regularly sews 60 pairs of gloves per day, and employee B regularly sews 40 pairs of gloves per day. Employee A is more productive than employee B in this comparison. However, assume employee A is paid $180 per day and employee B is paid $80 per day. The labor cost for a pair of gloves is quite different. Employee A made a pair of gloves for $3.00, while Employee B made a pair for gloves for $2.00.

Employee A:
$180 per Day ÷ 60 Pairs per Day = $3.00
(Labor Cost for One Pair)

Employee B:
$80 per Day ÷ 40 Pairs per Day = $2.00
(Labor Cost for One Pair)

Automation is the use of machines to perform tasks normally performed by people. In the manufacturing industry, robotic machines now do many of the tasks (assembling, painting, and sorting goods) that people used to do. Automation is less common in other types of businesses, but it does occur. Examples include automatic car washes and ATMs at banks. Automation is used when machines can do the same job as people. Of course, sophisticated machines are very costly. The extra cost of automation has to be weighed against the potential savings.

Most businesses, no matter what kind, rely on equipment to some degree. This includes industrial machines, electrical tools, company vehicles, computers, and other electronic devices. **Maintenance** is the upkeep and routine care of equipment to keep it in good working order. All

◀ **Figure 19-4**
Automation
Robotic machines now do many tasks that people used to do.
Comparing/Contrasting. *What are the benefits of robotic machines? What are the disadvantages?*

Ideagoras—New Ways to Solve Problems

When an entrepreneur had a problem to solve in the past, she might have chosen to hire a consultant to solve it. Now this may not be necessary. In an increasingly global and connected marketplace, business owners can turn to talent outside the company by using an innovation called "ideagoras."

Ideagoras are online destinations for the exchange of ideas, like an eBay for problem-solving. The term comes from the Greek *agora*, which means "marketplace." Examples of ideagoras include InnoCentive, crowdSPRING, YourEncore, and yet2.com. Gathering places for scientists, thinkers, freelancers, computer programmers, and inventors from around the world, ideagoras are changing research and development from the bottom up. The pioneers of these sites would like to see users form "virtual groups" to solve problems and communicate solutions. They want to ensure contributor loyalty and satisfaction by making sure problem solvers are recognized. As ideagoras grow, mature, and become the norm for innovation, co-creation will be part of the business plan for many organizations.

THINKING CRITICALLY

Communicating. Form an ideagora in your classroom and come up with two problems for the collective to work on. Communicate the solutions in a larger group.

To read more about ideagoras, go to "Entrepreneurship Issues" on the Student Center at entrepreneurship.pearson.com.

businesses want to keep their equipment working productively. A maintenance schedule helps ensure that equipment gets the attention it needs to keep serving the business.

Quality

Controlling quality is one of the primary functions of business managers. Most entrepreneurs strive to provide high-quality goods and services to satisfy customers. However, quality can be difficult to define and measure. High quality may mean different things to different people. Production managers set quality standards for their businesses based on the types of goods and services they are providing. These standards are part of their overall quality control program. Regular quality inspections ensure that standards are being met.

Quality inspections can be conducted at stages during the production process or when a service or product is completed. Manufacturing businesses use quality inspections to make sure their goods meet specified production standards. For example, a product may need to meet certain standards for appearance or strength. Service business managers conduct inspections to make certain that a task has been performed properly. For example, a car wash employee may inspect a vehicle after it has been washed to make sure the job met the company's standards.

Quality control is not just the responsibility of managers. Employees sometimes take an active role in quality-control programs. A **quality circle** is a group of employees who provide input and suggestions about ways to improve the quality of the goods or services they produce. Although quality circles are most often associated with manufacturing businesses, they can benefit any type of business.

READING CHECKPOINT *What are the three issues on which production management focuses?*

Distribution Management

Distribution management is the management of materials and processes associated with incoming and outgoing products. The goal of distribution management is to ensure that products are handled, stored, and transported in an organized, safe, and cost-effective way.

Distribution Chain or Channel

A **distribution chain** (or **distribution channel**) is a series of steps through which products flow into or out of a business. A typical distribution chain begins with a manufacturing business producing a product. That product is sold to a wholesaling business and then resold to a retailing business. Each business is a link that serves a specific purpose in the chain.

The price of a product increases as it goes along the distribution chain. A **markup** is a price increase imposed by each link in the chain. For example, manufacturers set a price based on their expenses and desired profit. Wholesalers pay that price and then set a higher price to cover their costs and to earn a profit. Retailers then add a markup to cover their costs and to earn a profit. These markups can be substantial. The price of a product in a retail store is typically much higher than the original manufacturer's price.

▼ **Figure 19-5**

Distribution Chain for Jeans

A distribution chain is a series of steps through which products flow into or out of a business.

Analyzing Data. *What was the markup from the manufacturer to the wholesaler? From the manufacturer to the retailer? From the wholesaler to the retailer?*

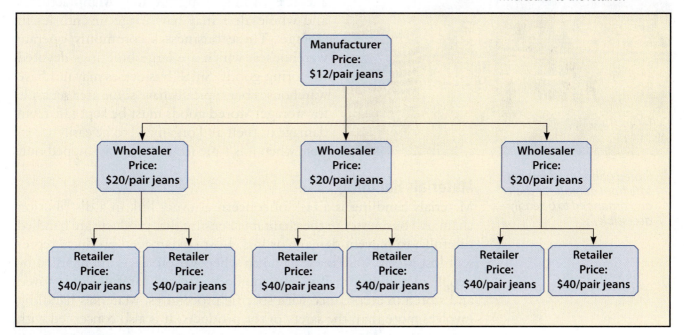

Transportation

Transportation of goods is a vital service in any distribution chain. Most goods are not manufactured and sold to consumers in the immediate area. Some goods travel vast distances, even around the world, to reach their final buyers. **Logistics** (luh-JIS-tix) is the handling and organizing of materials, equipment, goods, and workers. Transportation logistics is complex for some businesses, particularly larger ones. Goods can be transported by ship, airplane, train, or truck. Distribution managers make transport decisions based on the cost and scheduling needs of their companies and their clients.

Shipping and Receiving

Most large businesses have a department devoted to the shipping and receiving of goods. A shipping department handles outgoing goods. These are goods moving to the next link in the distribution chain or to final buyers. A receiving department handles incoming goods. These are goods sent to the business by suppliers. In a small business, one individual may handle all shipping and receiving duties. Whatever the size of the business, it is vitally important that incoming and outgoing shipments are monitored and tracked carefully and that accurate records are kept. The products in incoming shipments should be checked against purchase invoices to ensure that everything has been received as ordered and is in good condition. Outgoing shipments should also be checked to ensure that orders have been properly filled.

Stored goods must be kept safe from damage or theft and organized to be easily accessible.

Storage and Warehousing

Many products do not flow immediately along a distribution channel. They spend time in storage at each link along the way. Manufacturers and wholesalers may have large inventories in storage. These businesses commonly operate warehouses, which are large buildings devoted to storing goods. Small businesses may not have warehouses but typically have some area set aside for storage. Stored goods must be kept safe from damage or theft and organized to be easily accessible when it is time for them to be shipped out.

Materials Handling

Materials handling is a task of concern at every link in a distribution chain. All businesses in the chain must ensure that products are handled carefully, to prevent damage or loss. Lost or damaged products represent lost profit. Care must be taken whenever products are handled by people or equipment. Products should be treated carefully and moved and stored in accordance with specific procedures. Materials handling involves more than the safety of the products. It is also concerned with moving them in an orderly, efficient, and cost-effective manner.

Delivery Terms

Large products and large-shipment orders are considered freight, meaning that they are transported by large trucks, trains, or ships.

Manufacturing and wholesaling businesses use specialized terms to describe their freight-delivery options. One of these is "free on board." **Free on board** is a delivery term that is followed by a word or group of words that specify a location at which the ownership responsibility for the shipment switches from the seller to the buyer. Free on board may be abbreviated as F.O.B., FOB, fob, or f.o.b.

For example, a wholesaler in Chicago may indicate "FOB Chicago." This means that as soon as the goods are loaded onto a transport vehicle in Chicago, they become the responsibility of the buyer. Thus, the buyer will ultimately be responsible for the shipping expense and bear responsibility for the goods while they are in transit. If they become damaged or lost en route, the buyer will be responsible for filing an insurance claim.

An FOB location identifier is not always a city. The more general term, "FOB origin," is also used. This indicates that responsibility for the shipment switches to the buyer as soon as the goods are loaded on a transport vehicle at their point of origin. Likewise, the term "FOB destination" means that responsibility for the goods switches from seller to buyer when the goods reach their destination. If the goods become damaged or lost during transit, the seller will be responsible for filing an insurance claim.

The term FOB has a different meaning outside the United States and Canada. Entrepreneurs engaged in international trade need to research the proper delivery terms for freight transport to or from their specific destinations.

READING CHECKPOINT *What is distribution management?*

◀ **Figure 19-6**
F.O.B.
An F.O.B. location isn't always a city.
Solving Problems. *A wholesaler loaded five stoves onto this freight car in Albuquerque, NM. The stoves were intended for a retailer in Los Angeles, CA, "F.O.B. destination." The car derailed and the stoves were damaged in Flagstaff, AZ. Who will file the insurance claim?*

Your Business Plan. Continue developing your standard business plan. Go to "Section 19.1" of the *Business Plan Project* in your *Student Activity Workbook*, or "Section 19.1" of the BizTech Software.

ASSESSMENT 19.1

Reviewing Objectives

1. What is the difference between site selection and layout planning?
2. What are three issues production managers focus on?
3. What is the purpose of distribution management?

Critical Thinking

4. **Solving Problems.** Natasha operates a successful baked goods business out of her home in a quiet neighborhood. Lately, her neighbors have been complaining about Natasha's customers parking on the street when they come to pick up their orders. Describe some possible solutions for this problem.

5. **Relating Concepts.** How is productivity related to profit?

Working Together

Work with three classmates. Imagine you are a group of entrepreneurs with a paper airplane business. Each of you will make a paper airplane. Form a quality circle and work together to make a list of ways each airplane could be improved. The improvements must be practical and doable. Each of you will then make the improved model. Prepare a presentation for the class in which each member of the quality circle shows his or her original airplane and the improved model, explaining what improvements were made and why.

Science
Honeybee Logistics

The honeybee is one of nature's hardest-working creatures. Research the logistics involved in a wild honeybee hive and write a brief paper about it. Be sure to mention the site selection, layout, production, and distribution tasks that the honeybees perform.

SECTION 19.2 Managing Operations

OBJECTIVES
- Define operations
- Study general operating policies
- Learn the importance of customer service policies

VOCABULARY
- credibility
- operations
- operations management
- policy
- repeat customers
- rework
- warranty
- word of mouth

? *Think about this question:*

Has a sales clerk or cashier ever been rude to you?

Write you answer (yes or no) on a piece of paper. Be prepared to describe your experience to the class.

What Are Operations?

Operations are the everyday activities that keep a business running. So **operations management** is the management of the everyday activities that keep a business running. Large businesses often devote an entire department to a single operation, such as sales, human resources, or production. Small businesses may have only one person overseeing all operations. In businesses that have employees, the operations manager will likely delegate some operational responsibilities to one or more employees. This gives the manager more time to devote to tasks that only he or she can handle.

 *What are operations?*

General Business Policies

A **policy** is a procedure or set of guidelines that specifies exactly how something should be accomplished or handled. Many business policies are in written form. To ensure that operations proceed smoothly, a business develops policies that govern how specific operational activities should be conducted. Operations managers are responsible for making sure these policies are followed for the overall good of the company.

Businesses develop policies for many kinds of operations. However, some operating policies are very general, and common to most small businesses. These policies involve hours of operation, extending credit to customers, handling returns and rework requests, and delivering products.

Hours of Operation

An important component of overall policy is the hours of operation. Some large manufacturing plants operate around the clock because keeping the machines running continuously can be more economical and productive than stopping and restarting them. Some wholesalers, retailers, and service businesses are also open around the clock—"24/7"—especially in large cities. However, most choose to limit their hours to what best serves their customers' needs as well as their own. They may also be bound by local laws that prohibit businesses from operating at certain hours (for example, late at night).

BUSINESS HOURS:

MONDAY	TO	
TUESDAY	TO	
WEDNESDAY	TO	
THURSDAY	TO	
FRIDAY	TO	
SATURDAY	TO	
SUNDAY	TO	
HOLIDAYS	TO	

▲ Businesses must set their hours of operation.

Extending Credit to Customers

Many businesses establish a credit policy as part of their operations management. A clear policy helps make sure customers understand the conditions (if any) under which credit will be extended. Businesses often rely on "the three C's" when deciding whether to extend credit to a particular customer. These are:

- **Character.** Character refers to the financial trustworthiness of the customer. A customer's past credit history is considered essential here. Someone who has made credit payments on time and in full in the past is likely to do so again.

- **Capacity.** The customer's current cash inflow is referred to as the customer's capacity. A customer's current income is the best measure of this. People with good, steady income are more likely to pay their bills.

- **Capital.** The customer's total financial assets are referred to as the customer's capital. A customer who owns financial assets—a house, a business, corporate stock, a savings account—is usually more likely to pay bills on time than an individual who has few or no assets.

Returns and Rework Requests

Companies that sell products need to establish policies for handling situations when products are returned by dissatisfied customers. Returns due to product defects may be handled differently than returns due to other reasons.

Rework is a manufacturing term that refers to work performed to correct defects in a product. Manufacturing businesses often set rework policies that clearly state the conditions under which they will correct defective products, and how customers can go about getting products reworked. All businesses should establish policies that establish whether or not they will exchange, repair, or replace returned products, and whether they will refund a customer's money.

Service businesses don't typically sell products as their primary function, but some do sell items related to their business. For example, a landscape designer might sell plants or a dog groomer might carry a line

◀ **Figure 19-7**

Returns
Companies need to establish policies for returns.

Inferring. *Why might a company establish different procedures for returns for product defects than for returns because the customer is dissatisfied?*

of dog brushes and shampoos. These businesses also need return policies. In addition, service businesses need to establish policies regarding how they will handle requests from dissatisfied customers who want a service redone or money refunded.

Delivery Policy

Businesses that sell products need a delivery policy. These guidelines make customers aware of their delivery options and the costs and timetables involved. Manufacturers and wholesalers commonly use freight delivery services to ship large orders. Retail businesses, who sell much smaller orders, may offer customers a choice of several delivery options including the U.S. Postal Service or commercial delivery services (such as Federal Express or UPS).

A delivery policy may specify the amount of time between order placement and order shipment—for example, 24 hours. The policy should cover situations in which an order cannot be filled within the

E-mail retailers may offer customers a choice of delivery options.

specified time, such as when items are out of stock. In addition, some policies include notifying customers by e-mail when orders are shipped, providing a link so the customer can track the shipment online. A delivery policy should also make clear any conditions or restrictions imposed by the seller. Some businesses will not ship outside of the country, for example, or will not deliver to post office boxes.

 **READING CHECKPOINT** *What is a policy?*

Customer Service Policies

Customer service is one of the most important aspects of operating a business. There is a well-known saying that it costs more to gain a new customer than it does to keep an existing one. The goal of every business is to get **repeat customers**—that is, people who come back again and again. Satisfied customers are likely to be repeat customers. People tell their friends about experiences, both positive and negative, with businesses and products. **Word of mouth** is verbal publicity. Positive word of mouth about a company can bring in new customers. Negative word of mouth can be extremely harmful to a business. A customer service policy is designed to make sure that people have only good experiences when dealing with the company. Businesses set policies detailing how customers should be treated, both on a general basis and when problems arise.

YOUR BUSINESS CAREER

Integrity

Some people say you demonstrate your integrity when no one is watching. This may be a good way to think of this important personality characteristic. Being a person with integrity implies that you mean what you say, you follow through with what you start, and you keep your promises. You have a high moral code: you would never do something you believe to be wrong, no matter what the circumstances may be.

When you conduct your life with integrity, it almost always follows that you have a good reputation. People trust and believe the words and actions of a person with integrity. They know such a person means what he or she says and strives to make the right choices.

People with integrity aren't perfect and will certainly make mistakes. But when this happens, they own up to it. They try to make things right. They take their good name seriously so others will too. They know it can take years to build a good reputation but just a minute to ruin it.

THINKING CRITICALLY

Relating Concepts. Would you say you are working toward being a person of integrity? Why or why not? Think about people in your life whom you feel have integrity. In what ways can you learn from them?

To read more about integrity, go to "Your Business Career" on the Student Center at entrepreneurship.pearson.com.

There are five fundamental elements governing the treatment of customers: courtesy, respect, prompt attention, knowledgeable employees, and credibility.

- **Courtesy.** All customers should be treated politely, even if they are angry and not behaving in a courteous manner.

- **Respect.** Businesses show respect to customers through various means. Examples include a dress code and code of conduct for employees to follow while they are at work. In addition, businesses should respect the personal and financial information of their customers by safeguarding it.

- **Prompt Attention.** Customers do not like to be kept waiting, either on the phone or in person.

- **Knowledgeable Employees.** Customers want correct answers when they ask questions. Businesses must make an effort to handle every customer promptly and make sure that employees are knowledgeable about the company's business so they can answer questions and handle requests properly.

- **Credibility.** The quality of being believable, trustworthy, and keeping one's promises is called **credibility**. A business with good credibility builds customer loyalty, because people know that the business will keep its promises. A **warranty** is a statement from a seller, usually in writing, that promises that goods or services meet certain standards. It describes the conditions under which particular problems will be taken care of by the seller at no cost to the buyer. Because a warranty is a legally binding document, it should be written with the help of an attorney.

Every customer service policy should include procedures for handling customer complaints. Even a company with high standards for quality and service will have a few dissatisfied customers. The basic components of everyday customer service—courtesy, respect, prompt attention, knowledgeable employees, and credibility—also apply to handling complaints.

 *What is a customer service policy designed to do?*

▲ *Happy customers are often repeat customers.*

Your Business Plan. Continue developing your standard business plan. Go to "Section 19.2" of the *Business Plan Project* in your *Student Activity Workbook*, or "Section 19.2" of the BizTech Software.

ASSESSMENT 19.2

Reviewing Objectives

1. What is operations management?
2. Name four operations for which a business develops general policies.
3. What are repeat customers?

Critical Thinking

4. **Drawing Conclusions.** Why do you think companies typically have one policy for the return of defective products and a different policy for the return of products for other reasons?

5. **Writing.** Write a warranty for your teacher regarding your performance as a student over the remainder of the school term. What promises can you make? What are you willing to fix if there is a problem?

Working Together

Working as a team, role-play five situations that an entrepreneur might face in dealing with an unhappy customer. Base the situations on the five fundamental elements governing the treatment of customers. In each case, demonstrate to the class a wrong way and a right way to treat the customer.

Social Studies
Identity Theft

Identity theft is a serious crime and can occur when businesses do not protect the personal and financial information they collect about their customers. Research the problem and then write a brief paper about identity theft. Include the responsibilities that businesses have to safeguard customer information.

Saving Memories with Technology

When Eric Mund was 12 years old, he got a new PC that allowed him to convert old video tapes into digital files on his computer. Unfortunately, when he looked at a tape of his first birthday, only the first five minutes were visible! The rest of the tape was gray, the images lost. Eric said, "Seeing the ravages of time destroy my tape, I pledged that I would not allow this to happen to my little sister, who was just 3." Eric decided that he would convert all her videos onto DVDs so she would be able to see them in the future.

▲ *Eric Mund*

For several years, Eric did conversions of old videos and slides onto DVDs for family and friends. When he was 16, he decided to do it as a business, calling his company Digital Video Xpress. "I really like that name," said Eric. "It's a little catchy. It's got digital, video, fast, go, express. It flows together." He entered a South Florida business competition and, with the money he won, bought himself an iMac that allowed him to make more professional DVDs with labels and menus.

Meeting Expectations

Eric's parents helped him get his first customers through their friends, relatives, and acquaintances. At the beginning, though, there were some misunderstandings.

One customer sent her video to Eric by way of his dad. "My dad was expecting me to produce a masterpiece in seven hours. It usually takes me days to do it," explained Eric. Not knowing the realities of the process, both Eric's father and the customer were upset, wanting the video almost instantly. Eric was in a difficult situation. "I was like, I'm sorry, Ma'am, but there's nothing I can do. It's not my computer's fault, it's no one's fault. It's just not possible."

Eric now makes sure customers know how long the process takes and draws a distinction between friends and customers. He recognizes that friends have different expectations when dealing with him than they would with a larger company. "Friends tend to expect you to do it in an instant, whereas if a really big company was to say it will take two weeks, they'd be okay with this."

Pleasing Customers

Eric has learned how to please his customers. He makes sure they are fully involved in the production of their DVDs—something his competition doesn't offer. "I can post their work in progress on my Website and allow them to see what the actual slide show or video will look like on their DVD from the comfort of their home," said Eric. "They have full control of their projects. They can make comments, request changes, and see the progress. All the work can be seen online, including the DVD labels and the main menus for the DVD." Using the Internet this way is, for Eric, what makes his business, Digital Video Xpress, unique from all others.

Thinking Like an Entrepreneur

1. Eric's parents helped him get his first customers. What are the good and bad points about having your family help you get business?
2. What are some differences between working for friends and for clients you don't know personally?
3. Eric gives customers control over their projects. Could this ever be a bad thing?

CHAPTER SUMMARY

19.1 Managing Production & Distribution

Before a business begins operating, it must choose a site and plan its layout. Production management is concerned with the processes that produce goods and services. Three major tasks are scheduling, controlling productivity, and controlling quality. Gantt charts and PERT charts are common scheduling tools. Products typically travel along a distribution chain (channel) that includes a manufacturer, wholesaler, and retailer. Distribution management is concerned with materials handling, logistics, shipping and receiving, storage and warehousing, transportation, and terms of delivery for products.

19.2 Managing Operations

Operations management is concerned with the daily activities that keep a business running. Policies are developed that specify procedures for handling particular operations. General operational policies address the hours of operation, extending credit to customers, handling product returns and rework claims, and delivering goods to customers. Customer service is one of the most important components of daily operations. The five fundamental elements governing the treatment of customers are courtesy, respect, prompt attention, knowledgeable employees, and credibility. Good customer service builds customer loyalty and spreads positive word of mouth about a business.

REVIEW VOCABULARY

You want to hire a manager to be in charge of production, distribution, and operations for a new company you are starting. Write a job description that includes at least 12 of the following terms.

- automation (p. 515)
- credibility (p. 525)
- distribution chain (p. 517)
- distribution channel (p. 517)
- distribution management (p. 517)
- free on board (p. 519)
- Gantt chart (p. 513)
- layout (p. 512)

- logistics (p. 518)
- maintenance (p. 515)
- markup (p. 517)
- milestone (p. 513)
- operations (p. 521)
- operations management (p. 521)
- PERT chart (p. 514)
- policy (p. 521)

- production management (p. 513)
- productivity (p. 514)
- quality circle (p. 516)
- repeat customers (p. 524)
- rework (p. 523)
- warranty (p. 525)
- word of mouth (p. 524)
- zoning laws (p. 511)

CHECK YOUR UNDERSTANDING

Choose the letter that best answers the question or completes the statement.

1. An operations manager delegates when he or she
   a. ships freight free on board
   b. uses a Gantt chart to schedule an operation
   c. puts an employee in charge of an operation
   d. writes a warranty for a business service

2. What are the "three C's"?
   a. character, capacity, and capital
   b. charts, channels, and customer service
   c. capability, courtesy, and credibility
   d. credit, costs, and customers

3. Zoning laws affect
   a. quality circles
   b. credit policies
   c. price markup
   d. site selection

4. A receiving department is responsible for
   a. scheduling outgoing shipments
   b. writing warranties for products
   c. handling incoming goods
   d. assigning employees to quality circles

5. The purpose of maintenance is to
   a. repair machines that have broken down
   b. add a link to the distribution chain
   c. ensure that deliveries are shipped on time
   d. keep equipment in good working order

6. A warranty is a(n)
   a. tool used for scheduling
   b. promise that a product or service meets certain standards
   c. inspection technique used in a quality-control program
   d. method for transporting freight

7. A PERT chart is useful for
   a. showing which tasks must be completed before others can be started
   b. keeping track of daily employee productivity
   c. delegating responsibility for customer service
   d. illustrating the types of zoning laws in a community

8. How does the price of a product change as it moves along a distribution chain?
   a. the price decreases to provide each business in the chain with a profit
   b. the price increases to provide each business in the chain with a profit
   c. the price decreases because the product quality decreases
   d. the price increases because the product quality increases

9. Which of the following best describes productivity?
   a. a courteous way to deal with a customer complaint
   b. a method for shipping products free on board
   c. a measure of business output compared to business input
   d. a price markup on a product

10. The importance of courtesy is most likely explained in a
    a. customer service policy
    b. scheduling policy
    c. production management policy
    d. maintenance policy

11. Which of the following describes a typical distribution chain for a shirt?
    a. manufacturer to wholesaler to customer
    b. manufacturer to wholesaler to retailer to customer
    c. wholesaler to manufacturer to retailer to customer
    d. manufacturer to retailer to wholesaler to customer

12. Production management is concerned with
    a. scheduling
    b. productivity
    c. quality control
    d. all of the above

Business Communication

13. Imagine that an unknown person calls your store one day and wants to buy an expensive item on credit. Make a list of at least five questions you would ask to help you determine whether you should extend credit.

14. Imagine you are planning to open a business. Create a PERT chart and include at least seven steps you will need to take before you can open your business.

15. Imagine that your classmates are new employees recently hired to work at your business. Prepare a presentation in which you go over your company's customer service policy with them.

Business Ethics

18. Your business is running low on cash. A friend with her own business offers to pay you a large amount of money for a list of your customers' names and addresses so she can contact them about an investment opportunity. Your friend is reputable, has a very good business, and is often very helpful to people. You could really use the money right now because you have some expenses you could not otherwise pay. Should you sell her the list of your customers' names and addresses? Explain your answer.

Business Math

16. You have a 12-pound package to ship to a customer who lives 500 miles away. Delivery company A charges $0.80 per pound plus $0.06 per mile. Delivery company B charges $10 per package for the first 8 pounds and first 400 miles. Additional pounds are $0.30 each and additional miles are $0.25 each. What is the total shipping price for each delivery company?

17. A manufacturer sells pens for $0.50 each. If the wholesaler adds a markup of 60% and the retailer adds a markup of 120% of the manufacturer's price, what is the final price of the pen?

Business in Your Community

19. Research local zoning laws in your community regarding home businesses. Are home businesses allowed? Are there any restrictions? Report your findings to the class.

20. Draw a map with your school at the center. Show the locations of at least five businesses that receive shipments from suppliers or ship packages to customers.

ENTREPRENEURS & TECHNOLOGY

Spam

Almost 97 percent of all e-mail sent is spam. **Spam** is unsolicited bulk e-mail—"junk" e-mail that's usually advertising a product and sent to hundreds of thousands of recipients. On any given day, a person with an e-mail account could get hundreds of spam messages. Usually these spam e-mails end up in a separate **spam folder**. Your e-mail account probably has a **spam blocker**, which is also called a **spam filter**. The spam blocker is a program that stops spam from going into your e-mail inbox.

Spam is so common because it is inexpensive to send. Compare the cost of sending spam to the cost of sending this kind of mail through the U.S. Postal Service. With junk mail, the advertiser has to pay to print the ad and then pay for postage. With spam, there's relatively no cost. A **spammer**, a person who sends out spam, can send out a million e-mails for the same price as sending out one. Although only a very small percentage of the people who get spam actually buy the products associated with it, it's enough to make it worthwhile. This is why spam is so common and probably not going to go away any time soon.

How Do Spammers Get E-Mail Addresses?

Spammers use **spam bots**, programs that crawl through the Internet to collect e-mail addresses. Spam bots can get addresses from Web pages, newsgroups, and chat-room conversations. This information can then be used to put together a mailing list.

Online Scams

Spam can be used to steal information or cause damage to a computer. One spam scam is **phishing** (pronounced "fishing"). With phishing, you receive an e-mail that appears to be from a legitimate business, such as your bank, requesting that you verify certain information, such as your Social Security number or bank account number by clicking on a hyperlink. The information can then be used for identity theft, a crime where someone else pretends to be you and uses your credit card and financial information to make

purchases. Phishing e-mails often appear to be legitimate. They have the look of the institution, including the logo, and the From field appears to have the correct name. Hiding the origin of an e-mail message—the information in the From field—is called **spoofing**. It's commonly used for spam e-mail and phishing.

Protecting Yourself

To protect yourself from spam, make sure you have a spam filter installed. Avoid giving out your e-mail address, or have several e-mail addresses and use one for trusted friends and the other for unfamiliar sources. When a Website asks for your e-mail address, check to see that it has a **privacy policy** that states it won't give, sell, or rent your e-mail address to other companies or people. Avoid opening e-mail from sources you don't know. But if you do, don't click on any attachments. There's no way to completely avoid getting spam, but taking certain precautions can reduce your chances of having your computer damaged by malware contained in spam or of you becoming a victim of identity theft.

Tech Vocabulary

- phishing
- privacy policy
- spam
- spam blocker
- spam bots
- spam filter
- spam folder
- spammer
- spoofing

Check Yourself

1. What is spam?
2. What does a spam filter do?
3. What is a spam bot?
4. What is phishing?

What Do You Think?

Solving Problems. What do you do to avoid spam?

CHAPTER 20

MANAGING PURCHASING & INVENTORY

20.1 Managing Purchasing

OBJECTIVES
- Define purchasing
- Explore factors in purchasing management
- Learn about the process of purchasing

VOCABULARY
- buying in bulk
- cash discount
- demand forecasting
- e-procurement
- green procurement
- lead time
- nonperiodic reordering
- packing slip
- periodic reordering
- procurement
- product specification
- purchase order
- purchasing
- quantity discount
- sales forecasting
- sourcing
- trade discount
- value analysis
- vendors
- volume buying

Think about this question:

What is your favorite store?

Write your answer on a piece of paper. Be prepared to provide at least two reasons for your choice.

What Is Purchasing?

Purchasing is buying materials, products, and services for business purposes. **Procurement** is the act of purchasing. Businesses have many purchasing needs. All businesses buy products for their own use—for example, office supplies, raw materials, or other items needed for everyday operations. Wholesale and retail businesses also purchase merchandise to resell.

Large companies typically have an entire department devoted to procurement. Individuals who have purchasing responsibilities are called buyers, or purchasing managers. In small companies, the business owner is likely to do all the purchasing. Whatever the case, buyers must be knowledgeable about the goods and services they purchase and the companies with which they do business. **Vendors** (suppliers) are businesses that sell products or services to other businesses.

What is purchasing?

Managing Purchasing

The goal of procurement management is to buy goods and services of the right quality in the right amounts at the right time, and at the right cost and payment terms from the right vendors. Managing purchasing is extremely important, because every purchase has a cost, which directly affects the profitability of a business.

Goals of Procurement Management
- Right quality
- Right amount
- Right time
- Right vendors
- Right cost
- Right terms

Selecting the Right Quality

Quality covers many aspects of a product or service. For material things, quality can involve appearance, function, artisanship, or other properties of importance to the buyer. Wholesale and retail buyers may care about who produces the merchandise (for example, brand-name companies), where the merchandise is produced (for example, locally made or American made), or how the merchandise is produced. **Green procurement** is the act of purchasing goods and services that are environmentally beneficial in some way. Examples include recycled-content printer paper or a cleaning service that uses all natural products.

One of the tools used by procurement managers to make decisions about quality is called **value analysis**. This is a process for assessing the performance of a product or service relative to its cost. Performance includes any quality characteristic that is important to the buyer. Value analysis is particularly helpful when comparing products. When two items are equivalent in performance, the less costly item should be purchased.

Selecting the Right Quantity

Sales forecasting (**demand forecasting**) is predicting future sales based on past sales data (or other available information) and expected market conditions in the future. Purchasing managers use sales forecasting to help them determine the right quantities to purchase. They also rely on inventory data—that is, information on the number of such items the business already has in stock. The purchase quantity may also be influenced by vendors. Manufacturers and wholesalers typically sell merchandise in very large batches. Purchasing managers must consider all of these factors when deciding what quantities to buy.

Timing Purchases

Sales and inventory data help purchasing managers schedule the best times to place reorders. Items that are used or sold at a relatively constant rate are likely be reordered at regular time intervals. This is called **periodic reordering**. Other items may be reordered at irregular time intervals. This is called **nonperiodic reordering**.

Lead time is the period between starting an activity and realizing its result—for example, the time between order placement and receipt of shipment. In this case, lead time includes how long it will take for a vendor to process an order, pack it, and ship it. Purchasing managers should keep records of the lead times associated with every purchase they make from every supplier. This information will be useful for timing future purchases from these vendors.

Some businesses make purchasing decisions based on seasonal factors. Retail stores, for example, may time their purchases to have certain types of merchandise on hand for cold weather, hot weather, or holiday shopping. Most businesses should also consider cash flow and tax consequences when timing their purchases.

Choosing the Right Vendors

Sourcing is choosing appropriate vendors to supply desired goods or services. Numerous factors are involved in choosing a vendor. They include:

- Price
- Quality
- Lead time
- Location (local, foreign, etc.)
- Delivery and shipping options
- Reliability (for example, filling orders accurately)
- Customer service (during and after order placement and after delivery)

Purchase managers find and research potential vendors at trade shows and conferences and by using the Internet, business directories, trade journals, and industry publications. Purchase managers handle all communications with vendors and may negotiate contracts or agreements for particular prices and payment terms. Some buyers choose to work with

▲ **Figure 20-1**
Seasonal Factors
Some businesses make purchasing decisions based on seasonal factors.

Recognizing Patterns. *Name other products that retail stores might have on hand for different seasons.*

▲ *Buyers may receive a volume discount for purchasing a large quantity of products.*

a large number of vendors, while others prefer to develop close working relationships with a small number of vendors.

Getting the Right Price

Many buyers planning to make a purchase, particularly a large or expensive one, ask several vendors to provide a price quote showing what they would charge to fill the order. Some companies require their buyers to obtain and compare price quotes from a minimum number of suppliers before placing an order.

Buyers also strive to get discounts from vendors. A **quantity discount** is a discount given to buyers for purchasing a large quantity of a product or service from a vendor. Generally, the larger the order, the larger the quantity discount. **Volume buying** (**buying in bulk**) means purchasing a large quantity from a vendor, typically to take advantage of a quantity discount.

A **trade discount** is a discount given to resellers who are in the same trade, industry, or distribution chain as a vendor. Trade discounts often vary with the quantity purchased. In other words, a trade discount may also be a quantity discount.

Many small businesses are unable to take advantage of very large quantity discounts because they lack the cash to make a volume purchase, or they don't have the storage space for the goods, or they cannot possibly sell them in a reasonable amount of time. Small businesses should negotiate with vendors to get the best discount possible. For example, a vendor might give a quantity discount to a small business that commits to placing a large number of small orders over a long time period.

Getting the Right Payment Terms

Businesses that sell to the general public typically demand payment at the time of purchase. However, business-to-business purchases are often handled differently. Many vendors allow established business customers extra time to pay for purchases—for example, 30 days or 60 days.

As we have learned, trade credit is extended payment time given by one business to another business for purchased goods or services. A common trade credit term is "Net 30," which means payment is due within 30 days of purchase. If the buyer pays after that time, the vendor may charge extra fees or refuse to give trade credit to the buyer in the future. Another trade credit term is "Net EOM." EOM is an abbreviation for "end of month," meaning payment is due at the end of the month.

Buyers must be very clear about when a trade credit period begins. The starting date is often called the reference date. The reference date may be the date the goods or services are purchased or received by the buyer, the last day of the month, or some other date designated by the vendor.

Vendors who allow trade credit often provide a small discount to the buyer if full payment is made early and in cash. A **cash discount** is a discount given to buyers who pay for purchases in cash, either at the time of purchase or within a set time period after purchase. A cash discount typically ranges from 1 to 3 percent of the total.

For example, the term "2/10 Net 30" means full payment is due within 30 days but a 2 percent discount is given if the bill is paid within the first 10 days of that period. If the amount due is $1,000, a 2 percent discount totals $20. The buyer can pay $980 to satisfy this debt as long as payment is made within the first 10 days. The following table gives examples and definitions of some common trade credit terms.

TRADE CREDIT TERMS

Term	Meaning
Net 10	Payment is due within 10 days.
1/10 Net 30	Payment is due within 30 days. A 1 percent discount is given for full payment within the first 10 days.
2% EOM	A 2 percent discount is given for full payment before the end of the month.
3% EOM 10	A 3 percent discount is given for full payment before the 10th day after the end of the month (that is, the 10th day of the following month).
1% prox 10	A 1 percent discount is given for full payment before the 10th day of the following month. The abbreviation prox is short for proximo, which means "in the next month."

Receiving and Following Up on Purchases

Purchasing managers are responsible not only for making good purchase decisions but also for making sure that purchased goods and services

Career Planning

Career planning, in its most general sense, means thinking about and moving toward a satisfying job that will showcase your unique strengths and talents.

Career planning begins with thinking about what you enjoy doing. Friends, colleagues, and guidance counselors may be able to help you with choosing an occupation. The career you choose for yourself will be something you work toward. Many careers require a college degree. Others need technical training of some type. Career planning involves figuring out how you will obtain the education or training to become qualified for the job you want.

A good career plan will also include finding an appropriate position and considering how you intend to advance and be promoted—from the beginning of your work life to the end. High school students need to start planning now for their future careers.

THINKING CRITICALLY

Predicting. What type of work do you hope to be doing in the future? How do you plan to get into that field?

To read more about career planning, go to "Your Business Career" on the Student Center at entrepreneurship.pearson.com.

are received on time and in the proper quantity and condition. When goods are received, the buyer should double-check the shipment to make sure that all items ordered were received. Any problems, such as delivery delays or incorrect shipments, should be discussed with the vendor as soon as possible. Bills received from vendors should also be carefully checked to make sure they match what was ordered and that payment terms are those agreed upon before the purchase.

What is the goal of procurement management?

The Process of Purchasing

Proper purchasing management requires good recordkeeping. Several types of paperwork are common to the purchasing process.

- **Product Specification.** A <mark>product specification</mark> is a written, detailed description of the characteristics (size, shape, capabilities, etc.) of a product. Businesses may develop product specifications for items they intend to purchase, particularly those that are expensive or crucial to their operations. Buyers use product specifications to guide their purchases and vendor selections and make sure that products meet their quality standards. Suppliers develop product specifications to provide buyers with information about products they have for sale.

- **Purchase Order.** A <mark>purchase order</mark> is a document issued by a buyer to a vendor that lists the items to be purchased, their quantities and prices, and other relevant information, such as delivery or payment terms. Once a vendor accepts a purchase order, it becomes a binding agreement between the two parties to complete the purchase. A purchase order is a financial commitment. Businesses with employees should have policies that specify exactly who within the company has the authority to issue purchase orders and whether there are any spending limitations.

- **Invoice.** An invoice (bill of sale) is a document issued by a vendor to a buyer on fulfillment of a purchase order. An invoice typically lists the items purchased, their quantities and prices, and other information such as date of shipment and payment terms. Vendors should issue a receipt after each invoice is paid.

- **Packing Slip.** Another vendor-issued document is the **packing slip**, which is a list of all items in a shipment. Purchasing managers should make sure that invoices, receipts, and packing slips are accurate and match the original purchase orders.

Prior to the computer age most purchasing was accomplished through paper catalogs and phone calls. Purchasing conducted through electronic means, such as Internet Websites, is called **e-procurement**. Many vendors operate e-procurement systems that allow buyers to access product information and specifications, fill out purchase orders, and make purchases online.

▲ Figure 20-2
Packing Slip
Purchasing managers should make sure a packing slip is accurate and matches the original purchase order.
Solving Problems. *What would you do if the packing slip didn't match the original purchase order?*

 *What is a purchase order?*

 Your Business Plan. Continue developing your standard business plan. Go to "Section 20.1" of the *Business Plan Project* in your *Student Activity Workbook*, or "Section 20.1" of the BizTech Software.

ASSESSMENT 20.1

Reviewing Objectives

1. What is procurement?
2. Why is managing purchasing important to a business?
3. Name three documents associated with the purchasing process.

Critical Thinking

4. **Applying Concepts.** How could a business use value analysis to compare and choose one of three products that all have the same price?
5. **Inferring.** Which is preferable, a short lead time or a long lead time? Why?

Working Together

Working as a team, come up with a list of five office supplies commonly used by businesses. Research vendors that supply these items and obtain at least three price quotes for each item for two purchasing situations: (1) you wish to buy only one of the item and (2) you wish to buy the item in bulk. Present your findings to the class.

Social Studies

Government Procurement

The U.S. government is the world's largest purchaser of goods and services. Research U.S. government policies and practices regarding purchasing from small businesses and write a brief paper about those policies and practices.

20.2 Managing Inventory

OBJECTIVES

- Learn why managing inventory is important
- Investigate ways to plan inventory levels and investments
- Research methods for controlling inventory levels

VOCABULARY

- inventory investment
- inventory level
- inventory shrinkage
- inventory system
- inventory turnover
- inventory turns
- inventory value
- just-in-time (JIT) inventory system
- obsolescence
- partial inventory system
- periodic inventory system
- perpetual inventory system
- pilfering
- safety stock
- stock-out
- visual inventory system

Consider the following question:

Is there anything in your closet that you don't wear?

Write your answer (yes or no) on a piece of paper. Be prepared to discuss how you manage your "inventory" of clothes.

Why Manage Inventory?

As you learned in Chapter 11, inventory is the amount of merchandise a business has available for sale at a given time. The term inventory actually has several meanings in business, depending on the context in which the word is used. Inventory can be the merchandise itself, the quantity of the merchandise, or the monetary value of the merchandise. In this chapter, inventory refers to physical merchandise. The quantity of merchandise is called the **inventory level**, and the monetary value of the merchandise is called the **inventory value**.

Inventory management is concerned with the physical condition of inventory and the amount of space it takes up. The inventory level is important because it determines how well a business can meet customer demand. Inventory is a business asset; it has monetary value that affects a company's profitability. Inventory also has a cost. In addition to the money paid for inventory (called the **inventory investment**), there are expenses associated with keeping inventory. Inventory managers try to maintain inventory at a level that satisfies customer demand but minimizes expenses.

▲ Figure 20-3

Stock-Out

A stock-out occurs when an item in inventory is completely gone.

Predicting. *How would you expect customers to feel about a store that has a stock-out?*

The goal of inventory management can be summed up in one simple phrase: not too little and not too much. Too little inventory can be disastrous for a business. A **stock-out** occurs when an item in inventory is completely gone. A stock-out leads to lost sales and can cause disappointed customers to go elsewhere to shop. Desperate businesses may be able to place emergency orders with vendors when stock-outs appear likely, but they will probably pay much higher prices than usual to get rush service and delivery.

Too much inventory is also a problem. Excess inventory ties up money that could be used for other purposes. Keeping inventory involves material-handling, labor, tax, and insurance expenses. Inventory that becomes damaged during handling or storage may have to be discarded, adding a waste-disposal expense. **Obsolescence** (ahb-suh-LESS-ence) is the process of becoming obsolete, which means no longer useful or desirable. Retail inventory can go out of style, for example, as fashion trends change. Obsolete inventory has to be sold at a discount, maybe even for less than was paid for it. Obsolescence is more likely to occur when excess inventory is kept, particularly for long periods.

Why should inventory be managed?

Planning Inventory Level and Investment

Maintaining the right amount of inventory is an important task for a business. Useful data sources include purchasing records, sales figures and forecasts, and recorded lead times. Inventory managers must also consider the amount of storage space available and the expense of buying and storing inventory.

Calculating Inventory Level for Business Start-up

Start-up businesses do not have previous sales data on which to base inventory-level decisions. However, wise entrepreneurs conduct market research, analyze their competition, and develop a marketing plan and pricing strategy before they go into business. These are all critical components of a good business plan. Proper planning allows new business owners to make reasonable estimates about expected sales during the first weeks or months after start-up. They also know how much cash and storage space they can devote to inventory. From all this information, they can estimate how much inventory they should have for opening day.

Calculating Inventory Level for an Ongoing Business

An ongoing business that keeps good records can rely on many data sources for inventory-planning purposes. These include sales and cost data, vendor lead times, and losses of inventory due to damage or other reasons. Inventory managers can use this data to predict how inventory levels are going to decrease over time and decide when to reorder merchandise. Obviously, inventory management and purchasing management are closely linked activities.

▼ **Figure 20-4**

Inventory Level Planning
This graph illustrates inventory-level planning based on past sales and purchasing data.

Interpreting Graphs. *Identify the points on the timeline at which shipments are received.*

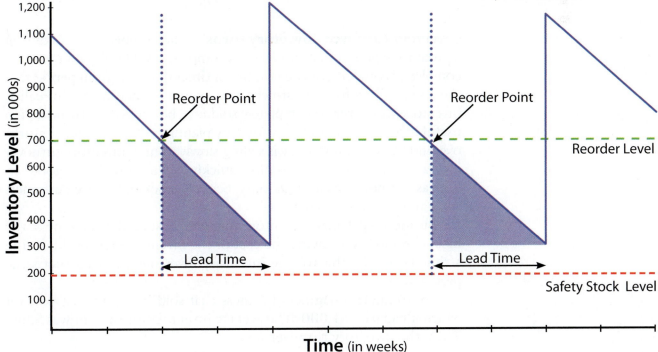

Businesses often choose to maintain a certain minimum inventory level. This level is chosen to cover typical sales and delivery situations, and perhaps unusual scenarios. **Safety stock** is the minimum amount of inventory kept to protect against a stock-out due to unusually high demand or unusually long lead times on delivery.

Imagine a business that expects to sell an average of 10 items per day and expects to experience a 14-day lead time when they place an order. From past data, the company knows that demand sometimes spikes to 30 items per day and some orders have been 4 to 5 days late arriving from the vendor. They choose a safety-stock level and reorder-point level to protect the business against a stock-out when these unusual events occur. Every business has to determine its own risk of stock-out and the measures it is willing to take to prevent one from occurring.

Calculating Inventory Investment

Inventory investment is money spent on inventory. Imagine a company that invests $1,200 per year in inventory. It may buy all its inventory at once or spread the purchases over the course of the year. Each purchase represents an inventory investment. The average inventory investment for the year is calculated by dividing the total investment for that year by the number of inventory purchases. For example, if the company makes 10 inventory purchases in a year, the average investment would be $120.

$$\frac{\text{Total Investment}}{\text{Number of Investment Purchases}} = \frac{\text{Average Annual}}{\text{Inventory Investment}}$$

$$\frac{\$1,200}{10} = \$120$$

Inventory turnover (**inventory turns**) is the number of times during a given time period that inventory is completely sold out (and therefore completely replaced), or the number of times during a given period that the average inventory investment is recouped (earned back). In reality, inventory will never be completely sold out, but inventory turnover is a useful mathematical tool for inventory planning. A low inventory turnover indicates that inventory is selling slowly. A high inventory turnover indicates that inventory is selling quickly. Selling quickly is good, so long as it is not causing stock-outs, because stock-outs drive customers away and hurt future sales.

Businesses calculate inventory turnover in several ways. One of the most common is to divide the cost of the inventory items sold during a time period by the average inventory investment during that same period.

For example, imagine a business that sold inventory last year for which it had paid $1,000. The average inventory investment was $250. Thus, the inventory turnover was 4.

$$\frac{\text{Cost of the Inventory}}{\text{Average Inventory Investment}} = \text{Inventory Turnover}$$

$$\frac{\$1,000}{250} = 4$$

The business's owner likes this inventory turnover rate and wants to achieve the same rate next year. The sales forecast for next year is $2,000, with $1,600 expected to be spent on inventory. The average inventory investment will be $1,600/4 = $400.

 *What data sources are used to plan inventory levels?*

Controlling Inventory Level

Inventory shrinkage is any loss of inventory that occurs between the time the inventory is purchased and the time it is sold or otherwise removed from the shelves. Inventory levels shrink for a variety of reasons. Items may become damaged during handling or storage and have to be discarded. In businesses with employees, there is also a risk of losing inventory to **pilfering** (PILL-fur-ring), which is stealing, particularly

ENTREPRENEURSHIP ISSUES

Inventory Optimization

Many kinds of businesses have to maintain the right amount of inventory. Retail stores, restaurants, and manufacturing plants all closely track inventory levels. If you don't have enough inventory, customers will buy from your competitors or production will stop because of missing parts. If you have too much, the inventory might become out-of-date or spoil while still on the shelves. Getting inventory under control is essential for entrepreneurs.

Very large retail operations, such as Wal-Mart, have fine-tuned the art of inventory optimization. To keep prices down and stores stocked, Wal-Mart has a system called "Retail Link." It uses bar codes to track products and then supplies information to product makers about how much of an item—such as a certain brand of cat food—has sold over the past two years. The individual product suppliers use this information to keep Wal-Mart shelves stocked at 98.5

percent at all times. This way, inventory is managed not by the store but by the companies who want their products on its shelves. As a result, Wal-Mart is rarely short on inventory. If a supplier falls behind on restocking, the retail giant simply gives another supplier an opportunity.

THINKING CRITICALLY

Communicating. In small groups, discuss opening a retail store. What types of products would you sell? Discuss inventory optimization for your store. What are some ways you would make sure to optimize your inventory at all times? Would a system similar to Wal-Mart's work for you?

To read more about inventory optimization, go to "Entrepreneurial Issues" on the Student Center at entrepreneurship.pearson.com.

of small amounts over time. Retail businesses with walk-in customers may lose inventory to shoplifting.

Inventory management involves two important values: the recorded inventory level and the actual inventory level. The recorded inventory level is the amount of inventory that exists according to accounting records—such as purchase and sales records. The recorded inventory level can differ from the actual inventory level for a variety of reasons, including human error, inaccurate recordkeeping, and shrinkage. One of the chief goals of inventory control is reconciling (comparing and bringing into agreement) the recorded and actual inventory levels.

Inventory Systems

An **inventory system** is a process for counting and tracking inventory so inventory value can be calculated. Large companies often use electronic means of tracking inventory. For example, bar codes are scanned when items enter or leave inventory. Electronic inventory systems often feed data to accounting software programs.

- **Visual Inventory System.** Small businesses may rely on people to physically count inventory items. This is known as a **visual inventory system** and is probably the system of choice for most new small-business owners. Even companies using electronic inventory

▼ **Figure 20-5**

Visual Inventory System
Small businesses often rely on a physical counting of inventory.

Relating Concepts. *Why might a company that uses an electronic inventory system use a physical inventory count occasionally?*

systems rely on occasional physical inventory counts to reconcile recorded inventory levels with actual inventory levels. Most businesses perform a physical inventory count at least once a year.

- **Perpetual Inventory System.** For accounting purposes, some businesses choose to update inventory value continually, and others choose to update it periodically. A **perpetual inventory system** is a system that tracks inventory on a continual basis and calculates the inventory value, for accounting purposes, after each inflow or outflow occurs. In other words, inventory is valued after every transaction. Large companies use electronic means, such as bar-code scanning and sophisticated computer programs, to conduct perpetual inventory tracking. These systems provide a running total of both inventory level and value.

- **Periodic Inventory System.** A **periodic inventory system** is a system that calculates inventory value for accounting purposes at periodic times—for example, at the end of the month or end of the year—when a physical inventory count is performed. A periodic inventory system does not keep a running total of inventory value.

- **Partial Inventory System.** A **partial inventory system** combines elements of the perpetual inventory system and the periodic inventory system. Businesses may use the perpetual inventory system to value their most important or most expensive items and use the periodic inventory system for their other items.

- **Just-In-Time Inventory System.** The **just-in-time (JIT) inventory system** is a system in which the goal is to maintain just enough inventory to keep the business operating, with virtually no inventory kept in storage. The JIT system first became popular in the manufacturing industry but has since been embraced by other industries. This system requires precise planning and scheduling, and very close cooperation with vendors, to achieve a condition in which virtually no inventory has to be stored.

Warehousing

Some businesses use warehouses to store inventory, particularly if inventory levels are high. Warehouses must be well organized and integrated into the inventory control system to make sure the inventory is counted properly. Inventory arriving at the warehouse should be logged into the inventory control system and then positioned in storage areas. Inventory leaving the warehouse to fill customer orders, supply manufacturing processes, or restock store shelves must also be carefully tracked.

What is an inventory system?

Your Business Plan. Continue developing your standard business plan. Go to "Section 20.2" of the *Business Plan Project* in your *Student Activity Workbook*, or "Section 20.2" of the BizTech Software.

ASSESSMENT 20.2

Reviewing Objectives

1. What is the goal of inventory management?
2. How is inventory turnover calculated?
3. Name four inventory systems.

Critical Thinking

4. **Comparing/Contrasting.** Compare and contrast the following businesses in terms of their likely inventory turnover rates during one week: an automobile dealership, a produce stand, and a bakery.

5. **Analyzing Information.** What are the difficulties involved in predicting how much inventory a business should keep?

Working Together

Working in a group, imagine that you have to count and list every item of school property in your classroom. Design a plan for achieving this visual inventory system. Describe your plan to the class.

Science

Food Preservatives

Preservatives allow many foods to stay edible and tasty even after long periods in storage. Compile a list of 10 food preservatives and research their chemical properties. Identify which are natural and which are artificial. Describe their uses in the food industry. Present your findings to the class.

Helping Buyers Find Their Dream Home

The Academy of Entrepreneurship Program at Buchholz High School in Gainesville, Florida, offers students the opportunity to learn about entrepreneurship during high school. The program is similar to those offered in high schools across the nation, with courses in the principles of entrepreneurship and business ownership.

Preparing for the Future

For Eric Hunt, the Academy of Entrepreneurship was the opportunity of a lifetime. "I was immediately taken with the freedom and excitement of being my own boss," he said. "I threw myself into it full force. I became the program's vice president my junior year and CEO—Chief Executive Officer—my senior."

After graduating from Buchholz, Eric went on to college. "I didn't look at entrepreneurship as an alternative to higher education," said Eric. "On the contrary, it was just the supplement necessary to make my college experience exactly what I needed." Eric earned a degree in public relations and acquired a real estate license on his own time.

Putting It All Together

When Eric's grandmother, who owned a real estate agency, wanted to retire, Eric felt ready to take over. He already had a real estate license and he used his experience from Buchholz, as well as what he had learned about public relations in college, to make the transition to running his own business.

Eric took advantage of both local television and real estate publications in his marketing strategy. He put up a Website where prospective buyers could see his inventory of available homes and lots. The Website shows photographs of the houses and lots, with short descriptions. Additional photos and information about each property are available with a single click. The Website also offers links to

▲ Eric Hunt

community information, from financing to education. Prospective home buyers can find just about everything they need to know. Eric offers many of the services of larger firms, but with personal attention and flexible commissions. His company motto is "Finding Your Dreams."

With a marketing strategy that shows off his inventory as well as providing additional information, Eric has become a multimillion-dollar producer in just four years. His future in Florida looks sunnier every day. Eric's advice for high school students is, "If you have the opportunity to get involved in an entrepreneurship program, don't hesitate. Even if it isn't your ultimate educational goal, it will enhance whatever path you choose in remarkable ways. It did for me and it can for you."

Thinking Like an Entrepreneur

1. How can entrepreneurship courses help you decide what you want to do?
2. What marketing strategy would you use to promote a real estate business?
3. Eric put his inventory of available properties—houses and lots—on his Website. How could you translate this concept to other types of businesses?

CHAPTER SUMMARY

20.1 Managing Purchasing

Managing purchasing is vital to a business, because purchasing directly affects profits. Purchasing managers strive to buy goods and services of the right quality in the right amounts at the right time, and at the right costs and payment terms from the right vendors. Buyers use sales and inventory data, sales forecasts, and information on lead times to help them make purchasing decisions. Price and payment terms are particularly important factors. Discounts are often offered to buyers who buy large quantities, pay their bills early, or are in the same trade as the vendor. Good recordkeeping is an essential element of the purchasing process.

20.2 Managing Inventory

Inventory management is concerned with having the right amount of inventory—that is, neither too much nor too little. Inventory managers strive to maintain inventory at a level that satisfies customer demand but minimizes expenses. They use purchasing records, sales data and forecasts, lead-time records, and space and cost considerations to plan inventory levels and investments. Inventory obsolescence and shrinkage due to damage or theft are also concerns. Inventory counting and control can be performed by people or by electronic and computerized systems. For accounting purposes, inventory value may be calculated continually or periodically.

REVIEW VOCABULARY

Imagine you are planning to start a wholesale business in which your purchasing and inventory departments will work together in a large warehouse. Write a plan describing the role each department will play in your business and how they will work together. Include 20 of the following terms in your plan.

- demand forecasting (p. 534)
- e-procurement (p. 539)
- green procurement (p. 534)
- inventory investment (p. 541)
- inventory shrinkage (p. 545)
- inventory turnover (p. 544)
- inventory turns (p. 544)
- inventory value (p. 541)
- just-in-time (JIT) inventory system (p. 547)
- nonperiodic reordering (p. 535)

- obsolescence (p. 542)
- partial inventory system (p. 547)
- periodic inventory system (p. 547)
- periodic reordering (p. 535)
- perpetual inventory system (p. 547)
- pilfering (p. 545)
- procurement (p. 533)
- product specification (p. 538)
- purchase order (p. 538)

- purchasing (p. 533)
- quantity discount (p. 536)
- safety stock (p. 544)
- sales forecasting (p. 534)
- sourcing (p. 535)
- stock-out (p. 542)
- trade discount (p. 536)
- value analysis (p. 534)
- visual inventory system (p. 546)
- volume buying (p. 536)

CHECK YOUR UNDERSTANDING

Choose the letter that best answers the question or completes the statement.

1. The trade credit term 1/10 Net 15 means
   a. full payment is due within 30 days
   b. full payment is due within 10 days
   c. a 1 percent discount is given for payment within the first 15 days
   d. a 1 percent discount is given for payment within the first 10 days

2. Why is a stock-out bad for business?
   a. it indicates that there is too much inventory in storage
   b. it disappoints customers
   c. it encourages pilfering
   d. it indicates that the safety-stock level is set too high

3. Which of the following is a vendor?
   a. a purchasing manager
   b. a wholesale business that sells merchandise to a retail store
   c. a retail store that buys merchandise from a manufacturer
   d. a buyer who uses trade credit

4. Obsolescence occurs when
   a. items in inventory increase in value over time
   b. inventory turnover is a large number
   c. items in inventory are no longer popular with customers
   d. inventory gets stolen

5. A cash discount given to a business for paying a bill early is an example of
   a. safety stock
   b. e-procurement
   c. value analysis
   d. trade credit

6. Choose the best example of green procurement.
   a. buying goods that are environmentally friendly
   b. purchasing services at very low prices
   c. buying merchandise by using trade credit
   d. purchasing goods from many different vendors

7. Safety stock is
   a. the rate at which sales are made
   b. a value used to calculate the number of inventory turns per year
   c. a minimum level of inventory that prevents a stock-out
   d. the best inventory to have on hand to prevent pilfering

8. Inventory shrinkage occurs because
   a. inventory becomes damaged
   b. inventory gets stolen
   c. inventory has to be thrown away
   d. all of the above

9. Which is included on a purchase order?
   a. a receipt
   b. a packing slip
   c. a list of the items to be purchased and their prices
   d. a list of the items that were shipped to the buyer

10. A perpetual inventory system
    a. provides a running total of inventory level and value
    b. calculates inventory value at periodic time intervals
    c. helps inventory become obsolete and more valuable
    d. ensures that pilfering and shoplifting will take place

11. A quantity discount is a discount
    a. for paying the bill early
    b. for buying a large amount of an item
    c. for conducting a value analysis of an item
    d. for using trade credit

12. A physical inventory count is
    a. performed by people during a visual inventory
    b. an inventory level calculated from accounting records
    c. conducted by computers using bar-code scanners
    d. the number of inventory turns per accounting period

Business Communication

13. Imagine you are planning to buy a computer for your start-up business. Write a detailed product specification that includes all the features you believe the computer should have.

14. Draw an inventory-level planning graph covering 35 days for a new business that is open every day of the week. Assume starting inventory and reorder quantity is 8,000 items, sales forecast average is 500 items per day, reorder level is 3,000 items, lead time is 7 days, and safety stock is 1,000 items.

15. Deliver a presentation to the class in which you describe the green procurement policy that you would use in your business. Include at least three products or services.

Business Ethics

18. Imagine you are the purchasing manager for a new small business that plans to order large quantities of merchandise. You have interviewed three vendors who all have very similar prices. One of the vendors offers you two free tickets to the Super Bowl (or other event that is very expensive and that you would enjoy) if you will order all the merchandise from that vendor's company. Should you accept the offer? Why or why not?

Business Math

16. A vendor charges a regular price of $1 per pen but offers these quantity discounts: 10% discount for an order of 500 to 1,000 pens and 25% discount for an order of more than 1,000 pens. What is the total bill for an order of 750 pens? What about an order for 3,000 pens?

17. Your company recently made two purchases. The first invoice is for $800 and has a payment term of 3% Net 30. The second invoice is for $950 and has a payment term of 2/10 Net 15. If you take the discounts and pay both invoices within a week, what is the total amount of money you will pay?

Business in Your Community

19. Imagine that a large company wants to relocate its offices to your community and hire local businesses to provide the services it will need. Working in a group, make a list of at least 10 business services that this new company might need. Use a phone directory or business listing to find and identify businesses in your area that could provide these services.

20. Interview a small-business owner in your community whose business maintains an inventory. Find out what type of inventory management and control techniques are used at the business and report your findings to the class.

Auction Sites

Auction sites are Websites where buyers and sellers come together to buy and sell goods and services, mostly by **bidding**, or making an offer on the item. For many people, auctions are a way to save money on products, find used products online, or sell products they no longer need. For other people, it's a business. An auction can be a stand-alone e-business or an extension of a brick-and-mortar company that wants to reach more customers throughout the world. There are dozens of well-known auction sites, with the biggest and best-known one being eBay. It has almost 85 million active members worldwide and more than 50,000 categories of goods and services.

Bidding

Buyers are required to register before bidding. On some sites, the seller must pay a fee or commission only when an item is sold, and on other sites, sellers are required to pay a listing fee as well as a commission. With most auction sites, bidding is done in a limited time period and the highest bidder wins the item. Generally, a good idea is to start with a low price to attract the highest number of bids and promote a bidding war. Sellers can set a **reserve price**, which is the minimum price the seller will take for the item. It means that the item will not be sold unless it meets that price. There's also an option for a fixed price, which is sometimes called "Buy It Now." With a fixed price, the buyer can immediately buy the item. The seller may have a number of the same items and will let the bidders know how many are left.

Auction Site Tips for Entrepreneurs

If you're thinking about starting an e-commerce business by using an auction site, you will need to take into account some of the same techniques necessary to be successful in a brick-and-mortar business. You'll want to sell something that interests you. You need to know where you're going to get your products— whether they're items you make, items you buy new online at wholesalers or at discount stores, or collectibles you own or find at garage sales. According to one

expert, the best eBay businesses sell unusual, hard-to-find items at a discount. You need to research the competition. What are other people selling? How are they pricing their products? As well as researching your potential market and competition, you also need to pay attention to the way you advertise and safely ship your products. As in any business, building trust with your customers is essential.

Posting on an Auction Site

Photographs, along with your ad copy, are crucial to selling online. You'll need a high-quality digital camera to take pictures that you can upload to the auction site. If the product is damaged, show it clearly in your photos.

Include the facts of your product in the title of your listing. Be totally honest, especially if you're selling a used product. You'll be required to include your return policy and the payment and shipping options in your listing. It's best to offer more than one payment option—PayPal, credit and debit cards, checks and money orders are the usual possibilities. Do not ship the item until you receive payment.

Tech Vocabulary
- auction site
- bidding
- reserve price

Check Yourself
1. What is an auction site?
2. What is bidding?
3. What is a reserve price?
4. Why are photographs important?

What Do You Think?
Analyzing. What are the similarities and differences between operating a retail business through an online auction site or in a physical store?

MANAGING FOR SUCCESS

After four years, business is booming at Eva's Edibles. Eva Tan and Sylvia Watson came up with a long-range plan that involved leasing a commercial kitchen that had a small storefront. Watch as Eva's Edibles moves into its new space and continues to grow.

The Big Picture

To begin their fourth year, Eva and Sylvia worked together to develop a strategic, or "big-picture," plan for the business. They made a list of their goals for the company over the next five years.

Both women pictured Eva's Edibles becoming a large commercial kitchen with a small storefront for retail. This would enable them to expand their offerings of packaged meals. Sylvia also wanted a place where she could showcase her cakes to the public. She wanted to sell cakes both whole and by the slice.

To help accomplish this, Eva and Sylvia divided the business responsibilities. Eva focused on hiring and directing employees, handling business promotions, and building a favorable company image.

Sylvia, a talented pastry chef, was responsible for the baking. Sylvia also had experience in purchasing and inventory management, so she handled those areas.

Eva and Sylvia developed a day-to-day operational plan for achieving their overall objectives. They also resolved to review their strategic progress every year.

"Let's make sure we are always happy with our direction," said Sylvia. "If we don't plan it, it won't happen!"

Location, Location, Location

The first step in achieving their goal was to locate a commercial kitchen with a small storefront. To encourage walk-in customers, the partners wanted an easily accessible site with parking. An area near both the Ohio State University and the downtown Columbus business center seemed best.

They discovered the perfect location. It was a two-story brick building with a storefront, a modern commercial kitchen, and a large walk-in refrigerator. The building was in an area zoned for commercial use. They wanted to lease the building and use the upstairs as an office.

Although they had been putting away money for the initial payments (first and last month's rent and security deposit), they needed more funding. Sylvia had some savings and she agreed to lend the company the necessary cash. Eva and Sylvia hired a lawyer to write an agreement that specified the repayment terms.

Moving into the building brought new management challenges. Eva and Sylvia created Gantt and PERT charts to plan and monitor the tasks they needed to complete before opening. They changed the layout to maximize the kitchen's efficiency and created a small, cheery front retail space where walk-in customers could buy prepared meals and bakery items.

They posted their hours of operation: Monday through Saturday from 10 a.m. to 5 p.m., and Sunday from 12 p.m. to 4 p.m.

Eva's Edibles had found a place of its own.

Buying Smart

When Eva's Edibles began, four years earlier, purchasing was pretty easy. Eva bought what was needed to make each customer's meals for a week. She had no storage or inventory issues. Now that the company had grown, Eva and Sylvia wanted to start buying in volume to reduce costs.

Because she was responsible for inventory management, Sylvia had to consider the lead time required for certain foods. Groceries needed to arrive in time to fill orders but not too long before that. Spoilage was an issue with fresh ingredients. Sylvia couldn't afford to order too much at one time.

Storage space was also limited. So Sylvia adopted a just-in-time inventory system for fresh items and a periodic inventory system for dry ingredients that had a long shelf life.

Controlling costs was also important. Eva suggested they could save money by doing their own cutting and trimming of meat, poultry, and fish instead of paying a higher price for items that were already prepped. "We have this huge walk-in refrigerator," Eva said. "Let's use it."

Sylvia began buying whole poultry, fish, and large cuts of meat. Frank, the cook they hired to help them, learned how to butcher. Eva's Edibles reduced its costs and increased its profits.

Things were definitely going well.

What Would You Have Done?

1. **Predicting.** Imagine you were Eva or Sylvia beginning the fourth year of Eva's Edibles. What would be your goals for the company?

2. **Relating Concepts.** What other production, distribution, or operation issues might Eva or Sylvia have needed to address after moving to their new location and selling prepared foods and bakery items to walk-in customers?

3. **Solving Problems.** During a holiday season, Eva's Edibles ran out of a key ingredient used to make its specialty cakes. What would you have done to solve this problem and prevent it from happening again?

UNIT **8**

GROWING YOUR BUSINESS

YOUR BUSINESS PLAN

In this unit, you'll focus on the **Plan for Growth** section of the business plan and answer these questions:

- How can I plan for business growth?
- What are the challenges of growth?
- Can I franchise or license my business?
- When and how should I leave my business?

CHAPTER **21**

MAKING YOUR BUSINESS GROW

21.1 Planning for Business Growth

OBJECTIVES

- Examine business growth
- Learn when to grow a business
- Explore product life cycles
- Investigate business growth strategies

VOCABULARY

- core business
- diversification growth strategy
- horizontal diversification
- horizontal integration strategy
- integrative growth strategy
- intensive growth strategy
- market development
- market penetration
- market share
- organic growth
- perpetual life cycle
- product development
- product life cycle
- synergistic diversification
- vertical integration strategy

Answer this question:

Do you have hobbies?

List your hobbies on a piece of paper. Be prepared to discuss in class how you spend your free time.

What Is Business Growth?

To grow a business means to make changes that result in greater sales. A business grows, or expands, in two ways: internally and externally. **Organic growth** is growth achieved by expanding a business internally—for example, adding new products or services for sale. External growth is achieved by buying other businesses or merging with them. Most small businesses experience organic growth rather than acquiring other companies.

When a business thrives, the owner must eventually decide whether to maintain the original strategy or take a bold step to grow the business. Because entrepreneurs are ambitious by nature, the question is often not whether to grow, but when and how to grow.

Growth, like any business move, must be carefully thought out. A smart entrepreneur develops a carefully researched business plan before launching a business. Business growth also requires a great deal of planning. The original business plan should be updated or an entirely new one developed. In either case, the plan should outline steps for implementing the growth strategy and look at the possible consequences on the business.

Deciding When to Grow

Three factors affect the decision to grow a business:

- **Condition of the Business.** A business is ready to grow when it has a solid base of customers and makes sales that meet or exceed forecasts and contribute to a satisfactory net profit. The business has become good at what it does. It makes a consistent profit and achieves quality standards and customer-satisfaction targets. The owner does not struggle to keep up with the day-to-day demands of the business but has enough time to devote to growth.

- **Economic Climate.** The economic climate in which the business operates is also important. Owners planning for growth must consider economic conditions at the local, national, and perhaps even global levels. Economies tend to follow cycles of upturns and downturns. A downturn is not necessarily a bad time to expand a business. It depends on the business and its markets.

- **Life Goals of the Business Owner.** Growing a business is not only an economic move, it's a personal one as well. An owner who decides to grow a business takes on new pressures and demands. Growth will require more time and money and introduce new risks. Owners who want to grow their businesses should schedule growth with their life goals in mind.

Figure 21-1 ▶

Life Goals
The decision to grow a business also depends on the life goals of the business owner.

Predicting. *How would various life goals, such as marriage, children, or relocation, affect the decision to grow a business?*

Product Life Cycles

A **product life cycle** is a series of stages—introduction, growth, maturity, and decline—that a product may pass through while it is on the market. This concept can be applied to a product type or industry (for example, automobiles), to a specific brand (for example, Ford), and to a particular product (for example, the Ford Explorer).

Product Life-Cycle Stages

Each stage in a product life cycle has specific cost and profit considerations. A conventional product life-cycle curve is shown in Figure 21-2.

- **Introduction.** When a product is introduced, the marketing effort is devoted to building product awareness—that is, making consumers aware of the product. This is typically an expensive phase with high advertising and promotional expenses. Profits may be low at first.

- **Growth.** Sales and profit increase steadily as the product is embraced by consumers. Competitors may be few at this stage, allowing the business to expand distribution and take advantage of strong demand.

- **Maturity.** This is the stage during which sales and profits stop growing. They level off and may begin to decline. By now, the product probably faces stiff competition. The business may have to lower prices or enhance the product in some way to give it a new competitive advantage and extend its life.

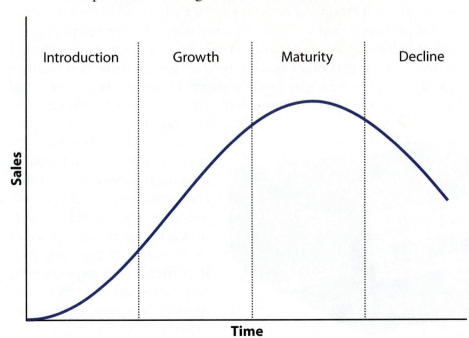

◀ **Figure 21-2**

Product Life-Cycle Curve
A product life cycle typically includes various sales stages.

Interpreting Graphs. *During what stage do sales reach their peak?*

- **Decline.** During the decline stage, product sales and profits fall steeply and don't recover. The product loses its appeal to consumers. In some cases, the decline is due to technological advances or governmental regulations. For example, the VCR has given way to the digital video recorder.

Product life-cycle curves have many variations. Some products are immensely and immediately popular. Their sales rocket upward but then decline quickly. This cycle is common in the fashion and entertainment industries.

Other products endure for long periods. A **perpetual life cycle** is a product life cycle in which a product never undergoes a final decline, because it remains in the maturity stage forever. Basic food products, such as bread and other items in everyday use, are said to have a perpetual life cycle. However, individual brands and products within the bread industry can certainly decline.

Product Life Cycle in Growth Planning

The product life cycle is a useful concept for planning growth strategy. One way for a business to grow is to provide a product (or service) that it has not offered before. This product will be new to the business but may not be new to the market. It could be similar to other products already being offered. If you want to add a new product to your company's offerings, you must understand the product group's stage in the product life cycle. This knowledge will help you determine the level of competition you will face and the costs and marketing strategies that will be required to make the new offering successful.

The product may be completely new and different, with no competition. This is an introductory stage offering. The product may be similar to others that are in a growth phase. In this case, the new offering probably needs to be innovative to set itself apart from competitors. A business may decide to introduce a copycat product when the overall life cycle for that product group is in the maturity stage. At this point, price or product enhancements may be the competitive advantage. Introducing a product that is part of an existing product group in the decline stage typically wouldn't be a wise business move. However, the decline stage is an excellent time to introduce a replacement product for the one that is in decline.

Businesses also have to consider the costs and risks of introducing a new product that competes against their existing products. For example, a business with an existing product in the maturity stage may find it difficult and expensive to lure customers away from that product to a new, but similar, offering.

▼ **Figure 21-3**
Product Life Cycles
A business must understand a product group's stage in the product life cycle.

Drawing Conclusions.
A company is considering offering a VHS recorder that is new to the company. Would this be a wise move in relation to the product group's stage in the product life cycle?

Increasing Use of Online Surveys

Online surveys help take the guesswork out of decision-making for entrepreneurs. Instead of hearing comments from only a handful of vocal clients, e-surveys allow a business owner to find out what hundreds—or thousands—of consumers think. Small companies can often respond to survey data quickly and make immediate improvements to their services or products, their Websites, or their customer service operations.

Online survey tools are easy to use. Firms that sell these tools to small businesses let their customers design custom surveys and analyze results in easy-to-read graphs. Small businesses can offer online surveys on their Websites or ask customers to respond in an e-mail invitation.

Since its founding in 1999, one survey tool—SurveyMonkey (www.surveymonkey.com)—has grown quickly. According to Alexa, an Internet-watch firm that measures Web traffic, SurveyMonkey ranks among the top 800 most-visited sites on the Internet. You can find other examples of online survey tools at www.questionpro.com and www.zoomerang.com.

THINKING CRITICALLY

Applying Concepts. Imagine you are a small-business owner designing an online survey. What are three questions you would ask your customers?

To read more about online surveys, go to "Entrepreneurship Issues" on the Student Center at entrepreneurship.pearson.com.

What are the four stages of a typical product life cycle?

Growth Strategies

Businesses can follow many growth strategies when they wish to expand. These strategies typically focus on new products and/or new markets. (In this discussion, services are referred to as the products of a service business.) Three broad categories of growth strategies are:

- Intensive growth strategies
- Integrative growth strategies
- Diversification growth strategies

Intensive Growth Strategies

An **intensive growth strategy** is a growth strategy that focuses on cultivating new products or new markets, and sometimes both. Businesses use an intensive growth strategy when they believe they haven't fully realized their strengths or their markets. This strategy is best described as "doing more of what you are good at doing." The three most common types of intensive growth strategies are:

- Market penetration
- Market development
- Product development

Market penetration is an intensive growth strategy that emphasizes more intensive marketing of existing products. This strategy has two goals: sell more to existing customers and sell to new customers in existing markets. Both goals require extensive, and expensive, marketing (advertising, promotions, and so on). However, market penetration is a way for a business to increase its profits by taking advantage of its existing skills, experience, and knowledge about its target markets. It is a popular growth strategy for small businesses.

Existing customers may be convinced to buy more of a product if the business advertises new uses for that product. The makers of dry soup mixes could, for example, publish recipes for party dips made from their products. Businesses can also try to convince existing customers to buy a product more often. Toothbrush manufacturers advertise that dentists recommend replacing a toothbrush every three months. Existing customers may also buy more and buy more often if they are offered incentives, such as frequent-buyer programs.

Market penetration can also involve pursuing new customers in current target markets. Basically, the business uses marketing tactics to try to gain customers from its competitors. This increases a business's market share. **Market share** is the percentage of the total sales captured by a product or a business in a particular market. In other words:

$$\frac{\text{Sales by Business}}{\text{Total Sales in Market}} \times 100 = \text{Market Share Percentage}$$

If a company sells \$1,000 worth of tennis rackets in a town where total sales of tennis rackets are \$5,000, the company has a one-fifth, or 20%, market share.

$$\frac{\$1,000}{\$5,000} \times 100 = 20\%$$

Once a business has the largest market share it believes it can capture, the next step is usually to find new markets.

Market development is an intensive growth strategy that focuses on reaching new target markets, such as customers in another geographic area or customers who have different demographics from current customers. A retail store might open a branch in a new city or develop a Website to sell its products online.

Product development is an intensive growth strategy in which businesses develop new products or enhance their existing products. Enhancements may include bonus features or new packaging for products. For example, they could add small toys as extras to cereal boxes. Product development is typically costly for a business but can be a successful means of growth if the new or enhanced offering is popular with customers.

Integrative Growth Strategies

An **integrative growth strategy** is a growth strategy that emphasizes blending businesses together through acquisitions and mergers.

Integrative growth strategies are typically more expensive than intensive growth strategies and are usually practiced by mature businesses with large cash flows. There are two types of integrative growth strategies:

- **Vertical Integration.** An integrative growth strategy in which one business acquires another business in its own supply chain, *but not at the same supply chain level,* is a **vertical integration strategy**. An example of this type of growth strategy is when a retail store buys a wholesaler. Another example is when a manufacturing business buys a retail store in which its products are sold.

- **Horizontal Integration.** An integrative growth strategy in which one business acquires another business *at the same supply chain level as itself* is a **horizontal integration strategy**. When one manufacturing company buys another manufacturing company, that's a horizontal integration strategy. The acquired business may be a competitor or a business in a completely different industry.

▲ *A product development strategy enhances existing products.*

Diversification Growth Strategies

Every business has a **core business**, which is the most important focus of the business. For example, the core business of McDonald's is selling fast food. A **diversification growth strategy** (die-ver-sih-fih-KAY-shun) is a growth strategy in which a business grows by offering products or services that are different from its core business. There are two types of diversification growth strategies:

- **Synergistic Diversification**. A growth strategy in which a business adds new products or services that are related to its existing products or services is a **synergistic diversification** (sin-er-JIS-tic). A clothing store that begins selling shoes practices this type of growth. So does an event-planning business that begins to offer catering services.

- **Horizontal Diversification**. A growth strategy in which a business adds new products or services that are not related to its existing products or services but appeal to its existing target market is called **horizontal diversification**. Recently some large grocery stores have begun offering credit cards to their customers. This is an example of horizontal diversification. Another example would be a gasoline station that sells food.

Name three broad categories of growth strategies.

Figure 21-4 ▶

Horizontal Diversification
A grocery store that offers credit cards to its customers is practicing horizontal diversification.

Recognizing Patterns. *Can you name other types of products or services that a grocery would offer that would be examples of horizontal diversification?*

 Your Business Plan. Continue developing your standard business plan. Go to "Section 21.1" of the *Business Plan Project* in your *Student Activity Workbook*, or "Section 21.1" of the BizTech Software.

ASSESSMENT 21.1

Reviewing Objectives

1. What are two general ways in which a business grows?

2. Name three factors that affect the decision to grow (expand) a business.

3. What are the four stages of a product life cycle?

4. How does an intensive growth strategy differ from an integrative growth strategy and a diversification growth strategy? Give your own examples of each.

Critical Thinking

5. **Classifying.** Classify each of the following plans as to type of growth strategy: a) a retail shoe store that wants to buy the manufacturing plant that makes its shoes; b) a bookstore that wants to sell packs of flavored coffee; c) a landscaping business that plans to advertise in another part of the state.

6. **Recognizing Patterns.** Draw product life-cycle curves for a) bread; b) ticket sales for a highly anticipated movie that soon disappointed moviegoers.

Working Together

Working with three classmates, develop a poster showing the four stages in a product life cycle, with two products, product groups, brands, or industries that currently fall into each one.

Science
Perpetual Motion

For centuries, inventors have tried to create perpetual motion machines—mechanisms that, once started, continue to run indefinitely with no additional energy inputs. Research perpetual motion machines, the many claims that have been made about them, and the scientific laws that relate to them. Is there any relation to perpetual life cycle? Explain your findings to the class.

OBJECTIVES

- Examine how personal feelings affect business growth
- Study the practical challenges of growing a business
- Investigate the chances for business growth

VOCABULARY

- debt capital
- entrepreneurial mindset
- equity capital
- micromanager
- self-financing

Consider this question:

Do you believe the saying, "If you want something done right, do it yourself"?

Write your answer (yes or no) on a piece of paper. Be prepared to explain your answer to the class.

Personal Feelings about Business Growth

Entrepreneurs excel at identifying business opportunities and finding resources to transform innovative ideas into reality. An **entrepreneurial mindset** is the mental attitude common to entrepreneurs. It typically includes an optimistic, can-do outlook and the personal ambition necessary to create a business. This is ideal for starting a business but may not be as useful when it comes to growing the business.

Business growth often requires the owner to give up some personal control over the business. This may be difficult for someone who has been the driving force and creative center of the business and largely responsible for its success. A **micromanager** is an individual who interferes too much in the decisions and tasks of associates or employees. He or she constantly scrutinizes and criticizes everything they do, or automatically dismisses their ideas and opinions as inferior. A micromanager does not trust others to get things done or do them right. A business owner prone to micromanagement, or reluctant to delegate responsibilities, may become overwhelmed by the added demands of business growth. Entrepreneurs must truthfully examine their personal feelings about

▲ Figure 21-5

Successful Growth

Successful growth can be rewarding to a business owner.

Inferring. *People say that the greater the risk, the greater the reward. How would you relate that to growth that was very rewarding?*

giving up some control for the chance to grow the business.

Also, business growth increases risk. The growth effort may fail; it may even put the overall business in jeopardy. Entrepreneurs who are considering growth should carefully examine the risks involved and weigh them against their personal capacity for taking on that risk.

Obviously there are personal challenges and potential negative consequences associated with business growth. However, growth that is successful can be rewarding to a business owner. It will probably bring greater personal income and financial stability and a sense of accomplishment. Business owners must ultimately make the decision about whether to grow or not, based on their life goals.

READING CHECKPOINT ✓   *What is a micromanager?*

Practical Challenges of Growing a Business

Growing a business involves six practical challenges. Each should be addressed in the revised business plan you will develop.

- **Space.** A growing business usually requires more physical space. If the existing building or rooms are not large enough to handle the expansion, you will have to find additional space.

- **Business Structure.** You may need to change the organizational structure of your business—for example, from a sole proprietorship to a limited liability company or corporation.

- **Materials and Equipment.** Growth may require you to purchase more materials, equipment, and office furniture and supplies. A manufacturing business that wants to grow must be sure the supply chain will be able to accommodate the new demands.

- **Information Technology (IT).** This is the use of computer systems, hardware, and software to store and manage information. IT demands for accounting, purchasing, inventory, payroll and other operations will increase as the business grows and expands its recordkeeping.

- **People and Skills.** A growing business almost always needs more employees, especially at the management level. Existing staff may have to be trained in new skills that will be necessary to make the growth effort successful.

- **Money.** Business growth requires financing. This money may come from the company itself or from outside sources.

▲ *Growth often requires purchasing more office furniture and supplies.*

Motivation

If you thought about it, you'd probably say that motivation can be either internal or external—and you'd be right. Young children are motivated almost entirely by external forces (for example, a promise of extra play time if they get their homework done). Adults don't typically rely as much on external motivators to get things done. They are more often motivated from within.

Developing ways to motivate yourself takes practice and time. Here's one way to begin developing the ability to motivate yourself from within: Think of what you need to do, and decide why it needs to be done. Just recognizing why you need to complete a task can act as an inspiration to do it. And when it is finished you will have the personal satisfaction that you were able to do it—and you can move on.

Sometimes you can also give yourself an external reward for completing a job. This could include treating yourself to a movie or doing something else you find enjoyable. When you can combine an internal and an external motivator, you will increase your chances of finishing the job.

THINKING CRITICALLY

Recognizing Patterns. Think about what motivates you most effectively. When you have had projects and assignments to complete, what has helped you get them done? Do you think you are able to motivate yourself well? Why or why not?

To read more about motivation, go to "Your Business Career" on the Student Center at entrepreneurship.pearson.com.

Self-financing means obtaining the funds for growth from existing operations, for example, by reinvesting cash reserves (profits). External sources of money include **debt capital**, which is money obtained by a business through a loan, and **equity capital**, which is money obtained by a business from an investor in exchange for a share of ownership (equity) in the business. Whatever the source, you must carefully consider the financial risks and obligations as part of your strategy for growth.

READING CHECKPOINT *Name six practical challenges associated with business growth.*

▼ **Figure 21-6**
Multiple Locations
The factors that made one location a success may not exist in a new location.

Comparing/Contrasting. *What kinds of factors might exist in one location but not in a second location?*

Can a Business Grow?

The success of business growth will be more certain if you follow a strategic plan. It is also important to know as much as possible about your business: what works well, what could be improved, what drives profitability, and so forth. An effective tool for accomplishing this task is a SWOT analysis.

The SWOT analysis introduced in Chapter 6 was used for evaluating the prospects of starting a business. A SWOT analysis assesses strengths, weaknesses, opportunities, and threats for a start-up company. However, a SWOT analysis is also useful for established businesses when analyzing growth opportunities. An established business that keeps good records should be well aware of its strengths and weaknesses. Customer surveys can also provide valuable feedback. The threat component of the SWOT analysis is, in large part, the competition. Business owners need to learn as much as possible about the strengths and weaknesses of potential competitors and the market share their actual competitors have. It's also important to be aware of any new or potential regulations that may impact growth.

When you know your business's capabilities, limitations, and threats, you can better select an appropriate growth opportunity. Many small businesses choose to grow by opening a new location that offers the same products or services as their original location. But the factors that made one location successful may not work in another location. A business owner with multiple locations must also be careful that the original customers are not ignored during the growth process. Another possible choice is to expand the product offerings in the existing location. No matter what strategy a business owner selects, a completely new business plan should be prepared to assess all aspects of the situation.

 *How is a SWOT analysis used to analyze a growth opportunity?*

 Your Business Plan. Continue developing your standard business plan. Go to "Section 21.2" of the *Business Plan Project* in your *Student Activity Workbook*, or "Section 21.2" of the BizTech Software.

ASSESSMENT 21.2

Reviewing Objectives

1. What is an entrepreneurial mindset?
2. What are the six practical challenges associated with growing a business?
3. Which four characteristics does a SWOT analysis assess?

Critical Thinking

4. **Predicting.** Imagine that the student population at your school is going to double next year. Review each of the practical challenges of growth and predict how your school cafeteria might cope with each challenge.
5. **Relating Concepts.** Explain how a SWOT analysis for a growth opportunity might differ from the original SWOT analysis that was performed at start-up.

Working Together

Working in a group of three, role-play for the class three situations that demonstrate a business owner who is micromanaging employees.

Social Studies
Groupthink

Groupthink is a sociological phenomenon that occurs when a group of people develop a particular mindset. Research groupthink and write a brief paper explaining whether it is a good or bad means for making business decisions.

Making InnerLeaf Grow: Spreading the Seeds

When Kathleen Jeanty was at Babson College, she realized she "had a real knack for marketing." Although she started a company as a student, she found "it was difficult to have people take me seriously." Kathleen decided to focus on school and get more experience in the industry after she graduated.

She did get more experience in the industry after graduation—and was laid off three times in three years! That was when she decided it was time to return to her entrepreneurial inclinations. Kathleen founded InnerLeaf Communications, a marketing and public relations company.

Starting from Seed

Kathleen began InnerLeaf with practically no money, getting by on unemployment benefits from her previous job. She moved into a rooming house to save on expenses, bought used equipment, and printed business cards. She found work through word-of-mouth, and her business grew.

Kathleen didn't have a brochure when she started out. "At the time, there was no track record, no portfolio, no work. We needed to build samples."

But she wanted the image of being a business and not an independent consultant, so she moved her office to a space in the back of a retail store. From there, Kathleen has expanded through two office spaces to her current 2,000-square-foot location in Center City, Philadelphia. She has a staff of five and hires contract employees when needed. Having this much space and a staff to pay has made Kathleen look for business in a different way.

Finding a Niche

When Kathleen first started, she only needed to meet expenses for herself. She was happy to work on single projects. "Now, we definitely have to have clients secured for a couple of years," she said. She also needs to plan for the future in case she loses a contract.

▶ *Kathleen Jeanty*

There's a lot of competition in the marketing and public relations field. "I realized very early on that for us to be known and to remain in the mindset of folks, we needed to be known for something."

When Kathleen looked at her portfolio of clients, at her business relationships, and at her own lifestyle, the right market became clear. Kathleen was born and raised in Haiti. The Afro-Caribbean market was the perfect place to position her company. "It's a huge, untapped market that's growing all over the country," she says. To help serve clients, InnerLeaf has satellite offices in Miami and Boston, and Kathleen has plans to expand to even more cities.

Thinking Like an Entrepreneur

1. How important is it to have a business office?
2. Kathleen didn't have a brochure when she started out. Would you make the same decision? Why?
3. Kathleen targeted a specific market, the Afro-Caribbean segment. Identify 10 other market segments that might use the services of a company like Kathleen's.

CHAPTER SUMMARY

21.1 Planning for Business Growth

Growing a business means making changes that are expected to result in increased sales. Growth should be well planned and timed based on the condition of the business, the overall economy, and the life goals of the business owner. When introducing a new product to the market, it is important to know the product's life-cycle stage for the product group. Growth strategies fall into three broad categories: intensive, integrative, and diversification. Intensive growth strategies include market penetration, market development, and product development. Integrative growth strategies include horizontal and vertical integration. Diversification growth strategies may be synergistic or horizontal.

21.2 Challenges of Growth

Growing a business poses both personal and practical challenges to the business owner. The personal challenges include less control but more risk for the entrepreneur as a business grows. Any plans for growth must be carefully timed with the entrepreneur's life goals in mind. Practical challenges relate to space, organizational structure, materials and equipment, information technology, people and skills, and money. The funds needed for growth can be raised through internal or external means—from cash reserves (profits) or by borrowing or selling equity. A SWOT analysis should be performed to assess the strengths and weaknesses of the business, the threat posed by competitors, and the growth opportunity.

REVIEW VOCABULARY

Imagine that you are going on the "Business Help Line" television show. It provides information to entrepreneurs. You've been asked to give a short talk titled "Growing Your Business." Present this talk to the class. Use at least half of the following terms.

- core business (p. 565)
- debt capital (p. 569)
- diversification growth strategy (p. 565)
- entrepreneurial mindset (p. 567)
- equity capital (p. 569)
- horizontal diversification (p. 565)
- horizontal integration strategy (p. 565)

- integrative growth strategy (p. 564)
- intensive growth strategy (p. 563)
- market development (p. 564)
- market penetration (p. 564)
- market share (p. 564)
- micromanager (p. 567)
- organic growth (p. 559)

- perpetual life cycle (p. 562)
- product development (p. 564)
- product life cycle (p. 561)
- self-financing (p. 569)
- synergistic diversification (p. 565)
- vertical integration strategy (p. 565)

CHECK YOUR UNDERSTANDING

Choose the letter that best answers the question or completes the statement.

1. Obtaining debt capital to grow a business can also be described as
   a. self-financing
   b. micromanagement
   c. SWOT analysis
   d. borrowing money

2. A micromanager is
   a. a manager in charge of information technology
   b. a manager in charge of the product life cycle
   c. a manager who interferes too much in the decisions and tasks of employees
   d. a manager who interferes too little in the decisions and tasks of employees

3. Which of the following is an example of organic growth?
   a. a business that sells more to existing customers than to new customers
   b. a business that buys a competitor
   c. a business that practices integrative growth
   d. a business that buys its supply company

4. A company that begins advertising its existing products in another state is practicing
   a. market penetration
   b. market development
   c. vertical integration
   d. horizontal integration

5. How could a SWOT analysis be used when planning business growth?
   a. to assess the threat posed by the competition in a new market
   b. to assess a company's existing strengths and weaknesses
   c. to assess a specific growth opportunity
   d. all of the above

6. The stages of a product life cycle are
   a. introduction, growth, maturity, and decline
   b. space, materials, people, and money
   c. vertical and horizontal
   d. intensive, integrative, and diversification

7. Information technology is a practical concern of business growth because a growing business
   a. needs more computers for recordkeeping
   b. needs an entrepreneurial mindset
   c. needs more physical space
   d. needs more people

8. Which of the following indicates good timing for business growth?
   a. the owner has trouble meeting the day-to-day demands of the business
   b. the business does not make a consistent profit
   c. the business is meeting its customer satisfaction standards
   d. the owner is worried about the survival of the business

9. Market penetration is
   a. an integrative growth strategy
   b. an intensive growth strategy
   c. synergistic diversification
   d. information technology

10. A fast food restaurant that begins selling toys is following which growth strategy?
    a. market development
    b. vertical integration
    c. horizontal diversification
    d. micromanagement

11. A product with a perpetual life cycle is
    a. a product in the introduction stage of the product life cycle
    b. a product in the growth stage of the product life cycle
    c. a product with rapidly declining sales
    d. a product with relatively constant sales

12. An integrative growth strategy is best described as
    a. developing new markets for existing products
    b. buying other companies in the same industry
    c. developing new products for existing target markets
    d. introducing products in the decline stage of the product life cycle

Business Communication

13. Using the Internet, find five large companies that offer products or services that differ from their respective core businesses. Present your findings to the class.

14. Work in a group of five. One person plays the owner of a successful pet-sitting business and the others are employees in the business. The owner wants to expand by offering dog obedience classes but doesn't want to hire anyone new. Role-play the situation when the owner tells the employees that they will need to become dog trainers.

15. Imagine that you operate a successful retail store and wish to grow your business by using an intensive growth strategy. Choose one of the strategies and write a letter to your local bank manager explaining how you plan to grow.

Business Ethics

18. Your family gave you money to start your business five years ago. In exchange, you gave them 20% ownership in your company and a share in the decision-making. The business is doing well, and you want to add some new products to your line. Your family is opposed to the idea because of the risk. An outside investor will provide the cash you need to grow, but only if you buy back your family's share of the business, putting them out of the decision-making process. Should you take the money from the outside investor? Explain your reasoning.

Business Math

16. Total sales of athletic shoes amounted to $3 million last year. Tip Top Shoes had a 30% market share, while Might-ee Shoes had a 45% share. The remaining market share was split evenly between Super Glide and Hoopster Shoes. Calculate last year's sales amount for each company.

17. A small car-wash business makes $5 in profit for each car washed. It performs an average of 200 car washes per month. For the past 20 months, the owner has been saving 50% of the profit. She wants to buy a new machine that costs $12,500. How much money has she saved so far? How many more months until she has enough to buy the machine?

Business in Your Community

19. Interview a local small-business owner who has a physical store in your community and also operates a Website from which customers can order the business's products. Find out how the company's marketing efforts differ in targeting its potential walk-in and online customers.

20. Working with a group of classmates, choose a small business in your community. Think of seven specific ways that the business might be able to grow—using three intensive growth strategies, two integrative growth strategies, and two diversification growth strategies. Present your ideas to the class.

Affiliate Marketing

One way Website owners can use their sites to make money or increase traffic is through affiliate marketing. With affiliate marketing, online entrepreneurs can earn a commission by posting a link to a merchant's site and sending traffic to that online merchant. Online merchants can increase traffic to their own sites by using affiliates to post ads. For example, let's say you became an affiliate of Amazon and advertised Amazon books or products on your site through the Amazon Associate Program. Each time a purchase is made on Amazon that originated at your site, you'd receive a percentage of the sale, while Amazon does the work of storing and shipping the item. Amazon receives exposure and more opportunities for sales through its affiliate program. Amazon has hundreds of thousands of affiliate Websites. This type of affiliate marketing opportunity exists for all types of products from autos to Web hosting.

How Does Affiliate Marketing Pay?

The most common method of payment for affiliate marketing is **revenue sharing**, which is also known as **pay-per-sale** or **cost-per-sale**. This is the commission the merchant pays the affiliate when a customer actually buys an item. Another method of payment is **pay-per-lead**, which occurs when the visitor registers or fills out a form on the merchant's site. With this arrangement, the customer doesn't have to actually buy anything for the affiliate to receive a commission. **Pay-per-click** is when the affiliate receives a commission for each visitor who clicks on the link at the affiliate's site to get to the merchant's site. The pay is based on the number of visitors sent.

Becoming an Affiliate Marketer

Depending on the type of business, a Website owner can decide to become an affiliate, acquire affiliates, or do both. You may want to become an affiliate and promote other companies on your Website to earn extra income. Or, if you have an e-commerce site and want to increase sales or brand recognition, you might want to acquire affiliates who can spread your name and merchandise.

To become an affiliate for a specific brand, go to the product's Website. You'll often see a link on the page saying "Become an Affiliate" or "Join our Associates Program." Another option is to join an **affiliate network**. Affiliate networks act as intermediaries between affiliates and merchants with affiliate programs. For Websites wanting to become affiliates, the affiliate network will help set up links, track the activity, and send out checks. Affiliate networks exist for all types of products, but you'll probably have the best success if you pick those that offer products relevant to your Website. Research the affiliate network to see its commission rate, payment guidelines, and linking options. Affiliate networks may review your site before they accept you.

If you want to acquire affiliates for your e-commerce business, you can set up an affiliate program on your own or join an affiliate network. Because setting up your own affiliate program can be complicated and time-consuming, small businesses often join affiliate networks that help find affiliates and do the necessary recordkeeping. There are online directories of affiliate networks for both becoming an affiliate and acquiring affiliates.

Tech Vocabulary
- affiliate network
- cost-per-sale
- pay-per-click
- pay-per-lead
- pay-per-sale
- revenue sharing

Check Yourself
1. What is revenue sharing?
2. What are affiliate links?
3. What is pay-per-lead?
4. What is pay-per-click?

What Do You Think?
Forming a Model. How would you become an affiliate?

CHAPTER 22

FRANCHISING &
EXIT STRATEGIES

Franchising & Licensing

OBJECTIVES

- Investigate franchising a business
- Learn about franchising documents
- Examine the advantages and disadvantages of being a franchisor
- Explore brand licensing

Consider the following question:

Are fast food restaurants dependable?

Write your answer (yes or no) on a piece of paper. Be prepared to compare the dependability of a fast food restaurant with a nonfranchised, locally owned restaurant.

Franchising a Business

As you learned in Chapter 3, a franchise is a business arrangement in which an established company sells others the right to use the company's name and operating plan to sell the products or services in other locations. The franchisor is the owner of the established company. A franchisee is an individual who uses the company's name and operation to run the same business in another location. The franchisee pays the franchisor for this privilege. These payments typically include:

- **Franchise Fee.** The **franchise fee** is an upfront charge that is usually sizeable—from many thousands of dollars to more than a million—and allows the franchisee to join the franchisor's system.

- **Franchise Royalty.** The franchisee pays the franchisor a regular, ongoing payment called a **franchise royalty**. This is typically a percentage of the sales the franchisee earns. Basically, royalty fees are payments made to stay in the franchisor's system. They may be made monthly, quarterly, or on some other time schedule set by the franchisor.

Figure 22-1 ▶
Franchises
Franchises are replica businesses in various locations.
Predicting. *Do you think there is a limit to the number of franchises a franchisor can establish?*

- **Franchise Advertising Fee.** Many franchisors operate an advertising fund on behalf of their franchisees. This fund pays for the creation and distribution of marketing, advertising, and promotional materials that benefit all franchisees. For example, a franchisor might buy national radio or television commercials. Franchisees are often required to pay into this advertising fund based on a percentage of their sales.

 *What are three types of payments associated with franchising?*

Franchising Documents

Franchisors must provide three documents to any franchisee:

- Franchise disclosure document
- Franchising agreement
- Operations manual

Franchise Disclosure Document

A **franchise disclosure document** is a legal notice that provides detailed information to potential franchisees about the franchisor. Typically, the document must be given to a potential franchisee at least 10 days before the franchisee signs a franchise agreement or pays the franchise fee.

The **Federal Trade Commission (FTC)** is a U.S. government agency that administers consumer protection laws and regulates certain business practices. A federal law called the Franchise Rule regulates business practices. A federal law called the Franchise Rule regulates what must be included in a franchise disclosure document. State laws may include additional requirements. The FTC requires the document to include:

- Background information about the franchisor

- The costs of entering the franchisor's system

- The legal obligations of the franchisor and franchisee

- Notice of any recent lawsuits filed against the franchisor

- Statistics and detailed financial information about the franchisor's company (including all locations)

If the franchisor makes any statements about the existing or projected financial performance of the company, the statements must be backed up with specific information.

Franchise Agreement

A **franchise agreement** is a legally binding contract between a franchisor and franchisee that lists the rights and responsibilities of each party. A well-written franchise agreement includes:

- Detailed information about fees, royalties, and other payments (such as taxes or rent) to be paid by the franchisee

- Information regarding the use of the franchisor's patents, trademarks, service marks, copyrights, signs, and systems by the franchisee

- Description of the geographic territory in which the franchisee will operate

- Indication of the term of the franchise agreement (for example, 10 years)

- The availability of training, technical support, marketing and advertising support, and other services to be provided by the franchisor

- Any requirements regarding specific vendors the franchisee must use

- Other financial and operational considerations

- Legal requirements, including the terms for renewal or termination of the agreement

Franchise Operations Manual

A **franchise operations manual** is a manual produced by a franchisor that gives detailed instructions to a franchisee about how to operate, staff, and manage a franchise unit. The manual should cover hiring and

Figure 22-2

Training
A franchise operations manual must be very detailed and precise so franchisees can closely duplicate the practices and systems that have made the franchisor's business a success.

Drawing Conclusions. *Why is it important to duplicate the practices and systems of the original franchisor?*

training employees, management practices, marketing, and operating procedures and systems (such as computer software). Because a franchise operations manual is considered the property of the franchisor, the franchise agreement will probably include a requirement to keep its contents confidential.

The operations manual must be detailed and precise so that franchisees can closely duplicate the practices and systems that have made the franchisor's business a success. Franchisors typically update the operations manual frequently.

 *What are three types of documents associated with franchising?*

Advantages and Disadvantages for Franchisors

A business can expand geographically in two ways: either by opening multiple company-owned units or by franchising the business. Franchising represents a great opportunity for business owners who want to expand their business but lack the money, time, or personnel to open numerous company-owned units.

Advantages for Franchisors

Franchising provides five major advantages to a franchisor:

- **Increased Revenue.** The franchisor earns a substantial upfront fee and regular royalty payments from each franchise.

- **New Locations without Financial Responsibility.** The franchisee, not the franchisor, takes on the financial responsibilities for loans, leases, and other expenses needed to get a franchise unit up and running.

- **Franchisee Investment.** Because franchisees invest their own money, they are highly motivated to make their franchise units profitable. This may not be the case for company-hired managers who run company units. Also, company-hired managers may quit at any time. A franchise agreement requires a franchisee to commit to a specific number of years.

- **No Liability.** A franchisor is not directly liable (legally and financially responsible) for the acts of the franchisee's employees, or accidents that take place on franchisee premises.

- **Builds Brand Awareness.** Franchising builds brand awareness for the franchisor's products or services.

▲ *Franchises build brand awareness.*

Disadvantages for Franchisors

Franchising has five major disadvantages for a franchisor:

- **Regulatory and Legal Requirements.** There are substantial government regulations and legal restrictions.

- **Extensive Preparation.** Preparing a business for franchise, assembling the needed documents, and finding and training qualified franchisees can be time-consuming and expensive. Many franchisors hire professionals to help with the legal and accounting matters associated with franchising.

- **Substantial Upfront Investment.** All of the expenses involved in setting up a franchise have to be made *before* a single franchise fee is ever earned. This represents a substantial investment from the franchisor.

- **Time-Consuming.** Franchising is also time-consuming. The franchisor must prepare a thorough and detailed operations manual and provide technical, marketing, and other forms of support throughout the franchise arrangement. Franchisors risk spending so much time and money on their franchising activities that they neglect their original business. An established business should have more than one company-owned location before attempting to franchise. This helps prove to potential franchisees that the business concept and operations are repeatable.

- **Requires Certain Types of Businesses.** Franchising can only be successful for businesses that are in solid financial condition, easily duplicated, and not dependent on the personal characteristics of their owners. A business owner with a struggling business shouldn't consider franchising. Likewise, a business whose success is due primarily to its owner's personal contacts, charisma, or skills isn't a good candidate for franchising.

 *What are five major advantages and disadvantages to a franchisor in relation to franchising a business?*

READING CHECKPOINT

▼ *Brand licensing has been popular for years.*

Licensing a Brand

A brand is more than a name. It's a name with a specific worth in the marketplace. It has this worth because of the reputation of the product, company, or individual associated with the brand. **Brand equity** is the perceived monetary value of a brand. Entrepreneurs who build brand equity can benefit financially by selling the right to use their brand name to other businesses. This is referred to as licensing a brand, or brand licensing. **Brand licensing** is granting permission to some person or company to use your brand. The purpose of brand licensing is to associate a new product with an existing and popular brand name.

The company or person who owns the brand is the **brand licensor**. The company or person who is granted permission to use the brand is the **brand licensee**. A brand licensee pays the brand licensor for the privilege of using the brand name. The licensee is then responsible for producing and marketing the branded product. The licensee may pay an upfront fee and then pay regular royalties based on sales of the branded product. The licensor retains control over how the licensee can use the brand name and image.

Brand licensing has been popular for years in the entertainment and sports industries. Marketing new products can be expensive and time-consuming for companies. Associating a new product with the name or image of celebrities past or present (Babe Ruth and Michael Jordan are good examples), fictional characters (such as Mickey Mouse), or company brands (Harley-Davidson, Levi, Caterpillar) helps gain recognition and acceptance in the marketplace. Basically, licensees are renting brand names to give their products a particular image and a marketing advantage. Licensees hope that customers who are already

Market Saturation

In 2004, Starbucks seemed to be on an unending growth spurt, opening new stores at a rate of 4 per day for a total of 1,344 new stores. But in 2008, the company announced the closing of 600 stores across the United States. What happened?

One possibility is market saturation. Market saturation means that a product has been completely distributed in its market. For example, most households in the United States own a stove and only need one. So future growth in the stove industry will only come from population growth or from one manufacturer of stoves taking away business from another. In many cities, it is the same with coffee. Starbucks opened new stores quickly. They were followed by competition such as Caribou and Barnies, and now even McDonald's is getting into the premium coffee market. Everyone who wants fine coffee is covered. So what does a savvy entrepreneur do in the face of saturation? Starbucks is getting back to basics, eliminating its line of breakfast sandwiches and focusing on the quality of its core product. It is also pursuing growth overseas in newer markets, such as China.

Product innovation is also a core strategy in saturated markets. For example, it is true that most households have a washer and dryer. But not every household has a high-efficiency front-load machine—in red.

THINKING CRITICALLY

Predicting. With a partner, create a list of products you feel are experiencing market saturation. What would you do if you were responsible for these products?

To read more about market saturation, go to "Entrepreneurship Issues" on the Student Center at entrepreneurship.pearson.com.

familiar with an existing brand will have positive feelings toward new products bearing the same name.

Licensing Agreements

Brand licensing is accomplished through a written licensing agreement between a licensor and a licensee. The licensing agreement grants limited rights to the licensee. The licensor maintains ownership of the brand name and any trademarks or other marks associated with it.

The typical components of a licensing agreement are:

- **Time and Termination.** A licensing agreement specifies the length of time the agreement will be in effect and the conditions under which it can be ended.

- **Financial Terms.** These are the amounts and payment schedules for upfront fees and royalties.

- **Licensee Performance Standards.** The licensee may need to meet specific business performance standards during the licensing term—for example, sales or earnings targets.

- **Licensing Restrictions.** The licensor may impose restrictions on the licensee in such areas as pricing, the markets in which the licensed brand can be sold, distribution methods (for

Figure 22-3

Non-Exclusive License
A non-exclusive license allows
the licensor to lease the brand
to multiple licensees.

Relating Concepts. *Why do you
think a non-exclusive license is
less expensive than an exclusive
license?*

example, the types of retailers or resellers that can be used),
and marketing techniques (such as how and where the licensed
brand may be advertised and how much will be spent on advertising them).

- **Quality Control Criteria.** The licensee may have to provide
  regular samples of the branded products so the licensor can make
  sure they meet quality-control standards.

- **Indemnification.** The licensor typically requires protection in
  the agreement from any legal action, fines, or other damages
  resulting from the licensee's actions. This is referred to as **indemnification** (in-dem-nih-fuh-KAY-shun).

- **Ownership Assurances.** The licensor must provide reasonable
  assurances to the licensee that the licensor is actually the legal
  owner of the brand name or trademark being licensed.

- **Confidentiality.** The licensee must keep confidential any trade
  secrets, quality standards, or other technical information provided
  by the licensor.

- **Multiple Licensees.** Many licensors want to be able to lease their
  brands to multiple companies. A nonexclusive licensing agreement
  is one in which a licensor maintains the right to lease the brand

to other licensees. An exclusive licensing agreement stipulates that only the licensee has the right to use the brand.

Advantages and Disadvantages of Licensing

Successful companies that have worked hard to build a positive brand name or image in the marketplace can benefit greatly from licensing. The two biggest advantages are:

- **Increased Revenue.** The licensor typically receives substantial upfront fees and royalties from licensees.

- **Brand Enhancement.** Ideally, the branding process should increase customer awareness and enhance the positive reputation of the original brand.

These advantages will only be realized if the licensor chooses reliable licensees and makes wise decisions about which products to license. Some of the potential problems with licensing are:

- **Misbranding.** Some brand concepts do not transfer well across industries or across product groups. Misbranding is choosing the wrong product to brand. There are many famous examples of misbranding, including the failed efforts of the Harley-Davidson motorcycle company to extend its brand name to a cake decorating kit!

- **Over-Branding.** Over-branding occurs when licensors sell a brand name to so many licensees that the original brand concept becomes muddied and unclear to consumers.

- **Risk to the Brand.** Licensors risk losing the good name and image associated with their brand if they license it to products or services that disappoint consumers.

- **Lack of Marketing.** Licensees may mistakenly assume that a well-known brand name will sell their products on its own. As a result, they may shortchange their advertising campaigns. The licensor needs to be knowledgeable about the marketing techniques and intentions of licensees and should insist on minimum advertising standards and expenses as part of the licensing agreement.

- **Expense.** Licensors often hire brokers to find and qualify potential licensees for their brands. This can be an expensive process.

 *What is brand licensing?*

 Your Business Plan. Continue developing your standard business plan. Go to "Section 22.1" of the *Business Plan Project* in your *Student Activity Workbook,* or "Section 22.1" of the BizTech Software.

ASSESSMENT 22.1

Reviewing Objectives

1. Name three types of payments associated with franchising.
2. Name three documents associated with franchising.
3. What are some of the advantages and disadvantages for franchisors?
4. What does it mean to license a brand?

Critical Thinking

5. **Drawing Conclusions.** Why do successful businesses try to license their brands?
6. **Communicating.** Choose one well-known person, living or dead, whose name and/or image you would most like to associate with your business. Explain your choice to the class.

Working Together

Together with three other students, use real-life companies, brand names, and products to create a list of 10 bad brand-licensing ideas. Present your list to the class and explain why each idea was an example of misbranding.

> **Social Studies**
> **Fast Food in the '50s and '60s**
> Research the popularity of franchising fast food restaurants such as McDonald's during the 1950s and 1960s. Based on your research, give a brief presentation describing how—and why—this period in history witnessed the birth of fast food in America.

22.2 Exit Strategies

OBJECTIVES

- Examine when the timing is right to leave a business
- Study methods for valuing a business
- Investigate exit strategies for business owners
- Understand how to build wealth

VOCABULARY

- book value
- compounding
- diversification
- emergency fund
- employee stock ownership plan (ESOP)
- future value of money
- goodwill
- harvesting
- Individual Retirement Account (IRA)
- initial public offering (IPO)
- liquidation
- liquidity
- management buyout
- multiple of earnings method
- net worth
- owner's equity
- Rule of 72
- volatile

Consider this question:

Will you ever stop working?

Write your answer (yes or no) on a piece of paper. Then write down the age at which you think you'll stop working. Be prepared to explain your answers to the class.

When to Leave a Business

One of the goals of owning a business is to build personal wealth. In fact, business ownership provides a unique opportunity for doing so. Regular profits earned during the lifetime of a business can provide a very good income and a comfortable living for the owner. But when an entrepreneur leaves his or her business, a much more valuable asset is involved. It's the accumulated and potential worth of the business itself.

Liquidity is the ease of converting a non-cash asset (such as a business) into cash. A successful business is a very valuable asset, but actually selling it is not always an easy process and must be timed carefully. The owner should consider three factors when deciding to sell a business:

- Personal considerations
- Condition of the business
- Condition of the economy

Entrepreneurs thrive on creating and growing innovative businesses. However, there may come a time when a business owner decides to sell the business. This decision is often prompted by personal reasons.

The entrepreneur may wish to retire or pursue other business opportunities, or may have health or family issues. Selling a business can take months or even years. The new owner may insist that the old owner stay for a while after the deal is closed to help smooth the transition process. A business owner must consider these possibilities when selling a business.

The condition of the business and the economy are also important in timing when to sell. The business will be worth more if it's growing and thriving when it goes up for sale. It needs to be operating smoothly and should not be dependent on the owner's extensive day-to-day involvement. Overall economic conditions are also important. A business will probably sell more quickly and for more money when the national and local economies are doing well.

▼ **Figure 22-4**
Personal Factors
The decision to sell a business is often prompted by personal reasons.

Communicating. *What types of personal reasons might make an entrepreneur want to sell an existing business?*

 **READING CHECKPOINT** *What are three factors to consider when deciding to sell a business?*

How to Value a Business

Determining the value of a business can be difficult. You need to consider such factors as the business type, the length of time the business has been operating, its sales and profits, its cash flow, its liabilities or debts, its tangible assets (such as buildings, furniture, inventory, and equipment), and its reputation and prospects for growth. Obviously some of these factors are easy to express in numbers, but others, such as reputation, are not as easy to calculate.

There are no simple formulas for calculating the value of a business. There are, however, methods for calculating amounts that are considered benchmarks or reference points in the valuation process. These methods usually use numbers from the income statement or balance sheet. They don't completely give the worth of a business, but they do provide a starting point from which to begin an analysis of the business's value.

A business that is not doing well may be valued purely on

the tangible assets it owns. **Liquidation** is a process in which the tangible assets of a business are sold. Liquidation often occurs when a failing business declares bankruptcy, or the owner decides the business itself is not worth selling. The owner (and any investors or creditors) may be able to recoup some of the money they have put into the business over its lifetime.

◀ **Figure 22-5**
Liquidation
Liquidation is the process in which the tangible assets of the business are sold.
Inferring. *When would a business liquidate its assets? When wouldn't a business want to do this?*

Another business valuation method is based on the book value of the business. **Book value** (also known as the **net worth** or **owner's equity**) is an accounting term that means the total assets minus the total liabilities according to a company's balance sheet. Experts believe that the book value isn't generally a good indication of the overall value of a business, but it does serve as a point of reference.

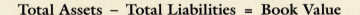

Total Assets − Total Liabilities = Book Value

The **multiple of earnings method** is a method of valuing a business in which the amount of business earnings over a specific time period (usually one year) is multiplied by a number, typically 3 to 5, to determine a reasonable sales price for the overall business. Use the annual net income as "earnings" in this calculation. For example, if the annual net income for a business is $230,000 and you are using a multiplier of 3, the value of the business would be $690,000.

Net Annual Income × Multiplier = Value of Business

$230,000 × 3 = $690,000

Other business-valuation methods use multiples—for example, multiples of cash flow or multiples of book value.

Some business-valuation methods consider both historical earnings and tangible assets. The value of tangible assets is also important to an owner who wants to leave a successful business. A prospective buyer may be more interested if the business owns a substantial amount of tangible assets. Additional methods for business valuation include estimating future earnings or future cash flow, the known value, or sales price for similar businesses in the industry.

All the valuation methods described here deal with aspects of a business that can be easily calculated. But one thing in the valuation process can't be calculated: goodwill. **Goodwill** is a business term that encompasses the intangible positive aspects of a business, such as location, employee knowledge and skills, brand awareness, intellectual property, relationships with suppliers and customers, and reputation in the community and the industry. The actual value of a business, therefore, depends on both factors that can be calculated and those that cannot be calculated.

In all cases, the business will be more valuable if a new owner is confident that the business already includes both the tangible and intangible aspects needed for success.

 *What are two specific methods used to financially value a business?*

Exit Strategies

Planning how to sell a business is just as important as planning how to start one. The process of exiting a business and gaining the

YOUR BUSINESS CAREER

Setting Boundaries

Your parents have probably been setting boundaries for you for most of your life. These boundaries may have included enforcing a curfew, indicating acceptable and unacceptable behaviors, and even establishing rules concerning your friends. These boundaries were designed to give you a clear sense of what was expected and to make you feel secure, protected, and safe. There were probably agreed-upon consequences if the boundaries were not respected.

As you move into the work world, you will have to set your own boundaries. That means making guidelines about how you will balance your personal and work life. Because you probably won't have anyone checking to see whether you are following these guidelines, it is important to take them seriously and be completely committed to them.

Staying out late at night with friends, getting little sleep, and then going to work the next day may sound like fun. You probably know already that this type of lifestyle will cause your job performance to suffer. Don't forget that when someone is paying you to do a job, he or she will expect you to be awake, motivated, and ready to work each day. Setting boundaries can help ensure that you're always doing your best work, that you're living a healthy lifestyle, and that you feel good about yourself.

THINKING CRITICALLY

Comparing and Contrasting. What are some ways your life may change after high school? Are there any boundaries your parents have set that you may keep in force even though you will be policing yourself? What are they?

To read more about personal boundaries, go to "Your Business Career" on the Student Center at entrepreneurship.pearson.com.

value of the business in cash when you leave is referred to as **harvesting** the business. It's sometimes called cashing in or cashing out because it involves turning a non-cash asset (the business) into cash.

An exit strategy should be part of an entrepreneur's initial business plan. Thinking about exiting a successful business someday helps entrepreneurs focus on their goals for the business and determines the measures they will use to define business success. Potential investors will be keenly interested in an entrepreneur's exit strategy. It represents a future opportunity for them to recoup their investment and potentially gain additional profit beyond their initial investment.

> **Thinking about exiting a business helps entrepreneurs focus on their goals.**

Harvesting Value from a Business

Several methods exist for harvesting value from a successful and growing business. Most methods account not only for the past success of the business but also for its future potential to make money. For most entrepreneurs, the desired exit strategy is selling the business, or at least selling their ownership interest in the business.

Some successful business owners choose to sell their business to another company, merging it into the other company in the process. Often, competing businesses have an interest in such sales. The terms acquisition and merger are often used interchangeably to describe the financial union of two companies. However, the first indicates the outright purchase of one company by another, and the second is a mutual decision by two companies to join together. In both cases the deal results in an exchange of money (or stock) and changes in ownership control. An owner that chooses to sell to, or merge with, another company must be prepared for close scrutiny by the other firm.

Most small businesses, and many large ones, are privately held, meaning their shares are held by a small number of people—maybe only by one individual (the owner) or by the owner and family members or a handful of investors (and not traded publicly). Typically the company's founder/owner is the sole or majority shareholder. By selling those shares, the owner gives up ownership in the company in exchange for a cash payment.

A **management buyout** is an exit strategy in which a business owner sells his or her ownership shares to the business's managers. The managers then take over ownership of the business. The management buyout is popular with entrepreneurs who wish to transfer business ownership to people they already know and trust to lead the company in the future.

An **employee stock ownership plan (ESOP)** is a fund established when a business owner sells his or her ownership shares to a retirement fund for the employees. Although an ESOP can offer substantial tax benefits to an exiting owner, the plans are expensive to establish and subject to many legal regulations.

An **initial public offering (IPO)** is the first sale of shares of stock to the general public by a privately held company. IPOs are not always exit strategies. Sometimes they are undertaken to raise money for business expansion. In either case, an IPO can be risky. The stock may be popular with the general public, or it may not. There's no way to tell until the IPO is actually executed. An exiting business owner is also bound by government regulations that restrict company executives from selling their shares within a certain time period after an IPO is initiated.

 *What are three exit strategies for leaving a business?*

Building Wealth

Building a successful small business is a fine achievement. What you do with your earnings, however, determines whether you will have a secure financial future or will be always struggling to get by.

The key to a secure financial future is saving money and investing it. Whether you have a career as an entrepreneur or work as an employee, you need to learn how to invest your money so it can earn more money.

Importance of Saving

When you earn money, what do you do with it? If you're like most people, you use it to pay bills and buy things. Here's an idea: pay yourself first. Get into the habit of automatically saving ten percent of your income. This is the first step toward building wealth.

If you don't make a great deal of money, this may sound hard—even impossible. But try it. You'll discover ways to get by without that ten percent. Let's say that you pay yourself $200 from sales made by your small business this month. First thing, put $20 into your savings account. Don't even think about it. You'll still have $180 to use for bills and purchases.

Time Value of Money

If you start saving now, you'll have money for such goals as buying a house or financing a comfortable retirement. Investing some of your savings will help you, too. Safe investments usually grow slowly. Riskier ones may grow faster, but you could lose your money. If you are counting on your investment for your future, a good policy is to invest most of your funds in a relatively safe way.

Remember, all investments involve some risk, meaning that you could lose money. And remember this principle as well: The greater the potential reward of an investment, the more risky it is likely to be.

High Reward = High Risk

This implies that if an investment has little or no risk, the reward will probably not be high.

Low Risk = Low Reward

Invested money grows by **compounding**, which means that you earn interest on your interest. The younger you are when you start saving and investing, the more compound interest you will accumulate.

The **Rule of 72** is a quick way to figure how long it will take to double your money at a given rate of return. Here's how it works: Divide 72 by the interest rate (or return rate) to find the number of years needed to double your money.

For example, how long would it take for you to double $1,000 if you were earning 8% interest?

72 ÷	**Interest or Rate of Return**	= **Number of Years to Double Money**
72 ÷ 8		= 9 Years

Figure 22-6

The Rule of 72
The Rule of 72 is used to calculate how long an investment will take to double.

Solving Problems. *How long will it take to double your money at a growth rate of 5%?*

THE RULE OF 72

Growth Rate	Years to "Double"
4%	18 Yrs
6%	12 Yrs
8%	9 Yrs
10%	7.2 Yrs
12%	6 Yrs

The government allows you to set up a retirement account called an **IRA (Individual Retirement Account)**. This type of investment is tax free, meaning that you typically won't have to pay taxes on the money in the account until you withdraw it. The goal is to save this money, allowing it to compound, so you'll have money after you retire.

One type of retirement account, the Roth IRA, can be a good choice for a young person because it allows you to make a one-time withdrawal of funds to buy a house. With the Roth, you can save not only for your retirement but for buying a house as well.

The government establishes a maximum amount of money that you are allowed to save in an IRA each year. To encourage people to save, the government has been steadily increasing that figure.

Future Value of Money

The **future value of money** is the amount to which a given sum will increase over time through investment.

The Future Value of Money chart on the opposite page shows you how much one invested dollar will be worth over time at a given interest rate. Take a look at the chart. Can you see that $1 invested for ten years at ten percent will grow to $2.59? (So $100 invested at ten percent for ten years will increase to $259.)

Risk Factors: Time and Liquidity

Two factors affect the risk associated with an investment:

- **Time.** The longer someone has your money, the greater the chance that your investment could somehow be lost. The longer you have to wait for the payback on your investment, the greater the return should be.

- **Liquidity.** As you remember from Chapter 12, liquidity refers to the ability to convert assets into cash. You always want to know how liquid your investment is. Can you get your money out in 24 hours? Or do you have to commit your investment for a specified period?

FUTURE VALUE OF MONEY

Periods (in years)	1%	2%	3%	4%	5%	6%	7%	8%	9%	10%	11%	12%
1	1.0100	1.0200	1.0300	1.0400	1.0500	1.0600	1.0700	1.0800	1.0900	1.1000	1.1100	1.1200
2	1.0201	1.0404	1.0609	1.0816	1.1025	1.1236	1.1449	1.1664	1.1881	1.2100	1.2321	1.2544
3	1.0303	1.0612	1.0927	1.1249	1.1576	1.1910	1.2250	1.2597	1.2950	1.3310	1.3676	1.4049
4	1.0406	1.0824	1.1255	1.1699	1.2155	1.2625	1.3108	1.3605	1.4116	1.4641	1.5181	1.5735
5	1.0510	1.1041	1.1593	1.2167	1.2763	1.3382	1.4026	1.4693	1.5386	1.6105	1.6851	1.7623
6	1.0615	1.1261	1.1941	1.2653	1.3401	1.4185	1.5007	1.5869	1.6771	1.7716	1.8704	1.9738
7	1.0721	1.1487	1.2299	1.3159	1.4071	1.5036	1.6058	1.7138	1.8280	1.9487	2.0762	2.2107
8	1.0829	1.1717	1.2668	1.3686	1.4775	1.5939	1.7182	1.8509	1.9926	2.1436	2.3045	2.4760
9	1.0937	1.1951	1.3048	1.4233	1.5513	1.6895	1.8385	1.9990	2.1719	2.3580	2.5580	2.7731
10	1.1046	1.2190	1.3439	1.4802	1.6209	1.7909	1.9672	2.1589	2.3674	2.5937	2.8394	3.1059
11	1.1157	1.2434	1.3842	1.5395	1.7103	1.8983	2.1049	2.3316	2.5084	2.8531	3.1518	3.4786
12	1.1268	1.2682	1.4258	1.6010	1.7959	2.0122	2.2522	2.5182	2.8127	3.1384	2.4985	3.8960
13	1.1381	1.2936	1.4685	1.6651	1.8057	2.1329	2.4098	2.7196	3.0658	3.4523	3.8833	4.3635
14	1.1495	1.3195	1.5126	1.7317	1.9799	2.2609	2.5785	2.9372	3.3417	3.7975	4.3104	4.8871
15	1.1610	1.3459	1.5580	1.8009	2.0789	2.3966	2.7590	3.1722	3.6425	4.1773	4.7846	5.4736

▲ *This chart shows the future value of $1 over a period of years at a specified growth rate.*

The longer the time frame, the riskier the investment. The less liquid, the riskier the investment. The easier your money is to retrieve, the lower your return will probably be.

Tolerating Risk

Here is one more factor to consider when deciding on the risk and potential reward an investment offers: How do you feel about risk?

Everyone has a different tolerance for risk, and there is no level of tolerance that is "right" for everyone. Some people prefer safe investments that offer lower rates of return and minimal risk. Others prefer to take greater chances with their money in hopes of earning higher returns.

You need to know how you feel about risk before you make a decision about investing. You don't want to enter into investments that will keep you awake at night worrying!

Investing

Once you have saved some money and have determined your risk tolerance, you are almost ready to invest.

Before you actually make the investment, be sure you have enough cash saved to cover your personal expenses (food, clothes, rent, transportation, and so on) for at least three months. This is your <mark>emergency fund</mark>. It will protect you from having to sell off investments if an emergency prevents you from being able to earn money for a while. Keep your emergency fund in a savings account (or in some investment that can be turned into cash within 24 hours).

Once you have established an emergency fund, you are ready to invest. Choose from these possibilities:

- **Cash.** Cash investments can be retrieved in 24 hours. There is almost no risk that you will lose money in a savings account, so savings accounts typically pay a very low rate of interest. Treasury bills are another cash investment. Treasury bills are short-term loans issued by the U.S. government. The government pays you a fairly low interest rate but guarantees your money. You can sell treasury bills on the market for cash within 24 hours. You can also turn stocks and bonds into cash fairly quickly by selling them, but the price may be lower than what you paid. Securities (stocks and bonds) are riskier than cash.

- **Bonds.** Bonds are also riskier than cash, but less risky than stocks. Bonds are interest-bearing loans. Corporations issue bonds to borrow money that they agree to pay back on a specific date. If you buy a bond, you will be paid interest. When the bond comes due, the money you paid for it will be returned to you. Bond prices fluctuate and can be traded (bought and sold) on the bond market.

- **Stocks.** Stocks represent equity shares of a company. If you own stock in a corporation, you own a piece of the business, however small. Stocks may pay dividends, which are a share of the company's profits. You can trade stocks on the stock market. Stocks tend to be more risky (and potentially more rewarding) than bonds or cash.

Volatile Investments

Investments can be affected by world events. If war breaks out, stock prices usually fall. Bad news often drives the stock market down. A stock's price may also change in reaction to news about the company that issued the stock. Because stock prices change in reaction to information, they are considered to be ==volatile== investments. This means they can change frequently and unpredictably.

When there is uncertainty, people tend to move their money into cash and other low-risk, highly liquid investments, even if it means taking a loss.

Diversification

Protect yourself from volatility by spreading your money over different types of investments. This method of decreasing risk is called ==diversification==. It is the opposite of "putting all your eggs in one basket."

If you have $10,000 and you invest it all in the stock of one company, you will lose all your money if that company goes out of business. It is wiser to diversify: buy small amounts of many different stocks. When you own $1,000 worth of each of ten stocks, you'll only lose a small part of your investment if one company fails. Because the stock market and the bond market tend to behave differently, it is good to diversify by owning both. When the stock market goes down, bonds usually rise, and vice versa.

What Would You Do with Wealth?

This chapter has provided an overview of the strategies for exiting a successful business and suggested ways to build personal wealth. Your decisions in building a business and in building your wealth will cause you to think about your long-term life goals. If you do accumulate wealth—from the continued performance of your business or from exiting the business one day—what would you do with that wealth?

Many entrepreneurs use their wealth to start a second business. In this way, over time, individuals have built great fortunes. Others use their money to go back to school. Still others become philanthropists and focus on helping others.

The most important lesson entrepreneurship can teach is that you have the power to think for yourself and to create an exciting and fulfilling life. When you use your imagination and skills to grow a small business, you prove to yourself that you can create something real and valuable from an idea.

Whether you become a lifelong entrepreneur or choose another career entirely, remember that you will *always* be stronger by thinking and behaving entrepreneurially.

Never stop asking:

- What kind of life do I want?
- How can I make my community a better place?
- What makes me happy?
- How can I help others be happy?

> ## Use your imagination to grow
> ## not only the business of your dreams,
> ## but also the *life* of your dreams.
> ## Dare to dream!

 **READING CHECKPOINT** *How can you use the Rule of 72 to calculate when you will double your investment?*

 Your Business Plan. Continue developing your standard business plan. Go to "Section 22.2" of the *Business Plan Project* in your *Student Activity Workbook*, or "Section 22.2" of the BizTech Software.

ASSESSMENT 22.2

Reviewing Objectives

1. Name three factors an owner should consider when making a decision to sell a business.
2. Name two methods used to quantify the value of a business.
3. What does it mean to harvest a business?
4. How do you use the Rule of 72 to calculate when you will double your money?

Critical Thinking

5. **Solving Problems.** You found the perfect buyer for your thriving small business, but she only has half the cash needed to buy it. What could you do to help her complete the deal?
6. **Inferring.** How might an exit strategy help an entrepreneur focus on the business?

Working Together

Working in a group, use the Internet to identify companies that, over the past 10 years, have gone through an acquisition or merger, a management buyout, the establishment of an employee stock ownership plan, or an initial public offering. Find at least one company in each of the categories.

Social Studies
Public Perception of Technology

Many of the most important technology companies were started by entrepreneurs. These businesses issued IPOs when they "went public" and began to be traded on the stock market. Research a technology company and find out what newspapers and magazines said about it at the time it was first offered on the stock market. Were the publications right in their evaluation of the company's prospects? Present your findings to the class.

The Sweet Taste of Success

When Cassandra Collazo, Dalila Flores, and Tiffany Fuentes came up with a plan for a chocolate business in their junior class at William H. Turner Technical Arts Senior High School in Miami, Florida, no one took them seriously. They had previously made and sold chocolate-covered Oreos as a class project, but now they wanted to turn their chocolate expertise into making a healthy snack using fruit. "Most people doubted us," said Tiffany. "All ideas look really good on paper, but paper is one thing and the real thing is different." At the school's Entrepreneurship Expo, all the doubts disappeared. Cassandra, Dalila, and Tiffany spent the day before the Expo hand-picking over 1,000 strawberries from a local farm and coating them with chocolate. They sold out the first day.

▲ *Les Dames de Chocolat*

Les Dames de Chocolat

The girls named their company Les Dames de Chocolat, French for "The Ladies of Chocolate." "We wanted a business name that was distinctive and elegant," said Dalila, "and Les Dames de Chocolat is owned by all of us." The three partners were good friends and knew each other's strong points. Tiffany became the CEO, organizing the work and overseeing operations. Cassandra was the CFO, in charge of the financing, negotiating for the best prices, and making sure everyone was paid equal amounts. Dalila was named the Vice President of Marketing and Production, getting the word out and coming up with new products.

Our Passion, Your Satisfaction

With a slogan of "Our passion, your satisfaction," Les Dames de Chocolat aims to please. Over the past two years, they've tried almost every type of chocolate. "So far, the best is a vegan chocolate that we buy at a wholesaler that only sells to restaurants," said Dalila.

Les Dames de Chocolat's products include chocolate-covered fruit—such as strawberries, bananas, and pineapples—and chocolate-covered Oreos. For parties and weddings, they have chocolate fountains in which guests can dip pieces of fruit, and they'll provide any type of chocolate—dark, milk, or white—the customer wants. Their success is due to the quality and freshness of their products and their willingness to meet their customers' needs. "We always adapt to what the event is going to be," said Dalila. "We don't just sell one product and give it out to everybody. It's always what they want." For example, at one child's Halloween party, Les Dames de Chocolat decorated the chocolate-covered Oreos with pumpkins and ghosts.

They market through flyers and brochures and by word-of-mouth. They've had media coverage in the Miami area, appearing on Telemundo and other networks. They also have a MySpace Website, which they've found is the best way to reach the teenage market. And, Les Dames de Chocolat participated in the International Chocolate Festival in Coral Gables.

Their plans for the future include finding a store location where they can sell Les Dames de Chocolat products and bring their chocolate treats to an even wider clientele.

Thinking Like an Entrepreneur

1. In a partnership, how important is it that the partners have a variety of skills?
2. Les Dames de Chocolat adapts its products to the desires of its customers. Can every company do this? Why or why not?
3. Can you think of other business opportunities in the food industry?

CHAPTER SUMMARY

22.1 Franchising & Licensing

Setting up and running a franchise operation is expensive for the franchisor but can provide significant benefits if the franchise units are successful. The franchisor earns cash from fees and royalties paid by the franchisees, and benefits from wider brand awareness in the marketplace. Franchising does pose substantial legal, accounting, and regulatory challenges to the franchisor. Brand licensing is the granting of legal permission to others to use your brand name to sell something. The licensor maintains ownership over the brand name but earns income by leasing its use to other companies that wish to take advantage of the brand's existing public name awareness and good reputation.

22.2 Exit Strategies & Building Wealth

Exit strategies are ways of leaving a business and harvesting as much cash as possible. You should include an exit strategy in your original business plan. Exit timing will be governed by personal considerations and the state of the individual business and the economy as a whole. The value of a business can be roughly estimated by using financial records, such as the income statement or balance sheet. The actual evaluation should take into account the intangible, goodwill aspects of the business. Owners often exit unsuccessful businesses by selling off tangible assets. Possible exit strategies for owners of thriving businesses include acquisitions and mergers, management buyouts, establishing employee stock ownership plans, or making an initial public offering of stock. When you invest money, it compounds and builds wealth. The future value of money is the amount to which it will increase over time.

REVIEW VOCABULARY

Imagine you are a successful entrepreneur who has decided to leave your business and sell it to a younger entrepreneur. Write a letter to this individual and include at least half of the following terms:

- book value (p. 589)
- brand equity (p. 582)
- brand licensee (p. 582)
- brand licensing (p. 582)
- brand licensor (p. 582)
- compounding (p. 593)
- diversification (p. 597)
- emergency fund (p. 596)
- employee stock ownership plan (ESOP) (p. 592)
- Federal Trade Commission (FTC) (p. 578)
- franchise agreement (p. 579)
- franchise disclosure document (p. 578)
- franchise fee (p. 577)
- franchise operations manual (p. 579)
- franchise royalty (p. 577)
- future value of money (p. 594)
- goodwill (p. 590)
- harvesting (p. 591)
- indemnification (p. 584)
- Individual Retirement Account (IRA) (p. 594)
- initial public offering (IPO) (p. 592)
- liquidation (p. 589)
- liquidity (p. 587)
- management buyout (p. 592)
- multiple of earnings method (p. 589)
- owner's equity (p. 589)
- Rule of 72 (p. 593)
- volatile (p. 597)

CHECK YOUR UNDERSTANDING

Choose the letter that best answers the question or completes the statement.

1. A franchise royalty is
   a. the same as a franchise fee
   b. the fee for filing a franchise disclosure document
   c. a regular ongoing payment based on the franchisee's sales
   d. a regular ongoing payment made to the Federal Trade Commission by the franchisor

2. Using the image of Donald Duck to sell raincoats would be an example of
   a. franchising
   b. brand licensing
   c. indemnification
   d. liquidation

3. The Rule of 72 tells you
   a. how much a dollar is worth over a specified amount of time at a given return rate
   b. how much to save for an emergency fund
   c. when your money doubles at a given return rate
   d. when to cash in stocks and bonds

4. Which of the following is an advantage of franchising to the franchisor?
   a. selling a franchise can help a struggling business
   b. the franchisor must pay legal fees to prepare a franchising document
   c. the franchisor collects a fee and royalties from the franchisee
   d. selling a franchise is an inexpensive process

5. The book value of a business is equal to
   a. the overall value of the business
   b. net worth minus owner's equity
   c. a multiple of business's earnings
   d. total assets minus total liabilities on the company's balance sheet

6. Which of the following must be completed before the franchise agreement is signed?
   a. a franchise disclosure document
   b. a franchise royalty payment
   c. the indemnification
   d. the FTC

7. One of the primary goals when exiting a business is to
   a. have exclusive licensing agreements
   b. have nonexclusive licensing agreements
   c. convert the business to cash
   d. prepare a franchise disclosure document for the new owner

8. An initial public offering occurs when
   a. a business owner decides to franchise his or her business publicly
   b. a privately held company first offers its stock for sale to the public
   c. a privately held company conducts a management buyout
   d. a liquidation is caused by bankruptcy

9. Which of the following is the result of a management buyout?
   a. an initial public offering
   b. an employee stock ownership plan
   c. the owner buys shares from the managers
   d. the managers of the company take over ownership

10. An owner may choose to fund an employee stock ownership plan
    a. to prepare for bankruptcy
    b. as part of an exit strategy
    c. to quantify goodwill for the valuation process
    d. as part of the multiple of earnings method

11. Goodwill is a business valuation term that refers to
    a. liquidation
    b. the franchise operations manual
    c. the tangible assets of the business that can be sold
    d. reputation, employee knowledge, and relationships with customers

12. Which of the following is a disadvantage of franchising to the franchisor?
    a. the franchisor is legally liable for accidents that occur at the franchise unit
    b. the franchisor must pay the franchisee's lease and loan payments
    c. the franchisor may have difficulty finding a suitable franchisee
    d. all of the above

Business Communication

13. Research the Federal Trade Commission's Franchise Rule and create a table showing a list of the items that must be included in a franchise disclosure document and a brief description of each item.

14. Write an exit strategy for an imaginary business. Include both the business and personal goals you hope to fulfill when you leave.

15. Working with 3 or 4 classmates, develop a written list of 15 branded products for which the industry or product group associated with the original brand name is different from the present industry or product group of the branded product. Share your list with the class.

Business Ethics

18. You are an entrepreneur with a successful and profitable business that employs 25 people, some of whom have been with you for many years. You want to sell the business and invest the cash in another opportunity. Should your employees be a consideration in your decision? Should you tell your employees you are planning to sell the business? If so, when? Describe your decision and the steps you would take with your employees.

Business Math

16. You must pay a franchise royalty of 5% on monthly sales up to $20,000 and 7% on monthly sales greater than $20,000. (For example, if your sales were $23,000, you would pay 5% on $20,000 and 7% on $3,000.) If your monthly sales for the past 3 months were $18,500, $20,100, and $27,200, how much did you pay in franchise royalties per month and in total?

17. You have received two offers to buy your business, which has a book value of $93,500 and annual earnings of $108,500. Company A has offered to pay $20,000 plus four times the book value. Company B will pay $23,500 plus three times annual earnings. How much is each company offering? Which offer will you take?

Business in Your Community

19. Working with a group of three classmates, research three existing franchises that do not have units in your community but which you believe would be successful. Report your findings to the class and explain why these franchises might do well in your locality.

20. Interview a successful entrepreneur in your community and ask for a description of the goodwill aspects of his or her business.

Outsourcing

Outsourcing is hiring another company or individual to handle part of a business's everyday operations or to do special projects. In the e-commerce marketplace, outsourcing is common. Though some Websites have an entire office staff working behind the scenes, many do not. Jobs that can't be done in-house are outsourced to other professionals or companies that are often called **third-party providers**. When the work is being done in a different country, outsourcing may be referred to as **offshoring**. Whether the providers are in the same country or not, they will often work with the Website through telecommuting—working online and communicating via e-mail and phone rather than coming to the actual place of business. Outsourcing allows Website owners to take advantage of expertise from other people and companies. It also creates opportunities for entrepreneurs who want to work in technology.

Constructing a Website

Generally a Web designer takes the Website owner's concept and designs a site to match it. Developers program the site. A producer coordinates the design and technical teams and may also be responsible for overall site-performance tracking and optimization. Producers may write and edit copy, but usually writers and editors write and fine-tune the various types of content on a Website. These may include articles and blogs, advertisements, and **calls to action**—the part of the ad copy that tries to get the Website visitor to perform a specific action, such as registering for the site or buying a product. Copyeditors check the copy for grammar and style.

Customer Service

A Web business needs many of the same features as a brick-and-mortar company. A **customer service operation** provides a way for the customer to get help, whether it's for placing an order, getting information, or making a complaint. Outsourced customer service often takes the form of a **call center**, where a group of people answer phone calls and offer help. **Chat room support** is a type of online customer service in which the support staff communicates with the customer by using instant-messaging software. Other customer support is handled through e-mail. Often, an outsourced customer service company provides all of these options.

Payment Processing

Accepting payment on a Website can be done through third-party providers. An outside business that handles payment processing will also handle **inventory management**—keeping track of the items for sale, storing them, and shipping orders—in addition to storefront creation. **Storefront creation** is designing a Website that can list products, prices, payment terms, and shipping costs and then process orders.

Outsourcing can be expensive, but if a Website owner doesn't have the necessary expertise or knowledge to do a specific job, it can be worth the money. Outsourcing makes it possible to set up an Internet business almost overnight.

Tech Vocabulary

- call center
- call to action
- chat room support
- customer service operation
- inventory management
- offshoring
- outsourcing
- storefront creation
- third-party providers

Check Yourself

1. What is outsourcing?
2. What is offshoring?
3. What happens in chat room support?
4. What is storefront creation?

What Do You Think?

Analyzing Information. What sort of outsourcing do you think is most useful?

EXITING THE BUSINESS

Eva's Edibles has been in existence for eight years. It has had its share of ups and downs. But, with detailed planning, lots of hard work, and strategic adjustments along the way, the company is making a good profit. Continue the journey with Eva Tan as she decides to leave the company she founded.

New Opportunities for Growth

Eva's Edibles had a solid base of customers. It had a satisfactory, consistent net profit. It had a loyal, efficient group of employees. But Eva and Sylvia wondered if the business could continue its growth. Maybe they had grown it as much as they could.

Then something happened.

In a routine staff meeting, people began mentioning the lack of cuisines that reflected their various backgrounds. Eva missed Filipino food. Frank, the cook, complained about not being able to find good Jamaican food. Sylvia wished she could have French bistro fare. Paul, another cook, said that there was no Brazilian food in the area. Suddenly Sylvia said, "This might be a business opportunity!" After some discussion, they agreed that there might be a market for prepared foods for national and cultural groups whose preferred cuisines weren't locally available.

Eva and Sylvia began researching this idea in more detail. They became convinced that there were real possibilities in this market. They thought they could maintain their current successful menus while gradually creating new ones that were more ethnically diverse. These new products could also be marketed to current customers who might want to try new foods.

Another idea for growth was to sell packaged frozen meals to gourmet supermarkets. Sylvia pointed out that if they were successful in establishing a recognizable brand in the Columbus area, they could then possibly expand statewide and perhaps even nationally.

Eva also proposed the idea of providing cooking classes, a service that was outside their core business. She had discovered that training their employees in cooking techniques was a personally satisfying task, and she wanted to do more of this type of work. She could conduct classes in the kitchen at Eva's Edibles or in clients' homes.

Knowing When to Leave

After much research and planning, and some additional investment, Eva's Edibles began adding a few new specialty meals every month. Products that were successful were included in their future product offerings. Those that weren't successful were dropped.

Eva also began conducting cooking classes. She loved the work, but in Sylvia's opinion, it took Eva away from the more profitable aspects of the business that needed her help and expertise. Sylvia strongly believed that Eva's Edibles should focus on what it did best: making great packaged meals for a reasonable price.

Over time, Eva saw the wisdom of Sylvia's views about the cooking classes. Promotional costs and Eva's time investment in teaching them weren't in the best interest of the company. Reluctantly, Eva agreed to discontinue the classes and turn her attention back to promoting the company's new line of prepared meals.

But Eva just wasn't happy. She remembered how she and Sylvia had always said they needed to be happy with the direction of the company. She wondered if continuing to run Eva's Edibles was the best choice for her, personally.

When another entrepreneur, Daniel Ross, approached Sylvia and Eva about selling the company's frozen meals on a national basis, Eva found that her heart just wasn't in the business anymore.

After much thought, Eva talked with Sylvia. She told her that her real interest was teaching cooking. She wondered how Sylvia would feel if she left the business. Sylvia wanted Eva to be happy and suggested they might ask Daniel if he had any interest in Eva's part of the business.

Eva and Sylvia approached Daniel and asked him if he wanted to buy Eva's share of the company. Daniel was interested and figured out a fair value for Eva's percentage. Eva agreed and sold him her share. As part of the negotiation, Eva agreed to continue working at Eva's Edibles part-time for six months to help make the transition easier.

While working part-time, Eva returned to school. She transferred her credits to the Ohio State University and eventually earned a four-year degree in Technical Education and Training. After graduating, Eva was hired as a full-time teacher at a vocational school, teaching entrepreneurship and culinary skills.

Eva is happy teaching, but she has another dream now. It's an idea for starting another business: her own culinary school. And Eva knows that, to make it a reality, the only thing she needs to do—the only thing any entrepreneur needs to do—is dare to dream.

What Would You Have Done?

1. **Drawing Conclusions.** In your opinion, did Eva do the right thing in discontinuing the cooking classes? Explain your answer.
2. **Relating Concepts.** What methods would you have recommended for Eva to determine the value of her portion of the business?

PHOTO CREDITS

Thomas D. Altany, 161

American Foundation for the Blind, Inc., 351

Kyle J. Califf, 259

CES International, 150

Kim Cole, 453

Comstock Complete, 18, 20, 50, 52, 62, 84, 95, 110, 117, 140 Bottom, 146, 154, 224, 227, 231, 237, 240, 243, 268, 357, 370, 404, 510

Ronald R. Craft, 187

Doctor's Associates, Inc., 578

Dorling Kindersley
(c) Judith Miller / Dorling Kindersley / Wallis and Wallis, 584 Left and Right
Susannah Sayler\Rough Guides Dorling Kindersley, 580

Julene Fleurmond, 337

Margaret Fox, 283, 599

Freed Photography, 21

Getty Images
Asia Images Group/Getty Images, 138
Steve Cole\Getty Images/Digital Vision, 556-557
Digital Vision\Getty Images/Digital Vision, 90, 94
DreamPictures/Blend Images/Getty Images, 558
Jon Feingersh Photography Inc.\Getty Images, Inc. - Blend Images, 2-3
Getty Images/Digital Vision, 35
Getty Images, Inc - Purestock Royalty Free, 29
Patrick Lane/Getty Images, 346
Ray McVay\Getty Images/Digital Vision, 42
PhotoDisc/Getty Images URL: http://www.photo-disc.com, 15
Plush Studios/DH Kong/Getty Images, 166
Plush Studios/DH Kong/Blend Images/Getty Images, 458
Monica Rodriguez\Getty Images/Digital Vision, 488-489
Ariel Skelley/Getty Images, 58
SW Productions\Getty Images, Inc.- Photodisc., 123
Klaus Tiedge/Getty Images, 26, 288, 320
Vico Collective/Alin Dragulin\Getty Images, Inc. - Blend Images, 4
Todd Wright\Getty Images, Inc. - Blend Images, 72-73

Mike Greenberg, 315

Eric Hunt, 549

iStockPhoto, 11, 31, 53, 104, 111, 113, 175, 178, 334, 421, 440, 450, 452, 535, 539, 542

Kentucky Fried Chicken Image Courtesy of KFC Corporation, 581

Selda Kurtuldu, 427

Library of Congress, 108 Top, 112, 460

Iris Mund, 527

Sino A. Munoz, 65

National Archives and Records Administration, 472

Jose Luis Pelaez Inc /Blend Images/Jupiter Images, Front Cover

Pepsi-Cola North America, 582

Photos.com, 6, 60, 118, 140 Top, 152, 239 Right, 282, 341, 362, 425

PRNewsFoto/Nike, 215

PureStockX, 120, 185, 359

Martin Regusters, 571

Shutterstock 8, 156, 197, 208, 217, 270, 271 Top, 272, 274, 276, 277, 279 Top and Bottom, 372, 494, 536
Yuri Arcurs \Shutterstock, 239 Left
Yuri Arcurs/Shutterstock Images LLC., 576
Tammy Allen\Shutterstock, 478
Andresr\Shutterstock, 82, 568 Top
Maricin Balcerzak/Shutterstock Images LLC, 532
Laura Clay Ballard\Shutterstock, 446
Max Blain\Shutterstock, 417
Gualtiero Boffi\Shutterstock, 467
Lori Monahan Borden\Shutterstock, 350
Gary L. Brewer\Shutterstock, 449
Ken Brown\Shutterstock, 589
Caruntu\Shutterstock, 568 B
Diego Cervo\Shutterstock, 69, 566
Stephen Coburn/Shutterstock images LLC, 490
Stephen Coburn\Shutterstock, 70, 134, 192, 264, 342, 486, 554, 604
WilleeCole\Shutterstock, 327 Top
HD Connelly\Shutterstock, 564
Zhu Difeng\Shutterstock, 461
George Dolgikh\Shutterstock, 331
Estelle\Shutterstock, 168
ExaMedia Photography\Shutterstock, 438
Wendy Farrington\Shutterstock, 413 Top
János Gehring/Shutterstock images, 432
Samantha Grandy\Shutterstock, 522
Jeff Greenberg\Photolibrary.com, 183
Greywind\Shutterstock, 121
Jeff Gynane\Shutterstock, 474
JHogan\Shutterstock, 560
Anthony Hall\Shutterstock, 451
Hannamariah\Shutterstock, 447
Peter Hansen\Shutterstock, 524
David Hilcher\Shutterstock, 468
Ifong\Shutterstock, 518
Rafa Irusta\Shutterstock, 322
Eric Isselee\Shutterstock, 479
Brian A. Jackson\Shutterstock, 435
Sergey Kamshylin\Shutterstock, 462
Dan Kaplan\Shutterstock, 422
Karkas\Shutterstock, 326
Sergey Karpov\Shutterstock, 181
Kash76\Shutterstock, 592
Sebastian Kaulitski\Shutterstock, 305, 381

Kiselev Andrey Valerevich\Shutterstock, 136-137
Maxim Kulko\Shutterstock, 35
Blaz Kure\Shutterstock, 515
Olga Kushchena\Shutterstock, 409 B
Kuzma\Shutterstock, 519
Svetlana Larina\Shutterstock, 184
Karin Lau\Shutterstock, 41
Lepas\Shutterstock, 330
Andrew Lever\Shutterstock, 445
Lowe Llaguno\Shutterstock, 477
Luchschen\Shutterstock, 423
Robyn Mackenzie\Shutterstock, 329, 377
macumazahn\Shutterstock, 335
Arkady Mazor\Shutterstock, 463
Mauro\Shutterstock, 420
Stephen Mcsweeny\Shutterstock, 476
Felix Mizioznikov\Shutterstock, 523
Monkey Business Images\Shutterstock, 344-345, 588
Nicholas Moore\Shutterstock, 49
Nubephoto\Shutterstock, 413 B
objectsforall\Shutterstock, 102
OPIS\Shutterstock, 407
Padal\Shutterstock, 503
Paul Paladin\Shutterstock, 409 T
Pandapaw\Shutterstock, 406
Zoltan Pataki\Shutterstock, 562
PhotoBarmaley\Shutterstock, 328
Lukas Pobuda\Shutterstock, 327 B
Tatiana Popova\Shutterstock, 302
Leigh Prather\Shutterstock, 35
prism_68\Shutterstock, 74
Radarreklama\Shutterstock, 132, 133
ragsac\Shutterstock, 205
Steve Rosset\Shutterstock, 512
Sergey Rusakov\Shutterstock, 323
Dmitry Shironosov\Shutterstock, 208-209, 266-267
Gina Smith\Shutterstock, 569
James Steidl\Shutterstock, 434
Donald R. Swartz\Shutterstock, 352
Charles Taylor\Shutterstock, 465
Irina Tischenko\Shutterstock, 501
Paul Tobeck\Shutterstock, 546
Miroslav Tolimir\Shutterstock, 333
Yobidaba\Shutterstock, 271 Bottom
Feng Yu\Shutterstock, 108 Bottom
Zimmytws\Shutterstock, 444
Zoom Team\Shutterstock, 525

Sanueldo Spaldings, 45

Starbucks Coffee Company, 583

James Steidt\Stock Photo/Black Star, 10

Tom Rosenthal\SuperStock, Inc., 17

Dian Thomas, 233

T.B. Harry S. Truman Presidential Library, 108 Middle

Marissa Weekes-Mason, 127, 481, 505

Matthew Williamson, 365

John Xie, 399

www.indexopen.com, 106

360° marketing Approach to marketing that communicates with your prospects and customers from all directions; it blends low-tech methods and high-tech methods to carry your message to customers in as many ways as possible. (p. 228)

A

Accounting System of recording and summarizing business and financial transactions and analyzing, verifying, and reporting the results. (p. 376)

Accounting controls Checks and balances established to provide accounting personnel with procedures that will avoid potential problems. (p. 382)

Accounts payable Amount of money a business owes to its suppliers for purchases made on credit. (p. 306)

Accounts receivable Amount of money owed to a business by its customers for credit sales. (p. 305)

Accreditation Certification by a professional group that an individual possesses certain skills or a specific level of expertise. (p. 417)

Active content Web content that changes frequently, such as the current time and temperature. (p. 287)

Active listening Listening consciously and responding in ways that improve communication. (p. 85)

Adulterated Containing substances or processed in ways that may be harmful to health, or modified to mask poor quality. (p. 476)

Advertising Public, promotional message paid for by an identified sponsor or company. (p. 232)

Affiliate marketing Process used by Website owners who sell items from another store and take a percentage of the profits. (p. 69)

Affiliate network Intermediary between affiliates and merchants with affiliate programs. (p. 575)

AIDA (attention, interest, desire, and action) Popular communication model used by companies to plan, create, and manage their promotions. (p. 223)

Angels Equity investors who finance start-up ventures in which they have a particular interest. (p. 359)

Antitrust laws Laws that forbid anticompetitive mergers and business practices. (p. 477)

Applications End-user programs. (p. 457)

Apprenticeship Internship in which a technical or trade skill is taught. See also internship. (p. 7)

Aptitude Natural ability to do a particular type of work or activity well. (p. 14)

Asset Everything owned by the business that has a monetary value. (p. 305)

Attitude Way of viewing or thinking about something that affects how you feel about it. (p. 14)

Auction site Website where buyers and sellers come together to buy or sell goods and services. (p. 553)

Auditor Accountant who examines a company's financial records and verifies that they have been kept properly. (p. 383)

Authoritarian (aw-thor-uh-TEHR-ee-un) leadership style Practiced when a leader tells employees what needs to be done and how to do it, without seeking their advice. (p. 494)

Automation Use of machines to perform tasks normally performed by people. (p. 515)

B

Balance sheet Financial statement that summarizes the assets and liabilities (debts) of a business. (p. 304)

GLOSSARY

Bank debt ratio Your monthly income compared to your debts. (p. 356)

Bank reconciliation Process of verifying that a checkbook balance is in agreement with the ending balance in the checking account statement from the bank. (p. 373)

Banner ad Ad at the top or side of a Web page. (p. 431)

Bargaining in good faith An honest intention to resolve differences in a way that is acceptable to all. (p. 87)

Barter financing Trading of items or services between businesses. (p. 361)

Benefits Reasons customers choose to buy a product. (p. 215); Types of compensation other than salary or wages. (p. 412)

Bidding Making an offer on an item. (p. 553)

Blog Personal journal. Short for "weB LOG." (p. 287)

Book value Accounting term that means total assets minus total liabilities according to a company's balance sheet. Also referred to as net worth or owner's equity. (p. 589)

Bootstrapping Starting a business by yourself without any outside investment. (p. 352)

Bounce rate Percentage of visitors who visit the landing page and exit without visiting another page. (p. 509)

Brand Marketing strategy that can create an emotional attachment to your product(s). (p. 215)

Brand equity Perceived monetary value of a brand. (p. 582)

Brand licensee Company or person who is granted permission to use the brand. (p. 582)

Brand licensing Granting of legal permission to someone or some company to use your brand. (p. 582)

Brand licensor Company or person who owns the brand. (p. 582)

Brand mark Symbol or other graphical design that can be used to identify a brand. (p. 216)

Breach of contract Failure to carry out the required conditions of a contract. (p. 441)

Break-even analysis Examination of the income statement that identifies the break-even point for a business. (p. 333)

Break-even point Point at which the total at the bottom of the income statement is zero because the business has sold exactly enough units for sales to cover expenses. (p. 333)

Break-even units Number of units of sale a business needs to sell to arrive at the break-even point. (p. 335)

Bundling Combining the price of several different services (and/or physical products) into one price. (p. 221)

Burn rate Rate at which a company spends cash to cover overhead costs without generating a positive cash flow. (p. 303)

Business Organization that provides products or services, usually to make money. (p. 5)

Business broker Someone who is licensed to sell businesses. (p. 154)

Business environment Any social, economic, or political factors that could impact your business including global, national, and industry-related factors. (p. 167)

Business ethics Moral principles applied to business issues and actions. (p. 106)

Business interruption insurance Covers losses if a business can't operate due to a covered event, such as a storm or fire. (p. 446)

Business opportunity Consumer need or want that potentially can be met by a new business. (p. 147)

Business plan Statement of your business goals, the reasons you think these goals can be met, and how you are going to achieve them. (p. 139)

Business-to-business (B2B) company Company that sells to other companies. (p. 170)

Business-to-consumer (B2C) company Company that sells to individual people. (p. 169)

Buying in bulk Purchasing a large quantity from a vendor, typically to take advantage of a quantity discount. Also referred to as volume buying. (p. 536)

C

C corporation Corporation that is taxed as an entity by the federal government. (p. 60)

Calculated risk Risk in which potential costs and benefits are carefully considered before starting a business. (p. 157)

Calendar year January 1 to December 31. (p. 290)

Call center Operation where a group of people answer phone calls and offer help—often part of an outsourced customer service. (p. 603)

Call to action Part of the ad copy that tries to get the Website visitor to perform a specific action, such as registering for the site or buying a product. (p. 603)

Capital Another name for the cash and goods a business owns. (p. 30)

Capitalism Another name for a free enterprise system. (p. 30)

Carbon footprint Amount of carbon you use and thus release into the atmosphere. (p. 122)

Carbon offset Practice of "buying" a certain amount of carbon to help offset your carbon footprint. (p. 122)

Carrying capacity Maximum number of companies an industry can support based on its potential customer base. (p. 169)

Cash budget Record on which a business owner forecasts (predicts) incoming and outgoing cash flows for an upcoming period (typically a month) and later compares actual cash inflows and outflows to the forecasted amounts. (p. 502)

Cash discount Discount given to buyers who pay for purchases in cash, either at the time of purchase or within a set time period after purchase. (p. 537)

Cash flow Money received minus what is spent over a specified period of time. (p. 300)

Cash flow statement Financial document that records inflows and outflows of cash when they actually occur. (p. 300)

Cash value Actual worth of a property. (p. 445)

Catastrophic risk Risk of an unpredictable event that causes severe loss to many people at the same time. (p. 446)

Catch phrase Slogan or phrase that is repeated so often that people use it without knowing its original context. (p. 237)

Cause-related marketing Partnership between a business and a nonprofit group for the benefit of both. (p. 123)

Central processing unit (CPU) Unit that does all the actual computing in the computer. (p. 49)

Chart of accounts Shows all the accounts used in a business, including assets, liabilities, owner's equity, income, and expense accounts. (p. 376)

Chat room support Type of online customer service in which the support staff communicates with the customer using instant-messaging software. (p. 603)

Checking account Bank account against which the account holder can write checks. (p. 372)

Click-through rate Shows how many customers who saw a Web ad actually clicked on it. (p. 431)

GLOSSARY

Co-signer Individual who signs a loan agreement to guarantee the loan payments in case the first signer is unable to make them. (p. 357)

Cold call Sales call to someone not known, and without prior notice; also called canvassing. (p. 242)

Collateral Property or assets pledged to a bank to secure a loan. (p. 356)

Command economy System in which the government controls the production, allocation, and prices of goods and services. (p. 28)

Commerce server Type of server that runs commerce-based applications, such as credit card processing and inventory management. (p. 69)

Commission Amount paid based on the volume of products or services that a salesperson sells. (p. 252)

Company image Perception (thoughts, attitudes, opinions, and beliefs) that the public holds about a company. (p. 496)

Compensation Money and benefits that an employee receives in exchange for working. (p. 411)

Competent In the legal sense: capable of understanding the terms of a contract and the consequences of entering it. (p. 440)

Competition-based pricing Pricing method that focuses on what the competition charges. (p. 220)

Competitive advantage Something that puts your business ahead of the competition. (p. 179)

Competitive intelligence Data you collect about your competitors. (p. 177)

Competitive matrix Grid used to compare characteristics of your business with those of your direct competitors. (p. 179)

Compounding Way in which invested money grows by earning interest on the interest. (p. 593)

Compromise An agreement arrived at when all sides have made concessions. (p. 91)

Computer virus Software program that can cause damage to the data on your computer by erasing files, creating new ones, changing files, or moving them. It can easily spread from computer to computer. (p. 341)

Concession Something you are willing to give up. (p. 89)

Conditions Events or circumstances that must occur for the contract to be binding. (p. 439)

Conference call Three or more parties in different locations speaking to each other over the same phone line. (p. 83)

Confidentiality agreement Agreement that binds parties to secrecy and usually concerns employees, investors, and others with whom a business owner needs to share a trade secret or other sensitive information. Also called nondisclosure agreement. (p. 441)

Conflict of interest Situation in which personal considerations and professional obligations interfere with each other. (p. 113)

Consideration Benefit that each party in a contract provides for the other. (p. 440)

Consumer credit Extended payment time given by a business to consumers for purchased goods or services. (p. 500)

Contact information Information about potential customers, such as name, address, phone number, and e-mail address. (p. 485)

Content Management System (CMS) System that provides the software or programs needed to put content onto a site. (p. 287)

Contract Agreement between competent parties in which each party promises to take or avoid a specified action. (p. 439)

Contribution margin Amount per unit that a product contributes toward the company's profitability before the fixed expenses are subtracted. (p. 276)

Controlling Ongoing process of setting performance standards, measuring actual performance, comparing it to the standards, and taking corrective action if actual performance does not meet the standards. (p. 496)

Conversion rate Percentage of Web traffic that translates into sales. It is a measure of how many potential customers actually buy. (p. 69)

Cookies Short messages that are given to a Web browser (such as Internet Explorer) by a Web server when you visit that site. (p. 509)

Cooperative Business owned, controlled, and operated for the mutual benefit of its members—people who use its services, buy its goods, or are employed by it. (p. 62)

Cooperative advertising When two companies share the cost of advertising. (p. 232)

Copyright Exclusive right to perform, display, copy, or distribute an artistic work. (p. 111)

Core business Most important focus of the business. (p. 565)

Corporate social responsibility Acting in ways that balance a business's profits and growth with the good of society. (p. 115)

Corporation Legally defined type of business ownership in which the business is considered a "person" ("entity") under the law, and limited liability is granted to the business owner(s). (p. 60)

Cost of goods sold (COGS) Variable expense that is associated with each unit of sale, including the cost of materials and labor used to make the product or provide the service. (p. 272)

Cost-based pricing Pricing method that sets a product's price based on what it costs the business to provide it. (p. 220)

Cost-per-sale In affiliate marketing, commission that the merchant pays the affiliate when a customer actually buys an item. Also known as pay-per-sale or revenue sharing. (p. 575)

Cost/benefit analysis Process of adding up all the expected benefits of an opportunity and subtracting all the expected costs. (p. 157)

Coverage Protection provided by the policy. (p. 445)

CPM (cost-per-thousand) Amount it will cost to reach 1,000 potential customers with a particular advertising type and time slot. (p. 231)

Creative thinking Thought process that involves looking at a situation or object in new ways; also called lateral thinking. (p. 150)

Credibility Quality of being believable and trustworthy, and keeping one's promises. (p. 525)

Credit Granting of extended time to pay off a debt. (p. 500)

Credit bureau Business that collects and maintains credit history records and sells the information under certain circumstances. (p. 501)

Credit history Record of credit transactions that includes information about whether or not they were repaid in accordance with the credit terms set by the creditor. (p. 500)

Credit terms Particular conditions set by creditors when they grant credit. (p. 500)

Credit union Nonprofit cooperative organization that offers low-interest loans to members. (p. 357)

Creditor Person or business that grants credit. (p. 500)

Critical thinking Logical thought process that involves analyzing and evaluating a situation or object; also called vertical thinking. (p. 151)

Current assets Short-term assets that can be converted into cash within one year. (p. 305)

Current liabilities Short-term debts that must be repaid within one year. (p. 306)

Current ratio Current assets divided by current liabilities. (p. 331)

Customer financing Type of financing in which the customer provides either debt or equity financing for your business. (p. 361)

Customer profile Detailed description of your target market's characteristics. (p. 169)

Customer service operation Part of a business that provides a way for the customer to get help, whether it's for placing an order, getting information, or making a complaint. (p. 603)

Cyberspace Virtual world of computers. (p. 509)

Cyclical (SIK-lih-kul) Refers to cash flow that varies according to the time of year. (p. 302)

D

Damages Payment to reimburse an injured party for loss. (p. 441)

Data mining Using a computer program to search large collections of electronic information and look for patterns or trends. (p. 242)

Debt capital Money obtained by a business through a loan. (p. 569)

Debt financing Obtaining money by borrowing it, thereby increasing your company's debt. (p. 355)

Debt ratio Ratio of a business's total debt divided by its total assets. (p. 329)

Debt-to-equity ratio Ratio of the total debts (liabilities) of a business divided by its owner's equity. (p. 330)

Dedicated server Server that gives a Website its own space. (p. 263)

Deductible Amount the insured must first pay before the insurance company is required to chip in. (p. 445)

Deduction Item or expense subtracted from gross income in a tax return, with the effect of reducing one's taxes. (p. 468)

Delegating leadership style Practiced when a leader gives employees complete freedom to decide what tasks need to be done and how to do them. (p. 495)

Demand curve Curve on a graph that shows the quantity of a product or service consumers are willing to buy across a range of prices over a specific period of time. (p. 32)

Demand forecasting Predicting future sales based on past sales data or other available information and expected market conditions in the future. Also referred to as sales forecasting. (p. 534)

Demand Quantity of goods and services consumers are willing to buy at a specific price and a specific time. (p. 30)

Demand-based pricing Pricing method that focuses on customer demand—how much customers are willing to pay for a product. (p. 220)

Democratic leadership style Practiced when a leader seeks input from employees about what tasks need to be done and how to do them but ultimately makes the final decisions. (p. 494)

Demographics Objective social and economic facts about people. (p. 170)

Depreciation Accounting method of spreading the total cost of the equipment a business buys over the amount of years it will be used. (p. 270)

Depreciation expense Amount of depreciation calculated per year. (p. 270)

Derivative Artistic work based on one or more existing works, such as a movie sequel or a translation in another language. (p. 435)

Differentiator Unique characteristic that distinguishes your business from other businesses. (p. 180)

Direct channel Distribution pathway in which a product goes from the producer straight to the consumer. (p. 216)

Direct competitor Business in your market that sells a product or service similar to yours. (p. 177)

Direct mail Form of print advertising that uses one-to-one communication. (p. 225)

Direct sales force Salespeople who work directly for you as full-time employees; also called internal salespeople. (p. 250)

Directing Ongoing process of leading, influencing, and motivating employees so they will work together to achieve specific goals. (p. 493)

Disposal value Amount for which equipment can be sold at the end of its business life. Also called salvage value. (p. 270)

Distribution chain Series of steps through which products flow into or out of a business. Also referred to as a distribution channel. (p. 517)

Distribution channel Way in which a product can reach the consumer. (p. 216); Series of steps through which products flow into or out of a business. Also referred to as a distribution chain. (p. 517)

Distribution management Management of materials and processes associated with incoming and outgoing products. (p. 517)

Diversification Spreading money over different types of investments as a protection against volatility. (p. 597)

Diversification growth strategy Growth strategy in which a business grows by offering goods and services that are different from its core business. (p. 565)

Dividend Payment corporations make to their shareholders, being a portion of the corporation's profit. (p. 60)

Domain name Primary part of a Website's address (as in www.name.com), which may be the name of the Website itself. (p. 191)

Domain name registration Way to reserve a Web address. (p. 237)

Domain registrar Site that manages domain names. (p. 191)

Domain suffix Part of a Website's address (such as .com) that refers to the largest groupings of domains. Also called the Website's top-level domain (TLD). (p. 191)

Double-entry accounting Accounting system where every business transaction affects at least two accounts. (p. 376)

Drop-down menu Menu at the top of a Webpage that allows users to navigate through the site. (p. 165)

Duality Key accounting concept. In a single-column method, duality means that for any transaction, all changes on the asset side minus all changes on the liability/owner's equity side must equal zero. In the double-column method, duality means that for any transaction posted to the general journal (and any special journals), all debits must equal all credits. (p. 380)

E

E-commerce Process of buying and selling goods online. (p. 69)

E-procurement Purchasing conducted through electronic means, such as Internet Websites. (p. 539)

Economic system Method used by a society to allocate goods and services among its people, and to cope with scarcity. Also referred to as an economy. (p. 28)

Economics Social science concerned with how people satisfy their demands for goods and services, when the supply of those goods and services are limited. (p. 27)

Economics of one unit Calculation of the profit (or loss) for each unit of sale made by a business. (p. 36)

GLOSSARY

Economy Method used by a society to allocate goods and services among its people and to cope with scarcity. Also referred to as an economic system. (p. 28)

Economy of scale Cost reduction made possible by spreading costs over a larger volume. (p. 274)

Embedding Process of incorporating audio and video content into a Website by using HTML. (p. 287)

Embezzlement Crime of stealing money from an employer. (p. 382)

Emergency fund Amount of money a business should have available in the first three to six months for the emergencies that often arise when a company is just beginning. (p. 348); Cash saved to cover personal expenses for at least three months. (p. 596)

Emoticon Symbol or combined punctuation marks used to convey an emotion. (p. 85)

Employee Person who works in a business owned by someone else. (p. 5)

Employee stock ownership plan (ESOP) Fund established when a business owner sells his or her ownership shares to a retirement fund for the employees. (p. 592)

Enterprise Another name for business. (p. 30)

Enterprise zone Geographic area in which businesses receive economic incentives to encourage development there. (p. 462)

Entrepreneur (on-tra-prih-NER) Someone who creates and runs their own business. (p. 5)

Entrepreneurial (on-tra-prih-NER-ee-uhl) To think or act like an entrepreneur. (p. 5)

Entrepreneurial mindset Mental attitude common to entrepreneurs that typically includes an optimistic, "can-do" outlook and the personal ambition necessary to create a business. (p. 567)

Entrepreneurship (on-tra-prih-NER-ship) Process of being an entrepreneur. (p. 10)

Equilibrium point Point at which the supply curve and the demand curve intersect. It is the point at which supply and demand are balanced. (p. 32)

Equilibrium price Price at which supply equals demand. (p. 33)

Equilibrium quantity Quantity at which the supply equals the demand. (p. 32)

Equity capital Money obtained by a business from an investor in exchange for a share of ownership (equity) in the business. (p. 569)

Equity financing Method of financing a start-up business by selling shares of ownership in the business. (p. 358)

Ergonomics Study of designing environments to fit the people who use them. (p. 452)

Ethical sourcing Buying from suppliers who provide safe working conditions and respect workers' rights. (p. 115)

Ethics Set of moral principles that govern decisions and actions. (p. 105)

Excise tax Tax on a specific product or commercial activity. (p. 466)

Exclusive distribution Type of distribution that gives a specific retailer, or authorized dealer, the sole right to sell a product in a particular geographical area. (p. 218)

Executive summary One- or two-page summary of the business plan's highlights and the key selling points of the investment opportunity. (p. 142)

Exporting Business activity in which goods and services are sent from a country and sold to foreign consumers. (p. 39)

Express contract Contract in which the terms are explicitly stated either orally or in writing. (p. 440)

External sales Sales obtained by hiring another company, or an outside individual, to do selling for you. (p. 249)

F

Facilitated giving Type of cause-related marketing in which a business makes it easier for customers to contribute to a cause. (p. 124)

Fair Labor Standards Act Federal law that guarantees most hourly workers a minimum hourly wage, a maximum number of hours worked, and extra pay for working overtime. (p. 474)

Fair trade Policy of ensuring that small producers in developing nations earn sufficient profit on their exported goods to improve their working, environmental, and social conditions. (p. 42)

Fair use Doctrine that provides for the limited quotation of a copyrighted work without permission from or payment to the copyright holder. (p. 112)

Fax (facsimile) (fak-SIM-uh-lee) Exact copy of something. (p. 80)

Feasibility How possible or worthwhile it is to pursue an idea, to see if it is actually an opportunity. (p. 157)

Features What a product does and how it appears to the senses (sight, sound, taste, smell, and touch). (p. 215)

Federal Deposit Insurance Corporation (FDIC) Independent agency of the federal government that insures savings, checking, and other types of deposit accounts. (p. 371)

Federal Trade Commission (FTC) U.S. government agency that administers consumer protection laws and regulates certain business practices. (p. 578)

FICA Acronym for Federal Insurance Contributions Act, the law that requires employers and employees to share the cost of the federal government's insurance and retirement program through deductions from wages and income. (p. 464)

File sharing Ability of computers to share files so everyone involved can look at the same files without having to store copies on their individual computers. (p. 319)

Financial ratio Relationship between important financial data that is expressed as a fraction or percentage. (p. 321)

Financing activities In relation to the statement of cash flows, these primarily consist of debt and equity financing. (p. 394)

Financing Raising money for a business. (p. 347)

Firewall Software program or hardware device designed to prevent unauthorized electronic access to a networked computer system. (p. 319)

Fiscal year Any 12-month period you choose to treat as a year for accounting purposes. (p. 290)

Fixed expense Expense that isn't affected by the number of items a business produces. (p. 269)

Flash animation Software program used to create animated graphics. (p. 165)

Flextime Flexible work schedules. (p. 421)

Floating ad Ad that floats or flies over the Web page for 5 to 30 seconds. (p. 431)

Focus group Small number of people who are brought together to discuss a particular problem, product, or service. (p. 173)

Fonts Styles of typefaces. (p. 131)

Foreign exchange rate Value of one currency unit in relation to another. (p. 42)

Franchise Business arrangement in which an established company sells the right for others to use the company's name and operating plan to sell products or services. (p. 54)

Franchise agreement Legally binding contract between a franchisor and franchisee that lists the rights and responsibilities of each party. (p. 579)

Franchise disclosure document Legal notice that provides detailed information to potential franchisees about the franchisor. (p. 578)

Franchise fee Upfront charge that is usually sizeable—from many thousands of dollars to more than a million—and allows the franchisee to join the franchisor's system. (p. 577)

Franchise operations manual Manual produced by a franchisor that gives detailed instructions to a franchisee about how to operate, staff, and manage a franchise unit. (p. 579)

Franchise royalty Regular, ongoing payment paid by the franchisee to the franchisor. It is typically a percentage of the sales the franchisee earns. (p. 577)

Franchisee Franchise buyer. (p. 154)

Franchisor Franchise seller. (p. 154)

Free enterprise system Another name for the market economy, also known as capitalism, where people are free to become entrepreneurs and own and operate an enterprise (business). (p. 30)

Free on board Delivery term that is followed by a word or group of words that specify a location at which the ownership responsibility for the shipment switches from the seller to the buyer. (p. 519)

Free Web host Opportunities that allow you to set up a Website for free. (p. 263)

Future value of money Amount to which a given sum will increase over time through investment. (p. 594)

G

Gantt chart Bar chart that shows schedule goals for a list of tasks and the duration (length of time) of each task and the progress made at achieving each task. (p. 513)

General journal Accounting record that shows all the transactions of the business. (p. 379)

General partnership Partnership in which all partners have unlimited liability. (p. 58)

Geographics Market segments based on where consumers live or where businesses are located. (p. 170)

Global economy Flow of goods and services around the whole world. (p. 39)

Goodwill Business term that encompasses the intangible positive aspects of a business, such as location, employee knowledge and skills, brand awareness, intellectual property, relationships with suppliers and customers, and reputation in the community and the industry. (p. 590)

Green company Company that adopts business practices aimed at protecting or improving the environment. (p. 11)

Green procurement Act of purchasing goods and services that are environmentally favorable in some way. (p. 534)

Greenwashing Trying to appear environmentally responsible by overstating one's commitment. (p. 123)

H

Hackers People who write and often use programs that enable access to computers and networks by unauthorized users. (p. 341)

Harvesting Exiting a business and gaining the value of the business in cash as one leaves. (p. 591)

Headers Lines of text that appear at the beginning of paragraphs or at the head of sections of your Website copy. (p. 369)

Homepage Website's main domain. (p. 191)

Horizontal diversification Growth strategy in which a business adds new products or services that are not related to its existing products or services, but appeal to its existing target market. (p. 565)

Horizontal integration strategy Intensive growth strategy in which one business acquires another business at the same supply chain level as itself. (p. 565)

HTML Stands for Hypertext Markup Language. It is the language that programmers use to identify how text is used on the Web page. It also controls the appearance of a Web page. (p. 25)

Hubs Devices that connect computers both to each other and to the Internet. (p. 319)

Human resources People who work in a business. (p. 405)

Hyperlinks Another term for links that take you to other pages on the site. (p. 287)

I

Implied contract Contract made when the parties' actions demonstrate their agreement. (p. 440)

Importing Business activity in which goods and services are brought into a country from foreign suppliers. (p. 39)

In-kind donation Donation of a good or service. (p. 125)

Income statement Financial document that summarizes a business's income and expenses over a given time period and shows whether the business made a profit or took a loss. Also called a profit and loss statement. (p. 289)

Incorporate Set up a corporation in accordance with the laws of the particular state where the business is located. (p. 61)

Indemnification (in-dim-nih-fuh-KAY-shun) Protection from legal action, fines, or other damages. (p. 584)

Indirect channel Distribution pathway in which the product goes from the producer to one or more intermediaries before it reaches the consumer. (p. 217)

Indirect competitor Business that sells a different product or service from yours but fills the same customer need or want. (p. 178)

Individual Retirement Account Type of investment on which you won't have to pay taxes until you withdraw the money in the account. (p. 594)

Infomercial Product demonstration, usually produced as a cable television show, that typically lasts from 30 minutes to an hour in length. (p. 226)

Information technology (IT) Study, design, development, implementation, support, and management of computer-based information systems. (p. 49)

Infrastructure System of physical structures and services that a society needs to function and be productive. (p. 459)

Infringement Violating a copyright or patent holder's rights. (p. 112); Violating the rights provided by a copyright or patent. (p. 441)

Initial public offering (IPO) First sale of shares of stock to the general public by a privately held company. (p. 592)

Injunctive relief Order for the violator of a contract to stop the illegal activity. (p. 441)

Instant messaging (IM) Immediate communication using typed text over the Internet. Also called texting. (p. 84)

Intangible Nonmaterial. (p. 157)

Intangibles Things that have value but are not material goods. (p. 433)

Integrative growth strategy Growth strategy that emphasizes blending businesses together through acquisitions and mergers. (p. 564)

Intellectual property Artistic and industrial creations of the mind. (p. 111)

Intensive distribution Type of distribution that makes a product available at as many sales outlets as possible. (p. 218)

Intensive growth strategy Growth strategy that focuses on cultivating new products or new markets, and sometimes both. (p. 563)

Intermediary Bridge between a producer and a consumer – may include agents, brokers, wholesalers, distributors, and retailers. (p. 217)

Internal audit Audit performed by an accountant hired by a company to check their books. (p. 383)

Internal sales Sales obtained by you or your employees who sell your products/services exclusively. (p. 250)

Internet Global system of interconnected networks. (p. 25)

Internet protocol (IP) address Unique string of numbers that identify the domain. (p. 191)

Internship Work program that provides practical, on-the-job training in a business setting. See also apprenticeship. (p. 7)

Interpersonal skills Skills used by people as they interact with others, particularly in a one-on-one setting. (p. 493)

Interstitial ad Ad that appears in its own window before a Web page loads. (p. 431)

Intrapreneurship (in-tra-prih-NER-ship) Practice of giving employees opportunities to be creative and try out new ideas within a company. (p. 19)

Intrastate sales Sales made within the state where the company is physically located. (p. 466)

Inventory investment Money paid for inventory. (p. 541)

Inventory level Quantity of merchandise. (p. 541)

Inventory management Process of keeping track of the items for sale, storing them, and shipping orders. (p. 603)

Inventory shrinkage Any loss of inventory that occurs between the time the inventory is purchased and the time it is sold or otherwise removed from the shelves. (p. 545)

Inventory system Process for counting and tracking inventory so inventory value can be calculated. (p. 546)

Inventory turnover Number of times during a given time period that inventory is completely sold out (and therefore replaced), or the number of times during a given period that the average inventory investment is recouped (earned back). Also referred to as inventory turns. (p. 544)

Inventory turns Number of times during a given time period that inventory is completely sold out (and therefore replaced), or the number of times during a given period that the average inventory investment is recouped (earned back). Also referred to as inventory turnover. (p. 544)

Inventory value Monetary value of merchandise. (p. 541)

Investing activities In relation to the statement of cash flows, these involve buying assets that will last more than one year. (p. 394)

J

Job description Explanation of a position's purpose, tasks, and responsibilities and the qualifications needed to perform it. (p. 411)

Job enlargement Adding responsibilities to a position. (p. 422)

Job enrichment Increasing the depth or involvement of a job. (p. 422)

Job shadowing Process of learning a job by watching an employee perform the job over a period of time. (p. 417)

Just-in-time (JIT) inventory system System in which the goal is to maintain just enough inventory to keep the business operating, with virtually no inventory kept in storage. (p. 547)

K

Keyloggers Programs used for surveillance by companies to make sure their employees are only using their computers for business. Keyloggers are also used to spy on unsuspecting users by recording the letters and numbers (keystrokes) made on a keyboard.(p. 341)

Keywords Words or phrases that represent a Web page's content. (p. 369)

L

Landing page Page that appears when the visitors click on an advertisement or search engine link. (p. 509)

Law of large numbers Theory that says if you want to predict how likely an event is to occur, you will get the most accurate answer by looking at the largest number of cases where it might. (p. 444)

Layout Physical arrangement of objects in a given space. (p. 512)

Lead generation Process of obtaining leads. (p. 485)

Lead lists Contact information for potential customers that is sold by lead-generation services to Website owners. (p. 485)

Lead time Time period between starting an activity and realizing its result—for example, the time between order placement and receipt of shipment. (p. 535)

Lease Written contract in which a property owner gives temporary use of that property to another party. (p. 440)

Liability Legal obligation of a business owner to use personal money and possessions to pay the debts of the business. (p. 56); Any outstanding bill or loan that must be repaid. (p. 305)

Liability insurance Provides protection when a business's actions or lack of action injures another party. (p. 446)

License Providing rights to use intellectual property. (p. 439); Legal document issued by the government that allows a business to provide a regulated product or service. (p. 477)

Limited liability Business owner cannot be legally forced to use personal money and possessions to pay business debt. (p. 56)

Limited liability company Legally defined type of business ownership similar to a C corporation but with simpler operating requirements and tax procedures, and greater liability protection for the business owners (who are called members). (p. 61)

Limited partnership Partnership in which at least one partner has limited liability for the debts of the business. (p. 58)

Line organization Direct chain of command through levels of personnel who are directly involved in a business's main activity. (p. 408)

Line-and-staff organization Expanded version of a line organization. (p. 408)

Link Method used to connect to a related Web page or another Website. (p. 25)

Link trades Site owners agreeing to link to each other's sites. (p. 369)

Liquidation Process in which the tangible assets of a business are sold. (p. 589)

Liquidity Ability to convert assets into cash. (p. 330); Ease of converting a non-cash asset (such as a business) into cash. (p. 587)

List-rental company Company that provides names and contact information for specific groups of consumers or businesses. (p. 173)

Local area network (LAN) Network used in a limited area such as an office, school, or other building. (p. 319)

Local economy Economy that covers a limited area, such as a community or town. (p. 43)

Logistics (lo-GIS-tix) Handling and organizing of materials, equipment, goods, and workers. (p. 518)

Long-term assets Assets that usually take longer than one year to turn into cash. (p. 305)

Long-term liabilities Debts that usually take longer than one year to repay. (p. 306)

M

Main domain Homepage of a Website. (p. 191)

Maintenance Upkeep and routine care of equipment to keep it in good working order. (p. 515)

Malware Various types of malicious software, including computer viruses, Trojan horses, and spyware. (p. 341)

Management Skillful use and coordination of all the business's resources—money, facilities, equipment, technologies, materials, employees—in a systematic and effective way to achieve particular goals. (p. 491)

Management buyout Exit strategy in which a business owner sells his or her ownership shares to the business's managers. (p. 592)

Manufacturer Business that converts materials into goods suitable for use and sells those goods to others. Also referred to as a manufacturing business. (p. 51)

Manufacturing business Business that converts materials into goods suitable for use and sells those goods to others. Also referred to as a manufacturer. (p. 51)

Markdown price Price created when a retailer wants to reduce the price of an overstocked product. (p. 220)

Market Group of potential customers—people or businesses—who are willing and able to purchase a particular product or service. (p. 167)

Market development Intensive growth strategy that focuses on reaching new target markets, such as customers in another geographic area or customers who have different demographics from current customers. (p. 564)

Market economy System in which suppliers and consumers control the production, allocation, and prices of goods and services. (p. 28)

Market penetration Intensive growth strategy that emphasizes more intensive marketing of existing products. (p. 564)

Market research Organized way to gather and analyze information needed to make business decisions. (p. 167)

Market segment Small group of consumers or businesses within a particular market that has one or more things in common. (p. 170)

Market share Percentage of a given market population that is buying a product or service from a particular business. (p. 212); Percentage of the total sales captured by a product or a business in a particular market. (p. 564)

Marketable securities Investments, such as stocks or bonds, that can be converted to cash quickly. (p. 330)

Marketing Way of presenting your business to your customers that clearly communicates the value of your product or service. (p. 211)

Marketing mix "Recipe" for reaching and keeping customers that combines five marketing elements called the Five P's: people, product, place, price, and promotion. (p. 213)

Marketing plan Detailed guide with two primary parts: marketing goals and strategies for reaching those goals. (p. 211)

Markup Price increase imposed by each link in a distribution chain or channel. (p. 517)

Markup price Price created when a retailer adds an additional amount to the cost of a wholesale product to make a profit. (p. 220)

Mass market Market that includes as many customers as possible. (p. 169)

Media Communication channels. (p. 225)

Memo Brief note that informs employees about a business-related matter (short for memorandum). (p. 79)

Mentor Person who provides free guidance, tutoring, and suggestions for achieving your goals. (p. 18)

Message thread Series in an e-mail that shows every previous message. (p. 80)

Metatags HTML tags that provide information about a Webpage. (p. 369)

Micromanager Individual who interferes too much in the decisions and tasks of associates or employees. (p. 567)

Milestone Significant point of progress in a process or timeline. (p. 513)

Milliseconds Thousandths of a second, which is the unit of measurement used to determine the time it takes to access information on a hard drive. (p. 49)

Mind share Awareness or popularity a certain product has with consumers. (p. 216)

Mixed economy Economic system that blends elements of the command economy and the market economy. (p. 28)

Monopoly Single supplier who is a market's only provider of a certain product. (p. 477)

Multi-user license Legal document allowing multiple users to use software in a networked hardware environment. (p. 403)

Multiple of earnings method Method of valuing a business in which the amount of business earnings over a specific time period (usually one year) is multiplied by a number (typically 3 to 5) to determine a reasonable sales price for the overall business. (p. 589)

N

Nanoseconds Billionths of a second, which is the unit of measurement used to determine the time it takes to access information in primary storage. (p. 49)

Need Something that people must have to survive, such as water, food, clothing, or shelter. (p. 147)

Negotiation Process in which two or more parties reach an agreement or solve a problem through communication. (p. 87)

Net worth Accounting term that means total assets minus total liabilities according to a company's balance sheet. Also referred to as book value or owner's equity. (p. 589)

Network server Computer that stores files used by the networked computers. It may also store programs. (p. 319)

Networking Process of meeting new people though current friends and business contacts. (p. 228)

Newsgroup Online message board where people post information about a particular topic. (p. 228)

Nondisclosure agreement Legal document in which a person or group agrees to keep certain information confidential. (p. 157); Agreement that binds parties to secrecy and usually concerns employees, investors, and others with whom a business owner needs to share a trade secret or other sensitive information. Also called confidentiality agreement. (p. 441)

Nonperiodic reordering Ordering items at irregular intervals. (p. 535)

Nonprofit corporation Legally defined type of business ownership in which the company operates not to provide profit for its shareholders but to serve the good of society. (p. 61)

Nonprofit organization Organization that operates solely to serve the good of society. (p. 37)

North American Industry Classification System (NAICS) Classification system that assigns a numerical code to every industry in North America based on its primary business function. (p. 55)

O

Objections Reasons why a customer may be reluctant or cautious about buying. (p. 239)

Obsolescence (ahb-suh-LESS-ence) Process of becoming obsolete, which means no longer useful or desired. (p. 542)

Occupational Safety and Health Administration (OSHA) The federal agency responsible for setting and enforcing standards of safety in the workplace. (p. 473)

Offshoring Outsourcing and giving the project to a company or individual in another country. (p. 603)

One-user license Legal document giving one user the right to use the program, which is sold with the stand-alone version of the software. (p. 403)

Operating activities In relation to the statement of cash flows, these are the day-to-day activities. Most cash changes fall into this category. (p. 394)

Operating ratio Percentage of each dollar of revenue, or sales, needed to cover expenses. (p. 327)

Operational plan Details the everyday activities that will achieve the goal of the tactical plan (and ultimately, the strategic plan). (p. 492)

Operations Everyday activities that keep a business running. (p. 521)

Operations management Management of the everyday activities that keep a business running. (p. 521)

Opportunity cost Value of what you will give up to get something. (p. 158)

Opt-out Option to deny permission for a business to make contact via the Web. (p. 485)

Order getting Sales role in which the primary responsibilities are finding prospects, presenting the product/service, and helping to "close" sales. (p. 250)

Order taking Sales role in which the primary responsibility is recording and processing orders from customers who seek out your product/service. (p. 251)

Organic growth Growth achieved by expanding a business internally—for example, adding new products or services for sale. (p. 559)

Organizational structure System for dividing work, authority, and responsibility within a company. (p. 408)

Organizing Ongoing process of arranging and coordinating resources and tasks to achieve specific goals. (p. 492)

Orientation Process of gradually integrating an employee into a workplace. (p. 417)

Outsourcing Hiring another company or individual to handle part of a business's everyday operations or to do special projects. (p. 603)

Owner's equity Value of the business on a specific date if all the assets were sold and all the liabilities were paid. (p. 305); Accounting term that means total assets minus total liabilities according to a company's balance sheet. Also referred to as net worth or book value. (p. 589)

P

Pacioli check column Column in an accounting worksheet that ensures that the accounting equation always balances after each transaction. (p. 387)

Packing slip List of all items in a shipment. (p. 539)

Parked domain Web address that has been bought but remains unused. (p. 191)

Partial inventory system Combines elements of the perpetual inventory system and the periodic inventory system. (p. 547)

Partnership Legally defined type of business organization in which at least two individuals share the management, profit, and liability. (p. 58)

Partnership agreement Legal document that clearly defines how the work, responsibilities, rewards, and liabilities of a partnership will be shared by the partners. (p. 60)

Pass-through business Business in which the business owner is taxed in the same way as income earned as an employee since the business's income is the owner's personal income as well. (p. 466)

Patent Exclusive right to make, use, or sell a device or process. (p. 111)

Pay-per-click In affiliate marketing, commission the affiliate receives when visitors on the affiliate's site click on the link to get to the merchant's site. (p. 575)

Pay-per-lead In affiliate marketing, commission the affiliate receives when the visitor registers or fills out a form on the merchant's site. (p. 575)

Pay-per-sale In affiliate marketing, commission that the merchant pays the affiliate when a customer actually buys an item. Also known as cost-per-sale or revenue sharing. (p. 575)

Payback Amount of time, measured in months, that it takes a business to earn enough in profit to cover the start-up investment. (p. 349)

Payee Person to whom a check is written. (p. 372)

Periodic inventory system System that calculates inventory value for accounting purposes at periodic times—for example, at the end of the month or end of the year—when a physical inventory count is performed. (p. 547)

Periodic reordering Ordering items at regular time intervals. (p. 535)

Permanent cookie Cookie that is stored on the hard drive. Also called persistent cookie. (p. 509)

Permit Legal document that allows a business to take a specific action. (p. 478)

Perpetual inventory system System that tracks inventory on a continual basis and calculates the inventory value, for accounting purposes, after each inflow or outflow occurs. (p. 547)

Perpetual life cycle Product life cycle in which a product never undergoes a final decline, because it remains in the maturity stage forever. (p. 562)

Persistent cookie Cookie that is stored on the hard drive. Also called permanent cookie. (p. 509)

Personal selling Direct (person-to-person) effort made by a company's sales representatives to get sales and build customer relationships. (p. 225)

PERT chart Scheduling diagram that shows tasks as a sequence of steps and illustrates how steps are dependent on each other. (p. 514)

Philanthropy Donating money and other resources for a socially beneficial cause. (p. 124)

Phishing Spam scam in which you receive an e-mail that appears to be from a legitimate business, such as your bank, requesting that you click on a hyperlink to verify certain information, such as your social security number or bank account number. (p. 531)

GLOSSARY

Pilfering (PILL-fur-ring) Stealing, particularly of small amounts over time. (p. 545)

Pitch letter Cover letter that's often sent with a press release to introduce it. (p. 227)

Planning Ongoing process of setting goals, deciding when and how to accomplish them, and determining how best to accomplish them. (p. 492)

Policy Written contract between the insurer and the policyholder. (p. 445); Procedure or set of guidelines that specifies exactly how something should be done or handled. (p. 521)

Pop-up Ad that appears, or "pops up," in its own window on top of a Web page. (p. 431)

Posted Act of writing a transaction in the accounting worksheet. (p. 384)

Premium "Give-away" item or free gift that usually has the company's name, address, and telephone number printed on it. (p. 227); Amount of money the policyholder pays for coverage. (p. 445)

Press release Written statement, typically consisting of several paragraphs of factual information, that's sent to the news media about a product or business. (p. 226)

Price discrimination Charging competing buyers different prices for the same product. (p. 477)

Price fixing Competitors agreeing to set the price of goods or services, or the terms of business deals. (p. 477)

Primary data New information that is collected for a particular purpose. It is obtained directly from potential customers. (p. 171)

Primary storage One of two types of storage used by the computer. It is contained in the computer and is directly accessed by the central processing unit (CPU). The data stored in primary storage is wiped clean when you turn off your computer. Also known as random access memory (RAM). (p. 49)

Privacy policy Policy that a Website has saying it won't give, sell, or rent your e-mail address to other companies or people. (p. 531)

Procurement Act of purchasing. (p. 533)

Product development Intensive growth strategy in which businesses develop new products or enhance their existing products. (p. 564)

Product life cycle Series of stages—introduction, growth, maturity, and decline—that a product may pass through while it is on the market. (p. 561)

Product mix Combination of products that a business sells. (p. 215)

Product placement When a company pays a fee to have a product displayed during a movie or television show. (p. 226)

Product positioning Process of creating a strong image for your product; a way of influencing customers to distinguish your brand's characteristics from those of the competition. (p. 216)

Product specification Written detailed description of the characteristics (size, shape, capabilities, etc.) of a product. (p. 538)

Production management The oversight of the processes that produce goods and services. (p. 513)

Productivity Measure of business output compared to business input—for example, the number of items produced per employee or the number of customers served per day. (p. 514)

Profile A user's own Web page placed on a social or business networking site (p. 457)

Profit and loss statement Another name for an income statement. (p. 316)

Profit motive Incentive that encourages entrepreneurs to take business risks in the hope of making a profit. (p. 35)

Project organization Employees from more than one department working together as a team on a specific goal. (p. 409)

Promotion Process used to make potential customers aware of your product/service and to influence them to buy it. (p. 214)

Promotional campaign Group of specific promotional activities built around a particular theme or goal. (p. 229)

Promotional mix Combination of promotional elements that a business chooses (advertising, visual merchandising, public relations, publicity, personal selling, and sales promotions). (p. 224)

Property insurance Protects a business's possessions in the event of fire, theft, and damage from the weather. (p. 445)

Prospect Person or company with many of the characteristics of the target market, including some key characteristics. (p. 242)

Protégé Person who receives guidance in a mentoring relationship. (p. 418)

Prototype Model on which future reproductions of an invention are based. (p. 156)

Psychographics Psychological characteristics of consumers, such as attitudes, opinions, beliefs, interests, personality, lifestyle, political affiliation, and personal preferences. (p. 170)

Public domain Status of creative works for which the copyright or patent has expired. (p. 112)

Public relations (PR) Activities aimed at creating goodwill toward a product or company. (p. 224)

Publicity Form of promotion for which a company does not pay; sometimes referred to as "free advertising." (p. 224)

Purchase order Detailed, written record of a business's request for supplies or inventory, often referred to as a PO. (p. 374); Document issued by a buyer to a vendor that lists the items to be purchased, their quantities and prices, and other relevant information, such as delivery or payment terms. (p. 538)

Purchase-triggered donation Practice in which a business contributes a certain amount of money or a certain percentage of an item's purchase price. (p. 124)

Purchasing Buying materials, products, and services for business purposes. (p. 533)

Pure risk Chance of loss with no chance of gain. (p. 444)

Q

Quality circle Group of employees who provide input and suggestions about ways to improve the quality of the goods or services that they produce. (p. 516)

Quality control program Program used by a business to ensure that its products or services meet specific quality standards. (p. 496)

Quantity discount Discount given to buyers for purchasing a large quantity of a product or service from a vendor. (p. 536)

Query Question or phrase that you type into a search engine when looking for information. (p. 369)

Quick ratio Comparison of cash to debt, based on the concept that a business should have at least enough money on hand to pay its current debts. (p. 330)

Quota Limit on the quantity of a product that can be imported into a country. (p. 41)

R

Random access memory (RAM) Another name for primary storage. (p. 49)

Rapport (ra-POR) Emotional connection between people based on feelings of mutual trust and respect. (p. 244)

Recall Notice for customers to return a product that poses a risk of injury or illness. (p. 476)

Receipt Detailed written proof of a purchase. (p. 374)

Recruit To find and hire qualified candidates for a job. (p. 410)

Referral One person providing contact information for another who may be interested in your product/service. (p. 242)

Repeat customers Customers who come back again and again (p. 524)

Replacement cost Cost of replacing property at current prices. (p. 445)

Request for proposal (RFP) Formal way of asking a company to make a bid for a sale; includes details about what the prospect wants. (p. 246)

Reseller's permit Special permit, required by most states, that retailers must have to purchase goods tax-free from wholesalers and collect sales tax from end buyers. (p. 52)

Reserve for fixed expenses Money that a business should have set aside to cover their fixed expenses for at least three months. (p. 348)

Reserve price Minimum price the seller will take for an item. (p. 553)

Résumé Written summary of work experience, education, and skills. (p. 407)

Retailer Business that buys goods, often from wholesalers, and resells the goods in small quantities directly to consumers. Also referred to as a retailing business. (p. 52)

Retailing business Business that buys goods, often from wholesalers, and resells the goods in small quantities directly to consumers. Also referred to as a retailer. (p. 52)

Return on investment (ROI) Profit on an investment expressed as a percentage of the total invested. (p. 331)

Return on sales (ROS) Financial ratio calculated by dividing net profit by sales. (p. 327)

Revenue sharing In affiliate marketing, commission that the merchant pays the affiliate when a customer actually buys an item. Also known as cost-per-sale or pay-per-sale. (p. 575)

Rework Manufacturing term meaning the work performed to correct defects in a product. (p. 523)

Rider Amendment to policy that changes the benefits or conditions of coverage. (p. 449)

Risk Possibility of loss. (p. 444)

Risk transfer Shifting risk to another party. (p. 444)

Royalty fee Regular, ongoing payment to a franchisor based on a percentage of the sales a franchisee earns. (p. 155)

Rule of 72 Quick way to figure how long it will take to double your money at a given rate of return. (p. 593)

S

Safety stock Minimum amount of inventory kept to protect against a stock-out due to unusually high demand or unusually long lead times on delivery. (p. 544)

Salary Fixed amount of money that an employee is paid on a regular basis, such as weekly, biweekly, bimonthly, or monthly. (p. 252); Weekly, bi-monthly, or monthly payment to employees for jobs where the hours and schedule vary. (p. 411)

Sales account Established customer. (p. 246)

Sales call Contacting a sales lead, prospect, or established customer by telephone or in person. (p. 243)

Sales contract Agreement that includes the items sold, the selling price and how it will be paid, and the date and location of the transaction. Also describes each party's right and obligations. (p. 440)

Sales force Employees in a company who are directly involved in the process of selling; another term for salespeople or sales representatives. (p. 239)

Sales forecast Prediction of the amount of future sales your company expects to achieve over a certain period of time. (p. 255)

Sales forecasting Predicting future sales based on past sales data or other available information and expected market conditions in the future. Also referred to as demand forecasting. (p. 534)

Sales invoice Itemized list of goods delivered or services rendered and the amount due. (p. 375)

Sales lead Person or company with some characteristics of your target market. (p. 242)

Sales promotion Short-term activity or buying incentive, such as providing coupons or free samples or conducting product demonstrations. (p. 225)

Sales quota Target amount of sales per month or quarter that a salesperson is expected to achieve. (p. 252)

Sales support Positions that mostly involve assisting others with selling activities. (p. 251)

Sales tax The most common consumption tax required by some local and state governments on goods that are used, or consumed. (p. 465)

Sales territory Specified geographical area for which a salesperson is responsible, such as a city, county, state, or region. (p. 253)

Salutation "Greeting" that begins a letter. (p. 77)

Salvage value Amount for which equipment can be sold at the end of its business life. Also called disposal value. (p. 270)

Same-size analysis Comparison of total revenue or other financial data against that same data converted into percentages of sales. (p. 325)

Savings account Bank account in which money is deposited and on which the bank pays interest to the depositor. (p. 372)

Scarcity State when there are not enough goods or services to meet the demand. (p. 28)

Screen recorder Type of spyware that takes a picture of your computer screen. (p. 341)

Search engine optimization (SEO) Variety of techniques that improve a site's ranking. (p. 369)

Search engine ranking Order of specific words or groups of words in a particular search engine. An e-business owner's goal is to be on the first page of search results. (p. 101)

Secondary data Existing information that was previously gathered for a purpose other than the study at hand. (p. 171)

Secondary storage One of two types of storage used by the computer. It is a more permanent type of storage, not directly accessed by the central processing unit (CPU), and does not lose data when the computer is turned off. The most common type of secondary storage is a computer's hard drive. (p. 49)

Secure sockets layer (SSL) Security measure that "locks" the site, making it secure so it cannot be read by outsiders. It is important for credit card processing online. (p. 69)

Seed money Another term for start-up capital or start-up investment. (p. 347)

Selective distribution Type of distribution that allows a product to be sold at a moderate number of sales outlets, but not all, in a particular geographical area. (p. 218)

Self-assessment Evaluating your strengths and weaknesses. (p. 14)

Self-financing Obtaining the funds for growth from existing operations, for example, by reinvesting cash reserves (profits). (p. 569)

Server Computer that contains all the information you see on the Website. (p. 25)

Service business Business that provides and sells services to customers for a fee. (p. 52)

Service contract Agreement that includes the service provided, the price and how it will be paid, and the date and location of the transaction. Also describes each party's right and obligations. (p. 440)

Service mark Word, phrase, or symbol a service provider uses to identify its services. (p. 438)

Session cookie Cookie that is erased when you close the browser. (p. 609)

Severance pay Amount of money given to employees when they are terminated for reasons other than performance. (p. 474)

Share of stock Unit of ownership in a corporation. (p. 60)

Shared Web hosting Process of sharing server space with other Websites. (p. 263)

Shareholders Owners of a corporation. Also referred to as stockholders. (p. 60)

Shopping cart A type of payment system used by e-commerce sites to process orders. Shoppers place selected items in the "cart" and pay for them when they finish shopping. (p. 69)

Sidebar ad Ad that appears in a vertical format at the side of a Web page. (p. 431)

Sidebar Area on the left or right side of a Web page where there are links to pages within the site or to other Websites. (p. 165)

Signature In an e-mail program, text that is added to a letter along with your name. (p. 131)

Site registration Signing up to a site by providing an e-mail address. (p. 485)

Site traffic Number of visits a Website gets over a specified period. (p. 101)

Site traffic analyzer Tool that shows the number of visitors who came to the site on a hourly, daily, and monthly basis, as well as a visitor's location and type of browser. (p. 509)

Site-ranking portal Web company that lists top-ranking Websites. (p. 101)

Skill Ability that's learned through training and practice. (p. 16)

Social media Interactive electronic forms of communication. (p. 108)

Social networking sites Sites where people can share information. (p. 457)

Sole proprietorship (pruh-PRY-uh-tur-ship) Legally defined type of business ownership in which a single individual owns the business, collects all profit from it, and has unlimited liability for its debt. (p. 57)

Source document Original record (source) of a transaction, including receipts, cancelled checks, invoices, bank deposit slips, and other records. (p. 376)

Sourcing Choosing appropriate vendors to supply desired business goods or services. (p. 535)

Spam Junk e-mail. (p. 341); Unsolicited bulk e-mail—"junk" e-mail that's usually advertising a product and sent to hundreds of thousands of recipients. (p. 531)

Spam blocker Program that stops spam from going into your e-mail inbox. Also called a spam filter. (p. 531)

Spam bots Programs that crawl the Internet to collect e-mail addresses. (p. 531)

Spam filter Program that stops spam from going into your e-mail inbox. Also called a spam blocker. (p. 531)

Spam folder Separate folder in which spam e-mails accumulate. (p. 531)

Spammer Person who sends out spam. (p. 531)

Speculative risk Risk that holds the possibility of either gain or loss. (p. 444)

Spiders (search engine robots) Computer robots that scan individual Web pages. (p. 369)

Sponsorship Sponsoring a community event or service in exchange for advertising. (p. 123)

Spoofing Hiding the origin of an e-mail message—the information in the "from" field. (p. 531)

Spyware Software that lets computer users spy on other users. (p. 341)

Start-up capital Another term for seed money or start-up investment. (p. 347)

Start-up investment One-time sum required to start a business and cover start-up costs. Also called seed money or start-up capital. (p. 347)

Static content Web content that stays the same over time. (p. 287)

Stationery Pre-set selection of fonts, font color, background color, and graphics that resemble printed stationery and make your e-mails look more finished and attractive. (p. 131)

Stock-out Item in inventory is completely gone. (p. 542)

Stockholders Owners of a corporation. Also referred to as shareholders. (p. 60)

Storefront creation Designing a Website that can list products, prices, payment terms, and shipping costs, as well as process orders. (p. 603)

Straight-line method of depreciation Method used to calculate the depreciation of equipment based on how long the equipment will last. (p. 270)

Strategic plan Lays out a broad course of action to achieve a long-term goal, typically three to five years in the future. (p. 492)

Subchapter S corporation Corporation that differs from a C corporation in how it is taxed. Its income or loss is applied to each shareholder and appears on their tax return. (p. 61)

Subdomain Domain within a Website, such as an individual product page. (p. 191)

Subsidy Financial aid from the government to support an industry or public service. (p. 460)

Supply Quantity of goods and services a business is willing to sell at a specific price and a specific time. (p. 30)

Supply and demand curve Graph that includes both a supply curve and a demand curve. It shows the relationship between prices and the quantities of a product or service that is supplied and demanded. (p. 32)

Supply curve Curve on a graph that shows the quantity of a product or service a supplier is willing to sell across a range of prices over a specific period of time. (p. 31)

Sustainability Another term for sustainable economic development. (p. 43)

Sustainable Meeting the planet's current needs while preserving resources for future generations. (p. 120)

Sustainable economic development Economic development that does not harm society or the environment. It ensures that human and natural resources are maintained for future generations. (p. 43)

SWOT analysis Business evaluation method that draws its name from the four areas it evaluates: Strengths, Weaknesses, Opportunities, and Threats. (p. 158)

Synergistic diversification Growth strategy in which a business adds new products or services that are related to its existing products or services. (p. 565)

T

T-account Double-sided presentation that shows credits and debits. (p. 379)

Tactical plan Outlines specific major steps for carrying out the strategic plan. (p. 492)

Target market Limited amount of customers who are most likely to buy a specific product or service. (p. 169)

Tariff Fee, similar to a tax, that importers must pay on the goods they import. (p. 41)

Tax avoidance Using legal strategies to reduce one's tax liability. (p. 467)

Tax credit Dollar-for-dollar reduction in taxes owed. (p. 469)

Tax evasion Trying to avoid paying taxes through illegal or deceptive means. (p. 464)

Tax-increment financing (TIF) Strategy of spending taxpayer money to encourage businesses to locate in an area or improve their property there, with the goal of starting a cycle of growth and prosperity. (p. 462)

Taxes Money required by the government to support its various functions. (p. 459)

Team building Motivating individuals in a group to work together to achieve a shared goal. (p. 493)

Telecommuting Working from a location other than the business site, linked by telecommunication technology. (p. 421)

Telemarketing Promoting or selling products/ services one-to-one over the telephone. (p. 228)

Texting Another name for instant messaging. (p. 85)

Third party transaction Occurs when a third party collects the money from the buyer and then pays the seller. (p. 403)

Third-party providers Professionals or companies to which jobs are outsourced. (p. 603)

Top-level domain (TLD) For a Website, this is identified by the domain suffix (such as .com). (p. 191)

Trade barrier Governmental restriction on international trade. (p. 41)

Trade business Term used to refer to a wholesale business or a retail business. (p. 52)

Trade credit Extended payment time given by one business to another business for purchased goods or services. (p. 500)

Trade discount Discount given to resellers who are in the same trade, industry, or distribution chain as a vendor. (p. 536)

Trade secret Information that a business or individual keeps confidential to gain advantage over competitors. (p. 439)

Trade show Convention where related businesses come to promote their products or services. (p. 150)

Trade-out As a promotion strategy, a bartering practice whereby you trade your company's products or services for free air time on a radio station. (p. 231)

Trademark Symbol that indicates that the use of a brand or brand name is legally protected and cannot be used by other businesses. It is a type of intellectual property. (p. 111)

Traffic log Record of the raw traffic data that a server collects. (p. 509)

Transaction Any payment or income received. (p. 376)

Transparency Openness and accountability in business decisions and actions. (p. 107)

Trojan horse Software program that takes control of your computer without your knowledge. (p. 341)

Typeface Design of a printed character (font). (p. 237)

U

Unicast ad TV/Web commercial that appears in its own window. (p. 431)

Unit of sale What a customer actually buys from you. It's the amount of product (or service) that you use to figure your operations and profit. (p. 275)

Universal values Values shared by all cultures throughout history. (p. 106)

Unlimited liability Business owner can be legally forced to use personal money and possessions to pay the debts of the business. (p. 56)

Uptime Amount of time that a Website is online. (p. 263)

V

Value analysis Process for assessing the performance of a good or service relative to its cost. (p. 534)

Values Intangible things that you believe are worthwhile and important. (p. 93)

Variable expense Expense that changes based on the amount of product or service a business sells. (p. 272)

Vendors Businesses that sell products to other businesses. (p. 533)

Venture capital Money invested in a potentially profitable business by a specialized company whose purpose is to invest in start-ups. (p. 359)

Vertical integration strategy Intensive growth strategy in which one business acquires another business in its own supply chain, but not at the same supply chain level. (p. 565)

Videoconference Meeting in which participants in different locations see and hear each other through monitors, cameras, microphones, and speakers. (p. 83)

Viral marketing Word-of-mouth promotion on the Internet. (p. 431)

Vision "Picture" of what you want the future to be. (p. 19)

Visual inventory system Physically counting inventory items. (p. 546)

Visual merchandising Use of artistic displays to attract customers into a store and visually promote products inside a store. (p. 224)

Volatile Changing frequently and unpredictably—stock prices that change in reaction to information are volatile. (p. 597)

Volume buying Purchasing a large quantity from a vendor, typically to take advantage of a quantity discount. Also referred to as buying in bulk. (p. 536)

Volume discount Discount for buying greater quantities. (p. 274)

Voluntary exchange Transaction in which both suppliers and consumers believe they benefit. (p. 30)

W

Wage Payment to employees per hour worked or piece of work completed. (p. 411)

Want Product or service that people desire. (p. 147)

Warranty Statement from a seller, usually in writing, that promises that purchased goods or services meet certain standards and describes the conditions under which particular problems will be taken care of by the seller at no cost to the buyer. (p. 525)

Web 2.0 For the first time, allowed interaction between Websites and Web surfers on the Internet, opening the door to commerce. (p. 457)

Web analytics software Various programs that measure and monitor the traffic to a Website. (p. 509)

Web analytics tool Tool used by e-commerce Website owners to track daily traffic, length of stay on the site, sales, and conversion rates. (p. 69)

Web banner Electronic advertisement that you pay other companies or organizations to embed on their Web sites. (p. 226)

Web browser Software that enables you to navigate the Web. (p. 25)

Web designer Professional who designs Websites that will stand out from other Websites. (p. 165)

Web domain Primary part of a Website's address (as in www.domain.com) (p. 191)

Web hits Number of visitors to a site, tabulated by the Web host. (p. 263)

Web host Business that stores all the information for a Website on its servers. (p. 69)

Web page Document on a Website. (p. 25)

Web search engine Way of finding information online. (p. 237)

Web surfing Process of visiting one Website after another. (p. 25)

Web template Pre-made Website that includes already-created graphics and an established layout. (p. 165)

Web traffic Number of visitors a site gets over a specific time period. (p. 69)

Webcasts Web presentations where there is no interaction (p. 485)

Webinars Short for Web-based seminars or lectures. (p. 485)

Webmaster Person who manages a Website. (p. 369)

Website Collection of Web pages (p. 25)

Website slogan Short phrase that describes what the company does. (p. 237)

Whistle-blower One who reports illegal or unethical conduct to superiors or to the public. (p. 108)

Wholesaler Business that buys goods in large quantities, typically from manufacturers, and resells them in smaller batches to retailers. Also referred to as a wholesaling business. (p. 52)

Wholesaling business Business that buys goods in large quantities, typically from manufacturers, and resells them in smaller batches to retailers. Also referred to as a wholesaler. (p. 52)

Wide area network (WAN) Network that connects large geographic areas such as one city to another or one country to another, through the Internet. (p. 319)

Wikis Collaborative Websites where anyone can edit, delete, or modify content. (p. 457)

Window of opportunity Period of time in which you have to act before a business opportunity is lost. (p. 148)

Wireless network Network that operates on a radio frequency, in much the same way that cell phones work. (p. 319)

Word of mouth Verbal communications or publicity. (p. 524)

Workers' compensation insurance Covers losses to employees due to job-related injury or illness. (p. 447)

Workplace climate General feeling in a business shaped by the psychological state and attitudes of the people who work there. (p. 496)

World Wide Web Important part of the Internet—huge set of documents, pictures, and other elements that are linked together. (p. 25)

Z

Zoning laws Local laws that specify the types of development and activities—residential, commercial, industrial, or recreational—that can take place on particular pieces of property. (p. 511)

INDEX

INDEX

C

C corporation, 60–61, 63
capital
    debt capital, 569
    equity capital, 569
carbon credits, 272
carbon footprint, 122
carbon offset, 122
career
    career exploration, 17
    career orientation, 53
    career planning, 538
carrying capacity, 169
cash discount, 537
cash flow, 299–303
    burn rate, 302–303
    cash budget, 502
    forecasting, 502–503
    improving, 503
    keeping cash flowing, 301–302
cash flow statement, 300–301, 394
cash flow statement, parts of
    beginning cash balance, 300
    cash inflow, 300
    cash outflow, 300
    net cash, 300
    total available cash, 300
cash reserves
    emergency fund, 348
    reserve for fixed expenses, 348
chart of accounts, 376–381, 387–391, 394
checking account, 372–373, 387
co-signer, 357
cold call, 242
collateral, 356
commerce server, 69
communication, 75–96, 239
    nonverbal, 254
community, 123
    awareness, 8, 17
    community resources, 172
    events, 227
company
    best companies to work for, 497
    business-to-business (B2B) company, 170
    business-to-consumer (B2C) company, 169

company image, 496–497
    list-rental company, 173
compensation
    commission, 252
    salary, 252, 411–412
    severance pay, 474
    wage, 411–412
competition, 33–34, 101, 168
    competitive advantage, 177–187
        competitive matrix, 179–180
        determining yours, 179–182
        differentiator, 180
        SWOT analysis, 182
    competitive intelligence, 177–182
    direct and indirect competitors, 177–178
    fair competition, 476–477
    identifying your competition, 177–178
    information on the competition, 254
compromise, 91
concession, 89
confidentiality, 113–114, 441
conflict of interest, 113
contract, 439–441
    agreement between parties, 439
    breach of contract, 441
    competence, 440
    consideration; mutual exchange, 440
    express contract, 440
    implied contract, 440
contract, types of
    confidentiality agreement, 441
    lease, 440
    nondisclosure agreement, 441
    sales contract, 440
    service contract, 440
contribution margin, 276–282, 295
controlling, 496, 545–546
cooperative, 62, 214
copyright, 111, 435
    infringement, 441
corporation, 60–62
    corporate social responsibility, 115–126
corporation, types of
    C corporation, 60–61
    employee-owned corporation, 59
    limited liability company, 61
    nonprofit corporation, 61–62
    subchapter S corporation, 61

personal selling, 225
public relations (PR), 224
publicity, 224
sales promotion, 225
visual merchandising, 224
promotional plan, 229–230
promotional responses, 242
property
property tax, 466–467
securing property, 450–451
prospect, 242
protecting
your works, 434–439
copyright, 435
patent, 435
registered trademark, 439
service mark, 438–439
trademark, 438–439
public domain, 112
public relations (PR), 224
purchase order (PO), 374, 538
purchasing, 533–540
purchasing management, 533–540
doing the paperwork, 538
following up on purchases, 537–538
getting right payment terms, 536–537
getting right price, 536
goals of procurement management, 534
purchasing online, 539
receiving purchases, 537
selecting right quality, 534
selecting right quantity, 534
selecting right vendors, 535–536
timing purchases, 535

Q

quality, 516
quantity discount, 536
quota, 41, 252

R

receipt, 374
recordkeeping, 371–383

recruiting employees, 410–415
referral, 242
relationships
personal, 18, 239, 337
resiliency, 351
respect, 151
responsibility, 105–126, 309
corporate social responsibility, 115–116
to community, 123
to environment, 119–123
to individuals, 116–119
return on investment (ROI), 331
revenue sharing, 575
reward versus risk, 593
rewards
of being an entrepreneur, 7–8
risk
calculated risk, 157
catastrophic risk, 446
managing risk (insurance), 444
pure risk, 444
reducing risk, 450–452
risk transfer, 444
risk versus reward, 593
speculative risk, 444
tolerating risk, 596
risks
of being an entrepreneur, 8–9
royalty fee, 155
Rule of 72, 593–594
résumé, 407, 413–414

S

safety and health, 451
employee protection, 473
product safety, 476
sales
closing a sale, 245–246
cold call, 242
data mining, 242
estimating sales, 249–258
external sales, 249–250
internal sales, 250
order form, 246–247
prospect, 242
referral, 242

INDEX

T

tariff, 41
tax credit, 469–470
taxes, 57–62, 459–470, 463
  business, 462–463
    contribution to the federal budget, 467
    contribution to the state budget, 467
  deductions, 468
  defense, 461–462
  Employer Identification Number, 58
  Federal Insurance Contributions Act (FICA), 464
  infrastructure, 459
  public services, 459–460
  reason businesses pay taxes, 459
  social programs, 460–461
  subsidy, 460, 463
  tax avoidance, 467
  tax credit, 469–470
  tax evasion, 464, 467
  tax I.D. number, 58
  tax-increment financing (TIF), 462
  tax-saving strategies, 467–468
taxes, types of, 463–467
  consumption taxes, 465
  excise tax, 466
  Federal Unemployment Tax (FUTA), 465
  payroll tax, 464–465
  property tax, 466–467
  sales tax, 465
team building, 493
teamwork, 184
technology
  e-commerce, 69
  global economy, 40
  information technology, 49
  skills, 254
telemarketing, 228
testimonial, 232
thinking creatively, 150–153, 495
thinking critically, 151
third-party providers, 603
third-party transaction, 403
trade
  fair trade, 41, 120
  international trade, 41–42
  trade barrier, 41

trade credit, 500, 537
trade discount, 536
trade secrets, 439
trade show, 150
trading partners, 361–362
trademark, 111, 438
training employees, 416–419
transaction, 376
transparency, 107–108
transportation, 218, 517–518
  logistics, 518

U

U.S. Constitution, 434
unit of sale, 275–282

V

value analysis, 534
values, 93, 106
variable expenses, 272–273, 276–282
vendor, 535, 538
venture capital, 359–360
vision, 19–20
volume buying, 536
volume discount, 274
volunteers, 125

W

warehousing, 547
warranty, 525
wealth, building, 592–593
  compounding, 593
  future value of money, 594–597
  Rule of 72, 593–594
  time value of money, 593
whistle-blower, 108–109